PERSPECTIVES IN AUDITING
Readings and Analysis Situations

C.P.A.*

T. Tucker

Son of the Wheel,
Brother of fire,
Consort of balanced accounts,
I tell the feet of wire and call them dollars;
Twenty-nine cents for a pint of safflower oil.

No one knows the pound of copper,
Its price fluctuates
While I make inventory;
One end of the bright rainbow of worth
Trapped in my ledger,
The other, struggling to be free,
Bends nicely to my art;
The fee, that measure of myself,
Is named openly in every client's books.

A ten pound goose
Is worth the hire of an apprentice carpenter
No more, no less than an hour,
Whether he drive a nail
Or sever a timber,
Or it lay a thousand golden eggs,
Which make a separate entry
Whose question lies in the fiscal years of laying
And depreciation schedules.

A stockroom kiss
Has cost and value in the broken bottle,
The crushed head of lettuce,
The leakage, spoilage, shrinkage, tearage
Of what is bought or sold.
People do not appreciate,
They earn pension rights
Or incur casualty losses
Covered, in main, by workman's compensation,
Blue Cross, Blue Shield,
Aetna, Equitable,
And M.O.N.Y.

I cheat on my income tax,
Enter fifty fewer orgasms,
Two geese less,
A hundred feet of copper wire forgot,
No stockroom kiss,
Yet claim depreciation on my wife;
Physician and actuary say: expected life
One point seven years,
A large, anticipated carry-over loss
In straight-line tears.

*An original poem published here from *Poet and Critic* by special permission of the author and publisher. Artistic impressions of the accounting profession are so rare that we are especially pleased to include this unique example of contemporary art.—D.R.C. & J.J.W.

PERSPECTIVES IN AUDITING

READINGS AND ANALYSIS SITUATIONS

D. R. Carmichael, PhD, CPA
Auditing Research Consultant
American Institute of Certified Public Accountants

John J. Willingham, PhD, CPA
Professor of Accounting
The University of Texas at Arlington

McGraw-Hill Book Company
New York   St. Louis   San Francisco   Düsseldorf
Johannesburg   Kuala Lumpur   London   Mexico   Montreal   New Delhi
Panama   Rio de Janeiro   Singapore   Sydney   Toronto

This book was set in News Gothic by University Graphics, Inc.,
and printed and bound by The Maple Press Company.
The designer was Barbara Ellwood;
the drawings were done by John Cordes, J. & R. Technical Services, Inc.
The editors were Jack R. Crutchfield and Cynthia Newby.
Sally Ellyson supervised production.

PERSPECTIVES IN AUDITING
Readings and Analysis Situations

Library of Congress Catalog Card Number 71-163300

07-070601-8

234567890MAMM79876543

CONTENTS

PREFACE

In the past few years auditing has begun to enjoy a rebirth as an academic interest area. Part of the renewed interest must be attributed to the press coverage of audit activities; however, it is the activities themselves—the work of auditors and repercussions of this work—that are the root cause. This integrated set of readings and analysis situations is designed to provide the auditing instructor with materials that are either not included or not covered in depth in auditing textbooks.

The book is divided into four sections:
I The Audit Profession
II The Audit Process
III Audit Reports
IV Contemporary Issues in Auditing

Almost all auditing textbooks include materials that fit these classifications. Our intention is to provide additional depth through presentation of integrated sets of materials that cover subareas of the four general areas listed. Some of the pieces we include are original, but most are not; some are uncommon and some common; a few have not been included in previous sets of auditing readings; all, we believe, are important to the understanding of auditing.

The book's chapters are organized around a given subject. We strongly recommend that students be assigned chapters rather than individual readings or analysis situations. Each selection in the book is, we hope, interesting in and of itself. But each will assume additional pertinence if accompanied by the associated materials. This book can be used to supplement any standard auditing textbook. However, most such texts are lengthy enough to prohibit inclusion of supplementary materials. Therefore, the instructor will find that these materials will better supplement one of the shorter texts. On the other hand, *Perspectives in Auditing* may be used as the basic text in a graduate-level course. If, however, some materials included in one of the longer texts can be omitted, *Perspectives* should make a relevant and useful substitute.

Readings and analysis situations are distinguished both in the Contents and in the body of the book by the following symbols:

○   Reading
▷   Analysis situation

The readings will provide a base for useful class discussion of the topics but no specific written analysis is required of the student. The analysis situations do require solutions, positions, or other thoughtful effort on the part of the student.

We are indebted to all the authors whose work appears in *Perspectives in Auditing* and take this opportunity to thank them for enriching the literature of auditing.

D. R. CARMICHAEL
JOHN J. WILLINGHAM

PERSPECTIVES IN AUDITING
Readings and Analysis Situations

PART ONE

THE AUDIT PROFESSION

CHAPTER 1

THE ATTEST FUNCTION: EVOLUTION AND PURPOSE

Historical perspective is essential to understanding auditing as a profession. The objectives and techniques of auditors have changed during the four hundred years of recognizable existence of auditors. These changes are synthesized by Brown through a historical analysis.

CHANGING AUDIT OBJECTIVES AND TECHNIQUES
R. Gene Brown*

A review of the history of auditing provides a basis for analyzing and interpreting the changes which have taken place in audit objectives and techniques. Even more important, this review reveals a significant recent trend toward increased reliance on internal controls and a decrease in detailed testing. Auditing in the future will probably consist primarily of a procedural (or system) review, with the analysis of effectiveness of internal controls providing the major basis for the procedural appraisal. Several arguments seem to support this view:

1 Rising costs in public accounting and the consequent additional emphasis on economy and effectiveness.

2 Requests received by the auditor from management, owners, and other parties-at-interest for additional information.

3 The increased complexity of the business enterprise resulting in geometric compounding of data control problems.

4 The development of new communication and information systems and introduction of extremely reliable data processing machines.

It is interesting to view present auditing objectives and techniques in terms of their evolution, as tabulated below.

ANCIENT TO 1500

Prior to 1500, accounting concerned itself with governmental and family units. The use of two scribes who kept independent records of the same transactions was designed to prevent defalcations within the treasuries of the ancient rulers. A secondary objective was assurance of accuracy in reporting. Inventories

* From *The Accounting Review*, Vol. XXXVII, No. 4 (October, 1962), pp. 696–703. Reprinted by permission of the American Accounting Association.

Period	Stated Audit Objectives	Extent of Verification	Importance of Internal Controls
Ancient–1500	Detection of fraud	Detailed	Not recognized
1500–1850	Detection of fraud	Detailed	Not recognized
1850–1905	Detection of fraud Detection of clerical error	Some tests, Primarily Detailed	Not recognized
1905–1933	Determination of fairness of reported financial position Detection of fraud & errors	Detailed and Testing	Slight recognition
1933–1940	Determination of fairness of reported financial position Detection of fraud & errors	Testing	Awakening of interest
1940–1960	Determination of fairness of reported financial position	Testing	Substantial emphasis

were periodically taken to prove the accuracy of the accounting records; auditing was not relied upon for this function. The "hearing" of accounts during the time of the Roman Empire was also primarily concerned with preventing fraudulent acts by the quaestors.

Subsequent to the fall of the Roman Empire, auditing developed hand-in-hand with the Italian City States. The merchants of Florence, Genoa and Venice used auditors to assist in the verification of the accountability of the sailing-ship captains returning from the Old World with riches bound for the European Continent. Auditing was primarily fraud-preventive during this era.

The audit of the City of Pisa in 1394 was designed to test the accounts of the governmental officials to determine whether defalcation had taken place. Accuracy was sought in most of these cases, but only insofar as it might indicate the existence of fraud. Mr. L. Fitzpatrick commented on the early audit objective as follows: "Auditing as it existed to the sixteenth century was designed to verify the honesty of persons charged with fiscal responsibilities."[1]

[1] L. Fitzpatrick, "The Story of Bookkeeping, Accounting, and Auditing," *Accountants Digest,* IV (March 1939), 217.

A review of the literature pertaining to the early history of auditing reveals nothing concerning the existence of internal controls (or indeed accounting systems). Early auditing techniques consisted almost exclusively of a detailed verification of every transaction which had taken place. As an audit procedure the concept of testing or sampling was unknown.

1500 TO 1850

There is little in the period of 1500 to 1850 which would distinguish audit objectives from earlier times. Auditing was expanded in scope to include the earlier manufacturing activities arising during the early days of the Industrial Revolution. Audit objectives were still directed to detection of fraud, achieving more importance as it became common for owners to be separated from management and their capital investment. Detailed checking was still the rule and the accepted approach.

However, rather significant changes in attitude occurred during this period. The first was the recognition that an orderly and standardized system of accounting was desirable for both accurate reporting and fraud prevention. The second important change was a general acceptance of the need for an independent review of the accounts for both large and small enterprises.

Examples of this latter attitude are found in the English Companies Act of 1862 as well as certain bookkeeping texts of that era.

> The fundamental principles of Double Entry are as infallible in their application to every species of accounts as their operation is extensive; in practice, however, they are exposed to all the moral and mental imperfections of the accountant: They are neither exempt from the defects of ignorance — the errors of indolence — or the practice of fraud, — and frequent and careful investigations on the part of the proprietor himself are scarcely sufficient to render him secure from such evils.[2]

> . . . the Italian Method, by a double entry of Debtor and Creditor, by way of eminence, is now always distinguished by the appellation of Bookkeeping as being of all others the most perfect, the most elegant and the most satisfactory, either for the Merchant's own information . . . or otherwise for the inspections of others. . . .[3]

The recognition of the importance of a standardized system is also well covered in Jackson's book.

> In conducting of business, Order and Method contribute very much to lighten the care, facilitate the despatch and ensure the success thereof. The advantages

[2] B. F. Foster, *Commerical Bookkeeping* (Philadelphia: Perkins & Marvin, 1836), p. 4.
[3] William Jackson, "In the True Form of Debtor and Creditor," *Jackson's Book-keeping* (New York: Evert Duyckinck, Daniel Smith and Others, 1823), p. iii.

of regularity are not more sensibly experienced by the extensive trader, in any part of his transactions, than in the orderly stating and keeping of his books of account.[4]

The understanding that internal control was a desirable product of an accounting system came sometime after this. It was not specifically identified with any audit processes. The strength or weakness of the accounting system, and thereby of internal control, did not influence the amount of detailed checking accomplished.

1850 TO 1905

The fifty-five years following 1850 encompassed the period of greatest economic growth in Great Britain. The large-scale operations that resulted from the Industrial Revolution provided the impetus necessary to bring the corporate form of enterprise to the foreground. As management passed from individual owners to hired professionals, the owners in absentia became concerned over the proper protection and growth of their capital investment. The time was ripe for a profession of auditing to emerge.

Shortly after the middle of the nineteenth century, teams of stockholders, making periodic visits to the corporations, attempted to verify the recorded data. It soon became evident that a reliable audit required specialized training. This recognition, coupled with the suggestions for auditing in the Companies Act of 1862, increased substantially the demand for trained accountants who could perform professional, independent audits.

Internal control was recognized as existing in standardized systems of accounting, but little attention was paid to it in auditing. Little interest was shown in any systems of controls for assets other than cash. The built-in control inherent in double entry accounting was often the only cross check recognized as significant for all accounts. Because of this, the audits during the period 1850 to 1905 usually involved rather complete reviews of transactions and the preparation of corrected accounts and financial statements. This was inefficient, expensive, and did not satisfactorily provide for strengthening of weak areas in subsequent periods. The need for changes in the accounting system to improve the accuracy of reported amounts and reduce the possibilities for fraudulent acts was obvious. As the accounting system and the organizational structure were strengthened, the technique of sampling became accepted practice for auditors.

The implementation of testing as an auditing procedure can be traced to

[4] *Ibid.*

the last ten years of the nineteenth century. By 1895 there was evidence of sampling in Great Britain. In the London and General Bank case of that year, the following statement was made by the presiding judge:

> Where there is nothing to excite suspicion, very little inquiry will be reasonable and quite sufficient; and, in practice, I believe business men select a few cases haphazard, see that they are right and assume that others like them are correct also. [5]

The new technique of sampling was not peculiar to English auditing; it also appeared in the United States about this time:

> With the rapid growth of American business following the Spanish-American war, the increase in size of many enterprises and the auditing of larger concerns, there developed the necessity for making the audit one of selected tests of the accounts rather than an endeavor to examine all of the transactions of the period. [6]

Evidence of sampling in auditing can also be seen in one of the pre-1900 New York CPA Examination Questions which asked, "In an audit where an exhaustive detailed examination . . . is not stipulated or practicable, what examination is necessary to assure . . . general correctness?" [7]

One would expect to see some evidence of a change in audit objectives during this period which would account in part for the acceptance of the new technique of testing. Techniques implement objectives; a change in techniques normally results from a corresponding change in objectives. However, in the literature relating to auditing in this period, there is no argument to support this assumption. The primary objective of auditing was still the detection of fraud; the reason that the auditor switched from detailed verification to testing was simply because he could no longer check every transaction of the ever-growing corporate entities.

Prior to 1905, a natural basis for deciding to limit the amount of testing to be done in auditing would have been the improvements in accounting systems, and consequently in internal controls, which existed in the larger corporations. Surprisingly, it was sometime later, during the period 1905 to 1933, that auditors realized the importance of internal controls and the relation of strengths and weaknesses therein to their testing programs. The first true recognition of internal control as a foundation for deciding on the amount of detailed verification to be done appeared in the American version of Dicksee's *Auditing,*

---

[5] E. D. McMillan, "Evaluation of Internal Control," *The Internal Auditor,* XIII (December, 1956), 39.

[6] Walter A. Staut, *Auditing Developments During the Present Century* (Cambridge: Harvard University Press, 1942), p. 10.

[7] C. A. Moyer, "Early Developments in American Auditing," *Accounting Review,* XXVI (January, 1951), p. 5.

". . . a proper system of internal check [will] frequently obviate the necessity of a detailed unit."[8]

Despite this statement in a leading auditing book of the era, detailed testing was still the rule. Testing did exist, but was limited in application. This same book summarized the audit objectives at that time as follows:

The object of an audit may be said to be three-fold:

1 *The detection of fraud.*

2 *The detection of technical errors.*

3 *The detection of errors of principle.*[9]

1905 TO 1933

The auditing objectives and techniques of Great Britain formed the basis for the development of the American auditing profession in its early years. However, in the ten years after the turn of the twentieth century, the American auditing profession progressed independently of its origins. The objectives and approach of the British auditors were found to be unsuitable for American business. British audits designed to discover defalcations did not continue long into American auditing. The first major American work on auditing characterized this change in objectives in this manner:

> *In what might be called the formative days of auditing, students were taught that the chief objects of an audit were:*
>
> 1 *Detection and prevention of fraud*
>
> 2 *Detection and prevention of errors, but in recent years there has been a decided change in demand and service. Present-day purposes are:*
>
> 1 *To ascertain actual financial condition and earnings of an enterprise.*
>
> 2 *Detection of fraud and errors, but this is a minor objective.*[10]

Accompanying this change in objectives was a rather significant change in techniques. The transition from British to American auditing was characterized by a change from detailed verification to testing. Auditors decided that ". . . . it was not necessary to make a detailed examination of every entry, footing, and posting during the period in order to get the substance of the value which resulted from an audit."[11]

[8] Lawrence R. Dicksee, *Auditing,* ed. Robert H. Montgomery (New York: Ronald Press, 1905), p. 54.
[9] *Ibid.,* p. 22.
[10] Robert H. Montgomery, *Auditing Theory and Practice* (New York: Ronald Press, 1912), p. 13. This identical statement appeared in the second (1923) and the third (1927) editions.
[11] Frank G. Short, "Internal Control from the Viewpoint of the Auditor," *Journal of Accountancy,* 70 (September, 1940), 226.

The literature of this period began to recognize more fully the importance of internal control and its relation to the extent of audit testing to be done. An English book published in 1910, *Audit Programmes,* pointed out that the first step in any audit was to "ascertain the system of internal check."[12]

Typical of the American authors' treatment of this subject were the following:

> *Systems of operating accounts and records should be formulated with a single guiding principle—that they must furnish means of control.*[13]

> *Where there is a satisfactory system of internal check, the auditor is not expected, and should not attempt, to make a detailed audit.*[14]

> *If the Auditor can satisfy himself that the work of record keeping is done in such a way as to furnish a system of internal check . . . he can accept the results [of the system] as being correct, subject to tests. . . .*[15]

Unfortunately, the literature was far ahead of actual practice. The auditor continued to expand his use of the technique of testing, but his decision as to the extent of testing was not directly tied to an appraisal of internal controls. This direct relationship was not to come until some years later. The stated audit objectives changed; the techniques changed; but the attitude of the auditor was slow to change.

> *The adoption of sampling procedures probably represented the most important development in auditing during the early 1900's. Account analysis was done, but this seems to represent no departure from the point of view of the detailed auditor's, merely a substitution in the quantity of the work formerly done.*[16]

1933 TO 1940

The period encompassed by 1933 and 1940 is interesting not only because of the influence of the New York Stock Exchange and various governmental agencies on auditing, but also because of the relative confusion that existed regarding audit objectives. At the inception of this period some writers were begin-

[12] E. V. Spicer and E. C. Pegler, *Audit Programmes* (London: H. Foulkes Lynch & Co., 1910), p. 4.

[13] F. R. Carnegie Steele, "The Development of Systems of Control," *Journal of Accountancy,* 4 (October, 1913), 282. This excellent article was the first on the subject of internal control to appear in an American professional accounting magazine. Most of Mr. Steele's comments could be lifted verbatim from context and be as timely today as they were in 1913.

[14] Montgomery, *op. cit.,* p. 82.

[15] DeWitt Carl Eggleston, *Auditing Procedure* (New York: John Wiley & Sons, 1926), p. 19.

[16] Moyer, *op. cit.,* p. 7. It is interesting also to note that an auditing text published in 1919, *Auditing Procedure,* by William B. Castenholz made no mention of internal control or check, yet suggested that less than detailed testing was permissible.

ning to discount the significance of detection of fraud as an objective of auditing while others emphasized its importance. By the end of the eight years there was a fair degree of agreement that the auditor could not, and should not, be primarily concerned with the detection of fraud. This attitude was undoubtedly influenced by the McKesson Robbins case.

This transition in attitude is well demonstrated in successive editions of Montgomery's Auditing text during this period which stated: "An incidental, but nevertheless important, object of an audit is detection of fraud." (Fifth Edition, 1934, page 26.) "Primary responsibility . . . for the control and discovery of irregularities necessarily lies with the management." (Sixth Edition, 1940, page 13.)

Prior to 1940, uniform agreement as to audit responsibility for the detection of fraud did not exist. Other authors had stated: "It is well established that one of the main objects of an audit is the detection and prevention of fraud."[17] "The partial checking, or testing of a group of items is firmly established in audit procedure as a means of discovering the presence of fraud."[18] ". . . in the testing process, the auditor has a powerful weapon against fraud—one perhaps more potent than has heretofore been realized."[19]

The question of the importance of fraud detection during this period was a relative one; most authors agreed that the normal audit was primarily concerned with determining the fairness of reported financial statements but disagreed as to the role of tests designed to detect fraud.

Despite the disparity in defining audit objectives, there was nearly uniform agreement on audit techniques. By this time, testing was the rule, not the exception. The degree of testing decided upon was largely dependent on the effectiveness of internal control. Fairly typical of the acceptance of internal control as the basis for testing decisions are these three quotations:

> The first step to take when planning an audit by test methods consists of a thorough investigation of the system on which the books are kept. . . . It is not the auditor's sole duty to see that the internal check is carried out but to ascertain how much it can be relied upon to supplement his investigations.[20]
>
> It has been the accepted practice of public accountants to consider the adequacy of the system of internal check in determining the extent of the examination required.[21]

[17] L. F. Foster, "Internal Check," *Accountants Digest,* 1 (March 1936), 236.
[18] Lewis A. Carman, "The Efficacy of Tests,"*American Accountant,* 18 (December, 1933), 360.
[19] *Ibid.,* p. 366.
[20] Anonymous, "Test Methods in Auditing," *Accountants Digest,* 1 (March, 1936), 240.
[21] Victor H. Stempf, "Influence of Internal Control Upon Audit Procedure," *Journal of Accountancy,* 62 (September, 1936), 170.

> . . . audits consist largely of samplings, tests and checks. Their value depends on what are known as "internal checks and controls." Auditors are supposed to satisfy themselves that these internal checks and controls are adequate and, if they are, not to make a more complete examination. [22]

1940 TO 1960

Audit objectives and approach changed only slightly between 1940 and 1960. Emphasis continued to be placed on the determination of the fairness of financial statement representations with a corresponding deëmphasis on fraud detection. This was the attitude expressed by the American Institute of Certified Public Accountants and most accounting writers. Officially the Institute was on record as follows:

> The primary purpose of an examination of financial statements by an independent Certified Public Accountant is to enable him to express an opinion as to the fairness of the statements. . . .
>
> The ordinary examination incident to the issuance of an opinion respecting financial statements is not designed and cannot be relied upon to disclose defalcations and other similar irregularities. [23]

However, many audit techniques in this period were specifically designed to assist in the detection of fraud.

In addition to this disparity between stated audit objectives and certain techniques used in implementing those objectives, there was some disagreement in the literature as to the auditors' responsibility for performing tests to disclose fraud. Typical of the prominent accountants who accepted the position of the Institute with reservations was Samuel J. Broad: "The discovery of error and irregularities is still an objective [of auditing], but not the primary one." [24] Considering the importance placed on fraud detection in the history of auditing and the disagreement in the literature as to the subject, it was not surprising that much of the general public viewed the auditor as a detective.

1960 TO DATE

In "Statement on Auditing Procedure Number 30," published in the January 1961 *Journal of Accountancy*, The American Institute's Committee on Auditing Procedure undertook a clarification of the position quoted above from the

---

[22] Johnson Heywood, "Are Auditors Hard of Hearing?", *Nations Business*, January, 1940, as reviewed in *Accountants Digest*, 5 (March, 1940), 203.

[23] American Institute of CPA's, *Codification of Statements on Auditing Procedure* (New York: A.I.C.P.A. 1951), pp. 11, 12.

[24] Broad, *op. cit.*, p. 39.

1951 Codification. The general comments at the outset of Statement 30 serve primarily as a reaffirmation of the official Institute attitude communicated in the earlier Codification. In the latter paragraphs of the more recent Statement the Committee becomes somewhat more specific. They state that the auditor

> . . . recognizes that any fraud, if sufficiently material, may affect his opinion on the fairness of the presentation of the financial statements, and his examination made in accordance with generally accepted auditing standards gives consideration to this possibility.

And further,

> When an independent auditor's examination leading to an opinion on financial statements discloses specific circumstances which arouse his suspicion as to the existence of fraud, he should decide whether the fraud, if in fact it should exist, might be of such magnitude as to affect his opinion on the financial statements. If the independent auditor believes that fraud may have occurred which could be so material as to affect his opinion, he should reach an understanding with the proper representatives of the client as to whether the independent auditor or the client, subject to the independent auditor's review, is to make the investigation necessary to determine whether fraud in fact has occurred and, if so, the amount involved.

It is somewhat questionable whether this statement has provided the proper solution. Another look at current auditing objectives is necessary. The objective of the independent review of financial statements is the expression of an opinion as to the fairness of the representations included in those financial reports. In order to be in a position to form a professional opinion regarding the financial statements, the auditor must do sufficient work so as to be reasonably assured that there are no errors of commission or omission of sufficient materiality to misstate reported amounts. This is necessary regardless of the source of those errors. To deny responsibility for testing to determine if material fraud may exist because of any consideration of time or cost involved or because of the difficulties of detection is to reduce the value of the professional opinion.

The suggestion that a portion of the testing be shifted to the client creates many new problems. In line with generally accepted auditing standards, the auditor must determine that the client personnel performing the work are technically equipped and proficient, maintain the necessary independent attitude, and exercise the same professional care that the auditor himself would use. Further, it could be easily argued that in order to meet these professional standards, the auditor must actively supervise such tests and not confine his interest to a post-test review. Short of this, if material fraud is suspected there is little justification for rendering an opinion on the fairness of . . . statements.

Additional clarification relative to professional responsibility as to testing for defalcation is necessary. This can be accomplished best by a redefinition and restatement of audit objectives. Such a redefinition must include audit responsibility for performing tests designed to disclose all material misstatements of financial statements, whatever the source. Only then can the auditor's opinion be accorded the respect it deserves.

For some reason whenever the subject of fraud detection arises, special rules for audit responsibility are felt necessary. This is an unduly defensive position to assume. . . . the general rules governing audit responsibility in other areas . . . incorporate material fraud. As to any possible material misstatement of financial statements . . . the auditor's responsibility is to *perform tests* in line with generally accepted auditing standards. . . . The auditor is not responsible for detecting fraud, for example, but cannot and should not disclaim responsibility for *testing* for it within the course of his normal examination. That this is an existent consideration within most engagements few auditors will deny.

The final paragraph of Auditing Procedure Statement Number 30 is related to this argument:

> *The subsequent discovery that fraud existed during the period covered by the independent auditor's examination does not of itself indicate negligence. . . . He is not an insurer or guarantor and, if his examination was made with due professional skill and care, in accordance with generally accepted auditing standards, he has fulfilled all of the obligations implicit in his undertaking.*

Despite the existence of differences in opinion as to audit objectives, there is widespread general acceptance of the approach wherein the review of internal control is the starting point of the audit and the results of that review the basis for determining the extent of testing required.

> *In more recent years the independent auditor has gradually changed from a program of detailed auditing to one of test and analysis. It is no longer practical in large or even medium-sized companies to examine in detail the increased volume of transactions; nor is it necessary in view of the improvements in the organization of the clients' accounting and allied internal operations.*[25]

Summary

In most professions it is rather difficult to predict the future, but there are some significant trends revealed by the history of auditing which should carry forward into succeeding years. Interpreted in line with changing audit objectives and techniques these trends seem to indicate:

---

[25] Victor Z. Brink, "The Independent Auditor's Review of Internal Control," *Journal of Accountancy,* 73 (May, 1942), 430.

1 The first and foremost audit objective will remain the determination of the fairness of financial statement representations.

2 Reliance on the system of internal controls will increase. The audit will be primarily a system of audit of procedures. Detailed testing will take place only insofar as it is required to detect irregularities, errors, or to evaluate the effectiveness of the internal controls.

3 Since the fairness of the financial statement representations is affected by all material misstatements, there will be acceptance of the general responsibility of the auditor to perform tests to detect material defalcations and errors if they exist. This will be incorporated as a supplementary audit objective.

The evaluation of internal control effectiveness is destined to become the most important part of the auditor's program for evaluating fairness of financial statement presentations. The four conditions cited at the start of this article offer support to this conclusion. Auditing in the future will place a greater emphasis on system control techniques designed to insure reasonable accuracy and less emphasis on what has happened in the past. ". . . the modern audit . . . has shifted from a review of past operations to a review of the system of internal control."[26]

With the changes in objectives and techniques have come changes in auditor's reports. Report changes should logically follow changes in audit objectives. Brown's analysis of changing objectives can be juxtaposed with the following summary of changes in American auditors' reports in order to determine if this has been the case in the development of auditing in the United States.

THE AUDITOR'S REPORT:
ITS EVOLUTION IN THE U.S.A.
George Cochrane*

BACKGROUND: EVOLUTION OF THE REPORT

Reference will be made in the course of this paper to seven examples of auditor's reports which have been used at different periods in the United

* FCA, CPA, Partner, Haskins & Sells. This article is reproduced (in part) from a speech given by the late George Cochrane before the Institute of Chartered Accountants of England, Scotland and Wales and later reproduced in The Accountant, Vol. 123, No. 3959 (November 4, 1950), pp. 448–460.
26 Oswald Nielsen, "New Challenges in Accounting," Accounting Review, XXXV (October, 1960), 584.

States of America. The year given for each report indicates approximately the time when such report came into general use.

The forms of reports are those generally which have been used in connection with accounts submitted to stockholders by corporations engaged in industry and commerce.

Reports Nos. 4, 5, 6 and 7 have been used not only in connection with accounts submitted to stockholders but also in reporting on financial statements filed by companies with the Securities and Exchange Commission.

BASIS OF AUDITOR'S RESPONSIBILITIES

Since accountancy as a profession was introduced into the United States of America by British accountants during the second half of the nineteenth century, [British] auditing procedures were adopted by the early professional accountants in the United States. At the same time, the [British] report used in those days was generally adopted, even though neither the American auditor's responsibility nor his duties had any statutory background. . . .

Under the Federal laws there is no provision for the formation of public companies. Thus a public company must be organised under the laws of one of the states—and not necessarily the state in which it operates. While these laws, in general, are similar, they vary in a number of important particulars, but in one particular omission they are nearly all identical; except in one or two states, the corporation laws do not require accounts to be audited. Audit requirements generally arise from stock exchange listing agreements and regulations of the Securities and Exchange Commission.

In the absence of statutory provision, the responsibilities of professional accountants in examining accounts issued to stockholders depend for their definition on:

1 Acceptance of responsibilities imposed through codes of ethics adopted by the professional societies.

2 Pronouncements by the professional societies and the Securities and Exchange Commission of accepted principles of accounting and procedures and standards of auditing.

3 Court decisions under the general statutes.

Until well after the end of the first world war there were practically no court decisions dealing with the duties and responsibilities of the auditor, other than British decisions, which latter largely influenced the American accountant's thinking and, consequently, his procedures.

The absence of statutory provisions requiring the issuance of accounts to stockholders or the audit of accounts where they were required to be submitted, resulted in examinations which varied from a balance sheet audit to a full detailed examination, although the auditor's report might be couched in the same words. Usually the auditor was engaged by the directors or managing officers and the report was directed to them.

WORLD WAR I

The period of world war I, an eventful one for the public accountant everywhere, was particularly eventful for those practising in the United States of America. Roughly, that war marks the introduction of our first income-tax law (in 1916 the rate was 2 per cent, which to-day seems unbelievably low) and also the beginning of a great change in the investment habits of our citizens.

The rapid increase in the number of individual stockholders widened extensively the area in which corporate accounts carrying auditors' reports were circulated. As a result, there was a disproportionate increase in the number of those receiving such reports who were ignorant of their significance. Misunderstanding as to the object of the auditor's work was common, not only on the part of the average citizen but also on the part of bankers, credit grantors and business men.

It was widely believed, and to some extent still is, that the auditor's examination imbued the figures contained in financial statements with meticulous accuracy; that the auditor's opinion was a guarantee.

In an effort to correct these misunderstandings, a booklet known as 'A memorandum on balance sheet audits' was prepared by the American Institute of Accountants[1] at the request of the Federal Trade Commission, a government bureau, which approved the booklet and transmitted it to the Federal Reserve Board.

The Federal Reserve Board, after giving the document its provisional endorsement, published it in the Federal Reserve Bulletin of April, 1917. Reprints under the title 'Uniform accounting: a tentative proposal submitted by the Federal Reserve Board' were distributed for the consideration of banks, bankers and banking associations; merchants, manufacturers and associations of manufacturers; and auditors, accountants and associations of accountants.

The bulletin was reissued in 1918 under the same sponsorship with a new title—'Approved methods for the preparation of balance sheet statements'.

[1] In 1957 the name of the American Institute of Accountants was changed to American Institute of Certified Public Accountants.

There was practically no change from the 1917 issue except as indicated by the respective titles and a change in preface. The material contained in these bulletins was similar to that which is comprised in audit programmes.

This generally was the background of the independent public accountant in the United States of America in his auditing practice at the end of world war I.

ORIGIN OF 'CERTIFY'

Report No. I, used from about 1900 until well after world war I, was worded as follows:

> *We have audited the books and accounts of the ABC company for the year ended December 31, 1915, and we certify that, in our opinion, the above balance sheet correctly sets forth its position as at the termination of that year, and that the accompanying profit and loss account is correct.*

The description of the auditor's examination as an audit of the books and accounts, and the use of the words 'we certify', doubtless was due to the continuing influence of the English form of certificate. . . .

A profession, new in the United States, was growing up and the new accountant was willing to give his client what he wanted, i.e. a certificate, even in many cases capitalising the words 'WE HEREBY CERTIFY'. To this day we have not entirely overcome the effect of this practice on the public mentality.

By the end of world war I the United States had changed from a debtor to a creditor nation. The huge accumulation of wealth, extensively represented by government war bonds, released by the government policy of national debt reduction in the early 1920's, introduced a period of reinvestment, speculation and inflation encouraged by methods of financial reporting which, in some cases, as the period ran its course, became fantastic.

Efforts were continually made by outstanding accountants to discourage these misleading accounting and reporting methods but, unfortunately, the professional accountant was not then clothed with authority either by statute or by public acceptance. Corporate management frequently depended on its legal advisers for accounting advice and the efforts of accountants to obtain acceptance of the accounting principles involved were nullified by advice that the presentation desired by the company was legal.

Under the statutes of many of the states, it was, and still is, legally possible to carry out transactions having accounting results not in accord with accepted accounting principles. Accounting principles were not then well defined and there was authoritative support for many practices which are banned to-day. The accountant now would look through the legal concept and insist on the applicable accepted accounting concept.

As the 1920's progressed, accountants more and more frequently objected to the practices used and many insisted upon qualifications in their reports. The qualifications were made by use of the words, 'Subject to such and such, in our opinion,' or 'On the basis indicated, in our opinion'.

It was not until many years later that the American Institute of Accountants recommended that an opinion should not be given where the qualification was sufficiently material to negative the expression of an opinion.

During the entire period 1900 to 1929 the opinion paragraph of auditors' reports included, as alternatives to 'correctly sets forth', such phrases as 'exhibit a true and correct view', 'accurately record conditions', 'represent the true financial position'. The foregoing phrases implied a condition of exactitude which to-day is recognised as non-existent, in view of the conventions and philosophies which are the background of financial statements.

In the majority of instances only balance sheets were published during this earlier period and the auditor's work was generally confined to an examination known as a 'balance sheet audit'. The profit and loss account, referred to in Report No. I as correct, was usually one figure, shown on the balance sheet as the amount added to prior year's surplus, without any supporting statement.

THE SITUATION IN 1929

During the year 1929 the bulletin 'Approved methods for the preparation of balance sheet statements', which had been in use over ten years, was revised by a committee of the American Institute of Accountants. The revised bulletin, entitled 'Verification of financial statements', was issued by the Federal Reserve Board for the consideration of bankers, merchants, manufacturers, auditors and accountants. Issuance to accountants was necessary because the membership of the American Institute of Accountants in 1929 totalled only 2,185 and other accountants, who were not members, numbered over 11,000. Even as late as 1929 the authority of the profession to speak on accounting matters had not reached a level where its pronouncements were accepted without the support of other authority.

The preface to this bulletin stated that

> the scope of the work indicated in these instructions includes a verification of the assets and liabilities of a business enterprise at a given date; a verification of the profit and loss account for the period under review and, incidentally, an examination of the accounting system for the purpose of ascertaining the effectiveness of the internal check. . . . The extent of the verification will be determined by the conditions in each concern.

While emphasis on the verification of the assets and liabilities was still retained, the verification of the profit and loss account was now added and was much more detailed than before.

The additional concepts recorded in the 1929 bulletin were:

1 That the profit and loss (or income) account is of primary importance and, in consequence, that more audit work needs to be applied to profit and loss (or income) accounts.

2 That the auditor properly places reliance on internal control (where it exists) and need not check in detail each transaction.

Instructions were given in the bulletin as to the scope of the examination and the manner in which it should be carried out, if a report and opinion were to be issued.

It was also recommended that the profit and loss account should be prepared in very much greater detail than formerly, so as to reveal the operating results for the period under review. Corresponding figures for one or more prior years also should be furnished, as being valuable information for the stockholder, prospective investor and the prospective credit grantor.

Report No. 2, still referred to as a certificate, was devised to meet the requirements of this bulletin and read as follows:

We have examined the accounts of the ABC company for the period from January 1 to December 31, 1929.

We certify that the accompanying balance sheet and statement of profit and loss, in our opinion, set forth the financial condition of the company at December 31, 1929, and the results of operations for the period.

It will be noted that this report did not refer to an examination of the books but only of the accounts, and the opinion covered not only the balance sheet but the statement of profit and loss, as setting forth the financial condition and the results of the operations for the period.

THE ULTRAMARES CASE (1931)

As pointed out above, the corporation laws do not provide definitions of auditors' duties or responsibilities as such. Up to this time it had seemed to accountants self-evident that, if they were challenged, their liability would be measured by the principle of law that anyone who holds himself out to be skilled in any trade or profession and who is negligent in the performance of his work, becomes responsible for damages only to his client. In the case of an auditor, the client was the board of directors or the management that engaged him.

In the year 1931 there occurred an event which jarred the accountants' complacency and caused the adoption of Report No. 3 (page 25).

A suit, dealing with their responsibilities and liabilities as auditors, was brought against a firm of professional accountants. This suit has become known as the *Ultramares* case. After being heard in the lower courts, the suit finally reached the Court of Appeals of the State of New York, the highest court in that state. The court held that an auditor's obligation under his contract is to his client only and to him he is responsible for negligence. Third parties not privy to the contract cannot hold the auditor for negligence. There must be a greater degree of culpability than mere negligence, as liability of the auditor to third parties must lie in tort, and, therefore, gross negligence or fraud must be shown. The court said:

> . . . *although bankers, other credit grantors and investors may predicate their actions upon auditors' reports, it is obvious that no privity of contract can exist between the auditor and the public. The auditor's liability to third parties is based upon the law of torts.*

Negligence upon the part of an auditor,

> *creates no liability to third parties unless the negligence is so great as to be deemed equivalent to fraud. In that case there must be a false representation of a material fact known to be false by the party making it, or else recklessly made; the misrepresentation must be made with intent to deceive and for the purpose of inducing the other party to act upon it; the other party must, in fact, have relied upon it to his injury or damage.*

The court continued:

> . . . *our holding does not emancipate accountants from the consequences of fraud. It does not relieve them if their audit has been so negligent as to justify a finding that they had no belief in its adequacy, for this again is fraud. It does no more than say that if less than this is proved, if there has been neither reckless mis-statement nor insincere profession of an opinion, but only honest blunder, the ensuing liability for negligence is one that is bounded by the contract and is to be enforced by the parties between whom the contract is made.*

This decision was the most important rendered up to that time in the United States of America involving the duties and responsibilites of an accountant to his client.

Substantially, the question was whether or not the audit had been so grossly negligent as to constitute constructive fraud. If less than that were proved, the ensuing liability was one for negligence and could sustain a cause for action only by the party by whom the accountant had been engaged. The case was referred back to the trial court for rehearing but, unfortunately for the profession at large, was settled before retrial.

The Journal of Accountancy for July, 1931, made the following editorial comment:

> *If we interpret this decision as the language seems to justify and if we may attempt to put it into an ordinary straight-forward statement, it seems that the sum of the whole matter is this: Gross negligence may be regarded as evidence that fraud may have existed.*

The Journal of Accountancy also asked the rhetorical question: 'What is the accountant to do?' and supplied an answer indicating further changes which were later made in accountants' reports:

> *Every accountant's report will be addressed to the client only . . . the accountant will divide his report into two sections, one dealing with fact (that is, scope of examination) and one with opinion. . . . The accountant perhaps should abandon certificates and merely make reports. . . . The world "certify" which has been used for many years is quite inappropriate and should be abandoned. . . . It is absurd to speak of certifying an opinion.*

Accountants, therefore, by again changing the wording of their reports, endeavoured to make clear that the report was an opinion and not a guarantee. The word 'certify' was eliminated and words indicating agreement with the books were removed. Report No. 3 read:

> *We have examined the accounts of the ABC company for the year ended December 31, 1931. In our opinion the accompanying balance sheet and statement of profit and loss set forth the financial condition of the company at December 31, 1931, and the results of its operations for the year ended that date.*

CORRESPONDENCE WITH THE STOCK EXCHANGE (1932–34)

NEED FOR IMPROVEMENT IN FINANCIAL REPORTING

The period of the 1920's ended with the stock market crash of October, 1929.

Demands arose from the public, professional and laymen alike, that methods be formulated which would avoid the repetition of the misleading financial reporting practices of the past years.

Recognising the need for leadership, conferences were instituted between the special Committee on Co-operation with Stock Exchanges of the American Institute of Accountants and the Committee on Stock List of the New York Stock Exchange. The latter committee reviews applications from corporations for trading privileges on the exchange. The conferences commenced in September, 1932, and continued to January, 1934. They were conducted in an atmosphere of political change, economic confusion, financial disruption and suspicion, all of which brought about the far-reaching economic and social changes symbolised by the term 'The New Deal'.

On September 22, 1932, the Institute's committee, in a letter to the Committee on Stock List, stated that the nature of a balance sheet or an income account was quite generally misunderstood, even by writers on financial and accounting subjects. Consequently there were two major tasks to be accomplished:

1 to educate the public in regard to the significance of accounts, their value and their unavoidable limitations; and

2 to make the accounts published by corporations more informative and authoritative.

Alternatives for improving the existing situation were suggested. First, the selection by competent authority, out of the body of acceptable methods in vogue, of detailed sets of rules which would become binding on all corporations of a given class. This procedure had been applied broadly to railroads and other regulated utilities. The committee felt, however, that there were overwhelming arguments against any attempt to apply this procedure in industrial corporations.

The second alternative and, in the committee's opinion, the more practical one, was to leave every corporation free to choose its own method of accounting within very broad limits—but to require disclosure of the methods employed and consistency in their application from year to year.

DETAILED SUGGESTIONS BY AMERICAN INSTITUTE OF ACCOUNTANTS TO THE NEW YORK STOCK EXCHANGE

The letter from the American Institute of Accountants listed a limited number of suggestions designed in part to carry out the general objective expressed above.

The committee advised the stock exchange that the principal objects which should be kept constantly in mind were:

1 To bring about a better recognition by the investing public of the fact that the balance sheet of a large modern corporation does not and should not be expected to represent an attempt to show present values of the assets and liabilities of the corporation.

2 To emphasise the fact that balance sheets are necessarily to a large extent historical and conventional in character, and to encourage the adoption of revised forms of balance sheets which disclose more clearly on what basis assets of various kinds are stated (for example, cost, reproduction cost less depreciation, estimated going-concern value, cost or market whichever is lower, liquidation value).

3 To emphasise the cardinal importance of the income account, such importance being explained by the fact that the value of a business is dependent mainly on its earning capacity; and to take the position that an annual income account is unsatisfactory unless it is so framed as to constitute the best reflection, reasonably obtainable, of the earning capacity of the business under the conditions existing during the year to which it relates.

4 To make universal the acceptance, by listed corporations, of certain broad and generally accepted principles of accounting, and within the limits of such broad principles to make no attempt to restrict the right of corporations to select detailed methods of accounting which they consider best adapted to the requirements of their business, but:

   a To ask each listed corporation to formulate a statement of the methods of accounting and reporting it employed in sufficient detail to be a guide to its accounting department; to have the statement adopted by its board so as to be binding on its accounting officers; and to furnish the statement to the exchange and make it available to any stockholder on request and upon payment, if desired, of a reasonable fee.

   b To secure assurances: (1) that the methods so formulated will be followed consistently from year to year; and (2) that if any change in the principles or any material change in the manner of application is made, the stockholders and the exchange shall be advised when the first accounts are presented in which effect is given to such change.

   c To endeavour to bring about a change in the form of audit 'certificate' so that the auditors would specifically report to the shareholders whether the accounts as presented were properly prepared in accordance with the methods of accounting regularly employed by the company, defined as already indicated.

REQUEST TO LISTED COMPANIES

In January, 1933, the President of the New York Stock Exchange addressed a letter to the presidents of all corporations listed on that exchange, as follows:

The New York Stock Exchange has recently announced its intention of requiring audited listing applications after July 1, 1933. The public response to this announcement indicates clearly that independent audits are regarded by investors as a useful safeguard.

If, however, such a safeguard is to be really valuable and not illusory, it is essential that audits should be adequate in scope and the responsibility assumed by the auditor should be defined. . . .

The letter went on to say:

. . . in furtherance of this end we should be greatly obliged if you will secure from your auditors upon the completion of the audit for the year 1932 and furnish to the Committee on Stock List for its use and not for publication, a letter which will contain information on the following points:

1 *Whether the scope of the audit conducted by them is as extensive as that contemplated in the Federal Reserve bulletin, "Verification of financial statements".*

2 *Whether all subsidiary companies controlled by your company have been audited by them. If not, it is desired that the letter should indicate the relative importance of subsidiaries not audited as measured by the amount of assets and earnings of such companies in comparison with the total consolidated assets and earnings, and should also indicate clearly on what evidence the auditors have relied in respect of such subsidiaries.*

3 *Whether all the information essential to an efficient audit has been furnished to them.*

4 *Whether in their opinion the form of the balance sheet and of the income, or profit and loss, account is such as fairly to present the financial position and the results of operation.*

5 *Whether the accounts are in their opinion fairly determined on the basis of consistent application of the system of accounting regularly employed by the company.*

6 *Whether such system in their opinion conforms to accepted accounting practices, and particularly whether it is in any respect inconsistent with any of the principles set forth in the statement attached hereto.*

This request made it necessary for the auditors of all listed companies to review their procedures. In those cases where the procedures had not been as full as were required by the bulletin 'Verification of financial statements', arrangements were made for such work to be carried out in future.

A letter dated December 21, 1933, addressed by the American Institute of Accountants to the Committee on Stock List said, in part:

While agreeing with your committee that in the case of large companies the safeguarding of transactions is primarily a matter of internal organisation, we should like to make it clear that we fully appreciate the value of the detailed audit in appropriate cases. Where the internal check and control are necessarily limited or severly restricted, the detailed audit serves a most useful purpose, though no audit should be regarded as taking the place of sound measures of internal check and control, except in cases where the organisation is so small as to make adequate internal check impracticable.

The letter then referred to the bulletin 'Verification of financial statements', as revised by the American Institute of Accountants in 1929, the first sentence in the general instructions of which read, in part:

The scope of the work indicated in these instructions includes . . . an examination of the accounting system for the purpose of ascertaining the effectiveness of the internal check.

In commenting on this excerpt from the bulletin, the Institute added:

We would, however, point out that it is always a matter of judgment on the part of corporate management to weigh the risks against which safeguards are desirable in comparison with the cost of providing safeguards. The whole matter lies in the field of discretion, and if in any case a defalcation should occur and escape detection, the accountants cannot be expected to accept any financial responsibility, but only to accept such blame as may attach to a possible error of judgment on their part with respect to their review of the methods and extent of the internal check and control.

THE AUDITOR'S NEW REPORT

Arising out of the correspondence above referred to, Report No. 4 was suggested:

> We have made an examination of the balance sheet of the ABC company as at December 31, 1933, and of the statement of income and surplus for the year 1933. In connection therewith, we examined or tested accounting records of the company and other supporting evidence and obtained information and explanations from officers and employees of the company; we also made a general review of the accounting methods and of the operating and income accounts for the year, but we did not make a detailed audit of the transactions.

> In our opinion, based upon such examination, the accompanying balance sheet and related statement of income and surplus fairly present, in accordance with accepted principles of accounting consistently maintained by the company during the year under review, its position at December 31, 1933, and the results of its operations for the year.

This report was submitted by the Committee of the American Institute of Accountants with the following suggestions:

> It is contemplated that before signing a report of the type suggested, the accountant should have at least made an examination of the character outlined in the bulletin, "Verification of financial statements".

> The report should be addressed to the directors of the company or to the stockholders, if the appointment is made by them.

> The statement of what has been examined would, of course, conform to the titles of the accounts or statements reported upon.

> In the second sentence, any special forms of confirmation could be mentioned, e.g. "including confirmation of cash and securities by inspection or certificates from depositaries".

> This certificate is appropriate only if the accounting for the year is consistent in basis with that for the preceding year. If there has been any material change, either in accounting principles or in the manner of their application, the nature of the change should be indicated.

> It is contemplated that the form of report be modified when and as necessary to embody any qualifications, reservations or supplementary explanations.

While the requirements here outlined could only be enforced against companies listed on the Stock Exchange and their auditors, it immediately became
evident that the accounts of unlisted companies and the examination thereof
by accountants might well be considered inadequate unless the requirements
had been met.

THE SECURITIES ACT AND OTHER
LEGISLATION (1933–40)

SCOPE OF THE ACTS

The conferences between the committee of the American Institute of Accountants and the New York Stock Exchange during the two-year period, 1932–34,
were carried on against a background of severe public criticism of the financial
community and corporate management throughout the United States.

The Congress of the United States passed a series of Acts, i.e. the Securities
Act of 1933, the Securities Exchange Act of 1934, the Public Utility Holding
Company Act of 1935 and the Investment Company Act of 1940.

While the scope of these Acts is nation-wide and they regulate many matters
which previously had been considered the exclusive field of state legislation,
the number of companies required to register under these Acts is but a small
proportion of the companies doing business in the United States.

A commission composed of five commissioners appointed by the President of the United States of America was given authority to make, amend and
rescind rules and regulations necessary to carry out the provisions of the Acts.

The commission was authorised to prescribe the form in which should be
set forth the items or details in balance sheets or earnings statements to be
submitted to the commission. It was also to prescribe the methods to be followed in the preparation of the accounts, in the appraisal or valuation of assets
or liabilities, in the determination of depreciation and depletion, in the differentiation of recurring and nonrecurring income and of investment and operating income and other matters.

The Acts also reversed the rule that the burden of proof should be on the
accuser and, where the Acts were operative, placed this burden on the accused.
The only other Acts where this is so are the Income Tax Acts.

The accounting and auditing procedures required by the Securities and Exchange Commission and the penalties for failure to follow these procedures
do not apply to balance sheets and accounts submitted by corporations to their
stockholders or to the accounts of corporations not registered with the commission.

Nevertheless, if statements submitted to stockholders become the subject of litigation, it is believed the courts will take judicial notice of the accounting requirements of the Securities Acts and the type of disclosure required by these Acts. Consequently, great attention is now given to disclosure in corporations' accounts to stockholders, and such statements are little, if any, more condensed than similar statements supplied to the Securities and Exchange Commission. However, the detailed schedules required by the commission, as a rule, are not issued to stockholders.

Considerations of disclosure frequently cause the addition of notes to stockholders' accounts. Such notes may be added for the purpose of elaboration, but an item which is incorrect cannot be corrected by a note. When correction is needed it must be given effect in the statement. . . .

AUDITORS' LIABILITIES UNDER SECURITIES ACT

The civil liabilities affecting auditors under the Securities Act of 1933, as amended, are:

Section II (a)

In case any part of the registration statement, when such part became effective, contained an untrue statement of a material fact or omitted to state a material fact required to be stated therein, or necessary to make the statements therein not misleading, any person acquiring such security (unless it is proved that at the time of such acquisition he knew of such untruth or omission) may . . . sue . . . every accountant, . . . who has with his consent been named as having . . . certified any part of the registration statement, . . . with respect to the statement in such registration statement, . . . which purports to have been . . . certified by him.

The suit may be to recover damages representing the difference between the amount paid for the security and (1) its value at the time the suit was brought, or (2) the price at which the security had been disposed of in the market before the suit was brought, or (3) the price at which the security had been disposed of after the suit.

Liability may attach to an auditor under the Act for an error of judgment regarding the extent of the examination which he should have made, or through honest error or oversight on the part of an assistant normally competent and reliable. Obviously the cost, if an accountant is held liable, may amount to a very substantial sum.

The liability is somewhat complicated by the provision of the code, that reasonable belief by an expert as to truth and material fact must extend in point of time until the statements filed with the commission have become effective. This latter date almost invariably is later than the date of the auditor's report.

The standard of reasonableness when applied to the investigation to be made shall be that required of a prudent man in the management of his own property.

The Act, of course, placed a new and heavy responsibility on the professional accountant and, of necessity, increased his authority.

Consideration by the commission's staff, of the accounting principles used by the companies filing reports and of the audit procedures undertaken by the independent accountant in such cases, has led to a much wider knowledge of what is and is not, being done by corporations and accountants. Accounting principles and auditing procedures in specific cases are the subject of frequent conferences between the appropriate committees of the American Institute of Accountants and the commission's staff, in order to arrive at definitions satisfactory to both or an understanding of differences, when they exist.

BULLETIN—'EXAMINATION OF FINANCIAL STATEMENTS'—(1936)

The American Institute of Accountants, as the authoritative representative of a profession now well established in the business community, undertook the responsibility of revising earlier pamphlets and in 1936 issued a bulletin known as the 'Examination of financial statements by independent public accountants'. The preface stated that 'developments of accounting practice during recent years have been in the direction of increased emphasis on accounting principles and consistency in their application and a fuller disclosure of the basis on which the accounts are stated'. These developments had been accelerated by the prominence given to them in regulations of the Securities and Exchange Commission dealing with financial statements and also in the correspondence between the American Institute of Accountants and the New York Stock Exchange.

The bulletin pointed out that the suggestions were intended to apply to examinations by independent public accountants of financial statements prepared for credit purposes and for annual reports to stockholders.

A MAJOR FRAUD CASE (1939)

FEATURES OF THE CASE

American accountants had but commenced to practise in accordance with the 1936 bulletin when a serious fraud was disclosed in the accounts of *McKesson*

& *Robbins, Incorporated,* which, for many years, had been audited by a prominent firm of independent accountants.

In the consolidated balance sheet of the company with a total of about $87 million of assets, approximately $19 million were found to be entirely fictitious —fictitious inventory items amounting to $10 million and fictitious accounts receivable amounting to $9 million. The case had a number of unique features: invoices, advices, shipping and other documents using fictitious names; recording fictitious transactions; forged contracts, guarantees and supposedly independent credit rating reports.

The president of the company had been living under a false name and was assisted in his malpractices by three brothers, also using false names, and occupying, respectively, the positions of assistant treasurer, manager of receiving, shipping and warehousing, and manager of offices, mailing, bank accounts and other activities. The president of the company had previously been convicted of commercial fraud, carried out in co-operation with his brothers. Before the investigation had proceeded far, the president committed suicide.

S.E.C. HEARING

After a great deal of ill-informed discussion in the public press and investigation by both federal and state officers, a hearing was held before the Securities and Exchange Commission with three particular objectives. First, the ascertainment of the character, detail and scope of the audit procedure which had been carried out. Second, the extent to which prevailing and generally accepted standards of audit procedure had been adhered to and applied. Third, the adequacy of the safeguards inherent in the generally accepted audit procedure to assure reliability and accuracy of financial statements. Many expert witnesses were called and the whole matter was very thoroughly reviewed. There is no point, at this time, in reviewing all the matters taken up but, because of their relative size and the outcome, particular attention may be directed to inventories and accounts receivable.

The Securities and Exchange Commission, in regard to accounts receivable, found that, as a whole, the audit programme conformed to then generally accepted procedures for an examination of financial statements, although confirmation of the accounts receivable by direct communication with the debtor was not included in the programme. The facts of the case demonstrated the utility of circularisation and the desirability of this procedure.

However, there seemed to exist a difference of opinion among accountants as to the extent of the auditor's duties and responsibility in physical verification of quantities, quality and condition of inventories. A substantial proportion of the profession took the position that investigation of quantities, quality and condition should be confined to the records. An equally authoritative opinion supported the view that auditors should make physical inspection of the inventory, either by test-counts, by observation of inventory-taking, or by a combination of these methods.

The outcome of this inquiry was to make the confirmation of receivables and contact with inventories by observation of inventory-taking mandatory audit procedures.

AMERICAN INSTITUTE RECOMMENDATIONS

The report of the Securities and Exchange Commission was not released until 1940 and by that time the American Institute of Accountants had adopted modifications of the bulletin 'Examination of financial statements' issued in 1936. The modifications were published in a pamphlet called 'Extensions of auditing procedure', which became the first of a series of twenty-four statements on auditing procedure subsequently issued by the Institute.

Recognising the obvious requirements of the evidence before the commission, there was introduced into a new Report, No. 5, the statement that a review of the system of internal control had been carried out and that the examination had been made 'by methods and to the extent deemed appropriate'. The report, recommended by the American Institute of Accountants, read:

> We have examined the balance sheet of the ABC company as of December 31, 1939, and the statements of income and surplus for the fiscal year then ended, have reviewed the system of internal control and the accounting procedures of the company and, without making a detailed audit of the transactions, have examined or tested accounting records of the company and other supporting evidence, by methods and to the extent we deemed appropriate.

> In our opinion, the accompanying balance sheet and related statements of income and surplus present fairly the position of the ABC company at December 31, 1939, and the results of its operations for the fiscal year, in conformity with generally accepted accounting principles applied on a basis consistent with that of the preceding year.

The use of this report (in the light of 'Extensions of auditing procedure') required the auditor to satisfy himself, by suitable observation and inquiry, as to the effectiveness of the methods of inventory taking and the measure of reliance which could be placed on the inventory records and the clients' representations as to quantity and condition. The American Institute's recommendation, however, laid special emphasis on the fact that the auditor did not hold himself out as a general appraiser, valuer or expert in materials. Implicit in the new report also was the representation that accounts receivable had been confirmed by direct correspondence where appropriate.

The finding and conclusions of the Securities and Exchange Commission upon the conclusion of the inquiry into the *McKesson and Robbins* case eventually were made effective for the purposes of the commission by amending their rules. In issuing this amendment, the commission stated that the auditor's Report No. 5 recommended by the American Institute of Accountants was defective for the purposes of the commission, in that the report did not state whether the examination had been made in accordance with generally accepted auditing standards applicable in the circumstances and did not state whether any procedures deemed necessary by the auditor had been omitted.

In order to meet the commission's view, Report No. 5, recommended by the American Institute of Accountants, was amended by the addition of the following words to the first paragraph:

> *Our examination was made in accordance with generally accepted auditing standards applicable in the circumstances and included all procedures we considered necessary.*

So Report No. 6 became the report in general use and read:

> *We have examined the balance sheet of the ABC company as of February 28, 1941, and the statements of income and surplus for the fiscal year then ended, have reviewed the system of internal control and the accounting procedures of the company and, without making a detailed audit of the transactions, have examined or tested accounting records of the company and other supporting evidence, by methods and to the extent we deemed appropriate. Our examination was made in accordance with generally accepted auditing standards applicable in the circumstances and it included all procedures which we considered necessary.*

> *In our opinion, the accompanying balance sheet and related statements of income and surplus present fairly the position of the ABC company at February 28, 1941, and the results of its operations for the fiscal year, in conformity with generally accepted accounting principles applied on a basis consistent with that of the preceding year.*

THE REPORT TO-DAY

Finally, in 1949, Report No. 7 was introduced, after nearly twenty years of practice under conditions which had grown out of the correspondence with the Stock Exchange and the creation of the Securities and Exchange Commission. This report read:

> *We have examined the balance sheet of ABC company as of December 31, 1949, and the related statements of income and surplus for the year then ended.*

Our examination was made in accordance with generally accepted auditing standards, and accordingly included such tests of the accounting records and such other auditing procedures as we considered necessary in the circumstances.

In our opinion, the accompanying balance sheet and statements of income and surplus present fairly the financial position of ABC company at December 31, 1949, and the results of its operations for the year then ended, in conformity with generally accepted accounting principles applied on a basis consistent with that of the preceding year.

Auditing standards had now been established through the issuance of the American Institute of Accountants' 'Tentative statement of auditing standards' and the auditor's report was required to state that the examination had been carried out in accordance with such standards.

As it was now widely known and accepted that an auditor relied, and was entitled to rely, on the internal control in existence and on testing and sampling, rather than detailed examination, reference to these facts in the report was no longer required.

About 1948, the 1936 bulletin 'Examination of financial statements' was recognized as obsolete, in view of the numerous important developments since its publication, and was allowed to go out of print. In June, 1950, the American Institute of Accountants published a new pamphlet, 'Audits by certified public accountants' which summarises all the auditing standards and procedures agreed upon up to that time.

INDUCTIVE ANALYSIS
OF PROFESSIONAL EVOLUTION

 The expression of an opinion by an auditor on financial statements contemporarily represents the outcome of the attest function. This attest function serves to satisfy a social need. Throughout history the nature of the attest function has changed to satisfy the needs of the time. Below are four descriptions or manifestations of the work of auditors at different times in history. From a reading of them, answer the following questions:

1 What changes have occurred in the nature of the attest function from the year 1400 to the present? Indicate any weaknesses present in Brown's analysis.

2 If the past changes in the audit function are projected into the future, what might the role of the auditor be in the year 2000?

I. AUDITING IN THE FIFTEENTH CENTURY

The following is excerpted from: Barbara Ross, "The Accounts of the Stewards of the Talbot Household at Blakemere: An Example of Medieval Accounting Practice," *Abacus* IV, 1 (August, 1968), pp. 51–72.

By the third decade of the fifteenth century, the Talbot family, largely through judicious marriages, had accumulated valuable and extensive English estates, both in Yorkshire in the north, and in Shropshire, Gloucestershire, and Herefordshire on the Welsh Marches. The manor of Blakemere, the ancient seat of the Le Strange family, is near the small country town of Whitchurch in north Shropshire, and was added to the Talbot holdings by the marriage of Richard, fourth Lord Talbot, to the heiress Ankaretta Le Strange.

The surviving documents relating to Blakemere are accounts of various officials there, namely, the rent collectors of the vills, the receiver, the bailiff of the manor and the steward of the household; as well, there are court rolls of the manor and hundred courts held at Whitchurch. Although the account documents are not numerous nor in an unbroken sequence, they are nevertheless informative about conditions and administrative procedures in the household for the period c. 1390–1420. . . .

The items which are disallowed by the auditors in the accounts of the bailiff or any other Blakemere ministers are always those where the accountant acted on his own responsibility and either had no evidence of the transaction such as a tally or indenture, or else could not produce any authority from the lord in the shape of warrants, letters, or writs.

The audit process, incidentally, is mentioned only briefly in the extant Blakemere accounts. The only indication of the time of the year at which it was held is in the receiver's account of 14–15 Henry VI when 17's is allowed for:

the expenses of Richard Legett receiver-general of the lord and auditor of said lord staying here (Blakemere) for hearing and completing the accounts of the ministers, of this lordship with members, together with the expenses of the said ministers and others coming there on behalf of the lord for six days in October at the end of this account.

There are no receiver-general's accounts in existence, but the anomaly whereby the official who was the ultimate receiver of the cash profits of his lord's lands was also the auditor would no doubt be removed when he himself would be called upon to answer for his own 'stewardship' before the lord and his council.

There are several indications that the lord was present at the audit and was called upon to verify statements made by the accountant. For instance in the account of Thomas Clerc, receiver for 17–18 Richard II (he also held the position of household steward), under the heading liberacio denariorum, *there is the entry:*

And paid to the lord on various occasions as appears in detail in a certain schedule reserved at this account and shown before the lord and which the lord acknowledges that he has received, 24. 7s. 7d.

This is crossed out, the considerably smaller sum of 53s 4d is substituted, and above is written 'because the lord repudiates this'. The next entry has a similar turn of phrase except that it is the lady who is involved; in this case the amount is acknowledged and allowed to stand. . . .

Once the auditors had allowed an item at the audit it was presumed that the transaction was fair and just and the amount consumed reasonable and fitting. The economizing which such an attitude would imply is quite foreign to medieval notions of generosity, largesse and munificence, which were regarded as necessary attributes for any person of rank. . . .

Du Boulay's remark that an audit was more like a plea or a court hearing than a piece of arithmetic reveals the basic reasoning behind these and many other medieval accounts. The official rendering the account must give a true statement of his stewardship of the powers and assests invested in him by his lord, complete with all the warrants and authorities which his activities required. The lord and his auditors wished to know what the official had done, by what authority he had done it, and what the results of his actions were. If he had erred and the results were unfortunate, the official nevertheless had to stand by his actions and eventually make them good.

Then, as now, there may well have been fraudulent office holders, and there may well have been varying types of malpractice. But it is surely misleading to assume that the procedures as described developed only in response to the need to detect such frauds. The primary purpose of the accounting practices, culminating in an audit, was to investigate whether the holder of an office was serving his lord's interests in a proper and diligent manner, and to record his actions and their consequences within a clearly defined area of responsibility. As a result, weak and unsatisfactory officials, as well as any fraudulent activities, would become known to the lord.

II. A GUIDE TO PRACTICE, CIRCA 1910

The following admonishment to prospective auditors is reproduced from: *Auditing (Lesson XII of Volume II, Higher Accounting)* (332), The Business Man's Publishing Co., Ltd., Detroit, 1910.

The Object of an Audit

Periodical examinations of the accounts of commercial and financial institutions, special examinations for prospective investors, investigations on behalf of creditors and trustees in bankruptcy, examinations to ascertain the cause of decreasing profits, exhaustive audits preparatory to installing improved systems of financial cost accounts and investigations of the accounts of public officials at the behest of dissatisfied citizens, are but a few of the many purposes which clients have in mind when desiring to have accounts of an undertaking audited.

The object of the auditor should be, in the main, threefold: (1) Detection of fraud. (2) Discovery of errors of principle. (3) Verification of the mechanical accuracy of accounts. As has been pointed out by many writers, the attempted concealment of fraud must be accomplished by commission of either an error of principle or one in the mechanical work of the accounts; owing, therefore, to its importance, and often its predominating importance, the detection of frauds is conceded a separate place among the objects of an audit. From first to last it is the auditor's duty to be on the lookout for fraud. Nine times out of ten the client who determines upon an audit suspects no one in his employ in the slightest of dishonesty, and yet experience teaches that in nine cases out of ten it is where they are least expected that fraud and dishonesty are discovered. This should not be taken to mean that all the employees in a client's office are to be suspected of being rogues masquerading as honest men — on the contrary, every man is held to be innocent until proven to be otherwise — but it does mean that the auditor must be vigilant and not forget that occasionally, or we may even say frequently, "appearances are deceitful." Errors of principle are as often found to be errors of omission as of commission, and it is here that an initial audit most often bears its fruit. As regards verifying the mechanical accuracy of accounts, it is, of course, preposterous to suppose that an auditor in the limited time at his disposal could be expected to verify every footing, every posting, and all the other routine details of a set of accounts. The verification incident to and necessitated by the attainment of the first two objects is usually sufficient to reasonably satisfy him of the correctness of the accounts from this standpoint.

III. A REPRESENTATIVE AUDITOR'S OPINION IN 1920

PRICE, WATERHOUSE & CO.
Union Trust Building

Detroit, Mich.,
March 26, 1920.

To the Stockholders of
The Willys-Overland Company,
Toledo, Ohio.

We have examined the books and accounts of The Willys-Overland Company and of its subsidiary and affiliated Companies for the year ending on December 31, 1919, and certify that the attached Consolidated Balance Sheet at that date and relative Income Account are correctly prepared therefrom.

We have satisfied ourselves that only actual additions and extensions to the properties during the year have been added to the capital accounts, and that adequate provision has been made out of the earnings for accruing renewals and depreciation.

Having regard to the serious setback in production caused by the strike in the summer of 1919, a further interruption of manufacturing operations for the purposes of stock-taking at December 31, 1919, was deemed undesirable and no physical inventory was, therefore, taken at the factories at that date. The Materials, Supplies, and Finished and Partly Finished Parts on hand at the factories are accordingly included at the book valuations which the responsible officials have certified to the best of their knowledge and belief to be correct and conservatively stated. The stocks at the distributing branches shown by certified inventories have been carefully valued at or below cost prices, and we have satisfied ourselves that all inter-company profits have been eliminated.

We have verified the cash and securities owned by actual inspection or by certificates from the depositories, and have satisfied ourselves that full provision has been made for Bad and Doubtful Accounts Receivable and for all ascertained liabilities; and

WE CERTIFY that, in our opinion, the Balance Sheet is properly drawn up and on the basis indicated above, shows the true financial position of the Company and its Subsidiary Companies on December 31, 1919, and that the relative Income Account correctly sets forth the Earnings for the year ending on that date.

PRICE, WATERHOUSE & CO.

IV. THE STANDARD SHORT-FORM OPINION CURRENTLY IN USE

TO THE BOARD OF DIRECTORS OF X COMPANY:

We have examined the balance sheet of X Company as of

December 31, 19X6, and the related statements of income and retained earnings for the year then ended. Our examination was made in accordance with generally accepted auditing standards, and accordingly included such tests of the accounting records and such other auditing procedures as we considered necessary in the circumstances.

In our opinion, the accompanying balance sheet and statements of income and retained earnings present fairly the financial position of X Company at December 31, 19X6, and the results of its operations for the year then ended, in conformity with generally accepted accounting principles applied on a basis consistent with that of the preceding year.

/s/ SMITH & SMITH
Certified Public Accountants

CHAPTER 2

CPA PROFILES:
PAST, PRESENT, AND FUTURE

Until the second half of this century, the general public knew little about CPAs. However, as early as the 1930s, the investing public began to take an interest in them. The auditing function and the men who performed it in America were first discussed in the following 1932 profile of the audit profession.

CERTIFIED PUBLIC ACCOUNTANTS
(Anon.)*

Towards the turn of the century, there sprang up in this country a new profession. Already established abroad, it followed English investments to the U.S., watched over them, took root. Today it is no overstatement to say that there are preëminently three professions upon whose ethics as well as upon whose skill modern society depends: law, medicine, and Certified Public Accounting. Yet this third profession, which is no heritage but a creation of our necessity, is so little known that certainly 100,000 of our free, white, educated American contemporaries will die in A.D. 1932 without ever having the vaguest notion of what manner of men Certified Public Accountants are. They walk in the shadow of virtual anonymity. So discreet are they that at times it seems as though their aim were to become a disembodied function, almost without proper name. Yet upon the expert opinion of these abstract beings—who pit their judgment against the unbelievably subtle economic forces of this generation—the financial structure of our greatest industries is founded.

A man with a secret, mobile face walked past the *concierge* of his Paris apartment last March without speaking to him, went upstairs and shot himself. Next day stocks fell, bankers' hair turned white. A week later a committee invited certain gentlemen to come from Paris to Stockholm. Three weeks later these gentlemen issued a report: missing securities, false entries, grossly overstated profits, fraud.

The dead man was Ivar Kreuger; his name filled headlines the world over. The gentlemen from Paris were public accountants, and people generally forgot the name of their firm, Price, Waterhouse & Co., as soon as they had read it. Accountants, to the world in general, are old gentlemen with green eye-

* Reprinted from the June, 1932 issue of Fortune Magazine by special permission; © 1932 Time Inc.

PLUMS

A roster, more or less according to size, of the chief accounting firms of the U.S. Seven hundred corporations whose securities are listed on the New York Stock Exchange publish balance sheets certified by public accountants who audit their books. The list below gives the names of the leading accounting firms, each preceded by the number of such corporations whose accounts it audits and followed by the name of its most notable client.

146	Price, Waterhouse & Co.	U.S. Steel
71	Haskins & Sells	General Motors
71	Ernst & Ernst	Chrysler
56	Peat, Marwick, Mitchell & Co.	International Shoe
49	Arthur Young & Co.	Swift
48	Lybrand, Ross Bros. & Montgomery	A.T. & T.
27	Touche, Niven & Co.	Fox Film
24	Arthur Andersen & Co.	Montgomery Ward
15	Deloitte, Plender, Griffiths & Co.	American Sugar Refining
12	Barrow, Wade, Guthrie & Co.	Texas Gulf Sulphur
11	Audit Co. of New York	Woolworth
10	Loomis, Suffern & Fernald	Adams Express
10	F. W. Lafrentz & Co.	Corn Products
8	Miller, Donaldson & Co.	American Chicle
7	Leslie, Banks & Co.	American Brake Shoe & Foundry

136 All others
————
701

355 *Companies not reporting names of auditors*
————
1,056 *Total listed on Stock Exchange*

shades who sit on high stools and add up other people's figures—a secret fraternity, buried beneath books. Yet if we dig below those books, as the gentlemen from Price, Waterhouse (an English firm with branch offices in New York, Paris, Calcutta, Johannesburg, Bucharest, and many other places) dug into the books of Ivar Kreuger, we shall find not human adding machines but the youngest, least-known, and most responsible of professions; we shall find 12,000 men, certified by state boards after pitiless examinations, whose duty it is to strain through the sieve of their art and skill the chief facts of business and rearrange those facts so as to form a true picture of what has happened and may therefore happen again; we shall find, hidden under incomes modest out of all proportion to the importance of their services, a race of watchdogs guarding the corporation from its hopes, guarding the stockholder against misstatement; we shall find the men who substantiate the truth of the reports of two-thirds of the companies listed on the New York Stock Exchange; the men whose say-so determines the basis of many great mergers; the men who vouch for earnings per share of the stock you buy; the men whose opinion—a certified opinion, but an opinion nonetheless—determines all important borrowing and lending; the only men not lawyers allowed to plead before the Board of Tax Appeals in Washington, a body which has the standing of a U.S. court.

Certified Public Accountants (who call themselves C.P.A.'s) may descend like a swarm of locusts upon a manufacturer, explode his delusion that he is solvent. C.P.A.'s charge by the day—regardless of the amount of money involved. C.P.A.'s sometimes become millionaires—usually because they perform other services as well. C.P.A.'s practice in partnerships, almost never corporations. C.P.A.'s fly in large flocks, in huge offices with branches, as many as fifty-four, all over the U.S., employing up to 1,200 men. One mistake and a C.P.A.'s career is ended. C.P.A.'s as a rule do not think they ought to own stock in, or become directors of, the companies of their clients. It was C.P.A.'s —and their $46,000,000 disagreements—who figured so largely in the failure of the Bethlehem-Youngstown merger. C.P.A.'s have gone beyond their functions as auditors and accountants and are turning up as advisers to business and as management experts. C.P.A.'s are by nature skeptical, cool, cautious, and conservative; to them understatement is a golden virtue and overstatement almost the equivalent of fraud. C.P.A.'s spend years at their apprenticeship and are still learning. C.P.A.'s have been trying for eight years or more to agree upon a definition of earned surplus. C.P.A.'s are keepers of their own counsel, and not one of them has been a public booster or a Cassandra either before or since the crash—which they saw coming, though no one would have listened to them anyhow in 1929. It is contrary to the professional ethics of C.P.A.'s to solicit business or to advertise; their self-effacement goes down to their roots, which were transplanted from England. Up to fifty years ago there were no American public accountants: the oldest firm in the U.S., Barrow, Wade, Guthrie & Co. (once of England), celebrates the fiftieth anniversary of its American firm this November.

Never forget that English background: it explains much about the American C.P.A. Up to the '80's we had bookkeepers, but no public accountants. American industry was expanding mightily then, and shrewd Englishmen poured their capital into the veins of the new giant. But they poured carefully—and sent over the dour, watchful members of their ancient and honorable profession, the Chartered Accountants, the best of whom were Scottish, to feel the giant's pulse and explore his financial anatomy. American breweries, so accounting history would have it, were their first concern. Then millions of pounds in American railroad securities were floated on the London market, which meant more Chartered Accountants crossing the sea. A few American accountants sprang up, but the more important firms—and the flavor of accounting—remained English. This is partly true even today. Gradually, American companies began to make use of accountants; the first American industrial organization to incorporate and offer its securities to the public with an accountant's certification was the John B. Stetson Co., manufacturer of hats.

In 1886 the gross earnings of the twenty-five men who were professional public accountants did not exceed $250,000; today there are many thousands, with a gross income of some $60,000,000. There are now a dozen large American firms (among the largest: Haskins & Sells; Ernst & Ernst; Lybrand, Ross Bros. & Montgomery; Peat, Marwick, Mitchell & Co.), but the largest of all, Price, Waterhouse, auditors of U.S. Steel, was born in London and today employs 2,500 men in the offices of its several partnerships, from the Pacific Coast to India, via Buenos Aires. And English blood and tradition are common in other firms: the English and senior partner of Touche, Niven & Co. (accountants for Macy), Sir George A. Touche, has been Lieutenant and Sheriff of the city of London; the head of Deloitte, Plender, Griffiths & Co., the first Lord Plender, is a Knight of Grace, Order of St. John of Jerusalem in England.

The real growth of public accounting took place in this century. There were two things that made it grow: (1) the immense expansion of American industry that very soon knit its vast machinery together in gigantic mergers, requiring the most intricate accounting; (2) the federal income tax, according to the rules of which individuals and corporations had to learn to play, for the protection of their profits, an ever more and more complicated game. The accounting of small industrial units in a simple society is simple also; the immense modern complex of parent and subsidiary companies, of vast stock flotations, of no-par stocks, of reorganizations and loans requires accounting by accurate, subtle, and imaginative minds. The machinery of American business has grown so fast that old definitions of capital, of earnings, of assets, surplus, and profits, in all their infinite subdivisions and ramifications, have become invalid and questionable overnight. The giant has outgrown his ability to talk intelligently about himself; it is the accountant's job to discover and define and speak the words that will describe him. Accountants say that accountancy is the language of business. Not an exact, mathematical science, mind you, but a growing, debatable, living language; not a question of formulas but of style.

What are the functions of an accountant? Here again we must compare America and England. The English Chartered Accountant's first duty is to the stockholders who elect him in open meeting. The C.P.A., though sometimes so elected, is almost always (proxies being what they are) appointed by the management, paid by it, and first of all obligated to give it a clearer picture of its status and operations than it can form itself. A secondary obligation is to the creditors of that company, who want to know how safe their money is. Of late quite as important is the implied duty to the future security holders, to the investing public that buys stock upon a statement, certified to by the accountant, of so much earned per share, of so much net current assets, of so much net worth. Were those dollars really earned? Are those current assets really there? Stock may quite frequently be priced according to the skill and mental honesty of the accountant.

The accountant has primary functions, beyond which the public usually does not see. Everyone knows that a C.P.A., like a bank examiner, goes into his client's office to audit his books, to count his cash, to check his bank deposits, to evaluate his computation of goodwill and other intangible assets. This is only the first and the simplest step, no matter how arduous it may be or how many weeks or months it takes. Second step: when the mass of detailed figures, the contents of a hundred ledgers, have been found correct, the accountant must sort out those figures into piles, into classifications—as few as possible—that are clear and relevant to the main issue: the client's desire to know what has happened and where he stands. The accountant is concerned with far greater things than columns of figures and petty frauds: frauds are incidental excitements that relieve his monotony; figures are not his end—they are his means.

As a frame for its picture, accountancy invented—centuries ago—that brief, almost mystical double set of figures, of figures in total always exactly even no matter how much money the company is making: the balance sheet. An eternal equation that always puzzles the layman—and yet its theory is very simple: assets should always equal property interest in those assets; assets should always equal liabilities plus capital and surplus. Just as a watermelon should always equal the sum of the slices cut by those who have a right to eat it. But companies, like the contents of fruit stands, cannot instantly be added up; besides fixed assets, cash, inventory, and accounts receivable, their contents include things intangible as well as tangible which must be translated into terms of money; they include grounds for hope and possibilities of decay which must be reduced to figures. So one of the functions of the accountant is that of translator. There are no cribs, no trots for an accountant, and if he makes too literal a translation he will be unfaithful to the original. It is a matter of art, of common sense, and of opinion. Accounts receivable, for instance: they stand on a company's books at $500,000. But the accountant knows that things hoped for are not always received, and among those receivables he spots some uncollectibles. On the records of past years he notes a yearly average in losses of gross sales of one-half of 1 per cent, and he reasons that in times of depression this will probably rise to 1 per cent. He therefore subtracts from the $500,000 an allowance for doubtful accounts, and reduces the total of receivables to $450,000. A slightly less conservative accountant would reach a slightly different total. It is a matter of opinion. That almost all accountants are conservative by nature, that all accountants take delight in discounting chickens before they are hatched, is what stabilizes the opinion.

But opinions differ; accountants disagree. Their standards—their definitions of what shall or shall not constitute an asset, of what is a proper rate of depreciation—change, and often remain matters of debate. These debates read to the laymen like something out of the Talmud, like the medieval discussions of how many angels could dance on the point of a needle. Yet, unlike the Talmud and the angels, the outcome has a direct bearing upon a management's policy and upon how the public invests its savings.

For example: a company wins an old tax suit from the government, and recovers $1,000,000. It is obviously a nonrecurring item, yet the company in its report has lumped this windfall with earnings from operations, thereby showing earnings of $5 per share. The public accountant might be tempted to incline toward his client's wishes and to save his own face by a footnote, calling attention to the nonrecurring nature of the refund so included. But he lives up to his duty as painter of a true picture, insists upon rearranging the balance sheet to report the $1,000,000 separately. Result: the public reads that earnings are only $2 per share.

Here is the accountant in his function as watchdog (complaints are heard, even from their own ranks, that accountants don't bark as loud or as often as they should; that some of them have even been known to wag their tails at the burglar). A historical watchdog, who warns against distortion of past events. Sometimes, however, the accountant is forced, against one of the strongest instincts of his profession, to abandon history and become a prophet. Some six or seven years ago an accountant audited the books of an ice plant. The accountant, with his pencil poised at the item "depreciation," realized that electric refrigerators were becoming all the rage. He wrote against his ice plant a drastic depreciation rate that wiped it out in 1928. Came 1928 and electric iceboxes were booming, to be sure, but so was the ice business: the standard of living had gone up and the ice habit was growing. Today, in writing off for depreciation on an ice plant, in the light of his mistaken pessimism, what in the world is going to help him fix the proper rate?

The greatest debate among public accountants, practically a battle, was held in the arena of the Bethlehem Steel–Youngstown Sheet & Tube merger controversy between Price, Waterhouse and Ernst & Ernst. Price, Waterhouse, engaged as accountants by those who desired the merger, was asked to determine a fair basis for exchange of the two corporations' stock. Ernst & Ernst was engaged by the minority stockholders of Youngstown, led by Cyrus Eaton, who opposed the merger. The accountants disagreed chiefly on rates of depreciation for the two companies—a matter, said Price, Waterhouse, ultimately "of opinion." The gap between the two opinions amounted to $46,000,000. Both opinions were certified. The merger fell through. Who can decide when accountants disagree?

This—like many other cases that never reach the public—makes one ask what, if the margin of doubt and opinion be so wide, is any published balance sheet worth? If it be true, as accountants say, that ten different accountants may, after working upon the books of one company, draw up ten slightly different balance sheets, what is the public, the investor, to believe? It is all a highly difficult and technical matter to him anyhow. He does not understand the language; he is impressed by the accountant's "certification" that "in his opinion" so-and-so is true (as if one could certify to an opinion); he does not realize how much more of an accountant's skill and courage are required in auditing the books of a company that is losing money than the books of one that is making money. And much of the time he does not see the original statement of the accountant: that report to his client which he sprinkles with skeptical footnotes, which he certifies to with reservations and expressions of when and if the company does thus and thus, then so and so is true. Accountants may—and do—comb a company's books with rigorous honesty, and give its directors an accurate, certified balance sheet, full of doubts and danger signals, only to have the company thank them, pay them, summarize the report, and pass this midleading summary, without a word about auditors, on to the investing public. For a certification is more for the client's benefit and remains, if the client chooses, a private document. Unhappily there is nothing at present in law or custom that forces the company to tell the investors what the accountants said. That, however, is a condition that soon may change.

For the profession of accounting is keenly aware of itself, and has organized a general staff which is constantly trying to adopt accounting procedure and philosophy to a chaotic, changing business world. Unlike lawyers, accountants are not the interpreters of already existing rules: they must largely make their own. The definitions, the terminology, the conduct, the building of their profession are in their own hands, in the hands of a unique professional organization, the American Institute of Accountants. The Institute—known until 1916 as the American Association of Public Accountants—was formed in 1887, and includes partners or principals from a thousand firms, more than nine-tenths of whom are C.P.A.'s. It has the most complete library on accounting in the world. Through active committees, it sets the ethical and technical standards for the profession, gives candidates for membership examinations, builds up a literature, supports legislation to recognize and protect the C.P.A. certificate, and tries to teach the public something about what accountants have to offer. The professional code is strict: members of the Institute must not solicit business or split commissions with the laity or take contingent fees or cut the corners of good accounting to meet a client's wishes. Members who sign inaccurate statements or are proved grossly negligent are subject to severe penalties —the Institute has tried forty-two of its members for various infractions in the past sixteen years. Its minimum audit program has been adopted by the Federal Reserve Board. Its special committee on coöperation with stock exchanges is only one of the many important Institute activities.

The New York Stock Exchange requires, of all applicants for listing on the Big Board, certain information, and its tendency as time goes on is to require more accurate and detailed information, set forth in accordance with the best accounting practice. Accountants and Exchange officials sometimes disagree— there is some difference of opinion now as to consolidated statements and stock dividends. The New York Stock Exchange, be it noted, does not require a company's statement to be certified to by a public accountant: only two-thirds of the reports of the companies on the Big Board are so certified. Here again there is disagreement. There is more than one point of view as to the attitude of the Exchange in this respect. Some accountants would regret to see an absolute requirement along these lines until differences of opinion among accountants themselves have been worked out to a greater degree. Others would welcome the most stringent regulation on the subject.

It will probably happen—accountants hope before long—that the public accountant's certification is insisted upon, even that all company reports are required by law to be so certified.

But the picture will yet be incomplete, and the ultimate investor must still beware. For the accountant's report perforce deals not with entire industries but with individual companies, not with economic trends and personalities but with a particular picture in its individual frame. The most conservative and honest accountants may certify to a cheerful, prosperous statement of a company whose stock may be the worst of investments—may later prove to be headed for worthlessness. For the accountant's province is at present limited. He cannot, in his balance sheet, make an accounting of the management or of economic conditions in a particular industry which may make all of its units go on the rocks; he cannot deduct from assets an allowance for bad weather that everyone in the industry as a whole knows is blowing up; he cannot add to liabilities the plain fact that the president of the corporation is drinking himself to death. His functions—which are constantly developing toward

stricter definition of the items of his balance sheet in accordance with industrial change and fundamental economic law, toward advice and management,
toward a closer relation with the ultimate investor—are still in the process
of evolution.

A LONG LADDER: A SMALL POT OF GOLD

The ambitious young man who is keeping the books of the Oak Forks Ice, Wood
& Coal Co. is reading the annual report of Fox Film, 1930, and the fascinating
disagreements of two firms of public accountants as to the proper rate of depreciation for talkie negative attract him more than ever to accounting as a
profession. He wonders, incidentally, how much money there is in it. Turning
the page whereon are recorded Fox Film's expenses during a year of phenome-
nal suits, disputes, and battles, he reads:

Legal expenses $2,038,711
Accounting fees   168,281

But money isn't everything, and the young man loves figures and the secrets figures can reveal—or hide. He decides to become an accountant. Let us
briefly trace his career, its rewards, its rigors, its possibilities, and its blind
alleys.

The young man, like all bright young men, goes to the city, keeps books
again, studies at night. On his twenty-second birthday the periodic auditor
(member of a firm of C.P.A.'s), who was impressed with the way the young
man kept his books, offers him a job. He becomes a "junior" in the firm, and
audits, in turn, the books of shoe companies, milliners, drug stores, sawmills,
for $25 a week. He counts petty cash, checks "postings" from ledger to journal,
verifies bank balances. His dispassionate, skeptical gaze sweeps into every
corner of a strange business; he records the main items upon his working papers (which are yellow to save his eyes), in pencil (Price, Waterhouse & Co. is
the only firm of accountants whose working papers are written in ink). Three,
four months of exacting work, almost drudgery, relieved by the excitement of
a whiff of fraud; rewarded by the growth of experience, of insight into the main
springs of industry. The experience makes up for the pay.

And then suddenly both pay and experience cease. For accountants work
furiously upon annual statements for a few months of the year. Staffs are doubled, partners burn midnight oil. In April or May staffs are cut to normal size,
and our young man is let out. He joins the great army of junior accountants
who, for over half the year, get jobs where and as best they can. I might as well,

he thinks (a trifle bitterly), be in the Christmas card business, or a strawberry picker. But in December the firm takes him back, this time permanently. He is still a junior, at $30 a week. From here on the steps in his career, unless he has extraordinary ability or lack of it, are well defined:

Junior assistant (about two years) averaging	$30 a week
Semisenior assistant (one year)	50–60
Senior (depending)	80–100
Supervisor	100–150
Partner	20,000–100,000 a year

A semi-senior has graduated from the drudgery of auditing, and his satisfactions are keener; a senior is in close contact with the client and feels some of the joys of an engineer completing a difficult job. Our young man will remain a senior unless he is exceptional, unless he has the spark of creative imagination which is as necessary to top-notch accounting as to any other profession.

Anyone who pleases can call himself an "accountant" and print the title on his letterhead and practice his craft, but only after passing a state examination is our young man entitled to call himself a "Certified Public Accountant." The examinations for C.P.A.'s are horribly difficult. There is probably no other professional examination half so rigorous, and the examination papers seem, to a layman, like the nightmares of some Einstein of American business.

Our young man is now over thirty. He is pleased with his choice of a career —no other could have given him such a profound grasp of the machinery of modern civilization, about which he knows far more than most of the business-men whose books he examines. The work—though still exacting, though he offers up a prayer each time he signs a certification—is absorbing and full of intellectual question marks. He is a pioneer, often moving ahead into unexplored territory. As he takes stock, there is only one thing to trouble him: money.

He has spent some thousands of dollars in professional education—perhaps, if he includes five years at the low pay of apprenticeship, as much as $10,000. Ahead of him is a possible partnership, but he remembers that Fox Film report, and has heard the rumors that there are few millionaires among accountants—Colonel Carter, Colonel Montgomery, J. E. Sterrett, Samuel Leidesdorf, G. O. May, perhaps, some of whom have received fees as lawyers, executors, and special counsel as well. There are three paths open to him.

He may give up his professional practice and accept the offer of the knitting mills to become its comptroller at twice his present salary. There is precedent for this: indeed, it is a matter of some melancholy to leaders of the profession that so many of its members look upon it chiefly as a marvelous side door into big business. He remembers that Mr. William J. Filbert scaled the high walls of Steel on the long ladder of accountancy: that Mr. Erskine, president of Studebaker, Mr. Reay, comptroller of International Harvester, Mr. Oakey, comptroller of New York Life, Mr. John Henry Schneider, auditor of Montgomery Ward, Mr. John A. Will, comptroller of the Chase National Bank; all rose to these summits with the aid of a C.P.A.'s certificate. Our young man glances at the roster of the New York State Society of Certified Public Accountants, and finds it studded with the names of men who are not "in practice," who have become the auditors, comptrollers, treasurers, cost accountants, tax counsel, even presidents, of powerful corporations. But he decides to remain a professional, and free, for he feels that if he joins the ranks of business, demands may be made upon him, compromises expected of him which his professional pride might not stand for.

He also decides against going into practice on his own — at least until he can take some of the important clients away with him, for banks demand a well-known name attached to the certification of balance sheets.

So he remains where he is, and eventually becomes a partner. His responsibility increases vastly, as does the interest and delicacy of the work; he is involved in questions of management, of policy — sometimes has to run a business himself. Yet the accountant, for no just or sufficient reason, is practically never appointed as receiver, a function he could perform most admirably — far better, he is convinced, than the vast majority of the lawyers into whose laps courts drop these frequently juicy plums. Though deprived of such plums, he is by now making more money. The firm, let us say, takes in a million dollars in fees. The expenses of accounting — mainly clerical wages and the salaries of the assistants — cut away all but 25 to 33 1/3 per cent, leaving $300,000, let us say, to distribute among the partners. As a junior partner his yearly income is about $20,000. A lawyer in his position with a law firm of corresponding prominence would be getting $50,000 to $75,000. For the ancient profession of the law has accustomed the public to paying — and paying well — for its services, while American accountancy is not two generations old, is unknown to the public, and is still regarded by its clients as something comparable to the annual visit of the vacuum cleaner. The lawyer charges what the traffic will bear; the accountant is almost always paid by the day, according to the cost of the job, regardless of the size of the corporation or how many millions of dollars are involved. The accountant sends his men out on the job and, some months later, bills his client for the time spent and the grades of accountancy engaged, approximately on the following basis:

Juniors	$20 a day
Semi-seniors	25–30 a day
Seniors	35 a day
Supervisors	50–75 a day

For his personal attention, a partner charges $100, $200 and, on the highest summits of the profession, occasionally as much as $1,000 a day. Work done according to these standard fees—with individual jobs ranging from a few hundred dollars to tens of thousands—yields the bulk of accountants' revenue. Work done upon a contingent fee basis is rare, even in accounting for income tax purposes, and is generally frowned upon. And the contingent fee men are— or rather used to be—those racketeers who got jobs with the Internal Revenue Department in Washington, learned the slippery ropes, resigned, set up shop, and hooked clients with the bait of inside knowledge. And then there are accountants who receive more than the usual fees for acting as executors, for helping to run a business, for performing special advisory functions. But the majority of accountants are on a per diem basis. And there is no such disparity between the fees charged by inconspicuous firms and those charged by famous firms as there is in the legal profession. There is no Max Steuer to be found in the ranks of public accountants. The accountant's abilities and responsibilities are out of all proportion to the money he receives for exercising them.

ARCHITECTS OF THE U.S. BALANCE SHEET

C.P.A.'s themselves: a portfolio of brief biographies. In terms of firms rather than individuals, for that is the tradition in this most secret guild.

PRICE, WATERHOUSE

The accountants who certify that, in their opinion, the balance sheet of U.S. Steel is properly drawn up so as to present a true and correct view of its financial position are to accountancy what Steel is to business, what sterling is to silver. Price, Waterhouse is easily the world's foremost accounting firm in size, in reputation, in number of clients. Price, Waterhouse men went to Stockholm from Paris, and found the holes in Ivar Kreuger's dream. Price, Waterhouse audits the books and makes up the balance sheets for Steel, Case, Eastman, I.M.M., Goodyear, Packard, Goldman Sachs, Shell Union Oil, and hundreds of others. It employs, in the U.S. and Canada alone—in nineteen offices scattered from Montreal to Los Angeles, from Seattle to Atlanta—more than a thousand men, whose fees may bring into the office well over $6,000,-000 a year.

Of course, Price, Waterhouse was born in England. S. H. Price and Edwin Waterhouse, independent Chartered Accountants, joined forces in London in 1860. For a time the firm name was Price, Holyland & Waterhouse. A son of one of the founders, Sir N. E. Waterhouse (M.A., New College, Oxford), and a nephew of the other, Mr. S. N. Price, are among the partners in the London office. Four of the partners are K.B.E.'s. Including its head London office, it has six in England; 500 men. Famous reorganizations and cases in which the London branch took part: Hatry, Marconi, Lipton's—and the Royal Mail Steam Packet.

There are really three firms of Price, Waterhouse: the English, the American, and the Continental, with a head office in Paris. When the Kreuger & Toll affair arose, the Swedish Government applied to the Continental office of Price, Waterhouse, which appointed Mr. Seatree, Continental senior partner, who traveled to Sweden with a staff of incorruptible skeptics and soon discovered that Ivar Kreuger, by some miracle of concealment, had managed to keep the secret of his manipulations in his various companies from the accountants of three nations, no one of whom audited all his books.

All told, 2,500 men work under the name of Price, Waterhouse in the fifty-seven branch offices of its various partnerships. The New York office, now the largest and most powerful of all, began life as Jones, Caesar & Co., which amalgamated with the London firm some thirty-odd years ago. The connection between London and New York is one of interlocking independence. The senior partner is Mr. George O. May (adviser to the Stock Exchange on all matters of accounting). Mr. May, whose distinctions and whose contributions to his profession are numberless, is so retiring by nature and so reluctant to stand in the glare of publicity that his name is not even to be found in *Who's Who*. With Mr. May, the men chiefly responsible for the fortunes of the American Price, Waterhouse are Mr. William Bynner Campbell and Mr. Joseph Edmund Sterrett.

Mr. Sterrett—if one may pick one man in a world-wide firm, all of whose members are overshadowed by the greatness of its name—is an example of the accountant who has taken part in affairs commonly considered beyond the realm of accountancy. He was born at Brockway, Pennsylvania, sixty-two years ago. He became a partner in the firm of John W. Francis at twenty-three. Later the firm—by then his own firm—was consolidated with Price, Waterhouse. Since then the list of his services both to his profession and to the machinery of a disordered world has been colossal, and most distinguished. Mr. Sterrett (it was while the late Senator Morrow was Ambassador) helped investigate the finances and economy of the Mexican Government. In 1917 he was one of a group of advisers who explored the territory opened up by the excess-profits tax. He has been an administrator of that law, and an adviser to the U.S. Treasury on tax matters. In 1919 he took part in the organization of the Reparation Commission, was later appointed American member of the Transfer Committee for Reparation Payments under the Dawes Plan, and acted as principal assistant to the Agent General of Reparations. His career is prophetic for the profession, and foreshadows the larger and larger part accountants' brains, training, and imagination will and should play in a society which is perforce overhauling its economic system. Foreign governments know Mr. Sterrett's worth (though his name may be unknown to an American who could name ten famous bankers and twenty notable lawyers), and have rewarded him with the Order of Leopold of Belgium, of which he is a Commander; with the First Order of the German Red Cross; with the Crown of Italy (Grand Officer).

Price, Waterhouse is as unapproachable as royalty, intrenched in tradition and pride as well as professional ethics. The Price, Waterhouse letterhead, with splendid simplicity, says: "Price, Waterhouse & Co., 56 Pine Street, New York — nothing more.

LYBRAND, ROSS BROS. & MONTGOMERY

Colonel Robert H. Montgomery's abilities have entitled his colleagues to consider him the chief figure in the American accounting profession — they are the kind of abilities that would place him in the front rank of any other profession than the two he follows (he is a lawyer as well as a C.P.A.). He has a decisive, penetrating, analytic mind — a kind of razor-edged wisdom that is forever probing the question of what accountancy is, and forever pushing back the limits of what accountancy should become. His honors are practical as well as theoretic. A former professor of accounting at Columbia and the author of innumerable textbooks and pamphlets, he is also known and respected in Washington as a man who can turn government tax claims for $500,000 into refunds of $4,000,000; as the man whom Albert Lasker told to sign his (Lasker's) name to any measure that would straighten out the Shipping Board mess, "the worst accounting mess in all history."

Born fifty-nine years ago, the son of a Pennsylvania Methodist minister. At sixteen he became office boy to a notable Philadelphia accountant, John Heins — and at twenty-four he was a partner. Went to Porto Rico as a private of artillery, came back and studied law at night. Opened the New York office of his present firm in 1902; personnel: Robert H. Montgomery and one secretary. During the War — whence the "Colonel" — he was invaluable to the government as an appraiser, a price fixer for the War Industries Board. He is a teacher of his profession to others, and a writer upon its problems. His *Auditing, Theory and Practice* is virtually the young accountant's Bible. He was president of the International Congress on Accounting in 1929; he is most active in the work of the American Institute of Accountants, and a holder of C.P.A. certificates in five states. Tall, with a bronzed face much younger than his graying hair; with a broad-shouldered, athletic frame; a lover of horses and golf. He owns the Montgomery Evergreen Nursery, Inc. at Cos Cob, Connecticut, where he watches the growth of 400 kinds of trees. His keen blue eyes look at a complicated world with courage and skepticism, settle on facts and about those facts his tongue asks questions.

The firm of which Colonel Montgomery was a founder has thirty partners, employs hundreds of men in three foreign and twenty-two American offices. It has the largest Washington office of any public accountant. Tax work is its specialty, a natural by-product of its general accounting practice, particularly the Colonel's specialty, as results accomplished for taxpayer clients will testify. The government tried to collect $12,000,000 from the estate of Rodman Wanamaker; Colonel Montgomery appeared as a witness, and the government didn't get a nickel. The government tried to collect $600,000 from the American Cigar Co., but after Colonel Montgomery had dealt with the case—as public records show—it was the American Cigar Co. that was waiting for a check.

Some of the corporations listed on the New York Stock Exchange whose published statements bear the certificate of Lybrand, Ross Bros. & Montgomery: American Telephone & Telegraph, American Metal, American Chain, Associated Dry Goods, Baldwin Locomotive, Curtiss-Wright, Electric Storage Battery, Freeport Texas, Hudson Motor Car, Manhattan Shirt, U.S. Pipe & Foundry, United Gas Improvement.

ERNST & ERNST

Birthplace: Cleveland, where Mr. A. C. Ernst formed his own firm in 1903. Habitat: fifty-four cities in the U.S., none elsewhere, a record for American accounting firms. Specialty: everything from Coca-Cola to Chrysler Motors. Particular attention to cost accounting, installation of cost and budget systems, and organization and personnel work. One of the few firms which have come into real prominence in the last twenty years: one of the few large additions to the rather static picture of accountancy. A firm that has gone beyond the traditional limits of its craft, for Ernst & Ernst believes in advertising and does advertise.

Ernst & Ernst (which looks upon accountancy commercially as well as professionally) is not orthodox; Ernst & Ernst is not a member of the Institute. Mr. Ernst deplores the assumption that the public accountant is dry as dust, deplores the readiness of the accountant to hide behind his figures. "Without personality," he says, "a public accountant may be likened to a nourishing food without flavor." It is the definite policy of Ernst & Ernst to advertise, not so much for itself as for the good of the profession which, as enlightened accountants admit, has suffered much from hiding its light under a bushel. Ernst & Ernst has taken the bushel off its light, and it is one of the biggest bushels in accounting. As may be seen from a partial list of clients (which includes between 500 and 600 department stores): Coca-Cola, Chrysler, Columbia Gas & Electric, Continental Motors, Eaton Axle & Spring, Firestone, Glidden, Gotham Silk Hosiery, International Match, Lambert, Motor Wheel, Murray Corp. of America, New York Air Brake, Otis Steel, Republic Steel, R. J. Reynolds Tobacco, Sherwin-Williams, Transamerica, Timken Roller Bearing, United American Bosch Corp., White Motor.

BARROW, WADE, GUTHRIE AND MR. COUCHMAN

It is not common for an accountant to begin life as a writer of detective stories. Yet for a number of years Mr. Charles Bennington Couchman, fifty-two, president of the American Institute of Accountants and since 1928 general partner in Barrow, Wade, Guthrie & Co., thought fiction was the one thing he wanted to do — and did it well. Today Mr. Couchman is an accomplished writer, though not of fiction — for his articles have appeared in the *Wall Street Journal* and *Nation's Business;* today Mr. Couchman is a man of eloquence and accurate, rounded language, though upon a different theme. His books, in fact, concern accounting; his talks, frequently delivered before fellow accountants, bankers, and students, concern fine points of the profession. He is the head of accountancy's highest professional fellowship, the Institute, yet his first love calls strong within him: he is still a member of the Authors' League. His ambition is to achieve, through the practice of his profession, a leisure that will enable him to write.

Mr. Couchman was born in Missouri; worked on a farm, with threshing gangs and for cattlemen; took three years' high-school work in one. Taught mathematics and history, hated it, wrote short stories in his spare time. Checked cars in a railroad yard, kept books in Kansas City, drifted into public accounting because he needed the money. As soon as he became successful at that, his stories began to sell. Helped form the firm of Crockett, Couchman & Co. Opened his own office in New York in 1921. In 1924 published *The Balance Sheet,* for which he has refused requests for translation into Spanish, Japanese, and German, characteristically fearing that mistakes and misstatements would creep in. Reads philosophy, economics, and detective stories. Smokes a pipe, likes tramping, belongs to the Gipsy Trail Club, is a trustee of the Broadway Presbyterian Church. In 1928 merged his firm with Barrow, Wade, Guthrie & Co., which was formed in 1883, a firm English in origin (established by Edwin Guthrie and Charles H. Wade, members of the firm of Thomas Wade, Guthrie & Co., Chartered Accountants of London and Manchester), but now entirely American, with fourteen branches in the U.S.; sixteen in Canada, Europe, South America. The firm represented the British Government during the War, on contracts for war materials and supplies in the U.S. Among the clients of Barrow, Wade, Guthrie are: Atlas Powder, Congoleum-Nairn, Phillips Petroleum, Texas Gulf Sulphur, Rolls Royce, Clark Thread, De Forest Radio, Scribner's, Hudson Bay, Roxy Theatre, Yale & Towne, Fidelity & Casualty, John B. Stetson.

S. D. LEIDESDORF

The traditional accountant gives his client the figures about his business and then departs from the scene, leaving the client to translate those figures into action as best he may; the firm of S. D. Leidesdorf & Co. — young, progressive, energetic, with a practice centered largely in New York City — combines accounting with advice, can prescribe remedies as well as diagnose a case. The traditional accountant's work is finished with the drawing up of the balance sheet and profit and loss statement: S. D. Leidesdorf & Co. performs this service for countless New York manufacturers; cotton, fur, silk, and woolen houses; commission houses and factories; for real estate, hotels, banks, brokers, shoes, rubber boots, jewelers, chain and department stores, milliners, perfumers. But S. D. Leidesdorf will also help to cut those losses and increase those profits by suggesting a tonic, by helping a business out of its accustomed rut, by acting as experts to the management.

The 200 men of the S. D. Leidesdorf staff are employed — again contrary to the universal practice of a profession that has a seasonal boom followed by seasonal slack and unemployment — for twelve months of the year. S. D. Leidesdorf has persuaded its clients to have continuing accounts rather than year-end balance sheet accounts; its men are constantly at work on clients' books — on a monthly basis. From this ceaseless routine work the Leidesdorf men can be withdrawn and hurled, like shock troops, into the breach of a special job, checking, verifying. Fifty, a hundred strong, on a few hours notice, in they march. And if, as once happened when taking inventory, they find that those packing cases seem heavy only because they are nailed to the floor, out of the place they walk again, fifty or a hundred, silent and stern. For S. D. Leidesdorf & Co., like all good accountants, will quit rather than go on with work if a client goes too far in suppressing essential facts.

These men are accountants primarily; their special functions as advisers and physicians have grown logically out of accounting. They are pioneers of a growing tendency among the more progressive accountants to help clients do something with the figures brought to light by the audit. This help goes far beyond mere financial advice: S. D. Leidesdorf & Co. is able to suggest to a client new merchandising methods, and is frequently engaged to install such new methods and supervise their operation for a year or more. S. D. Leidesdorf points to the day when business will look to the accountant as a permanent ally and technical counsel and not merely as an annual and somewhat academic auditor of books.

Mr. Samuel D. Leidesdorf, heavy-set, agreeable, and energetic, was born in New York of German stock. Started in as a shipping clerk, got into accounting, made a deal with the head bookkeeper to teach him bookkeeping at night for $15, envied the visiting auditor, cultivated him, picked up from him the essential facts. Became a first-class bookkeeper, turned down a $5,000 a year salary, plus 5 per cent interest in the business, in order to work with an auditing company at $20 a week, an act for which his mother wanted his sanity examined. Three years later, however, he was getting $5,000 plus 10 per cent of the profits. Shortly afterwards he was in business for himself.

Today the S. D. Leidesdorf practice is growing mightily, and is one of the most interesting features in the rather static landscape presented by accountancy as a whole.

HASKINS & SELLS

Accountants who marry the boss's daughter are rare—Arthur Hazelton Carter is perhaps the only example. But it is mainly as a result of his own brains and effort that Colonel Carter, graduate of the class of 1905 at West Point, finds himself the head and one of the thirty-nine partners of the greatest of the strictly American accounting firms, Haskins & Sells. In spite of a vague youthful interest in financial records he decided to become a soldier. Soldiering—if begun at the United States Military Academy—has its by-products, among them a rigorous training in mathematics and economics: in precision, mental as well as physical. While Colonel of Ordinance in the early days of the War, Colonel Carter—at thirty-two—organized the property accounting section, linking property accountability with the purchase of new material. A more purely military task was his organization of the officers' Field Artillery School at Camp Zachary Taylor, which he administered until the end of the War, with such distinction that he was awarded the D.S.M.

In 1919 he was honorably discharged, and joined the firm of which his wife's father, the late Elijah Watt Sells, was senior partner. Colonel Carter, with a keen accounting mind, plus his qualities of energy, fairness, and sincerity, has seen Haskins & Sells grow and maintain its place in the front rank of accountancy. His particular care is the training of the firm's junior accountants, chosen for character and personality as well as for brains, from college graduates and seasoned in New York for work in the seventeen branch offices (England, France, Germany, China, Mexico, South America, and Africa—not to speak of many branches in the U.S.), most of which have been added to the firm since Colonel Carter joined it and internationalized it.

Yet Haskins & Sells was famous before Colonel Carter. Founded in 1895 by Elijah Watt Sells of Iowa and Waldo Emerson Haskins at a time when few accountants, even fewer firms, were anything but British. What brought Mr. Sells and Mr. Haskins together was their common service in revising the accounting system of the U.S. Government—a job that needs to be done all over again now.

One of the firm's first assignments (in 1895) was an examination of the methods of accounting at Vassar College. Some years later the city of Chicago employed it to install a uniform system of accountancy (another job that might well be overhauled), and in 1906 Haskins & Sells saw service in the big insurance scandal—and analyzed the books of Mutual, New York Life, and Equitable, which settled it permanently in the public eye. Ever since, Haskins & Sells has been called in frequently to straighten out public books and tangles: the Bureau of Audits of the Alien Property Custodian, the Red Cross, the Cook County Highway Department, the Maryland State Roads Commission, the State of Tennessee.

The firm is, where private business is concerned, anything but a specialist, as will be seen from a partial roster of its clients: American Smelting & Refining, International Harvester, American Beet Sugar, American International, Borden, Canada Dry, Crucible Steel, Chicago Pneumatic Tool, Cluett, Peabody, Reliance International, Davison Chemical, General Motors, Grigsby-Grunow, Hudson & Manhattan Railroad, Houston Oil of Texas, Hartman, Mid-Continent Petroleum, Pacific Lighting, Philadelphia & Reading Coal & Iron, Pacific Gas & Electric, Quaker Oats, Standard Brands (1929, 1930, 1931), Simms Petroleum, St. Joseph Lead, Standard Gas & Electric, Texas Pacific Coal & Oil, U.S. Rubber, United Railways & Electric Co. of Baltimore, Westinghouse Electric, Westinghouse Air Brake.

AND MANY, MANY A WORTHY OTHER

Arthur Andersen & Co. (chiefly of Chicago) which is now—as everyone knows—deep in the auditing of some of Mr. Samuel Insull's utility companies; whose founder, Mr. Andersen, came of Norwegian parents and is president of the board of trustees of Northwestern University; whose clients include Montgomery Ward, Marshall Field, International Telephone & Telegraph, Hershey Chocolate . . .

Touche, Niven & Co., whose English partner, Sir George A Touche, has been Lieutenant and Sheriff of the city of London; which has nine branch offices in the U.S.; whose New York partner, Mr. John B. Niven, was born in Scotland and is a willing friend and adviser to every young public accountant; whose clients include R. H. Macy (and half a dozen other department stores), Studebaker, Endicott Johnson, Arundel, Fox Film, Kelly-Springfield, Underwood Elliott Fisher, Worthington Pump . . .

Patterson, Teele & Dennis, one of the oldest American firms, which audited, under Mayor Gaynor's administration, every Catholic charity in the city of New York; whose co-founder, Arthur W. Teele, has personally conducted the yearly audit of the Southern Railway since 1901 . . .

Deloitte, Plender, Griffiths & Co., English to the core, whose senior partner, Lord Plender, was Commissioner under the Welsh Church Act, and is a Knight of Grace, Order of St. John of Jerusalem in England, and a member of Brooks's; whose clients include American Sugar Refining, Tri-Continental, and Selected Industries . . .

Scovell, Wellington & Co., which was organized in Boston, and employs a staff of engineers; whose services have been employed by the makers of books, typewriters, carpets, vanilla, and deviled hams; whose Mr. Wellington graduated from Harvard; whose founder, the late Clinton H. Scovell, was a member of the old firm of Harvey Stuart Chase of Boston (and thereby partner of the man who put depreciation on the map—the man whose son, Stuart Chase, is a C.P.A. as well as the author of *Mexico, Tragedy of Waste*) . . .

Peat, Marwick, Mitchell & Co., one of the four or five largest firms in the country, whose clients include Borg-Warner, Consolidated Cigar, General Railway Signal, International Shoe, Pittsburgh Coal, Pere Marquette Railway . . .

Arthur Young & Co., another ancient powerful, and growing firm, whose clients include Commercial Solvents, Mack Trucks, Radio Corporation of America, Sinclair Consolidated Oil, Socony-Vacuum, Swift, and Pullman . . .

The Audit Co. of New York, one of the very few public accountants that is organized not as a partnership but a corporation, whose clients include American Car & Foundry, Diamond Match, International Business Machines, Woolworth, and Sears, Roebuck . . .

A current profile of the audit profession would reveal changes since 1932. The following one is ten years old, but it is, on the whole, an accurate image of the profession today. Indeed, many of the problems unsolved in 1960 remain so.

THE AUDITORS HAVE ARRIVED
T. A. Wise*

It is a curious and noteworthy fact that the tremendous growth of the U.S. accounting profession in the postwar years has taken place almost unnoticed by most Americans. In the same years, other proliferating white-collar types—advertising and public-relations men, union and corporation lawyers, stockbrokers, research scientists—have impinged heavily on the national consciousness; news stories about such men are often in the papers, and their prototypes appear regularly in novels and television dramas. But the rise of the accountants has occurred quietly. To most businessmen, the names of the big accounting firms are familiar, principally because of the way the names recur at the end of published annual reports; but not many businessmen know, or have even heard of, the men portrayed on the following pages, who are the senior partners of the nation's largest accounting firms. They are among the most powerful men anywhere in business today.

In a way, their anonymity is in keeping with the traditions of the profession, which have always called for a rather aloof public posture. Elbert Hubbard's description of "the typical auditor" many years ago had him "cold, passive, noncommittal, with eyes like codfish . . . minus bowels, passion or a sense of humor." The modern auditor is likely to have all three, but he is still unlikely to step out of the shadows very often. One reason for this reticent posture is that an auditor is privy to the secrets of many businessmen, and they naturally feel easier about this relationship if the auditor seems to be a man of reserve and discretion. Moreover, an auditor must preserve his independence in dealing with present or prospective clients. The chiefs of the profession—the leading lights of the Big Eight firms—live very much in a world of their own. Six of the eight have their main offices within a few blocks of one another in New York's Wall Street area; they see a lot of and know a lot about one another. Their firms audit about 80 per cent of all the corporations listed with the Securities and Exchange Commission. But not many line executives know how these eight men operate: how much money they make, and how much their firms make, how they have been steadily taking on new functions, how they get new business, and how they have been coping with an extraordinary range of ethical and intellectual problems.

These operations do not constitute all the news about the auditors these days. The profession today is fighting a number of quiet but intense battles to clarify and make consistent the accounting principles used in the U.S. It

* Reprinted from the November and December, 1960 issues of *Fortune Magazine* by special permission; © 1960 Time Inc.

is a truism in the profession, though it still seems a bit shocking to many businessmen, that two different accountants in possession of the same figures may construct two considerably dissimilar balance sheets. The principal issues in the battles between accountants, and the profession's prospects for resolving them, will be described in a second article next month.

A few figures and definitions are in order at the outset. When some of the more prestigious members of the profession are asked whether they consider themselves auditors or accountants, they may take a deep breath and reply that they are "independent certified public accountants." On the other hand, the Census Bureau just lumps "accountants and auditors" together (there were 376,459 in the U.S. in 1950). The difference between an accountant and an auditor is a chronic source of confusion, but the operational distinction is a simple one. All accountants assist in the preparation of financial statements according to the principles they believe to be generally accepted by the profession. An audit is an *examination* of such a statement, and an auditor is simply an accountant checking the work of someone else—often another accountant. The great majority of those listed by the Census Bureau are not recognized as accountants by the profession, and most of them are, realistically, plain bookkeepers, untrained in the many rigorous disciplines, the concepts, and the case lore of modern accountancy, and unrecognized by any state authorities. Just about 108,000 have acquired this recognition: these include the 71,000 certified public accountants in the U.S. (about 11,000 work for the Big Eight) and 37,000 who have "licenses" issued in thirty-one states to do public accounting.

Not all the C.P.A.'s have the same qualifications—these vary from state to state—but all of them have, at least, passed a rigorous examination that is given twice each year and is prepared by the American Institute of Certified Public Accountants. The examination covers accounting practice and theory, auditing, and commercial law; it is given in several installments, each of which begins at the same moment in every state, and all together it usually consumes about nineteen hours, spread over a Wednesday-to-Friday period. Before the examination, the questions are kept under close security; they are delivered in armored trucks to the examination centers and opened in the examination rooms before witnesses.

The C.P.A.'s competition is not limited to other C.P.A.'s. The 37,000 "licensed public accountants" can legally do everything the C.P.A.'s can do, even though many have not passed an examination (they got into business before the enactment of the present laws regulating accounting). In nineteen states (including Massachusetts and Pennsylvania) *anyone* can call himself a public accountant—i.e., no license is issued. There are perhaps 15,000 such unlicensed, uncertified public accountants in these states, and they too are entitled to do anything a C.P.A. can do.

The growth of the profession has taken place in less than a century. As recently as 1900, there were exactly 243 C.P.A.'s in the U.S., and no more than 1,000 persons employed in all the nation's accounting firms. And the rate of growth is still accelerating: the profession expects to pick up an additional 40,000-odd C.P.A.'s by 1970. Accountants' numbers and influence are increasing in other countries as well as in the U.S.; but the scope and diversity of U.S. capitalism have made this country the modern center of the profession, and the American Institute of Certified Public Accountants is always playing host to droves of visitors from Italy, Japan, Israel, and many other nations who are eager to learn how auditing, and accounting in general, are practiced here.

A BEGINNING IN BREWERIES

The steadily expanding influence of the auditors derives, in general, from two sources: (1) the increasing complexity of the modern industrial world, and (2) its greater emphasis on *accountability,* meaning the need of one man to refer his actions to judgment by standards he shares with other men. The classical nineteenth-century entrepreneur had little need for an accountant in the modern sense; he was accountable to the law of the land and his own conscience, but beyond that he was the sole judge of whether his performance was meritorious. A very different situation is that of professional managers controlling the property of unknown stockholders, dealing with institutionalized creditors, and entrusted with a host of social tasks from the generation of taxable revenues to the production of essential weapons. Under these circumstances, it becomes a matter of the utmost public importance to know how the management of a public corporation is performing. Accountancy has created several concepts that are useful in evaluating these performances. "Depreciation" is one such concept, "earned surplus" is another, and "net working capital" is a third. Aside from the help such measurements give the public, it is important *within* any top management group to be able to evaluate objectively the performance of subordinates, and accountancy contributes many techniques to the discharge of this responsibility.

The accounting profession in this country can be traced back to about 1880, when some English and Scottish investors began to put their money into U.S. securities. The securities they picked were mostly brewery stocks, which were then regarded in Great Britain as the worthiest of blue chips. The investors who bought heavily into American breweries sent their own auditing firms over here to check on the health of these investments. Two members of the Big Eight, Price Waterhouse and Peat, Marwick & Mitchell, were originally British firms that got their start in the U.S. this way. Today, of course, they are entirely American-owned but have working relationships with the British partnerships.

By the time of World War I, the ownership of public securities had become fairly widespread, and there was a growing awareness of the need for more uniformity in financial reporting. The nation's first Secretary of Commerce (in the Wilson Administration), William C. Redfield, was a businessman who had been engaged shortly before taking office in an effort to merge several companies. The merger collapsed when he realized that some of the companies involved were substantially overvalued. He discussed the generally chaotic state of financial reporting with officials of the Federal Reserve Board, and persuaded several of them to take the lead in setting down some guidelines for businessmen. In 1917, with the help of the accounting profession, the board produced a memorandum, subsequently published in booklet form, called "Approved Methods for the Preparation of Balance Sheet Statements." This booklet did a lot to systematize financial reporting, and also to make businessmen aware of the need to employ accountants who understood what was required in making reports.

THE MORAL OF MCKESSON & ROBBINS

During the 1920's the New York Stock Exchange also boosted the accountants' business by waging a continuous campaign to get corporations to provide more financial information. In 1933, after the crash, the Exchange, with advice from the institute, initiated a whole new series of standards for the treatment of unrealized profit, capital surplus, earned surplus, and other corporate financial items. The standards were incorporated into the accounting principles approved by the American Institute of Certified Public Accountants. That same year the Exchange also began requiring of all listed corporations an audit certificate by an independent C.P.A. Both of these developments did a lot to enhance the prestige and acceptance of the independent accountant.

The sensational revelations of the McKesson & Robbins case in 1939 temporarily impaired the profession's new prestige, but in the end, by showing the need for much more careful auditing practices, the case brought the profession a great deal of new business. When it was first revealed that the head of the drug company had swindled it of millions, principally by carrying fictitious inventories on the books, it was obvious that the profession had to revise completely many of its accepted methods of verification. The SEC investigation showed that the audit of McKesson & Robbins by Price Waterhouse had "conformed . . . to what was generally considered mandatory."

While the case was still warm, the A.I.C.P.A. set up a review committee, which proposed that future audits include direct verification of inventory, by personal inspection of warehouses where that seemed necessary; direct communication between auditor and debtor on a corporation's receivables; and the selection of auditors by directors, with the approval of the stockholders, who, in addition, should be entitled to a description of the scope of the auditor's work, and to read his opinion in a separate section of the annual report.

E.P.T. GETS THE BUSINESS

The profusion of taxes, and tax complications, have also accelerated the growth of the profession. Many Americans had their first contacts with accountants in the period just after 1913, the year when the first income-tax law was passed. Four years later, in 1917, the government passed its first excess-profits tax. Manufacturers now found that they had to calculate their profits in relation to the capital invested in their firms—a new and burdensome chore for many firms that had never systematically distinguished between, say, maintenance costs and new investment, and now found themselves obliged to reconstruct their books from the ground up. The first E.P.T., like those during World War II and the Korean war, generated a lot of business for the accountants.

Their tax practice is still growing. All of the Big Eight firms have tax departments staffed by anywhere between 100 and 250 specialists. Their clients today include not only corporations and wealthy individuals, but an increasing number of upper-middle-income citizens who find it necessary or convenient to pay $100 or $200 to have their accountancy chores handled by a national firm. No one knows just how many such people there are, but some accountants figure the total market for individuals at about 750,000—this being roughly the number of individuals whose taxable income is over $20,000, and who can expect that the Internal Revenue Service will probably audit their returns.

In building their tax business, the accountants have got into a battle with the legal profession. Back in 1913, lawyers generally shied away from tax work because it was highly technical and involved accounting concepts with which many of them were unfamiliar. But in the 1930's, as the tax rates mounted and tax problems entered increasingly into business and personal decisions, lawyers began to feel that they had let the accountants get too firm a hold on something good. The dispute came to a boil in 1943, when a client in New York balked at paying his accountant a $500 bill on the grounds that, in preparing his tax return, the accountant had given *legal* advice, which he was not professionally qualified to do. The accountant sued. The legal profession sensed an opportunity and the New York County Lawyers Association entered the case on behalf of the defendant. In alarm, the New York State Society of C.P.A.'s rushed to support the plaintiff. Later, a similar case cropped up in California. In both cases the courts ruled that the accountants were illegally engaging in the practice of law.

Both professional groups felt that the dispute was unseemly. In 1957 they agreed not to engage in any more court contests on such disputes, but instead to refer any cases that came up to a special mediating committee made up of representatives of both professions. However, neither profession has yielded an inch on its own asserted right to practice in the field of taxes.

ACCOUNTING TO ROYAL LITTLE

In the postwar years the rise of the accountants has been accelerated by three rather special phenomena: a vast wave of corporate mergers; the need for better accounting on the financial affairs of labor unions, pension and welfare funds, foundations, and other institutions; and the push of the big auditing firms into a vast, sprawling area they call "general management services."

The first two of these new phenomena are well known. During the 1950's the number of mergers involving manufacturing companies, for example, rose from about 300 to about 500 a year. Furthermore, mergers that do not come off—that bog down over some disagreement—also represent a substantial volume of accounting business. Royal Little of Textron, Inc., has had his auditor, Arthur Young & Co., do preliminary investigations of over 100 companies during the past five years alone; only twenty-five of the companies were eventually merged into Textron.

It seems likely that the market for noncorporate accounting services will continue to be expanded. The 1959 disclosure law requires labor unions to file financial statements with the Department of Labor but does not require these to be audited unless the Secretary requests an audit. Over 50,000 unions are affected, and most of them have by now filed their statements—mostly unaudited. The value of such statements is questioned in many quarters, and eventually, it seems likely, auditing of these statements will become widespread. Auditing of the nation's 150,000 welfare and pension funds has improved considerably since the passage, in 1958, of a law which requires that the funds' administrators account to the Secretary of Labor for all contributions, salaries, and fees, the rates given insurance carriers, and a variety of other data on investments and loans. Finally, there is a mounting pressure to get better audits of charitable and philanthropic funds. It was intensified by the scandal earlier this year over the finances of the Sister Elizabeth Kenny Foundation. When this foundation's finances were first audited back in 1951, Arthur Andersen & Co. refused to certify the financial statement attached to the report because the executives did not want to disclose that it had cost $975,000 to collect $1,240,000. It later turned out that these executives had prevented the Andersen audit from reaching the foundation's board of directors. And eight more years passed before the public learned what was happening to the money it had contributed to the foundation.

BREAD AND TOLL BOOTHS

The "management service" business has burgeoned in the accounting profession during the past few years. Many accountants find it confusing and hard to justify, but others consider it a logical and lucrative extension of what they have been doing in the financial field all along.

In effect, the auditors are going into competition with the management consultants. The independent auditor called upon to examine a corporation's financial records often becomes aware of the full range of problems facing the company—sometimes more acutely aware than management itself. Moreover, many auditors are real experts in some fields—e.g., a man who has spent twenty years auditing department stores often knows more about merchandising than some of his clients—and it was probably inevitable that such auditors, observing the surge of business to professional management-consultant firms, would feel a desire to sell their own expertise too. Moreover, many clients of auditors were requesting their help in developing systems to keep track of affairs and of records that were growing increasingly complex.

Some of the big auditing firms have committed themselves wholeheartedly to the management-services field. Ernst & Ernst, Peat, Marwick, and Price Waterhouse have staffs of 250 in their management-service divisions, and offer clients literally any management services they want. Ernst & Ernst, for example, will tackle any assignment in labor negotiations, personnel selection (it has its own staff psychologists available for consulting), new-product planning, and factory design and layout. Recently E. & E. took on the job of working out a control system for the New York State Thruway: it determined the number of men needed to man the toll booths at the heavy traffic periods, and it set up a record system to check the number of tickets sold. Arthur Young helped Becton, Dickinson & Co., the medical-supply firm, to determine the market for a disposable surgical needle it had developed, the price the needle should sell for, and the way it should be promoted. But many big auditing firms will handle only a few kinds of management chores. Recently a bakery firm asked

Lybrand, Ross to help it solve the problem of determining the optimum number of loaves to bake — i.e., so that it would not always have large amounts unsold and wasted on rainy days, and run short on sunny days. Lybrand, Ross considered the job to be primarily mathematical, and since the firm has its own research department, which is well able to apply mathematical techniques to inventory sampling and other accounting problems, it felt that it could take on the job.

An accounting firm's revenues are derived, or course, from renting out the services of its staff. Junior accountants in the big firms earn perhaps $5,500 a year, and senior accountants perhaps $7,500 to $12,500. These are the firm's "production workers" and, at the same time, its physical assets, and an idle junior or senior accountant is viewed with the same dismay a manufacturing company might view an idle plant. In general, a big firm feels that it can be profitable if its juniors and seniors are working for customers 75 per cent of the time. At this rate they would ordinarily generate revenues about two times their salaries, which would comfortably cover their own costs to the firm, and also the salaries of their superiors: the "managers" ($12,500 to $20,000), who run the offices, and the senior partners ($25,000 and up), who handle any large questions that arise with clients and in general devote most of their time to what might be called "diplomacy" — e.g., persuading clients that furniture cannot be written off in two years, or making recommendations on some other phase of the client's business, or pitching for new business.

This pitch is hampered by several kinds of restrictions. Not only is advertising unethical, but any competitive bidding is frowned on, and so is contacting a prospect without the knowledge of its incumbent auditing firm. Free-for-all competition is permissible only when a new company, which has never had an auditing firm, comes into the daylight. Then a direct approach can be made.

The elaborate procedures that surround the getting of new business can be seen in a switch in auditing firms recently made by Allied Stores, one of the nation's largest department-store chains. Several months ago, Allied broke the bad news to the firm of Touche, Ross, Bailey & Smart, that it was going to look for a new auditor. It then invited Ernst & Ernst and Arthur Andersen to visit its executive offices and make "presentations" for the account. Both auditing firms had meetings with several Allied executives in order to learn some of the particular requirements of the corporation. (As a matter of professional courtesy, Touche, Ross was kept notified of all these meetings.) Then the two firms sent delegations to Allied's offices on Fifth Avenue in New York and recited their own experience, made some promises about the time that their top men could personally give the account, and volunteered to discuss fees. The Ernst & Ernst delegation consisted of Hassel Tippit, the senior partner (see pp. 51–52), and William Stowe, the head of the New York office, who would be in direct charge of the account, and several staff men; the Arthur Andersen delegation was headed by senior partner Leonard Spacek. The results of these meetings were communicated to a committee of Allied's directors, which had been appointed by the board to make a recommendation.

Ernst & Ernst had several advantages in this competition. It had been Allied's auditor back in the 1940's, and was familiar with the company. It had pioneered the development of the last-in-first-out (LIFO) method of inventory valuation in the retail field. A substantial number of its ninety-five branch offices were near Allied's eighty-five stores, and E. & E. prepared a map that brought home the point forcefully at the presentations. The next day Ernst & Ernst was told it had the job—subject, of course, to the approval of the Allied directors.

PRICE CUTTING BY AUDITORS

As it happened, there was no detailed discussion of fees in these negotiations; Allied simply made it clear that it expected the fees to be in the normal range. But ordinarily such presentations do include some fairly explicit talk about costs and fees. Price competition between auditors can be intense—though price cutting in order to get an account is officially deplored in the profession. Auditing firms generally calculate their fees in relation to the time they expect their personnel to be occupied on an account; but a firm with a high proportion of its junior and senior accountants idle may submit a bid well under "the normal range" just to get them working again. Al Jennings, the senior partner of Lybrand, Ross Bros. & Montgomery, recalled recently that his firm had lost a big account to another of the Big Eight, which put in a "loss-leader" bid—after it had managed to wangle an invitation to make a presentation. Firms often submit such bids in the hope that after they get a foot in the door, they can gradually expand the volume of their work and their fees.

Another large influence on the bids that auditors submit, and on their costs in handling an account, is the extent of the client's own internal controls. A sizable number of large corporations have recently been building up their internal auditing staffs, in order to maintain consistent surveillance and control over their systems and procedures, to guard against fraud, etc. This internal auditing cuts down the independent auditor's case load considerably, and huge companies like General Motors and A.T. & T., which have such internal systems, are able to hold down the fees they pay their independent accountants.

In setting his fees, the independent auditor has to make a calculation about the length of time it will take him to familiarize himself with a company. Its sales volume is only a rough guide, but its "complexity"—the number of operations it performs, the number of branches or divisions—matters considerably. Merrill Lynch, Pierce, Fenner & Smith, possibly the most complex "service company" in the world, paid Haskins & Sells $164,000 last year.

In general, the auditing firm's work load is heaviest in the first year, when it is just getting to know the corporation, and some auditors expect to lose money on a big account in this year—even with normal fees. The loss should be recovered in the second year, when the work load drops by perhaps 25 per cent. In the third year the account pulls into the black. An auditor cannot very well submit a loss-leader bid if there is any danger of his losing the account within a few years, and many auditors are chary of bidding for business where there is a tendency to rotate auditors. For many years E. I. du Pont de Nemours & Co. has been the outstanding exponent of the rotation philosophy. The company used to change its auditors every three years; recently the time has been lengthened somewhat.

A QUESTION OF ROTATION

The rotation problem is a delicate subject in the auditing profession. Some corporations have formal policies calling for the rotation of auditors. They believe that their stockholders are entitled to receive fresh and objective views of their financial operations, and that an old, established auditor may begin simply to take the company's practices for granted. Some companies want to be sure that the auditor's loyalty is to his own organization and not to the officials he is supposed to be reporting on, who get to be his friends after a while. Finally, there is the problem that an auditor who has worked a long time on one account may develop a kind of vested interest in not uncovering any frauds or financial irregularities—i.e., any such discovery would reflect on his own handling of the account in the past.

Auditing firms do not have, to any great extent, the problem, usually associated with the advertising business, of the partner who "controls an account" and is able to walk off with it. The rotation of auditors on an account is one obvious deterrent. Even when some partners in auditing firms develop close and friendly relationships with the executives in client firms, it is hard for the client to justify giving them the account, because stability and manpower, rather than any special creative talent, are what auditing firms must primarily offer. One exception: in 1947, George Bailey, the partner in charge of the Detroit office of Ernst & Ernst, fell out with A. C. Ernst, and managed to take the Chrysler Corp. and many other clients away from the firm. Chrysler agreed to go with Bailey, but stipulated that he must have a large enough organization to service the account nationwide. Bailey then pulled together the firm of Touche, Niven, Bailey & Smart (now Touche, Ross, Bailey & Smart) today a member of the Big Eight, and still handling Chrysler's business.

How profitable are the big firms? For many big firms, in an average year, about 20 per cent of total revenues can be considered net income—i.e., it is available for distribution to the partners and for working capital. Auditing firms have one substantial expense that most other companies in "service" industries do not have. This is the cost of liability insurance—to protect the firm from any stockholder suit charging negligence in the event that a client suffers a substantial loss traceable to professional incompetence. (If such a charge were proved, the partnership would, of course, be fully liable for the entire amount.) Any of the Big Eight firms is likely to carry as much as $15 million of this insurance. (Coverage in such large amounts is offered only by Lloyds of London.) The auditing firms all prefer not to publicize the existence of this insurance on the ground that anyone contemplating a fraud is likely to be encouraged by the thought that everyone involved is insured.

THE PROBLEM OF "BIGNESS"

What sets the Big Eight apart from most other auditing firms is not only their size and influence, but also the fact that they are national—and international—in the scope of their operations. The bulk of public accounting in the U.S. is done by 25,000-odd small, local firms. In between these and the giants are a number of well-known semi-national firms, whose senior partners are also influential in the profession. These include Seidman & Seidman, Scovell Wellington, S. D. Leidesdorf, Main & Co., Horwath & Horwath, and Alexander Grant. Like the Big Eight, many of these firms are headquartered in New York; however, they characteristically have only a few branch offices and their gross revenues run below $10 million.

The problem of "bigness" agitates the accounting profession as much as it does many manufacturing industries. Virtually any member of the Big Eight or of the semi-national firms will say that the backbone of the profession is the small, local, independent accounting firm. Such firms still are the training grounds for the great majority of independent accountants. These firms have the great bulk of the personal tax business, and most of whatever auditing is done for the more than four million "small business" enterprises in the U.S. But these local firms have never been able to compete effectively with the national and semi-national firms for the business of big clients—e.g., those that generate over $10,000 a year in fees. The local firms face a continuing succession of tragedies as the small and medium-sized companies they have grown up with locally grow too big for them. It often happens that a local company separates from a local auditor when the company makes its first public offering of stock; at such times the underwriters are likely to insist that the prospectus bear the name of a national auditing firm—to ensure that a competent job will be done, and perhaps for reasons of prestige too.

Some small auditing firms have tried to cope with this problem by merging with other small firms. La France, Walker, Jackley & Saville, with sixty-three professional accountants, thirteen partners, and branch offices in seven cities, was formed last year in a merger of nine small firms—none of whom had more than seven professional employees before the merger. But more often the small firms are absorbed into the medium firms and the Big Eight. In July, 1959, for example, Alexander Grant merged four local firms into its organization.

Within the American Institute of Certified Public Accountants, the smaller firms have been pushing for a series of reforms that would help them to maintain their own identities and remain competitive. Many of them would like the institute's ethical code to include a ban on the vast "publishing activities" of big firms. The latter do, in fact, turn out a steady stream of booklets and magazines explaining and analyzing the operations of state tax codes, the functions of management service divisions, the problems arising out of new SEC regulations, etc. There is a vast amount of real scholarship in these publications, but the small firms feel that there is also a vast amount of promotion for their sponsors. The small firms would like the ethical code to ban the continued use of a deceased partner's name in a firm's name—i.e., they want to prevent the Big Eight from continuing to cash in on the immense prestige of some of their founders.

To help the small firms the institute is now sponsoring a professional training program designed for accountants in two-to-five-partner firms. The program includes, for example, training in the application of management services to small business. It also includes, oddly enough, a study of the special economic problems of small accounting firms—which are often considerable, principally because the partners are apt to be young and inexperienced, and trained in handling other companies' accounting problems, not their own.

THE FOOTING IS ELECTRONIC

The widespread introduction of electronic data-processing equipment in the accounting profession recently has left some auditors with a feeling that the profession's economics are about to be transformed. E.D.P. equipment has vastly increased the efficiency of many routine operations of the big clients, especially the so-called "posting and footing" operations. (This is what the profession calls routine bookkeeping work, e.g., checking classifications.) The new equipment will increasingly cut down the proportion of junior accountants required by the big firms. Haskins & Sells, for example, used twenty juniors back in 1950 to make a headquarters audit for one of the big farm-equipment firms. In 1960 they used only seven. Seidman & Seidman reports that the ratio of junior accountants to seniors in its firm has declined by 25 per cent in the past two years. One interesting application of the use of E.D.P. by a *small* firm is provided by Young, Skutt & Breitenwischer of Jackson, Michigan. The firm was approached last year by a local manufacturer who had bought a computer and then found he could not really keep it busy. He suggested that the accountants take it off his hands, use it in their own operations, and rent it out to their clients when they were not using it. This scheme has worked out nicely so far.

THE AUDITING BOOM IN WASHINGTON

The increasing influence of accountants and auditors has not been confined to private business. Accountants are proliferating furiously in the great public bureaucracies as well, and at all levels, from the municipalities to the federal government. Auditors and accountants are the fastest growing of all occupations in the federal government; there are now 16,845. Of the FBI's some 6,000 special agents, over 700 are trained accountants. In the General Accounting office there are 1,800 professional accountants—over 400 of these are C.P.A.'s, among them the Controller General himself.

The rise of accountants in government, as in private industry, is essentially a reflection of the endless complexity of the modern world. At many levels of government today, accountants are inextricably involved in the formation of policy—often because they are the only officials able to make sense of a modern government budget. Abraham Beame, the budget director of the City of New York, completely dominates many policy-making sessions of the city's Board of Estimate, principally because he is apt to be the only official present who knows what is possible within the scope of the city budget. Professor Wallace Sayre of Columbia University, who recently made a detailed study of the workings of the city government, says that Beame is "the single most powerful official in the city." At the national level, U.S. Budget Director Maurice Stans has played an important role in several major policy decisions, including a very controversial decision to cut back the B-70 program to the development of a single prototype. (Actually, Stans argued for a complete cessation of the B-70 program, but the Air Force finally got the President to agree to a prototype program.)

The whole federal system of accounting was overhauled ten years ago, with the passage of the Budget and Accounting Procedures Act of 1950. This called for much more complete disclosure of the government's financial operations, and authorized the establishment of new accounting and reporting systems for each executive agency of the government. It directed the Bureau of the Budget, the Secretary of the Treasury, and the Controller General, to conduct a joint program for the improvement of cost accounting in the government. Before 1950, federal accounting systems were dominated completely by the General Accounting Office and the Treasury Department, with the emphasis on "allotment accounting," which was designed to keep agencies' expenses and obligations under control. Few attempts were then made to use cost accounting so that agencies could present budgets that systematically related their costs to their proposed operations. The 1950 act required the Executive Department to project its requirements through the Bureau of the Budget. With the Eisenhower Administration's greater emphasis on balancing the budget, the bureau's power and prestige were steadily expanded. The budget director now receives an earlier and more detailed picture of the over-all operations of the executive department than any other individual; and this fact probably made a policy role for him inevitable.

WHY AUDITORS ARE UNEASY

Many accountants and auditors, although delighted with the volume of new business and new responsibilities they have acquired during the 1950's, will confess to a kind of uneasiness about their situation. Their uneasiness stems from a feeling that the profession has not yet done a satisfactory job of resolving all the uncertainties and ambiguities as to the proper ethical conduct of auditors in situations where their private interests seem to clash with their clients'. But there is an even larger ambiguity as to what constitutes "generally accepted accounting principles." And many auditors believe that it is an urgent matter to resolve these before the profession is inundated by the load of new business it expects in the 1960's. The ambiguities are more than mere details; they are numerous and fundamental, and many auditors believe that unless they are resolved, the interpretation of many financial statements will come down to an elaborate guessing game. The nature of these ambiguities, and the prospects for resolving them, will be discussed in a second article next month. . . .

"The beginning of wisdom," say the Chinese, "is to call things by their right names." The 71,000 certified public accountants in the U.S. are every year becoming more aware that finding the "right" names for business operations may be the most arduous part of the unending search for a more understandable, more rational, more honest, and more efficient business society. When the terms that measure business performance are used inflexibly, business practice may be unduly constricted. But when these terms are used too loosely, business practice may degenerate into confusion and mistrust.

At their convention in Philadelphia last September, the C.P.A.'s labored mightily to find a set of principles that would minimize both dangers. They need such principles as underpinnings for their professional code of ethics and to gain more respect for their professional independence.

One afternoon during the convention, about a thousand of the most distinguished C.P.A.'s in the U.S. gathered in the Rose Garden Room of the Bellevue-Stratford Hotel, to hear what was billed as a debate on the principles of their profession. An uninitiated visitor wandering into the room might have thought at first that they were arguing over some minor, tedious technicalities, and so might have been puzzled by the passions that were manifestly stirred up. The C.P.A.'s themselves knew that the debate concerned a lot more than technicalities. They knew that they—the members of the American Institute of Certified Public Accountants—were in a position to influence considerably both the financial reports of companies and the business practices to which the reports refer. In recent years the A.I.C.P.A. has, in fact, become a kind of private financial legislature; working within the limits imposed by tax and securities laws, its members advise businessmen as to correct and permissible procedures to be followed in reporting their financial affairs. What now bothers many members of the profession, and what occasioned the debate, is the fact that the limits of permissibility stretch pretty far these days.

The case against flexibility was argued by Leonard Spacek, the senior partner of Arthur Andersen & Co. Spacek is regarded within the profession as something of a rebel. He knew that he was speaking to a predominantly hostile audience, and he made no attempt to conciliate it; peering sternly from the lectern through thick glasses, never smiling, never raising or lowering his voice, he set forth the case for greater uniformity in accounting procedures. His opponent and opening speaker in the debate was Maurice Peloubet, the white-haired senior partner of Pogson, Peloubet & Co., whose benign and avuncular manner contrasted sharply with Spacek's. Peloubet argued forcefully that businessmen *should* have maximum flexibility in handling their financial affairs. In the ensuing question-and-answer period Spacek promised that his fight would continue; he said that eventually he would "tear to shreds" the case for flexibility. His firm had already done a lot to arouse the profession. Currently, for example, he is circulating a booklet citing twenty different issues on which the institute's own position differs from the practice of many of its members, or on which the institute's position is unclear, or on which new financial developments have raised new questions about the institute's position.

"THE TRUTH AS IT ACTUALLY IS"

The problems the profession is concerned about may be suggested, briefly at this point, by citing some figures:

> In the past nine years Texaco has reported earnings some $213 million below what it might have if it had adopted different (but also acceptable) methods of accounting for intangible costs involved in drilling operations.

> The Great Atlantic & Pacific Tea Co.'s balance sheet shows about $560 million (arbitrarily capitalized at ten times current rent payments) less of debt than it would if the company had followed a policy of owning its stores rather than one of sale and lease-back. Although the company is under a long-term obligation on the stores, these lease commitments do not have to appear on the balance sheet as debt.

> The American Electric Power Co. has been able to increase its stockholders' equity by some $67 million by crediting deferred federal income taxes to a restricted earned surplus.

> In 1958 the Transamerica Corp. increased its assets figure almost fourfold, to $149 million, by reporting its subsidiaries at book value instead of original cost.

The institute has been aware for several years that it will have to take a position either for continued flexibility in handling financial statements or for uniformity. C.P.A.'s have been zealous in their insistence that their work calls for a high degree of judgment; yet at the same time they have been apprehensive that their judgments, unless tied to some systematic set of principles, will come to seem arbitrary. Some members of the profession talk ambitiously of the "principles" on which accounting practices rest, and of the "postulates" on which the principles rest—as though the whole edifice had been constructed logically, like theorems in geometry. Yet there is no definitive list of principles or postulates, and many of the practices have simply evolved ad hoc.

In the debate in Philadelphia, Spacek made it clear that his quest for uniformity was related to a desire to help investors "find the truth as it actually is." Peloubet, by contrast, ridiculed the notion that there is "some sort of absolute truth. . . . This exists nowhere else and will not be found in the practice of accounting"—which merely requires "that the conventions and assumptions on which the accounts are prepared should be clearly stated." Peloubet's view on this matter has generally prevailed within the profession over the years.

George O. May, often identified as the dean of the modern U.S. accounting profession . . . , remarked many years ago that the "world of business . . . is subject to constant and sometimes violent change and full of uncertainties." He added that the works of accountants "cannot rise higher in the scale of certainty than the events which they reflect."

The effort to cut through all the ambiguities in modern accounting gained momentum at the 1957 convention of the A.I.C.P.A., with a speech by Alvin R. Jennings, the senior partner of Lybrand, Ross Bros. & Montgomery. Jennings proposed that the profession buttress its theoretical underpinnings, in part by organizing a sizable new research effort. Specifically, he persuaded the members to support a new research division, staffed by both academicians and practitioners, that would codify, analyze, and recommend changes in prevailing accounting practice. Also the organization of an Accounting Principles Board, which would work out an agreed-upon body of doctrine, was an indirect result of his proposals. The board was organized last year and, since Spacek is now on it, will be addressing itself soon to the issues he has raised.

THE ETHICS OF AUDITORS

The accountants' intensified concern about their principles is related to their consciousness that the importance and status of their profession have been rising rapidly; but that even so it lacks the independence and authority that come from having at its back a systematic body of solid and settled principles. The lawyer serves his client, but he takes his guidance from a body of law and knowledge on which the client's beliefs and wishes have no influence. The accountant occupies a much lower place on the scale of independency. His code will not, of course, allow him to put his name to an outright untruth. But he is sometimes caught in a position where there is no agreement in his profession about the way "the truth" shall be stated—and this makes it harder for him to be independent of his client's demands.

In 1959, for example, the Alaska Juneau Gold Mining Co. pressed its auditor, Arthur Andersen, to permit a revaluation (upward) of certain of the company's properties to offset partially a substantial net reduction in the over-all assets. The Andersen firm did not agree that any properties should be written up, although it conceded that the case was not clear-cut. Alaska Juneau thereupon switched to Arthur Young & Co., whose partners, after careful study, felt there was merit in the management's position. This sequence of events suggests the pressures that auditors are often under, and the range of ethical problems they face in the absence of agreed-upon accounting principles. In Philadelphia this year, the institute's efforts to clarify its rules about members' independence, and about their ethical obligations in general, consumed more time than, and created as much of a fuss as, the debate over accounting principles.

Some of the ethical prohibitions confronting C.P.A.'s are clear-cut. It is plainly a violation of the code to advertise or solicit new business, or to tell outsiders about clients' business transactions. But other situations are not easy to resolve. Consider two very sticky problems recently faced by auditors:

Not long ago a partner in one of the Big Eight national firms made the arresting discovery that some employees of one corporation he was auditing received payments from a supplier company that he was also auditing. The partner was ethically bound not to reveal this information to the executives of the first corporation (i.e., because it involved confidential information obtained in the course of auditing the supplier company). At the same time, he was found to protect the first corporation from repetition of the practice. He finally resolved the matter by asking the chief executive officer of this corporation to state the company policy on such payments. When he was told that they were forbidden, he disclosed that the policy was being violated—but left it up to the management to detect and halt these practices.

A partner in another Big Eight firm found, in checking the books of one client, that a high proportion of its assets consisted of receivables from another client—which, the auditor knew, was close to bankruptcy. He could not reveal this fact to the first company; yet he had to insist that larger reserves than usual be set up against possible losses on the receivables. The management of the first company made it clear that they thought his demand unreasonable. This left the auditor in a painful and precarious position, but he stuck to his guns, and eventually management accepted his recommendation.

INDEPENDENCE—BUT HOW MUCH?

The ethical problem that commanded most attention at Philadelphia concerned the "independence issue." This issue involves a lot more than the problem of the client exerting pressure on an auditor who wants to keep an account. The issue also embraces some questions about auditors' impartiality in handling secure accounts.

It is clear that an auditor must not have, or even seem to have, any motive for failing to disclose misleading information in his client's accounts. The SEC has ruled that no auditor can be considered independent if he has a financial interest in a client; and auditors practicing before the commission cannot own shares or serve as directors or officers in corporations whose financial statements they audit in connection with public offerings. The Big Eight firms generally have adopted this principle, and as a matter of policy bar their partners and managers from owning stock in or serving as directors of any client corporation. A partner in Price Waterhouse, for example, is barred from investing in about 400 listed companies.

Several leaders of the A.I.C.P.A. have been prodding the institute to require *all* C.P.A. firms to follow the Big Eight in barring such investments. The Illinois state society has already passed rules forbidding an auditor to express an opinion on the financial statement of a concern in which he has any financial interest or with which he is associated as a director, officer, or promoter. But at the Philadelphia convention the institute leaders ran into trouble when they tried to get the membership to bar such holdings formally.

Spokesmen for some of the small firms argued that the concept of independence could not be linked mechanically to the absence of such holdings. In some cases, they said, they had been asked to help out young enterprises, often when these were close to bankruptcy. In many such cases, these auditors argued, they had been willing to help the companies conserve cash by taking payment in stock; now it would be unfair to make them dispose of this stock in order to keep the accounts. Furthermore, they contended, only a small proportion of the nation's C.P.A.'s practice before the SEC, and it would be unfair to saddle a majority of the profession with standards that are relevant only for a minority.

The whole debate was intensely embarrassing to the leaders of the institute. Part of their embarrassment arose from the strong feeling of many members that the Big Eight, and the semi-national firms, too, already have too much influence in the institute—and the more rigorous standards were plainly modeled on Big Eight practice. The dispute accentuated the divided interest of the big and small firms and highlighted the fact that they have different standards of ethics. Supporters of the proposed standards, not anticipating a proxy contest, had done no campaigning or proxy soliciting. The small firms—the one-to-five-man outfits—did solicit proxies against the proposed rule, and apparently they got enough to make its adoption doubtful. As soon as it was doubtful, its proponents grew leery of bringing it to a vote at all; the one thing they did *not* want was a vote showing the institute membership against stricter standards. After a great deal of parliamentary maneuvering and a certain amount of unparliamentary chaos—at one point five overlapping and contradictory motions were being entertained by the chair—there was a vote to defer the issue until next year, and the session adjourned. The issue will undoubtedly be on the agenda for 1961.

HOW TO TRY A C.P.A.

The conduct of certified public accountants is subject to several different kinds of discipline. Some of it is imposed by state licensing authorities, which, however, have widely varying standards. Some of the discipline is exerted by state C.P.A. societies, whose standards are in principle — but not always in practice — as high as the national organization's. In addition, a C.P.A. who certifies financial statements concerning securities of any listed company must agree to observe the regulations of the SEC. Finally, he may join the American Institute of C.P.A.'s and agree to abide by its code of ethics. (The institute has about 38,000 of the 71,000 licensed C.P.A.'s in the U.S.) Of all these organizations, the American Institute exerts the tightest discipline.

Some of the state licensing authorities and associations have, in fact, been powerless to require accountants to adhere to their presumed standards. C.P.A.'s who have been expelled from the A.I.C.P.A. often continue to practice undisturbed by the state authorities. One C.P.A. was expelled by the institute after he pleaded *nolo contendere* in a federal tax-fraud case; he had been charged with allowing his client, a hardware retailer, to manipulate profit figures in such a way that he evaded $125,000 in income taxes over a four-year period. The auditor is still practicing in Pennsylvania.

The institute has three penalties it may invoke against transgressors. It may admonish, suspend, or expel them. Many of the admonitions are for borderline offenses — e.g., for seeming to violate the rule against self-advertisement by allowing a local bank to tell its depositors that a C.P.A. who is a "tax expert" will be available for consultation at certain hours. Suspensions and expulsions are for more serious offenses, are relatively rare, and cannot be invoked without a trial. In the period from May, 1956, to September, 1960, twenty-one members of the institute were brought to trial. Eleven were expelled, and eight were suspended, and two were acquitted.

The trial procedure is quite formal. First, a fifteen-member Committee on Professional Ethics establishes a prima-facie case that the rules of conduct have been violated. Then the case is handed over to a twenty-one-man trial board. The accused C.P.A. may be, and usually is, represented by counsel. The case is presented by the chairman of the Committee on Professional Ethics, and the whole trial rarely takes longer than a day — usually only two or three hours. It requires a simple majority of the trial board to suspend a member from the institute, and a two-thirds vote to expel him.

Despite all the parliamentary uproar over "independence," most of the men at Philadelphia were aware that the larger problem facing their profession was the fuzziness about the basic principles of accounting. The institute's current attempt to clarify these principles is not its first. Indeed, it had a Committee on Accounting Procedure before its new Accounting Principles Board was set up, and the former issued basic opinions for twenty years, beginning in 1939. There are now fifty-one bulletins outlining accepted accounting principles, and some regard them as a sort of catechism of the profession. They do, in fact, constitute the most authoritative written guides to good accounting practice. But accountants have had varying degrees of loyalty to these bulletins, at least one of them having been virtually ignored by the profession. (This stated the preferred method of writing off plant and equipment under the wartime rapid-depreciation laws.) A more recent bulletin, dealing with the procedure to be followed in treating welfare and pension plans, was two years in preparation, went through fifteen drafts, was finally exposed to the profession, then was revised, re-exposed, and then formally issued. It still has not gained complete acceptance.

Can the Accounting Principles Board gain a more widespread acceptance of *its* recommendations? The new board has at least one large advantage over the old committee: its members are aware that the confusions about acceptable practices cannot be ended merely by issuing a lot of specific recommendations—and they are resolved that the board shall clarify first principles first. With the principles clarified, it may be easier to get agreement on practices.

On the other hand, the new board has some new problems. One problem is simply that tax laws and securities regulations are much more complex than they used to be. In the complexity there is at least some room for businessmen to maneuver—to make decisions more freely—and any attempt to codify the handling of related financial data reduces the area of freedom, and will surely meet some resistance. A related difficulty has arisen from the steady shift in emphasis and interest away from the balance sheet and toward the income statement. Investors, security analysts, bankers, and even some creditors have grown more interested in the earnings capacities of companies than in their assets and liabilities. (It is almost forgotten today that until the passage of the Securities Act in 1933 many public corporations did not even issue income statements; the curious investor could deduce the income only from changes in net worth shown on successive balance sheets.) The tremendous premium placed by the stock market today on high earnings capacities suggests that reforms tending to lower some companies' reported earnings will meet with considerable resistance.

OILY FINANCIAL STATEMENTS

Perhaps the most spectacular example of the flexibility of modern accounting is provided by the disparate handling of the oil industry. At present there are several alternative procedures, all "generally accepted," that may be followed in accounting for the intangible costs of drilling productive wells—at least, in accounting to stockholders. In tax reports to the U.S. Government, almost all oil companies charge off their intangible drilling costs against income in the year the cost is incurred. But in their published reports, oil companies generally follow one of three procedures. The first, which seems to be the most conservative (because it results in lower reported earnings), is used by Amerada Petroleum Corp. Amerada charges all intangible drilling costs against income immediately. ("Tangible" costs, i.e., of equipment, are of course depreciated at varying rates.) Under the Amerada procedure, a company with, say, $200,-000 of income and $100,000 of intangible drilling costs would report the balance of $100,000 as taxable income. After paying the 52 per cent corporate income tax, the company would show a net profit of $48,000—exactly in line with its tax return.

The second procedure, perhaps the most liberal, is followed by Standard Oil of New Jersey and many other companies. Jersey does not charge any intangible drilling costs against income, at least not at the time the well is drilled. Instead, the intangible costs of productive wells are capitalized; and so they show up on the balance sheet as new assets, and not on the income statement as expenses. Under the Jersey method, therefore, the company with $200,000 of income would report all of this amount. However, companies using this method report to their stockholders only the actual taxes paid to the government—$52,000 in this case—which means that they can report a net profit of $148,000, roughly three times as much as a company using the Amerada method.

Midway between these two extremes, and increasingly popular with accountants, is a reporting procedure followed by Texaco and Shell Oil and others. Like Jersey, these companies immediately put the intangible costs of productive wells on their books as assets; and if they have the same $200,000 of income, they do not deduct these costs from it. But unlike Jersey, these companies suggest in their published reports that they pay taxes on the full amount —i.e., they show a provision of $104,000 for taxes and so report a net of $96,-000. Since they actually had to pay only $52,000 in taxes, they take the other $52,000—i.e., the taxes saved—as a reduction of the $100,000 cost of developing the well; and so the net asset that appears on the balance sheet is the $48,000 difference. This asset is charged against income over the useful life of the well—perhaps at the rate of $4,800 a year if the well is presumed to be good for ten years.

In sum, then, three different oil companies, each with revenues of $200,000, each with intangible development costs of $100,000, and each actually paying the U.S. Government $52,000 in taxes, might report three considerably different net-income figures to the public: $48,000, $96,000, or $148,000—and all three would be following "generally accepted accounting procedure." Furthermore, *none of the companies would be under any obligation to tell the public which procedure they were following;* they would only be obliged to indicate if and when and how they changed their procedures. Texaco, Shell, and Jersey Standard do not indicate in their annual reports how they account for intangible development costs. (Amerada does make its accounting practice clear.)

The businessman aghast at all this flexibility can be reassured on one point at least: Amerada's procedure results in lower earnings reports, and Jersey's in higher, only in the short run. In the long run, and *ceteris paribus,* the accounting procedure adopted will have little effect on earnings. Eventually, Amerada's reported earnings will be bolstered by revenues from wells it has already written off. And eventually, Jersey's reported income will be depressed by the amortization costs of its wells.

HOT WATER IN POOLS

Investors also have a problem in evaluating the financial data relating to mergers; and the New York Stock Exchange recently asked the American Institute of Certified Public Accountants to straighten out a large, continuing confusion about two different kinds of mergers: purchases and pools. In principle, a merger may take place *(a)* when one company purchases another, or *(b)* when two companies pool their interests. In either case, there is likely to be an exchange of stock. The difference is that in a purchase the smaller company becomes a part of the parent; in a "pooling of interests" the companies are simply blended into one, whose assets, liabilities, and net worth are the sum of these pairs of items on the two original balance sheets. Perhaps a half of all big mergers these days are pools.

Why should the distinction be of any interest to investors? Consider some recent examples:

Not long ago, C.I.T. Financial Corp. merged with the privately owned Home Finance Service. To swing the merger, C.I.T. had to give stock with a market value of $5,600,000 in exchange for Home Finance stock with a book value of $3,600,000. If the merger had been construed as a purchase, C.I.T.'s assets would have had to reflect an additional $2-million cost, and amortizing this amount might have created a steady drain on reported profits in the years following. Instead, C.I.T. reported a pooling of interests with Home Finance — and so it had no problem

The Automatic Canteen Co. of America was recently involved in two mergers. In one of them it exchanged 82,500 shares of its own stock for Nationwide Food Service, Inc. In the second merger, six weeks later, Automatic Canteen exchanged 40,970 shares for the stock of the A.B.T. Manufacturing Corp. In this second merger the stock exchanged was about equal in value, and the deal was called an acquisition. But in the first case the Automatic Canteen stock was worth some $2 million more than the book value of the company it merged with; and calling this deal an acquisition might have required a write-off of the differential. The deal was called a pooling.

Here again, the basic problem is that public corporations have considerable latitude in reporting on their earnings and financial position. The A.I.C.P.A. has, to be sure, outlined a number of standards that accountants are supposed to follow in determining whether a merger can be considered a pooling: the institute says, for example, that the relative sizes of two companies should not be wildly out of line, and specifically suggests that the smaller company's assets should not be less than 5 per cent of the larger company's. Actually, Automatic Canteen acquired Nationwide Food Service in exchange for only 1.6 per cent of its own stock. Yet it would be unfair to suggest that the deal violated accepted accounting procedure. For different C.P.A.'s assign different weights to the several standards, and no one of them is considered controlling.

PENSION RIGHTS AND WRONGS

Another large accounting problem, also unresolved by the profession, concerns the proper method of reporting on pension funds. Ever since the first great wave of corporate pension plans broke over the profession a decade ago, accountants have been trying to grapple with the two kinds of costs involved in pension planning. One cost, which has created few problems, reflects the pension credits built up by the employees in the current year. The other cost, which *has* created problems, is incurred in amortizing the employees' "past service liability." The main accounting questions were, and still are, how this liability should appear on the balance sheet, and how much of it should be charged against income every year.

Corporate responses to both questions have varied widely. When U.S. Steel inaugurated its pension plan in 1950, the corporation's unamortized past-service liability was estimated at $574 million—an amount equal to half the market value of all the common and preferred stock at the time! In most subsequent years U.S. Steel has made payments for past-service charges. But in 1958 the corporation contended that past-service charges were amortized adequately and that it did not have to make a payment that year. Price Waterhouse had no real grounds for rejecting the company's contention, but insisted on inserting in the annual report a long paragraph spelling out the change that had taken place. The effect of the change, in any case, was to increase the corporation's reported net profit that year from $200 million to $300 million (i.e., the pension cost was reduced by about $100 million). In 1959, U.S. Steel resumed its payments for past-service costs.

The institute has done little to clarify pension reporting practices. In 1956 it issued a bulletin to the effect that financial statements should at least indicate the present liability, actuarially calculated, of future pension commitments. But the institute has never got any agreement on the best way to charge for past-service costs, and some sizable corporations do not even make charges for current-service costs. Until this year, for example, American Tobacco has had an unfunded pension plan, and the only pension charges shown in its financial statements were actual payments to retired employees. At the other extreme, the Gillette Co. is one of the few large corporations that have funded substantially all their past-service liability. And in between are a fair number of corporations—e.g., American-Standard—that contribute to pension funds each year only the additional obligation incurred that year—with no contributions for past-service liability.

ACCOUNTING AND INFLATION

In general, many auditors believe, most of the big disagreements in their profession concern proper methods of allocating costs over periods of time. And some auditors believe that the biggest disagreement of all during the next decade will concern what they call "price-level depreciation"—a method of allocating costs over periods of time when prices are fluctuating.

The debate begins with the concept of depreciation itself. Originally, accountants thought of depreciation simply as an amortization of costs incurred in the past. But since World War II a second concept has become more widespread—the "shoebox" concept of depreciation charges as a reserve put aside for replacement of worn-out plant and equipment. This new concept brought a new problem with it. In a period when the purchasing power of the dollar has been declining, it obviously requires more dollars to replace worn-out plant and equipment. Some accountants, including Leonard Spacek of Arthur Andersen, contend that present depreciation charges are not realistic. They believe that annual depreciation charges, whether calculated on a straight-line or accelerated basis, should be increased (or, conceivably, decreased) as the cost of living changes. Thomas Higgins, the senior partner of Arthur Young & Co., suggests that the profession might get into price-level depreciation by encouraging its corporate clients to publish two sets of figures—one adjusted for prices, the other unadjusted. A strong body of opinion in the A.I.C.P.A. is still against any such change, however. Carman Blough, the institute's very influential research head, does not believe that inflation has yet been severe enough to distort the meaning of present depreciation figures. Anyway, he argues, why should price-level accounting be limited to depreciation? Blough points out, for example, that no auditor has proposed charging against income any figure for insurance costs higher than the actual costs, even though insurance premiums are sure to rise in an inflationary era. (Higgins is for using price-level reporting on any item that is "material"—which presumably excludes corporate insurance charges.)

While price-level depreciation is not an accepted accounting method in the U.S., it is accepted in Europe, and more U.S. investors are likely to begin encountering the problem as the securities of more foreign corporations are traded in U.S. markets. In 1956, for example, Simca, the French auto company, sold some capital shares in the U.S. In its prospectus, which was passed by the SEC, Simca noted that under French tax law it was permitted to account for the loss in purchasing power of the franc by putting a higher figure on its fixed assets. Simca has continued to depreciate its assets on the basis of the adjusted figures. Philips' Gloeilampenfabrieken, a Dutch electrical manufacturer with many U.S. shareholders, uses price-level depreciation regularly.

One large difficulty about price-level depreciation is that, in a time of rising prices, the additional charges against income might depress earnings. Five years ago, Professor Ralph C. Jones of Yale made a study of this problem for the American Accounting Association (an organization composed primarily of teachers of accounting). One of the companies Jones studied was the New York Telephone Co., a member of the Bell family. His figures show that in 1946–52, New York Telephone reported 50 per cent more income than it would have reported if depreciation charges had been inflated along with the dollar.

THE POWER TO DECIDE

It is clear that the profession's principal unresolved problems will have to be solved, ultimately, by the A.I.C.P.A. and its new Accounting Principles Board. It is also clear that the actual powers of the institute and the board are still undefined. The scope of these powers was tested early last year in a case raised by three subsidiaries of the American Electric Power Co., which sought a court injunction to prevent the institute from issuing an "interpretation" of one of its prior opinions. Much of the ammunition against the institute was supplied by Donald C. Cook, an executive vice president of A.E.P., who also happens to be a member of the institute. Cook and his company argued that the influence of the institute had already led the SEC to change its approved procedure on the recording of deferred tax payments, and that some state regulatory agencies had followed the SEC's lead. (Cook also happens to be a former chairman of the SEC.) Until the institute and the SEC acted, A.E.P. had been allowed to carry deferred tax payments on its books in a "restricted earned surplus," which technically forms part of the stockholders' equity. The change had the immediate effect of reducing this equity by $67 million; and Cook contended that the reduction made it harder for the company to borrow money, and obliged it to sell stock instead—which, he also contended, was more expensive in the long run.

The battle between Cook and the institute is not over yet. The U.S. Supreme Court has upheld the right of the institute to circulate its opinions. But in Kentucky, at least, A.E.P. is still fighting. Its subsidiary, Kentucky Power, points to a state utility regulation which specifies that deferred taxes *shall* be reflected in restricted earned surplus. The subsidiary is doing some financing now, which brings it into direct conflict with the SEC, and may enable it to take the issue back to the Supreme Court—this time on the question whether the state's rules or the SEC's should be governing.

The institute's powers are especially ambiguous as they relate to regulated companies—e.g., railroads, airlines, public utilities, whose rates are regulated, and also banks, savings-and-loan companies, insurance companies, and stockbrokers, where regulation is concerned mainly with protecting consumers against fraud. Perhaps because these companies are regulated in so many other ways—to protect passengers, depositors, policyholders, etc.—not much concern has been given to the problems of their *stockholders,* and many such companies are not required to have audited financial statements. It is often hard for investors to make any meaningful evaluation of these companies as business enterprises. Accounting in the banking and insurance fields, for example, shows a preoccupation with the companies' solvency but is weak on their earning power. Fewer than 20 per cent of the nation's 14,000 banks are audited by independent certified public accountants. Robert A. Eden, a savings-and-loan executive who has extensively studied the varying accounting methods in use, said recently, "Two otherwise identical savings banks might report net income differing by thousands and even hundreds of thousands of dollars . . . might differ in total assets over the years by possibly millions of dollars."

WHERE THE POWER ENDS

If accountants need some clarification of their powers, they also need a greater public awareness of where that power and responsibility end. Many businessmen are surprised to learn that a corporate financial statement is the responsibility of management, not of the auditing firm. The chief executive of a corporation must give his auditors a letter of representation in which he states that, to the best of his knowledge and belief, all the information in the report is true and fairly presented. Technically, and legally, the auditor is responsible only for the honesty of his own opinion certificate, in which he ordinarily says that his investigations have led him to believe that the company's assets, liabilities, and earnings reports are fairly presented.

Not, of course, that the certificate is an unimportant matter. Any qualifications that may be expressed in it are attentively noted by investors these days. Stockholders are questioning auditors more frequently and more intensively at annual meetings, and often demanding to know why corporations changed their auditors. Questions about conflict-of-interest situations, as at Chrysler Corp. (see "Behind the Conflict at Chrysler," *Fortune,* November, 1960), are increasingly directed at the auditors, as well as at management. The selection of independent auditors is more often being submitted for stockholder approval. Some auditors believe that the time may soon come when U.S. stockholders will have the same legal rights as British stockholders, who are entitled, at annual meetings, to have both the old and new auditing firms present when there is any change in auditors. One way or another, it seems likely that auditors in the U.S. will be answering a lot of questions in the next few years.

STANDINGS OF THE TEAMS

The Big Eight partnerships dominate the auditing world, and their senior partners, portrayed on the pages following, provide that world with most of its leadership and direction. These firms operate in a stately and dignified environment, mostly in the Wall Street area, and the competition among them often seems to be muffled by all the rules about "ethics." Nevertheless, the competition is real and intense.

Unlike advertising agencies and law firms, auditing firms do not consider it unethical to serve clients competing against one another, and several of the Big Eight firms have important specialties in certain industries. Arthur Young & Co. has been strongest in the oil and gas fields. Touche, Ross, Bailey & Smart does auditing for both Macy's and Gimbels, and for scores of other retail corporations. Arthur Andersen & Co. originally made its reputation unraveling

Firm	Partners	Offices	Est. Gross
			(in millions)
Peat, Marwick, Mitchell & Co.	190	60	$45
Arthur Andersen & Co.	171	28	40
Ernst & Ernst	132	95	36
Price Waterhouse & Co.	101	40	35
Haskins & Sells	176	36	33
Lybrand, Ross Bros. & Montgomery	126	35	28
Arthur Young & Co.	104	28	26
Touche, Ross, Bailey & Smart	71	27	17

the snarled affairs of the Insull utility empire, and still maintains a strong position in utilities: today Andersen audits perhaps a third of all U.S. utility companies. (However, it does not have the business of the world's largest utility, the American Telephone & Telegraph Co., which is audited by Lybrand, Ross Bros. & Montgomery.)

One firm that has expanded in almost all possible directions is Peat, Marwick, Mitchell & Co., which has got to be the largest in the profession through an aggressive program of mergers. Its biggest single lift came in 1950, when it absorbed the established old firm of Barrow, Wade, Guthrie & Co. Price Waterhouse has always had a broad client base, and although smaller today than several other firms, it still audits more listed corporations than anyone else. It also retains a substantial foreign business through its contacts with affiliated firms, working in an international P. W. partnership. Haskins & Sells, which was the first major auditing firm founded by American accountants—most of the early firms were British in origin—also has a broadly based clientele, which includes the largest U.S. industrial corporation, General Motors, and hundreds of very small clients too. (In the world of the Big Eight, a small client is ordinarily thought of as one whose fees do not get above $10,000 a year.) Ernst & Ernst has built up its business substantially by moving very heavily into the "management services" field, in which it pioneered.

Because they are private partnerships, none of the Big Eight firms are required to disclose any information about their size or revenues. The last time any such data were spread on the record was in 1939, when the Securities and Exchange Commission was investigating the McKesson & Robbins scandal, and auditing practices generally. At that time the SEC report indicated that Price Waterhouse was the largest firm in the U.S. Peat, Marwick then had twenty-five partners and Arthur Andersen fifteen. The figures on partners shown above are not strictly comparable, since some firms have several classes of partnerships and others do not; however, these and other figures do at least make it clear that the relative sizes of the firms have changed a lot since 1939. The figures are *Fortune's* estimates and are based on information from a wide variety of sources. None of the firms named have confirmed these figures, but several have acknowledged that they are in the right range.

Behavioral scientists have studied professions for many years. However, the accounting profession has been ignored until recently. The following reading summarizes the only study accomplished by a behavioral scientist. It presents a behavioral view of the contemporary profession and some insight into future development and change in it.

PROFESSIONALIZATION AND BUREAUCRATIZATION IN LARGE PROFESSIONAL ORGANIZATIONS[1]
Paul D. Montagna*

ABSTRACT: The conflict and interdependence of the processes of professionalization and bureaucratization are examined in large public accounting firms. The emerging pattern of professional bureaucracy reveals the complementarity of previously offered models and depicts a sequential development. Comparative analysis with professional organizations from other occupations indicates that professionalization is positively related to centralization and size of administrative component. The rate of development of the professional bureaucratic process can be affected by changes in organization size and complexity and in capacity to innovate or create new knowledge.

 In recent years, several sociologists have emphasized the professionalization of modern industrial society.[2] Professionalization is seen as the newest major process that is an "effect" of technological change on the occupational structure of the community, the other processes

* From *The American Journal of Sociology*, Vol. 74, No. 2 (September 1968), pp. 138–145. Reprinted by permission of the University of Chicago.
[1] This study was supported by National Science Foundation grant GS-804 and by a New York University fellowship. I wish to thank Harry Gracey, Marvin Koenigsberg, and Erwin O. Smigel for their comments and advice on earlier drafts of this paper.
[2] Nelson N. Foote, "The Professionalization of Labor in Detroit," *American Journal of Sociology*, LVIII (January, 1953), 371–80; Howard M. Vollmer and Donald L. Mills, "Nuclear Technology and the Professionalization of Labor," *American Journal of Sociology*, LXVII (May, 1962), 690–96; Harold L. Wilensky, "The

being industrialization, urbanization, and bureaucratization.[3] As the number and types of professionals in the work organization have increased, their conflict with the bureaucratic process has generally deepened.[4] However, it has been shown that a reconciliation can be achieved between the two,[5] that, in fact, the professionalization and bureaucratization processes are of necessity interdependent in bureaucratic organizations.[6]

For professional organizations[7] a similar interdependence has been suggested by Litwak, which he calls *professional bureaucracy,* a third model of organization which is, in effect, a synthesis of professional and bureaucratic models.[8] Upon examining large law firms, Smigel uncovered a pattern of bureaucracy which also is given the name of "professional bureaucracy."[9]

Professionalization of Everyone?" *American Journal of Sociology,* LXX (September, 1964), 137–58; William A. Faunce and Donald A. Clelland, "Professionalization and Stratification Patterns in an Industrial Community," *American Journal of Sociology,* LXXII (January, 1967), 341–50.

[3] Faunce and Clelland, *op. cit.* The authors acknowledge the classification of the latter three processes by Maurice Stein, *The Eclipse of Community* (Princeton, N.J.: Princeton University Press, 1960).

[4] Among the earlier examinations of this development are: Logan Wilson, *The Academic Man* (New York: Oxford University Press, 1942); Peter M. Blau, *The Dynamics of Bureaucracy* (Chicago: University of Chicago Press, 1955); Roy G. Francis and Robert C. Stone, *Service and Procedure in Bureaucracy* (Minneapolis: University of Minnesota Press, 1956); Harold L. Wilensky, *Intellectuals in Labor Unions: Organizational Pressures on Professional Roles* (New York: Free Press, 1956); Alvin W. Gouldner, "Cosmopolitans and Locals: Toward an Analysis of Latent Social Roles — Parts I and II," *Administrative Science Quarterly,* II (1957, 1958), 281–306, 444–80.

[5] For example, Mary E. W. Goss, "Influence and Authority among Physicians in an Outpatient Clinic," *American Sociological Review,* XXVI (February, 1961), 39–50; Ronald G. Corwin, "The Professional Employee: A Study of Conflict in Nursing Roles," *American Journal of Sociology,* LXVI (May, 1961), 604–15; Howard M. Vollmer, "Entrepreneurship and Professional Productivity among Research Scientists," in Howard M. Vollmer and Donald L. Mills (eds.), *Professionalization* (Englewood Cliffs, N.J.: Prentice-Hall, Inc., 1966), pp. 276–82; Richard H. Hall, "Some Organizational Considerations in the Professional-Organizational Relationship," *Administrative Science Quarterly,* XII (December, 1967), 461–78.

[6] William Kornhauser, *Scientists in Industry: Conflict and Accommodation* (Berkeley: University of California Press, 1962), p. 197; Blau, *The Dynamics of Bureaucracy* (rev. ed.; Chicago: University of Chicago Press, 1963), p. 9, describes an interdependence maintained in an environment of continual change.

[7] A professional organization is here defined as an organization in which: (1) members of one or more professional groups define and achieve the primary organizational goals (as compared with a professional association — a group organized to initiate and promote general professional objectives of the entire profession or segments thereof); (2) the majority of the people in the organization are professionals; (3) the administrative hierarchy of authority lies within the firm, whereas authority in professional matters is placed in the hands of the professional associations; (4) the profession promotes norms of personal autonomy and altruistic action in all matters relating to use of the body of knowledge.

[8] Eugene Litwak, "Models of Bureaucracy Which Permit Conflict," *American Journal of Sociology,* LVVII (September, 1961), 182. The author does not use the term "professional organization," but the examples he gives — a large hospital, a graduate school, a research organization — fit the definition (see n. 7, above). The third model is a "co-ordination" of the unlike efficiencies of the first two: the Weberian (bureaucratic) model of recurrent events and traditional knowledge and the human relations (professional) model of uncertainty situations — ever developing, non-recurring events involving new knowledge.

[9] Erwin O. Smigel, *The Wall Street Lawyer: Professional Organization Man?* (New York: Free Press, 1964), pp. 275–86. Utilizing Gouldner's rules criterion for distinguishing three patterns of bureaucracy (Alvin W. Gouldner, *Patterns of Industrial Bureaucracy* [New York: Free Press, 1954], pp. 216–17), Smigel depicts a fourth pattern, professional bureaucracy, which is composed of a system of rules external to the organization, is devised by professional associations and the government, and which conditions the behavior of the lawyer through a long socialization process.

In an analysis of the largest professional organizations extant, the "Big Eight" public accounting firms, I inquired into the relationship among the aforementioned processes. A form of professional bureaucracy was found which combined elements of the perspectives of both Litwak and Smigel, thereby indicating their complementarity, and which disclosed changes in the relationship as measured by organizational variables of size, centralization, and size of administrative component.

BACKGROUND AND PROCEDURE

The Big Eight are international public accounting firms[10] founded around the turn of the century as small, local partnerships to manage the bookkeeping and accounting of corporations. With the growth of these clients over the succeeding decades and with the federal requirements of taxation and annual audit set up in the 1930's, the firms expanded their auditing services. Each firm presently has an average of eighty offices located in forty foreign countries and fifty offices located in the major cities of the United States. Offices of the largest American cities contain upward of fifty, and in a few instances more than 1,000, public accountants. The average size of a firm, including all offices, is 5,500.

The focus for this study is the largest offices of the Big Eight, located in New York City.[11] Each office, averaging 1,500 personnel, contains three separate hierarchies: one of public accountants, one of non-accounting "management services" experts, and a non-professional supporting staff. The largest group, the public accountants, number about 1,000, of whom approximately half are in the beginning position of "junior." Another 300 are seniors, 100 are managers, and the 100 top positions are filled by partners. The average size of the management services hierarchy is 200. Slightly more than half of these are "associates," another quarter are at the next higher level of supervisor, and the remaining 15 per cent are at the highest level of "principal." The clerical staff of 300 constitutes the third major group of the firm, with a system of ordered positions similar to the clerical arrangement found in large bureaucratic departments.

[10] The eight firms, alphabetically, are: Arthur Andersen & Co.; Ernst & Ernst; Haskins & Sells; Lybrand, Ross Bros. & Montgomery; Peat, Marwick, Mitchell & Co.; Price Waterhouse & Co.; Touche, Ross, Bailey & Smart; Arthur Young & Co.

[11] The national and international executive quarters for these firms are, with two exceptions, located in New York City. This policy-making group functions independently of the operating or "line" offices in New York City, but is usually housed in the same building.

Each firm is also stratified according to four major areas of work. The largest area, auditing, is the primary function of the firm — examining the financial structure and processes of the client. The tax area includes tasks ranging from preparation of corporate and individual tax returns to tax advice on mergers, reorganizations, liquidations, estate planning, and special surveys. The accounting personnel perform the duties of these two areas.[12] In the third area, management services, are located most of the non-accounting specialists (engineers, mathematicians, social scientists), who inform and advise clients on data processing, operations research, general management, personnel, organizational structure, marketing, and other economic considerations. The fourth area, firm administration, is shared by partners and some managers. It consists mostly of recruitment of personnel and their assignment and of periodic meetings on serious client matters.

The work of these firms is extremely important to the financial and investment communities. Collectively, these eight firms audit nearly half the total corporate wealth of the United States. They audit 94 per cent of the 500 largest industrial corporations and the same percentage of the fifty largest merchandising firms, the fifty largest transportation companies, and the fifty largest utility companies.[13] The smaller organizations are not excluded; nor are those which are not required by law to be audited.[14] The average number of clients for a Big Eight firm is 10,000.

Initially, a pilot study was carried out at each firm. On the basis of these broad reviews, a self-administered questionnaire was developed, pretested, and mailed to a systematic random sample of the New York City offices of three Big Eight firms. The sample was stratified first on the basis of the four major work areas and then within each area by position in firm. A highly satisfactory return was received on the first mailing for a total number of 111.[15]

---

[12] Within each of these work areas there is further specialization by the CPA. Although a partner has a specialty within an area, e.g., corporate reorganizations or tax planning, he assumes responsibility for the entire audit of each of his approximately thirty-five clients. As a result, specialization is limited to that amount of time remaining after his examination and analysis of all financial and related aspects of the client organization.

[13] This amounts to $300 billion + in total sales and net revenues and $400 billion + in total assets, based on the lists in *The Fortune Directory* (1965) (as compared with mention of auditors in the 1965 series of Moody's industrial, public utility, and transportation manuals and *Poor's Register of Corporations, Directors and Executives* [1965]), and personal telephone calls. These percentages are relatively stable over the span of a few years, because clients rarely change their auditors, and rarely do they fall from their top listing during that time.

[14] One Big Eight firm alone audits more than 1,000 banks, 700 savings and loan associations, 700 insurance companies, and 1,200 non-profit institutions, including universities, hospitals, and local, state, and federal governmental bodies; from T. A. Wise, "The Very Private World of Peat, Marwick, Mitchell," *Fortune,* LXXIV (July 1, 1966), 91.

[15] The total return was 92, 85, and 66 per cent for the three firms. Homogeneity and, in some cases, size of the thirteen subsamples limited the disproportionateness of the stratification.

From purposive samples constructed based on position in firm, fifty-one standardized interviews were conducted at six of the eight firms.[16] At one of these six firms, observation was conducted of the entire work process at a client's offices and of the firm's recruitment procedures.

ORGANIZATIONAL SIZE, CENTRALIZATION, AND ADMINISTRATION

From the pilot studies it was obvious that the first task of the research was to detect how professional organizations of such large size manage to remain relatively free from increasing bureaucratization.[17] First, examination of apportionment of work time showed that total time of all professionals in firm administration averaged 12 per cent of total professional work time. This administrative work is spread among 40 per cent of the professional staff, and only 4 per cent spend the majority of their time in it. Clerical staff comprise 20 per cent of the firm. This produces a grand total of 32 per cent spent in nonprofessional work.

Second, the formal managerial decision-making structure of a Big Eight firm is highly centralized, with a senior partner as "president" of the firm and chairman of the executive or managing committee. The committee is composed of partner-directors for each of the firm's major areas of specialization, with lines of authority within each area and for each region of the country. Even though every partner is given personal responsibility over his audit for the client, the system of checks on his work, along with the formal structure, allows the firms to be classified as highly centralized. One executive partner succinctly stated: "The audit partner calls the signals on the job. He can consult on his problems with any specialists in the firm. One partner reviews all opinions [final report on the client], but this comes after the fact, after the opinion is issued. The partner is responsible to the partnership for his work, but he has complete autonomy within the firm."

How is it, then, that these firms spend so little of their professional man-

---

[16] For a total sample number of 162 for the eight firms. Thirty-nine interviews contained a majority of the items appearing on the questionnaire. The remaining twelve focused on areas of special knowledge of those interviewees in positions of senior partner, management services director, and executive partner. Two firms granted only a single lengthy interview and no questionnaires. Enough material was gathered on size and work apportionment to include it in the analysis. In these two cases, the problems of professional conservatism and secrecy outweighed the interest to participate any further. These problems of gaining access I have examined in my Ph.D. thesis, "Bureaucracy and Change in Large Professional Organizations: A Functional Analysis of Large Public Accounting Firms" (unpublished, New York University, 1967), pp. 36–46.

[17] Bureaucracy is in this instance defined as the process of rationalized efficiency, according to Weber's characteristics; H. H. Gerth and C. Wright Mills (eds.), *From Max Weber: Essays in Sociology* (New York: Oxford University Press, 1946), pp. 196–98.

hours in administration? First, administrative authority is located at the very top. General firm policy is decided by the executive commitee. Other administrative tasks such as recruitment and assignment are shared by the partnership as equally as possible. In two of the firms, personnel department positions are filled by a system of rotating partners every few years. As already evidenced, nearly all partners and professional employees remain active in client work. Otherwise, they feel the stigma of being known as a "kept accountant." Second, the public accountant's work is conducted at the client's offices in small groups of three to ten persons, thereby spreading lower-echelon administration throughout the organization. Informality within the work groups is the norm. For each client, the partner selects a work team of managers, seniors, and juniors on the basis of their technical background and their ability to work smoothly with both client and partner. These employees move from one work team to another and from one partner to another several times a year. Centralization therefore is compatible with these professionalized firms.

The comparison of the relation of size to administrative component and to degree of centralization for these firms can be made to only one other study without becoming methodologically inconsistent.[18] This is the analysis of professional organizations of public personnel agencies.[19] The relationship, according to size, is similar in both studies. Using the measurement bases for the agencies,[20] the largest personnel agencies and the largest accounting firms display a high degree of professionalization, high centralization, and a small administrative component. And the changed relationship for medium-sized agencies (approximately 200 personnel) and medium-sized accounting firms[21] remains alike: a high degree of professionalization and low centralization,

---

[18] William A. Rushing, "Organizational Size and Administration: The Problems of Causal Homogeneity and a Heterogeneous Category," *Pacific Sociological Review*, IX (Fall, 1966), 100–108, emphasizes that the many studies dealing with the relationship between organizational size and relative size of administrative component have reached inconsistent results because total administrative component is a heterogeneous category with respect to types of occupations; therefore, it is not significant as a single total measure. Rather, classes of personnel must be related. In the case of the studies under consideration, only one class is dealt with — large-firm professionals, social agency and public accounting.

[19] Peter M. Blau, Wolf V. Heydebrand, and Robert E. Stauffer, "The Structure of Small Bureaucracies," *American Sociological Review*, XXXI (April, 1966), 179–91; see especially Table 2, p. 183.

[20] *Ibid.*, p. 183:
   "The administrative apparatus ratio is *low* when the proportion of clerks among the total staff is less than 60 per cent; *high* when it is 60 per cent or more.
   "The managerial hierarchy is *centralized* when the ratio of non-clerical personnel in managerial positions to non-clerical personnel in non-supervisory positions, excluding those listed as neither, is less than one to three; it is *dispersed* when the ratio is one to three or more.
   "Professionalization is *low* when the proportion of the operating staff (excluding managers as well as clerks) who are required to have, at least, a college degree with a specified major, is less than 50 per cent; *high* when it is 50 per cent or more."

[21] For purposes of comparison by size, four medium-sized accounting firms (average size 200 personnel) were extensively interviewed. The hierarchy of job titles and occupational specialties is basically the same as that of the large firms, except that the Big Eight afford greater specialization in each work area.

whatever the administrative ratio. All twelve accounting firms, the eight large and four medium-sized, follow the pattern of the majority of personnel agencies of like size. More important, the eight largest firms show a much higher measurement on these three variables than do the personnel agencies. Further investigation uncovered factors that indicate the determining variable to be professionalization.[22]

PROFESSIONALIZATION VS. BUREAUCRATIZATION: CONFLICT AND INTERDEPENDENCE

Blau feels that the unusual combination of centralization and professionalization is possible because there are "substitute methods of modern administration," such as detailed statistical records of performance, which check on the work of subordinates and obtain information on operations without frequent direct supervision.[23] In the highly professionalized accounting firms, besides the annual opinions and other performance reports, additional substitute methods of administration are the rules and procedures external to the organizations. These are the responsibility of the professional association of CPA's, the American Institute of Certified Public Accountants. These external rules include an elaborate and much revised code of ethics, a newly codified volume of principles of accounting, and revised auditing standards and procedures. They are constructed and revised by Institute committees in which the views of the large firms are well represented. These rules serve as a foundation for the firms' more specific internal rules, a few of which are more stringent, others of which merely expand on the external rules. Nearly to a man, the total sample agreed that compared with internal rules, the external rules were the more important rules for their firms and for the profession as a whole. For the firms, the number of problems inherent in constructing and enforcing these professional standards are greatly reduced. And changes are

[22] All of the Big Eight have an administrative ratio of less than 30 per cent, are centralized at a ratio of less than one to six if all partners are included as managerial personnel, and are 100 per cent professionalized (using Blau's bases for measurement—see n. 20, above). It is obvious that for highly professionalized organizations more sensitive measures must be developed. For the accounting firms, professionalization is given a wider definition, which includes the attributes of: a body of knowledge with a developed intellectual technique, supported by a formalized educational process with standardized testing and licensing, a code of ethics governing relations with colleagues, clients, and other external organizations, and a professional association to facilitate the maintenance and development of all of the former. Attempts to empirically measure these and other ideal type attributes are found in Richard M. Lynch, "Professional Standards for Management Consulting in the United States" (unpublished Ph.D. thesis, Graduate School of Business Administration, Harvard University, 1959), pp. 30–31, 138–39; Montagna, op. cit. (see n. 16, above), chap. iv.

[23] Blau, The Dynamics of Bureaucracy (rev. ed.), chap. iii; Blau, Heydebrand, and Stauffer, op. cit., p. 185.

made without an opposing vested interest—there are virtually no full-time administrators whose jobs depend on an elaborate bureaucratic system of one specified routine based on the affected rules.

In the case of these organizations, then, bureaucratization, in the pejorative sense of dysfunction, that is, routine, rigidity, overconformity, is limited by the external rules and by personal autonomy. However, because of the tremendous increase in the number, extent, and specificity of these rules, CPA's fear a severe limitation on the scope of their professional judgment. What was once unwritten rule or mystique is now rationalized; in the process of formalizing its rules, the profession transforms that knowledge from an intellectual to a mechanical technique. As one senior partner put it, "The client asks not what to do but how to do it, as the body of knowledge becomes detailed and easier to interpret." The power of the expert disappears as soon as the area of uncertainty (professional judgment) can be translated into rules and programs.[24] As one partner concluded, "We could audit IBM [the ninth largest corporation in America] in almost one day with very little risk because their internal systems of control are so tight." Partly because of rule making, partly because of computerization, the traditional annual audit, required by federal law, is becoming what one executive partner termed "the annual nuisance." The CPA finds he must submit to detailed professional requirements when constructing reports and opinions for his client. Yet, he should be free of such encumbrances to properly exercise his professional judgment.

The public accountant's response to this threat has been to expand into new areas of uncertainty, especially management services[25] and taxes. Presently, each of these areas accounts for 20 per cent of the professional man-hours in a Big Eight firm. Many CPA's contend that, like taxes, management services were always an integral part of the audit process, and indeed there is very little that cannot be classified within the broad definition of "internal control"

[24] Michel Crozier, *The Bureaucratic Phenomenon* (Chicago: University of Chicago Press, 1964), p. 299: "The elimination of the 'bureaucratic systems of organization' in the dysfunctional sense is the condition for the growth of 'bureaucratization' in the Weberian sense." Also, Michel Crozier, "Crise et renouveau dans l'administration française," *Sociologie du travail*, VIII (July–September, 1966), 327; Peter M. Blau and W. Richard Scott, *Formal Organizations* (San Francisco: Chandler Publishing Co., 1962), pp. 240–42; Victor A. Thompson, "Bureaucracy and Innovation," *Administrative Science Quarterly*, X (June, 1965), 4; James D. Thompson, *Organizations in Action* (New York: McGraw-Hill Book Co., 1967). The writings of a leading public-accounting spokesman reflect this thinking: John L. Carey, *The CPA Plans for the Future* (New York: American Institute of Certified Public Accountants, 1965), pp. 191–92, 227. A theoretical perspective of uncertainty is given by Ralf Dahrendorf, *Essays in the Theory of Society* (Stanford, Calif.: Stanford University Press, 1968).

[25] More recently, there has been experimentation with the management attest, an audit conducted for stockholders and other interested third parties to determine management's compliance with certain of its own prearranged standards for information collection, decisioning, and control processes, but not of the results of these processes. Some in the profession are now suggesting that the CPA should begin to think about prearranging the standards for management.

(an audit term). Regardless, new developments in management services, such as computerization, offer CPA's the ability to integrate the planning, measuring, attesting, and communicating of the total information system of an economic organization.[26] Thirty-five per cent of the total sample voluntarily suggested this area (called "operations auditing") to be the only one where judgment and creativity are found to a significant degree. It is the person who is familiar with the computer process who *composes* an "automated audit."

The movement into management services provides the profession with new non-rationalized intellectual techniques. But at the same time, this knowledge is not integrated within the profession and has proved to be dysfunctional to the firms. If the management services work for a client is coordinated with the partner's audit, some administrative authority will tend to be legitimated in terms of incumbency of office. In this situation, obedience is stressed as an end in itself because the CPA as administrator is not able to judge the non-accountant expert on the basis of that expert's knowledge. Rules are initiated by one party (a CPA) — characteristic of "punishment centered" bureaucracy.[27] Added to this is the task of each firm having to organize independently and enforce a new code of ethics and procedures for this technical field until, in time, the professional organization takes over this function.

In sum, the move into areas of uncertainty provides an important basis for continued professionalization — an expanded body of knowledge which supports an intellectual technique and requisite judgment.[28] However, because of this, new bureaucratic problems rapidly emerge. The process can be examined beginning at any stage of its development. External rules form a *pattern* (to use Smigel's term) for professional bureaucracy. They inject uniformity into the social system. But the danger of uniformity and the normal rate of technological development spur the search for new areas of professional control. At any one time in the organizational process, there is a conflicting yet interdependent mixture of uniform and non-uniform events, of rationalization and uncertainty (to use Litwak's description).

---

[26] These functions of the economic organization are defined by leaders in the profession. For example, Herman W. Bevis, "The Accounting Function in Economic Progress," *Journal of Accountancy*, CVI (August, 1958), 27-34; John L. Carey (ed.), *The Accounting Profession: Where Is It Headed?* (New York: American Institute of Certified Public Accountants, 1962), p. 11.

[27] Alvin W. Gouldner, "Organizational Analysis," in Robert K. Merton, Leonard Broom, and Leonard S. Cottrell, Jr. (eds.), *Sociology Today: Problems and Prospects* (New York: Basic Books, 1959), p. 403. See also a summary discussion by Louis R. Pondy, "Organizational Conflict: Concepts and Models," *Administrative Science Quarterly*, XII (September, 1967), 314-17.

[28] This move takes place because of the rationalization of CPA knowledge in external rules. As Faunce and Clelland (*op. cit.*, p. 342) point out: "While industrialization, urbanization, bureaucratization, and professionalization may occur *simultaneously*, they do not ordinarily develop at the same rate. More typically, they form a *sequence* with a high level of development of one acting as a spur to development of the next. Increased professionalization is, *in part*, an outgrowth of the bureaucratic emphasis upon expertise and rationalism" (emphasis my own, P. D. M.).

CONCLUSIONS

On the basis of the analysis, three generalizations can be drawn concerning large professional organizations: (1) The more highly professionalized the organization, the more highly centralized it is and the smaller its administrative component. (2) As organizations become larger and more complex, technically, strong patterns of punishment-centered bureaucracy may form which are not found in smaller organizations.[29] (3) The collection, analysis, classification, standarization, and enforcement of external rules carried out by the professional association may involve the simultaneous occurrence of rationalization of one body of knowledge and the development of another.

With regard to (3), both occurrences tend to create dysfunctions. Even though the process of professional bureaucracy allows for change, there is concern that the change may be too rapid or far reaching, as well as too precise or narrow.[30] Also, with rapid innovation, the firms must solve the immediate problems of administration until the slower-moving professional association develops profession-wide norms and laws. The rate of change must somehow be regulated, or the process will be disrupted.

Ultimately of more concern is the problem caused by increased size in (2). If these largest firms are the prototype for the future organization,[31] the serious problems of bureaucracy may not be so easily overcome in a future accelerated process of professional bureaucracy generated by more rapid social and technological change.[32]

Where is the profession headed? Will it prosper or die? The future cannot be known, but extrapolations and predictions sometimes prove to be accurate. The following selections are representative of the possibilities and problems that will confront auditors of the future.

---

[29] This pattern was not a significant one in the twenty largest law firms in the United States (Smigel, *op. cit.*, p. 279), which are, on the average, only one-tenth the size of the large public accounting firms.

[30] Wilensky, "The Professionalization of Everyone?" (see n. 2, above), pp. 148–49, defines the problem as knowledge being too vague (e.g., social work) or too precise and that there may be an optimal base for professional practice.

[31] Warren G. Bennis, *Changing Organizations* (New York: McGraw-Hill Book Co., 1966), chap. 1. Bennis forecasts "on thin empirical ice" that the work organizations of the future will contain adaptive, rapidly changing, temporary systems of diverse professionals operating in complex and creative environments and will displace bureaucracy as the primary form of organizational structure. Also, Harold L. Wilensky, *Organizational Intelligence: Knowledge and Policy in Government and Industry* (New York: Basic Books, 1967), pp. 46–47. Galbraith's "technostructure" agrees with this description; John Kenneth Galbraith, *The New Industrial State* (Boston: Houghton Mifflin Co., 1967), pp. 57–71, 168–75.

[32] See Litwak's explanation for his assumption that "non-uniform events will constitute a major factor in organizational analysis in the foreseeable future" (Litwak, *op. cit.*, p. 181).

FUTURE OF THE ACCOUNTING PROFESSION
David F. Linowes*

General environment

To effectively project the accounting profession into the future, we must first examine the entire social-economic-political phenomena and its direction.

Unquestionably we are in a stage of great change; a turning point has been reached in world history. This turning point is evidenced by two signs:

1 The power struggle between two ideologies, represented by the United States on the one hand, and by the Soviet Union on the other. Here are two giants, each with nuclear power sufficient to destroy the entire civilized world. But, also, each a deterrent to the other. The stockpiles of nuclear destructive capability developed by these two mighty countries act as barricades against one another. Each mass thereby is locked into a fixed posture. Satellite countries and lesser political entities take on new and enlarged authority. Other forms of power, less destructive and in the hands of little countries become the focal point and main thrust for power struggles, witness Laos and Viet Nam and Africa. The giants, the U.S. and Russia, dare not move for fear of self-annihilation. Erwin D. Canham, Chief Editor of *The Christian Science Monitor*, observing this peculiar phenomenon of our time, suggests that maybe the day of outlawed international war is here. Maybe the very possession of nuclear power by each of the diametrically opposed philosophies of government is accomplishing what world peace conferences could not accomplish—namely, the prevention of great international conflagrations. Meanwhile, this status of locked-in atomic military power on opposite sides of the world has created an environment for tremendous global business expansion and intermingling never before achieved in the history of mankind. Hard-headed American businessmen are penetrating deep into the interiors of Africa, and the Middle East. At the same time Japanese, Italian and German business leaders are infiltrating our shores, and seizing significant slices of our own markets from the backyards of American industrialists.

2 The second sign of a turning point in history is the progress in American technology during the past couple of decades. This technology has relieved the laborer of the menial job, of the mechanical, routine, tedious work. Machine progress is not harming labor, as many people feared. It is substantially improving the working man's lot by increasing his productivity and giving him a higher level of work to do. The automaton in factory and in office is no longer a human being. It is a machine.

However, although this technological progress has resulted in greatly increasing our country's capacity to produce, much of it is not being used. It lies idle in the form of unused plant capacity and unused human capacity, unemploy-

* From *The Accounting Review*, Vol. XL, No. 1 (January, 1965), pp. 97–104. Reprinted by permission of the American Accounting Association.

ment. We must not permit this capacity to be unproductive because there is plenty of work to do not only throughout the world, but also right here at home.

Practically every large city in the United States has patches of deterioration within its very heart. Most core cities need new buildings and new facilities. Slum areas are still common sights in all metropolitan areas. City transportation systems everywhere are inadequate, antiquated, and inefficient. Schools and recreational facilities are severely in short supply.

The idle technological and manpower capacity already in existence and still being increased can be effectively put to use if some means could be developed to improve the cooperation of the public and private sectors of our economy. This does not mean more Government interference with business. It means more mutual respect and consideration for one another's problems and objectives, and cooperation one with the other when such cooperation is in the best interest of all. In the Federal Reserve System and the banking industry we have such a working together of the public and private sectors of our economy.

In a recent speech President Lyndon Johnson emphasized that the greatest challenge of all time now confronts the rebuilding of our "cities." The "city" must be reconstructed for convenience, for beauty, and for pride so that our society may become, what the President termed, the "Great Society." This is a new task for us all, and one which the technological advances of science and business have made possible to accomplish. The old task of our society was to use every effort to prevent the overthrow of Western civilization. The new task is to use our technological know-how to build the finest civilization the world has ever known. The "Great Society" is a responsibility of business as well as government, both cooperatively applying the latest in productive computerized techniques.

These two signs: international movements and technological progress which so affect our changing environment, at the same time are affecting and will continue to severely affect the accounting profession of the future.

Change necessary

In its May 1964 issue, Fortune Magazine said in effect: Today the human race is at the threshold of a new epoch in world history. The accelerating rate of change that man has achieved through science and technology has ushered in an era of unprecedented problems and opportunities. Fear of change holds danger for individual freedom. Fear of change holds danger for the democratic constitutional state. Fear of change holds danger for the business system.

The accounting profession today does not fear change. It welcomes it with optimism and deliberate enthusiasm.

Because of the developments of operations research and electronic data processing on the one hand, and of global business expansion on the other, all accounting mores are being challenged and attacked. Change—deep and basic change—is on its way.

Profession's response to change

Our profession's early approach to keep up with the developing changes in our environment during the past two decades was to attempt to relieve the problem by sponsoring and encouraging professional training courses—both indirectly through the various types of accounting schools, and directly by occasional technical programs of the American Institute of CPAs and various state societies.

When it was realized that this was hardly adequate, attempts were made to help force a higher level of education and preparation by increasing the educational requirements as a prerequisite to sit for the CPA exams, as well as to improve and make uniform the quality of the CPA examinations in all the states. By so doing it was felt that persons unqualified either by ability or by education would be screened out before entering the accounting profession.

Experience showed that society and technology were changing too rapidly; more was needed. Positive steps were then taken to upgrade and substantially revise the courses at universities; and to formalize and improve professional training programs for CPAs already in practice. The breeding grounds of CPAs were subjected to rigorous re-examination.

A couple years ago our profession realized that this was still inadequate. The headwaters of the streams of men entering the profession had to be reviewed. We began asking ourselves questions such as what background should a young man have in order to be able to successfully practice accountancy in this cosmic age. What kinds of abilities should he have? What subjects should he study in college? What common body of knowledge would best qualify a man to enter this dynamic profession? In an attempt to answer these questions, a Common Body of Knowledge Committee was established about a year ago. This committee is a research group jointly sponsored by the Carnegie Foundation and the AICPA. It is made up of 13 men—including CPA practitioners, business executives, bankers and educators. Dean Robert Roy, dean of the Engineering Science School of Johns Hopkins University, not an accountant, is directing this committee and we are all looking forward to the committee's findings.

LRO committee

The inciting element in back of the more recent self-evaluating and self-advancing programs is a small group known as the Long Range Objectives Committee. To my knowledge, never before in the history of any profession has there ever been the kind of forward-looking, long range planning represented by the Long Range Objectives Committee of the AICPA. The accounting profession is doing today, what no other profession has ever attempted to do. We are charting our course over the next decade or more. We hope to help guide our own destiny, and not wait for destiny to mold us. In this effort we hope to apply to our profession a basic Aristotelian concept. As you know, Aristotle gave to the world the concept that we should view a thing in light of the best it can become — not from the standpoint of the position it may have come to by reason of the doings of the lowest effort.

Now how are we going about it?

About three years ago the Long Range Objectives Committee, which is made up of four members of the AICPA plus John Carey, its Executive Director, who is ex-officio member, undertook a series of conferences with consultants of many different callings. We interviewed two corporation executives, three bankers, a behavioral scientist, a public relations man, a corporate lawyer, an economist, a sociologist, a psychologist, three accounting educators, a dean of a graduate school, the Commissioner of Internal Revenue, the Chairman of the Securities and Exchange Commission, and others. The results of most of these consultations have been written up in the form of position papers, and are available, free, upon request of the American Institute office. The substance and conclusions of all of these studies are being developed into a book, presently being completed by John Carey, and to be published soon.

The object of our efforts is to try to predict where the profession of accounting will be in 1975. In so doing, it was inevitable that we should identify directions and movements which will substantially mold our profession in the period well beyond 1975, into the next generation of accountants.

Accounting defined

One of the first things we asked ourselves is, what is "accounting"? In the past it has been described as the language of business. Definitions were all rather fuzzy, but essentially accounting was understood to be that body of principles underlying the keeping and the explanation of *business* records.

Later the definition was expanded to cover all *financial* data, not just business records. More recently the definition has been enlarged and somewhat formalized, describing accounting as the measurement and communication of *financial* and *economic* data.

Now we find important leaders of academia equating accounting with the entire measurement concept. Some even suggest that consideration should be given for accounting to be established in a separate school of measurement, thereby divorcing accounting from the business environment. Men such as Dr. Paul Lazarsfeld, internationally renowned sociologist, and Dr. John Gardner, president of the Carnegie Foundation, believe that there exists a bed of knowledge common to the accountant as distinct from that which is common to the businessman. The deeper one goes in accounting, the more he gets into basic measurement; and the deeper he goes into measurement, the farther out he reaches. The unusually capable, vital individuals in accounting must go in the direction of broad measurement. Qualified practitioners could be called upon to measure anything for which standards exist. They would cross disciplines in applying objective standards for evaluation.

This is exciting, and opens unlimited horizons for the coming generation of accountants.

Attest function

The extension of the attest function in the future holds great promise for our profession, as well as for all society.

The independent opinion giving credibility to financial statements has made a major contribution towards facilitating accumulations of great quantities of capital for major business undertakings, and for the orderly conduct of the financial markets. Basically the independent opinion or so-called "certified statement" has been the primary expression of the attest function in the past. There have been others, but they have been incidental. For example, not too long ago, a promotion man wanted to determine the odds of having a professional golfer hit a hole in one. To study the odds, he engaged a pro, two caddies, two cameramen, and a CPA. The job of the CPA was to count the strokes, and attest to the number. Incidentally, it came to 442 to 1. Another incidental application of the attest function, as we all know, is with the Academy Awards. Each year a CPA controls the ballots and presents the results of the Academy Awards voting—thereby lending credibility to the honesty of the selections, and secrecy of the results.

For the accounting profession as a whole in the future, however, these extensions of the attest function are not important. Not because we would not like to take part in such painstaking verifications, but because most of us cannot qualify as experts in golf, nor do we have the attractive physical features to make us TV idols.

There are several significant applications of the attest function which the future could very well demand.

Labor-management relations

The single greatest problem in our business economy today for which there does not appear to be any formula for solution is in the area of labor-management relations. As each union contract expires, in practically every industry there begins a round of talks, negotiations, demands, threats, and badgerings until finally new higher rates and terms are agreed upon. These new rates have no relationship to the productivity of labor, nor to the operating results of the business. This is so largely because labor does not believe the figures management presents; and management does not believe the statements, claims, and cost-of-living needs presented by the union. After each cycle of forced wage increases, our country goes off on another inflation cycle.

Labor basically claims it only seeks its share of increased productivity. Management basically indicates a willingness to pay out a portion of this increased productivity, if the business as a whole can continue to operate profitably by so doing.

Is there any reason why in the future, labor and management cannot agree on a formula for wage increases, tied into the increased productivity of labor, and the profitability of the business, all of which would be attested to by an independent certified public accountant? If all financial data and statistics admitted as bases for union negotiations were required to be examined and verified by a qualified CPA, much of the suspicion and distrust which now so frequently fill the conference room would be dispelled.

An extension of our attest function into this area alone could have a major impact on our society. To achieve this will require the dedicated efforts of capable, well-educated men who have imagination, resourcefulness, courage and patience. The rewards, however, will be great.

Government reports

Our Federal, state and local governments produce mountains of statistical and financial data. World-wide decisions are frequently based on the statistics developed by the agencies of our Federal Government. Actions significantly affecting our personal daily lives in areas of education, welfare, sanitation, and safety are taken by our state and local governments on the basis of statistical reports, the accuracy of which is sometimes questionable. Here is another area in which it has been suggested for us to extend our attest function. The CPA could verify and give credibility to economic data in this area of government reports—these same reports which are the bases for major decisions affecting our personal lives.

Income tax returns

In the income tax area, the Federal Government has already begun to look into the practicality of having CPAs attest to tax returns they prepare, thereby relieving the Internal Revenue Service from auditing those returns. How desirable such an extension of the attest function might be is open to question. Nevertheless it was suggested by Commissioner Caplin of the Internal Revenue Service, and discussions have been undertaken with representatives of the American Institute.

Prospective accounting

Our profession has always identified itself with historical data—looking back. In more recent years, as an aspect of our management services function, prospective accounting services have been rather generally performed.

Now, there appears to have developed a need for someone qualified in accounting and budgetary matters to examine business projections and plans and to express an opinion. This aspect of verifying the fairness of presentation of prospective business plans could very well be an important constructive contribution to business management of the future.

Management performance

As accounting increasingly becomes recognized as the profession of measurement, we may expect society to look to us to extend our attest function to cover management performance. As quantitative standards continue to be developed which may be used to indicate the effectiveness of management, the CPA will be called upon to apply these standards to management's performance. We will become evaluators of management itself.

This pattern is already evident in some auditing practices followed abroad. And even in this country, a number of companies have begun adopting the procedure of having the CPA appear before the Audit Committee, with management executives excluded, for a frank discussion of overall company business affairs.

International area

One of the most far-reaching opportunities of the future is in the international field. In the past our profession developed by responding to demands made of it by outside influences. The industrial revolution required extensive costs and record keeping to control newly amassed capital and productive facilities. The income tax laws required exacting profit and loss computations. The Securities and Exchange Regulations required extensive refinements in record keeping to facilitate full disclosures. In each instance, we responded to the extent our clients requested. Now a new demand is being thrust upon us.

Business is becoming world oriented. Many businesses no longer think and plan in national terms, but in global terms. The word "multinational" has been coined to identify such companies. Their needs are for world-wide thinking. Their posture must transcend national habits, different languages, strange monies, and all the flesh colors: white, black, brown, red, yellow. Business must be flexible and adaptable to Equatorial heat and Alaskan cold; high culture and savage tribes. Accounting usage and business practices throughout the world are anything but uniform. Standards vary greatly, currencies fluctuate, governments topple, yet business goes on.

Businessmen desperately need help in this international area. They need creditable financial statements, which are meaningful, timely, and comparable. They need to know about business practices in the foreign countries, about social mores, about government regulations and taxes, and they need to know it in language and terms they understand.

In this area they sorely require not only historical professional accounting help, but also planning guidance.

We as the profession which serves business have the responsibility to fill this global need, and some progress is being made. The AICPA has a Committee on International Relations studying the entire field. A number of larger accounting firms have set up International Departments. Broadly-educated, well-trained CPAs whose interests lie in international affairs may very well become the future statesmen of multinational business, being called upon to evaluate political, economic and social influences throughout the world.

Electronic data processing

Electronic data processing is just beginning, yet its impact has been overpowering. The changes effected in the information system of business are so great, that we must actually experience them to believe them. A tabulation and verification job in our own office which required 3,125 hours, or about seventy-eight 40-hour weeks before EDP now takes 2 ¼ hours.

An RCA expert estimates that two minutes on a computer — using its full capacity today — equal 50 years of pencil work, based on a 40-hour week.

The internal information system in a business includes the recording, accumulation, classification, analysis and transmission of financial data. Traditionally the accountant has been an integral part of that system. With the advent of EDP, engineers, statisticians, and other scientists have also become essential to the overall functioning of the information system.

The person in charge of this system will be the most important man in an organization, next to the president.

Through this system will flow the projections of proposed alternative courses of action as well as current operating data. These projections will be communicated to the top executive for his final decision by the man in charge.

For the accountant to qualify as the man-in-charge here, he must have a general understanding of the statistical and engineering aspects of computer operation. He must know what the computer can do and how it is programmed; as well as what needs of management may be furnished by this fantastic machine. As never before, the accountant must understand the client's organizational structure, its policies, and its objectives.

Especially in the EDP age the CPA must appreciate the need for effective communication. No amount of comprehensive data can serve an operational purpose unless it is expressed in meaningful terms and placed in the proper hands within an organization.

The need for guidance is so great in this fast-moving field, that CPAs in every level of public practice will increasingly be called upon to perform services related to the computerized internal information system.

Profession internally

All of what I have said thus far about our profession in the future relates it as an entity to business and society. That is, I have dealt with the external aspects of certified public accounting. But what about the profession internally? What does the LRO crystal ball indicate will be the nature of the CPA in 1975; what will the accounting firm be like; in what direction will our professional societies devote their major efforts; will educators be an integral part of our profession, or will they tend to sit on the periphery, as they have done all too frequently in the past?

More learning

The CPA of 1975 and beyond will have to understand much broader and deeper concepts of business, of economics, of politics, of all society. He must recognize fully that learning is a lifetime effort, and that education does not end with the college degree or CPA certificate. The degree and certificate even today are only licenses to qualify one for further learning. To some extent such learning should be in specialized areas, such as operations research, electronic data processing, merger evaluations. To some extent such learning must provide for a personal continuing interest in literature, economics, politics, and other cultural areas. This emphasis on intellectual activity must include the important function of research in our own field.

Research and educators

To intelligently explore our constantly changing needs requires vital basic research not only of technical accounting subjects but of the profession itself. For this research we need people of high intellect and of academic inclination. Most often such qualifications are found in institutions of higher learning.

The academic world will be cultivated and made an integral part of the practicing accounting profession. Not in the sense that professors will serve on accounting staffs, or practicing CPAs will serve as part-time professors (although this is helpful), but in the sense that AICPA will take the initiative for establishing the mechanism so that a continuing dialogue will take place between researchers and standard setters on the one hand; and practitioners and standard appliers on the other.

We will reach out physically and mentally to that end of our profession which nurtures our young and revitalizes our old. Professors, deans, research people will be drawn close to active practitioners, to nourish and stimulate, to bring fresh perspective, to raise the voice of dissent when dissent is necessary.

More executives, fewer technicians

It is obvious from my remarks that the CPA of the future must and will be a "learned" professional man, with executive capacity and training, and able to deal comfortably and effectively with well-rounded, highly-educated future officers of industry.

But, what of the Indians? What of the accounting technicians, those who are now performing the routine, the mechanical, the repetitive detail? These are being replaced even today by the computer, the man-made brain. The day of full mechanization of all administrative operations is rapidly approaching. Accounting firms of the next decade will have many chiefs, and very few Indians, and most of those will be computers, not humans.

Conclusion

In conclusion what I have been trying to say is that imagination and dynamism have seized our profession and its leaders. The spirit of renewal is alive. The cumulative effect of space age technology; world oneness; and social reawakening has placed its mark indelibly on the direction and path of the accounting profession.

For the new generation of accountants, a great challenge lies ahead. It is a challenge to serve society to an extent unmatched in all history. It is a challenge to each accountant to serve himself by applying all his capabilities towards rounded, intellectual growth in a socially necessary function.

CHAPTER 3 # PROFESSIONAL RESPONSIBILITY: THE CPA AND THE SEC

Auditors often deal with regulatory agencies, and the agency most often encountered is the Securities Exchange Commission. The influence of the SEC abounds in the auditing literature. In order to understand the scope of the SEC's influence, it is necessary to study its functions and accounting requirements. The following reading presents an overview of these aspects of this important agency.

ACCOUNTING UNDER SEC REGULATIONS
Charles B. Hellerson*

AN OVERALL LOOK AT THE SEC

The public accountant will not become involved in all areas in which the SEC functions. However, he should have some idea of the scope of its activities and the basis for its operations. This section will provide the information that comprises the background for the public accountant's work. It will also touch on some items of more general interest.

Specifically, we will discuss:

1 Origin and structure of the SEC.

2 Laws administered by the SEC.

3 Enforcement powers of the SEC.

4 SEC procedures.

ORIGIN AND STRUCTURE OF THE SEC

The SEC was created in 1934 by act of Congress. Its inception can be traced to the Senate investigations following the stock market crash of 1929. These investigations revealed the many abuses existing at the time in the distribution of and trading in securities, thus underlining the need for legislation to protect the public. Although many states had their own laws for the regulation of security transactions, these "blue sky" laws were in many cases ineffective and, furthermore, had no application to transactions in interstate commerce.

* From *Accountant's Encyclopedia*, Vol. 3, © 1962, pp. 1211–60, Prentice-Hall, Inc., Englewood Cliffs, N.J., "Accounting Under SEC Regulations," Charles B. Hellerson. Reprinted by permission of Prentice-Hall, Inc.

Therefore, during the 1930's and in the year 1940, Congress passed a series of laws designed to guard the public with respect to securities sold in interstate commerce or listed on a national securities exchange.

The SEC was established to administer these laws. An independent regulatory agency responsible to the Congress, it performs a quasi-judicial function in conjunction with its administrative function. Five men, appointed by the President with the consent of the Senate, serve as Commissioners for five-year terms. They are assisted by a professional staff, which is organized into appropriate operating sections. As will be seen later in the chapter, the public accountant will be concerned principally with (1) the Division of Corporate Finance, and (2) the Office of Chief Accountant.

LAWS ADMINISTERED BY THE SEC

The significance of the SEC becomes obvious upon even a brief review of the laws it administers. These laws are:

1 **Securities Act of 1933.** This law protects the investor by requiring the issuer of a security to make full disclosure of the material facts concerning the security and the company. A *material fact* is defined as a fact that the average prudent investor would be expected to rely on. Disclosure is accomplished by means of a registration statement and a prospectus that must be filed with the Commission for review. Copies of the prospectus must be furnished to potential investors, and the registration statement is available for examination by the public. In its review, the Commission determines whether there has been compliance with its rules, regulations, and instructions, and whether there has been full disclosure of matters of significance to potential investors. However, any decision as to the relative value of the security as an investment is left to individual buyers.

Section 3(b) of the Act allows the Commission to exempt from registration offerings of an aggregate value of less than $300,000. Certain special types of offerings are exempt under Section 3(a) of the Act. Furthermore, the jurisdiction of the Act is limited to securities to be sold in interstate commerce or through the mails in such a way as to constitute a *public offering.*

Warning   The determination of what is and what is not a public offering frequently involves complex legal considerations in individual cases. The accountant should not attempt to offer advice on this question, but should suggest that the matter be referred to a qualified lawyer.

Note   Before 1934, the 1933 Act was administered by the Federal Trade Commission.

2 **Securities Exchange Act of 1934.** Any company that desires listing on a national securities exchange, the securities exchanges themselves, and various brokers and dealers are required to file registration statements with the Commission

under the provisions of this Act. The 1934 Act, then, protects the public in the *trading* in securities, while the 1933 Act protects the public in the *distribution* of securities. The two Acts thus complement each other and form the backbone of the Commission's work.

The registration statements required by the 1934 Act are kept up-to-date by means of periodic reports that must be filed with the Commission subsequent to the date of registration. Companies that register under the 1933 Act may become subject to the reporting requirements of the 1934 Act even though their securities are not listed on a national exchange (see page 1222). The 1934 Act also gives the SEC jurisdiction over the registrant's proxy solicitation material.

3 **Public Utility Holding Company Act of 1935.** As the name indicates, this Act pertains to a special field. It provides for registration of companies included in holding company systems in the electric utility and retail gas fields. The Commission is granted broad regulatory powers with regard to the financial and operating structures of these companies.

4 **Trust Indenture Act of 1939.** The purpose of this Act is to protect corporate creditors by requiring that evidences of corporate indebtedness (bonds, notes, etc.) be offered to the public only under a trust indenture that has qualified with the Commission.

5 **Investment Company Act of 1940.** This law protects the small investor who attempts to obtain diversification by purchasing shares in an investment company. Investment companies must register with the SEC, which also has regulatory powers under the Act.

6 **Investment Advisers Act of 1940.** This law provides for the registration of certain individuals engaged in the business of advising others on investment matters.

ENFORCEMENT POWERS OF THE SEC

The Acts just described provide the Commission with considerable powers with which to enforce their provisions. In addition, where fraud or willful violation of an Act is involved, the Justice Department may institute criminal proceedings based on evidence supplied by the SEC.

Note If fraud is involved in the sale of securities in interstate commerce or through the mails, exemptions under the 1933 Act do not apply and the SEC has jurisdiction.

In order to carry out its functions, the Commission has the following direct powers:

1 It can prevent the distribution of a security being offered for sale.

2 It can stop the trading in a security.

3 It can take disciplinary actions (fines, suspension of privileges, etc.) against individuals and organizations.

However, the Commission's orders may be appealed to the courts.

SEC PROCEDURES

The SEC is authorized to define terms used in certain of the laws it administers, and it can prescribe the way in which the information required by the laws is to be reported. In this regard, the SEC has issued rules and regulations under the various Acts. These rules and regulations provide essential information concerning SEC procedures. Of particular concern to the accountant are:

1933 Act:

Rules of general applicability (Rules 170 and 171).

Regulation A—general exemption to registration.

Regulation C—rules applicable to registration.

1934 Act:

Sections of Regulation 12 pertaining to formal requirements and general requirements as to contents.

Sections of Regulation 13 pertaining to requirements of annual and other reports.

Regulation 14—rules relating to solicitation of proxies.

Sections of Regulation 15 relating to reports of registrants who have registered under the 1933 Act.

Registration procedures

The procedures to be followed in preparing and filing the registration statement are the major area of interest to the public accountant, since a registration statement must include a great deal of financial information. Furthermore, much of this financial data must be accompanied by an opinion of an independent public accountant. The nature of the financial information will be discussed later on in the chapter. Our concern here is with procedures relating to the filing of the registration statement itself.

Observation Detailed financial information is not required under the Trust Indenture Act of 1939 and the Investment Advisers Act of 1940, so the public accountant will not be concerned with these laws. Two of the Acts that do require the filing of detailed financial information—the Public Utility Holding Company Act of 1935 and the Investment Company Act of 1940—apply to special types of businesses. Therefore, most public accountants will be involved only with the Securities Act of 1933 and the Securities Exchange Act of 1934.

The rules governing the requirements for registration are set forth in Regulation C, the instructions to the form used, and Regulation S-X. Under the 1933 Act, the first step in the registration procedure is to file the appropriate form with the office of the SEC in Washington, D.C. This should be done twenty days before the anticipated effective date of the registration. The registration statement is thoroughly reviewed by the Division of Corporate Finance. As we have previously indicated, this review is aimed toward determining whether there has been full disclosure of matters of significance to potential investors; the Commission does not pass judgment on the merits of the security as an investment. In fact, the front page of a prospectus must contain a statement in bold-face type to the effect that the securities have not been approved or disapproved by the SEC.

Upon completion of its review, the Commission sends a letter of comments (popularly known as a *deficiency letter*) to the registrant. This letter sets forth the particular parts of the registration statement that the SEC believes require amendment. In order to minimize the number and the extent of such deficiencies, accountants and others experienced in SEC work make it a practice to discuss matters on which they have doubts or questions with members of the Commission's staff before the registration statement is actually filed. Often, a problem can be resolved over the telephone. In other cases, a conference is required. The SEC's staff is extremely cooperative and helpful and should be consulted whenever a problem cannot otherwise be solved. But it should be remembered that they are busy men and should not be queried indiscriminately.

Discussion with members of the staff may be advisable after the letter of comments has been received. There may be some questions or problems concerning the means or even the desirability of complying with the Commission's suggestions. Again, some matters can be cleared up over the telephone, while others can be resolved only through a conference. When agreement has been reached, an amendment must be filed. This amendment is handled by the Division of Corporate Finance in the same manner as the original registration statement was handled. The twenty-day waiting period starts all over again. However, the Commission can agree upon request to "accelerate" the amendment by treating it as if it were filed as of the filing date of the original registration statement. If an amendment does not correct the deficiencies to the satisfaction of the Commission, another letter of comments is sent and the cycle is repeated.

Normally, a registration statement becomes effective twenty days after it has been filed, but the Commission has the power to consent to an earlier effective date (Sec. 8(a), 1933 Act). Therefore, it is necessary to file an amendment as quickly as possible. When an amendment is not filed within the allotted time, the Commission can take the following courses of action, depending on the circumstances: (1) if the deficiencies are not material, it can allow the registration statement to become effective in deficient form but without acceleration, or (2) if the deficiencies are material, it can refuse to permit the registration statement to become effective, thereby prohibiting sale of the securities to the public. . . .

The registration statement must not contain an untrue statement or omission of a material fact *when it becomes effective* (Sec. 11, 1933 Act). Therefore, the accountant must remember to keep currently abreast of the financial affairs of his client after the registration statement has been filed. An authoritative discussion of the accountant's responsibility for disclosure of events subsequent to the date of the financial statements, with suggestions for making a review of the client's affairs, can be found in *Statement on Auditing Procedure No. 25,* issued by the Committee on Auditing Procedure of the American Institute of Certified Public Accountants.

Comfort Letter   Frequently, the underwriter will require a "comfort letter" from the accountant. In this letter, the accountant indicates that he has made a review, but not an audit, of financial statements for periods subsequent to the date of the statements filed, and that he has read minutes, made inquiries of officers, and the like; and that, based on this review, no knowledge came to his attention of any changes in capital stock or any material adverse changes in the financial position of the company.

The SEC also reviews registration statements and annual reports filed under the 1934 Act. In general, the procedure is the same as under the 1933 Act— deficiency letters are sent and, if necessary, amendments are filed. However, since there is usually no effective date involved in filings under the 1934 Act, delaying amendments are not required. In fact, deficiency letters relating to annual reports filed under the 1934 Act sometimes consist merely of suggestions by the Commission that should be incorporated in the annual report for the next year. . . .

THE SEC IN THE ACCOUNTING FIELD

BACKGROUND

Guides to SEC thinking on accounting matters   The public accountant engaged in SEC work must be conversant with the requirements of the appropriate law, and he must also have a thorough knowledge of the Commission's views on accounting and auditing theory and practice. These views are expressed through a number of media, as follows:

1 **Regulation S-X.** This is the major accounting regulation. It governs the form and content of the financial statements that must be filed under the various Acts. An up-to-date copy of Regulation S-X is the most essential tool for any accountant engaged in SEC work. Copies can be obtained by writing to the SEC, 425 Second Street NW, Washington 25, D.C.

2 **Accounting Series Releases.** Opinions of the Chief Accountant on major accounting and administrative questions are published in these releases. Notices of changes in Regulation S-X and other matters of interest to accountants are also made known through Accounting Series Releases. Past releases can be obtained from the Superintendent of Documents, U. S. Government Printing Office, Washington 25, D.C. You will be placed on the current mailing list if you send a written request to the main office of the SEC.

3 **SEC Decisions and Reports.** The Accounting Series Releases were not issued before 1937. For information on Commission decisions and opinions that were reached prior to that date, it is necessary to refer to the bound volumes of SEC Decisions and Reports. These are available from the Superintendent of Documents.

4 **Annual Reports of the SEC.** At the end of each fiscal year, the SEC sends its annual report to Congress. This report summarizes the Commission's activities for the year and provides a valuable insight into its procedures and policies. Copies can be obtained from the Superintendent of Documents.

5 **Speeches and articles by the Commissioners and members of the staff.** Those officially connected with the SEC are often called upon to give talks on accounting subjects. Professional publications frequently print these speeches and also publish articles by the Commissioners and members of the staff.

The SEC position on accounting principles and practices   The SEC has not invoked the authority given to it by Congress to the extent that it dictates the accounting principles to be applied in the preparation of the financial section of the registration statement. It has left this area primarily to the discretion of the accounting profession by requiring that financial statements be prepared in accordance with generally accepted accounting principles. However, the Commission reserves the right to use "its own judgment of what is sound accounting practice." In this connection, the Commission has had to point out many times that tax accounting does not necessarily represent generally accepted accounting practice. And in Accounting Series Release No. 56, the Commission stated that the standard is the accepted accounting practice at the date of the particular transaction, not at the filing date. This is especially important in cases where it is necessary to reconstruct accounts.

Observation   If there is "no substantial authoritative support" for the accounting principles on which the statements are based, the deficiency will not be corrected by mere disclosure of this fact in footnotes or in the accountant's report. This point was brought out in Accounting Series Release No. 4. . . .

FINANCIAL STATEMENTS REQUIRED BY THE SEC

The requirements as to what financial statements must be filed for registration are shown on the appropriate registration or reporting form and in the instruction booklet for the form. Certain terms defined in Regulation S-X are used in the instructions to the various forms; we will refer to these definitions in the following discussion when it is necessary for clarification. Also, reference will be made to various provisions, rules, and regulations under the Acts that are of particular significance to the accountant.

Most of the forms prescribed by the SEC are for use only by special types of issuers or apply only to particular kinds of securities. Our discussion will concentrate on those forms that have general applicability and, therefore, are most frequently used, as follows:

1 Form S-1, for registration under the 1933 Act.

2 Form 10, for registration under the 1934 Act, and Form 10-K, for annual reports under the 1934 Act.

1. Forms S-1   Companies registering under the 1933 Act that do not fall within the "special" categories should use Form S-1. Thus, commercial or industrial concerns will usually file on Form S-1. The form itself is divided into two sections: Part I is for information required in the prospectus; Part II is for information not required in the prospectus. In preparing the statements required for Form S-1 and other forms, the preparer should keep in mind the provisions of Rule 3-06 of Regulation S-X to the effect that information required with respect to any statement is a minimum requirement to which must be added any additional information necessary to make the financial statements not misleading. Also, attention should be paid to General Instruction D for Form S-1, which permits cross-referencing instead of repeating the same information in several parts of the prospectus.

Part I of Form S-1   The financial information required in Part I of Form S-1 is:

1 **Summary of earnings.** Item 6 on the form requires that a summary of earnings be furnished in comparative columnar form for the registrant or the registrant and its subsidiaries consolidated, or both, depending on for whom balance sheets must be filed. This summary, which is actually a condensed profit and loss statement, is probably the single statement most frequently referred to by investors. It should include, depending on the type of business, (a) net sales or operating revenues, (b) cost of goods sold or operating expenses (or gross profit), (c) interest charges, (d) income taxes, (e) net income, (f) special items (see page 1252), and (g) net income and special items. If common stock is being registered, the earnings applicable to common stock, earnings per share, and dividends declared should be shown; if long-term debt is being registered, the annual interest requirements on the debt should be shown; and if preferred stock is being registered, the annual dividend requirements on the stock should be shown.

However, the trend in recent years has been to present more and more information in the summary of earnings. In fact, there is a tendency to reflect all the required income, expense, and sometimes even earned surplus information in the summary of earnings, thus eliminating entirely the separate profit and loss and earned surplus statements.

The summary must cover the preceding five fiscal years, unless the company and its immediate predecessors have not been in business that long. It must also cover (1) the period between the end of the latest fiscal year and the date of the latest balance sheet filed, and (2) the corresponding period of the preceding fiscal year. These interim periods are commonly referred to as *short periods*. The SEC further requires that data for additional years should be furnished if such data are necessary to keep the summary "from being misleading." In the case of an initial offering, the underwriters frequently demand that the summary cover a ten-year period. . . .

2 **Balance sheet of the registrant.** Item 21 on the form, as supplemented by the instruction book for the form, sets forth the requirements as to what financial statements should be filed. The first of these is the balance sheet of the registrant. This should reflect the accounts as of a date within 90 days prior to the filing date of the registration statement unless [certain conditions are met]. . . .

3 **Profit and loss statements of the registrant.** These should be filed for each of the last three complete fiscal years and for the period between the end of the latest of these years and the date of the latest balance sheet filed. As pointed out previously, the information required in the profit and loss statement can be included in the summary of earnings.

Under Rule 5-02(35d) of Regulation S-X, a surplus statement must be filed for each period for which a profit and loss statement is required. It may be either a separate statement or it may be a continuation of the related profit and loss statement. The information relating to retained earnings can also be included in the summary of earnings.

4 **Consolidated statements.** A consolidated balance sheet and a consolidated profit and loss statement for the registrant and its subsidiaries should be filed as of the same dates as the corresponding statements filed for the registrant. . . .

5 **Statements of unconsolidated subsidiaries.** For each of its majority-owned subsidiaries not consolidated, the registrant should file the balance sheets and profit and loss statements that would be required if the subsidiary itself were a registrant. In Rule 1-02 of Regulation S-X, a *majority-owned subsidiary* is defined as a subsidiary that has more than 50% of its outstanding voting securities owned by the registrant and/or one or more of the registrant's other majority-owned subsidiaries. . . .

6 **Statements of 50%-owned persons.** The term *person,* as defined in the 1933 Act, covers not only individuals but also every form of commercial organization that can issue securities. A *50%-owned person* is one whose voting securities are owned directly or indirectly as follows: (1) approximately 50% by the registrant, and (2) approximately 50% by another *single* interest.

The registrant should file the same financial statements for any 50%-owned person that would be required if the person were a registrant. The other single interest should be identified on these financial statements.

Significant Subsidiary Rule The financial statements of all majority-owned subsidiaries and 50%-owned companies that do not in the aggregate constitute a *significant subsidiary* do not have to be filed. As defined in Rule 1-02 of Regulation S-X, a subsidiary is considered significant if it (or, if it is itself a parent, it and its subsidiaries) meets any *one* of the following conditions:

a The assets of the subsidiary exceed 15% of the assets of the registrant and the registrant's subsidiaries on a consolidated basis.
b The investments in and advances to the subsidiary by the registrant and the registrant's other subsidiaries exceed 15% of the assets of the registrant and the registrant's subsidiaries on a consolidated basis.
c The sales and operating revenues of the subsidiary exceed 15% of the sales and operating revenues of the registrant and the registrant's subsidiaries on a consolidated basis.

Note When the financial statements of majority-owned subsidiaries and 50%-owned companies are omitted, the reason for the omission must be given. This is usually done in a footnote to the financial statements.

7 **Statements of affiliates whose securities are collateral for the issue being registered.** For any of its affiliates whose securities are pledged as collateral for more than 20% of the principal amount of the securities being registered, the registrant should file the same financial statements that would be required if

the affiliate were a registrant. The measure of the value of the securities of the affiliate is the greatest of principal amount, par value, book value, or market value.

8 Special statements. Under certain special conditions, additional statements or information must be provided. . . .

Part II of Form S-1   The financial information includible in Part II of Form S-1—that is, information that does not have to be shown in the prospectus— consists of historical data and schedules that support items reported in the financial statements in Part I. . . .

Pro-forma financial statements   In addition to the financial state- ments required to be furnished in the registration statement, it is often ad- visable to include pro-forma financial statements in order to clarify an other- wise complicated situation; the SEC can require that such statements be provided if they are omitted. Pro-forma statements can be used to present many kinds of situations, such as the financial position that would result from a proposed recapitalization or merger, the acquisition of two or more com- panies, or the incorporation of a partnership. In the latter two situations, a pro-forma profit and loss statement might be appropriate as well as a pro- forma balance sheet. However, it is important to remember that what purports to be a pro-forma statement of income should not in fact be a projection of future earnings.

Rule 170 under the 1933 Act pertains to pro-forma statements. It reads as follows:

Financial statements which purport to give effect to the receipt and application of any part of the proceeds from the sale of securities for cash shall not be used unless such securities are to be offered through underwriters and the under- writing arrangements are such that the underwriters are or will be committed to take and pay for all of the securities, if any are taken, prior to or within a reasonable time after the commencement of the public offering, or if the se- curities are not so taken, to refund to all subscribers the full amount of all sub- scription payments made for the securities. The caption of any such financial statement shall clearly set forth the assumptions upon which such statement is based. The caption shall be in type at least as large as that used generally in the body of the statement.

What to Do   Study the underwriting agreement and ascertain if the under- writing commitment complies with Rule 170 before including in the prospectus a pro-forma balance sheet that gives effect to the sale of the securities being registered.

Post-effective amendments   In certain instances, such as the existence of warrants or convertible debentures, it is necessary to bring the prospectus up to date periodically—that is, a new prospectus must be filed with and processed by the SEC. This is so because of the requirements of Section 10(a) (3) of the 1933 Act: when a prospectus is used more than nine months after the effective date of the registration statement, the information it contains can be no more than sixteen months old.

The prospectus is brought up to date annually by filing a *post-effective amendment.* As far as the financial statements are concerned, this involves filing the required information for the most recent fiscal year and dropping out the information that, as a result of the new information, is no longer required under the instructions to the Form. . . .

Generally available statement   Because of the liability provisions under Section 11(a) of the 1933 Act, it is important that the accountant be familiar with what is commonly known as a *generally available statement.* Section 11(a) provides that an investor may sue various persons, including the certifying accountant, who were involved with the registration statement, if the investor can show that an untrue statement of material fact was made in the registration statement or that a required material fact was omitted from the registration statement. It is not necessary for the investor to show that he relied on the untrue statement or relied on the registration statement not knowing of the omission.

However, Section 11(a) further provides that if the issuer has made generally available to its security holders an earnings statement covering a period of at least twelve months beginning after the effective date of the registration statement, the investor's right of recovery is conditioned on his furnishing proof that he acquired the security relying on the untrue statement in the registration statement or on the registration statement without knowledge of the omission. The advantage of furnishing a generally available statement, then, is obvious. While the generally available statement does not need to be accompanied by an accountant's opinion, the accountant is usually requested to review it.

Regulation A offerings   As we have already pointed out, the 1933 Act gives the SEC the authority to exempt from registration offerings of an aggregate value of less than $300,000. Under this authorization, the Commission has issued Regulation A, which specifically provides for the exemption from registration of securities for which the gross proceeds from sale within any twelve-month period do not exceed the $300,000 amount. However, such securities must be qualified by filing four copies of a notification (Form 1-A) with the regional SEC office along with four copies of the offering circular. . . .

2. Forms 10 and 10-K   Most companies listing securities on a national securities exchange for the first time will use Form 10 to register with the SEC. A summary of earnings is not required on Form 10, but otherwise the requirements for financial statements are virtually the same as those previously described for Form S-1. However, the balance sheets on Form 10 should reflect the accounts at the close of the latest fiscal year, unless such fiscal year has ended within 90 days prior to the date of filing *with the exchange*. In this latter situation, the balance sheets may be stated as of the close of the preceding fiscal year. Profit and loss statements should be filed for each of the three fiscal years immediately preceding the date of the corresponding balance sheet that is filed.

Note   When statements as of the preceding fiscal year are filed, an amendment to the registration statement must be filed within 120 days after the date of filing. This amendment must provide the appropriate balance sheets and profit and loss statements as of the end of the latest fiscal year.

Observation   When a company wants to list additional classes of securities, Form 8-A should be used. The financial information required on Form 8-A pertains to businesses acquired by the registrant or any of its majority-owned subsidiaries.

Rule 12B-23 (1934 Act) permits the incorporation of financial statements required to be filed as part of Form 10 by reference to the financial statements included in an earlier 1933 Act filing (Form S-1). Material incorporated by reference must be clearly identified in the reference. If the material to be incorporated by reference includes the accountant's report, a current accountant's consent (see page 1234) must be filed.

Any company having securities registered on a national securities exchange, and certain companies registered under the 1933 Act must file an annual report with the SEC. Form 10-K is the form most frequently used for this annual report. The financial information required is similar to that required on Form 10 except, of course, that it covers only the latest fiscal year.

Comment   In addition to the requirements of the SEC, the listing company must also adhere to the rules of the particular exchange. These can be obtained from the exchange itself.

Forms 8-K and 9-K   From time to time, the accountant will also be concerned with Form 8-K, a current report of certain important events or changes within the company, and Form 9-K. Form 9-K is a mid-year report of sales and gross revenues, net income before and after taxes, extraordinary and special items, and charges and credits to earned surplus. Form 8-K requires financial statements only when the purpose of the report is to disclose the acquisition of a *significant* amount of assets. In such a case, a balance sheet as of a date reasonably close to the date of acquisition and profit and loss statements for each of the last three fiscal years and for the period between the close of the latest fiscal year and the date of the latest balance sheet filed are required.

Proxy statements   Regulation 14 under the 1934 Act contains the SEC's rules relating to the solicitation of proxies. Schedule 14A under Regulation 14 sets forth the requirements for proxy statements.

Ordinarily, financial statements are not required in the proxy statement unless the matters to be acted upon by the stockholders relate to (a) authorization or issuance of securities otherwise than for exchange, (b) modification or exchange of securities, or (c) mergers, consolidations, acquisitions, and similar matters. In such cases, the company must furnish financial statements such as would be required in an original application for the registration of securities under the 1934 Act. . . .

THE ACCOUNTANT'S DUTIES AND RESPONSIBILITIES

In general, the public accountant who follows the requirements as to accounting and auditing set forth by the American Institute of Certified Public Accountants will usually be meeting SEC standards. However, there are a number of significant factors in the area of duties and responsibilities that the independent accountant should be aware of when engaged in SEC work. We will discuss these, as follows:

1 What statements should be certified.

2 Who may certify the statements.

3 The accountant's certificate.

4 The accountant's consent.

What statements should be certified   More often than not, financial statements filed with the SEC must be accompanied by an accountant's report or opinion, which the Commission refers to as a "certificate." The specific instructions with regard to what statements must be certified are contained in the instructions to the various forms. We will briefly outline the certification requirements for the most frequently used forms—S-1, 10, and 10-K.

1 **Form S-1.** Balance sheets and profit and loss and surplus statements, including consolidated statements, should be certified. Ordinarily, the balance sheets required to be filed with the registration statement will be certified. However, if they are not certified, either (a) an additional balance sheet as of a date within one year prior to the filing date, or (b) an additional balance sheet for a fiscal year that ends within one year and 90 days prior to the filing date should be filed and certified.

Profit and loss and surplus statements should be certified up to the date of the latest corresponding certified balance sheet filed. The summary of earnings does not have to be certified. But if the summary includes the information required in the profit and loss statement and therefore a separate profit and loss statement is not filed the summary must be certified on the same basis as a profit and loss statement.

2 **Form 10.** The balance sheets and profit and loss and surplus statements that are filed in accordance with the instructions must be certified.

3 **Form 10-K.** Balance sheets and profit and loss and surplus statements must be certified.

Amendments If, after certified financial statements are filed, they, or any notes to them, are amended (as a result, for example, of an SEC letter of comments), the certifying accountant must certify to them in their amended form. This always requires signing a new consent that generally refers to the registration statement being "as amended." In addition, depending on the circumstances, a new certificate may have to be signed.

Schedules In all cases, supporting schedules should be certified if the statements they support are certified (Rule 5-04, Regulation S-X).

Who may certify the statements Certification of financial statements filed with the SEC must be made by an independent certified public accountant or public accountant. However, "independence" is governed by the requirements of the SEC, not those of state CPA societies or the American Institute of Certified Public Accountants. The SEC does not consider an accountant independent if during the period covered by his report he has any direct financial interest in the business of his client, or any material indirect financial interest, or is connected with the client as either a promoter, underwriter, director, officer, employee, or voting trustee. The SEC considers all relevant circumstances in determining the accountant's independence with respect to a particular client. Thus, circumstances and relationships that do not have any direct connection with the filing of reports with the Commission are taken into account. For example, failure to make adequate disclosure in reports other than reports filed with the SEC may be grounds for questioning the independence of the accountant.

In practice, the question as to whether an accountant is independent is one of fact, depending on the particular circumstances of the case.

The accountant's certificate   The technical requirements applicable to the accountant's report are set forth in Article 2 of Regulation S-X. The certificate must contain these elements:

1 **It must be dated.**

2 **It must be manually signed.** If the accountants signing the certificate are a partnership, the firm name should be signed.

3 **The financial statements must be identified.** The accountant is expected to identify in his certificate the financial statements covered by his opinion. A detailed enumeration is not required—for example, a statement or statements, to the effect that the balance sheets and the related statements of profit and loss and surplus and the supporting schedules have been examined, is sufficient.

4 **The scope of the audit must be revealed.** The accountant must state in the certificate whether the audit was made in accordance with generally accepted auditing standards. He must designate any auditing procedures recognized as normal, or considered necessary under the circumstances of the particular case, that have been omitted, and he must give the reasons for their omission.

5 **The accountant's opinions must be expressed.** The accountant must clearly state in the certificate: (a) his opinion as to the financial statements covered by the certificate and the accounting principles and practices reflected in those statements; (b) his opinion as to any material changes in accounting principles or practices, or in the method of applying them; (c) his opinion as to any material retroactive adjustments of the accounts; and (d) the nature of, and his opinion as to, any material differences between the accounting principles and practices reflected in the financial statements and those reflected in the accounts after the entry of adjustments for the period under review.

Important   As indicated above, the accountant must specifically and clearly identify any matters to which he takes exception. Furthermore, he must state the effect of each exception on the related financial statements. But in practice the SEC will not accept a filing in which the accountant states exceptions to an accounting practice or as to the scope of his examination.

The standard report recommended by the American Institute of Certified Public Accountants meets the SEC requirements. . . .

In the case of a registration statement, it is customary to furnish a separate opinion on the schedules. This is so because the schedules are included in Part II of the registration statement but not in the prospectus. Typical wording of such an opinion would be as follows:

In connection with our examination of the financial statements of X Company as of December 31, 19____ and for the three years then ended, which are included in the prospectus, we have also examined the supporting schedules.

In our opinion, these schedules fairly present the financial data required to be submitted under the regulations of the Securities and Exchange Commission.

It is not uncommon for more than one accounting firm to be involved in a single registration statement. When the principal accountant relies on an examination made by another accountant, the report of the other accountant must be filed. However, if the principal accountant accepts responsibility for the other accountant's examination, either through making no reference to it in his certificate or through an express statement in his certificate that he does accept responsibility, the other accountant's report need not be filed.

To show that he has relied on (but does not accept responsibility for) the examination of another accountant, the principal accountant should include in his certificate a statement similar to the following:

. . . The financial statements of the Company's Canadian subsidiary which are included in the consolidated financial statements were examined by Roe and Doe, Chartered Accountants, whose report appears elsewhere in this prospectus.

In our opinion, based upon our examination and the report of Roe and Doe referred to above, the consolidated financial statements enumerated above fairly present . . .

Observation   In its letter of comments to the registrant the SEC may cite the accountant's certificate itself for deficiencies. Thus, it is important to have a thorough knowledge of the Commission's requirements as to the form of certificate and the extent of the opinions and information that must be included.

The accountant's consent   The SEC requires that the certifying accountant "consent" to the use of his opinion(s) on the financial statements and schedules. In fact, this consent must cover any reference made to the accountant in the registration statement. The consent, which must be dated and signed, may be incorporated in the accountant's certificate. Usually, however, it appears separately in Part II of the registration statement. An example follows:

We hereby consent to the use of our opinion, dated February 24, 19 _____, *in the Prospectus constituting a part of the within Registration Statement. We also consent to the reference to our firm as set forth under the captions "Summary of Earnings" and "Experts" in said Prospectus.*

The SEC has issued well over 100 Accounting Series Releases. Subjects covered in these releases have varied widely. Many have arisen from specific problems with individual registrant companies, while others, such as the following, have been issued after extended experience with a recurring situation.

The concept of independence is of vital importance to the audit profession. This, in turn, makes it of vital concern to the SEC. The following reading is the major SEC pronouncement on this subject.

INDEPENDENCE OF CERTIFYING ACCOUNTANTS— COMPILATION OF REPRESENTATIVE ADMINISTRATRATIVE RULINGS IN CASES INVOLVING THE INDEPENDENCE OF ACCOUNTANTS*

Reg. § **211.81.** The Securities and Exchange Commission today announced the publication of an additional release in its Accounting Series dealing with independence of accountants. This release, which summarizes cases in the Commission's experience under the independence rule[1] since the publication of Accounting Series Release No. 47 on January 25, 1944, together with prior releases and Commission decisions reflects the development of policy regarding the practice of accountants before the Commission over a period of some twenty-five years. See Appendix.

[Certification Requirement]

The various laws administered by the Commission either require or give the Commission power to require that financial statements filed with it be certified by independent accountants, and with minor exceptions the Commission's rules require that such statements be so certified. The concept of indepen-

---

* Accounting Series Release No. 81, Securities Act Release No. 4002, Exchange Act Release No. 5829, Public Utility Holding Company Act Release No. 13877, and Investment Company Act Release No. 2801, December 11, 1958, 23 F.R. 9777.
[1] Rule 2-01 of Regulation S-X.

dence was well developed and the value of a review by independent accountants who are in no way connected with the business was established before the passage of the first Act now administered by the Commission — the Securities Act of 1933.

[Senate committee's views]

The passage of the Securities Act, however, is an important landmark in the development of the concept of the responsibility of the independent accountant to the investor and the public. The original draft of the Securities Act did not require certification by independent accountants. A representative of the accounting profession appeared at the hearings on the bill before the Committee on Banking and Currency of the United States Senate to suggest revisions of the bill.[2] He pointed out that the bill as drafted imposed "highly technical responsibilities upon the Commission as to accounting principles, their proper application and their clear expression in financial statements," and suggested the bill be revised to require that "the accounts pertaining to such balance sheet, statement of income and surplus shall have been examined by an independent accountant and his report shall present his certificate wherein he shall express his opinion as to the correctness of the assets, liabilities, reserves, capital and surplus as of the balance sheet date and also the income statement for the period indicated."

The committee considered at length the value to investors and to the public of an audit by accountants not connected with the company or management and whether the additional expense to industry of an audit by independent accountants was justified by the expected benefits to the public. The committee also considered the advisability and feasibility of requiring the audit to be made by accountants on the staff of the agency administering the Act.

In the report on the bill the Senate committee stated that it was intended that those responsible for the administration and enforcement of the law should have full and adequate authority to procure whatever information might be necessary in carrying out the provisions of the bill, but it was deemed essential to refrain from placing upon any Federal agency the duty of passing judgment upon the soundness of any security.[3] The proposal to require certification by independent public accountants was incorporated in the bill as passed.

---

[2] Statement of Col. A. H. Carter, President of the New York State Society of Certified Public Accountants, before the Committee on Banking and Currency, United States Senate, 73d Congress, 1st Sess., on S. 875, p. 55.

[3] Senate Report No. 47, 73d Congress, 1st Sess., p. 2.

[SEC determination of independence]

The requirement that industry furnish financial statements certified by independent accountants imposes upon the Commission the responsibility of ascertaining whether audits pursuant to its requirements are made by qualified independent accountants. Rule II(e) of the Commission's Rules of Practice and Rule 2-01 of Regulation S-X reflect this concern. Under Rule II(e) the Commission may disqualify, and deny, temporarily or permanently, the privilege of appearing or practicing before it to any accountant who is found by the Commission after hearing in the matter not to possess the requisite qualifications to represent others; or to be lacking in character or integrity; or to have engaged in unethical or improper professional conduct. These proceedings are conducted privately and may or may not result in a published opinion. They have been rare. Day-to-day problems arising under Rule 2-01 of Regulation S-X are largely concerned with determining whether particular relationships are of a nature which would prejudice the independent status of an accountant with respect to a particular client.

In administering Rule 2-01 the Commission has not attempted to set up objective standards for measuring the qualifications of accountants other than requiring that they be in good standing and entitled to practice as independent accountants in their place of residence or principal office. However, it is expected that they will have adequate technical training and proficiency and will conduct their audit in a workmanlike manner in accordance with generally accepted auditing standards.[4] Rule II(e) of the Rules of Practice recognizes that ethical and professional responsibility is founded upon character and integrity.

As stated in Accounting Series Release No. 47, the Commission has consistently held that the question of independence is one of fact, to be determined in the light of all the pertinent circumstances in a particular case, but it has not been practicable to identify all of the circumstances which might prevent an accountant from being independent. However, in Rule 2-01(b) of Regulation S-X, as recently revised[5] to recognize the increasing complexities in the business world, the Commission has stated that ". . . an accountant will be considered not independent with respect to any person or any of its parents or subsidiaries in whom he has, or had during the period of report, any direct financial interest or any material indirect financial interest; or with whom he is, or was during such period, connected as a promoter, underwriter, voting trustee, director, officer, or employee." In connection with this revision prac-

---

[4] See Rule 2-02 of Regulation S-X.
[5] Accounting Series Release No. 79, April 8, 1958. [¶ 72, 101].

ticing accountants indicated that an interpretive release similar to Accounting Series Release No. 47 would be a helpful guide to the profession. This release therefore summarizes previously unpublished rulings on independence which have arisen under the several Acts administered by the Commission. A finding in a particular case that an accountant is not independent under our rules does not necessarily reflect on his professional standing or qualification to serve other registrants with the Commission.

In Accounting Series Release No. 47 it was said that it was not feasible to present adequately in summarized form the circumstances existing in particular cases in which it was determined not to question an accountant's independence. The growth of the accounting profession since 1944 and the number of inquiries received from public accountants unfamiliar with the rules suggest the need for publication of rulings in this category.

Administrative rulings in this area have been reviewed and there are stated briefly herein the relationships which existed in select cases where an accountant was not denied the right to certify the financial statements because under the circumstances it was concluded that the independence of the accountant was not prejudiced. It is emphasized that these rulings were made after taking into consideration all known relevant circumstances and under changed circumstances the relationships stated in some of these examples could be disqualifying. Appropriate procedure in all cases where any doubt exists is to discuss the facts with the staff.

The following examples have been selected as representative of administrative rulings in specific cases:

NOT INDEPENDENT

Representative situations in which accountants have been held to be not independent with respect to a particular client:

I **Relationships Specified in Rule 2-01(b) of Regulation S-X**
  A **Financial Interest**

  1 An accountant took an option for shares of his client's common stock in settlement of his fee. The option subsequently appreciated in value. The question of independence arose in connection with a proposed merger and application for listing on a national securities exchange.

  2 Chartered accountants for a proposed registrant, a foreign corporation, owned a stock interest in the company.

  3 Company A proposed filing a registration statement for a securities issue, part of the proceeds of which were to be used to acquire the assets of Company B. The certificate of the accountants of Company B could not be ac-

cepted for inclusion in the registration statement because a partner of the firm owned stock of Company B.

4 Using their own funds, the wives of partners in an accounting firm purchased stock in a client of the firm immediately prior to registration.

5 Shares of stock in a proposed registrant held by an accountant's wife had originally been received by him in settlement of his audit fee.

6 Partners and staff members of a small accounting firm which had certified the financial statements included in a registration statement subsequently acquired shares of stock of the registrant. They were denied the privilege of certifying subsequent financial statements to be included in a post-effective amendment to the registration statement.

7 An interpretation was given that the S.E.C. does not recognize a difference between a corporation and a registered investment company which would permit the ownership of shares in the latter by the accountant certifying its financial statements filed with the Commission.

8 After the issuance of an offering circular, some partners of the accounting firm which had certified the financial statements acquired shares of the company. In connection with a subsequent listing application the registrant was advised that the accountants had lost their independent status.

B Director, Officer, Employee

9 From the time of organization of a proposed registrant in November 1952 until July 1954, an accountant served as assistant treasurer, comptroller and director with the responsibility of keeping the accounts of the company and also acted as co-signer of checks. He also owned shares of the registrant's common stock. In July 1954 arrangements were made for an issue of securities. Even though the accountant severed his affiliation with the company as officer and director and made a gift of his shares of stock to his daughter, his certificate was not acceptable.

10 A partner in the firm of certifying accountants was a director of a proposed registrant, a stockholder, and a trustee of a testamentary trust which controlled a substantial portion of the registrant's stock. Even though he were to resign as director and trustee and dispose of his stock interest, the accounting firm could not be considered independent in connection with the proposed registration. It was also held that another partner of the accounting firm acting individually and apart from the firm could not be considered independent.

11 A partner in an accounting firm acted as controller and exercised some supervisory powers with respect to the proposed registrant's accounting procedures.

12 Financial statements for the first two years of the three-year period required to be included in a registration statement had been certified by an individual

practitioner who gave up his practice to become an executive of the registrant.

II Other Relationships and Conditions Resulting in Lack of Independence

13 An accountant who certified the financial statements of a registrant was the father of the secretary-treasurer of the registrant who was employed by the registrant on a half-time basis. Prior thereto, the secretary-treasurer had been employed by the registrant as its full-time principal accounting officer.

14 The wife of a partner of the accounting firm certifying the financial statements of an investment company was secretary-treasurer of the company.

15 A partner of an accounting firm was the brother of the holder of 50 per cent of the stock of proposed registrant. The accountant was also counsel for the company, and his wife held $35,000 of its preferred stock. The audit of the registrant's accounts was to be made by a branch office of the accounting firm in which the partner had only a financial interest.

16 The wife of the accountant who had certified the financial statements of a proposed registrant was the sister of the widow of the founder of the company. The widow had inherited 60 per cent of the company's stock from her husband and her son 10 per cent.

17 An accounting firm which certified the financial statements of a registered investment company had exclusive custody of the key to the company's safe deposit box. Under these conditions the accountants were acting as custodian of the securities portfolio and were/in the position of auditing their own work.

18 An accountant and five persons who were the sole stockholders of the proposed registrant acquired a parcel of real estate for the purpose of selling or leasing it to the company. The total purchase price was $85,000, of which $26,000 was paid in cash and the balance by a note secured by a mortgage. In addition to providing his portion of the cash payment, the accountant loaned the others $21,000 on interest bearing notes to cover their share of the down payment. It was also provided that the accountant would receive 25 per cent of any profit arising from sale of the property to an outsider.

19 A certifying accountant, together with certain officers of the registrant, organized a corporation which purchased property from the registrant for $100,000, giving the registrant $25,000 cash and a purchase money mortgage for $75,000.

20 Accountants were advised that they would lose their independent status if a trust created by partners and their wives purchased a building, occupied by a client under a 21-year lease. The building was owned by an unrelated person and the transaction would have involved a substantial sum of money.

21 The partners of an accounting firm were considering investing in a finance company which operated a wholly-owned insurance agency to arrange insurance on the property financed. It was contemplated that a substantial part

of such insurance would be placed with an insurance company client of the accounting firm. They were advised that if the insurance was so placed they would not be considered independent with respect to their client.

22 Two of the partners of the accounting firm certifying the financial statements of a registrant were also partners of a law firm engaged by the registrant to pass upon the legality of the securities which were being registered.

23 A certified public accountant who was also a lawyer practiced both professions as a partner in separate accounting and law firms. Both firms were approached by an investment company to accept engagements in their respective fields.

24 The wife of an accountant had a 47½% interest in one of the three principal underwriters of a proposed issue by the registrant.

25 A partner of an accounting firm acted as one of three executors of the will of a principal officer of a registrant and as one of three trustees of a trust established under the will. The principal asset of the trust was a substantial proportion of the voting stock of the registrant.

26 A partner in an accounting firm which audited registrant's accounts was appointed agent in control of certain buildings by the trustee for the children of the controlling stockholder of the registrant. In such capacity the accountant negotiated a lease with the registrant which occupied office space in one of the buildings. The partner in the accounting firm also acted as trustee of a trust for the benefit of the wife and children of the controlling stockholder.

NO ACTION

Representative situations in which accountants have not been held to be not independent with respect to a particular client:

I Relationships Specified in Rule 2-01(b) of Regulation S-X
A Financial Interest

27 A large national accounting firm had certified the financial statements covering the first eight years of a ten-year summary of earnings to be included in a registration statement. Another firm of accountants certified the last two years. At the time of their last certificate, two years earlier, there was no indication that the former firm was not in full compliance with the independence rule. It was deemed unnecessary for the firm to circularize the partners to determine whether any had subsequently acquired stock in the registrant.

28 Members of an accounting firm acquired shares of stock of a company controlled by one of their clients, an individual. The accounting firm had never done any work for the company. Upon being engaged to certify financial statements of the company in connection with a proposed registration, they immediately sold their holdings.

29 An accounting firm was held to be not independent because the wife of a partner owned stock in the registrant which had been acquired out of community earnings, and another accounting firm was engaged to audit the years in question. The wife disposed of the stock, and the firm was told that no objection would be raised to their certifying in subsequent years.

30 An accounting firm and the individual practitioner who preceded it had audited the accounts of proposed registrant since 1949. At various times between 1954 and 1957 a partner and an employee on the audit each acquired small amounts of issues of debenture bonds and subordinated notes. The securities held by these persons were redeemed by the company in August 1957 prior to certification of financial statements to be used in a proposed registration statement.

31 The following interpretations of the independence rule were given to an accounting firm which submitted two hypothetical situations:

a Company A proposed to file a registration statement and merge with or acquire Company X, which has been entirely independent of Company A. Financial statements of each company certified by different accounting firms were to be included in the registration statement.

In this situation if partners of the firm of accountants for Company X had a financial interest in Company A, that accounting firm could be considered independent for the purpose of certifying the statements of Company X to be included in a registration statement filed by Company A. This conclusion assumes that Company A's shares are widely held and the partners' interest is similar to any public investor's. A different conclusion would be indicated if the partners of the accounting firm were in a position to influence the action of Company A.

If Company X were to continue as a subsidiary of Company A, the accounting firm would not be considered independent for subsequent audits unless the partners of the firm promptly disposed of their financial interest in Company A.

b In a situation similar to that described above, the accounting firm which had certified the statements of Company A generally would have no knowledge of the investments of its partners in non-client corporations such as Company X. In some large national accounting firms, the determination of such holdings can be a time-consuming and burdensome task. Under these circumstances Item 24 of the requirements of a registration statement under the Securities Act of 1933 (disclosure of relationships between registrant and experts whose opinions are included in the registration statement) may be answered in the negative with a disclaimer of knowledge as to whether or not the certifying accountants of Company A had any interest in Company X.

B Director, Officer, Employee

32 A partner of an accounting firm was a director and member of the executive committee of a company for six years. In the year following his resignation the firm was engaged to certify the company's financial statements, but the

audit did not cover any of the time during which the accountant served as a director.

33 A partner of an accounting firm who held shares of a registrant's stock was elected a director. Eight days later he was notified of his firm's appointment as accountants for the current year. He never attended any meetings of the Board of Directors and did not participate in the selection of his firm. Upon being notified of the appointment of his firm as accountants he immediately resigned his directorship and sold his stock.

34 Company A acquired Company B in January 1955. Financial statements of Company A for years ended, June 30, 1954 and prior and financial statements of Company B for the year ended July 31, 1952 had been certified by accounting firm X. Financial statements of both companies for subsequent years were certified by accounting firm Y. After completion of the last audits of the respective companies by accounting firm X, a partner of that firm became a director of each company. The statements certified by accounting firm X were accepted for inclusion in a registration statement of Company A because the accountants were independent at the time of their certification and more recent audits were made by accounting firm Y.

35 An accountant had certified the financial statements of a prospective registrant for twelve years prior to its consolidation with another company in February 1957. After completion of the 1956 audit his services were terminated. At the time of certification he was independent in all respects. In May 1957 the accountant was elected to the Board of Directors and thereafter purchased shares of the common stock of the company. Late in 1957 the company proposed filing a registration statement which would include certified financial statements of the last three years examined by the accountant and a subsequent period to be certified by another accountant.

36 An accounting firm took into its partnership an individual who had been vice president and comptroller of one of their clients. The individual's resignation from the registrant and affiliation with the accounting firm would occur subsequent to the filing of the registrant's annual report on Form 10-K but before the designation of auditors for the current fiscal year. Although he would be a general partner, sharing in income from all sources, he would have no part in any work done for the client-registrant and would not be located in the same city as the client's head office.

II Other Relationships and Conditions Prompting Inquiries as to Independence

37 Registrants A and B each own 50% of the outstanding stock of Company C, but are otherwise not related. The accounting firm which audits Registrant A would not be disqualified because of ownership of a small number of shares of stock of Registrant B. However, the accounting firm which audits Company C would not be considered independent if any of its partners had an interest in either Registrant A or B.

38 Partners in an accounting firm owned stock in a company in which a substantial minority interest was owned by a client. Both companies were large and their securities were listed on a national securities exchange.

39 One of two partners of an accounting firm formed in February 1955 and dissolved in February 1956 became secretary-treasurer of a company in July 1955. He retained no interest in the partnership. The accounting practice was continued by the other partner who was engaged to make a first audit of the company in June 1956.

40 An accountant was co-executor of an estate which held approximately 15% of the outstanding shares of stock of a registrant. He had audited registrant's accounts for several years prior to the latest fiscal year. Another accountant had been engaged to certify the financial statements of the latest year for inclusion in a registration statement. The estate was being terminated and the registrant proposed engaging the accountant as auditor for subsequent years.

41 A staff member who had prepared financial statements for a mining company in the development stage and had participated in the audit was offered a position as an officer prior to the filing of a registration statement. Acceptance of the position by the staff member would not of itself destroy the independence of the accounting firm in connection with the proposed registration statement.

42 Accountants had installed an accounting system and prepared tax returns for a registrant prior to being engaged to certify financial statements to be included in a registration statement.

43 In addition to certifying the financial statements of a registrant, the accountant reviewed certain transactions of prior years, prepared fixed asset subsidiary ledgers, prepared the annual report to the state of incorporation, made recommendations for adjustments, and when consulted gave his professional opinion on the accounting treatment of particular transactions.

44 Due to the unexpected resignation of registrant's comptroller at the end of the year, the accountant was called upon to provide assistance in closing the books for the year. The work performed did not involve making decisions on a managerial level.

45 Following the death of the registrant's bookkeeper, an accounting firm posted the general ledger from the books of original entry and prepared periodic financial statements for the last eight months of the fiscal year. Registrant's bookkeeping staff had full charge of accounting journals and subsidiary ledgers and recorded all transactions. Financial statements certified by the accounting firm were accepted, but the accountants were advised to discontinue the bookkeeping services immediately.

46 A company operating hotels requested an accounting firm to assign to a hotel one of their senior accountants, experienced in hotel auditing, to make a continuous audit of transactions from day to day. The individual assigned to this work was not to administer the accounting office or to sign checks of the company, and he would not be required to make any entries in the books of account. The hotel had on its staff another person with the title of chief accountant whose duty it would be to administer the accounting office and to maintain the books of account.

BROKER-DEALER REPORTS

The revision of the broker-dealer reporting requirements effective November 15, 1957,[6] requires that all but a limited number of these reports be certified by independent accountants. Certification is required primarily in the interest of safeguarding the funds and securities of customers and consequently a more detailed audit is required than that ordinarily made in a regular annual audit of a commercial or industrial company for preparation of the annual report to security holders.

Accountant held not independent

The following are examples of representative situations in which an accountant has been held to be *not independent* with respect to a broker-dealer client:

47 A partner of the accounting firm which certified the financial statements of a registered broker-dealer was a partner in the registrant.

48 An accountant certified the financial statements of a brokerage firm in which his father and uncle were officers and owners of substantially all the outstanding stock.

49 An accountant certified the financial statements of a small brokerage firm in which his brother was a partner.

50 An accounting firm which had certified the financial statements of a registered broker-dealer for several years took the son-in-law of an officer of the registrant into their partnership.

51 A partner of the accounting firm which had certified the financial statements of a registered broker-dealer loaned securities to a partner of the registrant. The latter was the brother-in-law of the accountant. The securities were put in the firm's capital account and were used as part of the collateral securing a bank loan.

52 An accountant certified financial statements filed with the Commission by securities dealers. While considering an offer to serve as salesman for one of the securities dealers he inquired as to whether this would affect his independence with respect to dealers other than his prospective employer as to whom he acknowledged his lack of independence. He was advised that accepting such employment would place him in the position of engaging in a line of endeavor incompatible with that of an independent public accountant.

53 An accountant certifying the financial statements of a registered broker-dealer was a co-signer on the broker's indemnity bond.

54 An accounting firm was advised that the effecting of cash transactions in securities with a broker-dealer client ordinarily would not be cause for questioning its independence with respect to such client. However, if as a result

[6] Securities Exchange Act of 1934 Release No. 5560.

of such transactions a partner becomes indebted to the broker-dealer or becomes a creditor of the broker-dealer by leaving funds or securities on deposit, then the independent status of the accounting firm becomes questionable.

APPENDIX

Principal References Concerning the Practice of Accountants Before the Commission Opinions and Orders of the Commission

Cornucopia Gold Mines, 1 SEC 364 (1936) [¶ 68,515.065]

American Terminals and Transit Company, 1 SEC 701 (1936) [¶ 68,515.07]

National Boston Montana Mines Corporation, 2 SEC 226 (1937) [¶ 68,517.04]

Rickard Ramore Gold Mines, Ltd., 2 SEC 377 (1937) [¶ 68,515.085]

Metropolitan Personal Loan Company, 2 SEC 803 (1937) [¶ 68,515.075]

Interstate Hosiery Mills, Inc., 4 SEC 706 (1939) [¶ 68, 515.08]

A. Hollander & Son, Inc., 8 SEC 586 (1941) [¶ 68,515.05, .75, .129]

Abraham H. Puder and Puder and Puder, Securities Exchange Act of 1934 Release No. 3073 (1941)

Southeastern Industrial Loan Company, 10 SEC 617 (1941) [¶ 75,225]

Kenneth N. Logan, 10 SEC 982 (1942) (Accounting Series Release No. 28 [¶ 72,046])

Associated Gas and Electric Company, 11 SEC 975 (1942)

Cecil Bryant, 15 SEC 400 (1944) (Accounting Series Release No. 48 [¶72,066])

Red Bank Oil Company, 21 SEC 695 (1946) [¶ 75,610]

Drayer-Hanson, Incorporated, 27 SEC 838 (1948) [¶ 72,083]

Cristina Copper Mines, Inc., 33 SEC 397 (1952) [¶ 76,113]

Coastal Finance Corporation, 37 SEC 699 (1957) [¶ 76,518]

Accounting Series Releases

No. 2 (1937) Independence of accountants—Relationship to registrant [¶ 72,003].

No. 19 (1940) McKesson & Robbins, Inc. [¶ 72,020]

No. 22 (1941) Independence of accountants—Indemnification by registrant [¶ 72,040].

No. 28 (1942) Kenneth N. Logan (10 SEC 982) [¶ 72,046]

No. 47 (1944) Independence of certifying accountants—Summary of past releases of the Commission and a compilation of hitherto unpublished cases or inquiries [¶ 72,065].

No. 48 (1944) C. Cecil Bryant (15 SEC 400) [¶ 72,066]

No. 51 (1945) Disposition of Rule II(e) proceedings against certifying accountant [¶ 72,069].

No. 59 (1947) Williams and Kingsolver [¶ 72, 078]

No. 64 (1948) Drayer-Hanson, Incorporated (27 SEC 838) [¶ 72,083]

No. 67 (1949) Barrow, Wade, Guthrie & Co., Henry H. Dalton and Everett L. Mangam [¶ 72,086]

No. 68 (1949) F. G. Masquelette & Co., and J. E. Cassel [¶ 72,087]

No. 73 (1952) Haskins & Sells and Andrew Stewart [¶ 72,093]

No. 77 (1954) Disposition of Rule II(e) proceedings against certifying accountant [¶ 72,079].

No. 78 (1957) Touche, Niven, Bailey & Smart et al. (37 SEC 629) [¶72,100]

Changes in the Independence Rule

Article 14, Rules and Regulations under the Securities Act of 1933, Federal Trade Commission, July 6, 1933

Article 14, Rules and Regulations under the Securities Act of 1933, Federal Amended, April 29, 1935

Rule 650, General Rules and Regulations under the Securities Act of 1933, January 21, 1936

Rule 2-01, Regulation S-X, Adopted February 21, 1940, Accounting Series Release No. 12 [¶ 72,013]

Amendments of Rule 2-01

Accounting Series Release No. 37, November 7, 1942 [¶ 72, 055]

Accounting Series Release No. 44, May 24, 1943 [¶ 72,062]

Accounting Series Release No. 70, December 20, 1950 [¶ 72,089]

Accounting Series Release No. 79, April 8, 1958 [¶ 72,101]

Pronouncements of the SEC always demand attention from CPAs. Evidence of this is presented in the following taken from the "Accounting and Auditing Problems" section of the *Journal of Accountancy* edited, at that time, by Carman G. Blough.

SEC RELEASE ON OPINIONS
AND OPENING INVENTORIES*

The position taken by the Securities and Exchange Commission in its Accounting Series Release No. 90 has been the subject of considerable discussion among accountants and lawyers having clients that are trying to register with the Commission or have been planning to register soon.

The heart of the matter is contained in the following concluding paragraphs in that release:

> *If, as a result of the examination and the conclusions reached, the accountant is not in a position to express an affirmative opinion as to the fairness of the presentation of earnings year by year, the registration statement is defective because the certificate does not meet the requirements of Rule 2-02 of Regulation S-X. If the accountant is not satisfied with the results of his examination he should not issue an affirmative opinion. If he is satisfied, any reference from the opinion paragraph to an explanatory paragraph devoted solely to the scope of the audit is inconsistent and unnecessary. Accordingly, phrases such as "with the foregoing explanation as to inventories" raise questions as to whether the certifying accountant intended to limit his opinion as to the fairness of the presentation of the results shown and should be omitted.*

> *A "subject to" or "except for" opinion paragraph in which these phrases refer to the scope of the audit, indicating that the accountant has not been able to satisfy himself on some significant element in the financial statements, is not acceptable in certificates filed with the Commission in connection with the public offering of securities. The "subject to" qualification is appropriate when the reference is to a middle paragraph or to footnotes explaining the status of matters which cannot be resolved at statement date.*

In our opinion, the position of the Commission set forth in the two preceding paragraphs is absolutely sound. Undoubtedly, this will result in hardship for some companies that have not had the foresight to employ certified public accountants to make complete financial examinations during the past three years and have failed to follow procedures and maintain records from which an independent CPA can satisfy himself as to the fairness of the amounts of the inventories reported at the beginning of each of the three-year periods for which statements must be filed.

Some auditors have expressed the feeling that this puts them "on the spot." If a CPA has failed to point out to his clients the importance of having an opinion audit or has been willing to issue a qualified opinion in cases in which he has not observed the physical taking of the inventory, he definitely is "on the

*From *The Journal of Accountancy*, Vol. 113, No. 5 (May, 1962), pp. 71–73. Reprinted by permission of the American Institute of Certified Public Accountants.

spot." However, if he has emphasized to this clients the desirability of an audit leading to an unqualified opinion and outlined the necessity of the physical observation of the taking of inventories in connection with such an examination, and his advice has not been taken, it is his client that is "on the spot," not he.

Our professional literature has been full of emphasis on the necessity for the observation of inventories ever since the adoption by the membership of the Institute in 1939 of "Extensions of Auditing Procedure."

Very few companies that are now ready to register securities have grown so fast in the past three years that they should not have been expected to have a complete audit during each of those years. To those that have been properly audited, Accounting Series Release No. 90 will cause no trouble.

Circumstances may at times make it impracticable or impossible for the independent auditor to follow certain auditing procedures which are customarily applied with respect to particular accounts. When this occurs, the independent auditor may be able to satisfy himself by the application of other auditing procedures.

The AICPA's committee on auditing procedure has been working on a proposed Statement on Auditing Procedure dealing with "The Independent Auditor's Opinion on Financial Statements." In considering the auditor's responsibility in a situation such as that described in the preceding paragraph, the various drafts of the proposed statement during the past year or two have indicated that the committee believes that if he is able to satisfy himself by the application of other auditing procedures there has been no limitation of the scope of the examination. In such cases, disclosure is not required, except in those situations in which the confirmation of receivables or observation of inventories has been omitted with respect to the latest balance sheet. In the latter instances the committee seems to be in agreement that the independent auditor should refer to the limitation in the scope paragraph even when he is able to satisfy himself by the application of other auditing procedures. However, in any case where he has been able to satisfy himself by other procedures, there is also agreement that he should *not* refer to the limitations or other procedures in the opinion paragraph of his report.

It is our understanding that, although the committee had not taken definitive action on the proposed statement, a copy of a preliminary draft was submitted informally to the accounting staff of the SEC for comment some time before the issuance of accounting Series Release No. 90 and that the staff and the committee were in complete agreement on this particular phase of the statement.

We believe that it has long been the policy of the SEC to let the AICPA take the lead in matters of accounting principles and reporting standards. We understand that certain situations had developed which caused the Commission to feel that action on this particular matter could not be delayed until the committee had completed its statement and, accordingly, it moved promptly by issuing Release No. 90. However, it is gratifying to know that the Commission acted with the realization that its views were in harmony with those of the Institute's committee.

The position of the profession ever since the issuance of Auditing Statement No. 23 has been that the auditor has a responsibility for making clear to the reader of his report just what responsibility he takes for the fairness of the financial statements with which he permits his name to be associated. When he has satisfied himself that the statements are fairly presented he should say so. If he is in doubt, he has an obligation to either qualify his opinion or deny an opinion as to the over-all fairness of the statements. There is no in-between. Furthermore, the SEC has long had a rule against the acceptance of financial statements in which the auditor's opinion contains a qualification, except in circumstances where the qualification had to do with some fully disclosed matter, the financial effect of which was as yet unknown and dependent on some future event.

It has been our opinion for many years, dating back to pre-SEC days, that the words "subject to" in an opinion paragraph were so ambiguous that they conveyed no clear-cut meaning to the reader. There is no way of telling whether they are intended to be a qualification of the opinion, or whether they are intended merely to direct the attention of the reader to some significant fact which has been more fully disclosed elsewhere. The circumstances in which Release No. 90 indicates that the SEC will tolerate the use of this expression in the opinion paragraph seem to us to be about the only ones in which we could justify its use. The same lack of clarity of intent is present when the phrase "with the foregoing explanation" is used in connection with the opinion. Is it intended that this expression shall merely indicate that the explanation itself is so important to a full understanding of the statement that special attention has to be drawn to it, or does it mean that the auditor is taking an exception to the fairness of the presentation of the financial statements themselves?

We have taken the position in this column on numerous occasions that if the auditor substitutes other procedures for satisfying himself with respect to the fairness of the amount of the inventory in place of the observation of the taking of the inventory he must decide either that he has sufficient grounds for an unqualified opinion or that he does not have sufficient grounds for any opinion. In our opinion, he has no right to shift to the reader of the report the burden of determining the possible importance of an inadequate examination. In other words, we believe there is seldom justification for a qualification in the opinion due to a limitation on scope of examination. While the observation of the taking of inventories at the beginning of a fiscal period at the time of a first audit is not "practicable and reasonable," and is therefore not required by the extended procedures so that the auditor need take no exception in his scope paragraph, he nevertheless has the responsibility of satisfying himself with respect to such inventories by other procedures. However, this set of circumstances does not excuse him from taking the responsibility of determining whether he has sufficient grounds for an unqualified opinion or not. If his professional judgment is satisfied to the point that he is willing to assume the risk which is inherent in expressing an opinion, we believe he should do so, otherwise, in most cases, he should disclaim an opinion.

There is often room for qualification of an opinion when the client and the CPA differ as to a matter of accounting principle (although SEC is not likely to accept such a report) or where some indeterminable future event is involved. However, it seems clear to us that the CPA has no right to expect the reader of the financial statements to decide how important his inability or failure to satisfy himself might be with respect to the fairness of the financial statements. That is the professional responsibility of the auditor and of no one else. Either he has obtained enough evidence to have reached a professional opinion or he has not. There may be situations in which disclosure of the size of the item will be sufficient to warrant a qualification rather than a disclaimer, but we believe these are so rare that the Securities and Exchange Commission has good grounds for its position that no qualification of scope would be acceptable. Certainly, the urgency of his client's needs is no substitute for "sufficient competent evidential matter."

We have heard the fear expressed that Accounting Series Release No. 90 might have the effect of causing clients wishing to register with the SEC to transfer their audit work to the big accounting firms rather than remain with the smaller firms which have been serving them. We can see no reason why this should be the result. Many small firms are just as competent to make an audit of moderate-sized companies as any of the large firms. If they have maintained their independence, if they have kept the confidence of their clients' bankers and if they have conducted their audits in accordance with the generally accepted auditing standards of the profession, Release No. 90 should have no significance for them. If they have never previously made an opinion audit for the client, they have no greater problem in satisfying themselves as to the fairness of the opening inventories than a large firm would have.

When a company seeks to register with the SEC for the first time and has been served by a small firm or an individual practitioner, investment bankers frequently question whether a better known firm should not be employed. They feel that a large firm would be likely to afford more protection to them for the responsibilities they undertake in connection with the issuance of securities and would probably carry more prestige among prospective investors. Sometimes the smaller firm or the individual has not observed the SEC's requirements for independence so that a change of auditors is required. These, however, are entirely different questions and are completely unaffected by Release 90.

Leaders of the profession and representatives of the SEC have urged for years that CPAs having clients who may conceivably seek registration with the SEC familiarize themselves with its requirements governing the acceptability of auditors and the financial information to be filed. CPAs have also been urged to pave the way to their being acceptable to all concerned by becoming acquainted with the bankers and underwriters who might be involved in such a registration with a view to establishing confidence in themselves on the part of such persons. All of this was important before Release No. 90 was issued and has not been affected by it.

We have been told by a few lawyers who have much to do with registration statements that they might be inclined to consider this release to be justification for urging their underwriter clients to insist on large accounting firms. However, their reasons ultimately boil down to the old question as to whether the smaller firm or individual practitioner will afford as much protection as the large firm. Satisfying oneself as to the validity of an opening inventory is certainly no technical hurdle that the small firm finds more difficult to cross than the large firm. We see no reason why more significance should be attached to this than to any of the other questions which constantly arise in the course of an examination with respect to which the independent auditor must make his decision on the basis of his responsibility to the public and not on what his client wishes him to do.

CONCEPTS OF INDEPENDENCE: COMPARISON OF THE AICPA AND SEC POSITIONS

▷ The SEC has strongly influenced auditing in both professional and technical matters. An illustration of this influence was presented in Accounting Series Release No. 81. In order to determine the full impact of the SEC position on independence, obtain a copy of the Code of Professional Ethics and Numbered Opinions of the AICPA and make a comparison of the positions of these two organizations. In so doing, indicate the areas of conflict and of agreement.

CHAPTER 4

PROFESSIONAL RESPONSIBILITY:
THE CPA'S LEGAL LIABILITY

The CPA's responsibility under the law can be divided into statutory responsibility and common law responsibility. Chapter 3 presented aspects of statutory responsibility. Anyone who enters into a contractual relationship has certain obligations to the other party to the contract. CPAs enter into contracts in which audit services are rendered. Often, the outcome of the auditor's effort, an opinion, has an impact on independent third parties. The following two readings together present the landmark case that established the scope of auditors' liability to third parties under the common law. The precedent established in this case has endured since 1930.

ULTRAMARES CORPORATION v. TOUCHE
New York 229 App. Div. 581

1. Negligence
Public accountants certifying erroneous balance sheet inducing plaintiff to make loan to client *held* liable to plaintiff for negligence.

Accountants knew result of audit would be used by client to represent financial condition to persons from whom it might seek to borrow money, but nevertheless prepared balance sheet in negligent manner as result of which it was incorrect. Accountants, if they do not wish audit to be used as basis for borrowing money, should qualify statement of balance sheet and certificate which accompanies it in such way as to prevent such use.

2. Fraud
Public accountants *held* not liable for "fraud" to one loaning money to accountants' client on strength of erroneous balance sheet.
Misjudgment, however gross, or want of caution, however marked, is not "fraud," nor is mere breach of duty or omission to use due care.

3. Fraud
Intentional fraud, as distinguished from mere breach of duty or omission to use due care, is essential in action for deceit.

4. Damages
Amount of loans to accountants' client with interest credited with moneys repaid or collected *held* approximate damage as against accountants for furnishing erroneous statement.

The present action was brought against accountants by one who loaned money to their client in reliance on erroneous balance sheet.
Finch and **Martin, JJ.**, dissenting.

Appeal from Trial Term, New York County.

Action by the Ultramares Corporation against George A. Touche and others. From an order granting defendants' motion to set aside a verdict in plaintiff's favor on the first cause of action and dismissing the complaint, and from a judgment entered thereon, plaintiff appeals.

Judgment and order modified by reversing so much thereof as sets aside the verdict and dismisses the amended complaint as to the first cause of action, and by directing that verdict be reinstated and judgment entered thereon, and, as so modified, affirmed.

Argued before **Dowling, P. J.**, and **Finch, McAvoy, Martin,** and **O'Malley, JJ.**

Limburg, Riegelman, Hirsch & Hess, of New York City (Herbert R. Limburg, of New York City, of counsel; Lionel S. Popkin and Joseph L. Weiner, both of New York City, on the brief), for appellant.

Guggenheimer, Untermyer & Marshall, of New York City (James Marshall, of New York City, of counsel; Abraham Shamos, of New York City, on the brief), for respondents.

Coudert Brothers, of New York City (Mahlon B. Doing, of New York City, of counsel; Frederic R. Coudert, of New York City, and J. Harry Covington and Spencer Gordon, both of Washington, D.C., on the brief), for American Institute of Accountants, amicus curiae.

Martin Conboy, of New York City (David Asch and Charles W. Tooke, both of New York City, on the brief), amicus curiae.

McAVOY, J.

[1] The defendants, public accountants, have been held liable to the plaintiff, to whom they owed no contractual duty through any contract of employment which the plaintiff entrusted to them. Whether a duty arises here, in the absence of direct contractual relation, out of the situation shown by the evidence, is the problem for solution.

The general principle involved, and upon which plaintiff relies for imposition of liability, is that, if one undertakes to discharge any duty by which the conduct of others may be governed, he is bound to perform it in such a manner that those who are thus led to action in the faith that such duty will be properly performed shall not suffer loss through improper performance of the duty or neglect in its execution. Thus in Glanzer v. Shepard, 233 N. Y. 236, 135 N. E. 275, 23 A. L. R. 1425, we have the buyers of merchandise given recovery against public weighers who were to make return of the weight and to furnish buyers with a copy. The public weighers certified the weight, and the buyers paid the sellers on that basis. Discovery that the weight had been incorrectly certified as a result of defendants' negligence was found to give the plaintiffs the right to the resulting damage.

It was decided there that the use of the certificates was not an indirect or collateral consequence of the action of the weighers; that it was a consequence "which, to the weighers' knowledge, was the end and aim of the transaction." The sellers ordered, but the buyers were to use, the certificates. Public weighers hold themselves out to the public as "skilled and careful in their calling." Glanzer v. Shepard, 233 N. Y. 236, 238, 135 N. E. 275, 276, 23 A. L. R. 1425.

The duty there was held not to be found in terms of contract, nor of privity; although arising from contract, its origin is not exclusive from that realm. If the contract and the relation are found, the duty follows by rule of law. Diligence—it was pointed out—was owing not only to the person who ordered the employment, but also to those who relied thereon.

Plaintiff here is in the business of factoring. The defendants were engaged by Fred Stern & Co., Inc., to audit its books and accounts and certify a balance sheet as of the end of the year 1923. They prepared a balance sheet and attached it to a certificate signed by them, which they dated February 26, 1924. This balance sheet stated that Fred Stern & Co., Inc., had a net worth amounting to $1,070,715.26, when the fact (as thereafter found) was that at the very time of this certification the firm was insolvent, with impairment of thousands of dollars in its assets and credit and much enhancement of its reported liabilities.

The finding of the jury would justify a conclusion that defendants were guilty of a gross degree of negligence in their audit, and it is even urged that the evidence also warranted the finding that the balance sheet was made up in fraud of the rights and obligations which accountants, engaged in public calling, would owe to those to whom they had reason to believe such balance sheets would be exhibited for purposes of obtaining loans, extending credit, or to induce the sale of merchandise.

The evidence showed that these accountants knew for four years that their client (Fred Stern & Co., Inc.) was a borrower from banks in large sums; that these banks required certified balance sheets as a basis for making loans; and that Fred Stern & Co., Inc., would require these certified balance sheets for continuing existing loans and securing new loans. So that this might be done, some thirty-two original counterparts of the certified balance sheet were requested by the client, Fred Stern & Co., Inc., and furnished by the accountants (defendants).

The jury's verdict thus imports that defendants knew that the certified balance sheets would be used by Fred Stern & Co., Inc., for the purpose of procuring loans, and that the very purpose of employment in the transaction between Fred Stern & Co., Inc., and Touche, Niven & Co., the accountants, was to allow Fred Stern & Co., Inc., to bring it about through these balance sheets. The result that loans on the faith thereof would be made by persons who would be governed by its declarations. Financial statements in the course of trade have come to be used customarily for the purpose of securing credit, and accountants indicate in their public advertisements that makers of loans should require the safeguard of an independent audit prepared by public accountants, so a correlative obligation is placed upon them. It is their duty—if they do not wish their audit to be so used—to qualify the statement of their balance sheet and the certificate which accompanies it in such a way as to prevent its use. One cannot issue an unqualified statement which will be so used, and then disclaim responsibility for his work.

Banks and merchants, to the knowledge of these defendants, require certified balance sheets from independent accountants, and upon these audits they make their loans. Thus, the duty arises to these banks and merchants of an exercise of reasonable care in the making and uttering of certified balance sheets.

The facts here are brought within the rule in the case of International Products Co. v. Erie Railroad Co., 244 N. Y. 331, 338, 155 N. E. 662, 664, 56 A. L. R. 1377, that "there must be knowledge, or its equivalent, that the information is desired for a serious purpose; that, he to whom it is given intends to rely and act upon it; that if false or erroneous, he will because of it be injured in person or property. The relationship of the parties, arising out of contract or otherwise, must be such that in morals and good conscience the one has the right to rely upon the other for information, and the other giving the information owes a duty to give it with care."

The certificate which these accountants attached to the balance sheet reads:

>Touche, Niven & Co.,
>Public Accountants,
>Eighty Maiden Lane,
>New York

>February 26, 1924.

>Certificate of Auditors.

We have examined the accounts of Fred Stern & Co., Inc., for the year ended December 31, 1923, and hereby certify that the annexed balance sheet is in accordance therewith and with the information and explanations given us. We further certify that, subject to provision for federal taxes on income, the said statement in our opinion, presents a true and correct view of the financial condition of Fred Stern & Co., Inc., as at December 31, 1923.

Touche, Niven & Co.,
Public Accountants.

From this certificate and the findings made by the jury which are entitled to be held conclusive in behalf of the plaintiff there is established: That the defendants knew that the result of the audit would be used by Fred Stern & Co., Inc., to represent its financial condition to persons from whom Fred Stern & Co., Inc., might seek to borrow money, and that the balance sheet would be relied upon by such persons as indicating the true financial condition of Fred Stern & Co., Inc.; that defendants, in exercising their public calling as auditors, did not exercise that care and skill required of them, but acted in a negligent and careless manner, as a consequence of which the balance sheet made by them was incorrect, and that such negligence was the proximate cause of the loss sustained by plaintiff, i.e., that there was a causal relation between the neglect and the loss sustained which could reasonably have been anticipated, and that the presentation of the balance sheets, as certified by defendants, was the inducing cause for making these loans to Fred Stern & Co., Inc., which plaintiff made, and that the loss was not caused by reason of any change in the financial condition of Fred Stern & Co., Inc., from the time of the presentation of the audit to the plaintiff, or because of any reliance of plaintiff on other intervening causes; and that plaintiff's conduct was free from contributory negligence, and we therefore conclude that a liability was properly found, arising out of a duty owed by the defendants to plaintiff not to misrepresent, willfully or negligently, the financial condition of Fred Stern & Co., Inc., and that the judgment for the plaintiff was correct and should not have been set aside.

That the particular person who was to be influenced by defendants' act was unknown to the defendants is not material to a right to recovery, for it is not "necessary that there should be an intent to defraud any particular person." In this case there was no mere casual representation made as a matter of courtesy; there was a certificate intended to sway conduct. There was "the careless performance of a service * * * which happens to have found in the words of a certificate its culmination and its summary." Glanzer v. Shepard, supra, 233 N.Y. 241, 135 N. E. 275, 23 A. L. R. 1425. Here is an act performed carelessly, intended to influence the actions of third parties, and one that reasonably might be expected, when carelessly performed, to cause substantial loss.

A duty exists towards those whom the accountants know will act on the faith of their certificates. The loss occurring here was the very result which reasonably was to be anticipated if the balance sheet was carelessly prepared.

[2, 3] While negligence was established and was the proximate cause of the loss, and, as we have seen, the duty arose out of this situation which, while not contractual, was, nevertheless, a ground of liability, yet we do not think that there was sufficient proof upon which to found a liability in fraud. We think that there was no error, at the close of the entire case, in the court's decision to dismiss the second cause of action based upon that ground. Misjudgment, however gross, or want of caution, however marked, is not fraud. The mere breach of duty, or the omission to use due care, is not fraud. Intentional fraud, as distinguished from a mere breach of duty or the omission to use due care, is an essential factor in an action for deceit. Kountze v. Kennedy, 147 N. Y. 124, 41 N. E. 414, 29 L. R. A. 360, 49 Am. St. Rep. 651.

[4] We think that there was a proper conclusion with respect to damages. The amount of cash loans made to Fred Stern & Co., Inc., with interest thereon, credited with all moneys repaid or collected by plaintiff, whether through voluntary action or suit, without deduction of costs of collection, was the approximate damage, and, while other proof of damage was excluded by the trial court, no appeal has been taken by plaintiff which raises a construction of that rule.

The judgment and order appealed from should therefore be modified by reversing so much thereof as sets aside the verdict and dismisses the amended complaint as to the first cause of action, and by directing that the verdict be reinstated and judgment entered thereon, with costs to the plaintiff, and, as so modified, affirmed, without costs.

Dowling, P. J., and **O'Malley, J.**, concur; **Finch** and **Martin, JJ.**, dissent.

FINCH, J. (DISSENTING)

Assuming that the defendants may be held liable for the negligence of their employees where they undertake a duty to a definite plaintiff (Glanzer v. Shepard, 233 N. Y. 236, 135 N. E. 275, 23 A. L. R. 1425), or to a definite class (Doyle v. Chatham & Phenix National Bank, 253 N. Y. 369, 171 N. E. 574), yet, for the following reasons the defendants are not liable to this plaintiff: First, because they undertook to make only a "balance sheet audit" at the request of their client; second, because in their certificate the defendants purported only to furnish their opinion based upon an examination in connection with "the information and explanations given us." But, even more important, the defendants furnished such a report and certificate without reference to any particular person or class of persons.

The plaintiff seeks to liken the facts in the case at bar to a case where the defendants were to make an audit which to their knowledge was for a definite plaintiff, to induce such plaintiff to make loans thereon. Glanzer v. Shepard, supra. This record does not sustain such a contention. The courts have not gone to the length of holding that defendants in a case like the case at bar can he held liable in negligence to the whole world, or, as has been aptly said, liable for "negligence in the air."

In other words, not only the purpose for which the statement is to be used, but the person or class of persons who is to rely thereon, must be definite to the knowledge of the defendants. The plaintiff relies upon the stipulation in the record that the defendants "knew generally that these reports would be used as financial statements to banks or to creditors or to stockholders or to purchasers or sellers." In accordance with the authorities, this general knowledge is not sufficient.

As Judge Andrews said in International Products Co. v. Erie R. Co., 244 N.Y. 331, 338, 155 N. E. 662, 664, 56 A. L. R. 1377, speaking of the information given: "That he to whom it is given intends to rely and act upon it; that, if false or erroneous, he will because of it be injured in person or property." In Courteen Seed Co. v. Hong Kong & Shanghai Banking Corporation, 245 N.Y. 377, 382, 157 N. E. 272, 274, 56 A. L. R. 1186, Judge Pound writes: "It [the defendant] did not deal with appellant, had no relations with it, and was under no duty of care to it." See, also, National Savings Bank v. Ward, 100 U. S. 195, 25 L. Ed. 621.

The professional man, be he accountant or otherwise, certifies for his client and not for all the world. If the client makes it clear to such a man that the statement is to be used in a particular transaction in which a third party is involved, such circumstance should create a duty from the professional man to such third party. If the accountant is to be held to an unlimited liability to all persons who may act on the faith of the certificate, the accountant would be obliged to protect himself by a verification so rigid that its cost might well be prohibitive and a limited, but useful, field of service thus closed to him. The smallness of the compensation paid to the defendants for the services requested is in striking contrast to the enormity of the liability now sought to be imposed upon them. If, in the case at bar, the plaintiff had inquired of the accountants whether they might rely upon the certificate in making a loan, then the accountants would have had the opportunity to gauge their responsibility and risk, and determine with knowledge how thorough their verification of the account should be before assuming the responsibility of making the certificate run to the plaintiff.

It also appears in the case at bar that the loss of the plaintiff resulted because of its own contributory negligence in failing to check the collateral. Craig v. Anyon, 212 App. Div. 55, 208 N. Y. S. 259, affirmed 242 N. Y. 569, 152 N. E. 431.

In so far as the claim of actual fraud is concerned, there is no proof in this record sufficient to support such a finding by a jury. The court, therefore, properly dismissed this cause of action. Civil Practice Act, § 457-a. This is so, even assuming that personal connivance and fraud on the part of the employees of defendants could be held within the scope of the authority given to these employees by the defendants, which at least is doubtful. Henry v. Allen, 151 N. Y. 1, 45 N. E. 355, 36 L. R. A. 658; Credit Alliance Corporation v. Sheridan Theatre Co., 241 N.Y. 216, 149 N. E. 837; Martin v. Gotham Nat. Bank, of New York, 248 N. Y. 313, 162 N. E. 91.

It follows that the judgment and order should be affirmed.

Martin, J., concurs.

ULTRAMARES CORPORATION v. TOUCHE
255 N.Y. 170 ff.

Ultramares Corporation, Appellant and Respondent, v. George A. Touche, et al., Copartners under the firm name of Touche, Niven & Company, Respondents and Appellants

STATEMENT OF CASE

1. Public accountants owe to their employer a duty, imposed by law, to make their certificate without fraud and a duty, growing out of contract, to make it with the care and caution proper to their calling. Fraud includes the pretense of knowledge when knowledge there is none. It may also include the expression of an erroneous opinion where the supporting grounds are so flimsy as to indicate that there were no genuine belief back of it. To creditors and investors to whom the employer may exhibit the certificate, the accountants owe a like duty to make it without fraud where there is notice in the circumstances of its making that the employer did not intend to keep it to himself. Liability for negligence, however, is bounded by the contract, and is to be enforced between the parties by whom the contract has been made.

2. The decisions on the subject of liability for negligent words collated and examined, and held to be inapplicable to the facts of this case. (*Glanzer* v.

Shepard, 233 N.Y. 236; *International Products Co.* v. *Erie R.R. Co.,* 224 N.Y. 331; *Doyle* v. *Chatham & Phenix Nat. Bank,* 253 N.Y. 369, distinguished.)

3. While the case does not sustain a liability found upon negligence, since a duty of active care was lacking, there was error in refusing to submit the case to the jury on the theory of fraud. A jury might reasonably find upon the evidence that the defendants certified as a fact true to their own knowledge that the balance sheet was in accordance with the books of account when they had no knowledge on the subject. (*Kountze* v. *Kennedy,* 147 N.Y. 124, distinguished.)

4. The fact that the wrong was not the personal act or omission of the defendants but that of their subordinates does not relieve them of liability. It does not appear that the interests of the subordinates were adverse to those of defendants, and, having delegated the performance of the work to agents of their own selection, the defendants are responsible for the manner in which their business was done.

Ultramares Corp. v. *Touche,* 229 App. Div. 581, reversed.

OPINION[1]

The action is in tort for damages suffered through the misrepresentations of accountants, the first cause of action being for misrepresentations that were merely negligent and the second for misrepresentations charged to have been fraudulent.

In January, 1924, the defendants, a firm of public accountants, were employed by Fred Stern & Co., Inc., to prepare and certify a balance sheet exhibiting the condition of its business as of December 31, 1923. They had been employed at the end of each of the three years preceding to render a like service. Fred Stern & Co., Inc., which was in substance Stern himself, was engaged in the importation and sale of rubber. To finance its operations, it required extensive credit and borrowed large sums of money from banks and other lenders. All this was known to the defendants. The defendants knew also that in the usual course of business the balance sheet when certified would be exhibited by the Stern company to banks, creditors, stockholders, purchasers or sellers, according to the needs of the occasion, as the basis of financial dealings. Accordingly, when the balance sheet was made up, the defendants supplied the Stern company with thirty-two copies certified with serial numbers as counterpart originals. Nothing was said as to the persons *to whom*

---

[1] Delivered by Judge Cardozo.

these counterparts would be shown or the extent or number of transactions in which they would be used. In particular there was no mention of the plaintiff, a corporation doing business chiefly as a factor, which till then had never made advances to the Stern company, though it had sold merchandise in small amounts. The range of the transactions in which a certificate of audit might be expected to play a part was as indefinite and wide as the possibilities of the business that was mirrored in the summary.

By February 26, 1924, the audit was finished and the balance sheet made up. It stated assets in the sum of $2,550,671.88 and liabilities other than capital and surplus in the sum of $1,479,956.62, thus showing a net worth of $1,-070,715.26. Attached to the balance sheet was a certificate as follows:

TOUCHE, NIVEN & CO.
Public Accountants
Eighty Maiden Lane
New York

February 26, 1924.

Certificate of Auditors

We have examined the accounts of Fred Stern & Co., Inc., for the year ending December 31, 1923, and hereby certify that the annexed balance sheet is in accordance therewith and with the information and explanations given us. We further certify that, subject to provision for federal taxes on income, the said statement, in our opinion, presents a true and correct view of the financial condition of Fred Stern & Co., Inc., as at December 31, 1923.

Touche, Niven & Co.
Public Accountants.

Capital and surplus were intact if the balance sheet was accurate. In reality both had been wiped out, and the corporation was insolvent. The books had been falsified by those in charge of the business so as to set forth accounts receivable and other assets which turned out to be fictitious. The plaintiff maintains that the certificate of audit was erroneous in both its branches. The first branch, the asserted correspondence between the accounts and the balance sheet, is one purporting to be made as of the knowledge of the auditors. The second branch, which certifies to a belief that the condition reflected in the balance sheet presents a true and correct picture of the resources of the business, is stated as a matter of opinion. In the view of the plaintiff, both branches of the certificate are either fraudulent or negligent. As to one class of assets, the item of accounts receivable, if not also as to others, there was no real correspondence, we are told, between balance sheet and books, or so the triers of the facts might find. If correspondence, however, be assumed, a closer examination of supporting invoices and records, or a fuller inquiry directed to the persons appearing on the books as creditors or debtors, would have exhibited the truth.

The plaintiff, a corporation engaged in business as a factor, was approached by Stern in March, 1924, with a request for loans of money to finance the sales of rubber. Up to that time the dealings between the two houses were on a cash basis and trifling in amount. As a condition of any loans the plaintiff insisted that it receive a balance sheet certified by public accountants, and in response to that demand it was given one of the certificates signed by the defendants and then in Stern's possession. On the faith of that certificate the plaintiff made a loan which was followed by many others. The course of business was for Stern to deliver to the plaintiff documents described as trust receipts which in effect were executory assignments of the moneys payable by purchasers for goods thereafter to be sold. When the purchase price was due, the plaintiff received the payment, reimbursing itself therefrom for its advances and commissions. Some of these transactions were effected without loss. Nearly a year later, in December, 1924, the house of cards collapsed. In that month, plaintiff made three loans to the Stern company, one of $100,000, a second of $25,000, and a third of $40,000. For some of these loans no security was received. For some of the earlier loans the security was inadequate. On January 2, 1925, the Stern company was declared a bankrupt.

This action, brought against the accountants in November, 1926, to recover the loss suffered by the plaintiff in reliance upon the audit, was in its inception one for negligence. On the trial there was added a second cause of action asserting fraud also. The trial judge dismissed the second cause of action without submitting it to the jury. As to the first cause of action, he reserved his decision on the defendants' motion to dismiss, and took the jury's verdict. They were told that the defendants might be held liable if with knowledge that the results of the audit would be communicated to creditors they did the work negligently, and that negligence was the omission to use reasonable and ordinary care. The verdict was in favor of the plaintiff for $187,576.32. On the coming in of the verdict, the judge granted the reserved motion. The Appellate Division affirmed the dismissal of the cause of action for fraud, but reversed the dismissal of the cause of action for negligence, and reinstated the verdict. The case is here on cross-appeals.

The two causes of action will be considered in succession, first the one for negligence and second that for fraud.

(1) We think the evidence supports a finding that the audit was negligently made, though in so saying we put aside for the moment the question whether negligence, even if it existed, was a wrong to the plaintiff. To explain fully or adequately how the defendants were at fault would carry this opinion beyond reasonable bounds. A sketch, however, there must be, at least in respect of some features of the audit, for the nature of the fault, when understood, is helpful in defining the ambit of the duty.

We begin with the item of accounts receivable. At the start of the defendant's audit, there had been no posting of the general ledger since April, 1923. Siess, a junior accountant, was assigned by the defendants to the performance of that work. On Sunday, February 3, 1924, he had finished the task of posting, and was ready the next day to begin with his associates the preparation of the balance sheet and the audit of its items. The total of the accounts receivable for December, 1923, as thus posted by Siess from the entries in the journal, was $644,758.17. At some time on February 3, Romberg, an employee of the Stern company, who had general charge of its accounts, placed below that total another item to represent additional accounts receivable growing out of the transactions of the month. This new item, $706,843.07, Romberg entered in his own handwriting. The sales that it represented were, each and all, fictitious. Opposite the entry were placed other figures (12-29), indicating or supposed to indicate a reference to the journal. Siess when he resumed his work saw the entries thus added, and included the new item in making up his footings, with the result of an apparent increase of over $700,000 in the assets of the business. He says that in doing this he supposed the entries to be correct, and that his task at the moment being merely to post the books, he thought the work of audit or verification might come later, and put it off accordingly. The time sheets, which are in evidence, show very clearly that this was the order of time in which the parts of the work were done. Verification, however, there never was either by Siess or by his superiors, or so the triers of the facts might say. If any had been attempted, or any that was adequate, an examiner would have found that the entry in the ledger was not supported by any entry in the journal. If from the journal he had gone to the book from which the journal was made up, described as "the debit memo book," support would still have failed. Going farther, he would have found invoices, seventeen in number, which amounted in the aggregate to the interpolated item, but scrutiny of these invoices would have disclosed suspicious features in that they had no shipping number nor a customer's order number and varied in terms of credit and in other respects from those usual in the business. A mere glance reveals the difference.

The December entry of accounts receivable was not the only item that a careful and skillful auditor would have desired to investigate. There was ground for suspicion as to an item of $113,199.60, included in the accounts payable as due from the Baltic Corporation. As to this the defendants received an explanation, not very convincing, from Stern and Romberg. A cautious auditor might have been dissatisfied and have uncovered what was wrong. There was ground for suspicion also because of the inflation of the inventory. The inventory, as it was given to the auditors, was totaled at $347,219.08. The defendants discovered errors in the sum of $303,863.20, and adjusted the balance sheet accordingly. Both the extent of the discrepancy and its causes might have been found to cast discredit upon the business and the books. There was ground for suspicion again in the record of assigned accounts. Inquiry of the creditors gave notice to the defendants that the same accounts had been pledged to two, three and four banks at the same time. The pledges did not diminish the value of the assets, but made in such circumstances they might well evoke a doubt as to the solvency of a business where such conduct was permitted. There was an explanation by Romberg which the defendants accepted as sufficient. Caution and diligence might have pressed investigation farther.

If the defendants owed a duty to the plaintiff to act with the same care that would have been due under a contract of employment, a jury was at liberty to find a verdict of negligence upon showing of a scrutiny so imperfect and perfunctory. No doubt the extent to which inquiry must be pressed beyond appearances is a question of judgment, as to which opinions will often differ. No doubt the wisdom that is born after the event will engender suspicion and distrust when old acquaintance and good repute may have silenced doubt at the beginning. All this is to be weighed by a jury in applying its standard of behavior, the state of mind and conduct of the reasonable man. Even so, the adverse verdict, when rendered, imports an alignment of the weights in their proper places in the balance and a reckoning thereafter. The reckoning was not wrong upon the evidence before us, if duty be assumed.

We are brought to the question of duty, its origin and measure.

The defendants owed to their employer a duty imposed by law to make their certificate without fraud, and a duty growing out of contract to make it with the care and caution proper to their calling. Fraud includes the pretense of knowledge when knowledge there is none. To creditors and investors to whom the employer exhibited the certificate, the defendants owed a like duty to make it without fraud, since there was notice in the circumstances of its making that the employer did not intend to keep it to himself (*Eaton, Cole & Burnham Co.* v. *Avery,* 83 N.Y. 31; *Tindle* v. *Birkett,* 171 N.Y. 520). A different question develops when we ask whether they owed a duty to these to make it without negligence. If liability for negligence exists, a thoughtless slip or blunder, the failure to detect a theft or forgery beneath the cover of deceptive entries, may expose accountants to a liability in an indeterminate amount for an indeterminate time to an indeterminate class. The hazards of a business conducted on these terms are so extreme as to enkindle doubt whether a flaw may not exist in the implication of a duty that exposes to these consequences. We put aside for the moment any statement in the certificate which involves the representation of a fact as true to the knowledge of the auditors. If such a statement was made, whether believed to be true or not, the defendants are liable for deceit in the event that it was false. The plaintiff does not need the invention of novel doctrine to help it out in such conditions. The case was submitted to the jury and the verdict was returned upon the theory that even in the absence of a misstatement of a fact there is a liability also for erroneous opinion. The expression of an opinion is to be subject to a warranty implied by law. What, then, is the warranty, as yet unformulated, to be? Is it merely that the opinion is honestly conceived and that the preliminary inquiry has been honestly pursued, that a halt has not been made without a genuine belief that the search has been reasonably adequate to bring disclosure of the truth? Or does it go farther and involve the assumption of a liability for any blunder or inattention that could fairly be spoken of as negligence if the controversy were one between accountant and employer for breach of a contract to render services for pay? . . .

Three cases in this court are said by the plaintiff to have committed us to the doctrine that words, written or oral, if negligently published with the expectation that the reader or listener will transmit them to another, will lay a basis for liability though privity be lacking. These are *Glanzer* v. *Shepard* (233 N.Y. 236); *International Products Co.* v. *Erie R.R. Co.* (244 N.Y. 331); and *Doyle* v. *Chatham & Phenix Nat. Bank* (253 N.Y. 369).

In *Glanzer* v. *Shepard* the seller of beans requested the defendants, public weighers, to make return of the weight and furnish the buyer with a copy. This the defendants did. Their return, which was made out in duplicate, one copy to the seller and the other to the buyer, recites that it was made by order of the former for the use of the latter. The buyer paid the seller on the faith of the certificate which turned out to be erroneous. We held that the weighers were liable at the suit of the buyer for the moneys overpaid. Here was something more than the rendition of a service in the expectation that the one who ordered the certificate would use it thereafter in the operations of his business as occasion might require. Here was a case where the transmission of the certificate to another was not merely one possibility among many, but the "end and aim of the transaction," as certain and immediate and deliberately willed as if a husband were to order a gown to be delivered to his wife, or a telegraph company, contracting with the sender of a message, were to telegraph it wrongly to the damage of the person expected to receive it (*Wolfskehl* v. *West-*

ern Union Tel. Co., 46 Hun, 542; *DeRuth* v. *New York, etc., Tel. Co.,* 1 Daly, 547; *Milliken* v. *Western Union Tel. Co.,* 110 N.Y. 403, 410). The intimacy of the resulting nexus is attested by the fact that after stating the case in terms of legal duty, we went on to point out that viewing it as a phase or extension of *Lawrence* v. *Fox (supra),* or *Seaver* v. *Ransom (supra),* we could reach the same result by stating it in terms of contract (CT. *Economy Building & Loan Assn.* v. *West Jersey Title Co.,* 64 N.J.L. 27; *Young* v. *Lohr,* 118 Iowa, 624; *Murphy* v. *Fidelity, Abstract & Title Co.,* 114 Wash. 77). The bond was so close as to approach that of privity, if not completely one with it. Not so in the case at hand. No one would be likely to urge that there was a contractual relation, or even one approaching it, at the root of any duty that was owing from the defendants now before us to the indeterminate class of persons who, presently or in the future, might deal with the Stern company in reliance on the audit. In a word, the service rendered by the defendant in *Glanzer* v. *Shepard* was primarily for the information of a third person, in effect, if not in name, a party to the contract, and only incidentally for that of the formal promisee. In the case at hand, the service was primarily for the benefit of the Stern company, a convenient instrumentality for use in the development of the business, and only incidentally or collaterally for the use of those to whom Stern and his associates might exhibit it thereafter. Foresight of these possibilities may charge with liability for fraud. The conclusion does not follow that it will charge with liability for negligence.

In the next of the three cases (*International Products Co.* v. *Erie R.R. Co., supra*) the plaintiff, an importer, had an agreement with the defendant, a railroad company, that the latter would act as bailee of goods arriving from abroad. The importer, to protect the goods by suitable insurance, made inquiry of the bailee as to the location of the storage. The warehouse was incorrectly named, and the policy did not attach. Here was a determinate relation, that of bailor and bailee, either present or prospective, with peculiar opportunity for knowledge on the part of the bailee as to the subject matter of the statement and with a continuing duty to correct it if erroneous. Even the narrowest holdings as to liability for unintentional misstatement concede that a representation in such circumstances may be equivalent to a warranty. There is a class of cases "where a person within whose special province it lay to know a particular fact, has given an erroneous answer to an inquiry made with regard to it by a person desirous of ascertaining the fact for the purpose of determining his course accordingly, and has been held bound to make good the assurance he has given" (**Herschell, L.C.,** in *Derry* v. *Peek,* (L.R.) 14 A.C. 337, 360). So in *Burrowes* v. *Lock* (10 Ves. 470), a trustee was asked by one who expected to make a loan upon the security of a trust fund whether notice of any prior incumbrance upon the fund had been given to him. An action for damages was upheld though the false answer was made honestly in the belief that it was true (cf. *Brownlie* v. *Campbell,* (L.R.) 5 A.C. 925, 935; *Doyle* v. *Chatham & Phenix Nat. Bank, supra,* at p. 379).

In one respect the decision in *International Products Co.* v. *Erie R.R. Co.* is in advance of anything decided in *Glanzer* v. *Shepard.* The latter case suggests that the liability there enforced was not one for the mere utterance of words without due consideration, but for a negligent service, the act of weighing, which happened to find in the words of the certificate its culmination and its summary. This was said in the endeavor to emphasize the character of the certificate as a business transaction, an act in the law, and not a mere casual response to a request for information. The ruling in the case of the *Erie Railroad* shows that the rendition of a service is at most a mere circumstance and not an indispensable condition. The Erie was not held for negligence in the rendition of a service. It was held for words and nothing more. So in the case at hand. If liability for the consequences of a negligent certificate may be enforced by any member of an indeterminate class of creditors, present and prospective, known and unknown, the existence or non-existence of a preliminary act of service will not affect the cause of action. The service may have been rendered as carefully as you please, and its quality will count for nothing if there was negligence thereafter in distributing the summary.

Doyle v. *Chatham & Phenix Nat. Bank (supra),* the third of the cases cited, is even more plainly indecisive. A trust company was a trustee under a deed of trust to secure an issue of bonds. It was held liable to a subscriber for the bonds when it certified them falsely. A representation by a trustee intended to sway action had been addressed to a person who by the act of subscription was to become a party to the deed and a *cestui que trust.*

The antidote to these decisions and to the over-use of the doctrine of liability for negligent misstatement may be found in *Jaillet* v. *Cashman* (225 N.Y. 511) and *Courteen Seed Co.* v. *Hong Kong & Shanghai Banking P. Corp.* (245 N.Y. 377). In the first of these cases the defendant supplying ticker service to brokers was held not liable in damages to one of the broker's customers for the consequences of reliance upon a report negligently published on the ticker. If liability had been upheld, the step would have been a short one to the declaration of a like liability on the part of proprietors of newspapers. In the second the principle was clearly stated by POUND, J., that "negligent words are not actionable unless they are uttered directly, with knowledge or notice that they will be acted on, to one to whom the speaker is bound by some relation of duty, arising out of public calling, contract or otherwise, to act with care if he acts at all."

From the foregoing analysis the conclusion is, we think, inevitable that nothing in our previous decisions commits us to a holding of liability for negligence in the circumstances of the case at hand, and that such liability, if recognized, will be an extension of the principle of those decisions to different conditions, even if more or less analogous. The question then is whether such an extension shall be made.

The extension, if made, will so expand the field of liability for negligent speech as to make it nearly, if not quite, coterminous with that of liability for fraud. Again and again, in decisions of this court, the bounds of this latter liability have been set up, with futility the fate of every endeavor to dislodge them. Scienter has been declared to be an indispensable element except where the representation has been put forward as true of one's own knowledge (*Hadcock* v. *Osmer*, 153 N.Y. 604), or in circumstances where the expression of opinion was a dishonorable pretense (3 Williston, Contracts, § 1494; *Smith* v. *Land & House Prop. Corp.*, (L.R.) 28 Ch. Div. 7, 15; *Sleeper* v. *Smith*, 77 N.H. 337; *Andrews* v. *Jackson*, 168 Mass. 266; *People ex rel. Gellis* v. *Sheriff*, 251 N.Y. 33, 37; *Hickey* v. *Morrell*, 102 N.Y. 454, 463; *Merry Realty Co.* v. *Martin*, 103 Misc. Rep. 9, 14; 186 App. Div. 538). Even an opinion, especially an opinion by an expert, may be found to be fraudulent if the grounds supporting it are so flimsy as to lead to the conclusion that there was no genuine belief back of it. Further than that this court has never gone. Directors of corporations have been acquitted of liability for deceit though they have been lax in investigation and negligent in speech (*Reno* v. *Bull*, 226 N.Y. 546, and cases there cited; *Kountze* v. *Kennedy*, 147 N.Y. 124). This has not meant, to be sure, that negligence may not be evidence from which a trier of the facts may draw an inference of fraud (*Derry* v. *Peek*, (L.R.) 14 A.C. 337, 369, 375, 376), but merely that if that inference is rejected, or, in the light of all the circumstances, is found to be unreasonable, negligence alone is not a substitute for fraud. Many also are the cases that have distinguished between the willful or reckless representation essential to the maintenance at law of an action for deceit, and the misrepresentation, negligent or innocent, that will lay a sufficient basis for recission in equity (*Bloomquist* v. *Farson*, 222 N.Y. 375; *Seneca Wire & Mfg. Co.* v. *Leach & Co.*, 247 N.Y. 1). If this action is well conceived, all these principles and distinctions, so nicely wrought and formulated, have been a waste of time and effort. They have even been a snare, entrapping litigants and lawyers into an abandonment of the true remedy lying ready to the call. The suitors thrown out of court because they proved negligence, and nothing else, in an action for deceit, might have ridden to triumphant victory if they had proved the self-same facts, but had given the wrong another label, and all this in a State where forms of action have been abolished. So to hold is near to saying that we have been paltering with justice. A word of caution or suggestion would have set the erring suitor right. Many pages of opinion were written by judges the most eminent, yet the word was never spoken. We may not speak it now.

A change so revolutionary, if expedient, must be wrought by legislation (*Landell* v. *Lybrand,* 264 Penn. St. 406).

We have said that the duty to refrain from negligent representation would become coincident or nearly so with the duty to refrain from fraud if this action could be maintained. A representation even though knowingly false does not constitute ground for an action of deceit unless made with the intent to be communicated to the person or class of persons who act upon it to their prejudice (*Eaton, Cole & Burnham Co.* v. *Avery, supra*). Affirmance of this judgment would require us to hold that all or nearly all the persons so situated would suffer an impairment of an interest legally protected if the representation had been negligent. We speak of all "or nearly all," for cases can be imagined where a casual response, made in circumstances insufficient to indicate that care should be expected, would permit recovery for fraud if willfully deceitful. Cases of fraud between persons so circumstanced are, however, too infrequent and exceptional to make the radii greatly different if the fields of liability for negligence and deceit be figured as concentric circles. The like may be said of the possibility that the negligence of the injured party, contributing to the result, may avail to overcome the one remedy, though unavailing to defeat the other.

Neither of these possibilities is noted by the plaintiff in its answer to the suggestion that the two fields would be coincident. Its answer has been merely this, first, that the duty to speak with care does not arise unless the words are the culmination of a service, and *second,* that it does not arise unless the service is rendered in the pursuit of an independent calling, characterized as public. As to the first of these suggestions, we have already had occasion to observe that given a relation making diligence a duty, speech as well as conduct must conform to that exacting standard (*International Products Co.* v. *Erie R.R. Co., supra*). As to the second of the two suggestions, public accountants are public only in the sense that their services are offered to any one who chooses to employ them. This is far from saying that those who do not employ them are in the same position as those who do.

Liability for negligence if adjudged in this case will extend to many callings other than auditors. Lawyers who certify their opinion as to the validity of municipal or corporate bonds with knowledge that the opinion will be brought to the notice of the public, will become liable to the investors, if they have overlooked a statute or a decision, to the same extent as if the controversy were one between client and adviser. Title companies insuring titles to a tract of land, with knowledge that at an approaching auction the fact that they have insured will be stated to the bidders, will become liable to purchasers who may wish the benefit of a policy without payment of a premium. These illustrations may seem to be extreme, but they go little, if any, farther than we are invited to go now. Negligence, moreover, will have one standard when viewed in relation to the employer, and another and at times stricter standard when viewed in relation to the public. Explanations that might seem plausible, omissions that might be reasonable, if the duty is confined to the employer, conducting a business that presumably at least is not a fraud upon his creditors, might wear another aspect if an independent duty to be suspicious even of one's principal is owing to investors. "Everyone making a promise having the quality of a contract will be under a duty to the promisee by virtue of the promise, but under another duty, apart from the contract, to an indefinite number of potential beneficiaries when performance has begun. The assumption of one relation will mean the involuntary assumption of a series of new relations, inescapably hooked together" (*Moch Co.* v. *Rensselaer Water Co., supra,* at p. 168). "The law does not spread its protection so far" (*Robins Dry Dock & Repair Co.* v. *Flint, supra,* at p. 309).

Our holding does not emancipate accountants from the consequences of fraud. It does not relieve them if their audit has been so negligent as to justify a finding that they had no genuine belief in its adequacy, for this again is fraud. It does no more than say that if less than this is proved, if there has been neither reckless misstatement nor insincere profession of an opinion, but only honest blunder, the ensuing liability for negligence is one that is bounded by the contract, and is to be enforced between the parties by whom the contract has been made. We doubt whether the average business man receiving a certificate without paying for it and receiving it merely as one among a multitude of possible investors, would look for anything more.

(2) The second cause of action is yet to be considered.

The defendants certified as a fact, true to their own knowledge, that the balance sheet was in accordance with the books of account. If their statement was false, they are not to be exonerated because they believed it to be true (*Hadcock* v. *Osmer, supra; Lehigh Zinc & Iron Co.* v. *Bamford,* 150 U.S. 665, 673; *Chatham Furnace Co.* v. *Moffatt,* 147 Mass. 403; *Arnold* v. *Richardson,* 74 App. Div. 581). We think the triers of the facts might hold it to be false.

Correspondence between the balance sheet and the books imports something more, or so the triers of the facts might say, than correspondence between the balance sheet and the general ledger, unsupported or even contradicted by every other record. The correspondence to be of any moment may not unreasonably be held to signify a correspondence between the statement and the books of original entry, the books taken as a whole. If that is what the certificate means, a jury could find that the correspondence did not exist and that the defendants signed the certificates without knowing it to exist and even without reasonable grounds for belief in its existence. The item of $706,000,

representing fictitious accounts receivable, was entered in the ledger after defendant's employee Siess had posted the December sales. He knew of the in-
terpolation, and knew that there was need to verify the entry by reference to
books other than the ledger before the books could be found to be in agreement
with the balance sheet. The evidence would sustain a finding that this was
never done. By concession the interpolated item had no support in the journal,
or in any journal voucher, or in the debit memo book, which was a summary
of the invoices, or in any thing except the invoices themselves. The defendants
do not say that they ever looked at the invoices, seventeen in number, representing these accounts. They profess to be unable to recall whether they did
so or not. They admit, however, that if they had looked, they would have found
omissions and irregularities so many and unusual as to have called for further
investigation. When we couple the refusal to say that they did look with the
admission that if they had looked, they would or could have seen, the situation is revealed as one in which a jury might reasonably find that in truth they
did not look, but certified the correspondence without testing its existence.

In this connection we are to bear in mind the principle already stated in
the course of this opinion that negligence or blindness, even when not equivalent to fraud, is nonetheless evidence to sustain an inference of fraud. At least
this is so if the negligence is gross. Not a little confusion has at times resulted
from an undiscriminating quotation of statements in *Kountze* v. *Kennedy*
(supra), statements proper enough in their setting, but capable of misleading
when extracted and considered by themselves. "Misjudgment, however gross,"
it was there observed, "or want of caution, however marked, is not fraud."
This was said in a case where the trier of the facts had held the defendant guilt-
less. The judgment in this court amounted merely to a holding that a finding
of fraud did not follow as an inference of law. There was no holding that the
evidence would have required a reversal of the judgment if the finding as to
guilt had been the other way. Even *Derry* v. *Peek,* as we have seen, asserts the
probative effect of negligence as an evidentiary fact. We had not thought in
Kountze v. *Kennedy* of upholding a doctrine more favorable to wrongdoers,
though there was a reservation suggesting the approval of a rule more rigorous.
The opinion of this court cites *Derry* v. *Peek,* and states the holding there made
that an action would not lie if the defendant believed the representation made
by him to be true, although without reasonable cause for such belief. "It is not
necessary," we said, "to go to this extent to uphold the present judgment, for
the referee, as has been stated, found that the belief of Kennedy . . . was based
upon reasonable grounds." The setting of the occasion justified the inference
that the representations did not involve a profession of knowledge as distinguished from belief (147 N.Y. at p. 133). No such charity of construction ex-
onerates accountants, who by the very nature of their calling profess to speak

with knowledge when certifying to an agreement between the audit and the entries.

The defendants attempt to excuse the omission of an inspection of the invoices proved to be fictitious by invoking a practice known as that of testing and sampling. A random choice of accounts is made from the total number on the books, and these, if found to be regular when inspected and investigated, are taken as a fair indication of the quality of the mass. The defendants say that about 200 invoices were examined in accordance with this practice, but they do not assert that any of the seventeen invoices supporting the fictitious sales were among the number so selected. Verification by test and sample was very likely a sufficient audit as to accounts regularly entered upon the books in the usual course of business. It was plainly insufficient, however, as to accounts not entered upon the books where inspection of the invoices was necessary, not as a check upon accounts fair upon their face, but in order to ascertain whether there were any accounts at all. If the only invoices inspected were invoices unrelated to the interpolated entry, the result was to certify a correspondence between the books and the balance sheet without any effort by the auditors, as to $706,000 of accounts, to ascertain whether the certified agreement was in accordance with the truth. How far books of account fair upon their face are to be probed by accountants in an effort to ascertain whether the transactions back of them are in accordance with the entries, involves to some extent the exercise of judgment and discretion. Not so, however, the inquiry whether the entries certified as there, are there in very truth, there in the form and in the places where men of business training would expect them to be. The defendants were put on their guard by the circumstances touching the December accounts receivable to scrutinize with special care. A jury might find that with suspicions thus awakened, they closed their eyes to the obvious, and blindly gave assent.

We conclude, to sum up the situation, that in certifying to the correspondence between balance sheet and accounts the defendants made a statement as true to their own knowledge, when they had, as a jury might find, no knowledge on the subject. If that is so, they may also be found to have acted without information leading to a sincere or genuine belief when they certified to an opinion that the balance sheet faithfully reflected the condition of the business.

Whatever wrong was committed by the defendants was not their personal act or omission, but that of their subordinates. This does not relieve them, however, of liability to answer in damages for the consequences of the wrong, if wrong there shall be found to be. It is not a question of constructive notice, as where facts are brought home to the knowledge of subordinates whose interests are adverse to those of the employer (*Henry* v. *Allen*, 151 N.Y. 1; see, however, American Law Institute, Restatement of the Law of Agency, § 506, subd. 2-a). These subordinates, so far as the record shows, had no interests adverse to the defendants', nor any thought in what they did to be unfaithful to their trust. The question is merely this, whether the defendants, having delegated the performance of this work to agents of their own selection, are responsible for the manner in which the business of the agency was done. As to that the answer is not doubtful (*Fifth Ave. Bank v. 42d St., etc., R.R. Co.,* 137 N.Y. 231; *Gleason v. Seaboard Air Line Ry. Co.,* 278 U.S. 349, 356; American Law Institute, Restatement of the Law of Agency, § 481).

Upon the defendants' appeal as to the first cause of action, the judgment of the Appellate Division should be reversed, and that of the Trial Term affirmed, with costs in the Appellate Division in this court.

Upon the plaintiff's appeal as to the second cause of action, the judgment of the Appellate Division and that of the Trial Term should be reversed, and a new trial granted, with costs to abide the event.

Pound, Crane, Lehman, Kellogg, O'Brien and **Hubbs, JJ.,** concur.

Judgment accordingly.

While the precedent established in the Ultramares case has substantially endured, auditors have been subjected to an increasing number of suits challenging them under both statute and common law. A discussion of recent liability cases and their implications follows.

RECENT LIABILITY CASES—IMPLICATIONS FOR ACCOUNTANTS
Henry B. Reiling and Russell A. Taussig*

For the accounting profession, the late 1960's was a time of prosperity and a time of peril. Each year accountants posted new highs in billings and earnings, but at the same time they were reportedly subjected to an unprecedented number of lawsuits. A staff reporter for *The Wall Street Journal* opined that nearly 100 lawsuits were pending against auditors in late 1966.[1] More recently an associate editor of *Fortune* reported that as many claims for damages were filed against accountants in 1968 as

* From *The Journal of Accountancy,* September 1970, pp. 39–53. Reprinted by permission of the American Institute of Certified Public Accountants.
[1] Lee Berton, "CPAs Under Fire," *The Wall Street Journal,* Nov. 15, 1966, p. 13.

in the previous 12 years.[2] While some are skeptical that the volume of cases is so high,[3] it seems clear that there has been an increase in volume of suits filed,[4] that these suits have frequently involved the profession's more prestigious firms and that four cases surfaced which were particularly qualified to capture the profession's attention: *BarChris, Continental Vending, Yale Express and Westec.*†

Many readers are familiar with these cases. Those who are not may refer to Appendix A, page 181, which summarizes the facts, issues and rulings as developed to the date of this article. Litigation is far from over. Indeed, *Yale* and *Westec* have yet to go to trial; nevertheless, enough is known at this time to make a tentative assessment of their characteristics and their potential implications for the public accounting profession. It must be kept in mind, however, that allegations are not synonymous with findings after trial, and lower court conclusions can be overturned on appeal. Subsequent developments may affect the tentative conclusions of this article.

In the authors' opinion these cases collectively have the following three significant characteristics:

1 Recent and pending interpretations of federal securities laws appear likely to give plaintiffs not in a contractual relationship with accountants easier access to accountants than was heretofore the case under common law.

2 Judges and juries composed generally of laymen, not experts in the field of accounting, are beginning to render decisions interpreting accounting principles as well as auditing procedures.

3 The responsibilities of officers, directors and other professionals for financial statements appearing in prospectuses and related documents have received judicial comment for practically the first time; the result is a new awareness of responsibilities and risks and a related request for accountants to expand their attest function.

These characteristics raise at least five long-range planning questions for the accounting profession:

1 Must fee structures be adjusted to reflect the greater potential liability which appears to be emerging from recent lawsuits against public accountants?

†Two additional suits, *Mill Factors* and *Revenue Properties,* were instituted too late to be assessed and possibly commented upon in this article. Both involve very substantial dollar claims and may warrant the reader's attention.

[2] Louis, "The Accountants are Changing the Rules," *Fortune,* June 15, 1968, p. 177.

[3] An attorney particularly competent in the area of accountants' liability has expressed this view privately to the authors. On the other hand Mr. Berton informed the authors that his conclusion in *The Wall Street Journal* represented a middle ground of estimates solicited in approximately 200 interviews with members of leading accounting firms, accounting organizations and their attorneys.

[4] It should be noted that accounting is not the only profession experiencing a flurry of litigation. There is a rash of malpractice suits pending against doctors, lawyers, architects and investment bankers. "Professional Liability and Malpractice," *Federation Insurance Council Quarterly,* Summer 1967, p. 8.

2 What are the dangers in allowing courts to assume leadership in the pronouncement of accounting principles?

3 How can the accounting profession properly restrict its legal hazards?

4 Should accountants extend their attest function to financial information not
now included in certified statements, and certify interim financial statements
that are presently unaudited?

5 What are the advantages and pitfalls for accountants in accepting a new role
regarding financial statements?

As background for the consideration of these questions let us examine the
features of recent cases of particular significance to accountants.

IMPACT OF RECENT CASES UPON RELATIONSHIP
OF ACCOUNTANTS TO SOCIETY

CIRCUMVENTION OF COMMON LAW DEFENSES

Three recent cases, *BarChris, Yale Express* and *Westec* include as plaintiffs
third parties who are not in a contractual relationship with the auditor. Until recently, third party actions against accountants generally failed because of the
limited scope of legal doctrines available to the plaintiffs. The plaintiffs either
had to espouse common law negligence or deceit doctrines, or they had to
assert statutory rights available under the Securities Act of 1933 or the Securities Exchange Act of 1934. The common law alternative brought them
face to face with *Ultramares Corp.* V. *Touche, Niven & Co.*[5] or the formidable
task of proving fraud[6]; the securities law alternative forced them to assume
the uncertainty and risk of pioneering in the interpretation of the statutes.

Judge Cardozo in *Ultramares* held that an accountant was ordinarily liable
for negligent misrepresentation solely to the person who retained him, or to
the person who was known to be the primary beneficiary of the information.
The Court went on to say, however, that an accountant could be held liable
by a broader group if his conduct was fraudulent or so grossly negligent as
to amount to fraud. A few subsequent cases have imposed liability on this
constructive fraud theory, but these cases have been inconsequential. *Ultramares* has been widely followed for more than three decades, and it has effectively blocked negligence actions by third parties under common law. However,
the vitality of the common law privity doctrine is once again being tested.
Security holders represented by the trustee in bankruptcy are using common

[5] 255 New York 170, 174 N.E. 441 (1931).
[6] The conditions under which misrepresentations are fraudulent are sent forth in note 51.

law negligence as an alternative theory for recovery in *Westec*. Today the prospects for a successful attack against accountants by security holders are better than in the past; there is evidence that the utility of the privity defense for accountants has begun to deteriorate.[7]

Westec itself may not pose any direct threat to privity. This will become clear only as the facts are developed at trial. Nevertheless, the case is a potentially important barometer of judicial attitude toward privity and the tone of any comment on privity even in dictum must be watched with care and with Holmes' prediction theory of the law[8] clearly in mind. Should the pressures on privity from dictum and articles continue to mount,[9] and the authors anticipate that they will, the probability of an adverse decision on the doctrine will at some point become sufficiently great that professional practices of individuals and firms should reflect the increased liability risks in advance of any actual adverse holding.

Recent developments also imply an expansion in the legal hazards facing accountants under statutory law. Since passage in 1933 and 1934, the federal securities laws have represented a potentially effective way for litigants to reach accountants when blocked at common law by *Ultramares* or the difficulty of proving fraud. Indeed, aside from the attractiveness of the federal securities laws as the potential means for circumventing common law doctrines, it contains several ancillary features which enhance its usefulness as an alternative legal weapon.[10] However, the securities laws have evolved slowly in areas governing the relationship between accountants and the in-

---

[7] A very good discussion of the English and American cases and articles questioning the privity defense is presented by District Judge Pettine in *Rusch Factors Inc.* v. *Levin* 284 F. Supp. 85, 90–93 (1967). Expressing considerable doubt regarding the wisdom of the privity defense in negligence action involving accountants, the Court nevertheless had to stop short of a holding on the subject since the plaintiff in *Rush Factors* came within the exception to privity available to those whose use is the very end and aim of the audit.

[8] Mr. Justice Holmes defined law as "[t]he *prophecies* of what the courts will do in fact. . . ." [Emphasis added.] Address by Oliver Wendell Holmes, Jr. then a Justice of the Supreme Judicial Court of Massachusetts, Dedication of the new hall of the Boston University School of Law, Jan. 8, 1897, published as "The Path of the Law," 10 *Harv. L. Rev.* 457, 461 (1897). Thus law is a prediction. And precedent constitutes a major but not the sole basis for that prediction. See *id.*, p. 457 and p. 467.

[9] Accountants accustomed to taking the privity defense for granted should also reflect on the fact that it has recently been virtually eliminated from its formerly entrenched position in the product liability area. See Prosser, "The Fall of the Citadel (Strict Liability to the Consumer)," 50 *Minn. L. Rev.* 791 (1966). There are of course many socially significant distinctions between that area and the accountants' liability area, one of the more important of which is the personal injury often attending defective products in contrast to the financial injury that can attend incorrect financial statements. The point is that privity is under attack generally and the mere citation of precedent may no longer be adequate. Accountants' continued insulation from third party negligence claims will in the authors' opinion turn on the marshalling of the social justifications for that insulation.

[10] For example, the 1933 and 1934 Acts reduce the problem of quantifying the amount of damage sustained, and the additional problem of establishing a causal connection between the allegedly improper conduct and the damage.

vesting public,[11] and its potential aid to investors has not yet been fully realized. This situation may be changing.

In *BarChris* plaintiffs finally used Section 11 of the 1933 Act[12] against accountants, and in *Yale Express* and *Westec* plaintiffs are testing the utility of Rule 10b-5 promulgated under the 1934 Act[13] as a means of reaching accountants.[14] The outcome of these cases and the accompanying legal rationales will probably do much to encourage or discourage other plaintiffs and define the legal environment for accountants during the 1970s.

Although the accountants were held liable for nonfraudulent conduct to third parties not in privity with them, *BarChris* produced no unexpected legal theories or statutory interpretations directly affecting accountants; it was clear from reading Section 11 that a privity relationship was not a prerequisite to recovery and it was also clear that conduct short of fraud would support a recovery. Nevertheless, *BarChris* is likely to have legal significance for accountants. It is the first important case decided under Section 11 and it involved a major firm. The authors anticipate that it may alert potential litigants to a previously little used statutory provision, and similar cases will soon follow.

In the authors' opinion the legal environment surrounding Rule 10b-5 is alive with prospects for an extension of legal doctrines which would increase accountants' risks. The march of cases under the frequently interpreted Rule 10b-5 has steadily enlarged the list of potential plaintiffs and defendants. This expansion has occurred along with the erosion of the privity defense, a common law concept which was judicially appended at an early date to the rule. The question today is whether the erosion of privity is sufficiently advanced and the absence of direct personal gain sufficiently unimportant so that ac-

---

[11] For example, prior to 1954 the total number of suits brought under the civil sections of the 1933 Act against defendants of all classes totaled only 38, an average of less than two per year. *L. Loss, Securities Regulation,* 989 (Supp. 1955).

[12] Sec. 11 of the Securities Act of 1933 at issue in *BarChris* provides for a civil action for damages against accountants caused by their material errors in a registration statement. The statutory language of Sec. 11 makes it clear that privity is not needed for a successful suit under that section.

[13] The courts have interpreted Rule 10b-5 to permit a civil action for damages caused by fraud and misleading statements made in conjunction with the purchase or sale of securities. This provision reaches conduct which Sec. 11 and Sec. 18 do not.

[14] The following two additional provisions though less important than Section 11 and Rule 10b-5 are also involved in one or more of the four cases treated in this article:

Sec. 18 of the Securities Exchange Act of 1934. In essence it provides for a civil action for damages against any person who makes or causes a fraudulent statement to be made in statements filed with the exchanges or SEC.

Sec. 17 of the Securities Act of 1933. This provision is used to secure criminal indictments and injunctions. It is a general anti-fraud provision, making unlawful any form of fraud, untruth, or omission of a material fact associated with the sale of securities. This provision has not yet produced any case law of special significance to accountants.

countants can be reached. Although *Westec* and *Yale Express* are still in the pretrial stage, they both involve 10b-5 and are capable of defining the relationship between accountants and the rule.[15]

ACCOUNTING PRINCIPLES

Current cases differ from past ones not only with respect to legal theories used but also with respect to allegations of accounting errors. Plaintiffs increasingly allege violations of generally accepted accounting principles, a marked departure from such classic cases as *Ultramares,* (above), and *McKesson & Robbins,*[16] in which the decisions were based largely on auditing deficiencies. Judges and juries not only are finding deficiencies in the way auditors examine financial records, but also are making statements on accounting principles and the way in which they should be applied.

In *BarChris* the Court ruled that profits on a sale-leaseback should have been eliminated; however, the AICPA statements on accounting principles at the time of the transaction were silent as to the need for eliminating such profits. Publication of Accounting Principles Board Opinion No. 5 resolved the question concerning the accounting for sale-leasebacks. Opinion No. 5 of 1964 provides that ". . . the sale and the leaseback usually cannot be accounted for as independent transactions. Neither the sale price nor the annual rental can be objectively evaluated independently of the other. Consequently, material gains or losses . . . should be amortized over the life of the lease. . . ." However, APB Opinion No. 5 did not exist in 1960, when BarChris entered into the sale and leaseback of its bowling alley. The applicable section of Accounting Research Bulletin No. 43 simply provided that: ". . . in the year in which the transaction originates, there should be disclosure of the principal details of any important sale-and-lease transaction."

Let us re-examine the BarChris sale-leaseback transaction in the light of then existing accounting principles to answer the claims of some commentators that the relevant principles were sufficiently defined before the case was brought to trial. One might advance several reasons to explain why BarChris should have eliminated the profit in its consolidated statements on its sale of a bowling alley to a finance factor after which the alley was leased back

---

[15] Indeed, Judge Tyler in *Yale Express* denied the accountants' motion to dismiss certain parts of the complaint which were premised on 10b-5 though he did so without prejudice to renewal of the motion at trial. Judge Tyler's stress upon the importance of the questions involved and his stress upon the Court's need for further factual and legal development of those questions suggests further important comment will be forthcoming from *Yale Express.* The importance of the case is underlined by the fact that the SEC is participating as *amicus curiae.*

[16] *McKesson & Robbins,* Inc., SEC Accounting Series Release No. 19 (1940).

by a subsidiary. One might argue that an arm's-length transaction was lacking and the auditor could therefore not attest to the amount of profit on the transfer. One might also claim that management could time the recognition of profit to suit its private needs. Moreover, BarChris still had the use of the property after the sale-leaseback, and to recognize profit portrayed legal form not economic substance. Furthermore, one might argue that recognition of profit violated the ancient principle of conservatism: "recognize all losses, but anticipate no gains." Finally, the overriding doctrine of fairness might be invoked; one might argue profit should be eliminated so that financial statements would fairly present the financial position and results of operations for BarChris.

But the doctrine of fairness is necessarily egocentric. He who espouses it presumes to know the one and only correct interpretation of a given transaction. Unfortunately, fairness like beauty exists in the eye of the beholder. What appears fair to one often appears unfair to another. No one denies the propriety of fairness, but accountants need more explicit guidelines.

A similar comment applies to conservatism. Understatement of earnings can be just as harmful as overstatement. An investor can suffer economic injury from selling a stock on understated earnings as well as he can from buying on overstated earnings. The doctrine of conservatism, a disappearing one,[17] by itself is not sufficient to dictate nonrecognition of gain on a sale-leaseback.

It appears that ambiguity as to the definition of the accounting entity existed at the time BarChris entered into its sale-and-leaseback transaction. Furthermore, a review of the pros and cons for eliminating the profit on the BarChris sale-leaseback discloses that reasonable doubt existed as to what was required in accordance with the generally accepted accounting principles circa 1960. In fact, the issuance of Opinion No. 5 would have been unnecessary if the principles regarding sale-leaseback transactions were unambiguous. In rebuttal, one might contend that the principles always existed; and that the opinions were mere codifications of existing practice. This argument runs contrary to fact, however, for the APB Opinions frequently have changed previous accounting methods, as they did with respect to earnings and losses on unconsolidated subsidiaries. It appears to the authors that generally accepted accounting principles for sale-leasebacks were not clearly stated at the time of the Bar-Chris audit, and because of this uncertainty, the Court, perhaps inadvertently, prescribed a method of accounting it considered proper under the circumstances.

Westec is another case in which the Court is asked to consider accounting

---

[17] Maurice Moonitz, *The Basic Postulates of Accounting,* Accounting Research Study No. 1, (American Institute of CPAs, 1961) pp. 46–47.

principles, and to rule on the way in which financial statements should have been prepared.[18] The complaint of Westec's trustee in bankruptcy charges, among other things, that reported earnings for 1964 and 1965 were inflated by the company's improper accounting for several acquisitions. The plaintiff claims that five acquisitions accounted for as a pooling did not meet the established criteria. The handling of these is also attacked on grounds that it was improper to consolidate earnings of companies acquired after the close of the financial period but before release of the period's audit report.[19]

The allegations concerning the acquisition of Seacat-Zapata Offshore Co. illustrate the difficult questions the Court may have to face. Westec's negotiations for Seacat allegedly produced a tentative agreement whereby Westec would acquire Seacat's assets other than $1.5 million cash in exchange for $9.5 million in stock; and Westec would subsequently lease the assets to Zapata, a company which owned 50 per cent of Seacat. The auditors, when asked if pooling could be used, said no. In their opinion the lease of assets prevented pooling since the surviving entity failed the continuity-of-business test. Seacat would have changed from an operating to a leasing company. Although, in the authors' opinion this interpretation is questionable, management was convinced and allegedly asked the auditors for help in revising the terms of the acquisition.

The complaint charges that the auditors then suggested the substitution of a "work contract" for the lease, which in their opinion would permit pooling. According to the terms of the contract, Westec retained legal ownership of the properties and Zapata operated them, receiving as its fee a percentage of profits which rose as profits increased. It was allegedly anticipated that the work contract would produce the same cash flow to both parties as the lease, though it was not a lease[20] and therefore would not prevent pooling. The suggestion was implemented and the auditors approved the use of pooling in the annual reports.

The Seacat aspect of Westec raises three basic accounting questions. Did the work contract differ sufficiently from the original lease to justify pooling? Did the auditors lose their independence by the depth of their involvement? Was it proper to include in the audited statements an acquisition made subse-

---

[18] The description of *Westec* is based on the original complaint of August 23, 1968 filed in U.S. District Court (Houston). It must be remembered that all of the comments concerning *Westec* are based only on allegations. The case had not gone to trial as of February 1, 1970.

[19] The complaint alleges that three acquisitions were consumated on March 26, 1965, the date of the 1964 audit report; it is further alleged that the 1965 audit report was held open until April 28, 1966 to enable three additional acquisitions to be effected for the purpose of inflating 1965 earnings.

[20] Should the level of operations have deviated from that which was expected, the work contract would have produced a cash flow higher or lower than the lease.

quent to the accounting period in question? In the author's opinion, answers to the first two questions are not available in the accounting literature to date.[21] Nevertheless, the Court must make its rulings, and rulings necessarily rendered in the absence of clear guidelines are fraught with risk for the accountants.

The Court in *BarChris* was confronted with accounting alternatives and, as a byproduct of its decision, a preferred treatment for sale-leasebacks was identified. Alternatives are present in *Westec* and the possibility exists that it will have a similar consequence. This raises the serious question of whether, as a practical matter, judges and juries can avoid selecting amongst alternatives. A related important question is whether accounting guidelines which emerge from the judicial process will be as well conceived as those resulting from the careful method of review and public exposure developed over the years by the AICPA.

DISCLOSURE OF PRIVILEGED INFORMATION

The plaintiffs in *Yale Express* are asking the Court to decide whether independent accountants, who have expressed an opinion on financial statements in a 10-K, must disclose to the public material errors and omissions from those statements which they have discovered during the course of a subsequent management services engagement.[22] The accountants' dilemma arose from the dual responsibilities it assumed. Judge Tyler observed in *Yale Express* that as auditor of the 10-K financial statements its responsibility "is not only to the client who pays his fee, but also to investors, creditors and others who may rely on the financial statements which he certifies. . . . The public accountant must report fairly on the facts as he finds them whether favorable or unfavorable to his client. His duty is to safeguard the public interest, not that of his client. [In the Matter of Touche, Niven, Bailey and Smart, 237 SEC 629, 670–671 (1957).] (Footnotes omitted)."[23]

On the other hand, when the accountant performed the subsequent special study his "primary obligations, under normal circumstances, were to [his] client and not the public."[24] The unique question posed in *Yale Express* is

---

[21] The Accounting Principles Board has promulgated a statement on this matter. American Institute of Certified Public Accountants, Accounting Principles, Current text, Sec. 1091.13 (1969). Consequently, if the plaintiff is seriously going to urge that retroactive inclusion was wrong, it appears he must argue that the Accounting Principles Board erred in creating the principle, or argue that the Westec situation represented an exception to the principle.

[22] The committee on auditing procedure of the American Institute of Certified Public Accountants recently issued Statement on Auditing Procedure No. 41 (October 1969), "Subsequent Discovery of Facts Existing at the Date of the Auditor's Report." The Statement establishes procedures to be followed by the auditor who, subsequent to the date of his report upon audited financial statements, becomes aware that facts may have existed at that date which might have affected his report had he then been aware of such facts.

[23] *Fischer* v. *Kletz*, 266 F. Supp. 180, 184 (S.D.N.Y. 1967)

[24] *Id.*

whether the duty to the investing public terminated once the financial statements were certified or alternatively whether a duty to the investing public existed after the certification, which duty dominated the obligation to the client.

The Court deferred until after a trial the question of whether a dominant post-certification duty to investors was imposed by one or more of the following: common law deceit doctrines; Section 18 (a) of the Securities Exchange Act of 1934; and Rule 10b-5. In its ultimate resolution of this question the Court must reconcile the needs of investors for unfavorable financial information against the possible benefits to companies from preserving a confidential relationship between consultants and clients. Should this question eventually go against the accountants, it seems reasonable to anticipate that for companies with less than normal financial strength accountants and clients may find it undesirable to have audits and special studies performed by the same firm.

THE THREAT OF CRIMINAL ACTION

Continental Vending adds the threat of criminal action to the legal hazards of accountancy. In this case, criminal action was instituted against the auditors by the U.S. Attorney for the Southern District of New York. Significantly, criminal actions against accountants, particularly major firms, have been infrequent in the past.[25] Instead, incidents of alleged wrongdoing and substandard accounting practices have been resolved by administrative proceedings within the SEC[26] or in civil suits brought by the injured parties.

The severity of the government's decision to pursue a criminal charge—particularly since the accountants were not alleged to have benefited directly from their wrongdoing—leads one to speculate as to its motivation. Perhaps an analogy to the antitrust area is valid. When the government sustains a judgment against a company for an antitrust violation, that judgment can be used to establish a *prima facie* case by a private party allegedly injured by the violation.[27]   Considerable help is given to the private litigant. A violation of

---

[25] Diligent research has uncovered no other criminal prosecution where the motive of personal gain was so lacking and the argument for conformity with generally accepted accounting principles so strong.

[26] The SEC brings disciplinary or "disbarment" proceedings against accountants under Rule 2 of its Rules of Practice. Those rules provide in part as follows:

"(e) Suspension and Disbarment. The Commission may deny temporarily or permanently, the privilege of appearing or practicing before it in any way to any person who is found by the Commission after notice of any opportunity for hearing in the matter

(1) not to possess the requisite qualifications to represent others, or

(2) to be lacking in character or integrity or to have engaged in unethical or improper professional conduct." 17 Code Fed. Reg. Sec. 201.2.

[27] 15 U.S.C. Sec. 15 (1964).

the law is tentatively established, substantially reducing the risk of an unsuccessful suit. The prospect of a criminal suit as well as a civil suit makes a company more willing to acquiesce to a consent decree or some other settlement short of prolonged litigation. Perhaps the government is attempting to facilitate civil suits by resorting to criminal action. The criminal judgment would not have *prima facie* civil power,[28] but evidence would have been gathered and much of the rationale for a civil case would have been developed. Alternatively, where civil suit has already been instituted, as in *Continental,* the threat of criminal action might encourage prompt settlement.[29]

EXPANDED RESPONSIBILITIES

Last but not least significant of the characteristics of the cases under review is that they result in a pressure for expansion of the auditors' responsibilities. Two forces may cause this expansion. Section 11 of the 1933 Act[30] has been interpreted to impose a broad responsibility for financial information upon underwriters and signatories of the registration statement. Consequently, they are asking auditors to attest to new financial data. Also, for the first time a court has articulated the responsibilities of independent accountants in S-1 reviews.

The demand for an expansion of the audit function is an outgrowth of the "due diligence" defense in *BarChris*.[31] At issue was that defense as embodied

[28] The successful securities law plaintiff cannot recover treble damages as could his counterpart in the antitrust area. See *Globus* v. *Law Research Service, Inc.,* 418 F.2d 1276 (2d Cir. 1969).

[29] The prospect of criminal action is particularly threatening to accountants because of its potential impact on their professional lives. AICPA Bylaws 7.3.1, as amended February 20, 1969, specify that membership shall be terminated without a hearing if there is filed with the Secretary of the Institute a judgment for conviction of a crime defined as a felony under the law of the convicting jurisdiction. The Trial Board of the Institute according to Section 7.4 of the Bylaws may expel a member if he has been convicted of a criminal offense which tends to discredit the profession. More significantly, state boards have the power to revoke a CPA's license to practice. However,it has been held that revocation was too severe a penalty where the improper conduct consisted of preparing and issuing certified statements in which the corporate client's liabilities were deliberately understated when the CPA's professional conduct had previously been unobjectionable and his motivation had been solely to give the corporation a chance to stay in business. *Shander* v. *Allen,* 28 A.D. 2d 1150, 284 N.Y.S.2d 142 (1967).

[30] The most significant prior case discussing Sec. 11 is *Shunts* v. *Hirlman,* 28 F. Supp. 478 (S.D. Cal. 1939). Although the accountants escaped liability in that early decision, it has been roundly criticized by Professor Loss because of ". . . the surprising low accounting standards which seemed to satisfy the court . . ." L. Loss, *Securities Regulation,* 1020 (Supp. 1955).

[31] The so-called "due diligence" defense is embodied in the following provisions of Sec. 11 of the Securities Act of 1933:

Section 11(b) of the Act provides that ". . . no person, other than the issuer, shall be liable . . . who shall sustain the burden of proof . . . (3) that (A) as regards any part of the registration statement not purporting to be made on the authority of any expert . . . he had, after reasonable investigation, reasonable ground to believe and did believe, at the time such part of the registration statement became effective, that the statements therein were true and that there was no omission to state a material fact required to be stated therein or necessary to make the statements therein not misleading; . . . and (C) as regards any part of the registration statement purporting to be made on the authority of an expert (other in Section 11(b). The statute indicates that underwriters and signatories generally must make a reasonable and good faith investigation according to a *prudent man standard;* however, if they make statements in good faith on the authority of an expert, a *lesser standard* is operative with regard to the expertised statements. They must then merely have no reasonable grounds for believing the statements to be incorrect. Applying these standards the Court even held new outside directors to be liable since their investigations consisted only of questions put to officers and tenured directors, individuals who were not experts. Accordingly, directors (on their own initiative and at the request of underwriters) are asking independent accountants (experts within the meaning of Section 11) to expertise a larger portion of the information filed with the SEC, such as sales backlog, plant capacity and floor space.

The Court in *BarChris* also discussed the particular responsibility of the accountants in an S-1 review.[32] The question arose because the accountants tried to establish the due diligence defense; and, therefore, had to prove that when the registration statement became effective they had, as a result of a reasonable investigation, reason to believe and did believe that the expertised statements, i.e., the audited annual statements, were not misleading. The Court observed that the objective of an S-1 review is "to ascertain whether any material change has occurred in the company's financial position which should be disclosed in order to prevent the balance sheet figures from being misleading."[33] Although the Court ruled that the scope of the S-1 program as written conformed to generally accepted auditing standards, it found that the program was not properly executed.[34] It failed because some of the steps in the program were not taken, because an inadequate amount of time (20½ hours) was spent on the job, and because the in-charge accountant was too satisfied with what the Court styled "glib answers" to his questions.

than himself) . . . he had no reasonable ground to believe and did not believe, at the time such part of the registration statement became effective, that the statements therein were untrue or that there was an omission to state a material fact required to be stated therein or necessary to make the statements therein not misleading. . . ."

Sec. 11(c) defines "reasonable investigation" as follows: "In determining, for the purpose of paragraph (3) of subsection (b) of this section, what constitutes reasonable investigation and reasonable ground for belief, the standard of reasonableness shall be that required of a prudent man in the management of his own property."

[32] An accountant carries out an S-1 review to discharge an obligation which arises by implication from the language of Sec. 11. Since the section makes the accountant responsible for his opinion upon the audited financial statements as of the effective date of the registration statements, and since the effective date will not occur until sometime after the accountant has completed his audit and issued his opinion, he must satisfy himself as of the effective date, that the audited financial statements still fairly present the financial position and results of operations as of the end of the audited period.

[33] *Escott* v. *BarChris Construction Corp.,* 283 F. Supp., 643, 701 (S.D.N.Y. 1968).

[34] This improper execution denied the accountants the due diligence defense: "[t]here had been a material change for the worse in BarChris's financial position. That change was sufficiently serious so that the failure to disclose it made the 1960 figures misleading. Berardi did not discover it. As far as results were concerned, his S-1 review was useless," *Id.,* p. 702.

Part of the program required that the auditors "inquire as to changes in material contracts." Although the in-charge accountant asked the controller about uncompleted contracts and secured a list of them, he did not actually examine each contract. The Court ruled this inquiry to be inadequate since in the Court's opinion the absence of prices from some examined contracts should have prompted further investigation. The Court's ruling illustrates the grave danger to the accounting profession of undefined standards. The Court in *BarChris* has in fact enunciated new and higher procedures for S-1 reviews, than would be considered necessary by many accountants. Although the Court stated that the auditors should not be held to standards higher than those recognized in their profession, the standards were undefined and the Court filled the void.

IMPLICATIONS FOR THE PROFESSION

Let us turn now from the characteristics of the recent cases to a consideration of their implications.

1 Insurance Accountants have realized for some time that increased legal hazards require greater liability coverage. Through the efforts of leaders in the profession higher limits have been obtained, but the uninsured exposure is still staggering. For example, the market value of a major conglomerate's common stock declined more than $250 million in the year from July 1, 1968 to June 30, 1969. The mind boggles at the thought of a class suit by the company's stockholders against its auditors alleging the drop was the consequence of negligent or fradulent auditing. The need for increased liability insurance is obvious.

To the extent that coverage is not available, accountants must either absorb the loss or pass it on as part of their cost of business. The authors believe that miscreants should bear the brunt of loss when liability is the consequence of fraud. However, the recent civil cases fall short of fraud; they do not involve false statements deliberately made with the intent to deceive. The authors are of the opinion that in such cases it is practical and reasonable for accountants to pass on the costs of an evolving and increasingly demanding standard of professional conduct—especially when, as in several current cases, the standard, extant at the time of the engagement, was at best vague. Indeed, as the courts broaden the reach of federal securities laws they are in effect forcing accountants, and others, to assure investors against damage sustained as a result of reliance upon incorrect financial data, a type of information which is inherently imprecise. The authors believe that because of considerations of social advantage, the losses due to the ordinary claims under the securities law should be spread as widely as possible throughout the economy. This spreading of the risk can most conveniently be implemented by accountants' liability insurance, the cost of which ultimately is diffused through the entities of the economy and their participants.[35]

2 Reference of Accounting Issues to a Master   One implication of the phenomenon whereby judges and juries are shaping accounting practice is that defendants may wish to give new consideration to the advisability of urging the Court to refer accounting questions to a special master.[36] It seems reasonable that a master learned in accounting would handle accounting questions more capably than a lay judge or jury.

The Federal Rules of Civil Procedure permit the District Courts to appoint a special master and to refer matters to him.[37] The judge has considerable discretion over the scope of the reference. For example, the master may be directed to report only on a particular issue, or he may be directed to receive and report on evidence only.

Judicial discretion over the use of a master as opposed to the scope of the reference is more limited. In a jury trial a judge is authorized to refer questions to a master only when they are complicated. In a trial without a jury the master may be used only when some exceptional condition requires it. Thus, although a master cannot be used at the whim of the litigants or of the court, the option generally is available since many cases involving accounting issues would qualify as "complicated" or represent "exceptional circumstances."

Reference of accounting issues to a master both solves and creates problems. Difficult questions receive the sophisticated consideration they deserve; but selection of the master becomes a point of contention among plaintiffs, defendants, and judge. In addition, reference to a master generally delays the case and adds to its cost. On balance, the procedure would seem to have particular merit in cases where the accounting questions are either particularly numerous and/or difficult.[38]

[35] A similar argument was made by Judge Traynor of the California Supreme Court in a famous concurring opinion in a case involving product-liability:

"The cost of an injury and the loss of time or health may be an overwhelming misfortune to the person injured, and a needless one, for the risk of injury can be insured by the manufacturer and distributed among the public as a cost of doing business." *Escola* v. *Coca-Cola Bottling Co.,* 24 Cal. 2d 453, 462, 150 P.2d 436, 441 (1944).

[36] *Fed. R. Civ.,* p. 53.

[37] Although the Federal Rules of Civil Procedure govern only procedure in federal courts, they are crucial because the diversity of citizenship and size of claims in cases against accountants qualify them for consideration by a federal civil court.

[38] An example of the use of a special master where accounting questions are involved is *601 West 26 Corp.* v. *Solitron Devices Inc.,* CCH Fed. Sec. Law Rep., paragraph 92,611 (S.D.N.Y. Jan. 1970). There the special master supervised the taking of 401 pages of minutes which produced findings on 14 accounting ques-

3 Probability Approach   Since cases increasingly concern accounting principles as well as auditing procedures, accountants should warn the readers of financial statements regarding the probabilistic nature of their contents. Section 11 of the Securities and Exchange Act refers to "material facts." Unfortunately, accounting statements are still prepared as though their contents were indeed "facts" capable of being measured exactly to the penny. Small wonder the auditors in *BarChris* were sued partly because they failed to require the establishment of a proper allowance for doubtful accounts.

Auditors should not express an opinion on financial statements without qualifications as to the level of confidence for the estimated amounts in those statements. Financial reporting would be greatly improved if a Bayesian probability approach[39] were applied to the financial statements. Confidence limits should be published for the principal items along with their expected values. For example, earnings per share should be reported as $4.02 with the probability that they are between $3.90 and $4.14 at the 95 per cent level of confidence. Many lawsuits would be avoided if auditors would simply indicate that they are not certifying to deterministic facts, but rather are expressing an opinion on estimates from a probability distribution. A caveat should be included in the auditor's opinion putting the reader on notice of the stochastic nature of the quantities covered by the report.

4 Marginal Companies   One characteristic common to all of the cases in this article is that they involve businesses which have failed. Clearly, as a matter of self protection, an auditor must perform a more extensive investigation when he suspects financial difficulties. Unfortunately, evidence of business failure may be more apparent in retrospect than at the time of an audit. Nevertheless, the current cases indicate the wisdom of expanding an audit program for a company with declining earnings or weak credit.

The accountant's dilemma in this area has implications for society at large. If it becomes commonplace for stockholders to sue the auditors of every failing company, those firms least able to pay will be hindered by above average audit costs. Additional barriers to competition will be introduced because the cost of raising money and doing business will be higher for marginal companies.

5 Extension of Attest Function   As a result of *BarChris*, directors, underwriters, and their attorneys recognize that for them to secure maximum

---

tions. The questions ranged from whether the accountants had subordinated their judgment to that of the client to the determination of whether earnings were artificially inflated or otherwise misrepresented. The District Court disposed of the case — vindicating the accountants — based on the findings and conclusions of law of the special master.

[39] See R. Schlaifer, *Probability and Statistics for Business Decisions*. (1959).

protection under the "due diligence" defense of Section 11(b) as much of the prospectus as possible must be covered by an opinion of independent accountants. This recognition has prompted them to pressure accountants to expand in several ways the scope of their work as it relates to registration statements. Counsel for some underwriters, accepting the accountant's premise that he should only attest to "financial data" have in effect argued that the term "financial" has evolved and today encompasses more data than in the past. For example, in one instance independent accountants were asked to attest to the total floor space in a plant. In another, they were asked to attest to the amount of unfilled orders. Nevertheless, auditors typically have been unwilling to expand their attest function to cover data in the text of the prospectus and new types of data sought to be added to the annual financial statements via footnotes.

In addition, underwriters are asking independent accountants to expand the scope of their investigation of events subsequent to the date of the certified balance sheet. This request is a consequence of the underwriters' increased awareness of the due diligence defense at issue in *BarChris.* It will be recalled that maximum protection under that defense is available to the underwriter if at the time the registration statement becomes effective he had no reasonable ground to believe the expertised portion of the registration statements (audited financial statements, for example) was misleading. In order to satisfy these statutory requirements, the underwriter, aware that accountants conduct S-1 reviews to maximize their own due diligence protection,[40] typically secures from the company's independent auditors, "comfort letters" which contain comments on financial developments during the stub period. These comments are secured either by requesting them from the accountants who provide them as an accommodation, or by requiring in their underwriting agreement that the comments be provided.

In the authors' opinion *BarChris* suggests that standards for S-1 reviews need to be re-examined and made more specific, despite the fact that the Court stated that "[a]ccountants should not be held to a standard higher than that recognized in their profession" and the additional fact that the Court stated that it did not hold them to a higher standard. In the authors' opinion the S-1 review program prepared by the auditors in *BarChris* would have been acceptable to many accountants; and it appears that at least some accountants are out of touch with the standards as perceived by the courts.

Since S-1 reviews and inquiries for comfort letters are generally done at the same time, the authors suggest that the profession re-examine its posture regarding those letters when it reconsiders S-1 reviews. Two basic options are available regarding comfort letters. Accountants can restrict the rendering of

---

[40] The reasons for conducting an S-1 review were discussed *supra* at note 32.

them, or they can increase the scope of the work for their preparation. Accountants, generally, have tended to resist an expansion of comfort letters. They prefer that the letters continue to refer only to changes in capitalization and to material adverse changes in financial position which occur subsequent to the latest financial statements in the registration statement. Furthermore, they traditionally state that an examination for the stub period has not been made, and that an opinion is disclaimed. They generally state explicitly that the procedures followed by the accountant would not necessarily disclose adverse changes in either financial position or results of operations and the assurances given are negative, couched in language such as ". . . nothing came to our attention which caused us to believe that the accounting information requires any material adjustment for a fair presentation. . . ."[41]

Anticipating that some reconsideration of S-1 reviews and comfort letters will be forthcoming, the authors suggest that the profession go far beyond the most pessimistic reading of *BarChris* and consider several radical changes in stub period practice. They believe that the expression of opinions on "adverse changes" should be discontinued since it is impossible for the accountants to determine whether a change was in fact "adverse."[42] They recommend that all unaudited statements be audited and that the auditor attest to such other data contained in the registration statement as is capable of being measured. A complete examination for the stub period, though it would take more time than the present review, could generally be accomplished during the interval between the registration and effective date of the prospectus.[43] The updating of information supplied on initial filing would be accomplished by an amendment. The incremental cost of this work would vary depending upon the length of the stub period; assuming for purposes of illustration that a company went into registration three months after the close of its fiscal period, the authors estimate that in most cases the cost would run between 20 and 40 per cent of the annual examination. If as a practical matter the audit can be carried to within a few days of the effective date of the registration statement, the underwriters will have more due diligence protection, prospectus readers will have more useful information, and the accountants will have avoided the difficult problem of articulating detailed standards for the statutorily implied S-1 review.

---

[41] Statements on Auditing Procedure No. 35, p. 23.

[42] For example, an increase in research and development expense with a consequent decrease in income might be beneficial for the company in the long run.

[43] Although Sec. 8(a) of the Securities Act of 1933 provides that the registration statement becomes effective 20 days after filing unless the SEC accelerates the effective date or determines that the statement is incomplete or inaccurate, almost invariably the registrant files a delaying amendment which postpones the effective date substantially. The average time difference between registration and effectiveness was 65 days during 1969.

6 Accounting Principles   The courts, through their judges and juries, are affecting accounting principles as well as auditing standards. For example, the Court enunciated a basis for reporting a sale-leaseback in *BarChris*. These developments challenge the method developed by the AICPA over the years whereby it issues statements on accounting principles only after comprehensive research, publication of exposure drafts, and extended deliberation by the Accounting Principles Board. The courts are in a difficult position and may, inadvertently or otherwise, bypass this careful procedure unless the Institute accelerates its publication schedule.

The authors believe that the development of accounting principles by judges and juries as a by-product of their disposition of a series of cases will not result in the most desirable formulation of guidelines for financial reporting. Present litigation typically involves unusual circumstances, which could prejudice a decision on general principles. For instance, in *Westec* officers of the company have been found guilty on a number of criminal counts, including improper security transactions. The moral taint from these convictions might affect the Court's regard for the defendants and might prejudice its ruling on whether a pooling of interest fairly presented acquisitions by Westec. The authors believe that accounting procedures should be generalized from the experience of going concerns run by ethical managers, not failing companies run by wrongdoers.

The recent cases on accountants' liability highlight the pressing need for a massive expansion in accounting research. The SEC no longer stands alone in pushing the AICPA to narrow the differences in accounting principles. Judges and juries not expert in financial reporting are wrestling with highly complex accounting problems, and there is little reason to hope that they will do any better than the APB in developing viable accounting standards.

The AICPA expended $353,000 on research in 1968,[44] an increase of 64 per cent over 1966; but an amount which constituted less than one-tenth of one per cent of the reputed annual gross billings of the eight largest firms. These figures do not reflect the enormous donation of time and labor to the Board by the individual members and their firms; however, the authors hypothesize that a massive increase in the AICPA research budget with a comparable increase in either donated or paid professional time would be of prime importance in combatting the increasing number of liability cases. In addition, government sponsored research, possibly in the form of support by a National Social Science Foundation, would be helpful.

Some critics of financial reporting take the position that further research and increased output by the APB is less necessary than the creation of an au-

[44] American Institute of Certified Public Accountants, *Annual Report, The CPA,* November 1968, p. 13; *Fortune, supra* note 2, p. 178.

thoritative panel to choose between conflicting accounting procedures. Leonard Spacek's 1958 recommendation for an accounting court was a suggestion in that direction.[45] It will be remembered that Spacek recommended that the AICPA establish a professional tribunal, which was not to be a court of law; hence its discussions would not affect the laws nor the administration of the laws by regulatory bodies. One reason why the proposal for an accounting court has languished is that the financial community has never been convinced of the wisdom of putting the supreme rule-making authority on accounting in the hands of three judges, however learned they might be. This skepticism regarding a professional accounting court seems equally applicable to our nation's civil courts.

An interesting parallel exists between formulation of accounting principles and the development of common law. It is desirable that law be equitable, yet it is also essential that particular principles of law be certain and the outcome of litigation involving them predictable. In some situations considerations of equity are inconsequential or competing considerations cancel each other. In such a case it is more important that *some* rule be adopted, rather than that any particular rule be adopted. For example, in contract law it is important that the act for accepting an offer be certain. It makes little difference whether that act be the mailing of a letter by the offeree, or its delivery to the offeror. Some research in accounting might usefully determine the sensitivity of the user to alternative methods of financial reporting. Where it is found that one method of accounting is not better than another, the APB should stipulate the rule in accordance with the principle of certainty discussed above. Eliminating the options available to management for choosing between accounting principles will facilitate intra-industry comparisons. It also will reduce the financial credibility gap that invites litigation under legal doctrines emerging from the cases under review.

The authors believe that by accepting responsibility for the principles underlying financial statements, CPAs will renew the stress on "public" in certified public accountant. The march of recent cases indicates that the courts believe independent accountants should accept a greater responsibility. The profession should respond to the challenge.

SUMMARY

Recent litigation has been characterized by a successful effort on the part of plaintiffs to reach accountants in heretofore untested situations. Occasionally where auditing standards and accounting principles were unclear, the Courts though stating that they adhere to generally accepted accounting principles have selected those which appear to them most reasonable. This expansion of

---

[45] Leonard Spacek, "The Need for an Accounting Court," *Accounting Review,* July 1958, p. 368.

the law and articulation of accounting principles when combined with requests for broader attestation makes it incumbent upon accountants to consider a positive approach to the new problems and opportunities facing the profession. The suggestions presented in this article constitute the thinking of the authors on how this might best be done.

APPENDIX A

BARCHRIS CONSTRUCTION CORP. (ESCOTT v. BARCHRIS CONSTRUCTION CORP.)[46]

Plaintiffs   Purchasers of 5½% convertible subordinated 15 year debentures.
Defendants   The defendants can be subdivided into three groups: (1) those who signed the registration statement, including officer-directors; the controller, not a director; outside directors, including the company attorney, and another who was a partner of the lead underwriter; (2) the underwriters, consisting of 8 investment banking firms led by Drexel & Co.; (3) BarChris' auditors, Peat, Marwick, Mitchell & Co.
Court   U.S. District Court, Southern District of New York (Manhattan). District Judge McLean. By agreement of the parties, Judge McLean, rather than a jury, decided the questions of fact.

Factual Summary

1 **Re: Certified financial statements as of December 31, 1960**   The Court concluded that earnings had been overstated by 14%, a figure not deemed material given that the securities involved were B rated convertible debentures and that the reported earnings per share on the underlying common would still have nearly doubled compared to the preceding year ($.33 to $.65).

The Court also concluded the current ratio was overstated 16%, a figure deemed material.

The Court gives little insight into why a 16% overstatement of working capital is material whereas a 14% overstatement of EPS is not.[47] Possibly it hinges on the intentional nature of the overstatement. An officer of BarChris persuaded a factor to temporarily release $147,000 of an unconsolidated subsidiaries' funds, —being held as security—to the subsidiary; $145,000 of this . . . money was then transferred to BarChris and was accounted for by a debit to Cash and credit to the non-current asset Investment in Non-Consolidated Subsidiary.

---

[46] 283 F. Supp. 643 (S.D.N.Y. 1968).
[47] A feature of the financial statements not discussed in the opinion tends to rationalize these conclusions. The effect of the balance sheet error was to exacerbate BarChris' violation of the 2:1 test of current ratio used by the financial community. In contrast, as the Court observed, earnings increased dramatically even without this overstatement. The authors conclude that it is worse to minimize violation of a financial standard than it is to overstate the dramatic amount by which a standard has been exceeded.

The overstatement of earnings was caused primarily by:
a   Overstatement of the percentage of completion on some contracts.
b   The recording of a loan to BarChris as a sale.
c   The recording of a sale-leaseback to a factor as a sale: a bowling alley sold to Talcott (a factor) who leased it to a consolidated subsidiary of BarChris was treated as a sale by BarChris in its consolidated statements.
d   The recording of a sale-leaseback to a customer as a sale: a subsidiary leased property to an operator but treated the transaction as a sale.

The overstatement of the current ratio was caused primarily by:
a   Overstatement of $145,000 transferred from an unconsolidated subsidiary. This cash was received by the subsidiary as a short-term loan from a finance factor. It was not disclosed that the subsidiary had to repay this money 25 days after acquiring it.
b   Reserve for bad debts was understated by $50,000.
c   Accounts receivable contained $150,000 due from a consolidated subsidiary.
d   All reserves held by a factor were treated as current despite the fact that some of them would in the normal course of events not be released qithin one year.
e   Regarding footnotes, contingent liabilities were understated by $375,795 and a direct liability of $325,000 should have been included in the recorded liabilities on the balance sheet.
Plaintiffs unsuccessfully questioned other items. These included:

a   The theoretical justification for the percentage of completion method of reporting sales.
b   The absence of a reserve for contingent liabilities.

2 Re: Unaudited income statement for first quarter 1961   Sales were overstated by the inclusion of two intercompany transactions.

3 Re: Unaudited backlog as of March 31, 1961   Backlog was overstated by $4,490,000 due to the inclusion of transactions for which BarChris had no enforceable contracts.

4 Re: Unaudited contingent liabilities as of April 30, 1961   Contingent liabilities were understated by $618,853, and a direct liability of $314,166 was omitted.

5 Re: Text of prospectus   Inaccuracies in the prospectus included the following:
a   It was incorrectly implied that there were no outstanding loans from officers (they amounted to $386,615).
b   It failed to indicate that substantial sums would be expended to pay prior debts incurred as a result of alley construction already undertaken.
c   It gave the incorrect impression that BarChris' problems with customers' credit and performance were minimal.
d   It failed to mention that BarChris was operating alleys as well as constructing them.

Legal Doctrines and Statutes Relied Upon by Plaintiffs   Section 11, Securities Act of 1933. A registration statement filed with the SEC allegedly contained material false statements and material omissions.

Status   The Court found that the registration statement contained false statements of material facts. It was decided that no defendant established his "due diligence" defense with regard to all the material errors although several established that defense with regard to some of them. The Court reserved decision on such defenses as causation, estoppel, waiver, release, and the statute of limitations. The Court also reserved judgment on the claims of defendants against other defendants; these included the underwriters' claims against Peat, Marwick based on its comfort letter. The case has since been settled.

CONTINENTAL VENDING MACHINE CORP. (UNITED STATES v. SIMON)[48]

Plaintiffs   United States through the U.S. Attorney's Office for the Southern Districts of New York.

Defendants   Carl Simon, a senior partner of Lybrand, Ross Bros. & Montgomery, partner in charge of the Continental Vending Machine Corp. audit; Robert Kaiser, partner; Melvin Fishman, audit manager.

Court   U.S. Court of Appeals for the Second Circuit. Circuit Judges Waterman, Friendly and Smith. Opinion by Circuit Judge Friendly.

Factual Summary   The appellate court upheld the criminal conviction of defendants for certifying to misleading financial statements of Continental at September 30, 1962. The case turned on the reporting of loans by Continental Vending to its affiliate, Valley Commercial Corp.

Harold Roth, president of Continental, dominated both Continental and Valley. He owned about 25 per cent of Continental which was listed on the American Exchange. He supervised day-to-day operations of Valley, which were conducted from an office on Continental's premises. Roth from 1958–62 borrowed large amounts of money from Continental for his personal stock market dealings, much of which he repaid by the end of each fiscal year. Instead of borrowing directly, he had Continental lend to Valley; Roth then borrowed from Valley.

At September 30, 1962, the receivable from Valley resulting from Roth's borrowing amounted to approximately $3.5 million; and during the 1962 audit Roth informed the auditors that Valley was unable to repay Continental since he was unable to repay Valley. Consequently Roth agreed to post adequate collateral. However 80 per cent of the collateral Roth produced consisted of holdings in Continental; moreover, the total had a value of only $2.9 million on February 15, 1963, the date of the opinion on the 1962 statements. Nevertheless, the auditors attested to a Continental footnote which stated, in effect, that the $3.5 million receivable from Valley, less the balance payable to Valley, was collateralized by marketable securities of an amount greater than the difference between the receivable and payable.

48 CCA Fed. Sec. L. Rep. ¶92,511 (2d Cir. Nov. 12, 1969), *cert. denied*, (March 30, 1970).

Actually, the reporting of the Valley receivable and its pledged security was complicated by the fact that Valley was used for transactions other than Roth's personal borrowings from Continental. From time to time, Continental secured financing by issuing negotiable notes to Valley which in turn discounted them at banks and transferred the discounted amounts to Continental. At September 30, 1962, these notes amounted to about $1.0 million. The $1.0 million notes payable to Valley could not be offset against the $3.5 million receivable from Valley since the holder of the notes payable (the bank) differed from the debtor on the accounts receivable (Valley and ultimately Roth). Nevertheless, the footnote to the September 30, 1962 statements indicated that the payable was deducted from the receivable in figuring the adequacy of the collateral.

The pertinent sections of the September 30, 1962 Continental balance sheet and related footnotes are as follows:

ASSETS
Current Assets:
. . . .
Accounts and notes receivable:
. . . .
Valley Commercial Corp., affiliate
(Note 2) $2,143,335
. . . .
Noncurrent accounts and notes receivable:
Valley Commercial Corp., affiliate
(Note 2)   1,400,000
. . . .

LIABILITIES
Current liabilities: ·
. . . .
Long-term debt, portion due within one year
                                                 8,203,788
. . . .
Long-term debt (Note 7)
. . . .
Valley Commercial Corp., affiliate (Note 2)
                                               486,130
. · . .

NOTES TO CONSOLIDATED FINANCIAL STATEMENTS

[2]The amount receivable from Valley Commercial Corp. (an affiliated company of which Mr. Harold Roth is an officer, director and stockholder) bears interest at 12 per cent a year. Such amount, less the balance of the notes payable to that company, is secured by the assignment to the Company of Valley's equity in certain marketable securities. As of February 16, 1963, the amount of such equity at current market quotations exceeded the net amount receivable.

[7]. . . . The amounts of long-term debt, including the portion due within one year, on which interest is payable currently or has been discounted in advance, are as follows:
. . . .
Valley Commercial Corp., affiliate $1,029,475

Legal doctrines and statutes relied upon by prosecution The indictment charged defendants with conspiring and adopting a scheme to violate federal criminal statutes prohibiting one or more of the following: (1) the filing of false statements with a governmental agency (18 U.S.C. Section 1001); (2) the use of the mails to perpetuate a fraud (18 U.S.C. Section 1341); and (3) the filing of false statements with the SEC (Section 32 of the Securities Exchange Act of 1934, 15 U.S.C. Section 78 ff.). The appellate court stated that the government's burden "was not to show that defendants were wicked men with designs on anyone's purse, which they obviously were not, but rather that they had certified a statement knowing it to be false."

Status The three accountants were found guilty by a jury in June 1968 after an earlier trial ended in a hung jury. Simon was fined $7,000. Kaiser and Fishman were fined $5,000 each. The Second Circuit upheld the conviction and the Supreme Court declined to review the case.

In related cases the defendants were Harold Roth, president of Continental; David Roth, his brother; and Clair Gans, his administrative assistant. Harold Roth entered a plea of "guilty," and was put on probation for three years after serving six months of an 18-month term. The case against David Roth and Gans had not gone to trial at December 1, 1969. In November 1967, Lybrand settled a civil suit against it for $1,960,936.

WESTEC CORP.
(CARPENTER v HALL)[49]

Plaintiff Trustee of Westec Corporation. The trustee either directly or indirectly represents the interest of (1) Westec Corp., (2) the Fraud Claimants Fund for Creditors Class Six as set forth in the Trustee's Amended Plan of Reorganization, (3) a class of people consisting in part of all persons who sustained a loss as a result of any purchase of or loan against Westec common stock between September 2, 1964 and August 5, 1966.

Defendants There are 93 defendants. These include: James W. Williams, formerly board chairman of Westec; E. M. Hall, Jr., formerly president of Westec; numerous business associates of Williams and Hall and the companies with which these associates were affiliated; the American Stock Exchange specialists handling Westec trading; a variety of brokerage houses and their employees; and Ernst & Ernst, together with Clarence T. Isensee and Newman T. Halvorson (partners), and John F. Maurer (Audit Manager).

Court U.S. District Court, Southern District of Texas (Houston).

Factual Summary The bulk of the 32-page complaint alleges that various defendants joined in or abetted an unlawful conspiracy to misuse the corporate funds of Westec and associated companies; and/or to victimize the company, its shareholders and the investing public through manipulating the company's

[49] Complaint, C. A. No. 68-H-738 (S.D. Tex., filed August 23, 1968).

stock. Several defendants are singled out for different or additional allegations. The complaint directed at Ernst & Ernst alleges:

1 The auditors made a superficial examination in 1964 which failed to detect (a) that the sale of a plant had not been completed ($90,000 profit), and (b) that the sale of a warehouse ($150,000 profit) made to a company controlled by one of the conspirators was fictitious.

2 The auditors' 1965 examination was inadequate in that it failed to discover (a) that the $1.3 million sale of a production payment by an acquired company was reported as 1965 income although the sale occurred prior to the nonpooling acquisition of the company; and (b) a fictitious sale of oil properties was superseded by a non-arm's-length sale of the properties at an inflated price.

3 The pooling of interest approach to the accounting for six acquisitions was improperly applied. The audit report was held open until March 26, 1965, the date when three of the six contested poolings were acquired, so that the prior year's earnings of such acquisitions could be included in the consolidated reports. The plaintiff alleges that earnings of six acquired companies for periods prior to acquisition should not be combined with the parent company. It is also claimed that five of the six acquisitions failed to meet established criteria for ooling.

4 Ernst & Ernst were so involved in the structuring of acquisitions that they lost their status as independent accountants.

5 The auditors deliberately concealed the material impact (23%) of the three pooling acquisitions upon the 1964 earnings. They should have disclosed that the five 1965 poolings produced net earnings of $5 million, whereas reported 1965 earnings were only $4.8 million for the company as a whole.

Legal doctrines and statutes relied upon by plaintiff   The accountants are charged with: (1) common law negligence for breaching contractual and fiduciary duties to Westec requiring professional care; and (2) engaging in fraudulent acts proscribed by the Securities Act of 1933 and the Securities Exchange Act of 1934.

Status   In pretrial stage at May 1, 1970.

YALE EXPRESS
(FISHER V KLETZ)[50]

Plaintiffs   Stockholders and debenture holders of Yale Express Systems, Inc. (Yale).

Defendants   Peat, Marwick, Mitchell & Co. (Peat), numerous officers and directors of Yale and underwriters for Yale debentures.

Court   U.S. District Court, Southern District of New York (Manhattan). Judge Tyler.

[50] 266 F. Supp. 180 (S.D.N.Y. 1967).

Factual Summary   Plaintiffs claim damages from errors and omissions in three sets of financial statements, namely: (1) the unaudited statements appearing in the prospectus for an August 20, 1963 debenture offering; (2) the audited statements for the year ending December 31, 1963; and (3) unaudited interim statements issued during 1964. These statements were distributed to the public and filed with the SEC and stock exchanges. The consolidated earnings for 1963, the interim earnings for 1964 and year-end assets, particularly receivables, appear to have been overstated.

In early 1964, Peat undertook several management service studies for Yale; thus Peat changed its relationship to Yale from that of "independent public accountant" with statutory duties under the 1934 Act to that of management consultant. In this new capacity Peat discovered that figures in the 1963 annual report were substantially false and misleading. The litigants differ on when this discovery was made; Peat contends discovery occurred after the report was filed while plaintiffs contend discovery occurred before the SEC and others received the annual report. Peat did not disclose its finding to the SEC or public until May 1965, when the results of its management studies were released.

Legal doctrines and statues relied upon by plaintiffs; procedural setting   . . . Peat moved to dismiss those parts of the complaint dealing with the 1963 annual report and the 1964 interim reports. This procedural setting required the Court to view the facts in the light most favorable to the plaintiffs and to deny the motion if there was any viable legal theory for sustaining the plaintiffs. Plaintiffs opposed the motion regarding the 1963 reports by arguing that the failure to disclose the inaccuracies as soon as discovered violated common law deceit doctrines,[51] Section 18(a) of the Securities Exchange Act of 1934 and Rule 10b-5[52] promulgated by the SEC pursuant to Section 10(b) of the Securities Exchange Act of 1934. With regard to the 1964 interim statements, plaintiffs argued that the failure to disclose the findings of its studies constituted a violation of Rule 10b-5. The motion to dismiss was denied.

Status   The case was in the pretrial stages as of May 1, 1970.

---

[51] The Restatement of Torts identifies the elements of deceit involving business transactions as follows:

Sec. 525—Liability for Fraudulent Misrepresentations. One who fraudulently makes a misrepresentation of fact, opinion, intention or law for the purpose of inducing another to act or refrain from acting in reliance thereon on a business transaction is liable to the other for the harm caused to him by his justifiable reliance upon the misrepresentation.

Sec. 526—Conditions Under Which Misrepresentation is Fradulent. A misrepresentation in a business transaction is fradulent if the maker (a) knows or believes the matter to be otherwise than as represented or (b) knows that he has not the confidence in its existence or nonexistence asserted by his statement of knowledge or belief or (c) knows that he has not the basis for his knowledge or belief professed by his assertion.

[52] Rule 10b-5 provides as follows: It shall be unlawful for any person, directly or indirectly, by the use of any means or instrumentality of interstate commerce, or of the mails, or of any facility of any national securities exchange, (a) to employ any device, scheme, or artifice to defraud, (b) to make any untrue statement of a material fact or to omit to state a material fact necessary in order to make the statements made, in the light of the circumstances under which they were made, not misleading, or (c) to engage in any act, practice, or course of business which operates or would operate as a fraud or deceit upon any person, in connection with the purchase or sale of any security.

We now briefly turn our attention to the circumstances that lead to a court appearance by an auditor and to the nature of the courtroom proceedings. The following fictional account of a liability case gives insight into the types of conditions that lead to suits against CPAs; it also reveals the nature of CPA testimony and the manner in which courtroom examination proceeds.

A CPA'S DAY IN COURT
Henry G. Burke and Robert W. Black, Jr.*

INTRODUCTION AND SUMMARY OF FACTS

The factual events [presented here] are purely fictional, and any similarities to real situations are unintended, however, the situation is vividly real. At this moment, there are millions of dollars in claims against certified public accountants awaiting a determination by court processes of the liabilities that accrue to the CPA in the exercise of his professional responsibilities. Never before have the CPA's functions been so publicly discussed and debated. The once hidden accountant now finds articles in financial journals, magazines and local newspapers almost daily. The subject matter has almost turned into a debate—for example: when the accountant assists in the installation of a computer system, has he lost his independence for the purposes of signing off on the annual financial statements; does the fear of losing big clients hinder the CPA in resolving differences in generally accepted accounting principles (which I might add are made very simple by the examples related in most newspaper articles); is the accountant responsible to the client or the financial community; do reporting requirements give enough information to potential investors; how are credit grantors using our statements; can a company go to another CPA who will not qualify his opinion in a borderline accounting problem; and other questions which I am sure all of you have read about. All of these things have made the CPA more visible to the public. Additionally, modern corporate structures and financial transactions have rapidly become more complex. The computer age has ushered in a fast moving, more sophisticated, highly competitive business environment and the CPA in his attest function must keep up with the pace. We are not referring only to large widely-owned corporate giants but to local and regional businesses. . . . Smaller companies are expanding, merging, and going to the money markets in order to stay competitive.

* From *The Maryland CPA*, June 1968, pp. 3–20. Reprinted by permission of the Maryland Society of Certified Public Accountants.

Our subject client, . . . , is just such an example—a company which is like ones which most [CPAs] have as clients. Let's you and I step into the world of make-believe (and yet so very real) and consider a very disturbing situation.

Our firm, located in Baltimore, has two partners and seven full-time professional staff personnel. We have audited the financial statements of our imaginary client, Boxco, for a number of years. It manufactures folding and corrugated boxes in four plants and markets these products throughout the East Coast of the United States. The Company is eighth, in terms of sales volume, in its industry for the marketing area. Its shares are traded on the over-the-counter exchange and there are approximately 800 stockholders.

A few important figures in the 1966 comparative financial statements are as follows: Sales were 15 million dollars, net income was 1 million two hundred thousand dollars; gross assets were 10 million dollars at December 31, 1966; its net assets at that date were 5 million dollars; the Company has five hundred thousand capital shares outstanding. Our report on Boxco's financial statements which was dated January 31, 1967, showed that the scope of our examination had not been restricted in any way. It presented an unqualified opinion as to the fairness of the presentation of the financial position and results of operations that they revealed.

Here are some events that led up to the case. Immediately following the issuance of our report on January 31, 1967, the Company reported its earnings to the press. At that time, its stock was being traded for about 12 dollars a share. Since the reported earnings for 1966 were 1 million two hundred thousand dollars as compared to eight hundred thousand dollars for 1965, security analysts in local brokerage houses were attracted to the stock and the shares were recommended widely. As a result, the market price of the shares increased rapidly and reached a level of 20 dollars within ten days. On Feb. 25, 1967, Boxco acquired the shares of XYZ Box Corporation for shares of its own stock. The financial statements for 1966 were included in the proxy material prepared in connection with this transaction. The number of shares issued in this merger, totaled 50,000 shares, were established by the market price of 18 dollars at the merger date. On March 3, 1967, it was discovered that net earnings for 1966 were not 1 million two hundred thousand dollars but, in fact, were only six hundred thousand dollars. These revised earnings represented a 25% decrease from those of the prior year. The reasons for the six hundred thousand dollar discrepancy in earnings will be explained later. Once the Board of Directors learned of the error, they informed the press, the local brokerage house handling their shares, and the Security and Exchange Commission. The stock was unable to open for trading in the morning of March 4, because of a rash of sell orders. When it did open later in the day, the price was 10 dollars, 12 dollars lower than it was on March 2. In the next week, the price dropped to 8 dollars, and unfavorable publicity had driven the price to a level of 5 dollars in May, 1967. A group of shareholders of the company, who purchased shares between January 31 and March 3, 1967, have brought suit against us claiming two million dollars damages.

These shareholders purport to sue on behalf of all persons who purchased shares during this period. Shares traded during the period aggregated 50,000 shares. The shareholders alleged that we did not conduct an examination in accordance with generally accepted audited standards and did not perform such tests of the accounting records as were necessary. Further, they contend that the statements did not fairly present the financial position and results of operations as our report indicated, that our report was false, and that we know or should have known that it was false. Damages were claimed for the difference between the price paid for the stock during the period and the current price of 5 dollars which, with the 50,000 shares traded, totals approximately seven hundred fifty thousand dollars. They also claim, punitive damages of $1,250,000. The second suit was brought by the former shareholders of the XYZ Box Corporation against Boxco and our firm. This suit alleges the XYZ Box shareholders relied on the financial statement of Boxco, and on our report in agreeing to merge with Boxco. It is contended that the statements were false, that we and our client know or should have known that they were false. The suit was brought to rescind the transaction, or in the alternate, to collect about $650,000, representing the amount the shares were overpriced. Each of these actions has been reported to the Wall Street Journal and local newspapers. This wide reporting has created much unfavorable publicity for our firm.

Now let's discuss the details of the misstatements of the financial statements. In May, 1966, an unfavorable sales trend of Boxco became apparent to the officers of the company. They considered the trend to be temporary, and as a group, decided to charge certain repairable materials and indirect manufacturing supplies to the inventory account. The officers expected to correct this mischarge as soon as the downward trend changed. By Sept. 15, 1966, when the initial meeting to plan our examination took place, the improper charges had grown to $1,000,000. The expected upward trend of earnings had not developed and consequently, the officers were in somewhat of a bind. To forestall the discovery of the improperly charged expenses to the physical inventory, the officers conceived a plan to process fictitious sales aggregating $1,200,000 in the months of Oct., Nov. and Dec. The fictitious inventory was removed to the cost of sales as the cost of the fictitious sales. These transactions had the effect of moving fictitious inventory to fictitious receivables. The officers felt quite secure in the transfer of the inventory shortage because accounts receivable were normally confirmed at October 31. They knew that our remaining procedures for auditing receivables did not concern detail accounts except for the examination of collectability. The net result of the improprieties, as I've described them, was an overstatement of accounts receivable and sales of $1,200,000, less the tax effect of $600,000 or a net effect of a like amount or $600,000.

Now a few words about how the audit was planned and organized. Joe Senior, who was an assistant on the job in 1965, was selected in early September to manage the 1966 audit. In a brief discussion with Harry Jones, the partner on this engagement, it was suggested that Joe visit the controller to plan the audit. No representatives of our firm had visited Boxco since the previous March. Joe made his visit on Sept. 15, 1966. An understanding of the important matters discussed and arranged in this visit will be helpful for you to understand the case. At the request of the controller, Joe agreed to use client employees wherever possible to cut down on schedule preparation and clerical effort. The controller related that Boxco's business was good and the heavy sales were expected in the final quarter. This was contra to the trend of the industry and was explained as the result of an effective sales effort. The importance of the message will become apparent as the case develops. The controller requested delivery of our report on January 31 to permit early publicizing of the expected increased earnings. Previous report deliveries were about February 15 of each year. The controller explained the good earnings should favorably affect the market price of the company stock. This, in turn, would work to the company's advantage in the pending merger transactions. Joe struggled against short timing of the final audit, but he acquiesced. The controller suggested that inventories be taken at December 31 rather than November 30 as in the past in order to reduce analysis by the auditors of the transactions subsequent to the physical inventory. Joe was reluctant to accept this change but he was persuaded. The controller suggested that accounts receivable confirmations be done at October 31 to relieve timing difficulties at year end. Joe agreed to the earlier confirmation date on the basis that internal control was adequate. Joe informed the controller that interim work could be started in October and he explained what he planned to accomplish in this period.

In mid-October, Joe Senior and his audit crew began their interim work. Joe had two assistants, one who had been out of college for a year and a half. He had majored in accounting, had sat for the CPA exam in May, 1966 and passed two parts. The second assistant was in his third year of accounting at a local business school in a night program, and had been with our firm since June, 1966, only four months. Joe, who is a CPA, had worked on the Boxco job during 1965 as the number one assistant to the senior, who has since left the firm.

The following are some of the procedures that were performed at that time. The monthly statements through September were compared; the tests of transactions in the period January through October were performed; the accounts receivables were confirmed as of October 31 and physical inventory was observed December 31, as I previously mentioned. The final work was done in the period of January 6 to January 31, 1967. The procedures in this period included the following: The monthly statements for October and November were entered on analysis of monthly statements by the assistants. Very little was done with them, other than entering them on the schedule. Inquiries, regarding changes in procedures in October, November and December were disregarded in lieu of tests of transactions in these last three months. The collectability of receivables was established in the ordinary fashion and all our receivables work followed the normal pattern. We checked cash receipts into the accounts and looked for unusual items through analysis of the control accounts and other normal steps. Inventory work was also very normal; we extended pricing, extensions, market values and traced quantities into the physical inventory. That gives you some picture of when the work was done on the job. Harry Jones, our partner, was not able to devote as much time to the audit in 1966 as he normally did because of the tighter time schedule for the report, and two new client prospects had requested proposals which had to be submitted in January.

We now turn our attention to the examination of Joe Senior. The actions brought by the new purchasers of Boxco shares and by former shareholders of XYZ Box Corporation against our firm were consolidated for trial. As was previously mentioned, the issue was whether the statements of our firm, in its reports on the financial statements of Boxco, were false. The attorney for the plaintiff requested that Joe Senior be called to testify. Our working papers and the financial statements have been entered as evidence in the case and they have been thoroughly studied by the plaintiff's attorney who intends to prove that a proper audit has not been conducted. The date of this examination is May 15, 1967. . . .

. . . it is not our intention to arrive at any conclusion. We are interested in presenting dramatically the cross-examination of a witness who has performed an audit, presumably in a conscientious manner, but is being charged with issuing a false statement. We shall not attempt to create the precise atmosphere of the court but rather to give an impression of the scope of questioning to which the accountant will be subjected. Although the lawyer representing the plaintiff is not likely to be an accountant, he may very well have an accountant at his side and might even use accountants as expert witnesses in order to prove that the work was not performed in an acceptable professional manner. Furthermore, suing an accountant for negligence is to the lawyer no different from suing a doctor or an engineer for failure to perform his assignment in a thoroughly competent manner. Just as the lawyer suing a doctor for malpractice may have to immerse himself in medical terms and medical theory, he will also (in representing his client against an accountant) strive to obtain a working knowledge of what goes into the making of a satisfactory audit. His attack on the accountant will be a carefully studied analysis of everything that was done in connection with the audit. In a sense, not only the defendant but the entire accounting profession is then on trial. While it may be true that, in most instances, statements issued would be fair and reliable and that fraud and material mistakes are comparatively rare, the principles of auditing must be sufficiently rigorous to uncover fraud, whether superficial or latent. It is these principles which also are on trial when the accountant attempts to prove by his evidence that the methods he used were reliable, but that the error, mistake or falsity which occurred in the statements was one that could not be disclosed by the general principles and procedures available to the auditor.

EXAMINATION OF JOE SENIOR

Ques: What is your position for the work you are doing?
Ans: I am a staff accountant for the firm of Smith & Jones, in Balto.

Ques: How long have you been employed by Smith & Jones?
Ans: I have been with them approximately five (5) years.

Ques: Were you the accountant charged with the audit of Boxco?
Ans: Yes, I was.

Ques: Had you ever previously been in charge of the audit at Boxco?
Ans: No sir.

Ques: Who had previously been in charge of the audit at Boxco?
Ans: Well, the previous accountant sir, who was in charge of this job has left the firm.

Ques: And you took charge of the job?
Ans: Yes sir, that's correct.

Ques: Have you ever been in charge of any other audit?
Ans: Yes sir.

Ques: How often have you been in charge of audits?
Ans: Well, I wouldn't want to estimate sir, I would say frequently.

Ques: But you couldn't be any more specific than that, could you?
Ans: Frankly sir, I was in charge of most of the audits that I do.

Ques: That's true, but how many audits do you do?
Ans: I would say twelve to fifteen in the course of the year.

Ques: And approximately how much of your time does that consume?
Ans: Well, I feel it consumes all of my time throughout the course of the year.

Ques: I see, then in all cases in which you are engaged in the audit you are in charge.
Ans: At the time, yes sir.

Ques: How long has that been true?
Ans: On a full time basis, I would say approximately one year.

Ques: Now, was any member of the firm in any way acting with you in the audit of Boxco?
Ans: Yes sir, Mr. Harry Jones is the partner in charge of the job and I was assisted by two assistants.

Ques: And, how much time did you spend on the Boxco job?
Ans: Well, I was there principally all the time since we started the engagement until the time we released the financial statements.

Ques: Can you tell us from your time sheet, how much time you spent on the job?
Ans: I don't know off hand sir, but I think it worked out to about two hundred (200) hours, three hundred (300) hours.

Ques: And about how much time did Harry Jones, the partner, spend on the job?
Ans: I wouldn't have that information available sir, I do not recall.

Ques: Any time that he spent on the job, was that spent with you?
Ans: Principally, yes.

Ques: Then shouldn't you at least have some idea of how much time Harry Jones spent on the job?
Ans: Well sir, he visited me twice in the client's office and he had conferences with me three or four times in our own offices, and in addition, he reviewed the statements and the audit program.

Ques: But you had no idea of how much he spent?
Ans: No sir, nothing specific.

Ques: Nothing specific. Now, you do say that you had two (2) assistants on this job with you?
Ans: Yes sir, that's true.

Ques: And will you tell us who those two (2) assistants were?
Ans: Yes sir, one was Joe Dokes, he is semi-senior with the firm, and the other is Dan Smith, who is a junior.

Ques: Will you tell us about Joe Dokes?
Ans: Well, sir, he has had a year and a half experience, he's taken the CPA Exam and passed two parts, which is a pretty good showing and he has been with our firm for a year and a half.

Ques: Why do you say passing two parts is a pretty good showing?

Ans: Well, the percentage of the people who pass the exam is pretty low sir.

Ques: Could you tell us how low that percentage is?

Ans: Well, I would say approximately 13%.

Ques: And do you think that is due to the unreasonableness of the examiners?

Ans: Well sir, I'm not in position to say.

Ques: And the other assistant that you have, Mr. Smith, what were his qualifications?

Ans: Well, he is an accountant who has not completed his accounting education. He has been with the firm for six months and is currently attending night school.

Ques: I would like to go, Mr. Senior, to part of your audit and your report of Boxco. Your balance sheets show accounts receivable of how much as of Dec. 31?

Ans: $5,000,000 approximately.

Ques: Approximately $5,000,000 on December 31.

Ans: Yes, sir.

Ques: How much of the accounts receivable were fictitious?

Ans: Approximately $1,200,000.

Ques: When did you first discover that they were fictitious?

Ans: This was discovered in March.

Ques: At the time you issued the statement, did you believe that they were sound?

Ans: Yes, sir.

Ques: Valid accounts receivable?

Ans: Yes sir, very definitely.

Ques: Now, what steps did you take in order to verify that they were sound valid accounts receivable?

Ans: Well, we confirmed the accounts receivable and we did other test work.

Ques: As of what date did you confirm those accounts receivable?

Ans: October 31.

Ques: And you confirm them as of October 31 although your audit professed to issue a statement as of December 31, is that correct?

Ans: That is correct.

Ques: And why did you feel that it was reasonable to confirm as of October 31 when you were issuing a statement as of Dec. 31.

Ans: Well, there are several factors, we had always used October 31 in the past and it had always proved adequate, we examined the system of internal control and it appeared adequate under the circumstances, and we also had a time schedule which was quite pressing and we did not feel that the time schedule would permit us to confirm at the end of December.

Ques: Do you believe that the demands of your time schedule justifies the inclusion of $1,200,000 of fictitious accounts receivable?

Ans: No sir, we did not include the receivables, they were already included.

Ques: But you issued a statement saying that they were being fairly presented.

Ans: Sir, under the circumstances at the time we thought that that was true.

Ques: Under what circumstances do you think it might not be true to issue a statement showing $1,200,000 fictitious accounts receivable?

Ans: Well sir, I would say that it was never true but it appeared to be at the time.

Ques: Do you believe at the time of your statement, it was true and part of your judgment was based on your examination of internal check as you call it, right?

Ans: That is correct.

Ques: Can you tell us what your examination of internal check covered?

Ans: We complied with the generally accepted principles.

Ques: Can you tell us a little bit about those principles?

Ans: Well, we issued internal control questionnaires to the treasurer prior to our engagement and we made test inquiries during the time to see these procedures were being carried out.

Ques: And what was the nature of those tests that you made?

Ans: Well, we made tests on the book of entry, as I stated previously, confirmed the accounts receivable as of October 31. We made inquiries of the employees.

Ques: The confirmation as of October 31 would in itself have nothing to do with the internal check, internal audit?

Ans: True, it would not.

Ques: Now, would you tell us how it was possible then, in view of your judgment, that the internal check was adequate, and that you accepted $1,-200,000 in ficititious accounts receivable.

Ans: Well, there is a general segregation of duties, the sales were generally put through by the sales department, approved through the credit manager and recorded by a clerk in the sales journal. They would usually check for shipping documents and verified each shipment.

Ques: Do these fictitious accounts receivable conform in every respect to the procedures that you had inquired about?

Ans: No sir, they were put through by the president, bearing his approval.

Ques: And that was not part of the procedure that your examination of internal checking revealed, was it?

Ans: No sir.

Ques: Where are the people that should have passed on these accounts receivable as they found their way to the accounts receivables of Boxco?

Ans: Well, generally the credit manager would approve the credit; however, he was informed beforehand by the president, that he had initiated the sales and checked the credit out, and everything was OK and that he'd put them through. The clerk saw the president's signature on the sales orders and did not question approval.

Ques: Would you consider this a satisfactory working of the system of internal check?

Ans: No sir.

Ques: You mentioned the credit manager, you've mentioned the bookkeeper, you've mentioned the President, did anybody else have anything to do with the accounts receivable?

Ans: The accounts receivables were generally aged and presented to the credit manager for monthly review and sending out notices.

Ques: And who presented those accounts receivable to the credit manager?

Ans: The clerk prepared the accounts receivable register.

Ques: Did you discuss the accounts receivable schedule with the credit manager?

Ans: Yes sir, we did.

Ques: Who did?

Ans: My assistant.

Ques: And what did your assistant learn from the credit manager about the accounts receivable?

Ans: The credit manager had informed him that the accounts represented potentially an increased volume of sales from these new customers and that they had no reason to believe that they would not be readily collectible.

Ques: How were these $1,200,000 worth of accounts receivable distributed among the sales of Boxco?

Ans: Could you be more specific?

Ques: Yes, tell me in which month these fictitious entries were made.

Ans: Well, in October there was approximately $200,000; in November there was approximately $400,000; in December approximately $600,000 worth of receivables put on the books.

Ques: And the entire $1,200,000 of accounts receivable appeared among the accounts receivable on December 31, is that correct?

Ans: That is correct.

Ques: And you stated that the accounts receivable outstanding were about $5,000,000.

Ans: That is correct, sir.

Ques: So that almost 25% of the accounts receivable, fictitious in character, were on the books and were not discovered by you or by your assistant as fictitious.

Ans: That is correct, sir.

Ques: Were any of these accounts receivable collected or purported to be collected during this period?

Ans: No sir.

Ques: Now $200,000 of the sales were put through in October.

Ans: Yes sir.

Ques: Therefore, when you sent out your confirmations on October 31 did you or did you not attempt to confirm any of these fictitious $200,000 of accounts receivables?

Ans: Yes sir, we included approximately 50% of the dollar amount and 50% of the accounts and it turned out that one of the customers involved was solicited by our correspondence and that customer did reply.

Ques: And what was the nature of that reply?

Ans: They positively confirmed the liability at the time, that they owed Boxco the $100,000.

Ques: And who verified those confirmations when the reply came in?

Ans: My semi-senior, sir.

Ques: Was there anything about that confirmation that might have created any suspicion in his mind?

Ans: It turned out later the confirmation was mailed to a New York Post Office Box and it did carry a Baltimore address on its return and a Baltimore Postage stamp.

Ques: But nobody felt that was worth pursuing further?

Ans: Apparently not, I don't think anybody noticed it.

Ques: Approximately how many invoices went into this $1,200,000 of accounts receivable?

Ans: There were approximately 400 invoices.

Ques: Out of the total of how many invoices during the month of October, November and December?

Ans: I would say approximately 3 times that amount, sir.

Ques: 3 times, so that in the light of what you consider to be the system of satisfactory internal check, $\frac{1}{3}$ of the sales invoices that were put through during this 3 month period were fictitious.

Ans: Yes sir, we felt at the time that the control was adequate.

Ques: Do you still think so?

Ans: Under the circumstances that existed at the time, yes sir.

Ques: Do you think its possible that the control was adequate but that the difficulty was with the people who were doing the work?

Ans: No sir.

Ques: Do you consider them all right?

Ans: Well, yes sir, they are all qualified men.

Ques: I'm talking now about the President, credit manager and bookkeeper . . .

Ans: Well sir, we did make inquiries of the credit manager and the book-keeper who did not inform us of anything unusual occurring during the period of time of the examination.

Ques: Would you consider them reliable people?

Ans: The treasurer and the bookkeeper certainly sir, yes.

Ques: How about the credit manager?

Ans: The credit manager, yes sir, we've always relied on his opinion in the past, he has had a good record of collections.

Ques: And yet he permitted sales to be put through which did not bear his approval and the bookkeeper entered those sales.

Ans: Yes sir, the president came around and cleared it with him and told him that he had prepared a credit check.

Ques: I'd like to pass on to another part of your examination, the verification of the inventory. Did Boxco maintain what is known as a perpetual inventory system?

Ans: Yes sir.

Ques: And did you reconcile the date in the perpetual inventory system with the physical inventory which you supervised as of Dec. 31?

Ans: Yes sir, we observed the inventory as of December 31 and we made the usual checks on it, and it was not uniquely outlined with what they had in the books, there were only minor adjustments.

Ques: Did your examination of internal checks also include the methods for maintaining the perpetual inventory record?

Ans: Well sir, the inventory is maintained in a stock room under a segregated area and is locked up and under the hands of the storekeeper. We did some heavy test work in the month of June and the items that appear in the voucher register were being inventoried, and everything appeared in order at that time. We also did some test work in later months but we did not encounter any irregularities.

Ques: Do you know any irregularities that entered into those inventory records?

Ans: Yes sir, we found later that the company had charged $1,000,000 of repair materials and other items into the inventory in the months up to October.

Ques: And who were the members of the staff of the client at Boxco who made these entries?

Ans: Well sir, the person who handles the inventory papers would make the entries and usually these entries are supported in the usual manner with receiving tickets and he would record them in the books of original entry.

Ques: Now I would like to ask you this question. You've testified that $1,200,-

000 of the sales put through this year were fictitious out of the total of $15,000,000 sales, is that correct?

Ans: Yes sir.

Ques: Now what about the profit that was made on sales for this year for which you made your report which we are now considering. Did the profit on the merchandise sold look fair and reasonable to you?

Ans: Yes sir, it did.

Ques: And why do you say it looks reasonable and fair?

Ans: It was in the line of prior years.

Ques: Did it vary from prior years at all?

Ans: Well, the gross profit varied slightly.

Ques: What do you call varied slightly?

Ans: Well, prior year's gross profit was about 30% and this year was 27%.

Ques: Well, that's a variation of about 10% in my judgment, is that correct?

Ans: Yes sir, you could say that.

Ques: Well, would you say anything else?

Ans: No sir.

Ques: Do you think that might have alerted you to the existence of an over-statement of sales, consequently an over-statement of profit?

Ans: Well, as a matter of fact, we did question that and we were told that the decrease in gross profit percentage was because the customer was taking on some additional sales that were of high material content and therefore had a low gross profit percentage.

Ques: Who told you that?

Ans: The controller of the company.

Ques: Did you attempt to verify that statement?

Ans: Well, it was brought out by the increase of purchases.

Ques: But, isn't it also true that some of this increase in purchases arose out of charging items to merchandise or inventory which shouldn't have been charged in the first place?

Ans: Yes sir, I'm afraid that's correct.

Ques: Do you think that if this difference between your gross profit in the prior year and your profit in the current year had been pursued that you might have discovered that you were dealing with fictitious sales as well as fictitious charges in the inventory?

Ans: Well, sir, as I said before, we questioned it and the explanation seemed adequate in my judgment at the time. It was borne out by the increase in purchases.

Ques: And part of your examination of the internal check of sales included an analysis of the flow of information into the accounts receivable, is that right?

Ans: Yes sir.

Ques: And yet, at least three (3) people had something to do with that flow which resulted in the over-statement of $1,200,000 in sales?

Ans: Yes sir, that's correct.

Ques: And yet you feel that this is a reasonable and fair evaluation of the adequacy of the internal check of Boxco?

Ans: Yes sir, we complied with all the standards, we made inquiries, the employee didn't call it to our attention, and we did test work as I pointed out previously.

Ques: Well, with the standards you were complying with or trying to comply with, would a more vigorous, a more aggressive examination have disclosed some of these discrepancies?

Ans: I don't think so sir, no.

Ques: To what extent did you actually verify this flow of information through the sales to the accounts receivable?

Ans: Well, sir, in connection with our inventory testing we checked the sales for the last five days and we checked back on the shipping documents to make sure that the goods actually had been shipped.

Ques: What had you done the year before?

Ans: Substantially the same work sir, except we took the inventory at an earlier date and we checked some of the flow back from November to December. November was the date we took the inventory last year.

Ques: Was is possible for the client, therefore, to anticipate that you had only checked the last five or six days?

Ans: It was possible sir, but at the same time our work had run on a test basis and the client does not decide how much we will test.

Ques: But yet, your test was inadequate because the client was able to get fictitious sales in before the period of your test, is that correct?

Ans: Well, we considered our test adequate under the circumstances sir, as I said before we did do test work in June.

Ques: Do you think the testing of five days' work out of the total of perhaps 300 business days or so, $\frac{1}{60}$ of the volume is an adequate and satisfactory test?

Ans: Yes, but you have to understand also that we were relying on the system of internal control that was employed at the time.

Ques: And you were also relying on the people who were operating that system of internal control, is that true?

Ans: Yes sir, that is correct.

Ques: And at least three (3) of the people whom you have identified have proved to be unworthy of that reliance, is that also true?

Ans: Well sir, yes, that's the way it turned out.

Ques: In addition to Mr. Joe Dokes, who passed as you say, two subjects of which you think is a rather creditable record, you also have a Mr. Smith, who had not yet completed his accounting work. Will you tell us the kind of work he was doing?

Ans: Well, primarily sir, he just added the books of original entry . . .

Ques: And you didn't ask him to do more than that?

Ans: Well, he did do some additional work, a very minimum amount. He prepared some schedules for us.

Ques: What sort of schedules did he prepare?

Ans: He prepared schedules for the comparison of prior years and prior months, financial statements that the client prepared himself.

Ques: Which prior month did you prepare?

Ans: Through September.

Ques: Through September, and then you also had the statement for December?

Ans: Yes sir, these were just schedules, they were schedules of the client's statements prepared for comparative purposes.

Ques: What terms does Boxco sell on? When does it expect to collect these accounts receivable?

Ans: Generally sixty (60) days.

Ques: And what is the average life of their accounts receivable?

Ans: Between sixty (60) and one hundred twenty (120) days, sir.

Ques: And therefore, for them to have $5,000,000 outstanding at the end of the year, of which $1,200,000 was fictitious, you would consider perfectly normal and proper.

Ans: Well sir, in view of the circumstances, the sales were quite high in the last three (3) months.

Ques: Was there any reason for the sales being so high in the last three months?

Ans: Well, the client sells to a lot of local stores, sir, and they do quite a lot of business around the end of the year, around December 25.

Ques: How much business could they do around December 25?

Ans: The retail store, sir?

Ques: No, the client.

Ans: Well sir, their build-up is just before that time. It's generally in November and perhaps the early part of December.

Ques: Isn't it true that the Xmas season begins early in November and all that the client has around Xmas time are returns?

Ans: Yes sir, I do think that is true, partly true.

Ques: Can you tell me to what extent it may be true or for which it may be false?

Ans: No sir, I didn't audit any Department stores.

Ques: I'm talking about the client.

Ans: I'm sorry sir, but could you word that question again?

Ques: No, we're talking about the client. You said that the client had a great many of department store customers who would be buying around December 25 and I was just wondering what they would be buying around December 25.

Ans: Their sales will be around December 25, they will be buying in November and December and the early part of December.

Ques: Early part of December? When did these fictitious sales stop?

Ans: December 20th.

Ques: December 20th, O.K. I think we'll also stop at this point Thank you.

THE AUDIT PROCESS

CHAPTER 5

AUDIT PROGRAM DESIGN

Audit firms develop programs for virtually all engagements, and the substance of audit programs is the subject of much professional discussion. Understanding the difficulties and problems of audit program design can be fully appreciated only when a program is undertaken. The following programming problem was presented to CPA candidates in 1955, but its comprehensive dimensions have not been challenged before or since.

BLACK BISCUIT COMPANY

Your firm has been reappointed to audit the accounts of the Black Biscuit Company for the year ended December 31, 19X5. You have been asked to design an audit program for each of several major portions of the audit. In programming the audit, assume you will do as much interim work as seems to be feasible.

Give your comments on the existing internal control and state procedures which you would apply in (1) your *interim* examination and (2) your *year-end* examination of each of the following:

a Accounts receivable and allowance for uncollectable accounts

b Inventories

c Current liabilities

d Sales

e Payrolls

f Manufacturing costs

The capital stock of the Black Biscuit Co. is owned by two brothers, one of whom is president (in charge of sales and finance) and the other vice president (in charge of production). Their wives and the secretary-treasurer each hold a qualifying share and act as directors.

This company owns a plant in a densely populated area and markets all of its biscuits within an area of 400 square miles, through fifteen salesmen who call on grocery, confectionery and chain stores. Apart from miscellaneous income, all of its revenue is derived from the sale of biscuits.

The following statements indicate the relationship of costs and revenue in this company.

CONDENSED COMPARATIVE STATEMENTS

Cost of Goods Sold

	December 31 19X4	December 31 19X5
Raw materials	$1,802,500 (50%)	$1,871,595 (49¾%)
Packing materials	450,625 (12½%)	432,630 (11½%)
Direct labor	432,600 (12%)	451,440 (12%)
Overhead	180,250 (5%)	178,695 (4¾%)
	$2,865,975 (79½%)	$2,934,360 (78%)

Operating

Sales	$3,605,000 (100%)	$3,762,000 (100%)
Cost of goods sold	2,865,975 (79¾%)	2,934,360 (78%)
Gross profit	739,025 (20½%)	827,640 (22%)
Selling expenses	290,200	299,300
General and administrative	184,300	186,500
Financial	58,000	65,000
Net operating profit	$ 206,525 (5.7%)	$ 276,840 (7.3%)

Comparative figures taken from the books are as follows:

Account No.	Assets	January 1 19X5	December 31 19X5
A-1	Cashier's office—cash	$ 3,540	$ 4,212
A-10	General bank account	215,403	249,321
A-15	Payroll bank account	7,328	10,209
A-16	Salary bank account	4,126	3,843

Accounts receivable

A-20	Salesmen's ledgers	308,114	341,225
A-30	House accounts	36,002	45,211
A-40	Doubtful accounts	7,554	8,632
A-41	Advances to salesmen	2,500	3,000

Inventories

A-50	Raw materials	348,201	375,312

Account No.	Assets	January 1 19X5	December 31 19X5
A-53	Packaging material	189,100	202,451
A-52	Finished goods	72,803	67,210
	Property accounts		
A-60	Land	30,000	30,000
A-61	Factory and office equipment	278,123	278,123
A-62	Machinery and equipment	566,921	623,212
A-63	Office furniture and equipment	60,410	65,420
A-62a	Machinery and equipment		
	(fully depreciated)	63,418	50,312
A-64	Trucks	15,401	17,112
	Prepaid expenses and deferred charges		
A-70/74	Insurance, taxes, stationery, advertising, tools and maintenance supplies	38,150	40,554
		$2,247,094	$2,415,359
	Liabilities		
P-1	Accounts payable	$ 241,310	$ 208,420
P-2	Taxes payable	5,978	6,210
P-3	Commissions payable	16,220	18,450
P-5	Accrued wages payable	9,120	7,667
P-7	Bonus payable	32,000	38,500
P-10	Miscellaneous	1,519	2,142
P-20	Dividends payable — preferred shares	12,500	12,500
P-21	Dividends payable — common shares	15,000	15,000
P-25	Provision for Federal and state income taxes	96,842	138,216
P-40	Allowance for loss on accounts	7,554	8,632
P-41	Allowance for cash discounts	5,450	6,212
P-45	Allowance for possible inventory losses	10,000	15,000
P-61	Factory and office building depreciation	80,852	86,414
P-62	Machinery and equipment depreciation	169,776	250,196
P-62a	Machinery and equipment (fully depreciated)	63,481	50,312
P-63	Office furniture and equipment depreciation	19,095	24,301

P-64	Trucks—depreciation	10,551	4,223
P-90	5% preferred stock	500,000	500,000
P-91	No par value common stock	500,000	500,000
P-93	Retained earnings	449,909	522,964
		$2,247,094	$2,415,359

The major policies of the company are summarized as follows:

Sales and Revenues

1 The company operates under the Federal Pure Food and Drug Act and packages are labeled as to contents and weight.

2 Out-of-town sales are f.o.b. shipping point. Local deliveries are made by two trucks which the company owns.

3 Terms are 2% ten days or net thirty days. There are no trade discounts but a yearly rebate based on dollar volume is credited to customers' accounts.

4 Sales are billed to customers on the date of bill of lading, or delivery receipt for local customers.

5 Comparative monthly sales statistics as to quantity and value are kept for each type of biscuit and each size of packaging, and by salesman. Comparative monthly dollar volume statistics are maintained for each customer.

6 Salesmen supply their own cars and are paid on a 5% commission basis, plus car and traveling expenses. They are given advances against expenses for out-of-town traveling.

7 Freshness of product is a major sales policy. All stocks of biscuits over seven days old are sold to institutions (hospitals, etc.) at a 10% or greater discount. These are house accounts handled by the president and no salesman's commission is paid.

Production

Production is planned on Friday morning for the following week. The plant superintendent has prepared recipes, batches, instructions to production departments, and requisitions to raw material and packaging stores. This information is in the hands of interested parties by 4:00 P.M. on Friday.

Raw material stores deliver materials to production departments one-half hour before production starts each morning.

Production departments deliver biscuits to finished goods stores at the end of each morning and afternoon.

Production and stores reports of transactions are prepared in triplicate each day. The original goes to the cost department, the second copy to the vice president and the third copy to the plant superintendent.

Raw materials and packaging stores operate on *maximum/minimum* quantities. Requisitions are sent to the vice president for approval and are then turned over to the purchasing department.

Internal Control and Accounting Procedures

The company maintains the following principal accounting records:

1 General ledger

2 Journal voucher register (all journal entries are approved by the secretary-treasurer)

3 Cash receipts and disbursements records

4 Payroll records

5 Accounts receivable subsidiary ledgers

6 Accounts payable subsidiary ledger

7 Cost accounting records

8 Perpetual inventory records

There is no internal auditor. Original data are used for the recording of transactions wherever possible.

All prenumbered forms must be accounted for. If spoiled they are stamped *cancelled.* All multiple forms are printed *original, first copy,* etc.

Sales Orders (Prenumbered)

Sales orders are prepared in quadruplicate by salesmen, showing shipping and billing instructions. Quantities are shown under *ordered* section, opposite printed list of biscuits and packagings. Unit prices are also marked by salesmen. Three copies are mailed to the company.

The president reviews the orders and checks with the collection department concerning questionable credit risks, or asks the secretary-treasurer for a credit rating on new accounts. He approves the orders and turns them over to the order department to verify unit prices. The order department retains one copy and turns two over to the finished goods stores shipping department.

Goods are prepared for shipment and the quantities are entered under the *shipped* section of the order, one copy of which is included with the merchandise as a shipping memo. The other copy is entered on a daily summary sheet which forms the basis for deductions from the stock cards in the stores department (and later in the cost department) and is then returned to the order department.

The order department prepares back-order forms in quadruplicate, if necessary. One copy is sent to the salesman.

A comptometer operator extends and adds the completed orders, which are turned over to the billing machine operator.

Telephone orders are handled in the same manner, with a copy mailed to the salesman.

Contacts with institutions are handled by the president. He, or his secretary, calls the institutions and advises them of items that are available and agrees on a price, if there is an excessive supply which the president believes will have to be reduced more than 10% in price. The president has these orders written up in triplicate and at the same time prepares the invoice. He retains one copy of the order, sending two to the finished goods stores shipping department.

Invoices

Regular invoices are prepared in quadruplicate on prenumbered invoice forms by a billing machine operator, whose automatic calculations must agree with the comptometer operator's figures. Three copies are returned to the comptometer operator and the remaining copy is filed in a tray under customer's name (one tray for each salesman). These trays are the accounts receivable ledgers. The operator keeps control sheets for each tray on which she lists (in total) debits and credits each day. Each tray contains about one hundred active accounts. Trays are locked when the operator is not there and nothing can be extracted from a tray without her making a record on her control.

A copy of invoices to institutions that are prepared in the president's office is filed in a separate accounts receivable tray by the operator.

The comptometer operator compares regular invoices with orders for typographical errors, sends the original to the mailing department and one copy to the statistical department. The third copy is added, the total for the day entered in a sales summary which forms the basis of the posting to the general ledger, and is then filed in numerical order with the related order form attached.

The statistical department puts its copy of the invoice, by salesmen, on pegboards. Quantities, packagings and values are cross-added and entered on sales summaries which balance with the total determined by the comptometer operator in the order department. Invoices are then filed by customers, the total dollar value for each customer is determined monthly and agreed in total with the sales summary. The former are the basis of commission calculations and the latter of rebate calculations.

Credit Memos

The receiving department prepares *returned goods* slips in quadruplicate. These are approved by the superintendent after inspecting the goods returned, and are then sent to the order department. The order, billing and statistical departments handle receiving slips and credit memos in the same manner as orders and invoices.

Returned goods that cannot be sold to institutions at a special price are ground to form the base for a cheaper quality of biscuits or are scrapped entirely. In this last case, their cost is charged to a *scrap* account.

Purchase Requisitions (Prenumbered)

These are prepared by the stores department heads, plant superintendent or office, and approved by the vice president.

Purchase Orders (Prenumbered)

These are prepared in quadruplicate (last copy without prices). The original is mailed to the supplier; a copy goes to the accounting department; a copy without prices to the receiving department and one copy is filed by suppliers in the purchasing department.

Receiving Slips (Prenumbered)

These are prepared in duplicate in the receiving department. One copy goes to the accounting department and one copy to the stores department.

Purchase Invoices (Prenumbered)

Suppliers are requested to use the invoice form supplied with the purchase order and to send an original and a copy. Most suppliers comply. The accounting department marks the distribution. The original is matched with the receiving slip and purchase order, and then sent to the purchasing department head for approval. Purchasing department retains the order and receiving slip, which are filed numerically. All numbers of the order and of the slip must be accounted for.

Original invoices form the basis of direct posting to the general ledger and to the voucher part of the check. Invoices and checks are filed in trays, by suppliers, under classification of due dates. On the due date, a check is completed on the bookkeeping machine and the total repeated by *check protectograph*. The check is then sent (with invoices attached) to the president or vice president and secretary-treasurer for two signatures and initialing of invoices. Checks are turned over to the mailing department by the president's secretary, and invoices are returned to the accounting department where they are filed numerically. All numbers must be accounted for. The proof sheets of the posting of invoices to voucher part of check, and of posting of the amount on the body of check, form the voucher register and cash disbursements record respectively, and are the bases for posting to the general ledger.

The second copy of the invoice is sent to the cost department for individual machine posting to perpetual inventory cards and for total posting to the cost ledger. It is then filed in that department, under names of suppliers.

Where a supplier does not use the specified invoice form, the president must approve payment. He prepares memos to serve in lieu of the invoice form.

Salesmen's expense advances, commissions and other disbursements are recorded on *cash disbursement* forms in duplicate. The original is approved by the president, numbered consecutively with invoices and posted in the same manner. The duplicate is filed alphabetically in the accounting department.

Credit Memos from Suppliers
These memos follow the same procedure as invoices.

Freight Bills
Bills for incoming freight are matched with bills of lading and sent to the purchasing department for comparison with receiving slips and for approval. They follow the same procedure as purchase invoices, with a copy going to the cost department. Outgoing freight is never *prepaid.*

Inventories
Perpetual inventory records are maintained by the cost department for raw materials, packagings and finished goods. Units and values are posted to the cards. The FIFO method is in use in all stores. Complete physical inventories are taken at the year end, by teams composed of a member of the cost department and a member from the respective stores department. The cost department makes a weekly test of physical inventories against perpetual inventory records. All adjustments for shortages or overages are approved by the vice president. The company values inventories at the lower of cost or market.

Cash Receipts
Payment for cash sales is made to the cashier, who records it on a cash register. Cash is balanced with the locked tape by a member of the accounting staff. A separate deposit slip is made. The total for the day is entered in a cash summary and posted monthly to the general ledger. Cash sales invoices are prenumbered and all numbers must be accounted for. A copy is given to the statistical department and to the cost department.

Customer's checks are turned over to the collection department, which reports to the secretary-treasurer. They type deposit slips on special forms, in triplicate. The original serves as the customer's cash receipts record on which cash discounts, etc., are marked. The totals are posted to the general ledger. Matching invoices and credit memos are extracted from the trays and attached thereto. The duplicate deposit slip is retained by the bank and the triplicate is receipted and returned. Adjustment slips, in duplicate, may be approved by the secretary-treasurer, for accounts not balancing out. The original of such a slip is placed in the tray under the customer's name and the duplicate is attached to the cash receipts record.

Monthly open-item statements are prepared by the collection clerk for those accounts having past due amounts. Uncollectible or doubtful accounts are transferred to a separate tray and have their own general ledger control. The secretary-treasurer approves all accounts to be written off, except for accounts with institutions which are approved by the president. Trial balances of the accounts receivable trays are prepared and aged monthly.

Factory Payroll

Factory employees are paid weekly, by check, at fixed hourly rates. Checks are given out each Thursday for the prior week's earnings. Time cards are picked up by a member of the payroll department each Friday after the employees have checked out. Total hours are calculated and rechecked. Employees' names are entered on voucher checks from addressograph plates. Clock number, total hours, rate, gross pay, deductions and net pay are posted on the voucher part of the check and on the employee's cumulative record card in one operation, by an accounting machine which makes the calculations. The proof sheet forms the payroll record and is used for transfers to the payroll bank account and for posting the general ledger. It is approved by the personnel manager, who compares it with his record as to names and rates. The net amount is inscribed on the checks by *protectograph*. The payroll department is notified by the personnel department of all changes in employees or hourly rates. Prenumbered forms are used, which are approved by the vice president.

Office Salaries

Officers, office employees and the plant superintendent are paid monthly by voucher check. They are not paid for overtime. The president's secretary prepares the checks and individual salary records on an accounting machine. The proof sheet is the monthly salary record, and is approved by the secretary-treasurer, who authorizes the transfer to the salary account.

Distribution of Payroll Checks

Factory payroll checks are turned over to the cashier in alphabetical order. Employees picking up their checks must wear their employment badges, the number on which the cashier compares with the employee's number shown on his check before handing it out.

Office payroll checks are distributed by the president's secretary.

(AICPA adapted)

CHAPTER 6

INTERNAL CONTROL: SCOPE OF REVIEW

Chapter 5 dealt primarily with audit programs, but, in addition, it illustrated the importance of internal control evaluation. The *nature* of internal control and the required *scope* of the auditor's review of internal control have enjoyed high priorities as subjects of professional discussion. The best exchange of viewpoints on this subject occurred in 1957. That three-part exchange of ideas follows.

THE INDEPENDENT AUDITOR AND INTERNAL CONTROL
Gilbert R. Byrne*

Beginning with the revised American edition of Dicksee's *Auditing* (Montgomery, 1909), which discussed "internal check" in relation to the audit program, there has been a very considerable body of accounting literature dealing with various phases of internal control as it affects the work of the independent auditor. Over the years, various expressions, such as "internal check and control," "accounting methods" and "accounting procedures" have been used to describe the general concept of internal control. In 1947, however, the *Tentative Statement of Auditing Standards,* issued by the committee on auditing procedure of the American Institute of Accountants, included the dictum that:

> *There is to be a proper study and evaluation of the existing internal control as a basis for reliance thereon and for the determination of the resultant extent of the tests to which auditing procedures are to be restricted.*

This statement was followed in 1949 by a report of the committee which defined and discussed "internal control." At present, therefore, official pronouncements of the American Institute seem to have settled upon the all-embracing term "internal control," although the committee itself suggested that its definition is "possibly broader than the meaning sometimes attributed to the term" and that "a 'system' of internal control extends beyond those matters which relate directly to the functions of the accounting and financial departments." The term "internal control" as defined by the committee is a very broad one, and it is suggested that unless it is clear what *kind* of internal

* From *The Journal of Accountancy,* Vol. 103, No. 1 (January, 1957), pp. 41–46. Reprinted by permission of the American Institute of Certified Public Accountants.

control is under discussion, conclusions reached as to the independent auditor's responsibility in certain of the areas relating to it may be misunderstood. This discussion presents the thesis that there are three major classifications of internal control, with respect to each of which the independent auditor's responsibilities differ materially, and accordingly nomenclature should be adopted which will clearly indicate which classification of internal control is under consideration.

The definition of internal control given by the committee on auditing procedure, especially if somewhat rearranged as below, offers a suggestion for making an analysis of the nature of internal control:

> *Internal control comprises the plan of organization and all of the co-ordinate methods and measures adopted within the business to promote operational efficiency, and encourage adherence to prescribed managerial policies; to check the accuracy and reliability of its accounting data; and to safeguard assets.*

Thus stated, the three kinds of internal control referred to above begin to appear, and are outlined under the descriptive headings which follow.

Internal Administrative Control

Broadly, the prime responsibility of successful management is to operate at a profit the business with which it is concerned. It must produce an acceptable product at lowest practicable cost; it must develop markets in which its products can be sold at proper prices; and because pressure of competition, changes in customer demand and other factors cause obsolescence of product lines, it must develop new or improved products to replace older ones. To accomplish these objectives, management must, among other things, develop proper policies leading to efficient production, distribution and research; implement these policies through proper personnel selection, training and compensation; communicate the means of effecting its policies through instructions, procedures manuals and conferences; and police the performance of personnel through operating supervision and controls of various kinds.

For example, the personnel department may have methods, standards and procedures designed to insure the hiring, training and retention of proper employees; time and motion studies may promote more efficient use of labor; quality control of product may implement a policy of selling only first-grade merchandise to customers; comparative shoppers may police a policy of maintaining competitive selling prices. It is suggested that "the plan of organization and all the co-ordinate methods and measures adopted within the business to promote operational efficiency and encourage adherence to prescribed managerial policies" may be captioned "internal administrative control."

Internal Accounting Control

Controls which "check the accuracy and reliability of the accounting data" or, to put it another way, those controls which are designed to bring about the accurate and suitable recording and summarization of authorized financial transactions, are quite logically described as "internal accounting controls." The responsibility for the installation, maintenance, and correction of faulty operation of such internal accounting controls is clearly that of the accounting (or financial) department, and equally clearly, such controls are of prime interest to the independent auditor who is to report on the fairness of the financial statements which result from the records these controls are designed to protect.

Internal Check

Internal check may be described as those accounting procedures or statistical or physical or other controls which *safeguard assets* against defalcations or other similar irregularities. To the extent that such controls may be exercised through accounting means, or by proper assignment of duties within the accounting department, or between the accounting department and other operating departments which furnish data as a basis for recording financial transactions, the accounting department is responsible for their installation and maintenance. Some of the more usual forms of internal check of a physical nature such as fences, gates, watchmen, inspection of outgoing material or personnel, are ordinarily the responsibility of other operating departments.

There seems strong reason for distinguishing these three types of internal control, because the independent auditor's responsibilities, as later described, differ greatly as regards each of these phases of internal control.

Internal administrative controls are distinguishable from either internal accounting control or internal check because they originate in and are usually conducted by operating departments other than the financial or accounting. Certain administrative controls may be based on data or information furnished by accounting or financial departments: for example, various types of operating budgets or the reports of expenditures under plant addition authorizations which management uses to aid in controlling its policy in that area. On the other hand, internal administrative controls, especially those of a physical nature, may be useful as acceptable substitutes for or supplements to internal accounting control or internal check procedures. While there are borderline cases, it is usually not difficult to distinguish between internal administrative controls which do, and those which do not, enhance internal accounting control or internal check.

DISTINGUISHING INTERNAL CHECK

There has been little attention given to a differentiation between internal accounting control and internal check and the following illustration may clarify the point.

Consider the small manufacturing concern which has but a single bookkeeper. Let us assume that this bookkeeper is completely honest; so far as the bookkeeper is completely honest; so far as the bookkeeper is concerned, there is no need to institute controls to safeguard assets against defalcations or other similar irregularities. However, the honest bookkeeper wishes to please his employer by keeping accurate accounts, so he introduces controls and procedures which will help him to do so. Such internal accounting controls would include double-entry bookkeeping, control accounts, cross-checking of debit and credit categories, taking off and balancing trial balances. He would check his books with outside sources where possible; this would include reconciliation of cash per books with statements from the bank, comparison of book inventories with physical counts, possibly even circularization of debtors' accounts. As business grows and personnel is multiplied, there is more necessity for official authorization and approval of book entries, and more staff available among whom to divide duties so that clerical accuracy is enhanced by double check and cross-check. In addition, the honest bookkeeper and his honest staff promote accuracy by numbering and accounting for documents such as sales orders and sales invoices, purchase orders and vendors' invoices, receiving reports, checks, and numerous others. Such procedures are representative of those internal accounting controls which are necessary or desirable to insure the accurate and suitable recording and summarization of authorized financial transactions, and if there were no dishonesty to be dealt with, convenience or efficient operation would be the sole criterion in assigning various duties.

Unfortunately, experience teaches that not every bookkeeper is honest; neither is every workman, storekeeper, salesman or other person who has access to business assets. It is therefore necessary to provide controls to safeguard assets from defalcations or other similar irregularities. Such controls are encompassed in the term "internal check." For example, duties of accounting and financial personnel may be assigned in such a way that not only is accuracy enhanced through internal accounting controls, but also the arrangement of such assignments provides deterrents to wrong actions. These arrangements provide for independent performance of functions which are incompatible in terms of security, and they are among the most important tools of internal check.

So much has been written on this phase of the matter that it should be necessary only to remind the reader that, broadly speaking, custodianship functions should not be combined with record-keeping for the property held; control account functions should be independent of keeping the related detail records; those who record and summarize financial transactions should be independent of other operating functions. Thus, the requirements of internal accounting control (to insure the accurate and suitable recording of authorized financial transactions) are satisfied when the signer of a check has before him written evidence that the payments liquidate liabilities recorded by means of approved vouchers and that the data on the checks have been compared with the voucher, and then cancels the request for payment by appropriate means. But internal check requires that the signer be independent of persons who prepare vouchers for approval, persons who approve vouchers for payment, and those persons who prepare checks.

There are a number of other procedures of internal check frequently encountered. Among them are the *independent* control of and accounting for the usage of prenumbered documents, independent surprise counts of cash and securities, and protective paper and writing devices for checks. They have the common characteristic that they are not needed to ensure the accurate and suitable recording of authorized financial transactions by the honest bookkeeper, but are desirable only to prevent or disclose defalcations or other similar irregularities.

Independence and Internal Check

The value of independence on the part of those persons who are performing many of the procedures of internal check is based upon the assumption that an independent person will report to knowledgeable authority deliberate errors, falsification or improper use of documents, forgeries or other matters coming to his attention. To be independent in this sense, the reporter must be free to report such matters both from the standpoint of the duties assigned to him and of his position in the line of organization. When there is such freedom, failure to report to proper authority should occur only if the independent person is incompetent, or if there is collusion between persons presumed to be independent.

A person may be considered functionally independent when his assigned duties do not include functions which are incompatible from the standpoint of internal check. For example, the function of listing incoming receipts would be incompatible with the functions of preparing the bank deposit, posting detailed customers' accounts receivable, or posting credits for cash received to general ledger accounts; the function of preparing invoices for payment is incompatible with the function of approval for payment and cancellation of basic documents. In weighing independence, therefore, the first consideration is whether there are among a person's assigned duties those which are incompatible.

The next consideration is the extent to which the persons to whom compatible functions have been assigned are in fact independent from the standpoint of their position in the line of authority. In smaller organizations, incompatible functions may have been assigned to different persons, but if these persons report to a common chief who has hire-and-fire or disciplinary control over them, their functional independence may be nullified by their job dependence on their chief. In other words, the chief may be able to direct actions which result in fraud, and to ignore its indications in the accounts when reported to him. In larger organizations, the extent to which functional independence is affected by the line of authority in which the function is placed may be difficult to appraise. Incompatible functions may be divided between subsections of accounting or financial departments, but their heads may report through intervening subchiefs to the head of the accounting or financial function. Since in the last analysis, all department heads report to the president, it could be argued that there can be no organizational independence at all. As this, in practice at least, is an absurdity, it follows that the line may be drawn at some point on the organization chart; it is not always a simple matter to determine just where it is appropriate that this should be in a specific case.

It seems clear that the independent auditor, in making an examination of financial statements for the purpose of rendering an opinion on them, is not expected to investigate and evaluate internal administrative control *as such.* It is no part of his responsibility to determine whether salesmen are making a reasonable number of calls per day, whether the truck maintenance department is adhering to job schedules, whether established criteria for hiring of personnel are being followed by the personnel department, whether the experiments being conducted by the research department are in an area consistent with management policy, or to determine whether administrative controls are present and whether those controls are effective in providing the answers to a host of other questions which arise from business operations.

INTERNAL ADMINISTRATIVE CONTROLS

The experienced independent auditor gains much knowledge of useful internal administrative controls during the course of his work, especially those which may provide effective alternates for certain internal accounting controls or internal check procedures. Among these are physical controls such as watchmen and gates, and statistical records which may be kept by production, maintenance, sales or other operating departments. There is no reason, of course, why he should not take into consideration the presence of acceptable alternative internal administrative controls when evaluating internal accounting control and internal check, and he often will suggest the use of such procedures when, in a particular case, he considers that they are appropriate. For the independent auditor, however, any review or evaluation of internal administrative control procedures is not a part of his responsibilities regarding internal accounting control and internal check.

Many accounting firms offer management advisory services to their clients which include investigation of and advice concerning improvement of internal administrative controls. Many cost systems, for example, have built-in features which provide management controls for various purposes in addition to the mere computation of current costs. But such investigation is not properly a part of the usual examination leading to a short-form report.

INTERNAL ACCOUNTING CONTROL

Internal accounting control, as described above, is by definition designed, in the absence of dishonesty on the part of those who operate and administer it, to promote the accurate and suitable recording and summarization of authorized financial transactions. Thus, if generally accepted accounting principles have been consistently applied in recording properly controlled financial transactions by completely honest persons, fair presentation of financial statements prepared therefrom would result. There is no question that the independent auditor is responsible for making an examination which will permit him to express a well-founded opinion as to whether financial statements do or do not fairly present financial position and results of operations. Accordingly, if the independent auditor finds that a particular client has poor internal accounting control, he has no alternative, if he is to give an opinion upon the financial statements, to making such examination as would supplement the absent controls with additional audit tests or over-all checks and comparisons.

In practice, of course, any business which uses double-entry bookkeeping in its accounting has the rudiments of internal accounting control, and most businesses have reasonable accounting control even though it may be lacking in some particulars; it is seldom, if ever, necessary to apply *all possible* audit procedures for the *entire* period under review in any one case in order that the independent auditor may form an opinion that the financial transactions have been accurately and suitably recorded and summarized so as to produce a fair statement of financial condition and results of operations. It is for this reason that it is a generally accepted auditing standard that the auditor's examination include investigation and evaluation of internal accounting control which is designed to give him the knowledge upon which he forms a judgment whether and to what extent his audit procedures may be restricted. (See *Generally Accepted Auditing Standards,* AIA, 1954, page 13.)

If, for example, there were no proper review of the initial account classification to which voucher charges are assigned, the independent auditor would extend his examination of voucher charges, and if numerous errors of significant dollar amount were thus disclosed, he might well carry his tests further. If inventories are not controlled through perpetual detail records, currently checked by comparison with physical counts, he would probably feel it necessary to broaden the scope of his physical tests when attending the annual physical inventory taken by the client, as compared with what would be appropriate if the client kept perpetual records which were periodically compared with physical counts.

The essential point is that, except as to defalcations discussed below, leading spokesmen for the accounting profession agree that the independent auditor has heavy responsibility when he gives his opinion whether financial statements fairly present financial position and results of operations. If internal accounting control is a vital factor in producing financial statements which meet this test of fairness, then it follows that the auditor has equal responsibility for investigating, evaluating and reflecting in his audit program the results of such evaluation.

INTERNAL CHECK

Internal check, as described in this paper, is by definition an adjunct to internal accounting control, and is designed to supplement the latter by furnishing means to safeguard assets against the manipulations of the relatively few dishonest persons concerned with the accounting functions of business. With respect to the independent auditor's responsibility for the detection of fraud and other similar irregularities, the accounting profession has taken the position that there are very definite limitations to this responsibility.

Codification of Statements on Auditing Procedure, (page 12) states that:

> *The ordinary examination incident to the issuance of an opinion respecting financial statements is not designed and* cannot *be relied upon to disclose defalcations and other similar irregularities, although their discovery frequently results.*

This statement, by itself, might be taken to imply that the independent auditor assumes no responsibility whatever for the discovery of defalcations; if this were so, there might well be lack of understanding why the auditor in making such an examination devotes *any* time and attention to investigating and evaluating internal check, as the term is used in this paper.

The statement does require some explanation. It does not mean that the independent auditor is indifferent to the possibility that fraud exists. On the contrary, his audit program is framed and his examination conducted in such a manner that material fraud, particularly one concealed in the balance sheet, is sought to be, and often is, discovered. In essence, the statement recognizes the fact that reasonable audit procedures made with due care should more often than not disclose material errors of fairness of presentation of financial statements resulting from poor internal check; however, when fraud has been concealed through improper charges to the income account, even substantial extension of audit tests might not disclose fraud because it might be concealed by the next unchecked entry. Further, extension of audit tests to complete coverage might not suffice when collusion is present. It is obviously impracticable, in most cases, to extend audit procedures to this extreme, because the cost would be out of proportion to any possible benefits in the very great majority of cases. Clients generally appreciate this, and will agree to accept limitations on the auditor's responsibility for the discovery of defalcations as stated above; moreover, as further discussed in the *Codification,* good internal check and surety bonds provide reasonable protection against defalcations at much less cost.

This limitation of the auditor's responsibility in relation to fraud has its corresponding effect upon his responsibility in relation to internal check. While he makes somewhat the same investigation of and evaluation of internal check as he does of internal accounting control, it does not follow that he must extend his audit program in the same manner or to the same extent that might be appropriate if the revealed weaknesses were those of internal accounting control. If internal check weaknesses are such that they might permit abstraction of assets resulting in a corresponding difference between controlling accounts and the detail records or the actual assets on hand, the auditor might conclude that his counts and reconciliation of cash and inventories or confirmation of accounts receivable should be done at the balance sheet date, possibly with extended coverage, rather than at an interim period. However, if it appears that the weakness might permit concealing the defalcation through fraudulent entries buried in cost or expense accounts, even a complete, detailed examination might not reveal the manipulations. Therefore, unless his suspicions are aroused by specific circumstances, the auditor need not unreasonably extend his examination, but may rely upon his understanding with his client, and the more and more generally accepted position of the accounting profession referred to above with respect to responsibility for discovery of defalcations and other similar irregularities.

The independent auditor rarely, if ever, includes in his examination a review of internal administrative control, except those features, usually physical, which are substitutes for or supplementary to internal accounting control or internal check. As to the reviews of internal accounting control and internal check, it is usually convenient to coordinate these investigations and the recording of the results, and there is no objection to this if the distinctions pointed out are kept in mind. It appears, however, that most of the discussions of the subject, and the questionnaires or other tools which are used by independent auditors in their reviews, emphasize the internal check features of internal control and minimize internal accounting control.

EXTENT OF AUDITOR'S RESPONSIBILITY

Since the independent auditor's heaviest responsibility relates to "fairness of presentation" of financial statements (which internal accounting control by completely honest personnel tends to promote), and the accounting profession has stated limitations of its responsibility for discovery of fraud (which internal check is designed to prevent), it would seem that the emphasis should be just the reverse. If the independent auditor pleads nonresponsibility or limited responsibility for discovery of fraud, how will he explain exhaustive investigation of internal check, but with much less apparent attention given to internal accounting control? Further, if it be granted that the independent auditor, as a recognized expert in the field, has a responsibility to assist management by bringing to the attention of the proper parties serious weaknesses in internal check which, if not corrected, could lead to diversion of assets, he surely has the same responsibility to bring to management's attention weaknesses in internal accounting control which may lead to improper recording and summarization of transactions.

It would, therefore, appear that if it is desirable to have a record of the auditor's investigation and evaluation of internal check, both to justify the resultant effect upon his audit program and as a basis for suggestions for improvements to the client, it is equally or more important to have such a record for these purposes as to internal accounting control. In either case, of course, it is management's responsibility to decide to what extent the suggestions made should be adopted.

The accounting profession has long accepted its responsibility for investigating and evaluating internal control, and to relating the extent of the audit program to the results of such review. *Internal Control,* a special report of the committee on auditing procedure of the AIA, however, discusses the subject in such a way that it could well be argued that the independent auditor's responsibility should be considered the same for all phases of internal control. It is suggested in this paper that there is a real distinction between the three phases of internal control designated as internal administrative control, internal accounting control and internal check, and that this distinction is of importance because:

1 As to internal administrative control he has no responsibility for investigation or evaluation, nor does its presence or absence (except to a minor degree and in exceptional circumstances) affect his audit program.

2 As to internal accounting control, he has great responsibility for investigation and evaluation and for the related effect upon his audit program, because these are the principal controls contributing to fairness of presentation of financial statements, which is the auditor's prime responsibility.

3 As to internal check, while he has similar responsibility for investigation and evaluation, the resulting effect on his audit program is limited because his responsibility in relation to discovery of defalcations and other similar irregularities is limited.

The subject is of sufficient importance that it is hoped the appropriate committee of the Institute will soon issue a clarification of the pronouncements on internal control so as to remove doubt as to what may properly be expected from the independent auditor when he investigates and evaluates it.

INTERNAL CONTROL AND LEGAL RESPONSIBILITY
Saul Levy*

It would be difficult to overstate the importance of the review and appraisal of internal control by the public accountant, and its use as the very foundation and justification for a program of testing and sampling. Moreover, while the public accountant's appraisal of the structure and effectiveness of internal control is the basis for the extent of his testing and sampling, that very testing and sampling serves also, in large part, as a means of satisfying the auditor that the existing system of internal control is functioning effectively in actual practice.

The realization of all this by the profession is implied in the adoption by vote of the membership of the AIA of this standard of field work:

There is to be a proper study and evaluation of existing internal control as a basis for reliance thereon and for the determination of the resultant extent of the tests to which auditing procedures are to be restricted.

This specific auditing standard ties in with and is embraced by the representation in our standard short-form opinion that:

---

* From *The Journal of Accountancy*, Vol. 103, No. 2 (February, 1957), pp. 29–33. Reprinted by permission of the American Institute of Certified Public Accountants.

Our examination was made in accordance with generally accepted auditing standards, and accordingly included such tests of the accounting records and such other auditing procedures as we considered necessary in the circumstances.

It should be noted, however, that we do not go so far as to express approval of the client's existing internal control. What we do is to represent that we have made a proper study and evaluation of it for the purpose of determining the extent of the tests that we have employed in our auditing program; and that in our judgment the existing internal control, in conjunction with our tests and other auditing procedures, has enabled us to reach the opinion to which we subscribe.

Whereas the above-quoted standard of field work does not expressly impose upon us the duty or obligation to communicate to the client the results of our internal control study where significant weaknesses are apparent, it has become the practice to consider it desirable to do so. Thus, the Special Report on Internal Control by the Committee on Auditing Procedure of the American Institute (dated November 1948 and hereinafter referred to as the Special Report on Internal Control) states:

The public accountant's review of the system of internal control serves two purposes: first, it enables him to formulate an opinion as to the reliance he may place on the system to the end that, by adjusting his audit procedures accordingly, he may express an opinion as to the fairness of management's financial statements; and, secondly, where the review indicates apparent weaknesses, recommendations for possible corrective measures may be conveyed to management. This secondary aspect of his review frequently enables the public assountant to render broader services than those generally associated with his capacity as an independent reporter to stockholders upon management's conduct of stewardship responsibilities. His aid to management in attaining more efficient operation can and should be an equally important function. . . .

When the system of internal control is found to be unsatisfactory in some respects, the auditor should advise his client of such observed weaknesses in internal control so that the client may take what action he thinks is appropriate. Where the observed weaknesses in internal control have resulted in the extension of audit procedures beyond the scope which otherwise would have been necessary, the client should be advised that the correction of those weaknesses would make it possible for the auditor to reduce the scope of his work.

Apart from its great value to the client, such a report on weaknesses or suggested improvements in internal control serves as a protective measure for the benefit of the public accountant. In the *Codification of Statements on Auditing Procedure* published in 1951 by the Institute, we stress the function of internal control as the client's principal safeguard against defalcations and other similar irregularities. In this connection, the *Codification* stated:

The ordinary examination incident to the issuance of an opinion respecting financial statements is not designed and cannot be relied upon to disclose defalcations and other similar irregularities, although their discovery frequently results. In a well-organized concern reliance for the detection of such irregularities is placed principally upon the maintenance of an adequate system of accounting records with the appropriate internal control.

DISCLOSURE TO THE CLIENT

Since we have unequivocally assumed an obligation to study and evaluate internal control as an integral part of our audit, it is obviously desirable to communicate to our clients any knowledge of significant weaknesses which we obtain and to give the client the benefit of our professional advice as to how these weaknesses can be corrected. The accountant will usually feel that where his recommendations concerning internal control are in his judgment sufficiently important, he will not content himself with an oral report to the client but will make an adequate written record thereof by addressing to a responsible official of the company or to the individual client himself a written memorandum dealing with the subject.

The occasion frequently arises for the issuance to the client of such a written memorandum or special report on internal control, and this fact of itself sometimes raises questions which have an important bearing on the CPA's possible legal responsibility.

In the case of a corporate client, it will ordinarily be sufficient to address the communication to the chief accounting officer who may be the treasurer, the comptroller, or perhaps a vice president. Where the report involves serious criticisms of such an official or when it can reasonably be considered a matter for official consideration on the highest level, the letter should be sent to the president or even to the board of directors. This often becomes a delicate matter of judgment for the accountant to decide. Obviously, protection for himself increases the higher up he goes. On the other hand, many recommendations for improvement are of a technical nature not warranting submission above the level of the chief accounting officer.

DISCLOSURE IN THE AUDIT REPORT

The question is often raised as to whether the accountant's critical findings concerning internal control should be disclosed in his audit report. The consensus is that there is no such requirement, except in extraordinary circumstances. This matter is discussed in Chapter 16 of the *CPA Handbook,* entitled "Reliance Upon Internal Control" by Norman H. S. Vincent (hereinafter referred to as the Vincent chapter). His discussion draws upon the results of a questionnaire sent out by the Institute seeking the views of practicing public accountants. Vincent quotes the following comment of one firm of accountants:

> *Reporting on deficiencies in internal control must depend on the significance of the deficiencies and the purposes of the examination. Unless the terms of the engagement require otherwise, deficiencies as to which audit procedures have compensated should not be included in a report made for public purposes. A separate letter or report on such matters should, however, be directed to management.*
>
> *On the other hand, if the deficiencies were so great as to require a complete check of transactions, obviously any report made by the auditor should disclose the situation. (Page 23, Vincent chapter.)*

Vincent adds his own comment, based on the questionnaire replies, that "many accountants do not agree with the opinion quoted that, based on the facts stated, 'obviously any report made by the auditor should disclose the situation.'"

There is also the further comment by Vincent:

> *While there seems to be general agreement that deficiencies in control should be reported to the client, very few of the accountants who replied to the questionnaire believed they had any responsibility to disclose such deficiencies in an audit report. The replies on the questionnaire appear to indicate that most practicing accountants hold the belief that acceptance of an added responsibility to disclose weaknesses in an audit report would not serve the interests of either the public or the client. However, the replies indicated that the practitioners' views in this respect might be different if:*
>
> 1 *Definite standards were to be evolved for the auditors' review of internal control; or*
>
> 2 *Specific types of deficiencies were established as being so significant as to make impossible an expression of opinion as to the fairness of financial statements. (Page 5, Vincent chapter.)*

It would be a disturbing situation if accountants refrained from disclosure merely because sufficiently definite standards had not been formulated by the profession. The absence of such definite standards has never been a valid defense where the matter should be resolved by the accountant on the basis of his judgment. The absence of definite standards only leads to a situation where the existence or nonexistence of a standard (and what its content is or should be) becomes a contested factual question for the jury to decide in any litigation in which it is involved. The result can be that a jury of laymen sets up its own standard which becomes the yardstick measuring the duty of the accountant.

INSUFFICIENT INTERNAL CONTROL

Conceivably, internal control could be so lacking that this state of affairs would have to be disclosed in the audit report. The situation might call for a qualified opinion or even the denial of an opinion. On the other hand, it might result in an audit sufficiently detailed to lead to an unqualified opinion but nevertheless require disclosure of the deficiency in internal control. Rarely would the internal control situation be so seriously deficient as to require disclosure in the audit report in addition to a special report to the management. Instances requiring disclosure in the audit report would be the rare exceptions which merely proved the general rule that disclosure to the management only in a separate report or memorandum was all that ordinarily might be expected of the public accountant. Even so, it would be prudent to scrutinize the report or memorandum to management to reassure the reviewer that it does not portray so flagrant a condition that its omission from the audit report opinion may be considered misleading. In this connection, reference is made to SEC rulings that where the accounting records of a company are in extremely bad shape, failure to disclose that condition may be misleading, regardless of how much audit work or writing up of records was performed in order to support the auditor's opinion. (See Accounting Series Release Number 13, February 20, 1940.)

RECORD OF COMPENSATORY PROCEDURES

Where a special report or memorandum is sent to the client dealing with significant weaknesses in internal control, it constitutes a record of the findings of the public accountant. It obviously raises the question as to what was done in order to compensate for the weakness in or lack of internal control. It may be that other procedures were followed by the client which satisfied the public accountant, whose report was intended merely to recommend more efficient methods of internal control. It may be that the public accountant extended his own procedures, expanded the scope of his tests and sampling, or employed alternative auditing procedures in the premises. For the accountant's own protection it would seem to be essential that, having made a record of the discovered weaknesses in internal control, he should include in his working papers a correlative record of what additional work he did in compliance with the generally accepted auditing standard relating to internal control.

It may not be feasible for the accountant to state precisely how much testing and sampling is a normal amount and how much additional work should be done in excess of that normal amount in any given instance. These are essentially matters of judgment. Case Studies on Internal Control, Number 2, published by the Institute, is merely illustrative of how such matters were dealt with in one instance. The point is that whatever may be the conclusion of the accountant as to how much his audit procedures should be extended, he should make an adequate record of those conclusions. For example, questionnaire forms in general use for the study and evaluation of internal control can easily be expanded so that, with respect to items where there is an adverse answer, there can be added comment indicating what was done about it or why it was deemed unnecessary to expand the audit procedures.

We should guard against overstating the case against existing internal control in our communication to clients. In many instances, it may be an exaggeration to speak of weakness, deficiency, or lack of internal control when it would be more accurate to speak of recommended improvements which would make internal control more efficient, more effective, more reliable, or more closely conforming to usual practice. Often in such special reports to clients, the recommendations are unduly dramatized. For example, it may be stated that existing methods make payroll padding easy, that sums could be extracted from petty cash without detection, that receipts from customers could be withheld and the records readily manipulated to cover up the embezzlement, etc. From the standpoint of the accountant's legal responsibility, such use of the shock treatment against a client may not be a good idea. Such a letter might later be used in an effort to persuade the average juror that the accountant found so bad a mess that he should have gone to great extremes in disclosing his findings even in the audit report, and that an unqualified opinion was unjustified in the circumstances. Often such letters to clients are drafted by systems specialists who may be so intent upon persuading the client to adopt the recommendations made that little thought is given to dangerous implications of the derogatory comments concerning existing internal control.

However, no suggestion is being made here that the report to the client on internal control should for any reason be watered down. Attention is merely being directed to an observed tendency often to dramatize the internal control situation in language which is likely to give an exaggerated impression of flagrant weakness. In any event, it is again stressed that the report on internal control must be viewed in relation to the planning of the audit and also must be reconciled with the content of the audit report and the opinion there contained.

PROPER STUDY AND EVALUATION

The auditing standard which we have adopted provides for "a proper study and evaluation of the existing internal control." The scope and meaning of "existing internal control" are seriously in need of further clarification. The

Institute's Special Report defines internal control so broadly that the scope of the public accountant's "proper study and evaluation" thereof would be more comprehensive than is currently the practice. In this connection, the Special Report states:

> *Internal control comprises the plan of organization and all of the co-ordinate methods and measures adopted within a business to safeguard its assets, check the accuracy and reliability of its accounting data,* promote operational efficiency, *and* encourage adherence to prescribed managerial policies. *This definition possibly is broader than the meaning sometimes attributed to the term. It recognizes that a "system" of internal control extends beyond those matters which relate directly to the functions of the accounting and financial departments. Such a system might include budgetary control, standard costs, periodic operating reports, statistical analyses and the dissemination thereof, a training program designed to aid personnel in meeting their responsibilities, and an internal audit staff to provide additional assurance to management as to the adequacy of its outlined procedures and the extent to which they are being effectively carried out. It properly comprehends activities in other fields as, for example,* time and motion studies *which are of an engineering nature, and use of* quality controls *through a system of inspection which fundamentally is a production function. [Emphasis supplied.]*

This would seem to indicate that a proper study and evaluation of internal control by the public accountant in conjunction with his audit work might go well beyond the controls which relate to the accounting records. Such a conclusion might seem consistent with the following quotation from the Institute's Special Report which requires the annual review of the accounting controls, if practicable, while suggesting that the comprehensive review of all control procedures (presumably those beyond the accounting controls) may be spread over a period of several years:

> *Determining the effectiveness of the organizational plan, division of responsibilities, and such special control procedures as budgetary controls, reports, analyses, and cost systems are among the areas which the public accountant should cover in his review. It is not anticipated that the independent auditor will be able to review all the control procedures within the course of any one audit. The review may very well be so arranged as to entail complete coverage over a period of several years. However, the review of those controls which relate directly to the accounting records should, if practicable, be conducted each year.*

The Vincent chapter makes several significant observations on this very question, bringing into the discussion the results of the Institute questionnaire which sought to obtain a consensus of practicing accountants concerning this matter. The following excerpts from the Vincent chapter are relevant:

Many public accountants believe there is a distinct difference between internal control as defined broadly from the standpoint of its general use by business organizations and as defined by public accountants from the standpoint of their review of internal control on auditing engagements. This was shown by analysis of responses to a survey questionnaire which was submitted to over one hundred accounting firms. Of the large and medium-sized firms that responded, over 75 per cent reported that their review of internal control dealt only with business controls which were exercised through accounting procedures and methods. Less than 25 per cent of the large and medium-sized firms reported that they extended their review of internal control beyond the financial and accounting departments to include such matters as:

1 *Budgetary control.*

2 *Standards costs.*

3 *Periodic operating reports.*

4 *Personnel training programs.*

5 *Internal auditing.*

6 *Time and motion studies.*

In part, these responses indicate that public accountants restrict their review of internal control to matters concerning the expression of an opinion on financial statements. Time and motion studies, for example, are business controls which have little direct bearing on determining the fairness of the financial statements. The responses also indicate a confusion in definitions. It should not be concluded that public accountants ignore all the broader aspects of internal control methods. Instead it would appear that such matters as the review of budgetary control and standard costs are dealt with as a problem which is separate and distinct from the review of internal control.

The answers of the small accounting firms which responded to the questionnaire showed a 50—50 division between use of the narrow and broad concepts of internal control. This greater acceptance of the broad definition of internal control by the small firms may be explained in several ways. (Page 4, Vincent chapter.)

We do not know how extensive and how representative the questionnaire replies were; but they do constitute a part of our recent literature as to the scope of internal control from the standpoint of our study and evaluate it in connection with our audit engagements. Approximately 25 per cent of the large and medium-sized accounting firms and 50 per cent of the small accounting firms interpret internal control broadly in their actual practice, and this fact would indicate that a substantial segment of the profession has assumed that the broad definition in the Institute's Special Report bears upon their responsibility in this respect.

LEGAL CONSEQUENCES

From the standpoint of legal responsibility there is an obvious danger in assuming so broad a responsibility. Internal control, as broadly defined, is intended not merely to prevent or to minimize fraud. It is also a safeguard against waste, inefficiency, and an assurance that operating policies are being followed by personnel who are competent and faithful. Our study and evaluation of internal control is intended primarily to aid us in planning an audit program which, in turn, will enable us to express a public accountant's opinion as to financial position and operating results. However, an audit is not the equivalent of a management survey. It is obvious, therefore, that our responsibility should be limited to a study of those controls which are directly related to the accounting records.

It is my opinion that this is and should be the normal concept of what we mean by "existing internal control" in terms of our generally accepted auditing standards. The questionnaires which we use in our audit work are consistent with this limited concept. If our literature leaves this question in any way open to doubt, it is unwise to let the matter rest until it becomes an issue in some litigation, for then the doubt might be resolved by a jury inclined to take a very liberal but unrealistic view of the duty of the public accountant in his "proper study and evaluation of existing internal control" in accordance with generally accepted auditing standards.

THE BROADER CONCEPT OF INTERNAL CONTROL
Paul Grady*

DEFINITION OF INTERNAL CONTROL: Internal control comprises the plan of organization and all of the co-ordinate methods and measures adopted within a business to safeguard its assets, check the accuracy and reliability of its accounting data, promote operational efficiency, and encourage adherence to prescribed managerial policies. This definition possibly is broader than the meaning sometimes attributed to the term. It recognizes that a "system" of internal control extends beyond those matters which relate directly to the functions of the accounting and financial departments. Such a system might include budgetary control, standard costs, periodic operating reports, statistical analyses and the dissemination thereof, a training program designed to aid per-

* From *The Journal of Accountancy*, Vol. 103, No. 5 (May, 1957), pp. 36–41. Reprinted by permission of the American Institute of Certified Public Accountants.

sonnel in meeting their responsibilities, and an internal audit staff to provide additional assurance to management as to the adequacy of its outlined procedures and the extent to which they are being effectively carried out. It properly comprehends activities in other fields as, for example, time and motion studies which are of an engineering nature, and use of quality controls through a system of inspection which fundamentally is a production function. — *Internal Control, a special report by the AIA Committee on Auditing Procedure*

In the January 1957 issue of *The Journal of Accountancy* ("The Independent Auditor and Internal Control," p. 41) Gilbert R. Byrne, who has played an important part in the preparation of recent editions of Montgomery's *Auditing,* proposed that internal control be separated into three different compartments, designated "Internal Administrative Control," "Internal Accounting Control" and "Internal Check." From the conclusions in the article, it appears that the purpose of his proposal is to provide a basis for limitation of the independent accountant's responsibility for the study and evaluation of internal control. The February *Journal* ("Internal Control and Legal Responsibility," p. 29) contained a plea that "our responsibility should be limited to a study of those controls which are directly related to accounting records," by Saul Levy, author of *Accountants' Legal Responsibility.* The sponsorship of a narrower concept of responsibility in the important area of internal control by these eminent authors is sufficient grounds for a reexamination of the subject.

The broader viewpoint to which they object is reflected in *Generally Accepted Auditing Standards,* first issued by the committee on auditing procedure in 1947, and in a special report on *Internal Control* issued by that committee in 1948. I was chairman of the committee when both reports were issued. For this reason and because it is my belief that the narrow viewpoint is not a sound position for the profession, this article is submitted in support of the broader concept of internal control.

The suggestions by Mr. Byrne as to the major division of internal control and the degree of responsibility for investigation or evaluation thereof by the independent accountant may be summarized as follows:

1 Internal administrative control comprises the plan of organization and all of the co-ordinate methods and measures adopted within the business to promote operational efficiency and encourage adherence to prescribed managerial policies. "As to internal administrative control he has no responsibility for investigation or evaluation, nor does its presence or absence (except to a minor degree and in exceptional circumstances) affect his audit program."

2 Internal accounting control comprises the methods and procedures designed and maintained by the accounting (or financial) department to bring about the accurate and suitable recording and summarization of authorized financial transactions. "As to internal accounting control, he has great responsibility for investigation and evaluation and for the related effect upon his audit program, because these are the principal controls contributing to fairness of presentation of financial statements, which is the auditor's prime responsibility."

3 Internal check comprises those accounting procedures or statistical or physical or other controls which safeguard assets against defalcations or other similar irregularities. "As to internal check, while he has similar responsibility for investigation and evaluation, the resulting effect on his audit program is limited because his responsibility in relation to discovery of defalcations and other similar irregularities is limited."

It is not known whether Mr. Levy would agree with Mr. Byrne's suggested division of internal control or the related ascription of responsibilities, but the following concluding paragraphs from Mr. Levy's article indicate a rather close association in their objectives:

> From the standpoint of legal responsibility there is an obvious danger in assuming so broad a responsibility. Internal control, as broadly defined, is intended not merely to prevent or to minimize fraud. It is also a safeguard against waste, inefficiency, and an assurance that operating policies are being followed by personnel who are competent and faithful. Our study and evaluation of internal control is intended primarily to aid us in planning an audit program which, in turn, will enable us to express a public accountant's opinion as to financial position and operating results. However, an audit is not the equivalent of a management survey. It is obvious, therefore, that our responsibility should be limited to a study of those controls which are directly related to the accounting records.

> It is my opinion that this is and should be the normal concept of what we mean by "existing internal control" in terms of our generally accepted auditing standards. The questionnaires which we use in our audit work are consistent with this limited concept. If our literature leaves this question in any way open to doubt, it is unwise to let the matter rest until it becomes an issue in some litigation, for then the doubt might be resolved by a jury inclined to take a very liberal but unrealistic view of the duty of the public accountant in his "proper study and evaluation of existing internal control" in accordance with generally accepted auditing standards.

EVALUATION OF RECOMMENDATIONS

The foregoing brief quotations from the articles are intended to give the substance of the authors' recommendations. Their full arguments should be considered and analyzed from three principal viewpoints:

1 Would the narrower view of internal control decrease or increase the effectiveness of our work and what would be the resultant effect on the risk in examinations of financial statements?

2 Is it possible or feasible to compartmentalize the examination and evaluation of internal control in auditing practice?

3 Is a narrow concept of responsibility for investigation and evaluation of internal control compatible with the present stature and future potentialities of public accounting?

The matter of compliance with the generally accepted auditing standard relating to internal control cannot be considered standing alone. All of the standards are interrelated and all of them must be kept in mind as quality bench marks pervading every step of the work. In order that the reader may see the inseparable nature of the general standards and the standards of field work, they are summarized below:

General Standards

1 The examination is to be performed by a person or persons having adequate technical training and proficiency as an auditor.

2 In all matters relating to the assignment, an independence in mental attitude is to be maintained by the auditor or auditors.

3 Due professional care is to be exercised in the performance of the examination and the preparation of the report.

Standards of Field Work

1 The work is to be adequately planned and assistants, if any, are to be properly supervised.

2 There is to be a proper study and evaluation of the existing internal control as a basis for reliance thereon and for the determination of the resultant extent of the tests to which auditing procedures are to be restricted.

3 Sufficient competent evidential matter is to be obtained through inspection, observation, inquiries and confirmations to afford a reasonable basis for an opinion regarding the financial statements under examination.

In actual practice a considerable amount of planning is desirable in advance of beginning field work, such planning being predicated on prior knowledge of the enterprise to be examined. In all other respects the three standards of field work are not to be fulfilled by separate and distinct chronological or procedural steps. Contributions toward compliance with all of the standards are likely to be present in most of the phases of work undertaken. The independent auditor should consider evidence as to the effectiveness of the important aspects of internal control in all transactions selected for examination. The proper study and evaluation of existing internal control is directed to the particular purpose of serving "as a basis for reliance thereon and for the determination of the resultant extent of the tests to which auditing procedures are to be restricted." Thus it is clear that the study of internal control does not purport to bring out all the ways by which management could be improved, as Mr. Levy seems to fear, but is a "proper evaluation . . . for reliance thereon by the auditor."

SOME BASIC POINTS OF INQUIRY

Therefore a basic question is whether the examinee's existing internal administrative control and internal check, as defined by Mr. Byrne, have a bearing on the independent auditor's "selection of the appropriate auditing procedures and his determination of the extent of the tests to which such procedures are restricted." I think they have a significant effect and that the auditor must have considerable knowledge of them in order to exercise his best judgment in determining the scope of his examination. To illustrate the point, consider the following questions:

Do the principal duties of the officers conform to charts of organization and to the provisions of the bylaws?

Are the duties of the principal accounting officer segregated from those of the treasurer?

Are accounting employees and records at all locations under supervision of the principal accounting officials?

Are operating expense budgets and capital budgets prepared and variations therefrom adequately explained?

Are all accounting reports prepared, checked or reviewed by departments or individuals other than those responsible for the operation reported upon, particularly reports comparing budgeted with actual expenses?

Is the cost data supplied by the operating departments reasonably accurate and complete and does it reflect operations as they presently exist?

Are employees who perform accounting and treasury functions required to take vacations and are their duties performed by others?

Is there some assurance that officers and employees are not connected with other business organizations with which the company deals or that officers or employees in key control positions are not related to one another?

Are the treasurer's and cashier's functions such that they neither maintain nor create posting media for general accounting records, accounts receivable ledgers, etc., other than detail cash records?

Are appropriate segregations maintained between the functions of purchasing, shipping, storekeeping, accounting, billing, collecting and depositing funds?

Are the persons responsible for approving credits independent of the sales department, accounts receivable department, cashier?

Are credit memoranda for returns and allowances approved by an employee who has no access to customers' remittances or other company checks or currency?

Are physical inventory counts supervised by persons independent of storekeepers and those keeping the perpetual records?

Are there adequate provisions for obsolete or damaged materials included in inventories?

If investment securities and other negotiable instruments are not in the possession of an independent custodian, are they kept in a safe-deposit vault or under lock and key?

Are two or more officials or responsible employees jointly responsible for the safekeeping of the securities and do they have only joint access to them?

Is a count of securities and notes made periodically by persons who do not have custody of or access to them?

Are the purchase prices reviewed periodically by a responsible official or employee not connected with the purchasing department with a view to ascertaining that such prices are the most advantageous to the company?

Are invoices not involving materials or supplies (such as advertising, fees, rentals, utility bills, traveling expense, etc.) approved by department heads prior to payment?

Are such invoices reviewed for reasonableness and necessity, and approved by a responsible employee outside of the originating department?

Is the distribution of charges reviewed in the accounting department by a person competent to pass on the propriety of the distribution?

Are the procedures for approval and collection of timecards at operating locations effective in maintaining the separation of approving and processing functions from payment functions?

Are the policies of management with regard to distinguishing between capital and maintenance adequately explained at the operating level where initial decisions are made?

Many of the foregoing questions relate to all three of the divisions of internal control suggested by Mr. Byrne: administrative control, internal check and accounting control. If these are questions of proper interest to the auditor, how is it possible to omit looking into them? Yet, the conclusions in the articles by Mr. Byrne and Mr. Levy suggest modification of authoritative professional literature to eliminate or substantially curtail the requirement for knowledge of internal control beyond the accounting department. They would do this even though the knowledge is for the purpose of aiding exercise of judgment by the auditor in deciding upon the scope of his examination.

Business is a dynamic, living institution. It is comprised of many people of diverse talents, organized by logical patterns of responsibility to accomplish the many individual or group tasks embodied in the fulfillment of the broad missions of the enterprise. Good internal control requires a reasonable independence between the operating, treasury (custodial) and accounting functions. Efficiency requires close co-ordination and co-operation in the performance of the respective functions and a reasonable minimum of duplicated effort. For this reason many basic controls as well as many decisions affecting the handling of transactions in the accounts occur outside of the accounting department.

Manufacturing and shipping products, billing customers, granting allowances to customers, purchasing and receiving materials, custody of cash and securities and inventories, engaging employees, reporting and distributing employees' time charges, paying employees and vendors are some of the functions which ordinarily are controlled outside the accounting department. The accounting department will require authorized approvals and needed information on appropriate forms to support the transactions. However, the auditor must go beyond these pieces of paper to the people who are exercising the controls and who are making the decisions on distribution of charges if he expects to have a sound basis for judging the credibility of the accounts and the extent of his examination. Certainly it would be the height of futility for the auditor to spend his time checking the clerical aspects of accounting records when the validity of the basic information shown in them is dependent on the controls exercised and the decisions made in other departments.

Possibly Mr. Byrne would consider that all of these matters controlled or decided in other departments come under the heading of internal check. He says internal check should be studied and evaluated, but that the resulting effect on the audit program is limited because the auditor has a limited responsibility for defalcations. There is full agreement in the accounting profession that the ordinary examination is not designed and cannot be relied upon to disclose defalcations even though they frequently are discovered in such examinations. Regardless of this factor, I do not see how an auditor could design the same scope of examination in a company having very poor internal check as would be followed if the internal check were of excellent character.

THE RESPONSIBILITY OF THE AUDITOR

The sounder view is that internal check affects the entire credibility of the recorded transactions and the auditor should design a program which in his judgment properly meets the risks in rendering an opinion on the financial statements. The risks, excluding defalcations, surely are not the same when internal check is poor as when it is good.

One of the principal reasons for the growth in stature and usefulness of the accounting profession has been its willingness to accept a broad view of its responsibilities and to take steps to educate and train sufficient numbers of able personnel to meet such responsibilities. Oswald Knauth, an outstanding business executive and economist, recently urged (JofA, Jan. 57 p. 32) that "accountants should take a broader view of themselves and their responsibility to the public. . . ." He was speaking of accounting and interpretation of financial statements but the advice is equally applicable to auditing. I take great pride in the fact that the committee on auditing procedure adopted the broad view in creating generally accepted auditing standards as quality bench marks to be lived up to in the examination of financial statements. A similar breadth of view was shown in the preparation of the special report on internal control, particularly in delineating the elements of a properly co-ordinated system and explaining its importance to management and the independent public accountant.

The suggestions of Mr. Byrne and Mr. Levy reflect their sincere view that *Generally Accepted Auditing Standards* and the special report have overextended the independent auditor's responsibility for investigation of internal control. Their rights to these views are fully respected, but I think they are very much in error. The responsibility of the auditor to inform himself as to organizational independence of departments, the effectiveness of physical and other controls of transactions and decisions affecting the accounting for such transactions, wherever made, is essential to the exercise of his professional judgment not only in setting the scope of audit but in rendering his opinion on the financial statements.

The suggested narrowing of viewpoint, in my opinion, would constitute serious retrogression and impair the foundation of independent auditing. It may sound paradoxical, but there are many endeavors wherein a broader concept of responsibility results in a lesser risk. In the present international situation the recently announced Middle East Policy obviously broadens our responsibility. We have undertaken it, however, in order to lessen the risk of war. Similarly, the broader view of investigation and evaluation of internal control lessens the business risk inherent in the work of the independent auditor.

RECONCILIATION NEEDED

The articles by Mr. Byrne and Mr. Levy will serve the very useful purpose of focusing the attention of the profession on the need for reconciling auditing practice with the existing concept of responsibility for studying internal control. Their suggestions would seek to adjust this concept to a common denominator of practice. While it is granted there may be need for some clarification in the special report, the real problem is to bring the general level of practice into line with authoritative standards. The internal administrative controls and internal checks described by Mr. Byrne as peripheral responsibilities of the independent auditor are those internal control features which are least subject to examination of records. It is perhaps this absence of customary audit documentation which underlies Mr. Levy's concern. Insofar as their quest relates to the need for clarification, it might be satisfied by the development of the definition of internal accounting control within the framework of internal control. The following is offered for consideration:

> *Internal accounting control comprises the plan of organization and the coordinated procedures used within the business to, (1) safeguard its assets from loss by fraud or unintentional errors, (2) check the accuracy and reliability of the accounting data which management uses in making decisions, and (3) promote operational efficiency and encourage adherence to adopted policies in those areas in which the accounting and financial departments have responsibility, directly or indirectly.*

The purpose of such a definition would be to indicate the areas in which the independent auditor is professionally qualified to improve the system in effect. Internal accounting control naturally would receive the primary attention (in man-hours) for "proper evaluation . . . for reliance thereon by the auditor." Even with this suggested broader definition, however, there are other phases of internal control which the independent auditor would need to decide whether, and if so to what extent, he deems necessary to investigate. We should recognize that these are areas which cannot be wrapped up in a neat package, but must be left to the discretion and judgment of the independent auditor. To me it is merely proof of professional attributes that we do have areas almost wholly dependent upon judgment and experience. This should be a source of pride and strength, not fear, because it is obvious that we do not need either knowledge or evaluation beyond that required to pass upon the fairness of the financial statements.

To illustrate the foregoing point, there is no requirement for the investigation and evaluation of such matters as training programs, time and mo-tion studies and quality controls, unless in the particular circumstances they have an important bearing on the financial statements. Furthermore, eval-uation of the efficiency of management is not included in the independent auditor's responsibility in examining and reporting on financial statements. Naturally he will be interested in observing evidence of efficiency, particu-larly in the accounting and financial departments, and will make such sugges-tions for improvement as he may judge to be worthy of consideration by the client.

From the viewpoint of bringing auditing practice into line with authoritative standards relating to internal control, it is my belief that the principal area for improvement is the examination of large business enterprises. As corpora-tions grow in financial complexity and diversification of operations, the in-vestigation of internal control becomes increasingly difficult to implement, and requires a larger proportion of the total auditing effort. In an article pub-lished in *The Journal* ("Special Techniques Needed in the Audit of Large Busi-ness Enterprises," May 51, pp. 678–685) I attempted to outline a suggested direction for auditing practice for large-scale enterprises. The thoughts in the article will not be repeated, except to say that further progress can be made if the accounting profession will undertake a more active program in convinc-ing clients of the importance of establishing and maintaining an effective system by formalizing their plan of organization and required procedures and policies in chart forms of presentation and in written manuals, as suggested in the special report on internal control.

A further constructive step by the profession would be the preparation of a number of representative audit case studies for large corporations. Such studies would do much to clarify audit practice in the relationship of the broad concept of internal control and examination scope, and also to illustrate var-ious alternative approaches to other audit problems. This would be an exten-sion of the decision made more than ten years ago by the committee on audit-ing procedure that to illustrate the application of auditing procedures by specific case studies of actual examinations is preferable to compilation of hypothetical procedures.

The preceding discussion probably had a significant effect on practicing audi-tors. In late 1958, the AICPA issued Statements on Auditing Procedure No. 29 in order to officially state the scope requirements of internal control evalua-tions.

STATEMENTS ON AUDITING PROCEDURE—NO. 29
Scope of the Independent Auditor's Review
of Internal Control*

1 The purpose of this statement is to clarify previous pronounce-ments relating to the scope of the independent auditor's review of internal control as it pertains to his examination leading to an ex-pression of opinion on the fairness of financial statements. No attempt is made in this statement to consider the scope of reviews of internal control by the independent auditor for other purposes, such as special engagements involving systems surveys, revisions, etc.

Background and Discussion

2   The standard short-form report[1] includes the following sentence:

Our examination was made in accordance with generally accepted auditing standards, and accordingly included such tests of the accounting records and such other auditing procedures as we considered necessary in the circum-stances.

3   The generally accepted auditing standard relating to internal control is summarized in the standards of field work[2] as follows:

There is to be a proper study and evaluation of the existing internal control as a basis for reliance thereon and for the determination of the resultant extent of the tests to which auditing procedures are to be restricted.

It is generally recognized that as a by-product of this study and evaluation, the independent auditor is frequently able to offer constructive suggestions to his client on ways in which internal control may be improved.

4   In practice, certain questions arise concerning the scope of the inde-pendent auditor's review of internal control because of the broad definition set forth in the Special Report on Internal Control issued by the committee on auditing procedure in 1949. The definition reads as follows:

Internal control comprises the plan of organization and all of the coordinate methods and measures adopted within a business to safeguard its assets, check the accuracy and reliability of its accounting data, promote operational effi-ciency, and encourage adherence to prescribed managerial policies. This defini-tion possibly is broader than the meaning sometimes attributed to the term. It recognizes that a "system" of internal control extends beyond those matters which relate directly to the functions of the accounting and financial depart-

---

*Committee on Auditing Procedure, American Institute of Certified Public Accountants, October 1958. Reprinted by permission of the American Institute of Certified Public Accountants.
[1] Codification of Statements on Auditing Procedure, page 16.
[2] Generally Accepted Auditing Standards, page 13.

ments. Such a system might include budgetary control, standard costs, periodic operating reports, statistical analyses and the dissemination thereof, a training program designed to aid personnel in meeting their responsibilities, and an internal audit staff to provide additional assurance to management as to the adequacy of its outlined procedures and the extent to which they are being effectively carried out. It properly comprehends activities in other fields as, for example, time and motion studies which are of an engineering nature, and use of quality controls through a system of inspection which fundamentally is a production function.

5   Internal control, in the broad sense, includes, therefore, controls which may be characterized as either accounting or administrative[3], as follows:

a   *Accounting controls comprise the plan of organization and all methods and procedures that are concerned mainly with, and relate directly to, the safeguarding of assets and the reliability of the financial records. They generally include such controls as the systems of authorization and approval, separation of duties concerned with record keeping and accounting reports from those concerned with operations or asset custody, physical controls over assets, and internal auditing.*

b   *Administrative controls comprise the plan of organization and all methods and procedures that are concerned mainly with operational efficiency and adherence to managerial policies and usually relate only indirectly to the financial records. They generally include such controls as statistical analyses, time and motion studies, performance reports, employee training programs, and quality controls.*

The extent to which organizational plans and control methods and procedures may be classified as accounting controls or administrative controls will, of course, vary in individual circumstances.

Conclusions

6   In the ordinary examination, the selection of auditing procedures, their timing, and the determination of the extent to which they should be followed will depend largely upon the auditor's judgment of the adequacy and effectiveness of the internal controls. This judgment is arrived at as the result of his study and evaluation (which may involve testing, observation, investigation and inquiry) of those internal controls which, in his opinion, influence the reliability of the financial records. In the course of his examination the auditor obtains appropriate knowledge of his client's organization and operations, on which he bases his selection of the internal control areas he proposes to evaluate. Accounting controls, as described in paragraph 5(a), generally bear directly and importantly on the reliability of financial records and would, therefore,

---

[3] In one sense all controls may be characterized as "administrative," even the accounting controls. The division being made here is for the purpose of distinguishing the accounting controls, with which the independent auditor is primarily concerned, from all other controls.

require evaluation. Administrative controls, as described in paragraph 5(b), ordinarily relate only indirectly to the financial records and thus would not require evaluation. However, if the auditor believes that certain administrative controls, in a particular case, may have an important bearing on the reliability of the financial records, he should consider the need for evaluating such controls. For example, statistical records maintained by production, sales or other operating departments may be considered by the auditor as requiring evaluation in a particular instance.

7   The committee has considered whether the part of the definition of internal control concerning the safeguarding of assets and the auditing standard concerning study and evaluation of internal control, taken together, are inconsistent with the statement in the Codification[4] to the effect that, in the ordinary examination, the auditor does not assume responsibility for the detection of defalcations and other similar irregularities. The committee sees no conflict in this regard since the objective of the audit program (which is designed, in part, as a result of the evaluation of internal control) is to provide a basis for the expression of an opinion on the financial statements, taken as a whole, and not to detect defalcations or similar irregularities. In developing such a program, the auditor has a responsibility for evaluating internal controls designed to safeguard assets, and when such controls are weak or lacking his program should take this condition into consideration. This consideration might lead either to the extension of audit tests, or to the shifting of emphases or timing of the audit procedures; for example, counts, reconciliations, confirmations, or observations of certain assets (such as cash, receivables or inventories) might be made at the balance-sheet date rather than at an interim date.

[4]Codification of Statements on Auditing Procedure, "Responsibilities and Functions of the Independent Auditor," pages 11–13.

CHAPTER 7

INTERNAL CONTROL: EVALUATION IN A COMPUTERIZED ENVIRONMENT

After 1955 when computers began to appear in client offices, CPAs started complaining about the presumed undesirable effects of machine-processed accounting data. Computers, it was often said, meant a loss of the audit trail and, therefore, rendered audits difficult if not impossible. But computerization could not be curtailed by auditors' complaints.

In the decade of the sixties, auditors not only learned to accept computers, but they also began to develop the techniques necessary to audits of computerized clients. Later we will learn that auditors have begun to develop ways of using the computer as an audit aid; however, our subject at hand is internal control. Computers have had an influence on all aspects of auditing, but internal control review has been most affected. The next two readings present some of the techniques that have been developed for internal control review in a computerized environment.

AN INTERNAL CONTROL CHECKLIST FOR EDP
H. Bruce Joplin*

Accountants, auditors, and other persons concerned with the establishment of good internal controls have long sought a method of evaluating the adequacy of controls incorporated into electronic data processing systems. Those without extensive experience in computer operations who have attempted to penetrate the labyrinth of EDP will readily appreciate the value of an objective basis from which to launch their inquiry into this phase of automation. An internal control check list such as is presented in this article can serve as an invaluable aid in this regard.

From the outset it should be stated that the use of a check list does not obviate the need for judgment and discretion on the part of the reviewer; it does provide a framework around which an informed decision may be reached regarding the adequacy of the system of internal control. For example, a negative answer to any question or group of questions is not prima facie evidence of a weakness in internal control but must be evaluated in the light of the entire system. To do this the reviewer should inform himself as to the nature, scope, and capabilities of this particular EDP system. This knowledge may be obtained by a review of flow charts and input and output formats; observation of compu-

* From *Management Services,* July–August, 1964, pp. 32–37. Reprinted by permission of the American Institute of Certified Public Accountants.

ter operations; discussions with computer manufacturers' representatives; and review of computer reference manuals.

Mastery of a certain amount of computer jargon is an additional requisite to the evaluation of EDP systems. Since the reviewer must communicate with computer-oriented people who typically do not understand more than a minimum of accounting terminology, it is incumbent upon him to enter the discussion as well prepared as possible. The check list presented herein assumes a reasonable knowledge of computer terminology.

To provide continuity of thought, certain assumptions have been made in developing the model check list. Generally, a fully integrated, tape-oriented system with no parallel operations and few, if any, intermediary printouts has been assumed. The reviewer should modify his procedures for evaluating the system of internal control to fit the equipment configuration and stage of conversion he encounters.

An internal control check list for EDP should be divided into logical segments to facilitate an orderly approach by the reviewer. The following sections have been selected as appropriate for our discussion:

1 Organization of the EDP department

2 Standardization of procedures

3 Computer program maintenance

4 Input procedures

5 Computer processing procedures

6 Magnetic tape control

7 Physical condition and maintenance

The importance of each section will be considered briefly, followed by examples of the type of questions that could be included in an internal control check list. Space does not permit a complete listing of all appropriate questions.

EDP department organization

The proper segregation of duties is just as important, if not more so, in an electronic data processing system as it is in a conventional accounting system. There is a greater concentration of responsibility for data processing lodged in the EDP department than in any other single unit. It is important that this department be so designed as to permit maximum co-operation between work units yet provide for physical and organizational separation. The reviewer should regard the absence of written instructions and manuals and/or the prevalence of oral instructions as weaknesses in internal control.

1 Is the EDP department independent of all operating units for which it performs data processing functions?

2 Are the following work units physically as well as organizationally separate?
   a Computer center
   b Control unit
   c Program and tape library
   d Systems and programing units

3 Is there a current operating manual for the department?

4 Are current organization charts and flow charts available?

5 Is there a schedule of all active programs, including a brief description of the function of each, date of approval, and identification number?

6 Is access to the computer center limited to persons having a legitimate mission therein?

7 Is access to control data restricted to employees of the control unit?

8 Is the control unit responsible for recording and expediting all data processed by the EDP section, including control over the number, due date, and distribution of reports?

9 Are approved copies of all computer programs and necessary supporting documents maintained in the library and issued to interested persons only upon written authorization?

10 Are systems and programing unit employees forbidden to operate computers on regular processing runs?

Standardization of procedures

Although each computer is unique in its purpose, there are many programing techniques and procedures which are common to all programs. It is desirable that these techniques and procedures be standardized and set forth in a programing manual. This manual will contain a written record of all policies, procedures, and techniques which are to be used throughout the data processing organization. Such a manual will facilitate communication among programers, assist in training of new personnel, and prevent the development of conflicting procedures.

1 Is there a standard format for the program file which should be assembled for each program?

2 Are flow charts and block diagram symbols and procedures standardized?

3 Are program testing procedures well established?

4 Are program techniques standardized for the following?
   a Table look-up or search methods
   b Use of program switches

   c Initialization routines
   d Tape record blocking

5 Are halt addresses standardized as to core location and use?

6 Are symbolic programing labels or tags standardized?

7 Have all standardized procedures been compiled in a programing manual and is the manual current?

Computer program maintenance

Complete and thorough documentation of computer programs is a requisite to controlling the operations of programing and systems units, to safeguarding the assets of the company, and to expediting changes in, and patching of, operating programs. In the early stages of development, computer programs are altered and patched so frequently that proper documentation is difficult to achieve. However, at the time a program becomes operational, the documents which support and explain the program should be prepared and filed in the library. As subsequent changes are made, the file must be revised accordingly.

1 Are program changes cleared through persons of authority other than programers directly involved in the preparation of programs?

2 Are program changes documented as to the following?
   a Reason for change
   b Effect of change
   c Prior period adjustments necessary

3 Is there a program file for each computer program containing the following information?
   a Specific program name and number
   b The purpose of the program
   c Agreements as to:
     1 When source data is to be ready for processing
     2 What output is required, format, etc.
     3 When reports are due
     4 How various transactions and exceptions are to be handled
     5 What coding will be used (Written documents containing this information should be reviewed and signed by all department heads concerned. This assures that the problem has been thoroughly investigated and agreement has been reached before programing begins.)
   d A narrative description of the program
   e A general block diagram
   f A detailed block diagram
   g Complete operating directions. These instructions should be clear and simple. They should be so complete that no oral instructions are required to operate the program. These instructions should:
     1 Identify tape units on which various input and output files will be mounted

    2 Describe any action required regarding external tape labels
    3 Specify console switch settings
    4 List all program halts with prescribed action for each
    5 Describe restart procedures if other than standard
    6 Describe any exception to other standard routines
h A description of all input data required
i A description of output data required: form numbers, approximate quantity, number of copies, etc.
j Disposition of input material, defining exactly what is to be done with all input material: where to deliver; how long to retain
k Detail layout of:
    1 Tape input records
    2 Tape output records
    3 Punched-card input and output format
    4 Printed output including samples
l Layout of storage locations:
    1 Input, output, and work areas
    2 Subroutines
    3 Constants and variables
m Description and example of any control card which may be necessary
n A sample of the printer carriage tape
o A dump of the program now in use

Input procedures

The exactness with which computers follow instructions requires that data entering the system be translated into machine language in correct form and content. If input is captured accurately and completely, the processing of data will be relatively simple once computer programs have been debugged. The development of formal procedures, the presence of written instructions, and the minimization of transactions requiring special treatment will increase input accuracy and strengthen internal control.

1 Is the number of basic types of input documents limited so as to facilitate control and processing efficiency?

2 Are all input documents press-numbered?

3 Are all numbered documents accounted for by the control unit?

4 Are data processed in serially numbered batches?

5 Are all source documents identified by batch number and canceled to prevent reprocessing?

6 Are data controlled by the number of documents processed and by hash totals as well as by dollar amount?

7 Does the control unit use a document register or other positive method of comparing machine run totals with control totals?

8 Is responsibility fixed, and are adequate procedures in effect, for tracing and correcting input errors?

9 Are corrections identified and recorded in such a manner that duplicate correction will not occur and subsequent audit will be possible?

10 Are all instructions to key punch operators (or bookkeeping machine operators preparing paper tapes) written in clear, concise form?

11 If the computer writes checks or other negotiable instruments, are the requisition and use of blank stock closely controlled?

Computer processing procedures

Processing, as used here, includes all functions performed from the point at which the computer receives data in machine language to the final report. During this time the method of storing and transmitting data may change many times. The nature of data may be altered by other data already in storage or by factors built into programs. The auditor should be familiar with how data are processed, in what form, and with what results. This he may learn from flow charts and block diagrams.

1 Do programs positively identify input data as to date, type, etc.?

2 Do programs test for valid codes in input data, and are halts or printouts provided when invalid codes are detected?

3 Are changes in program rate tables and other constants initiated in writing by persons authorized to do so, and are all such changes recorded and retained for audit?

4 Are all instructions to operators set forth in writing in clear and unequivocal language?

5 Are operators cautioned not to accept oral instructions or to contact programers directly when errors are detected?

6 Is there a positive follow-up to determine if corrections are made on errors found by the machine?

7 Are all halts (except end of job) and errors recorded and the record retained for audit?

8 Is the use of external switches held to a minimum, and are the instructions for their use set forth in writing?

9 Are the situations whereby data may be inserted or extracted by the use of the console set forth in writing and limited to circumstances which cannot be handled through the stored program?

10 Are console printouts controlled and reviewed by persons (other than operators) who are familiar with the activity being performed?

11 Are console printouts labeled so as to be reasonably intelligible?

12 Are account codes, employee numbers, and other identification data designed with self-checking test digits, and does the program test for these digits?

13 Are checkpoints provided in lengthy processing runs, and are program or external restart instructions provided in case a checkpoint fails to balance?

14 Is a computer usage recorded on a positive basis by program as to run-time and set-up time and by nonuse as to maintenance time and off time?

Magnetic tape use

In EDP, data processing activities are organized around files as opposed to functions as in most manual systems. For example, in the typical EDP installation the hash receipts processing function will be subordinated to the accounts receivable file maintenance. The proper control over, and maintenance of, these files is of major interest to the reviewer.

1 Are there physical controls to prevent inadvertent erasure of tapes?

2 Are there formal procedures for preventing premature reuse of tapes?

3 Do external tape labels contain the following?
   a Reel number
   b Serial number
   c Number of reels in the file
   d Program identification number
   e Date created
   f Retention date
   g Density
   h Drive number

4 Do header labels have the following data?
   a Program identification number
   b Reel number
   c Date created
   d Date obsolete

5 Do trailer labels have the following data?
   a Block account
   b Record count
   c Hash totals
   d End of reel or end of file designation

6 Do programs test for header and trailer labels each time a new tape is accessed or the end of the reel is sensed?

7 Has a policy been established for the retirement of tape reels which have excessive read or write errors?

Physical condition

Computer manufacturers have made considerable progress in insulating their equipment from environmental influences. Nevertheless, certain precautions are still necessary to prevent damage to hardware and tape files. In addition, regular maintenance by qualified engineers is an integral part of assuring continued computer performance and accuracy. The reviewer should inform himself of maintenance and other requirements applicable to the computer under review.

1 Has a policy been established regarding visitors, neatness, smoking, etc., in the computer center?

2 Is the hardware serviced by qualified engineers on a regular basis?

3 Are manufacturer's cleaning recommendations for the computer center strictly followed?

4 Are manufacturer's temperature and humidity requirements maintained?

5 Are magnetic tape reels stored according to manufacturer's specifications?

The use of an internal control check list will greatly facilitate the development of objective criteria for the evaluation of the system of internal control in EDP application. Separation of the different facets of an EDP operation into manageable units will speed the reviewer's understanding of the system as a whole and can provide him with a basis for controlling the activities of the EDP department.

EVALUATING INTERNAL CONTROLS IN EDP SYSTEMS
W. Thomas Porter*

The evaluation of the system of internal control is a point of departure in auditing. Such an evaluation serves as a gauge of the quality of the system. It also gives the auditor the foundation upon which he will construct his examination and build his conclusions. The importance and increased emphasis on the evaluation of internal control are clearly revealed by a review of auditing literature. R. K. Mautz and H. A. Sharaf wrote:

Because the extent and effectiveness of internal control is so important in audit programming and performance, a prudent practitioner will tend to give this

* From *The Journal of Accountancy*, Vol. 118, No. 2 (August, 1964), pp. 34–40. Reprinted by permission of the American Institute of Certified Public Accountants.

phase of the examination a full measure of emphasis. At best, internal control is a rather amorphous subject and difficult to comprehend and reduce to satisfactory work paper notes. Yet no part of the examination is more important than his review and evaluation of internal control. Also, there is no area in which he can be of more real assistance to his client than by scrupulously examining and reporting on the client's control procedures.[1]

Although internal control does not lend itself to any simple set of rules by which it can be evaluated, it has historically been evaluated by the auditor through:

I Observation, inquiries, and review of manuals and charts to determine whether:

    1 The formal and informal organization of the company clearly establishes and specifically prescribes a functional segregation of duties between people responsible for
    a Authorization of the transaction
    b Recording and processing of the transaction
    c Custody of the assets involved in the transaction

    2 The financial and accounting procedures are sufficient to assure that
    a Transactions are reviewed sufficiently to establish the propriety and accuracy of their recording.
    b Data processing flow permits detection and correction of errors in operating and financial data and reduces such errors to the level permitted by management.
    c Reports are required and prepared to reflect the responsibility for the authorization, performance, and review of financial and accounting transactions.

II The selection of actual transactions to determine whether the purported policies, procedures and controls are operating as described.

The effect of electronic data processing on the evaluation of the system of internal control largely centers on point II above, the testing of the system. In any system, EDP or otherwise, a review of the organizational aspects, procedural controls, and administrative practices is necessary to establish the extent of the audit examination and to make constructive suggestions about improving the system. But obviously, EDP affects the nature of such a review. The importance of systems development and programming practices and documentation, input-output controls, programmed controls, tape library procedures, and computer operating controls require the auditor to observe different activities, ask different questions, and review different manuals and documents than he would in his review of a non-EDP system.

---

[1] R. K. Mautz and H. A. Sharaf, *The Philosophy of Auditing,* American Accounting Association, Madison, Wisconsin, 1961, p. 146.

TESTING THE SYSTEM

Conventionally, the auditor has selected actual accounting transactions that have been previously processed by the client to test the system. Typically, this approach calls for the tracing of a "representative" number of transactions from the recording of the source documents through whatever intermediate records might exist to the output reports or records produced. Such an approach is taken without any regard to the manner in which the output was actually developed. It is based on the logic that if the source data or system input can be proven correct and if the results of the system accurately reflect these source data, then the output must be correct and the manner in which the system processed the data is inconsequential.

In an EDP-dominated situation, such an approach has been called the "around the computer" approach to testing the system. This approach is the one which, in the majority of EDP installations, has been taken by auditors. Auditors have been using this "around the computer" approach because:

1 It is a familiar method.

2 It does not require technical knowledge of the EDP equipment.

3 The relatively unchanged audit trail conditions encountered in the EDP installations have not required a different approach.

An often unstated but perhaps more significant reason for the auditor's use of the "around the computer" approach is the auditor's unwillingness to come to grips with EDP.

The other approach to the testing of the system is the "through the computer" approach, which follows the concept that, if the controls and procedures incorporated in computer programs are effective and if a proper control of computer operations is employed, then proper processing of proven and acceptable input is bound to result in acceptable output. Such an approach is entirely dependent upon the consistency of processing operations found in computer operations.

In addition to an over-all review of the EDP system, this approach obviously requires an explicit knowledge of input and master file record layout, a fairly comprehensive knowledge of computer operations and built-in and programmed controls, and a thorough understanding of the development and use of "test decks."

Test Decks

In my opinion, often the conventional audit approach of testing the system by selecting actual transactions previously processed by the client is incomplete and inexact. In some cases, the transactions selected do not include the unusual ones requiring exception handling. In addition, the auditor, even with "representative" tests, can never be certain that the individuals carrying out the system actually do what they say they do or are supposed to do.

But with the advent of electronic systems, the operations research concepts of "models" and "simulation" appear applicable in the auditor's testing approach. The "model" is the client's computer program:

> . . . complete and accurate in all respects, not subject to the deviations caused by human idiosyncrasies or human temptation . . . containing in very specific language the exact instructions as to what the machine is to do. You can tell just what happened to a transaction.[2]

"Simulation" can be performed by the auditor by experimenting and testing the procedural model. The auditor can feed it all sorts of good and bad transactions to see how the EDP system reacts. These simulated transactions are commonly referred to as "test decks." The test deck is developed by preparing machine-readable data (i.e., punched cards, magnetic tape) designed to simulate every feasible type of transaction and to test specific program controls. These transactions are processed using the existing computer program, and the results of the computer processing are compared with predetermined results. Obviously, the purpose of the test deck technique is to determine for the auditor exactly how a specific processing system will react to particular types of transactions.

> In effect, the auditor allows the automatic data processing system to audit itself by merely presenting the system with a set of test problems or situations which the system cannot distinguish from normal processing activity, and then ascertaining how these tests cases are handled. Since no . . . programming is required to implement a test of this type, the procedure is a relatively inexpensive one from the standpoint of operating costs, and the results obtained are both effectively presented and irrefutable.[3]

While it is true that the computer operating costs to process test decks are rather minimal, it is also true that the development of test decks can be a complex and time-consuming project, and the auditor should be cognizant of the problems involved.

Before discussing the development of test decks, it is important to make two points clear. First, some writers fail to differentiate between test decks and computer audit programs and, as a result, such writing discusses the use of "test programs" in auditing. Test decks, as defined above, are used to evaluate the *quality* of the data processing *system* in use. Computer audit programs are

---

[2] A. B. Toan, Jr., "The Auditor and EDP," JofA, June60, p. 44.

[3] Department of United States Air Force, *Guide for Auditing Automatic Data Processing Systems*, Government Printing Office, Washington, D.C., 1961, pp. 8-14 and 8-15.

used to determine the *quality* of *information* generated by the system. Such programs, to be sure, can perform detailed tests and computations. They are more often designed to elicit, from current master files, exception reports or sample selections based on criteria specified and programmed by the auditor. Such information is then used by the auditor in his evaluation of the evidence supporting the reasonableness and adequacy of disclosure of the accounts descriptions, balances, and footnotes in the financial statements under examination. Secondly, some writers and speakers have often mentioned another technique of auditing computer records—the review of computer programs. There are several reasons why this method is not very satisfactory:

1 It requires a higher level of programming skill than that required to write the original program. To go through a program which may contain thousands of instructions, complex logic, and numerous switches is an exceedingly difficult job. Even if the auditing profession had enough persons competent to make such an evaluation, it would be too costly.

2 It would not guarantee that the program reviewed is the most current version. Because of the numerous minor changes made over a period of time in the ordinary course of computer operations, the auditor would have to repeat the detailed review periodically, or control program changes, neither of which is very practical.

3 It would not guarantee that the program reviewed is the regular production program being used by the client. The auditor must have assurance that the program he is evaluating is the one which is being used to process transactions and produce financial information.

In my opinion, the only practical answer to evaluating the performance of a computer is utilization of test decks, not reviews of programs. However, a review of the client's documentation used to develop the applicable program is desirable in developing the test deck. Such documents include flow charts, block diagrams, input and output media, exception reports, and narrative descriptions of the procedures and controls in the system.

A review of these documents must be sufficient to give the auditor a complete knowledge of the procedural controls, both manual and programmed, in the EDP system so that the transactions included in the test deck check the existence and effectiveness of these controls.

In addition, this review must enable the auditor to determine whether the client's controls are adequate or necessary to achieve the client's control objectives.

In developing and using the successful test deck, there are several important factors which the auditor must take into consideration:

1 He must decide upon the exact point in the system where the test data are to be entered.

2 He must determine the types of transactions to be included in the test deck.

3 He must obtain the master records to process against the test transactions and to compute the predetermined results for comparison with the output resulting from the test processing.

4 He must carefully consider the effects that the processing of the test transactions will have on the results of the system produced under normal operating conditions.

5 He must obtain the client's regular processing programs and assure himself that the program is used to process the test data.

6 He must make whatever arrangements are necessary to get the test data prepared and processed and to get the output in the desired form.

Where the tests are to be entered in the system
Before developing the test deck, the auditor must first decide the point at which he wishes to enter the test data. If the operations and controls in the preparation of input are to be included in the test, the test-deck data must be fed into the input portion of the system as basic source documentation. If only computer operations are being tested, the data may be introduced into the computer operations in the form of punched cards or magnetic tape records.

Determining the types of transactions
The inherent advantage of the test deck over the selection of actual transactions is that the auditor may include every type—normal or abnormal—of conceivable transaction in his tests with relative ease. And theoretically, a sample of one for each type of transaction is as statistically sound as a large number because of the uniformity involved in the processing of data.

There are several methods which may be used to construct a simulated transaction deck, all of which require a review of systems and program documentation to gain a complete knowledge of the procedural controls in the EDP system. Although the auditor can prepare entirely imaginary transactions, it may be expedient to select transactions from the client's actual data or from the test data used by the client's programmer to check out the computer program. For example, the programmer's test deck was used in developing the auditor's test deck to evaluate payroll processing in a large manufacturer. Many of the programmer's tests were applicable from an audit standpoint and were readily included in the auditor's test deck. The review of the client's test data also uncovered some outdated tests and areas in the program which were not tested at all. The client's data processing management felt such a review was highly informative and beneficial to operations.

Selection of the client's input data or test data usually will not include all the possible variables, and additional transactions must be created. The determination of possible variables to be tested may be made by analyzing the input record layout. By analyzing the fields of data included on the input record, all combinations of data can be determined. In this connection, several observations should be made:

1 It is not necessary that all possible combinations within all fields be set out as separate problems. Distinction should be made between variables which merely represent identification data (i.e., account numbers, social security numbers) and those which involve alternate handling. In the case of the former, only a limited number of possibilities need to be included to test the identification routines in the program. To illustrate, Exhibit 1, below, shows the fields and their description for a rate change input card used in a payroll system of the large manufacturer mentioned earlier. The transaction will change an employee's hourly rate and pay code. The transaction is program edited for validity of dates, alpha name, old pay code and rate and whether the new rate is equal to the old rate. In addition, any new rate greater than $10 is excepted. The tests included in the test deck for this transaction were:
a Valid rate change with all other fields valid
b Rate change greater than $10
c Valid rate change, old rate wrong
d Valid rate change, old rate equal to new rate
e Valid rate change, alpha name wrong

To test sequence checking and identification comparison routines, a card with a valid transaction number or employee number and containing valid information could be placed out of sequence in the test deck. Additional tests for sequence checking and identification comparison would not be necessary.

EXHIBIT 1   RATE CHANGE CARD FORMAT

Card Field	Description
4–12	Social security number
13–14	Transaction code (03)
16	Division
18–22	New hourly rate
24–29	Rate change date
30	New payroll code
31–34	First four characters of last name (alpha name)
48–52	Old hourly rate
75	Old payroll code

2 It is necessary to include at least two of each type of variable requiring alternative handling in order to test the existence and effectiveness of programmed

controls. For example, in the above illustration, all rates equal to or less than $10 are handled by one processing routine; all rates greater than $10 are handled by an exception routine.

3 The tests should include transactions which determine the processing and handling of the following general conditions:

a Out of sequence conditions

b Out of limits conditions

c Routines arising from a major decision point where alternative processing takes place as a result of the comparison of transaction records with master records; i.e., where the transaction identification number can be greater, equal to, or less than the identification number on the master record.

d Units of measure differences

e Incomplete or missing input information

f Wrong tape files

g Numeric characters in fields where alphabetic characters belong and vice versa

h Characters in certain fields which exceed prescribed length (an overflow condition)

i Illogical conditions in fields where programmed consistency checks test the logical relationship in the same fields

j Conditions where transaction codes or amounts do not match the codes or amounts established in tables stored in internal memory

Obviously all these conditions cannot be tested with each type of transaction, but the majority of them, if not all, may be tested in processing all transactions included in the test deck.

One of the problems involved in developing a test deck is the difficulty of reviewing its substantive aspects. Apart from a detailed review, which is impractical and time consuming for the audit manager or partner, it is very difficult for the reviewer to get a general idea as to the scope and "rightness" of a test deck. For audit review purposes, it may be useful to construct a matrix during the development of the test data which would indicate the types of conditions tested by each transaction. Such a matrix is shown in Exhibit 2 below. Another device which is helpful in review and which is necessary for the audit workpapers is a transaction listing of the test deck. Such a listing indicates, in code sequence, the information punched or recorded on the transaction input record. This information can be sorted and listed by tabulating equipment. The listing should include a narrative description of the type of test, the objective, and what output will result from the test.

Obtaining the master records

The auditor must obtain the master records in machine-readable form against which the test transactions are to be processed and in visible form to compute

EXHIBIT 2

Type of Condition Tested	Test Transaction Number
	0 1 2 3 4 .... n
a	
b	
c	
d	
e	
f	
g	
h	
i	
j	

the predetermined results for comparison with output resulting from the test deck processing.

With sequential processing, there is usually not much of a problem in obtaining the master records in machine-readable form since the master file is not written over or destroyed in processing the test transactions. There is a problem in random processing since the master records maintained on random access equipment are written over or destroyed by processing transactions. To protect the client's master records, the test deck can be run immediately after the random access file "dump."[4] After the "dump," the master records are on both the random access master files and on magnetic tape. The test data can then be processed against the tape files as discussed above. In such a situation, the client's computer would have to be altered slightly to have the computer "read" and "write" tape rather than "read" and "write" random access files. In situations where the auditor must or wishes to run his test transactions between the "dump" cycles, the random access files may be protected by physically locking the files to prevent writing on them and altering the program so that the "write random access file" instruction becomes "write tape."

In some installations such as the large manufacturer referred to previously, test master records are used, against which the test data are processed by the company's programmers in testing the system. These masters, although comparatively few in number, represent actual masters. The advantage of these test masters is the ease with which they can be used and changed to reflect

[4] A file "dump" refers to the transfer or writing of the contents of the random access files on magnetic tapes, at realistic intervals, to provide the ability to reconstruct the file in the event the original file is accidentally damaged or destroyed.

certain conditions necessary for testing, and the ease with which they can be printed out for visible review. For example, the manufacturer uses twenty-four test master records, in punched card form, as a test model payroll master file. These twenty-four records are used instead of the 20,000 employee master record file to avoid time in selecting and printing actual master records. The use of test masters is based on the premise that the computer cannot tell the difference between the processing of a test master record and an actual master record. A variation of the use of client's test master records is the creation, by the auditor, of "dummy" master records for use in testing the system. Such was the case in the test of an automated labor recording system in this large manufacturer.[5]

Although actual master records may be readily obtained in machine-readable form in many systems, it is difficult to get the same records in printed form without advance planning. One method is to time the tests so they are processed with the output master file used to prepare a printed report such as the accounts receivable aged trial balance or an inventory report. Another method is to have an inquiry program prepared which will print out selected master records from the master file to be used in processing the test transactions. Most installations have the ability to inquire into any file, and the auditor may, with a little planning, have his file-searching needs met by a routine procedure.

The need to carefully consider the effects test transactions will have on the results of the system

Obviously, the auditor does not want to have his test transactions affect the results produced under normal operating conditions. Accordingly, he must carefully consider what effects the processing of the test data will have on the results of the system. For example, the output tape resulting from the processing of test data should be clearly labeled so as to prevent improper use and subsequent incorrect processing of operating data.

Any tests that are processed along with actual transactions must be carefully controlled so as to preclude undesired results from taking place. For example, in a test to determine that the open order file was reviewed periodically for unusual items in a medium-sized steel manufacturer, a valid order was transmitted by the auditor from a sales branch location and the shipping copy was destroyed. This order had to be controlled by the auditor to prevent shipping of the order and to insure subsequent removal from the open order file.

[5] R. M. Benjamin, "Auditing Automatic Source Recording," *The Quarterly*, Touche, Ross, Bailey & Smart, September 1963.

Obtaining and controlling the client's regular processing program

One of the important procedures of testing a company's EDP system is obtaining assurance that the program being tested is the one the company actually uses to process data. Basically there are two ways in which this can be achieved:

1 If the data processing organizational and administrative controls are adequate, the program can be requested, on a surprise basis, from the program librarian and duplicated for the auditor's control and use in processing test data. As a further measure, the auditor may request that test data previously processed with the auditor's copy of the program be processed with the client's operating program and then compare the end results. This method has the added advantage of checking any computer operator intervention.

2 The auditor may request, on a surprise basis, that the operating program be left in the computer at the completion of processing operating data so that he may process his test data with it. This method has an advantage over the method above in that it usually ensures a current version of the program. In many installations and particularly in earlier stages of conversion, program changes are made frequently. These continuing program changes may make it quite difficult for the auditor to review and check all significant changes in order to be satisfied with the operations performed by the program.

As a general rule, the auditor should observe the running of the test data with the computer program. In many installations, this may not be practical because of the "grave-yard shift" scheduling of test data processing. The adequacy of the controls in the EDP department, however, should be the dictating factor here rather than the time of day, or night.

Arranging to get test data prepared and processed

In addition to obtaining master records and the client's regular processing program, the auditor must carefully design test data, obtain the necessary key punching equipment and/or personnel, and obtain computer time from authorized personnel in order to get the test data prepared and processed, and to get the output in the desired form. Most of these arrangements are procedural and involve advanced planning with systems and computer operations people.

The design of test data is not procedural in nature but is something that the auditor will find worthy of his careful consideration. Essentially the test deck should be so designed as to limit the amount of work required of the auditor to review the results of the test. The use of special codings or distinctive names which allow invalid test transactions to be easily identified, sorted out of valid tests, and listed on separate output listings are devices which can be employed to make the auditor's job of interpreting and evaluating the test results more simple and less time consuming.

In some installations where the audit trail has been drastically altered, it is pure nonsense to argue for alternative methods of testing and evaluating the system. The only practical approach is auditing "through the computer" with the use of a well-conceived test deck. In some installations where the audit trail has not been altered with the use of EDP equipment, the "around the computer" approach may seem to be a valid alternative. But even in these electronic systems, the benefits accruing to the auditor using the "through the computer" approach appear to outweigh the problems and additional considerations involved in using such an approach. These benefits are:

1 Better knowledge of the client's system of procedures and controls—many computer installations are integrated management information systems providing operating, as well as financial, information. A review and evaluation of such a system will necessarily provide the auditor with a more complete understanding of the client's "total" system of data processing and controls than normally obtained by auditing "around the computer."

2 Better letters of recommendations—a detailed review of the computer system along with the design and use of effective tests will enable the auditor to evaluate the client's input-output controls, built-in machine controls, programmed controls, and operating controls. Such an evaluation will result in more informative and constructive letters of recommendations and, hence, increased service to clients.

3 More representative tests—through the use of well-designed test decks, the auditor is able to evaluate the system's ability to handle all types of transactions, both normal and abnormal. The kind of transactions included in the test deck is limited only by the auditor's imagination, rather than by the practical limitations of time and cost involved in obtaining the same types of transactions from a sample of actual transactions. This point is emphasized by an audit manager in writing about the use of the computer in the audit testing of an automated labor recording system: ". . . The number of unusual conditions which were tested with a few simple prearranged plans would have required thousands upon thousands of transaction selections had random sampling or any other conventional testing procedures been used."[6]

4 Continuous auditing more readily achieved—one of the objectives of auditing in recent years has been the smoothing of the work flow in an annual audit examination. This has been achieved to some extent by spreading the examination between the "interim" period and the "year-end" period. Since the test deck is designed around a series of business transactions that do not change in nature from day to day, its usefulness can survive minor and perhaps major changes in the computer program. As a result, the auditor can make more frequent tests

[6] *Ibid.*, p. 11.

and obtain "readings" of the client's activities at different operating periods during the year without expending more time, if as much, than previously spent in testing the system.

The use of EDP equipment in no way lessens the auditor's requirement for evaluating the system of internal control; in my opinion, it makes the evaluation increasingly important to the audit examination and to the concept of service to the client. The auditor must recognize the importance of electronic procedures and the significance of the work performed within the EDP equipment. Accordingly, he must resist the temptation of assuming that, if the input to the machine system is adequately reviewed and controlled and the output can be checked back to source documents, he can then be unconcerned with what went on within the machine system itself.

At present, rarely will exclusive use of either of the two approaches discussed above be applicable to an electronic accounting system. The unusually large volume of data handled by EDP systems makes the "around the computer" approach impractical except in unusual circumstances. On the other hand, the inconsistency of processing found in all but the most sophisticated "total" systems renders the "through the computer" approach ineffective except in equally unusual circumstances. Experience has shown that the most effective method of auditing electronic systems will generally be some combination of these two approaches. Accordingly, the auditor can still use conventional techniques in evaluating and testing the system of internal control to some extent. But to a large extent, a fresh approach to the problem combined with the effective use of the computer is necessary.

The preceding discussion provides background necessary for attempting the following problems. Try to apply the concepts and techniques presented by Joplin and Porter to them.

INTERNAL CONTROL IN AN EDP DEPARTMENT

 The audit of the financial statements of a client that utilizes the services of a computer for accounting functions compels the CPA to understand the operation of his client's electronic data processing (EDP) system.

a The first requirement of an effective system of internal control is a satisfactory plan of organization. List the characteristics of a satisfactory plan of organization for an EDP department, including the relationship between the department and the rest of the organization.

b An effective system of internal control also requires a sound system of records control of operations and transactions (source data and its flow) and of classification of data within the accounts. For an EDP system, these controls include input controls, processing controls, and output controls. List the characteristics of a satisfactory system of input controls. (Confine your comments to a batch-controlled system employing punched cards and to the steps that occur prior to the processing of the input cards in the computer.)

(AICPA)

SAN JACINTO SAVINGS AND LOAN ASSOCIATION

▷ You have been engaged by San Jacinto Savings and Loan Association to examine its financial statements for the year ended December 31, 19X6. The CPA who examined the financial statements at December 31, 19X5 rendered an unqualified opinion.

In January 19X6 the Association installed an on-line real-time computer system. Each teller in the Association's main office and seven branch offices has an on-line input-output terminal. Customers' mortgage payments and savings account deposits and withdrawals are recorded in the accounts by the computer from data input by the teller at the time of the transaction. The teller keys the proper account by account number and enters the information in the terminal keyboard to record the transaction. The accounting department at the main office has both punched card and typewriter input-output devices. The computer is housed at the main office.

You would expect the Association to have certain internal controls in effect because an on-line real-time computer system is employed. List the internal controls which should be in effect solely because this system is employed, classifying them as:

1 Those controls pertaining to input of information.

2 All other types of computer controls.

(AICPA adapted)

CHAPTER 8

INTERNAL CONTROL:
A BEHAVIORAL PERSPECTIVE

Internal control consists not only of forms and machines; more importantly it consists of people and the behavioral structure in which they work in complex organizations. A behavioral approach to internal control evaluation is presented in this chapter. Sociometric, or positional, analysis is not presently being used by practicing CPAs, but the following two readings present a behavioral perspective of internal control as well as a suggestion for useful evaluation of it.

INTERNAL CONTROL EVALUATION—
A BEHAVIORAL APPROACH
John J. Willingham*

The importance of internal control review is well established among the members of the auditing profession. Some type of a review is accomplished during the course of practically every internal or external audit. The evaluation of internal control is used as a basis for determination of the extent of audit procedures and as a source of information for advising management. The internal control evaluation methods now employed by public accounting firms and internal auditors include questionnaires and observations of particular records during the course of the audit work itself. These evaluation techniques have been used by auditors for many years with little modification. Research in this area apparently has been non-existent, as no new techniques have evolved.

The purpose of this paper is to present a preliminary and tentative exploration of the possibility of using sociometric analysis techniques to evaluate internal control. In order to accomplish this task, certain assumptions about the nature of internal control must be made. Therefore, the first part of this paper will be devoted to a redefinition, or more accurately a synthesis of accepted current definitions of the concept of internal control. The auditing implications of a behavioral concept of internal control, and discussion of the application of sociometric analysis techniques to internal control evaluation will then follow.

*From The Internal Auditor, Summer, 1966, pp. 20–26. Reprinted by permission of the Institute of Internal Auditors.

A BEHAVIORAL CONCEPT OF INTERNAL CONTROL

A definition of internal control quite adequate for this discussion appears in the American Institute's booklet entitled *Internal Control.*

Internal control comprises the plan of organization and all of the coordinate methods and measures adopted within a business to safeguard its assets, check the accuracy and reliability of its accounting data, promote operational efficiency, and encourage adherence to prescribed managerial policies.

This same source states that characteristics of a satisfactory system of internal control would include:

A plan of organization which provides appropriate segregation of functional responsibilities,

A system of authorization and record procedures adequate to provide reasonable accounting control over assets, liabilities, revenues and expenses,

Sound practices to be followed in performance of duties and functions of each of the organizational departments, and

A degree of quality of personnel commensurate with responsibilities.

Even though there is some disagreement as to the nature of internal control and the scope of the auditor's responsibility in this area, the foregoing is an adequate and generally accepted description for purposes of this discussion.

An analysis of the foregoing definition and requirements for internal control, in order to determine the one or few cardinal elements, is revealing. The writer suggests that the above centers about an adequate division of labor among individual employees and groups or departments of employees. In short, the concept of internal control centers around the *behavior* of the members of a business organization. Certainly a "plan of organization" is a manifestation of a division of labor, and likewise a "system of authorization and record procedures." The same can be said with respect to "sound practices to be followed in performance of duties and functions of each of the organizational departments."

"A degree of quality of personnel commensurate with responsibilities" is a more difficult association to observe. It can be recognized by noting the consequences of *not* having qualified personnel. If a person truly is not qualified for a particular position, the tasks comprising the position are not being accomplished. This situation suggests that only a portion of the tasks is performed, or that some other employee is completing a portion of them for the unqualified person. In either instance, it seems proper to conclude that the division of labor is inadequate. If the unqualified person is accomplishing all tasks required by the position, it can be assumed that some or all of the tasks comprising the total position are being inadequately performed. Again, this is a manifestation of an improper division of labor. The division of labor can be corrected by either redistribution of labor among existing or additional employees, or replacement of the particular employee not qualified. Both types of corrections are means of correcting the division of labor.

It is submitted that auditors attempt to determine the *operative* division of labor of an organization under audit. After it has been determined, it is examined for weaknesses, and subject to the number and importance of these, the extent of audit tests is determined. A plan or chart of organization provides information on the general responsibilities of the various departments, and in some cases, individuals. A questionnaire is used to determine who performs specific, critical tasks. Business documents, *i.e.,* pre-numbered checks, vouchers, sales tickets, etc., provide evidence of who is performing certain tasks, provide evidence of tasks performed, and in addition nicely set the boundaries of those tasks.

Generally, all of the present evaluation techniques emphasize the *tasks* performed. Usually a questionnaire approach employs many questions of the type, "Who is responsible for performing task X?" The tests and observations of records themselves are all undertaken from the same viewpoint.

An alternative approach to internal control evaluation is to place the emphasis on the *people,* groups and individuals, who perform the tasks. More specifically, one might determine the operative division of labor by examining the operative organizational structure, *i.e.,* interaction and relationships among and between individuals and groups within the total organization. Sociologists have fairly recently become interested in organizational structure. Thus far, they have not become interested in the accounting control aspect of it, as such, but findings in the area of determinants of organizational behavior bear directly on this crucial area of auditing.

The sociologist defines organizational behavior to include all interaction between members of an organization resulting from the organizational structure (*e.g.,* giving orders), plus activity resulting from such interaction (*e.g.,* carrying out orders), and activity emanating from the structural elements *per se* (*e.g.,* an accountant for an industrial firm taking night courses in accounting not because he is required to do so but because of his concept of responsibility). In varying degrees, auditors are interested in the same types of behavior.

DETERMINANTS OF ORGANIZATIONAL BEHAVIOR

Sociologists view organizational structure in terms of norms which are behavioral prescriptions and proscriptions. The determination of what one ought and ought not do can be traced to several sources. I would suggest that most auditors consider the formal rules and regulations of an organization to be the only legitimate source of information about the duties and responsibilities (prescriptions and proscriptions) of the various members of an organization. This is evidenced by the reliance placed upon charts of organization and job manuals by auditors. While this formal organization structure is the only truly legitimate one, sociologists have discovered many others operative in businesses as well as other types of organizations. They have discovered and classed determinants into formal and informal. Formal determinants, as previously suggested, are those prescribed in the organization chart, chart of accounts, rules, office memos, manuals, contracts, and in general, *all specifications developed and supported by most or all of the top echelon personnel or the founders of a business organization.*

Informal determinants are all other specifications influencing the behavior of a member of an organization. Among these determinants are the following:

1 **Group supported, non-official structure** — normative specifications developed or supported by a non-official, identifiable group composed of organization members.

2 **Non-official structure based on member consensus** — normative specifications developed or held in common by some or all of the organization members that have developed over time. The consensus may range from almost universal consensus to small group coalitions.

3 **Interpersonal structure** — normative specifications developed as members get to know each other and begin to respond to each other as unique persons.

4 **Other minor things affecting behavior** — personality characteristics, experience, knowledge, capabilities, and individualistic definitions of positions or roles on the part of individual members of an organization.[1]

In summary, the structure of an organization results from a composite of the above. Behavior is determined in every instance by some or all of them.

Inasmuch as most business organizations have been characterized as having an over-all operative structure not wholly determined by top echelon management, it would seem that steps should be taken to eliminate all but the official structure. To the contrary, it has been discovered that while some unofficially prescribed behavior is dysfunctional, some is functional and actually enables a business to operate more smoothly and efficiently than it would if the official regulations were closely followed. Therefore, the auditor's problem is one of discovering the dysfunctional aspects of the over-all structure and remedying them.

[1] The author is indebted to Dr. J. Eugene Haas, Professor of Sociology, The University of Colorado, for this analysis of informal organizational behavior determinants.

At this point the question can be raised concerning the effectiveness of present internal control evaluation techniques in discovering the weaknesses within a division of labor. Inasmuch as over-all operative structure determines, among other things, the division of labor, it appears that present techniques could lead to improper conclusions.

PRESENT EVALUATION TECHNIQUES

A reading of internal control questionnaires and audit programs indicates that these evaluation techniques are designed to determine the operative division of labor in a given organization under audit. While this fact tends to support the contention that division of labor represents the essence of the concept of internal control, the administration, and to a lesser extent, the construction of questionnaires, may not accomplish the desired result.

A questionnaire is usually administered to only one, or to a few persons in an organization. These few persons are usually chosen because they are supervisors and should have the knowledge to answer the questions. It is quite possible that the persons chosen have full and complete knowledge about the responsibilities of the various persons under their supervision. In addition, such persons might be quite informed about the volume and quality of work being performed in their departments or work groups. But they may not know who is actually performing the work. Further, it is even possible that the person who was chosen for interview doesn't in fact supervise the employees in his own department, even though he is held responsible for their work. He may lack the power, which may be concentrated in the hands of his superior, another person at an equal management level, or even a person *at a lower level of management*. Secondly, the wording of the questions themselves might produce misconceptions. Many times the questions are aimed at determining the person *responsible* for a particular task, when the important matter is the person who *actually performs* the task. In other words, the person responsible according to the official structure may be a different one than the person actually performing a given task. Authority is derived from the official structure of an organization, but power does not necessarily rest with authority, and likewise with responsibility and performance. However, this is a relatively minor criticism of the present questionnaire approach to internal control evaluation. It could be corrected by restating questions to emphasize actual performance rather than responsibility.

Turning to the evaluation technique of observation and examination of documents during the course of an audit, the chance of drawing an incorrect conclusion with respect to the division of labor is also present, although not to the degree it is in the use of a questionnaire. Independent auditors are insistent upon support in the form of documents in order to satisfy themselves that each transaction was handled by several relatively independent persons. If each transaction has passed through the required number of persons, and each person has accomplished his specific task, each transaction is considered valid, and is considered to be classified appropriately in the accounts. If this is the case, then the document itself, and all its authorizations, validations, employee initials, and account classifications, simply constitute evidence that the proper division of labor was employed in admitting the transaction to the accounts and in physically handling the tangible goods represented by the documents.

The difficulty encountered in the use of this technique arises due to the quality of the evidence. If, for example, the initials of the company treasurer appear on an invoice to indicate authorization for payment, it is generally assumed that this task was performed by this person. In this example, the secretary to the treasurer might be the person who in fact made the approval, or the treasurer may have approved the item after only superficial examination of the supporting documents. It is impossible by this method to obtain information concerning who, in fact, accomplished this task. Again, this evaluation technique *does* establish responsibility but does *not* necessarily establish performance.

Finally the writer suggests that auditors have turned more and more to the use of observation and examination of documents and away from internal control questionnaires because the former source of evidence is more reliable. The added reliability of observation and examination of documents comes about because the auditor is actually observing the documentary manifestations of company activity rather than taking the word of a company official concerning who in the organization is responsible for its various aspects. Although internal control evaluation is used to delimit an audit, the fact remains that sometimes questionnaires are completed after an audit, from information gained from the audit tests themselves. And although the audit tests do provide more reliable evidence concerning internal control, such information obviously cannot be used to establish the extent of the audit.

SOCIOMETRIC-TYPE ANALYSIS

A possible alternative method of testing or evaluating internal control is sociometric-type analysis. This is a relatively simple testing technique, used by sociologists and social psychologists to determine and analyze the social structure of organizations. It involves interviewing a sample or all of the employees of an organization. Auditors are not concerned with all employees of an organization, and therefore, the scope of such testing would be diminished.

The interview is certainly not the unique feature of this technique. Rather it is the method of interviewing and the kinds of questions asked of the interviewees. Each person in the sample would be asked such questions as, "What tasks do you perform?", "What tasks are performed by your immediate superior?", "What tasks are performed by the person or persons directly under your supervision or on the next level of management below you?" Coleman gives further insight into how such a survey might progress in the following: ". . . the incorporation of sociometric-type data into survey research allows the investigator to *locate* each interviewed individual within the networks of voluntary relations which surround him. In some cases, these networks of voluntary relations will be superimposed on a highly articulated formal structure. In a department of a business, for example, there are numerous hierarchical levels, and there are numerous work relations, which are imposed by the job itself. In such cases, sociometric-type questions can be asked relative to these formal relations, *e.g.:* 'Which supervisor do you turn to most often?' or, 'Which of the men in your own work group do you see most often outside of work?' or, 'When you want X type of job done in a hurry, to whom do you go to get it done?' or, 'When you need advice on such-and-such a problem, to whom do you usually turn?'"[2]

After these and other questions have been asked of each of the employees in a department, the operative division of labor should become apparent. In some cases, the entire population of a particular department or segment of an organization would have to be surveyed. In others, it should be possible to use only a scientifically selected sample.

It must be made clear that the specific questions noted above are not designed to provide internal control information. The most productive combination of questions for auditing purposes would have to be determined through intensive research. In addition, a satisfactory means of compiling the results would have to be derived, to bring forth the weaknesses crucial to the work of the independent auditor. Matrices are presently being used to report the findings of similar types of organizational studies. Perhaps this device could be employed in internal control analysis of the sociometric type.

The advantage of such an evaluation technique lies in the fact that several opinions or points of view are derived concerning the division of labor. By not only asking an employee what tasks he performs, but also what tasks selected

[2] Coleman, James S., "Relational Analysis: The Study of Social Organizations with Survey Methods," *Complex Organizations: A Sociological Reader*, Etzioni, Amaitai, (Ed.), Holt, Rinehart and Winston, Inc., New York, 1961, pp. 443–444.

fellow employees perform, and asking the fellow employees the same question, the questioner elicits much more reliable information than may be derived through the use of present procedures, as previously set forth.

IMPLICATIONS OF A PERFECTED EVALUATION TECHNIQUE

Assuming that a sociometric-type of analysis could be perfected, other, more fundamental questions arise. First of all, such a technique would obviously take more time to administer than the present techniques. It might, therefore, prove too time consuming, and thus too costly. Another question that would require an answer concerns the amount of additional conventional testing that would be needed, if such an evaluation technique determined internal control of a given organization to be adequate. It would seem very little, if any, would be necessary. But this is little more than conjecture at this stage. However, cost might not be a deterrent if this proved to be the case.

As a final observation, the perfection of such an evaluation technique might change the position of most public accountants with respect to auditing for fraud or responsibility for detecting fraud. It is possible such a method would enable accountants to detect fraud whether the magnitude of the dishonesty be large or small. At a minimum, potentially collusive relationships between employees could be discovered.

CONCLUSION

The evaluation of internal control is an essential part of most every audit performed today. Our present methods must be critically evaluated, and research must be undertaken to perfect evaluation techniques. In the foregoing discussion, the suggestion is made that present methods may be inadequate and the problem is to find a reliable technique to replace them.

Internal control is certainly related to organization structure and behavior, and research in this area should prove fruitful.

A POSITIONAL ANALYSIS OF INTERNAL CONTROL
Robert J. Swieringa and D. R. Carmichael*

Internal control evaluation has two distinct but related objectives. The primary objective is to ascertain the extent to which the internal control system may be relied upon and thus establish a basis for determining the selection, timing and application of auditing procedures. A related, but secondary, objective is to provide sufficient knowledge of a client's affairs to make timely suggestions for not only strengthening the system of internal control but, more importantly, for increasing its efficiency and effectiveness.

This article advocates the view that evaluation of internal control should be positional, with appropriate recognition given to the task relations, power relations and personal relations of specific positions.[1]

Flowchart techniques, for example, provide the auditor with methods for analyzing and representing the task relations that result from the specification and assignment of specific internal control tasks to organization positions. Moreover, an analysis of organization charts and procedure manuals provides him with a means for analyzing and representing the power relations that result from the setting of responsibility and authority relations between positions. At present, however, there are no objective and reproducible methods available to the auditor for analyzing and representing personal relations, the patterns of communication and interaction among persons occupying organization positions.

This article explores the potential of a positional analysis of internal control in which methods borrowed from the behavioral sciences are used to *supplement* traditional methods of internal control evaluation.[2] Methods which have been used extensively by behavioral scientists to measure relationships among members of a variety of groups offer significant opportunities for increasing the effectiveness of the auditor's evaluation of internal control. We believe these methods should be helpful for determining audit scope and

* From *The Journal of Accountancy,* Vol. 131, No. 3 (February 1971), pp. 34–43. Reprinted by permission of the American Institute of Certified Public Accountants.

[1] A need for positional analysis was suggested by R. K. Mautz and Donald L. Mini, "Internal Control Evaluation and Audit Program Modification," *The Accounting Review,* XLI (April 1966), p. 289: "Since irregularities are brought about intentionally or unintentionally, by individuals working within the limits of given organization positions, the auditor's primary concern in studying a client's system of internal control must be with the duties attached to these *positions* and the irregularities these duties permit." (Emphasis added.)

[2] The methods presented in this article are usually classified by behavioral scientists under the area of "sociometry," the measurement of interpersonal relations. Although the methods have a long history in the behavioral sciences, the suggestion that these methods could effectively be used to study internal control was first made by John J. Willingham, "Internal Control Evaluation—A Behavioral Approach," *Internal Auditor* (Summer 1966), pp. 20–26.

should expand an auditor's opportunities for offering constructive suggestions to increase the effectiveness of organization operations.

The methods focus on people — groups and individuals — who perform tasks rather than on tasks only, and on actual behavioral occurrences rather than on those merely prescribed. They include objective and reproducible methods for obtaining data from all organizational personnel rather than only one or a few persons and provide a full array of graphic and quantitative techniques for analyzing and representing basic data.

The specific focus of this article is on the use of these methods to study compliance with organizational aspects of internal control. The next section examines present methods of studying organizational aspects of internal control. The following section outlines a positional analysis which can be used to supplement present methods and describes a case study in which the proposed methods were applied in an actual internal control situation.

TESTS OF COMPLIANCE AND ORGANIZATIONAL ASPECTS OF INTERNAL CONTROL

Internal control evaluation consists of two phases. The first phase is a "review of the system" in which the auditor obtains a preliminary description of a client's record system and related controls for the purpose of determining what procedures and practices are supposed to be in effect. This description is obtained through a review of system documentation, including procedure manuals, charts of accounts, account descriptions, organization charts and job descriptions; the auditor's observation of recording processes; and inquiry of key personnel, including the controller or chief accountant.

The second phase is a "test of the system" in which the auditor applies certain "tests of compliance" to determine if procedures described are being complied with. Some tests of compliance rely heavily on the trail of documentary evidence — source documents, journals and ledgers — prepared as transactions are processed from original entry to final posting. For example, the preliminary description of an accounting system is normally clarified by tracing transactions from the source documents and initial recording, through whatever intermediate records might exist, to the output in the form of final records and reports. In some cases, extended samples of sales transactions, purchases, petty cash transactions, expense payments and the like may be drawn to statistically determine the reliability of the underlying accounting data so that the timing or extent of the tests to be made of account balances may be modified.

Some aspects of internal control vary in the extent to which they provide a trail of documentary evidence and the auditor has to supplement his review with corroborative inquiry of different management personnel as well as his own observations of office routine. Positional analysis is suggested as a supplement to traditional nondocumentary tests of compliance. These nondocumentary tests are often facilitated by internal control questionnaires which are designed to elicit information about what elements of internal control are present and what relationships are prescribed and restricted.

Both the source and nature of the information obtained by these questionnaires, however, may limit their usefulness for obtaining information about compliance with established practices. First, the questionnaires are often administered to only one person, or to a few supervisory personnel who are considered to have full and complete knowledge about the responsibilities of various persons under their supervision. Although these persons may be informed about the general nature of the work being performed in their departments or work groups, they may not know who is actually performing the work. In addition, questions included in the questionnaires often focus on persons *responsible* for certain tasks rather than on the persons *actually performing* the tasks. Thus, internal control questionnaires, in their present form, may provide information that is essential for clarifying preliminary descriptions of prescribed methods and practices but may not provide adequate information about actual performance of specific procedures. The questionnaires, therefore, may not provide an adequate basis for assessing compliance.

POSITIONAL ANALYSIS OF INTERNAL CONTROL

In this section we propose that a positional analysis of internal control based on the examination of reported working relationships can be used to supplement present evaluation methods. In testing compliance with certain organizational aspects of internal control, the auditor is interested in how the day-to-day working relationships among organization personnel compare with those relationships formally described in organization charts and procedure manuals and, if differences exist, what their implications are for existing internal control. The positional analysis we propose consists of (1) obtaining evidence of the reported working relationships in an organization, (2) comparing the reported relationships with those formally prescribed and (3) evaluating the degree of conformance between the reported and prescribed relationships for purposes of determining the extent to which audit tests should be restricted and for making recommendations to management.

A case study of the office departments of an integrated parts depot is used to illustrate how positional methods are applied. The parts depot studied is a suborganization of a sales branch of a multiproduct, multiplant corporation located in the Midwest. The depot has responsibility for the custody, administration and distribution of approximately 60,000 different parts and components, and maintains an inventory at cost of about $7 million. The parts depot performs certain record-keeping, stock control and custodial functions. At the time of the study, the parts depot employed 80 warehouse and office personnel. This study covered only the office personnel, *including* 21 women and 19 men. It was performed as a special project rather than as part of an audit engagement and required approximately 20 man-hours.

METHODS FOR OBTAINING EVIDENCE OF REPORTED AND PRESCRIBED RELATIONSHIPS

Methods used to obtain evidence of the prescribed and actual working relationships among depot office personnel included an analysis of organization charts and procedure manuals and interview — questionnaire techniques. Data indicating prescribed relationships among depot office personnel were obtained by an analysis of the latest available editions of the depot's organization charts and procedure manuals. These official documents were updated in interviews with top management personnel to reflect the formal structure of the depot at the time the analysis was made. The formal organization chart of the parts depot is presented in Figure 1. The depot is organized into seven units of organization: six units encompass accounting and computer services; one unit, the warehouse and its supervision. There are five levels of organization in the depot.

The primary flow of documents in the depot begins with dealer parts orders which are interpreted by the respective export and domestic order departments. The orders are then processed by the computer services department where dealer orders are keypunched and keyverified. The punched cards are used as input to a tabulator processing system which modifies and updates perpetual inventory records; prepares picking tickets and identification tags for parts presently in stock; updates back orders for items presently out of stock; and prints invoices, work copies and parts lists. The parts lists follow the picked items and are included with the shipped parts. Work copies are used by the export order department and are forwarded, after adjustments for price later and price correction items, to the export division of the home office for eventual billing. Invoices for domestic parts orders are sent to the billing section of the domestic order department where an accounts receivable control tape is prepared of invoices processed. An accounts receivable list summary is run and checked with the tape prepared earlier and the accounts receivable cards are then reproduced in modified form for branch accounting and billing

FIGURE 1   ORGANIZATION CHART OF PARTS DEPOT

Designation	Organization Unit	Description
1.0	1	Manager
1.1		Secretary
1.2		Office Janitor
2.0	2	Order Department Manager
2.1		Stenographer
2.2		Mail and File Clerk
2.30	3	Supervisor, Export Order Department
2.31		Export Expeditor
2.32		Typist Clerk—First Picking Desk
2.33		Clerk Typist—Invoicing
2.34		Clerk Typist—Invoicing
2.35		Clerk Typist—Factory Orders
2.36		Clerk Typist—Tally Desk
2.40	4	Supervisor, Domestic Order Department
2.41		Chief Order Interpreter
2.42		Order Interpreter
2.43		Order Interpreter
2.44		Telephone Order Clerk
2.45		Order Control Clerk
2.46		Factory Order Clerk
2.47		Typist Clerk—Invoicing
2.48		Typist Clerk
2.50	5	Stock Control Analyst
2.51		Parts Inventory Clerk
2.52		Parts Inventory Clerk
2.60	6	Supervisor, Computer Service
2.61		IBM Machine Operator
2.62		Card Punch Operator
2.63		Card Punch Operator
2.64		Card Punch Operator
2.65		Card Punch Operator
2.66		Card Punch Operator
3.0	7	Warehouse Superintendent
3.10		Shipping and Warehouse Foreman
3.11		Shipping and Traffic Clerk
3.12		Shipping Office Clerk
3.20		Stock Foreman
3.21		Receiving Clerk
3.30		Order Scheduler
3.31		Typist Clerk

FIGURE 1   ORGANIZATION CHART OF PARTS DEPOT

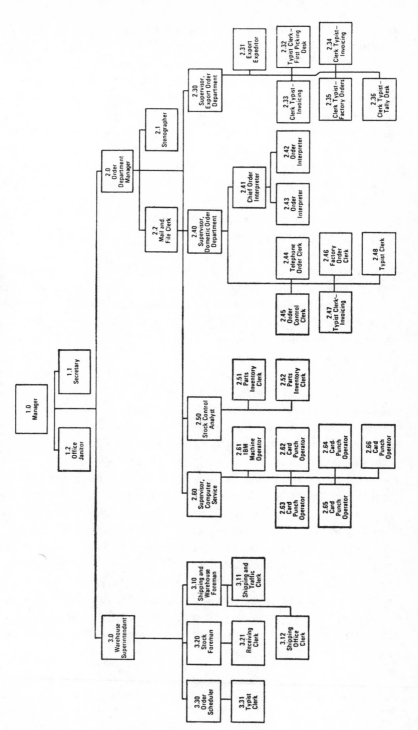

processes. Other document flows are, for the most part, confined to the designated export and domestic order processing departments.

Methods developed and tested by Stogdill and Shartle were used to obtain data about reported working relationships.[3] Depot office personnel were asked via a short one-page questionnaire to list names of other depot employees with whom they spend the most time in getting work done. Depot personnel were asked to reflect on the past month and to consider all other employees contacted during working hours. In indicating their choices, depot office personnel were asked to distinguish between employees under their supervision and employees not under their supervision. First, employees ranked (from most to least time spent) the names of their subordinates according to the amount of time spent with them on a working basis. They then listed the names of other employees not under their supervision. This second list included employees at levels of organization higher than that of the reporting employee, employees at about his own level, and employees at levels below him but not under his supervision. Finally, the reporting employee ordered all of the names included in both lists in a combined single ranking on the basis of with whom he spends the most time at work. This three-step process was designed to solicit a complete listing and ordering of names.

The methods for collecting evidence of working relationships supplement the effectiveness of present evaluation techniques. First, the methods focus on *people,* groups and individuals, *who perform tasks* rather than on what *tasks are supposed to be performed.* The methods are designed to provide the auditor with a sensitive and objective picture of the interpersonal relationships existing in an organization. Second, the methods focus on *actual* behavioral occurrences rather than on those relationships merely *prescribed.* The question used for obtaining data about actual work associations of respondents is: "With whom do you spend the most time in getting work done?" In a formal organization like a business enterprise, a person's working relationships may be brought about not by formal authority alone but also by the lines of communication, work flow, work proximity and the like. Third, the methods obtain data about working relationships directly from organization members in *all* levels of organization and are not based on inquiry from only one person or from only a few persons in the organization. The responses of persons in various levels of organization provide a relatively objective picture of the actual networks of working relationships that characterize daily interraction among individuals in the organization.

[3] Ralph M. Stogdill and Carroll L. Shartle, *Methods in the Study of Administrative Leadership,* Bureau of Business Research, Monograph No. 80 (Columbus: Bureau of Business Research, The Ohio State University, 1955).

METHODS FOR COMPARING REPORTED
AND PRESCRIBED RELATIONSHIPS

Various graphic and quantitative methods can be used to compare the reported working relationships with those relationships formally prescribed.[4] One method is to plot the reported relationships on top of the organization chart developed earlier. Figure 2, page 284, presents this now elaborated chart. The lines and arrows indicate the persons mentioned by each employee. Only the first two mentions of each person are shown (first mentions are in broken lines and second mentions are in dotted lines).

The chart shown in Figure 2 can be used to identify and compare the relative positions of certain persons in the formal and reported structures. The position of each employee in the formal structure can be described in a number of ways: his assignment to one department or work group rather than another; his relationship to other employees in his department or work group; his relationship to employees outside of his department or work group; and so forth. A person's position in the reported structure can be described by focusing on certain patterns or features. It will be observed in Figure 2 that some employees are the focus of many directed lines whereas others receive few or no mentions. Frequently chosen persons are referred to as "stars." Person 3.0, the warehouse superintendent, and person 2.30, the export order department supervisor, for example, received six and five mentions respectively and would be considered to be "stars." Person 2.46, the factory order clerk, is an "isolate," neither receiving nor giving mentions.

A "chain" consists of three or more persons connected by directed lines. One chain connects the receiving department with the warehouse superintendent and the depot manager. A second chain consists of persons who are all members of the export order department. A third chain connects the export order department, the order department manager, and the depot manager.

The chart in Figure 2 can be used to identify work subgroups or "cliques" and to compare their composition with that of the departments formally established. "Mutual pairs" consist of pairs of individuals who choose each other. Notice that the depot manager reciprocates the mentions of both the order department supervisor and the warehouse superintendent. Mutual pairs can be combined and used to identify other patterns such as "cliques." A "clique" consists of three or more persons who choose each other. Notice that there is a large number of mutual choices among the respective members of the

---

[4] A quantitative analysis of the reported working relationships can be made by plotting all of the mentions made in an *n* by *n* matrix where *n* represents depot employees. See Robert J. Swieringa, "An Inquiry into the Nature and Feasibility of a Sociometric Analysis of Internal Control" (unpublished Ph.D. dissertation, University of Illinois, 1969), for a description of how a matrix can be manipulated to analyze reported relationships.

FIGURE 2 ELABORATED CHART OF PARTS DEPOT

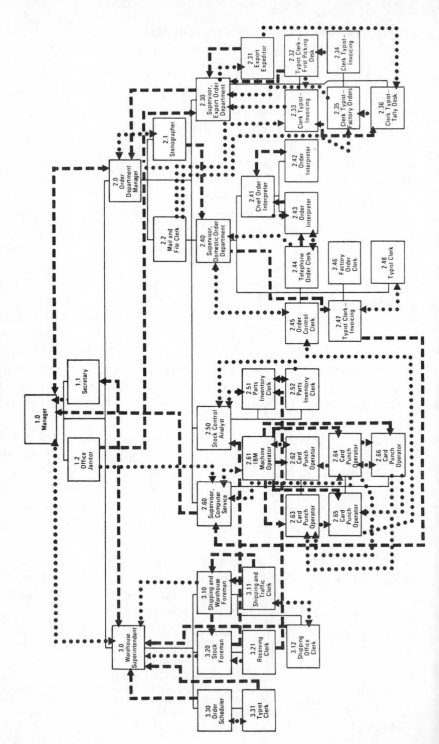

domestic order department, the stock control department and the computer services department.

The chart in Figure 2 can also be used to identify those relationships that seemingly differ from formal expectations, e.g., relationships that bypass immediate supervisory positions, relationships that cross interdepartmental boundaries of function and authority, etc. Notice that reported relationships between persons 2.65, the card punch operator, and 2.45, the order control clerk, between persons 2.60, the computer services supervisor, and 2.47, the invoicing typist clerk, and between persons 3.20, the stock foreman, and 2.50, the stock control analyst, and persons 3.21, the receiving clerk, and 2.51, the parts inventory clerk, cross interdepartmental boundaries of function and authority.

EVALUATION OF REPORTED
AND PRESCRIBED RELATIONSHIPS

Up to this point we have described methods for obtaining evidence of reported working relationships and for comparing these reported relationships with those formally prescribed. We now turn to the evaluation of the reported and prescribed relationships for purposes of determining the extent to which audit tests should be restricted and for making recommendations to management.

The evaluation of the reported and prescribed relationships consists initially of determining (1) to what other positions a given position is connected (to what other persons its occupant is connected) and (2) what the nature of the connecting bonds is (formal authority, functional dependence, proximity). A positional analysis of internal control focuses on specific positions and the relationships associated with those positions. Each member of the organization is viewed as occupying a designated position in the structure created by the division of labor, as performing the functions assigned to that position, and as interacting with members in certain other positions in ways designed to insure the additivity of their work. No position is considered to be intact and fully separable from other positions; instead, each position is defined in terms of its connections to (relationships with) other positions.

The positional analysis we propose differs significantly from present practice in its focus on positions and the connections between positions. The literature on internal control evaluation has typically emphasized the importance of internal control duties. Bower and Schlosser, for example, state that "without internal control duties specifically prescribed in the system there can be no internal control."[5] To focus on a position independent of the network of

[5] James B. Bower and Robert E. Schlosser, "Internal Control—Its True Nature," *The Accounting Review*, XL (April 1965), p. 340.

other positions to which it is connected, however, is like cutting a knot out of a larger net. A knot is no more than an intersection of bonds which is inseparable from the larger network of which it is a part. Similarly, a position is defined in terms of its connections to other positions and, if we abstract it out of the overall network of positions, we find that the duties, obligations and rights dangle from the position like the strands of a knot cut from a larger net.

The relationships reported by members of the parts depot indicate that the connections between positions extend beyond the dyad (each superior and each subordinate taken one at a time) and even beyond the group (each superior and his immediate subordinates) to include the various persons to whom an individual is connected whether by prescription, expectation or behavior. The relationships which connect one position with another have many antecedents, not formal authority alone. Two positions may be related because of the sequence of work flow or information, their organizational proximity, or a number of personal and interpersonal factors. The reported working relationships among persons occupying specific positions in the parts depot represent recurring patterns of interaction and behavior of one person toward another; imply that the occupant of one position is concerned with the behavior of another; is in some fashion dependent on that behavior; has ideas about what constitutes acceptable behavior; and acts to influence the occupant of the other position toward such behavior.

Both the prescribed and reported relationships provide evidence of the relationships which connect specific positions. The next step in the evaluation is to determine the nature of the connecting bonds. Both the graphic and quantitative methods described above only represent reported relationships; they do not explain them, their causes or their importance. It is only through subsequent investigation of the nature and content of the reported relationships that their significance for existing internal control can be assessed. Essentially, by using these techniques, the auditor is testing his preliminary description of a client's accounting procedures and related controls. Typically, the auditor will base his tests of the underlying accounting data on his evaluation of the extent to which a client's plan of organization, as contained in organization charts and procedure manuals, provides for a division of record-keeping and a separation of custodial and accounting functions.

A client's plan of organization is but one input to the evaluation of organization relationships for purposes of internal control review. The auditor is not only interested in the extent to which a client's plan provides for a division of record-keeping and a separation of custodial and accounting functions but also in the extent to which these aspects are reflected in actual organization functioning. To indicate how the evaluation proceeds, let us focus on the relationships reported by members of the domestic order department and to what extent control over order processing, shipping and billing are facilitated by a division of record-keeping and a separation of custodial and accounting functions.

RELATIONSHIPS REPORTED BY MEMBERS OF THE DOMESTIC ORDER DEPARTMENT

The domestic order department has primary responsibility for control over the receipt and filing of dealer parts orders and the preparation of sales invoices. Orders received from dealers are reviewed by the chief order interpreter (person 2.41) and by the order interpreters (persons 2.42 and 2.43) to determine what parts ordered are available and that the terms are acceptable. Factory orders for parts not currently in stock are prepared by the telephone order clerk (person 2.44) and by the factory order clerk (person 2.46); an order number is assigned to orders for parts currently available by the order control clerk (person 2.45). Records are then maintained in such a way that each order remains open until notification is received that the order has been shipped and billed.

Persons 2.47, the invoicing typist clerk, and 2.48, the typist clerk, make up the billing section of the domestic order department. The sales invoices are returned to the domestic order department and are processed by these two clerks. Adjustments are made for price later and price correction items, an accounts receivable tape is prepared of invoices processed and the original copy of the invoice is forwarded to the dealer. A posting copy of the invoice is used to prepare a deck of accounts receivable cards. An accounts receivable list summary is then prepared and compared with the accounts receivable tape prepared earlier.

The reported relationships indicate that the order and invoice processing sections of the domestic order department are relatively distinct in their functioning. Working relationships among members of the respective order and invoice processing sections are reflected in Figure 2. Notice particularly the close working relationships among the chief order interpreter (person 2.41) and the order interpreters (persons 2.42 and 2.43). The interpretation of dealer orders requires considerable coordination in the receipt of dealer orders, the checking of parts order numbers with standard parts lists and the current availability of the parts ordered. Note that the persons who prepare the factory orders and assign order numbers do not choose each other, reflecting in part the more individualistic nature of their task assignments. Also notice that there are few reported relationships between persons in the order and invoice processing sections, reflecting that even though these two sections are not organizationally independent, some degree of operational independence does exist.

Most of the working relationships reported by members of the domestic order department reflect intradepartmental processes. Those mentions which extend beyond departmental boundaries represent for the most part job-related interaction. Person 2.41, the chief order interpreter, receives information about the current status of back orders and parts on order from the stock control analyst (person 2.50) and from the parts inventory clerk (person 2.51) in the stock control department. Person 2.45, the order control clerk, forwards orders to be keypunched to person 2.65, the card punch operator, in the computer services department. Person 2.47, the invoicing typist clerk, maintains sales distribution records which are used by the export order department supervisor, person 2.30, and by person 2.52, the parts inventory clerk, in the stock control department. The reported relationship between the invoicing typist clerk (person 2.47) and the computer services department supervisor (person 2.60) arises from the comparison of the adding machine tape of invoices processed and the accounts receivable list summary, and the analysis of other quantitative data (e.g., sales distribution data) accumulated both before and after electronic data processing.

RELATIONSHIP BETWEEN POSITIONAL ANALYSIS AND AUDIT PROGRAM PLANNING

The relationship between a positional analysis of internal control and audit program planning is immediate and practical. First, analysis and representation of the reported relationships reveals the extent to which inter- and intradepartmental relationships exist among specific positions and how these relationships compare with those formally prescribed. The elaborated chart shown in Figure 2, for example, provides tangible evidence of the relationships and connections between positions. Moreover, the methods used to obtain this evidence are objective, reproducible and result in hard copy which can be placed in the permanent file and used by other audit personnel to familiarize themselves with depot operations.

Second, the auditor's investigation of the nature and content of the plotted relationships provides a basis for assessing the significance of specific relationships for existing internal control. As indicated earlier, the graphic and quantitative methods described above only represent reported relationships; their significance for audit program planning can only be assessed by an investigation of their nature and content. In some cases, the auditor may want to investigate all reported relationships. In most cases, however, the auditor will want to investigate those relationships which connect certain critical positions. In the parts depot, for example, the billing clerk occupies a critical position in the processing of dealer parts orders. As indicated by the earlier description, investigation of the nature and content of the relationships exported by depot personnel, both within and outside of the domestic order department, revealed that many of these relationships were closely related to the performance of specific internal control tasks. Moreover, this investigation disclosed that these relationships were, for the most part, consistent with the preliminary description of the division of record-keeping and the separation of accounting and custodial functions.

Thus, even though analysis and representation of the relationships reported by parts depot personnel provided evidence of the relative independence of departmental functioning, this independence was substantiated through subsequent investigation of the nature and content of specific reported relationships.

Finally, the auditor's investigation of the nature and content of specific reported relationships contributes directly to the auditor's search for weaknesses in internal control. Most business organizations cannot operate without a reasonably good accounting system. Consequently it will be rather unusual to find a situation in which a division of record-keeping is completely lacking. More often the auditor will be confronted with a series of minor weaknesses which he will need to evaluate in terms of the possible effects on his audit program. If the auditor's investigation discloses certain weaknesses in the division of record-keeping, the auditor has to consider the possibility of (1) extending his tests of transactions so that he can determine the reliability of the accounting system or (2) changing the timing of his tests so that he can assess the effect of any weaknesses on the balance sheet amounts. In some cases, his weakness investigation can increase substantially the audit time that is devoted to a particular engagement.

A separation of custodial and accounting functions, however, is difficult to achieve in most business organizations, and therefore it can be expected that weaknesses will be disclosed. As indicated by some of the reported relationships described above, the relative positions of any two persons within the depot's structure determine to a considerable degree the relationships and connections between them.

Every business organization is faced with the problem of dividing its activities into subsets which are of such a size and nature that they can be performed by individual persons. But this organizational division of labor creates a second problem—that of co-ordinating and controlling these activities with respect to the organization's goals. Out of attempts to solve such problems of differentiation and integration develop the relationships which connect one position with another. And it is these connections which are highlighted by a positional analysis.

Weaknesses in the separation of accounting and custodial functions will generally not increase substantially the audit time devoted to an engagement when the division of record-keeping is adequate. The auditor's major concern is to see that the financial statements are not materially misstated, and often he can shift his testing to the end of the reporting period to obtain greater assurance of the fairness of balance sheet presentations. For example, weaknesses in the separation of persons performing order processing, billing and shipping functions would, assuming an adequate division of record-keeping, only require shifting physical inventories and confirmations of receivables to the end of the period. It should be emphasized, however, that such changes need be made only when there are serious weaknesses in the separation of accounting and custodial activities. Weaknesses this serious were not disclosed in the parts depot case study.

CONCLUSIONS

We have proposed a positional analysis of internal control as an overall method which the auditor can use to test compliance with those organizational aspects of internal control which may not leave a trail of documentary evidence. Presently these aspects of internal control are tested by observation of office routine and corroborative inquiry. A positional analysis, as described in this article, is designed to supplement the effectiveness of present evaluation techniques. The methods used to obtain basic data focus on persons who perform tasks rather than on tasks only, focus on actual behavioral occurrences rather than those merely prescribed and obtain data from all organizational personnel. Moreover, a full array of graphic and quantitative techniques can be used by the auditor to analyze and represent the relationships which connect specific positions and to guide his investigation of the nature and content of the reported relationships.

CHAPTER 9

AUDIT TESTS: JUDGMENT AND STATISTICS

In the course of an audit, it is necessary to conduct many tests. The auditor cannot afford the luxury of examining *all* client transactions and resulting balances. When less than one hundred percent of any population can be audited, problems of both selection and evaluation are encountered. Traditionally, auditors have relied on their judgment in order to resolve these matters; but the application of statistical sampling to audit situations is gaining acceptance with auditors. Following are two views on audit tests and the applicability of statistical sampling to them.

SOME OBSERVATIONS ON STATISTICAL SAMPLING IN AUDITING
Howard F. Stettler*

The professional literature refers most frequently to three types of statistical sampling; acceptance sampling, discovery sampling and estimation sampling. The first two types can be effectively used only in sampling for what statisticians commonly refer to as "attributes." In auditing applications, these attributes will be whether a document has been processed correctly or incorrectly, or whether a transaction has been recorded correctly or incorrectly. Tests of transactions to arrive at a conclusion concerning compliance with a client's plan of internal control represent the most common application of sampling for attributes. The client's records are "accepted" if the number of defectives (errors) disclosed in the test does not exceed the number specified by the sampling plan—usually zero defectives, if the sample size is kept to a minimum.

Sampling for variables can be best handled by the use of statistical estimation, the variables typically being such items as the amounts of individual accounts receivable or the cost extensions for goods in inventory. A sample of the variables is "blown up" to arrive at an estimate of the total dollars represented by the class of items being sampled. Statistical estimation can also be utilized in attribute sampling to develop an indication of the proportion of defectives in the population.

*From *The Journal of Accountancy,* April, 1966, pp. 55–60. Reprinted by permission of the American Institute of Certified Public Accountants.

A CAVEAT ABOUT SAMPLING RESULTS

Sampling is intended to reveal information about a population of items by examining only a portion of the items in the population. A common assumption is that sampling yields positive information about the population, when in fact it can only yield negative conclusions. Thus a sample will *not* reveal the exact percentage of defective vouchers in a population consisting of all vouchers prepared during a year's time. (Assume that a defective voucher is being defined as one not containing the initials of a person who is expected to determine that prices on the supporting vendor's invoice agree with those on the related purchase order. A voucher could be defective for other reasons as well.) What the sample *will* do, if the number of defectives disclosed by the sample is equal to or less than the number specified by an acceptance sampling table, is tell the auditor that he can accept the population, with a stated amount of confidence, as *not having more* than a stated percentage of such defectives.

For example, the auditor may seek 95% confidence that the percentage of defective vouchers in the population does not exceed 2%. The sampling table in "A Simple Tool to Assist the Auditor in Statistical Interpretation of Test Checks," by the author in the January 1954 *Journal of Accountancy* (page 57), specifies a sample of 150 items with no defectives in the sample to give the results specified. Note, however, that the sample of 150 with zero defectives provides no basis for concluding that the population as a whole contains zero defectives, which would be a positive conclusion about the population. Instead, the only statement that can be made about the population (and the statement is a very useful one) is the negative conclusion that the sample affords 95% confidence that the percentage of defectives in the population *does not exceed 2%.*

The difference between defects appearing in the sample and the maximum percentage specified in arriving at the sample size is the *precision* of the estimate. The precision of the estimate can be improved by increasing the size of the sample. If the sample is increased to 300, with no defectives appearing in the sample, the precision changes from 2% to 1% with 95% confidence. Hence there is then 95% confidence that the defectives in the population do not exceed 1%, a more precise statement about what the population is not.

The approach just discussed may be referred to as a "one-sided" test, for it is concerned only with the single question of confidence that the population contains no *more* than a stated percentage of defectives. To accept the population on the stated basis, the sample must reveal no defectives or, for larger sample sizes, only a very limited number of defectives. Such a sample is likely to be obtained only if the population is substantially better than the specified maximum percentage of defectives. A sample of 200 revealing 4 defectives (2%) suggests a probable error rate of about 2%, but the caveat still applies that a sample offers no basis for a precise statement about what the population *is*. What the sample does offer is a basis for saying something about what the population *is not*. Based on the same table previously referred to, we can have 97% confidence that the error rate does not exceed 5%. We can also have 95% confidence that the error rate is not less than 1%, for we would only rarely obtain samples of 200 containing as many as 4 defectives from a population containing less than 1% defectives. Here we are in effect using our sample in a two-sided test, giving further indication of what the population *is not*: it is *no better* than 1% (95% confidence) and it is *no worse* than 5% (97% confidence). Thus in sampling we must disregard the urging of the once-popular song to "accentuate the positive; eliminate the negative" and, instead, place all our emphasis on the negative.

The same observations apply to conclusions based on estimation sampling. Assume the following facts:

10,000 individual accounts receivable

$25 standard deviation of the population of accounts receivable balances

625 accounts selected for positive confirmation

$98 mean of confirmed balances for 625 accounts

Based on the $98 mean calculated from the sample of 625 accounts, it would appear reasonable to estimate the total accounts receivable at 10,000 x $98 or $980,000. Actually, however, given the facts as stated above, the only appropriate statement to be made is the negative one that, with 95% confidence, the total of the receivables is not less than $960,000 and not more than $1 million.[1]

---

[1] Standard deviation of sample means:

$$\frac{\text{Standard deviation of population}}{\sqrt{\text{Sample size}}}$$

Standard deviation of sample means:

$$\frac{25}{\sqrt{625}} = \frac{25}{25} = 1.00$$

Two standard deviations of the sample means would encompass 95% (approximately) of all sample means.
    Hence, from a population whose mean is 96, only 2½% of samples of 625 would exceed a mean of 98, and for a population whose mean is 100, only 2½% of the samples of 625 would be less than a mean of 98, or 95% confidence that a sample mean of 98 came from a population whose mean was no less than 96 and no greater than 100.

Precision is again a factor in the results, and in this case would be stated as ±$20,000 of the total calculated from the sample mean. A larger sample size would give better precision (less than $20,000) or greater confidence based on the same precision of ±$20,000; a smaller sample size would give less precision (more than $20,000), or less confidence based on the same precision.

DISCOVERY SAMPLING: A DELUSION

Discovery sampling has been presented as a means of discovering at least one defective item in a population if defective items are present in excess of some stated percentage, thus giving the opportunity for the auditor to see an example of any serious breakdown of internal control or any evidence of fraud. A likely first impression on encountering the term is that discovery sampling holds the answer to discovering the "needle in the haystack"; i.e., the rare item in a population. The point that is easily overlooked is that the defective is likely to appear in a given size sample only if the defectives in the population exceed some stated percentage. Hence, what is "discovered" if a defective appears in the sample is not a rare item but rather an indication that the population may contain a percentage of defectives in excess of what the auditor is willing to tolerate; the maximum percentage that the auditor specified in order to determine the size of the sample to be taken, based on a confidence level that must also be specified.

On further examination, discovery sampling turns out to be little more than a different way of looking at the results of an acceptance sampling plan such as has already been discussed. Thus, with a sample of 150 specified to give 95% confidence that the percentage of defectives in the population does not exceed 2%, the presence of one or more defectives in the sample indicates that the population cannot be accepted, and the auditor has achieved the specified result of finding at least one of the defectives because the population may have more than 2% defectives.

LIMITED USEFULNESS OF ACCEPTANCE SAMPLING

Present day auditing relies heavily on a client's system of internal control to produce figures that fairly reflect the client's financial position and results of operations. The final figures are independently tested by such procedures as accounts receivable confirmation or inventory test counts. For very large clients with good internal control, the extent of receivable confirmation or inventory count tests in relation to the population being sampled suggests that the purpose may not be to provide information directly about the reasonableness of the total being tested, but rather to ascertain the efficacy of the client's internal control. By implication, auditors thereby place almost complete reliance on the client's system of internal control to produce acceptable figures when the verification of balances is limited to samples of nominal size.

It is commonly assumed that tests of transactions must be made to give assurance of compliance with the stated plan of internal control, and acceptance sampling is generally proposed as an effective means of satisfying the auditor of compliance with the client's internal control. Two objections can be raised, however, to such use of acceptance sampling.

First, it is extremely difficult, if not impossible, to set a meaningful maximum for the percentage of defectives that can be tolerated in the population being sampled. For example, at what point would it be assumed that material differences might exist in resulting figures for inventory, cost of sales and accounts payable if some vouchers are not initialed to show that receiving report quantities agree with the quantities invoiced and paid for? Would it be missing initials on 10% of the vouchers, or 40%, or even 100%?

The answer would have to depend largely on other internal controls present in the system: primarily, internal control over the year-end physical inventory and the maintenance of a book perpetual inventory. If the year-end physical inventory has been accurately taken, and if the difference between the book inventory and physical inventory is a reasonable figure, then even complete absence of initials evidencing the comparison of receiving report quantities and invoice quantities would seem to have had little effect on the client's figures. Consequently, there seems to be little or no reason to test the stated internal control over purchases and disbursements, or any other internal controls related to that area.

A better approach than testing transactions to ascertain compliance with internal controls is to ascertain what controls exist to give assurance that the basic internal controls are being followed. The development of differences between book and physical inventory figures is one such control. Others are the review and approval of invoices by a person who checks to see that all other required initials have been inscribed, tests by an internal audit staff, the existence of procedures manuals and written job descriptions that spell out each employee's responsibilities, and personnel selection and review procedures that assure a competent employee work force. In a computer-based system there may be many additional programed controls to test the validity and accuracy of input to the system and the appropriate processing within the computer.

UTOPIA AT LAST, OR THE MAGIC SAMPLE OF ONE

Given that a client's internal control looks good on paper, and that there is an indication of adequate controls over the controls, the auditor will still wish to know that he is not dealing with an imaginary empire that exists only on paper. Here it becomes necessary to ascertain that there are real ledgers, journals, documents, assets, and liabilities and that the procedures described to the auditor are actual procedures that are in effect. And it is here that the "magic sample of one" comes into its own. Even Noah had to obtain two of each kind, but one of each kind of transaction should be adequate for the auditor when the added support of good control over internal control is present!

What the proposal of a sample of one boils down to is that what is sometimes referred to as a "walkthrough" of one of each kind of transaction should suffice for the test of transactions. The walkthrough of a transaction involves following it from beginning to end, to show that each step in the procedures stated by the client as being in effect is actually being followed. For purchasing procedures the walkthrough would begin with the creation of the purchase order and extend through the writing and mailing of the check for payment to the reconciliation of the bank account against which the check was drawn. Other types of disbursements should similarly be subjected to walkthroughs, such as the reimbursement of petty cash funds, the payment for services such as utilities, and the payment for the acquisition of plant assets subject to capital budget appropriations and finance committee authorization.

Another way to look at such walkthroughs has been suggested by Gregory M. Boni of Touche, Ross, Bailey & Smart in a seminar on auditing EDP systems recently conducted by his firm for a group of college professors. Boni considers the walkthrough not as a test of the operation of a client's system, but rather as a means of assuring that effective communication with clear understanding has taken place between the auditor and the client's employees being questioned about company procedures. Thus, if the auditor asks whether prices on a vendor's invoice are compared with prices on the related purchase order, the auditor may be more certain that the employee understood his question and that the auditor understood the answer if follow-up of a selected transaction shows that (a) the audit block placed on the invoice contains a statement, "Prices charged agree with purchase order," (b) the employee's initials appear in the box that follows the statement, and (c) the related purchase order is attached to the invoice. Failure of the employee to make the stated comparison in every instance, or failure of the employee to detect existing discrepancies, need not concern the auditor if other controls exist to give assurance that the work was actually performed as prescribed.

Similar questions must be asked of a computer system, with the auditor taking a variety of samples of one by means of a "test deck" of hypothetical situations and asking how such input containing known exceptions is actually processed by the computer. The questions are "asked" by processing the test deck under the client's existing computer program (the equivalent of the employee who is questioned when manual procedures are involved) to see whether the program contains the necessary steps to recognize and report out such exceptions as an invalid account number, an employee's pay amount that would exceed a stated maximum, or a customer order that should be rejected because the customer's credit limit would be exceeded or because payments on past purchases are delinquent. The important point here is that a sample of one is taken of each different situation that the computer program is supposed to recognize and treat as an exception; each sample of one in effect "asks" the computer program what it actually does in the specified situation, in support of what an analysis of the client's program flow chart shows is supposed to be done.

If the test of one of each type of situation shows that the auditor's "question" was understood and the stated program check was actually incorporated in the program and functioning, the auditor relies on other controls, such as records of program changes during the year, to satisfy himself that the stated checking was being done throughout the year. The auditor also has the results of his balances verification work to further indicate whether the system was functioning effectively throughout the year.

SAMPLING WHEN INTERNAL CONTROL IS DEFICIENT

If tests of transactions are based on statistical measures, presumably the following guideline set down by the AICPA committee on statistical sampling applies: "Since samples taken for this purpose (to test compliance with internal control) are intended to provide a basis for relying on compliance with internal control procedures, the committee believes they should be evaluated at a reliability level the auditor considers reasonable in the light of factors other than the procedures themselves."[2] The committee does not identify the other factors, but second-level internal control over the internal control of the procedures being tested would seem to be one such factor. If such overall controls are good, reliability can apparently be set below the 90% to 95% range customarily used, and perhaps even 50% reliability would be reasonable in a test of transactions, thereby reducing sample size.

By contrast, it is my contention that the auditor may properly ignore the

---

[2] "Relationship of Statistical Sampling to Generally Accepted Auditing Standards," a special report by the AICPA committee on statistical sampling, *The Journal of Accountancy*, July 1964, p. 56.

question of sample reliability when adequate controls over internal control are present, reducing reliability practically to zero, so that only one of each type of item need be tested. On the other hand, if internal control is deficient, the auditor's modification of his examination should not be in the direction of increasing sample size for his tests of transactions to achieve increased reliability for his conclusions about compliance with the system of internal control. The sample of one of each type of transaction should suffice to indicate that the system such as it is, is operative, and a larger sample that would disclose the extent of compliance helps very little in assessing the fairness or propriety of the account balances produced by the system.

It is in the tests of the balances themselves against verifiable supporting evidence that the auditor must expand his sample to achieve increased reliability. Also, if internal control borders on the nonexistent, then the tests of balances may have to be supplemented by tests of the transactions that developed those balances to gain additional evidence of the credibility of the balances. In that case, the tests of transactions are not made to ascertain compliance with internal controls, but to gain direct support of the validity of the balances themselves.

ESTIMATION SAMPLING FOR TESTS OF BALANCES

The preceding discussion brings us to the conclusion that estimation sampling is perhaps the only statistical sampling approach that is valid and useful for auditing purposes. The application of estimation sampling to tests of account balances is not, however, the normal type of application for this form of sampling. Ordinarily under estimation sampling little is known about the population being sampled, and the sample is "blown up" to arrive at an estimate of the total variables in the population. The design of the sample affords some stated confidence that the estimate is accurate within a range of precision specified in the design of the sample.

An auditor, however, usually has a control balance or other total previously determined by the client that indicates what the total of the population is supposed to be. The sampling approach may then be considered as a test of the hypothesis that the sample taken could in fact have come from a population whose total is as represented by the client.

The statement has been made earlier that the auditor seeks to determine not what a population is, but what it is not. In applying estimation sampling under this concept, the objective is not to estimate the total of the population, but rather to gain a certain amount of assurance that the total of the population is no less than some figure that is not materially less than the client's total, and no more than a larger figure that is not materially greater than the client's total. Clearly this approach to estimation sampling requires the auditor to come to grips with the very elusive question of what is a material difference. Unlike the usual case, where the auditor evaluates a given difference and decides whether the difference is or is not material, here he must carry the matter of materiality to its extremes, and state rather precisely and in advance the maximum difference that would not be material in the given situation.

AN APPLICATION OF ESTIMATION SAMPLING

Here we may return to the example of estimation sampling given earlier dealing with accounts receivable. Note that if account balances are being sampled on the basis of confirmation results, there is no need to prove a trial balance as would be true in the usual auditing application, an important saving of the auditor's time.

We will assume that the client's control account for receivables has a balance of $1 million, that we have counted, or estimated by a test count, the number of ledger cards to be 10,000, and that further we have made the necessary estimate of the standard deviation of the population,[3] and have found it to be $25.

To calculate the size of the sample to be taken, we must specify the confidence desired from our sample, which we will assume to be 95% — a reasonable confidence level for most audit samples. Finally, we must set the minimum and maximum amounts by which the receivable total might differ from $1 million without the difference being material; i.e., without having to insist that the client change the $1 million figure in the financial statements or, alternatively, to insist that the client agree to a qualification or disclaimer of opinion. We will set the extremes at $900,000 and $1,100,000, or $1,000,000 ± $100,-000.

In proceeding to the next step, we must recognize that if repeated samples of a given size are taken from a population, the means of those samples if plotted will form a normal curve, and the sample means will be evenly distributed on either side of the true mean of the population. The standard deviation of the curve of the sample means will vary inversely with the size of the samples taken, because as larger samples are taken the effect of extreme values appearing in a sample is submerged, and there will be less variability in sample means from one sample to the next.

---

[3] A simple way to estimate the standard deviation is to select 49 balances at random, divide these into seven groups each containing seven items, calculate the dollar range between the highest and lowest balance for each group, calculate the mean of these seven ranges and divide the mean by 2.704.

The relationship of sample size, standard deviation of the population and standard deviation of the sample means is expressed by the formula given earlier, which can be transposed to read:

$$\frac{\text{sample}}{\text{size}} = \frac{(\text{standard deviation of the population})^2}{(\text{standard deviation of sample means})^2}$$

All that is necessary, then, to compute sample size is to set the standard deviation we seek for the sample means.

Here, let us consider the significance of possible sample means of $95 and $105, and let us assume that the sample size is such that if the true value of our population is actually $1 million, 95% of our sample means would fall within the range of $95 and $105. There would then be some possibility, although slight, that we might draw a sample with a mean of $95. Actually, however, we do not in fact know that the true value of the population is $1 million, but even if the true value of the population were only $900,000, there would be an equally slight likelihood of drawing a sample with a mean of $95 from such a population as from a population of $1 million. The same reasoning applies to the possible sample mean of $105, and an equally slight likelihood of the sample being drawn from a population of $1 million or $1,100,000. What has just been said may be shown graphically as below.

We are seeking a sample size such that if repeated samples were drawn, the curves would appear as shown if the populations from which the samples were drawn were $900,000, $1 million and $1,100,000, with corresponding population means of $90, $100, and $110. The curves have been specified as containing 95% of all sample means within ±$5 of the true mean of the population, which turns out to be approximately two standard deviations. That being so, the value of one standard deviation must be $2.50, and this value can be substituted in the preceding formula, giving a sample size of 100.

**DISTRIBUTION OF SAMPLE MEANS IN REPEATED SAMPLES
FROM POPULATIONS WITH MEANS OF $90, $100, AND $110**

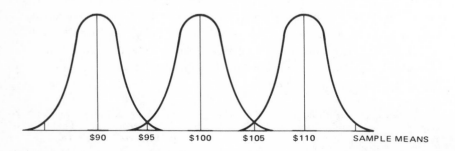

| $90 | $95 | $100 | $105 | $110 | SAMPLE MEANS |

Thus, when the sample of 100 is drawn, if the mean of that sample lies between $95 and $105, the auditor can state with 95% confidence that the true value of the accounts receivable is not less than $900,000 and not greater than $1,100,000. The reader should note that in the original example given earlier a sample of 625 accounts was stated to give precision of ±$20,000; by contrast, if precision requirements are relaxed to ±$100,000 as above, the sample size is reduced to 100 accounts.

SUMMARY

The major contentions that have been set forth are:

1 There is little justification for using either acceptance sampling or discovery sampling in making tests of transactions.

2 A sample of one of each type of transaction should constitute an adequate test of transactions.

3 When internal control is too weak to permit acceptance of account balances at face value as having been appropriately determined, tests of balances must be expanded to give increased reliability as a partial substitute for internal control.

4 A properly designed estimation sampling test of an account balance does not reveal what the balance is, but only a stated confidence in what the balance is not.

TESTS OF TRANSACTIONS—STATISTICAL AND OTHERWISE

D. R. Carmichael*

Statistical sampling is gaining increased acceptance as an audit tool. While much attention has been devoted to the characteristics of statistical sampling, sufficient attention has not been given to an integration of the characteristics of audit tests *and* statistical tests. In a previous article published in *The Journal*,[1] for example, Howard F. Stettler explained the meaning and relative merits of three approaches to statistical sampling: acceptance sampling, discovery sampling and estimation sampling. Although he presented a lucid explanation of these three sampling approaches,

* From *The Journal of Accountancy*, February, 1968, pp. 36–40. Reprinted by permission of the American Institute of Certified Public Accountants.
[1] Howard F. Stettler, "Some Observations on Statistical Sampling in Auditing," JofA, Vol. 121, April66, pp. 55–60.

his explanation of "tests of transactions" was not equally clear. In fact, there was inadequate recognition of the different types of tests made by auditors. His conclusions appear valid for one type of test, but not for all.

TYPES OF AUDIT TESTS

There are three types of audit tests, classified in terms of their usually recognized objectives:

1 *Those which provide the auditor with* prima facie *evidence of the existence and implementation of a system of internal control through observation and inquiry, and testing—usually of selected items from their inception through ultimate disposition.*

2 *Tests of items in quantities sufficient to obtain assurance that the functioning of the system of internal control is as planned and that the results of an examination of a portion of data are representative of the whole. These tests usually have the dual purpose of procedural tests and tests of* bona fides.

3 *Examination of especially significant items as to which the auditor may feel it necessary to require substantial assurance based on external evidence or detailed verification procedures.*[2]

These three types of tests will be referred to, respectively, as:

1 Single-purpose tests

2 Dual-purpose tests

3 Tests of *bona fides.*

It is submitted that the adequacy of the size of the sample of transactions is dependent upon the type of test, which, in turn, is dependent upon the objective of the auditor. Before the reasoning underlying this contention can be explained, the exact nature of each type of test should be clarified.

Single-purpose tests are audit tests designed solely to determine the existence of internal control procedures. The single-purpose test of transactions is frequently referred to as a "walkthrough." Such tests take the form of:

. . . *following typical transactions through from cradle to grave or, if one prefers, from grave to cradle. That is, in the first section, a few sales orders would be selected, traced to other copies of these same documents along the way, checked to shipping records, thence to corresponding sales invoices, their*

[2] Francis J. Schaefer, "Statistical Sampling—An Audit Tool," *The New York Certified Public Accountant,* Vol. 33 (November 1963), p. 777. For a similar analysis of types of audit tests see Charles T. Steele, "An Auditor Samples Statistics," JofA, Vol. 114, Sept.62, p. 52.

various copies, and ultimately to the sales journal and accounts receivable ledger. All along the way the auditor should discuss with each employee involved what his procedures are with these documents, where he receives and sends them, and what his approvals mean.[3]

A test of *bona fides* involves the direct verification of the balance of a specific account, usually by examination of evidence external to the internal control system. The comparison of the quantity of cash on hand, determined by a physical count, with the balance in the cash account is an example of a test of *bona fides.* This type of test is primarily applicable to the verification of assets and liabilities. However, a few revenue and expense accounts can be supported in this manner; e.g., verification of dividends by reference to independent reporting services.

Dual-purpose tests have characteristics of both single-purpose tests and tests of *bona fides.* They are tests which serve the dual purpose of providing assurance as to the effective functioning of the internal control system and of providing a degree of assurance as to the *bona fides* of the transactions supporting an account balance.

The three types of tests can be viewed as a continuum. Tests designed solely to determine the existence of internal control procedures—single-purpose tests—and tests designed solely to determine the integrity of the account balances—tests of *bona fides*—are the polar positions on the continuum of audit tests. Dual-purpose tests lie all along the continuum between the two polar positions. In fact, most of the auditor's tests are in the dual-purpose range.

Whether dual-purpose tests will lie closer to single-purpose tests or closer to tests of *bona fides* will depend on the intent of the auditor. The auditor may consider the tests to be examinations of internal control, although they are generally associated with determining the validity of account balances, or vice versa. The form of a test may resemble a test of *bona fides,* but the primary purpose may be to test internal control; e.g., interim confirmation of a sample of accounts receivable. Conversely, although the form of a given test may resemble a test of transactions, the purpose may be to add to the validity of an account balance when there is an internal control weakness; e.g., the tracing of book receipts to bank deposits, as shown by the cutoff bank statement at year-end.

Since a test of transactions may be either a single-purpose test or a dual-purpose test, Professor Stettler's conclusion that "a sample of one of each type of transaction should constitute an adequate test of transactions"[4] must be examined with respect to both types of tests.

---

[3] R. J. Anderson, "Analytical Auditing," *The Canadian Chartered Accountant,* Vol. 83 (November 1963), p. 323.
[4] Stettler, *op. cit.,* p. 60.

SAMPLE SIZE FOR SINGLE-PURPOSE TESTS

Single-purpose tests are used only in the review of internal control. By review-ing the procedure manual, chart of accounts and systems department memo-randums, and by discussing the system with the controller or chief accountant, the auditor can gather the preliminary information on internal control. This inquiry, however, is not sufficient to establish the existence of internal control procedures. Procedure manuals may be out of date or lacking in necessary detail; in addition, officials may be unaware of modifications of procedures made by operating personnel. It is at this point that single-purpose tests of transactions are necessary.

In applying single-purpose tests of transactions, the auditor traces each type of transaction from initiation to ultimate disposition. He discusses the proce-dures with the employee who performs them; he examines all documents on or related to the transaction he is tracing; and he notes any deviations from standard company procedure and any weaknesses in the procedures in effect.

The objective of this single-purpose test of transactions is to determine whether the internal control procedures which are supposed to be in effect are, in fact, in effect. The objective is not to determine if these procedures are in effect and functioning an acceptable percentage of the time.

Given the objective of single-purpose tests of transactions, Professor Stet-tler's conclusion is sound. A limited test of transactions will suffice because the auditor's objective does not include making valid statistical inferences about the population of all transactions of a given type.

The suggestion that single-purpose tests of transactions should be restricted to one of each type has merit. It cautions the auditor to avoid over-testing. A sample of 20 or 30 would generally be too small to establish the extent of compliance with procedures but would be far more than would be necessary to establish the existence of procedures.

The applicability of Professor Stettler's conclusion to dual-purpose tests of transactions is a separate issue. There are several differences between the two types of tests which must be made clear.

SAMPLE SIZE FOR DUAL-PURPOSE TESTS

One difference between dual-purpose tests and single-purpose tests is their timing. Dual-purpose tests follow single-purpose tests. The extent of dual-purpose tests is usually based on the apparent weaknesses in the internal control system which was diagnosed on the basis of the single-purpose tests.

In addition, single-purpose tests of transactions differ from dual-purpose tests of transactions in their inclusiveness and direction. Dual-purpose tests of transactions are generally less inclusive. The example cited in the explanation of a walkthrough proceeds from inception, sales order, to final disposition, sales journal and accounts receivable ledger. Emphasis is placed on the auditor's concern with all the documents and procedures along the path of the transaction. A dual-purpose test of transactions will, however, usually focus on the compliance with a specific procedure where an internal control weakness was found to be present. Shipping records, for example, may be traced to the accounts receivable ledger to assure the validity of the inference that an acceptable percentage of the orders shipped were billed. The direction of dual-purpose tests of transactions will be selected to meet a specific objective, rather than as a matter of the auditor's preference, as in single-purpose tests. If, for example, there is a system weakness which could create an understatement of sales, the auditor would trace a sample of sales orders to the sales journal. If the weakness permitted an overstatement, transactions would be traced backward from the sales journal.

Dual-purpose tests are not used solely as a follow up of weaknesses. A possibility of error in the auditor's judgment in evaluating internal control always exists. As a defense against this fallibility, dual-purpose tests are frequently applied on a rotating basis each year in areas where the control system seems satisfactory. This cyclical application of dual-purpose tests is usually planned to cover all key areas of the system over a three- or four-year period in a continuing engagement.[5] Application of dual-purpose tests would be more extensive in an initial examination.

In summary, dual-purpose tests of transactions are used by the auditor for investigation of internal control weaknesses established by single-purpose tests of transactions and for reinforcing the auditor's conclusions on the reliance to be placed on the internal control system. They provide assurance as to the effective functioning of the internal control system as well as to the *bona fides* of an account balance. For this purpose, a sample size sufficient to support statistically valid inferences would seem to be required.

---

[5] This is essentially the viewpoint expressed by Tietjen in his advocacy of rotation of audit procedures. See A Carl Tietjen, "A Suggested Change in Examination Approach," JofA, Vol. 101, April 56, pp. 47–49.

NECESSITY OF DUAL-PURPOSE TESTS

Professor Stettler seems to advocate the elimination of dual-purpose tests when he states:

> . . . The sample of one of each type of transaction should suffice to indicate that the system, such as it is, is operative, and a larger sample that would disclose the extent of compliance helps very little in assessing the fairness or propriety of the account balances produced by the system.
>
> It is in the tests of the balances themselves against verifiable supporting evidence that the auditor must expand his sample to achieve increased reliability.[6]

The audit would then proceed from single-purpose tests to tests of *bona fides*. A judgment of the validity of this contention involves two related issues: (1) the availability of tests of *bona fides* and (2) the auditor's reliance on the internal control system.

The auditor must express an opinion on the fairness of presentation of the financial statements as a whole. His opinion includes the fair presentation of the individual components of the income statement. Tests of *bona fides*, by the verification of net assets at the beginning and end of the year, could establish the fair presentation of net income, but the fair presentation of the individual components could not be verified in this manner. Tests of *bona fides* usually provide assurance that revenues and expenses are fairly presented, because the auditor determines that the internal control procedures which relate net assets with revenue and expense flows are functioning an acceptable percentage of the time; this relationship is ascertained, in part, by dual-purpose tests of transactions.

This argument is not meant to reject Professor Stettler's advocacy of second-level internal control;[7] his point is well taken. The auditor is not concerned with each and every internal control procedure. The "control points" must be determined. If an omission of a procedure or an error in the application of a procedure would be detected at a later point in the system, then the auditor is not concerned with adherence to that specific procedure. Once the second-level controls are determined, however, the auditor must still establish that these controls are functioning an acceptable percentage of the time.

The above argument is intended to state the case for dual-purpose tests of transactions. The relationship between types of audit tests and sampling approaches remains to be considered.

[6] Stettler, *op. cit.*, p. 58.
[7] *Ibid.*

SAMPLING APPROACHES AND AUDIT TESTS

This relationship—between types of tests and sampling approaches—must clearly identify the sample unit involved. The sample unit is the individual item which is chosen for testing and may be either quantitative or qualitative in nature.

A quantitative sample unit can be immediately observed in numerical form. In the audit of accounts receivable, for example, the actual dollar amounts of the account balances are quantitative sample units. These quantitative sample units are often referred to as variables.

Some observations, however, only provide information concerning the existing quality of an item. An observation may be that an account requires investigation, that a credit to an account has been properly approved, or that a sales transaction has been recorded in the correct period. Frequently these qualities are referred to as attributes. Each observation is tallied against a particular category and numerical data, necessary for statistical operations, emerge when the number in each classification is counted and expressed as a ratio of the total number of observations; e.g., the per cent of accounts requiring investigation.

Estimation sampling is the only statistical sampling approach which can be used to test for attributes or variables. Acceptance sampling and discovery sampling are confined to testing for attributes.

EXPLANATION OF THE THREE APPROACHES

For those unfamiliar with sampling terminology, a brief explanation of these sampling methods is offered.

The object of the estimation sampling approach is to make a quantitative estimate of a characteristic of the population being sampled within specified precision limits and with a specified level of confidence. Precision is a statistical term for the maximum probable difference between the sample estimate and the true, but unknown, population characteristic and is usually stated as a plus and minus range around the sample estimate. The confidence level is a number between 0 and 1 which measures the degree of confidence attached to the sample estimate and precision limits.

In an examination of 200 vouchers, for example, in which the auditor discovers eight procedural errors, the sample estimate of the procedural error rate is 4%. If precision has been specified as 2% and the confidence level has been specified as .95, the auditor can state that he has 95% confidence that the procedural error rate is not less than 2% and not more than 6%.

The object of acceptance sampling is to determine whether to accept or reject a group of items (the population) on the basis of the information provided by the sample. The auditor specifies a maximum acceptable error rate and the desired confidence level. By referring to an acceptance sampling table, the auditor can determine the number of errors which can be disclosed by the sample without "rejecting" the population.[8]

Assume, for example, that in an examination of vouchers for procedural error the maximum acceptable error rate is specified as 4% and the specified confidence level is .95, for a population of 1,250 vouchers. Assume, further, that an acceptance sampling table indicates an acceptance number of seven for a sample size of 120. If the auditor selects a sample of 120 vouchers and the sample contains seven or fewer procedural errors, the auditor can state that he has 95% confidence that the procedural error rate does not exceed 4%.

The discovery sampling approach is a means of selecting a sample and achieving a specified confidence that at least one error will be disclosed by the sample if errors exist in a specified proportion in the population. There are tables available which indicate the probability (confidence level) of finding at least one example of an event if the total number of events in the population are at various levels.[9] The auditor must specify the maximum allowable occurrence of errors and the confidence level desired. Reference to an appropriate table for the population involved will indicate the required sample size. If the sample does not disclose any errors, the auditor may conclude that the true error level does not exceed the specified maximum allowable error rate.

Since Professor Stettler considers only single-purpose tests and tests of *bona fides,* the polar positions on the continuum of audit tests, his argument leads him to the conclusion that "estimation sampling is perhaps the only statistical sampling approach that is valid and useful for auditing purposes."[10] Because a single-purpose test requires the observation of only one transaction, statistical sampling is not necessary. Since estimation sampling is the only sampling approach available to test variables, a test of *bona fides,* which involves verification of the dollar balance of a specific account, must use the estimation sampling approach.

Professor Stettler's conclusion ignores the relationship between sampling

---

[8] For Example: Harold F. Dodge and Harry G. Romig, *Sampling Inspection Tables,* John Wiley & Sons, Inc., New York, 1944.

[9] See the table illustrated in: Herbert Arkin, "Discovery Sampling in Auditing," JofA, Vol. 111, Feb.61, p. 53.

[10] Stettler, *op. cit.,* p. 59.

approaches and dual-purpose tests. He does not seem to notice that even the audit test chosen for his example, confirmation of accounts receivable, is frequently a dual-purpose test.

CONSIDERING THE TEST'S OBJECTIVE

In a study to investigate the applicability of statistical sampling techniques to the confirmation of accounts receivable, Professor John Neter concluded that this audit procedure had two purposes:[11] (1) "evaluating the effectiveness of internal controls and procedures" and (2) "evaluating the integrity of the account balances." His conclusion that "only one of these [purposes] would be used in some instances; in other cases, both would be employed simultaneously"[12] seems to support the contention that the objective of the test, rather than its form, determines the position of the test on the continuum of audit tests. Professor Neter's study involved two industrial companies and a public utility. Although the test of *bona fides* was emphasized for the industrial companies, the evaluation of internal control effectiveness was far more important for the public utility. He cautioned that "a sample size adequate for one purpose may not be adequate for another."[13] Professor Neter's study would seem to indicate that conclusions as to sampling approach should not be made without first considering the objective of the test.

CONCLUSION

While, as Professor Stettler explained, estimation sampling seems to be the most useful method for applying tests of *bona fides,* another sampling approach may be more appropriate for dual-purpose tests.

If the primary objective of the dual-purpose test is to evaluate the integrity of an account balance, the concern with a dollar amount, variable, would dictate the use of estimation sampling. On the other hand, if the primary objective is to evaluate the effectiveness of internal controls and procedures, the principal concern with an existing quality, attribute (e.g., that a confirmation reply indicates an account requires investigation), would allow the use of any of the three sampling approaches. Either estimation sampling, acceptance sampling or discovery sampling may be used in sampling for attributes.

[11] John Neter, "Applicability of Statistical Sampling Techniques to the Confirmation of Accounts Receivable," *The Accounting Review*, Vol. 31 (January 1956), p. 82.

[12] *Ibid.,* p. 84.

[13] *Ibid.,* p. 87.

Sample sizes required for acceptance sampling and discovery sampling are relatively small when compared to those required for estimation sampling. On the other hand, estimation sampling can be used to estimate error rates, while the other approaches only provide information that the rate of errors is higher or lower than a previously specified tolerable error rate.

The main point is that conclusions drawn about the adequacy of sample size of audit tests are directly related to the type of audit test. The conclusions that a severely restricted sample is adequate for single-purpose tests and that estimation sampling is most useful for tests of *bona fides* do not necessarily have a bearing on dual-purpose tests. Since the primary objective of dual-purpose tests is frequently to determine that internal control procedures are functioning an acceptable percentage of the time, acceptance sampling may be most suitable. This conclusion is, at this time, tentative, but any refutation should be directed to dual-purpose tests, rather than single-purpose tests or tests of *bona fides*. No matter what sampling approach is chosen for dual-purpose tests of transactions, the sample size must be large enough to support statistically valid inferences.

Formulation of a sampling plan in an actual situation can be a taxing experience. The following case is based on a situation actually encountered by an auditor.

CORSICANA ALUMINUM CORPORATION*

Corsicana Aluminum Corporation performs finishing operations on aluminum extrusions and sells them to wholesalers or contractors in the construction industry. Some of its more common products are aluminum framings for the exterior of multi-story buildings and window and door frames used in home and apartment construction. In addition to its product line, special orders for specific construction projects are undertaken.

* The authors are indebted to Robert W. Lambert of Peat, Marwick, Mitchell & Co., Dallas, for the original investigation and initial organization of the material.

FINANCIAL STATEMENTS

Condensed financial statements have been included as Figures 1 and 2 on the following pages. It is apparent that the two most significant assets are accounts receivable and inventory. These two items together comprise over 85 percent of the total assets. This case deals specifically with the audit process as related to the inventory. Therefore the assumption is made that tests of procedures have indicated an excellent system of billing and cash receipts, and through confirmation and subsequent collections the auditor is satisfied that any misstatement of receivables would be insignificant.

FIGURE 1   BALANCE SHEET

	Current Period	Prior Period
Assets		
Cash	$ 126,894	$ 4,967
Accounts receivable	776,905	649,823
Inventory	837,935	967,731
Reserve for obsolescence	(33,500)	(33,500)
Prepaid expenses	21,945	21,459
Total current assets	$1,730,179	$1,610,480
Property, plant and equipment	203,435	163,898
Less reserve for depreciation	(95,960)	(85,011)
Net property, plant and equipment	$ 107,475	$ 78,887
	$1,837,654	$1,689,367
Liabilities and equity		
Accounts payable	$ 39,241	$ 98,159
Accrued expenses	13,365	8,001
Total current liability	$ 52,606	$ 106,160
Stockholders' equity	$1,785,048	$1,583,207
	$1,837,654	$1,689,367

FIGURE 2   INCOME STATEMENT

	Current Year	Prior Year
Net sales	$4,741,016	$4,395,596
Cost of sales	3,825,794	3,640,479
Gross profit	$ 915,222	$ 755,117
Selling expense	$ 288,930	$ 215,463
General and administrative expense	227,536	217,971
	$ 516,466	$ 433,434
Operating income	$ 398,756	$ 321,683
Other income (expense)	$ 4,926	$ (941)
Net income	$ 403,682	$ 321,742

DESCRIPTION OF ITEMS AND PLANT

With the exception of some minor hardware items, the inventory consists of aluminum extrusions. There are countless different configurations of the extrusions, but the shape of the extrusion has little influence on the cost because most items are priced per pound. Although there is some variation in dimensions, most items measure approximately four inches by two inches on the end, and the length can vary from a few feet to twenty-four feet. The type of finish on the aluminum is a very important factor in valuation and is very easy to determine. The cost of an extrusion can double if the most expensive finish is used rather than the least expensive one. The actual quantities on hand can vary from one or two pieces to several hundred. The larger quantities are stacked on pallets and are easily located and counted.

The plant comprises a total area of approximately two city blocks. About one half of this amount is not covered and is used as a storage area for large quantities of aluminum. An attempt is made to stack all items with the same part number together and often such stacks are very large and require several pallets that can be easily moved by fork-lift trucks. The enclosed portion of the plant is primarily a work area. In addition, some plant space is used to store finished goods.

PHYSICAL COUNT PROCEDURES

In order to attain meaningful quarterly financial statements, a physical inventory is taken every three months. The actual count takes at least one day and often requires two days. Every item in the plant is physically counted. The plant has been divided into several areas, and one employee is responsible for the count in each area. The count is recorded on prenumbered tags that are distributed to the supervisors prior to the count. The entire tag is placed on the item it represents, and the product number, finish code, length and

**FIGURE 3 FREQUENCY DISTRIBUTION OF INVENTORY DATA
AND RELATION TO TOTAL VALUE**

Value of Individual Items	Number of Items	Total Value	% of Total Items	% of Total Value
$ 0–100	1973	$ 68,279	57.93	8.15
101–200	501	72,098	14.71	8.60
201–300	233	56,077	6.84	6.69
301–400	128	43,903	3.76	5.24
401–500	96	42,853	2.82	5.11
501–600	93	50,960	2.73	6.08
601–700	55	35,741	1.61	4.27
701–800	53	39,851	1.55	4.76
801–900	40	33,617	1.18	4.00
901–1000	32	30,247	.94	3.61
1001–1100	29	30,664	.85	3.66
1101–1200	27	30,970	.79	3.70
1201–1300	20	24,977	.59	2.98
1301–1400	17	23,125	.50	2.76
1401–1500	11	15,950	.32	1.90
1501–1600	15	23,345	.44	2.79
1601–1700	11	18,256	.32	2.18
1701–1800	7	12,199	.21	1.46
1801–1900	8	14,893	.23	1.78
1901–2000	4	7,863	.12	.94
Over 2000	53	162,067	1.56	19.34
	3406	$837,935	100.00	100.00

Mean = $246.02
Standard deviation = $516.19

quantity are entered on both sections of the tag. After the count is completed and after clearance from the auditor, one part of the tag is removed, and the numerical sequence is verified. The tags are then turned into the accounting department with any void or unused tags. The cost is then manually entered on the tag. The source of the cost data is discussed later. The information on the tag is then keypunched and processed by computer. It is assumed that the keypunch operators are independent of persons concerned with inventory valuation and that the cards are verified.

The cost by part number is developed on a per foot basis by the accounting department. There is an analysis sheet for every part number. It is assumed that the auditor has already performed test work on these cost sheets and is satisfied with their accuracy. The sheets serve the dual purpose of providing a method of pricing inventory and a basis for making bids on potential jobs.

INVENTORY DATA

At the end of the current fiscal year a physical inventory was taken. A preliminary computer run of inventory characteristics was undertaken for use by the independent auditors. Information from the computer output is summarized in Figure 3 on the preceding page.

Requirement: Design a sampling plan for inventory of Corsicana Aluminum clearly specifying the following:

1 The purposes of such a plan

2 The magnitude required to make a misstatement material

3 Audit procedures required

4 Method of selection of items

CHAPTER 10

AUDITING
WITH THE COMPUTER

Computers are capable of a huge quantity of work in a short period of time. Auditors have recently discovered this useful characteristic and are now putting computers to work. In many respects, auditors are turning the disadvantages of computers into advantages. One can still read articles that suggest that "auditing around the computer" is the only feasible approach; however, it is rapidly becoming an accepted fact that time, and therefore money and client billings, can be reduced by "auditing through the computer."

Almost all large CPA firms have now developed computerized auditing systems. Haskins and Sells Auditape was the first of these and is the central figure in the following analysis of generalized computer audit systems.

GENERALIZED COMPUTER-AUDIT PROGRAMS
W. Thomas Porter*

Much has been written about auditing electronic systems in the past few years. Most of the techniques recommended for the auditor who uses the computer require some specialized knowledge about computers and programing.[1]

The purpose of this article is to discuss the use of generalized computer-audit programs in evaluating and testing records produced by the client's system. In my discussion, some analysis will be made of the Auditape system, developed by Haskins & Sells, since this system is an important example of generalized computer-audit programs.

USES OF COMPUTER PROGRAMS IN AUDITING

A computer program can be used for any computational or comparison task for which quantitative criteria can be established. Examples of these types of tasks in auditing are:

* From *The Journal of Accountancy*, Vol. 127, No. 1 (January, 1969), pp. 54–62. Reprinted by permission of the American Institute of Certified Public Accountants.
[1] Many authors have advocated the use of test decks and specialized computer-audit programs by the auditor. Both these techniques require extensive knowledge about the computer and the programing process for the design and implementation to be effective.

1 Testing extensions and footings

2 Summarizing data and performing analyses useful to the auditor

3 Examining records for quality—completeness, consistency, invalid conditions, etc.

4 Selecting and printing confirmations

5 Selecting and printing audit samples

6 Comparing the same data maintained in separate files for correctness and consistency

7 Comparing audit data with company records.

A common characteristic of these applications is the fact that the auditor can define clearly and precisely what is to be computed, compared, summarized, printed, etc.

Testing extensions and footings

The computer can be used to perform the simple summations and other computations in order to test the correctness of extensions and footings. The speed and low cost per computation of the computer means that it takes only a small amount of extra time and expense to perform the test in all records rather than a sample.

Summarizing data and performing analyses useful to the auditor

The auditor frequently needs to have the client's data summarized in different ways for analysis. Examples are aging of accounts receivable, preparation of annual usage, requirements of parts and inventory, listing all credit balances in accounts receivable and all debit balances in accounts payable, etc.

Examining records for quality

The quality in visible records is readily apparent as the auditor makes use of them in his examination. Sloppy record-keeping, lack of completeness, and other conditions affecting the quality of the records are observed by the auditor in the normal course of the audit. If the auditor obtains a complete print-out for use in manual evaluation methods, the records can be tested for evidence of unsatisfactory record-keeping. If the records are in machine-readable form, the auditor has the option of using the computer for testing the records. In using the computer, a program is written to examine the records for completeness. For example, the customer file records might be examined to determine the number of records in which there is no credit limit specified. The records can also be tested for consistency between different items in valid conditions; e.g., account balances exceeding credit limit in unreasonable amounts (more than ten dependents for payroll deduction purposes on a man's payroll record).

Selecting and printing confirmations

Based on quantifiable selection criteria, the computer can select and print out the confirmation requests. As an example, one auditing firm has designed a multi-part form which is prepared on a computer. A single printing prepares a first request, a mailing envelope, a return envelope, a control copy and a second request should it be needed. The form is designed so that the first request is stuffed in the mailing envelope which contains the return envelope. The savings in audit time when preparing large numbers of confirmations is substantial. A computer program can be written to select the accounts according to any criteria desired and using any sampling plan.

Selecting and printing audit samples

A computer can be programed to select audit samples either through the use of random numbers or systematic selection techniques. The sample selection may be programed to use multiple criteria, such as random samples of items under a certain dollar amount plus all items having certain characteristics such as high dollar values. The samples selected in this way can be used for audit tests such as confirmation, price tests of inventory items, etc.

Comparing the same data maintained in separate
files for correctness and consistency

Where there are two or more separate records having data fields which should be the same, the computer can be used for testing for consistency. For example, the pay rates on the payroll master tape may be compared with the pay rates used in computing the payroll as shown on a transaction tape.

Comparing audit data with company records

Audit data such as inventory test counts can be compared to the inventory records by using computer programs. This requires that the audit data be converted to machine-readable records. Other examples of this use are tracing cash receipts to accounts receivable records or comparison of inventory costs with the master file cost data.

OBTAINING AN AUDIT PROGRAM

Three approaches have been used in obtaining suitable computer programs for use in the evaluation and testing of records: (1) programs written by the client, (2) programs written by or under supervision of the auditor and (3) generalized audit programs.

Programs written by client

Much analysis desired by the auditor is sometimes useful to the client. Therefore, the client will frequently write computer programs for his own use or will prepare the program for the installation if the auditor requests the analysis and there is also internal use for it. Examples are programs to age accounts receivable, analyze inventory turnover and obsolescence, review open order files, etc. Obviously, to use such programs the auditor will need to test the client's program. The extent of testing would depend, of course, on the reliance the auditor can place on the installation's control over programs and operations. As a general rule, the auditor should, at the minimum, obtain a copy of the run book for the application, review the documentation for the run and be present when the program is run.[2]

Writing an audit program

Since a computer-audit program is written in the same way as any other computer program and since the programing process is explained very well in other literature,[3] I will not discuss, in any detail, the steps involved in preparing a computer program to perform audit activities. Basically, there are four aspects of developing computer-audit programs: (1) determining audit objectives and procedures, (2) developing systems flowcharts, (3) developing program flowcharts and (4) coding, assembling and testing programs. The extent to which the auditor can or should perform each of these tasks depends upon many factors, such as the auditor's knowledge of data processing and competence in developing computer programs, the complexity of the programs being developed, the source language being used and the availability of client programing assistance.[4]

[2] For a discussion of programing documentation, see the author's "A Control Framework for Electronic Systems," JofA, Oct.65, p. 56.
[3] There are several excellent references available if one is interested in understanding the programing process. For example, Gordon B. Davis, *An Introduction to Electronic Computers*, McGraw-Hill Book Company; Gregory and Van Horn, *Automatic Data-Processing Systems*, Wadsworth Publishing Company, Inc.; Frederic G. Withington, *The Use of Computers in Business Organizations*, Addison-Wesley Publishing Company.
[4] For a detailed discussion of the development and use of computer-audit programs, see Chapter 5 of the author's book, *Auditing Electronic Systems*, Wadsworth Publishing Company, Inc.

Generalized audit programs

It has become apparent to auditors involved in computerized systems that there are many audit functions which change very little from client to client. This is not really a very novel observation. Indeed, public accounting firms have guides to the preparation of audit programs which are issued to all audit personnel. The guides suggest an outline of procedures to be employed in audit examinations and to be included in the individual audit programs prepared for each client.

The idea of generalized computer programs is also not a novel one. Equipment manufacturers and other organizations involved in supplying computer programs to clients have been involved in developing generalized programs or software for a number of years. These programs perform activities related both to the operation of the computer system (systems programs) and to the manipulation and processing of data used in the management of the business (applications programs). Generalized programs, such as assembly routines, utility routines and compilers, and application programs, such as payroll, inventory control and demand deposit accounting, find widespread use in many computer installations today. The availability of such programs is a great aid to personnel trying to use the computer in that these programs preclude the development of systems flowcharts, programing flowcharts, source language instruction and the assembling and testing of programs. Generalized programs, if developed, designed and tested properly, are available for use in performing functions designed to be performed by the computer with a minimum of preparation on the part of the user.

Until recently, generalized computer-audit programs have been used to a limited extent. One approach has been the use of an industry program which is applicable to all clients in an industry. The best example is the brokerage audit where generalized audit programs have been used to perform standard audit procedures having to do with confirmation, margin computations, etc. The client's files are transferred to a standard format on magnetic tape. The conversion program is unique for each client having a different computer; the data file in standard form is processed by an audit program used for all clients. The client's computer is used only if it fits the model and configuration specifications for which the audit processing program was written. It should be noted that even though two computer systems are not program compatible, they are probably data compatible if the data are put on magnetic tape.

THE AUDITAPE SYSTEM

The second approach is a generalized set of audit routines which can be useful for a variety of audit and management purposes and used on a restricted set of compatible computers meeting specified configuration requirements. Currently the best and most promising example of this approach is the Haskins & Sells Auditape system, designed to be used:

> By persons having no specialized knowledge of computers or programing languages, and having only a nominal amount of simple instruction.
>
> On a wide variety of records interchangeably, without any need for preparation of special programs for each type of application to be processed.[5]

The primary component of the system is Auditape itself, a series of audit routines written in machine language which are executed by virtue of specification cards developed by the auditor. In addition, the system includes an instruction sheet for computer operators, specification sheets and an operating manual. The operating manual includes a general discussion of the Auditape system, excerpts of which follow:

> The Auditape is in machine language, ready for immediate use, and includes several programs or what might be better referred to as routines to perform specific operations and a monitor routine to control the selection of these several operating routines.
>
> The instruction sheet for the computer operator includes all explanations necessary for operation of the equipment. The person using the Auditape system need not be concerned with any actions taken by the computer operator unless the application is being made for an audit purpose that requires control against possible manipulation of data by intervention of the operator.*
>
> The specification sheets are the means by which the person using the Auditape system adapts it to his purpose and to the input records available for each application. The specification sheets are used as a source document from which specification cards are key punched and read into the computer memory and combined with instructions read from the Auditape to complete the program for the particular routine being processed.
>
> The routines, other than the monitor routine, comprising the Auditape are:

---

[5] *Haskins & Sells Auditape System Manual*, Section 1, page 1.

* Author's Note: Haskins & Sells has recommended that the auditor using the system observe all processing with the system since it is possible for the operator to alter the contents of the computer core memory during processing by switches on the console of the central processing unit. The system as designed does not require any such manipulation during the auditor's processing of any routine. Accordingly, physical observation of the processing should be sufficient to maintain control.

1 *Edit routine, including the subtotal subroutine and an include-exclude subroutine*

2 *Print/punch routine*

3 *Summarize routine*

4 *Mathematical routine*

5 *Audit sample routine*

Edit Routine

The principal problem in developing the Auditape system, or any set of generalized programs, arises from the wide variety in the format of the computer records to be processed. This variety occurs not only in the records used by different companies for similar applications, but also for different applications by any one company. . . . In the absence of a generalized program, a separate program is required for each specific record format to be processed, even though the basic operation to be performed by each of the specific programs might be the same.

This problem is solved in the Auditape system by the use of the Edit Routine, which causes selected data to be read from any specified position in the input record regardless of its format and written in any specified field on an output tape in the Auditape record format. This output tape then becomes the input for any of the other routines in the system.

The Subtotal or Include/Exclude Subroutine can be processed simultaneously with the Edit Routine at the option of the person using the Auditape system. These subroutines can be used for special analyses and other purposes by providing subtotals of input data in certain specified classifications and by including or excluding input data based on certain specified criteria.

Print/Punch Routine

Aside from control totals and processing messages, the results from each of the other routines are written on an output tape in the Auditape record format. With any of these tapes as input, the Print/Punch Routine can be used to provide printed or punched card output or both. This routine also includes options to permit the fields in the Auditape record to be printed out in any desired order, and to print appropriate descriptive headings over each column of data.

Summarize Routine

The Summarize Routine can be used to summarize details of records by some identifying characteristic such as customer number or inventory part number.

Mathematical Routine

The Mathematical Routine performs addition, subtraction, multiplication, or division of amounts in any two quantitative fields in the Auditape record, or of amounts in one of such fields and a specified constant amount.

Audit Sample Routine

The Audit Sample Routine computes the approximate optimum sample size required to obtain the statistical precision and reliability specified for a particular sample and selects the items to be included in the sample.[6]

USE OF AUDITAPE SYSTEM

There is evidence that the Auditape system has been used very successfully by Haskins & Sells in performing audit tasks and by their clients in analyzing files for management purposes. My object in using the system was to confirm my understanding of the system and to compare it with the approach of using programs written by or under the supervision of the auditor. The situation I used was an accounts receivable application for which special computer-audit programs had previously been written to perform certain audit procedures. The audit procedures included in these specialized audit programs were accounts receivable year-end procedures in a medium-sized manufacturing company. The auditor's objectives were (1) to determine the validity of the client's year-end accounts receivable amount and (2) to evaluate the collectibility of the accounts.

The company processed accounting and operational data on an IBM 1401 data processing system. This system included a teletypewriter order entry network, 1011 paper tape reader, 7330 magnetic tape units, a 1402 card-read punch and a 1403 printer. The central processing unit had a storage capacity of 16,000 characters.

Trade accounts receivable, in the aggregate, averaged approximately $2,-500,000 and consisted of over 6,000 accounts, approximately 5 per cent of which represented about 80 per cent of the total dollar value. The accounts receivable were on two magnetic tape files, one being the basic record file that contained data records for each customer as shown in Figure 1, pp. 323–324; the other tape file was the item record file that contained the details—i.e., invoices, unidentified cash payments—which supported the basic record account balance (see Figure 2, p. 324, for item record of unpaid invoices).

[6]*Ibid.*, Section 3, pages 1 and 2.

FIGURE 1   ACCOUNTS RECEIVABLE BASIC RECORD

Data Field	Number of Characters
Customer number	7
Current A/R balance	9
Amount on order	
Steel	9
Tungsten	9
Sundry	9
Credit Limit	
Amount	7
Date limit established	6
Credit history	
Date account opened	6
Highest credit extended	9
Date highest credit extended	6
Original credit limit	9
Date original credit limit established	6
Previous credit limit	9
Date previous credit limit established	4
Number of months of previous credit limit	2
Number of items currently delinquent	3
Amount currently delinquent	9
Delinquency history	
Months reporting	2
Months delinquent	2
Consecutive months delinquent	2
Last month delinquent	4
Highest delinquency	
Number of items	3
Amount	9
Date	4
Date last sale	6
Sales history (material amount only)	
(By-product line—steel, tungsten, sundry)	
3rd prior year	9
2d prior year	9
1st prior year	9
This year to date	9
This month	9

FIGURE 1   ACCOUNTS RECEIVABLE BASIC RECORD (cont'd)

Data Field	Number of Characters
Potential	9
Profit at standard—year to date	9
Payment history	
Payment ratings (company establishes payment ratings 0–9 based on payments for each quarter):	
3rd prior year—by quarter	4
2d prior year—by quarter	4
1st prior year—by quarter	4
This year—by quarter	4
Dollars paid this quarter:	
By discount date	9
By due date	9
Customer name and address	136

FIGURE 2   A/R ITEM RECORD FOR UNPAID INVOICES

Data Field	Number of Characters
Item record code	1
Customer number	7
Date	5
Invoice number	12
Gross amount of invoice	9
Net amount of invoice	9
Cash discount	7

Audit procedures

In performing the year-end audit procedures for the accounts receivable files, the auditor developed certain computer programs using the client's accounts receivable basic record file and the item record file. These files were then processed with the computer-audit programs as shown in Figure 3. The procedures performed by the three programs were:

1 Select for positive confirmation and print, on the circularization report, accounts with:

a Balance $\geq$ $5,000 (type Code 1).

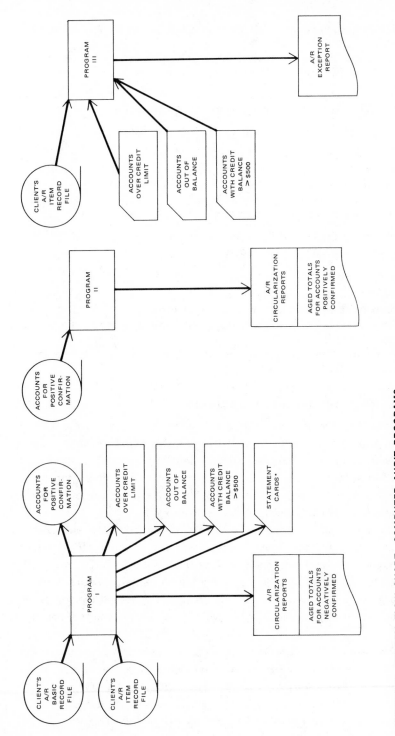

FIGURE 3   SYSTEM FLOW CHART—COMPUTER AUDIT PROGRAMS

Note: Statement cards are processed with the client's statement preparation program to produce customer statements for mailing with confirmation requests.

b Balance $\geq$ $1,000 but $\leq$ $5,000 and with any portion of the account 30 or more days delinquent (type Code 2).

c Balance $\geq$ $1,000 and with sales this year 500 per cent $\geq$ last year's sales or $\leq$ 20 per cent of last year's sales (type Code 3).

2 Randomly select for negative confirmation and print, on the circularization report, 10 per cent of the remaining accounts (type Code 0).

3 Age all accounts.

4 Select and print on the exception report all accounts:
  a Over credit limit (type Code 4).
  b Whose basic record balance is not in agreement with the total amount of all items in its item record (type Code 5).
  c With credit balance $\geq$ $500 (type Code 6).

5 Accumulate and print, on the circularization report:
  a Number of accounts in basic record file.
  b Aged totals of all accounts in basic record file.
  c Number of items in item record file.
  d Total balance of all items in item record file.
  e Total balance of all accounts with credit balances.
  f Number of accounts selected for negative confirmation and aged totals for these accounts.
  g Number of accounts selected for positive confirmation and aged totals for these accounts.

Developing computer-audit programs

After formulating the audit procedures for the accounts receivable work and the systems flowcharts, the auditor prepared program flowcharts and designed output records to include the required audit information.

Of the three programs shown on the system flowcharts, Program I includes most of the processing logic and decision criteria. Programs II and III merely print machine-readable output resulting from Program I.

The primary output from the computer processing is the accounts receivable circulation report (see Figure 4). The report was set up in working paper form ready for the auditor's analysis. The digit under the "T" column in the report corresponds to the type of confirmation request—that is, 1 represents a positive confirmation request. File totals are printed at the end of the report for comparison with file totals shown on the client's aged trial balance.

The Auditape system applied   In using the Auditape system to perform the audit procedures enumerated above, I completed the relevant specification sheets required to use the system. There were 38 separate computer runs required to perform the necessary audit procedures. Many of these runs were necessary to get the data into the Auditape record format for performing the

FIGURE 4   ACCOUNTS RECEIVABLE CIRCULARIZATION SEPT. 30, 19XX

Number	Name and Address	T	S	Balances	Difference	No Reply	Explanation and Disposition
0333500	ACE INC.	1	0	7,280.31	BALANCE		
	2105 WINSPEAR AVE.				937.41 30 DAYS		
	MADISON, ILL.				60 DAYS		
					90 DAYS		
0350000	ACME COMPANY	1	0	12,408.47	BALANCE		
	7055 BEST RD.				2,463.94 30 DAYS		
	LANSING 4, MICH.				60 DAYS		
					90 DAYS		
0514000	ADDER CO.	1	0	33,347.91	BALANCE		
	YAKIMA, WASH.				23,180.43 30 DAYS		
					60 DAYS		
					90 DAYS		
1161000	BOOM TOOLS	1	0	6,037.19	BALANCE		
	12360 ASPEN LANE				3,022.76 30 DAYS		
	BOULDER, COLO.				60 DAYS		
					90 DAYS		
1466000	CRISP FORGING MFG.	1	0	34,246.84	BALANCE		
	LOWELL, MASS.				23,082.57 30 DAYS		
					60 DAYS		
					90 DAYS		
2511000	DUNHILL SUPPLY	1	0	5,772.28	BALANCE		
	4890 SOUTH CANTON ST.				2,236.99 30 DAYS		
	CANTON, OHIO				60 DAYS		
					90 DAYS		
2620075	EARTH-MOVERS INC.	1	0	11,784.47	BALANCE		
	PUYALLUP, WASH.				7,121.74 30 DAYS		
					60 DAYS		
					90 DAYS		
2646000	ESTHER TOOLS	1	0	7,234.73	BALANCE		
	COLLEGE LANE				255.96 30 DAYS		
	WILLIAMS, PA.				60 DAYS		
					90 DAYS		
3170000	FIRST SUPPLY	1	0	8,098.33	BALANCE		
	6360 DIVISION RD.				75.20 30 DAYS		
	BATTLE CREEK, MICH.				60 DAYS		
					90 DAYS		
3262310	GUNN FORGING	1	0	6,738.26	BALANCE		
	BARNESVILLE, IND.				3,212.17 30 DAYS		
					60 DAYS		
					90 DAYS		

PAGE TOTAL   10 ACCOUNTS   BALANCE 132,948.79   30 DAYS 65,589.17   60 DAYS   90 DAYS audit procedures. The scope of this article does not permit any discussion of the technical aspects related to the completion of the specification sheets and details of operating the system.[7]

Based on my analysis, I concluded that the Auditape system can perform all of the significant procedures included in the specialized programs. It does not provide the same flexibility in report format—i.e., aged information on the circularization report, type code—but this seems to be a rather insignificant item.

As to a comparison of time requirements of both approaches, my analysis indicates:

	Specialized Programs	Auditape
Analysis of problem (including flowcharting, input-output design)	150.0	30–50 (estimated)
Programing (including coding, key-punching, assembly and testing)	70.0	
Completion and key-punching of specification sheets		12 (estimated 2 hours for key-punching)
Run time	.5	2.5
	220.5	44.5–64.5

One footnote to the above time analysis should be added. The actual time for the analysis of the problem originally was 230 hours; this reflected some developmental and learning time. Discounting this time, it is more realistic to think in terms of 150 hours, which I have shown above, for the analysis of the problem. Approximately 100–120 of the 150 hours would be required for flow-charting and input-output design and would be unnecessary when using the Auditape system; hence the 30–50 hours for analysis under Auditape.

CONCLUSIONS ABOUT AUDITAPE

Based on my knowledge of and experimentation with the Auditape system, my major conclusions are:

1 The Auditape system, by virtue of the Edit Routine, can be applied to a variety of EDP installations involving a variety of record and file formats "without any need for preparation of special programs for each type of application to be processed."

[7] For those who wish such details, they may contact the AICPA's professional development division about courses on the H&S Auditape system, Haskins & Sells, or me on the specifics of this research.

2 The system, by virtue of the Include/Exclude Subroutine of the Edit Routine, can be a very powerful auditing tool in a variety of auditing situations that require examination of records for qualitative characteristics and conditions. In relation to the auditing uses of computer programs discussed earlier in this article, my analysis indicates that the Auditape system can be used to:

  a Test extensions and footings through its Edit Routine and Mathematical Routine.

  b Summarize data and perform analyses according to specified criteria by virtue of the Include/Exclude or Subtotal Subroutines of the Edit Routine and the Summarize Routine.

  c Examine records for quality through the use of the Include/Exclude Subroutine.

  d Select and print audit samples through the use of the Audit Sample Routine and Print/Punch Routine.

At the present time, the Auditape system cannot print confirmation requests, and it cannot very easily compare data maintained in separate files. However, Haskins & Sells plans to develop routines in the near future which will print confirmation requests and which will handle multiple input files and permit comparisons of data in separate files.

3 The system has been developed for use with the following equipment:

  a Processing units—IBM 1400 series tape systems or system 360 with 1401 emulators, with memory capacity of at least 8,000 characters. Honeywell Series 200 tape systems, with memory capacity of at least 8,000 characters. IBM System 360 tape or disk systems, with memory capacity of at least 32,000. Certain other equipment for which 1401 simulators are provided by the manufacturers.

  b Card read-punch.

  c Printer or a console typewriter.

  d Input/output units—at least three units for applications requiring an output tape or disk; at least two units for other applications.

However, the nonavailability of the above equipment at a particular location may not be a limitation if the input data are available on tapes or disks that can be transcribed into punched card or IBM tape format and the required equipment is available at another location (such as a service bureau). For example, in using the system for internal audit purposes at the University of Washington, we analyzed, on the university's IBM 1401 computer system, files previously generated on the university's Burroughs B5500 computer system.

4 The system significantly reduces the time required by the auditor in using the computer in auditing as compared to the alternative approach of developing specialized computer programs for individual client situations without any significant decrease in effectiveness in performing audit procedures with a computer.

5 The system, although requiring no programing on the part of the auditor, does require some knowledge of the computer and programing to allow *efficient* completion of the specification sheets. For example, terms and activities such as low-order positions, data fields, record formats, control cards and character manipulation all require more than a basic knowledge of the computer and programing on the part of the user of the Auditape system to effectively and efficiently use the system. Haskins & Sells, in recognition of this problem, has designed and conducted an Auditape System Seminar sponsored by the AICPA's professional development division. This program provides instruction for practicing CPAs in the use of the system. This program coupled with a few on-the-job experiences in using the system should be sufficient to allow efficient use of Auditape.

6 The system requires that even auditors experienced in the use of the computer have a nominal amount of instructions about the system in addition to knowledge gained by reading the operating manual. This is extremely evident when trying to use the Include/Exclude Subroutine. This was borne out in a recent classroom experiment with M.B.A. candidates most of whom had previous knowledge of computers and actual programing experience. All of the students had difficulty in applying the Include/Exclude Subroutine to an auditing application. Comments on problems they encountered in using the system included:

I was not able to determine from the information provided in the operating manual how one indicates the information pertinent to the Include/Exclude operations on the specification sheets.

In relationship to the Include/Exclude Subroutine, it would appear advisable to include in the operating manual an appendix which demonstrates how a simple representative problem is worked out.

7 The system as currently designed is somewhat cumbersome to use and would be greatly improved if certain functions could be combined so as to minimize the number of runs. The current version of the Auditape system was designed for the IBM 1400 series with a minimum of 8,000 characters of memory. It is obvious to users of EDP equipment that such a small memory capacity places constraints on the design and running of computer programs, particularly generalized computer programs. Haskins & Sells is working on a new version of the system which will combine certain routines so as to minimize the number of runs required for some audit applications.

SUMMARY

This article has examined the development and use of generalized computer-audit programs with particular emphasis on the Haskins & Sells Auditape system. The idea of generalized audit programs is a good one. H&S has taken one approach; other but not mutually exclusive possibilities include:

1 Generalized industry programs to perform audit steps common to an industry.

2 Generalized programs to perform common tasks such as confirmation, aging, testing for obsolete items, examination of file quality, etc.

3 Standard COBOL subroutines which the auditor combines to develop an in-
dividualized program for a particular client.

4 An audit language, based perhaps on a special version of the RPG (Report Program Generator) language.

I believe that there will be considerable activity in the area of generalized
audit programs by different CPA firms and perhaps by software companies. In
view of the high costs involved in developing such programs, the duplication
of effort that may result from individual firms' developmental activities and the
relevance of such programs for the entire profession, it is comforting to know
that the AICPA has appointed a computer users committee which, among other
things, is looking into this entire problem area.

Auditing with the computer can take place on a smaller scale than that for
which Auditape and its counterparts were designed. In the following, Connolly
describes the development of a computer audit program designed for use in
only a segment of an audit.

ACCOUNTS RECEIVABLE SYSTEM: A CASE
STUDY
James J. Connolly*

The client's present system is basically an open invoice receivables
system on IBM cards grouped in controls by class of customer and
sales territory. A customer's account consists of a header card containing the customer's account number, name and address, and sales invoice
cards representing shipments made, with other cards provided for miscellaneous transactions such as discount not earned, unauthorized deduction,
unapplied cash, credit invoices, etc. Cash receipts are applied (posted) by
pulling from the customer's file (card deck) the applicable sales invoice card.
If the amount received is different from the invoiced amount by an amount
greater than the applicable discount, an adjustment card is prepared by an
accounts receivable clerk and checked by a supervisor. The card is inserted
in the customer's file, and a notice is sent to the customer. At the end of each
month, the accounts are run on the computer and an aged trial balance is pre-

* From *The Journal of Accountancy*, Vol. 125, No. 6 (June 1968), pp. 53–60. Reprinted by permission of
the American Institute of Certified Public Accountants.

pared, the total of which is agreed to the general ledger by the accounts receivable control group. The control group posts by hand the totals of the daily sales, cash receipts and miscellaneous posting media runs to their general ledger control figure (See Exhibit 1 below.)

EXHIBIT I   FLOW CHART OF ORDER PROCESSING, SHIPPING, BILLING, AND ACCOUNTS RECEIVABLE

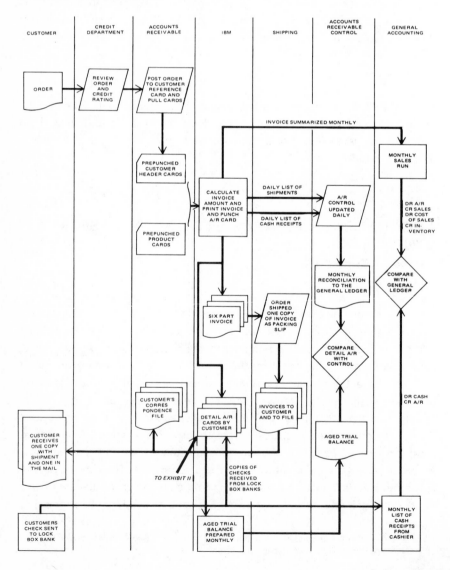

Originally, customers' accounts receivable records were maintained in a hand-posted Boston ledger; these records were converted to bookkeeping machine ledger cards. In 1964, the client converted the accounts receivable records from bookkeeping machine ledger cards to IBM cards as outlined above. This conversion was part of a long-range plan to place customers' accounts on magnetic tape. The change to bookkeeping machines did not involve a significant systems change or present a major problem to us as auditors nor did the conversion to IBM cards represent a radical change. Listing the cards on an IBM accounting machine would produce a printed ledger page not much different from the bookkeeping ledger page. The contemplated change from IBM cards to magnetic tape, which could not be read by the auditor without the use of electronic equipment, did promise a challenge for the future.

USE OF ELECTRIC ACCOUNTING MACHINES (EAM) EQUIPMENT TO ASSIST IN THE AUDIT

In 1964, it was decided that it was not feasible to write a sophisticated computer audit program for accounts receivable because the client's system was still in its first stages of operation and still being modified. However, it was decided that we could use the client's data processing equipment, under our control, to perform certain tests of footings (additions) that our Comptometer operator performed in prior years. By using the client's data processing equipment in this manner our staff acquired a better understanding of the operation of the equipment and the client's system. The personal working arrangements developed during these first small steps later proved invaluable when we began our accounts receivable confirmation program.

In all the following applications of the use of data processing equipment the intent was to use the speed and accuracy of the equipment to assist us in our audit. Our basic audit objectives have not changed; our audit procedures have not changed; we have used the equipment solely to increase the efficiency of our audit. Their potential is apparent when we are told that internal computer operations are now measured in picoseconds (one millionth of a millionth of a second,

$$\frac{1}{1,000,000,000,000} \text{ sec.}).$$

A. Electronic accounting machines used for test footing   The use of the client's data processing equipment to foot accounts receivable and payroll records enabled us to develop our accounts receivable program and are presented here as a guide to a few very simple ways in which data processing equipment may be used by the auditor to increase the efficiency of his examination. These specific applications illustrate footing by the use of the client's data processing equipment with some of the advantages and disadvantages. It should be understood that at this stage we were not attempting to do anything more than foot the selected records.

1. Accounts receivable—detail not normally printed out. In the client's accounts receivable system as outlined above the detail cards are not listed during the monthly updating run except for selected accounts to which statements are mailed. This was the first year that the accounts receivable records were on tabulating equipment and the alternative methods of footing the accounts receivable detail were very clear to us. We could request a special listing of the accounts receivable detail prepared on the IBM 407 accounting machine for the Comptometer operator to foot. This listing would be for our use only and would require several hours to prepare and a day and a half for our Comptometer operator to foot. Alternatively, we could control the IBM 407 during the processing of the selected controls, as outlined under B below, and *eliminate* the need for the Comptometer operator. It appears that a similar decision should be made wherever accounts receivable are on cards and that this may be an area for substantial audit economies.

We decided to use the client's IBM 407 to foot the accounts and, immediately after the monthly preparation of the aged trial balance, took control of the accounts receivable detail cards. We selected certain controls and sealed these card trays until we were able to obtain time on the IBM 407. By controlling the IBM 407 accounting machine during the processing of our selected controls, we effectively footed the selected accounts receivable detail.

2. Payroll—adequate hard-copy print-out available. The client maintains hard-copy payroll registers from which we selected certain payrolls to be footed as part of our normal examination in prior years. The machine data processing department also retained the IBM cards that were used to prepare these payroll registers. It appeared that we could effectively foot the selected payrolls either by the use of a Comptometer operator using the payroll register or by the use of IBM equipment using the applicable IBM cards, properly controlled by us as outlined in B below. However, after reviewing the payroll preparation, it was found that the processing of the payroll and subsequent disposition of IBM cards would make it costly to select an old pay period for our test. In subsequent processing the payroll cards are merged by man-number with other pay period cards and used in preparing quarterly reports to tax authorities; therefore, they were not available for use in our footing test without re-sorting by pay periods. The client was willing to start from the input data (timecards, etc.) of any old payroll which are kept intact and to reprocess the old input data on the punched card calculator and then run the payroll register from the cards produced from this pass.

Our choices were either to observe a current payroll processing run or request a complete rerun of old data. Because of the cost involved in the use of the machines for the time required, we decided to be present on a surprise basis during the processing of a current payroll. After the calculating pass was made for the factory payroll for the selected week we informed the IBM supervisor that we had decided to observe the subsequent processing of the payroll register, and we performed our footing tests at that time. The pay periods to be selected by us are not predictable by the payroll department because we can select payrolls processed during either our interim examination, the timing of which changes year to year, or our year-end examination. We can also select payrolls processed at the time of our observation of the annual physical inventory or at any other time during the year.

B. Controls over electronic accounting machine (EAM) equipment when used to foot   These were not complicated applications where sophisticated controls were necessary. *We were not attempting to do anything more than foot the selected records.* We intended to use the client's 407 accounting machine as an adding machine while satisfying ourselves that we had effective control over the input, output and machine operation by the use of the controls explained in the following paragraphs:

1 We observed the wiring of the program board used in the IBM 407 and ascertained the function of each wire. The board was wired by a machine operator and checked by a supervisor in machine accounting. In addition, a wiring diagram was prepared by the machine operator which was agreed by us to the program board used and later reviewed by one of our firm's computer specialists.

2 We processed a sample deck of cards on the 407 before we commenced processing the selected data to satisfy ourselves that the board was wired properly and functioning satisfactorily. This sample deck incorporated several control punches (any punch that is used to distinguish different types of punched card records) to test the machine's handling of cards with such punches.

3 We did not reveal our selection of accounts receivable controls or payrolls to be footed until we were ready to process the data and were present to maintain control over the program board and selected cards during the processing.

4 We requested a different machine operator from the one who normally operated the regular program.

C. Advantages of using EAM equipment for test footing

1 The understanding of the data processing system necessary to undertake and sustain a change in technique of this type should keep us abreast of the client's machine accounting system and internal controls.

2 The audit staff acquired firsthand experience in working with data processing equipment, which should improve their skills in other computer accounting areas.

D. Disadvantages

1 The timing of audit tests must be more exact because certain hard-copy listings which are normally footed at any time are only available in card form for a limited time. For example, as mentioned above we had to be present when the payroll was processed and our accounts receivable footing had to be made before the deck was updated by applying cash or inserting additional sales cards.

COMPUTER AUDIT PROGRAM

At our usual pre-examination meeting early in 1965 with the controller and chief internal auditor we requested their assistance in the accounts receivable area. We explained that their plans to place the accounts on magnetic tape would require us either to use a computer audit program or to audit around the computer. We explained that a computer audit program was necessary if we were to stay attuned to their system and that the program could also be used by the internal auditors. They agreed and set a date for a meeting at which time we would present a proposed accounts receivable audit program in English for the client's programers to write (program) in machine language.

EDP ACCOUNTS RECEIVABLE CONFIRMATION PROGRAM

The following program outline was used for our discussion with the internal auditors and the client's programers. The purpose of this program was to assist the auditor to select accounts receivable at random for confirmation and simultaneously establish that the field agreed with subsidiary ledger control accounts. The program also reviewed all accounts for unusual balances and footed and checked the aging of all accounts. The intention was that the internal auditors would control a copy of the program and we would control a copy, both programs in card form. The program could be modified at the time of processing by changing the variables marked N; this permitted us to guard the scope of our tests and confirmation requests until the actual time of processing when all input data was controlled by us.

Immediately after the normal monthly updating of the aged trial balance and the balancing of the accounts receivable detail with the general ledger (by the A/R control section), the client's personnel ran the following program under our observation:

1 Footed all accounts and listed on the console and on a magnetic tape for later off-line print-out the total dollars and number of accounts for each control. The totals of these controls were summarized and agreed to the general ledger.

2 Aged the accounts (the same routine already programed for the normal aging was used).

3 For every *Nth* account processed, starting at *X*, the computer listed these accounts on a control flag listing which was used as an audit workpaper and wrote the details of the account on tape for subsequent preparation of positive confirmation requests. Additional comments on our statistical sampling method are included below under Random Start. We indicated on all print-outs that the reason this item was selected was Code 1.

4 Listed on magnetic tape and prepared statements for all accounts that met the following criteria:

A. Balance at confirmation date over *N* amount.   Code 2
B. Balance at confirmation date of a credit amount over *N*.   Code 3
C. Account balance over *N* amount over *Y* days old.   Code 4
D. Inactive accounts with balances over *N* days which have had no
   activity during that time.   Code 5

5 Printed the code number indicated on each statement and the flag listing for identification of the reason the account was selected.

6 In order to have a complete sequential workpaper listing of each account selected at random for confirmation and each account selected because it fell outside our limit tests, we assigned consecutive audit numbers to each account listed. In addition, the applicable code number was placed next to each item selected to indicate why it was selected. The following information was printed on the audit workpaper flag listing:

Control	A/C No.	Store Name and Address	Audit Number	Code Reason	Amount
			1	1	$
			2	1	
			3	3	( )

This listing served as our audit workpaper schedule.

ADDITIONAL AUDIT STEPS DISCUSSED

Several other audit procedures were discussed including a comparison of the customer's account balance with the customer's history of purchases to agree the reasonableness thereof with the volume of business experienced. This step was not possible because the customer's history is not included in the magnetic tape record. Another audit procedure which would have been requested is a check to see that the credit limit has not been exceeded; but again, this information is not in the customer's magnetic tape record. However, the client has plans for including this data in the future, and we will then be able to include these additional steps in our program.

At the conclusion of our discussion we asked the internal auditors to follow up our request with the programer and keep us advised of results. It was emphasized that detailed documentation of the proposed program was an audit requirement and the representatives of Price Waterhouse & Co. and the internal auditors would review the documentation to establish the adequacy of controls.

USE OF THE PROGRAM IS NOT LIMITED TO AUDITING

The program is set up so that the criteria for selection of accounts are controlled by selection cards, which are set depending on the type of accounts within the control that are being run and which are key-punched at the time of the operation. The program can be used by four separate groups as listed below; consequently, a short payback period is expected for the cost of programing. Programing required approximately two man-weeks.

1 *Price Waterhouse & Co.*—will control a copy of the program in card form and use it to run audit tests and print customer statements for confirmation requests.

2 *Internal auditors*—will control their own copy in card form for use in their examination of accounts receivable.

3 *Customer service personnel*—may request print-outs with statements of any accounts in their controls depending on what they desire; e.g., accounts over $1,000 with no activity over 60 days, etc.

4 *Credit management*—before accounts receivable were maintained on EDP equipment it would have been expensive to select customers from the 35,000 to send statements monthly. With the use of the program, credit management can select economically those accounts that should receive statements.

Approximately six weeks after our initial discussions with the programer, who called us a half-dozen times with specific questions, we received the documentation and the actual programs in card form for the following programs:

Job No.	
723	Card to Tape—Accounts Receivable Aging and Detail
748	Accounts Receivable Confirmation Selection Program
749	Write Accounts Receivable Statements
751	Write Accounts Receivable Confirmation Flag Listing

REVIEW OF DOCUMENTATION OF PROGRAMS

In order to ascertain that the program's documentation was adequate for audit review purposes and also that the client's normal documentation complied with the Internal Revenue Service Guidelines for determining the adequacy of records maintained within an automatic data processing system, we referred to the IRS Guidelines and the IBM manual, "Management Control of Electronic Data Processing."[1] The following documentation is listed in the IBM manual as adequate for good operation of a system of average complexity and was supplied to us for all our audit programs:

1 A general, written description of the overall system, including a statement of its objectives, a description of the basic flow of information through the system, and a broad description of the separate processing steps and interrelationships between computer runs.

2 A general system diagram to accompany and illustrate the description. (See Exhibit 2, page 340, for a condensed system flowchart.)

3 For each computer program, a description of the functions performed by the program and a general description of how the program accomplishes them, with particular attention to features of the program or logic that would otherwise tend to be obscure.

4 Block diagrams showing the sequence of operations performed by the programs, with one or two levels of detail, as required, for clarity. The most detailed level should be less detailed than the source language listings.

5 Record descriptions showing the form and content of all inputs and outputs and memory locations.

6 Program listing in source language and in object code (a copy of a computer program used can replace the need for object code listing).

7 Program operating instructions for loading control cards, switch settings, halt procedure, sources of input and disposition of output.

The documentation for our audit programs was reviewed by the audit staff to acquire a general understanding of what the program does and how it does it as well as an understanding of what controls were included in the program. The program documentation was generally understood by the audit staff; however, for items 6 and 7 we consulted a computer specialist from our management advisory services (MAS) department for further information and explanation. The program listings and operating instructions were reviewed in depth as was the complete program. When the audit manager and computer specialist

[1] IBM Reference Manual, F20-0006, "Management Control of Electronic Data Processing," published by IBM Corporation, Data Processing Division, 1965, 33 pp.

**EXHIBIT II   GENERAL SYSTEMS FLOW CHART:
ACCOUNTS RECEIVABLE AUDIT PROGRAM**

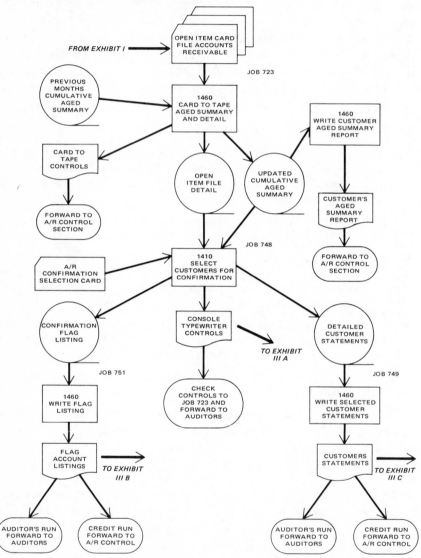

were satisfied that the program was sound and the controls built into the program were valid, we arranged computer time for a test run of live data.

RANDOM START

During the review it was noted that no provision had been included for a random start that would be required to insure the validity of our statistical selection. We requested the programer to provide for a random start, which was subsequently done. The complete details of our statistical sampling plan are not included here because of space limitations but a complete discussion of the technique is available in *Sampling in Auditing* by Hill, Roth and Arkin.[2]

Briefly the accounts which were selected at random on a systematic or every *Nth* basis comprised our statistical sample of accounts to be confirmed. Random as used in this article means that each of the accounts in the field had an equal opportunity for inclusion in the sample. We could have used random number sampling by loading random numbers into the computer and selecting those account numbers which matched up to the random number or we could have used a standard program developed by a computer manufacturer to select accounts completely at random.[3] Both systematic sampling and random number sampling are acceptable provided that in systematic sampling the starting point is a random selection and the entire field is covered. Care must be exercised that, because of the arrangement of the sequence of accounts, bias is not introduced into the sample. For this reason random number sampling is generally preferable.

We found that the assistance of the *computer* to select accounts for circularization using a *statistical sampling* plan and the subsequent statistical evaluation of the results proved to be a fruitful combination of two auditing tools.

TEST RUN OF OUR PROGRAMS

Two weeks after we received the programs the MAS computer specialist, the internal and external auditors visited the computer center to witness the test of our audit programs on the client's 1410 and 1460 computers. Job No. 723, the card-to-tape accounts receivable aging and detail, had been run the previous week and at our request observed by the internal auditors who controlled the selected tapes until this test run. At this time the selected customer accounts receivable files were written on magnetic tape for the three controls we had picked for our test run. Of course, when we subsequently ran our actual confirmation audit run we processed all controls. Details of our test run and the three audit programs follow.

A/R selection program—Job 748. A single selector (control) card—which controls the number of confirmations selected and the parameters of our tests, which were confidential until the last minute—was keypunched. The program

---

[2] *Sampling in Auditing*, by Hill, Roth and Arkin, The Ronald Press Company, New York City, 1962, 169 pp. including tables and appendix.

[3] IBM Reference Manual, C20-8011, "Random Number Generation and Testing," published by IBM Corporation, Data Processing Division, 1959, 12 pp.

card deck for Job 748, accounts receivable selection program, was loaded into the IBM 1402 card read punch. This program card deck, which consisted of approximately 500 autocoder condensed output cards, contained over 2,500 individual programed instructions. The program card deck consisted of two types of cards, each a different color for ease in handling—approximately 100 red cards which were an IBM software (standard) deck designed to clear all storage, load certain necessary tests, such as end of tape, etc., and 400 detailed program cards. We compared the switch settings on the 1410 console with the set-up instructions included in the program documentation and observed the computer operator run the job. The longest part of the whole operation was loading the program card deck because of the comparatively slow card reading speed. We requested our program in card form because it would facilitate changing the parameters of our tests and the fact that the storage of cards does not require the constant temperature and humidity conditions of magnetic tape. Once the proper magnetic tapes were mounted and the program card deck was read into core storage, the actual computer time used was less than a minute per control. The complete test was over in 15 minutes. The console print-out was obtained and a small sample is included in Exhibit 3, Part A. Each control group was read from one input tape and the selected accounts were written on two output tapes, one for a flag listing (Job 751) and the other containing the complete detail for customer statements (Job 749).

Program to write customers' accounts confirmation flag listing—Job 751. The output tapes from program Job 748 were mounted on the tape drive connected to the IBM 1460 computer and a flag listing was printed on the IBM 1403 at 1,100 lines a minute. The listing contained all the information necessary for an audit workpaper control sheet. A small sample is included in Exhibit 3, Part B.

Program to write customers' accounts receivable detailed statements— Job 749. The remaining output tape which contained the detail of the selected accounts receivable for preparing customer statements was also printed on the IBM 1403 using the IBM 1460 computer to read the tape. A statement for one customer is included in Exhibit 3, Part C.

What should our parameters be? After the results of the test run were analyzed, we decided to prepare six different selector cards to better apply our limit tests. The make-up of the accounts by control (some controls were large customers only, other controls small customers) was such that only by the use of six different selector cards could we obtain the desired results. For example, to ask that all accounts over $5,000 be printed out under Code 2 (balance at confirmation date over N) for a control containing large chain store accounts would be unrealistic as most of these accounts would probably have balances in excess of this amount. On the other hand, $5,000 for Code 2 on a neighborhood-type store would be excessive.

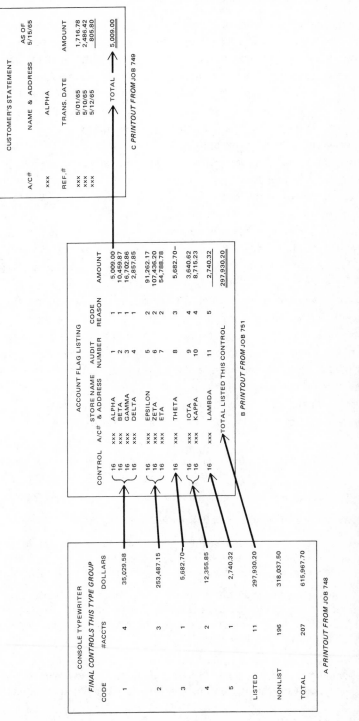

CUSTOMER'S STATEMENT

A/C#	NAME & ADDRESS	AS OF 5/15/65
xxx	ALPHA	

REF.#	TRANS. DATE	AMOUNT
xxx	5/01/65	1,716.78
xxx	5/10/65	2,486.42
xxx	5/12/65	805.80
	TOTAL	5,009.00

C PRINTOUT FROM JOB 749

ACCOUNT FLAG LISTING

CONTROL	A/C#	STORE NAME & ADDRESS	AUDIT NUMBER	CODE REASON	AMOUNT
16	xxx	ALPHA	1	1	5,009.00
16	xxx	BETA	2	1	10,459.87
16	xxx	GAMMA	3	1	16,702.86
16	xxx	DELTA	4	1	2,857.85
16	xxx	EPSILON	5	2	91,262.17
16	xxx	ZETA	6	2	107,436.20
16	xxx	ETA	7	2	54,788.78
16	xxx	THETA	8	3	5,682.70–
16	xxx	IOTA	9	4	3,640.62
16	xxx	KAPPA	10	4	8,715.23
16	xxx	LAMBDA	11	5	2,740.32
		TOTAL LISTED THIS CONTROL			297,930.20

B PRINTOUT FROM JOB 751

CONSOLE TYPEWRITER

FINAL CONTROLS THIS TYPE GROUP

CODE	#ACCTS	DOLLARS
1	4	35,029.58
2	3	253,487.15
3	1	5,682.70–
4	2	12,355.85
5	1	2,740.32
LISTED	11	297,930.20
NONLIST	196	318,037.50
TOTAL	207	615,967.70

A PRINTOUT FROM JOB 748

EXHIBIT III   EXAMPLES OF COMPUTER PRINTOUTS SHOWING INTERRELATIONSHIPS

ACTUAL RUN OF OUR PROGRAM

A month after we made the test run, our copy of the programs was run on a surprise basis with the actual live data and was a complete success. The planning and efforts of the prior months, together with the co-operation of the client's internal auditors and data processing and systems personnel, insured a successful conversion to a computer audit program. The following procedures were designed to review the accounts with unusual balances (Codes 2, 3, 4 and 5) which were printed out for further review.

Program to follow up exceptions printed out as a result of our EDP accounts receivable audit program. Through the accounts receivable EDP program we used the computer to review all of the accounts for certain conditions which, if encountered during our previous visual examinations, would have been followed up by us until we were satisfied that the accounts were correct. Because of the large number of accounts, in excess of 35,000, it had not been practical to review all of them visually; however, now that we were using the computer and reviewing them all we could have been faced with a large number of accounts printed out under one or more of the exception conditions as defined. If we did encounter such a large number of exceptions, it could have meant that we had not set our exception level correctly; therefore, it would have been necessary to again make a judgment of what the exception level should be and then complete the following audit procedures for those items printed out that still fell outside of our prescribed limits. The audit procedures listed below are only an indication of the type of audit work which was performed on exceptions and should not be considered complete or all-inclusive. The audit procedures did not apply to all types of exceptions:

1 On a limited random test basis we traced names and addresses of the accounts to a recognized credit service such as Dun and Bradstreet.

2 We ascertained that the customer's credit limit had not been exceeded.

3 We confirmed these accounts as considered desirable.

4 We noted any significant past-due items and followed them up in customer service department files and examined correspondence. Any large disputed items noted were investigated and discussed with credit department personnel.

5 Large credits in the accounts were traced to properly authorized credit memorandums filed in the customer service department, and selected large credits represented by returned goods were traced to the original receiving records in the returned goods section.

6 We discussed these accounts with customer service representatives and presented a copy of the listing to the customer service department manager with the request that he indicate thereon what was being done to effect collection.

7 We discussed any exceptions not adequately explained with appropriate company officials.

Controls over the computer audit program. The audit programs were operated by the client's personnel; consequently, the following controls over the equipment, data and print-outs were used to satisfy ourselves that the data were processed as we requested.

1 The actual program cards were controlled by the audit staff and remained in their possession when not in use.

2 The computer audit program was run under the observation of the audit staff at which time console switch settings were agreed to our copy of the "run book." The run book is a complete file of all program documentation which was reviewed in depth by the audit staff and a computer specialist of our MAS staff.

3 The console print-outs were controlled and examined by us.

4 Control totals were accumulated and printed out during all phases of the programs to insure that all of the records were processed. The total receivable balance for all control accounts was, of course, traced to the general ledger.

5 We supplied the selection card at the time of our processing, thereby keeping confidential the scope and limits of our tests.

6 We arranged to have our MAS computer specialist present during the processing of our test data and also had him review the documentation in depth. We did not feel that it was necessary for him to be present at the time of our actual run as we were satisfied that the other controls over the program and operation were adequate. Our knowledge of the EDP system had progressed to the point where auditing with the computer could be undertaken with complete confidence.

COMPUTER AUDIT PROGRAM SUPPLEMENTS NORMAL AUDIT PROCEDURES—IT DOES NOT REPLACE THEM!

In addition to the computer audit program, we completed the following audit procedures normally performed in the audit of accounts receivable:

1 Evaluated the reasonableness of the total accounts receivable balances by control in light of general industry and business conditions and the relationship of manufacturing activity to inventory levels and shipping activity.

2 Reviewed the system of internal control in the accounts receivable area including sales, shipping, billing, cash receipts and sales returns.

3 Tested sales invoices for proper pricing, terms and recording.

4 Tested credits issued, accounts written off, collectibility and the adequacy of the reserve for bad debts.

BENEFITS OF USING THE COMPUTER AUDIT PROGRAM

Expanded coverage and confidence. In addition to assisting us in selecting confirmation requests and proving the mathematical accuracy of the accounts receivable, the use of the computer enabled us to expand our coverage and confidence in the receivable balance by highlighting unusual balances.

The use of EAM equipment on simple footing applications enabled us to progress in one year to a fairly complex accounts receivable computer audit program. This demonstrates that once a start is made in the use of the EAM/-EDP equipment to assist in the audit other audit applications follow quickly.

Improved staff morale. Just as business uses computers to perform repetitive and routine clerical tasks, we found that the use of computers to perform certain of the necessary routine and tedious tasks of auditing increased staff morale considerably. The audit staff found the assignments where we used EDP equipment more challenging and rewarding.

Savings in audit time. In this first year, which included our start-up time, we reduced our audit time in this significant area by one-third and we expect even greater savings in the future. It should be emphasized that we did not develop the program solely for audit savings but also because we were at the crossroads; either audit around the computer or develop our own EDP program. In addition, and most important, are the increased efficiency and breadth of coverage now possible both to us and the internal auditors with the use of EDP.

What do the future advances in computer technology hold for the auditor? On-line, real-time computer systems are developing rapidly and will certainly be more numerous in the future. To date, except for isolated instances, auditors have not had to deal with them.

The following early encounter with an on-line, real-time system by an auditor suggests new audit methods that will be required as these "complete" business systems are introduced in companies.

AUDITING AUTOMATIC SOURCE RECORDING

Robert M. Benjamin*

Electronic data processing concepts have advanced so much that, if put into practice, they might make conventional auditing of automatic source recording physically impossible. Several writers on the subject have predicted that the conventional auditing techniques can be adapted to the EDP systems in current use as well as those of the future. These adaptations lean heavily on maintaining audit trails and getting readable input and output data.

But a recent case study of an automatic time clock system in a large industrial plant shows the need for a use of a fresh auditing approach. It solves the problem by emphasizing testing of procedures and controls rather than transactions. It appears to be a valid method for application to the "complete" business systems expected to be common in the future.

Before highlighting the case study, we will define the "complete" business systems as being on-the-line-real-time, translating business transactions when they physically take place. They have no audit trails. Input documents are unconventional, almost eliminated. Output information emerges in summary, not detail.

Steps toward the on-the-line-real-time systems taken now by many businesses involve use of either computer systems or semi-mechanized systems such as automatic source recording devices. Examples of such devices are time clocks, the subject of our study, point-of-sale recorders for retailers, the airlines' automatic reservations and ticketing networks.

In our case, the situation confronting the auditors was an automatic time clock system which records labor transactions in a major plant of a large manufacturer. Automatic time recording devices (IBM 357 "Transactors") are located throughout the shop areas. For the 11,600 employees covered by this system, these devices have completely replaced the human timekeepers and manually-prepared time cards.

Data from the system flows through to the company's payroll and job order cost accounting and control records. Basic timekeeping tools are: (1) the plastic employee badge, prepunched with identifying information, and (2) the job card, prepunched with the charge number and other information about a particular job.

The badges are permanently assigned to each employee. The job cards

---

*From *The Quarterly*, September 1963, pp. 8–11. Reproduced by permission of Touche, Ross and Company.

follow the parts or assemblies to be worked on. Exceptions are indirect labor and other special cards, which are located in racks adjacent to the Transactors. Clock-in on reporting for work requires only insertion of the badge into the Transactor, and depression of certain keys. Check-in on a job requires insertion of the badge and one or more job cards, and depression of other keys.

All Transactors are linked electronically to a central control box (IBM 358), a master clock, and an in-line key punch which creates a punched card for each entry. The cards are converted to magnetic tape for passing through computer processes on IBM 1400 Series equipment. The first of these, a match against an employee identification master tape, begins one-half hour after the beginning of each shift.

Within an hour after shift start, an exception report has been prepared for distribution to shop foremen. This report indicates absences, tardy clock-in, preshift overtime, and failure to check in on a job. Each exception must be approved by the shop foreman. Transactions accepted in this first processing routine plus transactions accepted for the remainder of the shift are "posted" to a 1410 random access file arranged by employee. Transactions rejected must be analyzed and corrected for re-entry into the processing cycle.

All labor transactions for the day are read out onto another magnetic tape which goes through a series of further computer processes:

1 Preparation of final daily report to shop foremen. Again prepared for exceptions only, this shows overtime, early clock-out, and other items for approval by foremen.

2 Daily report which balances job time by employee with time between clock-in and clock-out.

3 Daily labor tape prepared after (2).

4 Matching of job transactions against a random access file of job numbers. This processing involves application of labor standards on certain jobs, accumulation of time by classification, and preparation of output tapes for numerous reports. These include daily reports of actual and budgeted time to certain shops, summary management reports by type of labor, and job status reports.

5 Entry of the daily labor tape from (3) above into another computer (IBM 7080) for the payroll process. At this point the labor hour transactions are "priced" by application of pay rates. The labor is accumulated by employee for bi-weekly payroll processing and by job for weekly accounting distribution reports.

In pre-EDP days, an auditor was able to begin with either a payroll report or a labor distribution report and to trace individual time charges back through the system to underlying time cards or other source documents. This is obviously impossible when the labor transaction is initiated mechanically.

The auditors decided that their review of labor charges would consist of two phases:

1 Observance of actual labor charges being initiated, with subsequent tracing of these transactions through to final reports.

2 Test of the system itself in normal operations, by use of dummy but realistic transactions designed to test not only the routine processing but also the various exception editing and rejection procedures.

It was also decided that the second of these phases should receive greater emphasis because it enables many facets of the operation to be tested with only a small number of transactions. An alternate approach would be for the auditor to make a detailed examination of the computer program instructions. However, this would involve a massive translation and interpretation of many thousands of coded individual program instructions.

Consequently, the auditors decided upon the dummy transaction method as equally acceptable but easier than the alternate approach. Steps they followed in using the dummy transaction method included:

1 A thorough review of system and computer program flow charts was made.

2 Inquiry was made of responsible persons as to the various control points designed into the system.

3 Based on the system review, a set of situations was prearranged. These situations were designed to test many of the control points said to exist in the system. Several examples of these situations were:
   a Employee clocks in on time, works normally for full shift.
   b Employee checks in on job without clocking in.
   c Employee clocks in but fails to record a job transaction.
   d Employee is absent.
   e Employee is tardy.
   f Employee is tardy but within three-minute "grace period" allowed.
   g Employee leaves before shift ends.
   h Employee leaves early but returns.
   i Night shift employee clocks in on day shift.
   j Employee works overtime into next shift.
   k Employee is loaned to a different shop.
   l Employee charges jobs improperly (e.g. direct as indirect time).
   m Employee uses transactor keys improperly when checking in on job.

4 The necessary timekeeping documents were then arranged for and pre-set into the system. Since the auditors desired to perform the test under normal operating conditions, using actual shop locations and job cards, the only dummy items necessary were a group of employee badges. With one exception used for test purposes, the employee information was entered into the master records to agree with the badges. (Similar entry was not made into the payroll mas-

ter records in order that no paychecks would result. However, it would be possible to carry such a test through the payroll portion of the system.)

5 Using the situations outlined above, and a prearranged time schedule, the test was carried out in two shops during normal working hours. Both day and night shifts were used.

6 Data processing supervisors were made aware of the general nature of the test but not of the specific types of transactions being tested. Shop foremen were not informed until after they had questioned the dummy transactions which appeared as exceptions on attendance reports.

7 All transactions (42 in number) were traced through to reports which emerged from the data processing system on the same and following day. These included preliminary and final attendance exception reports, exception reports of erroneous job transactions, and the daily balance report of proper job and attendance transactions.

8 During the test, observation was made of several employees initiating job transactions. These were likewise traced to daily reports.

9 The auditors utilized the inquiry features of the data processing system to read out sections of the records and determine that the test items were being handled under normal conditions.

The results of the test proved highly satisfactory. The auditors identified, with two exceptions, every dummy transaction as being processed properly, and concluded that the system was generally functioning as it had been outlined. Two system discrepancies were noted.

Extended tests on a subsequent day were made in an effort to determine the reasons for these two discrepancies. The extended tests confirmed the errors and brought about an investigation which disclosed the reasons.

The first discrepancy resulted in the rejection of certain seemingly proper transactions as exceptions. This happened because the manufacturer had previously made a change in "leave early" cards but had failed to collect all the superseded cards from the rack placed in the shop.

The second discrepancy was rather unusual and brought to light a computer programming error. The program instructions said, in effect, "If the next to last employee in the processing cycle is an exception, do not process the last employee." Since the dummy employee numbers used by the auditors were the last on the employee list, this program instruction went into effect and the last item failed to process.

Although the procedures were not designed to test the payroll portion of the system, the auditors did note that all time accumulated for the dummy employees was rejected when the data reached the payroll cycle. This provided assurance that paychecks could be processed only for employees having payroll master records as well as master records in the timekeeping system.

PROGRAM 03621   MACCS LABOR BALANCE REGISTER   DATE 702-070

BUDGET LOAN	SHIFT	EIN PROCESS	S.S.N. STAT FWC	EMPLOYEE NAME / CC W.O. SUB SERIAL	OPN RES	CT CO	TIME	HOURS REG BON	DATE MO-DY-YR	L/D CARD COUNT	JOB COUNT
2-9251	1	159970	202-28-0826	MCLEAN GARY	7		09.47	7.0	10-31-62		
2-9251	1	037247Y	55 1331	16 7232-1027-237787			11.45	2.0		2	
2-1860	1	1309174	55 0000	8 25334-1860-000000	000		17.02	5.0			2
2-9251	2	159978	541-30-2792	MCLEAN GARY			17.88		10-31-62		
2-9251	2	159979	536-28-6570	MCLEAN GARY					10-31-62	ABSENT	
2-9251	1	159972	535-24-7310	MCLEAN GARY			08.5	8.0	10-31-62		
2-9251	1	1306013	55 0000	1-72823-0940-029251	000		10.93	2.4			
2-9251	1	044859W	55 1341	1-69591-1220-220050	3		13.85	.5			
2-9251	1	012614Z	55 1341	2-78800-0406-507508	675		13.85	.5			
2-9251	1	003865L	55 1341	1-72781-0322-072000	000		13.85	.2			
2-9251	1	003865L	55 1341	1-72141-0322-071000	000		13.85	.2			
2-9251	1	003865L	55 1341	1-72141-0322-072000	000		13.85	.3			
2-9251	1	003865L	55 1341	1-72141-0322-071000	000		13.85	.3			
2-9251	1	100436W	55 1341	1-78900-020-379106	000		13.85	.3			
2-9251	1	1369233U	55 4652	1-78103-0580-064007	152		13.85	.3			
2-9251	1	1369233U	55 4652		014		17.02	2.9			
2-9251	1	159971	518-30-7674								
2-9251	1	092586X	55 1323								
2-9251	1	092586X	55 1223								
2-9251	1	1309013	55 0000								
2-9251	1	1309013	55 0000								
2-9251	2	159977	513-20-9504								
2-9251	2	0999966									

GATE REPORT

FIRST SHIFT

SHIFT	BUDGET ORG'N	STA	SOCIAL SECURITY NO		CLOCK	NORMAL SHIFT START	ACTUAL TIME START	ACTUAL TIME STOP	HOURS PAID REG	HOURS PAID O.T.	EMPLOYEE NAME	EIN
1	2-9251	55	202	28	0826	085	0947	1702	7.0	00.8	MCLEAN GARY	599708
1	2-9251	55	518	30	7674	085	0827	178	8.0		MCLEAN GARY	599714
1	2-9251	55	535	24	7310	085	085	1702	8.0		MCLEAN GARY	559720

CLOCK IN · JOB CHECK IN · PRESHIFT O.T. · O.T. HOURS AUTHORIZED BY KEYBOARD · POST SHIFT O.T. · O.T. LUNCH S·NO O·YES · CLOCK OUT

SUMMARY

REMARKS:
LOAN TO 2-9251
LOAN TO 2-9251

A   - Absent
AP - Away but Paid
E   - Early Leave
F   - Failure to Punch
H   - Hospital Industrial Accident
JD - Jury Duty
LOA - Leave of Absence
NH - New Hire
SC - Shift Change
T   - Tardy
TB - Temporary Badge Used
TI - Transferred In
TO - Transferred Out
V   - Vacation

GRACE PERIOD G · TARDY T · RETURN R · EARLY LEAVE E · YES Y · NO N

DATE OCT 31, 1962

AUTHORIZED SIGNATURE

The auditor's name and dummy number appeared on reports produced by the daily data processing cycle. Above is segment of daily labor balance report. Below is final daily gate report indicating exception transactions to shop foremen.

Because the files and EDP equipment are physically and organizationally separated, payroll padding would require a considerable amount of collusion.

It should be mentioned here that the audit program for this manufacturer also includes tests which begin at the other end of the payroll cycle—the accounting records. The procedures include reconciling payrolls paid with distributed labor, tracing labor distribution from accounting entries to weekly and daily reports, and the normal testing of employees' payroll records and paychecks. It is felt that the system test of labor collection outlined above provides the auditors with a complete check on the labor system from the point of origin through to the general ledger.

Members of the manufacturer's management responsible for this phase of operations were extremely cooperative in assisting the auditors, and, in fact, welcomed the independent test of computer programs. While the programs were tested thoroughly during their design and implementation phases, this was the first test of the system in actual operation. The responsible persons were particularly interested in the system discrepancies disclosed, and took immediate corrective action.

This auditing project was in many ways experimental. Its success and in particular its comparative ease of performance were gratifying indeed. The number of unusual conditions which were tested with a few simple prearranged plans would have required thousands upon thousands of transaction selections had random sampling or any other conventional testing process been used.

The power of a fresh approach to the problem combined with the effective use of the computer in focusing on controls and exceptions is tremendous. By using his ingenuity and making the computer his tool, the auditor can meet the challenge of the future: maintaining his historically high standard of professional competence.

PART THREE

AUDIT REPORTS

CHAPTER 11

AUDIT REPORTING PROBLEMS

The format and wording of audit reports are based on a standard opinion that is widely accepted. Applications of the standard report, however, exhibit almost endless variety. We pursue this report variety in analysis form in this chapter.

GENERAL CONSIDERATIONS

REPORT FORMAT

The standard short-form report normally contains two paragraphs. In contrast, the report presented as Figure 11–1 contains only one paragraph.

Questions

1 What is the essence of the division of the short-form report into *two* paragraphs?

2 Is this report acceptable? Why?

FIGURE 11-1

OPINION OF INDEPENDENT ACCOUNTANTS

To the Board of Directors and Stockholders
of Bethlehem Steel Corporation:

In our opinion, the accompanying consolidated balance sheet and the related consolidated statement of income and income invested in the business and the consolidated statement of source and application of funds present fairly the financial position of Bethlehem Steel Corporation and its subsidiaries consolidated at December 31, 1969, the results of their operations for the year and the supplementary information on funds for the year, in conformity with generally accepted accounting principles applied on a basis consistent with that of the preceding year. Our examination of these statements was made in accordance with generally accepted auditing standards and accordingly included such tests of the accounting records and such other auditing procedures as we considered necessary in the circumstances.

New York, N.Y.
February 11, 1970   *Price Waterhouse & Co.*

ASSOCIATION WITH FINANCIAL STATEMENTS

The reports presented as Figures 11-3 and 11-4 identify financial statements by number and page number in the annual report. Figure 11-2, from *Accounting Trends and Techniques* (1969 edition), tabulates the location of auditors' reports in relation to financial statements.

FIGURE 11-2

Table 6-1: Location of Auditors' Report in Relation to Financial Statements

Location*	Number of Companies 1968	1969
Follows all statements covered by opinion:		
A: Follows notes to financial statements	451	450
B: Precedes notes to financial statements	54	47
C: Precedes all statements covered by opinion	48	46
D: Intermediate position	47	57
Total	600	600

* Refer to Company Appendix Section — A: 106, 284, 361, 481, 597, 686; B: 22, 157, 297, 321, 437; C: 29, 197, 259, 312; D: 126, 206, 408, 526.

Questions

1 What significance does the location of the auditor's report have?

2 Why would an auditor consider it important to identify statements by number?

3 When is an auditor "associated" with financial statements?

FIGURE 11-3

OPINION OF INDEPENDENT ACCOUNTANTS

To the Shareholders:

In our opinion, the accompanying statements 1, 2 and 5, and the statement appearing on page 10 present fairly (a) the financial position of Caterpillar Tractor Co. and consolidated subsidiaries at December 31, 1967, the results of their operations and the changes in their net current assets for the year, and (b) the financial position of Caterpillar Corporation at December 31, 1967 and the results of its operations for the year, in conformity with generally accepted accounting principles applied on a basis consistent with that of the preceding year. This opinion is based on an examination of the statements which was made in accordance with generally accepted auditing standards and accordingly included such tests of the accounting records and such other auditing procedures as we considered necessary in the circumstances.

(We have made similar annual examinations since incorporation of Caterpillar Tractor Co. and Caterpillar Credit Corporation and, in our opinion, statements 3 and 4 present fairly the historical financial data included therein.)

                                        Price Waterhouse & Co.

Chicago, January 17, 1968

FIGURE 11-4

Accountants' Report

Price Waterhouse & Co.   **60 Broad Street**

New York

To the Stockholders of   February 13, 1970

The National Cash Register Company:

We have examined the accompanying consolidated financial statements (pages 25 to 29) of The National Cash Register Company as of December 31, 1969. Our examination was made in accordance with generally accepted auditing standards and accordingly included such tests of the accounting records and such other auditing procedures as we considered necessary in the circumstances. We did not examine the financial statements of The National Cash Register Company (Japan) Ltd., a consolidated subsidiary, which statements were examined by other independent accountants whose report thereon has been furnished to us.

In our opinion, based on our examination and the report mentioned above of other independent accountants, the accompanying consolidated financial statements present fairly the financial position of The National Cash Register Company and its subsidiaries at December 31, 1969, the results of their operations and the supplementary information on changes in working capital for the year in conformity with generally accepted accounting principles applied on a basis consistent with that of the preceding year.

Price Waterhouse & Co.

REPORT EXPLANATIONS

▷ EXCEPTIONS TO SCOPE

Figures 11-6 and 11-7 both contain "exceptions to scope." However, Figure 11-6 is qualified, whereas Figure 11-7 contains an unqualified opinion. Figure 11-5 from *Accounting Trends and Techniques* (1969 edition) tabulates exceptions to scope in auditor's opinions.

FIGURE 11-5

Table 6-6: Exceptions to Scope

Auditing Procedure Omitted for*	1968	1967	1965	1960
Receivables not confirmed				
Due from U.S. Government	39	38	38	43
Due from others	7	8	9	6
Other procedures omitted	1	0	0	4
Total ommisions	47	46	47	53

Number of Companies				
Referring to omission of procedures	46	43	41	49
Not referring to omission	554	557	559	551
	600	600	600	600

Reference to Omission	1968
First part of sentence:	
A: "It was *not practicable (impracticable)* to . . ."	32
B: "We were *unable* to . . ."	7
C: Other explanations	7
Total	46

Second part of sentence:	
D: "We *satisfied* ourselves . . . other auditing procedures"	37
E: "We *carried* out . . . other auditing procedures"	8
Other descriptions	1
	46

* See Company Appendix Section — A: 71, 231, 345, 665; B: 222, 526; C: 276, 510; D: 131, 272, 360, 572; E: 293, 413.

Questions

1 Why is one opinion qualified whereas the other is unqualified?

2 What was the predominant reason for exceptions to scope in 1968 annual reports?

3 How many exceptions to scope resulted in qualification? Why did so few exceptions result in qualifications?

FIGURE 11-6

Accountants' Opinion

ALPHA PORTLAND CEMENT COMPANY:

We have examined the consolidated financial statements of Alpha Portland Cement Company and its subsidiary for the year ended December 31, 1968. Our examination was made in accordance with generally accepted auditing standards, and accordingly included such tests of the accounting records and such other auditing procedures as we considered necessary in the circumstances, except as stated in the next paragraph.

As explained in Note B, the Company's subsidiary is a participant with other contractors in long-term construction contracts undertaken as joint ventures. We have been informed that the financial statements of the joint ventures for the year ended December 31, 1968 have not been audited. Accordingly, we do not express an opinion concerning the equity in joint ventures, stated at $1,128,651 in the accompanying balance sheet, or in the income from joint ventures, stated at $158,459 (before income taxes) in the accompanying statement of consolidated income.

In our opinion, with the exception stated in the preceding paragraph, the accompanying consolidated balance sheet and statements of consolidated income and consolidated stockholders' equity present fairly the financial position of the companies at December 31, 1968 and the results of their operations for the year then ended, in conformity with generally accepted accounting principles applied on a basis consistent with that of the preceding year; and the accompanying statement of consolidated source and application of funds presents fairly the information shown therein.

Haskins + Sells

HASKINS & SELLS
Certified Public Accountants
Two Broadway, New York 10004
February 6, 1969

Note: Audits of the accounts of the joint ventures are now in process in order to permit Haskins & Sells to remove their exception, stated above, as to the scope of their examination. The Company will advise its stockholders upon receipt of the revised Accountants' Opinion.

B. Equity in Joint Ventures

The Company's subsidiary is a participant with other contractors in long-term contracts undertaken as joint ventures. The investment in joint ventures is stated at cost plus the equity in unremitted earnings of the various ventures. Summary information, based on unaudited balance sheets as of December 31, 1968, with respect to the joint ventures follows:

Assets	$8,835,983
Liabilities	5,524,605
Net assets	$3,311,378
Equity in net assets	$1,128,651

FIGURE 11-7

Accountants' Opinion

To the Shareholders and Board of Directors
Northrop Corporation
Beverly Hills, California

We have examined the statement of consolidated financial position of Northrop Corporation and subsidiaries as of July 31, 1969, and the related statements of consolidated income, shareholders' equity, and source and use of cash for the year then ended. Our examination was made in accordance with generally accepted auditing standards, and accordingly included such tests of the accounting records and such other auditing procedures as we considered necessary in the circumstances. We were unable to confirm by direct correspondence amounts receivable from the U.S. Government and certain other major customers, but we satisfied ourselves as to such amounts by means of other auditing procedures. We previously made a similar examination for the preceding year.

In our opinion, the accompanying statements of financial position, income, shareholders' equity, and source and use of cash, present fairly the consolidated financial position of Northrop Corporation and subsidiaries at July 31, 1969, and the consolidated results of their operations, changes in shareholders' equity, and source and use of cash for the year then ended, in conformity with generally accepted accounting principles applied on a basis consistent with that of the preceding year.

Ernst + Ernst

Los Angeles, California
September 15, 1969

EXPLANATORY MIDDLE PARAGRAPH

The explanatory middle paragraph in Figure 11-8 is not referred to in the opinion paragraph of the auditor's report.

FIGURE 11-8

Accountants' Report

THE BOARD OF DIRECTORS
DETECTO SCALES, INC.

We have examined the consolidated balance sheet of Detecto Scales, Inc. and Subsidiaries as at December 31, 1968 and the related consolidated statements of income and shareholders' equity for the year then ended. Our examination was made in accordance with generally accepted auditing standards, and accordingly included such tests of the accounting records and such other auditing procedures as we considered necessary in the circumstances.

Detecto Scales, Inc. has consistently followed the practice
of not including all labor and overhead in inventories.
However, the accompanying financial statements have been
prepared on the basis of including these elements and providing for taxes on income applicable to such adjustments.
The adjustment of inventories and the related taxes have not
been recorded on the books of the Company.

In our opinion, the accompanying financial statements present fairly the consolidated financial position of Detecto
Scales, Inc. and Subsidiaries at December 31, 1968 and the
consolidated results of their operations for the year then
ended, in conformity with generally accepted accounting
principles applied on a basis consistent with that of the
preceding year, except for the change in the classification
of deferred charges as described in Note 4 and the restatement of the consolidated financial statements for 1967 as
described in Note 6, both of which we approve.

The financial statements for the year ended December 31, 1967
were examined by other independent accountants.

LAVENTHOL KREKSTEIN HORWATH & HORWATH
Certified Public Accountants

April 2, 1969
New York, N.Y.

4. Deferred Charge:
   The balance of costs totalling $188,000 incurred in in-
stalling new operational and production control systems
which, in the opinion of management, will produce substantial cost savings, is being amortized over a sixty month
period effective January 1, 1968. During 1968, $37,600 was
charged to expense. The balance sheet for December 31, 1967
has been restated to reflect such costs as a deferred charge.

6. Taxes on Income:
   In 1967 the Company wrote off $414,623 representing the

cost of acquisitions in excess of the underlying net assets of the acquired companies. This was reflected in the consolidated statement of income as an extraordinary charge in the amount of $239,020, after provision of $175,603 for the related income tax benefit.

Federal income tax returns for 1965, 1966 and 1967 are presently being examined. The Internal Revenue Service has proposed to disallow the deduction of the item described in the preceding paragraph. While the Company intends to contest this proposed disallowance, provision has been made for the potential income tax liability in the amount of $175,603. The financial statements for 1967 have been restated to give effect to this provision.

Additional taxes on income in the amount of $990,904 have been provided for in connection with the adjustment of inventories described in Note 2.

Investment credits are reflected as a reduction of provision for federal taxes on income.

Questions

1 What is the general nature of the matter described in the middle paragraph?

2 Is the explanation required to conform to generally accepted auditing standards?

3 Why was the opinion not qualified with respect to this matter?

4 Why do you think the auditors disclosed this matter?

RELIANCE ON OTHER AUDITORS

The reports presented in Figures 11-10 through 11-13 all contain references to other auditors. However this reference is not uniform. The table reproduced in Figure 11-9 from *Accounting Trends and Techniques* (1969 edition) tabulates the various forms of reference to other auditors.

Questions

1 Of what significance is the statement in the scope paragraph in Figure 11-10 that the reports of other accountants have been "reviewed and accepted"?

2 Figure 11-10 makes no reference to other accountants in the opinion paragraph, although the other three reports do contain a reference. Why does this difference exist? Are the other reports qualified?

3 Figure 11-11 contains an explanatory middle paragraph which refers to the report of other accountants. Why did the matter explained not cause a qualification of the opinion paragraph? Since there was no qualification, why was the explanation necessary?

4 Figure 11-12 refers to chartered accountants while the other reports merely refer to "other" accountants or auditors. Why did the report specifically identify the other accountants as chartered accountants?

FIGURE 11-9

Table 6-7: Reference to Other Auditors*

Manner of Reference	1968	1967	1966
A: Adopting the *opinion* paragraphs referred to in par. 34 above	64	58	49
B: Adopting the *scope* paragraph referred to in par. 34 above	25	24	24
Reference to other auditors does not include specific statement that opinion is based on their report	5	6 ⎫	
C: Reference to examination by other auditors of prior year statements	8	4 ⎭	5

Number of Companies			
Auditor's opinion refers to other auditors	102	92	78
No reference to other auditors	498	508	522
Total	600	600	600

Examination by other Auditors covers:		
Current year statements for branch or consolidated subsidiary	81	77
Current year statements for unconsolidated subsidiary or affiliate only	12	10
Prior year statements only	9	5
Total	102	92

* See Company Appendix Section—A: 70, 186, 329, 497, 694, B: 177, 399, 582; C: 375, 606.

FIGURE 11-10

ACCOUNTANTS'
REPORT

Board of Directors
The Black and Decker Manufacturing Company
Towson, Maryland

We have examined the statement of consolidated financial
condition of The Black and Decker Manufacturing Company and
subsidiaries as of September 28, 1969, and the related
consolidated statements of earnings, capital in excess of
par value of Common Stock, earnings retained and used in the
business, and source and application of funds for the year
then ended. Our examination was made in accordance with
generally accepted auditing standards, and accordingly included such tests of the accounting records and such other
auditing procedures as we considered necessary in the circumstances. The financial statements of certain of the
foreign subsidiaries were examined by other independent
accountants resident in the foreign countries and copies of
their reports have been submitted directly to us. We have
reviewed and accepted the reports of these accountants. We
previously made a similar examination of the financial
statements for the preceding year.

In our opinion, the accompanying statements of financial
condition, earnings, capital in excess of par value of
Common Stock, earnings retained and used in the business,
and source and application of funds present fairly the consolidated financial position of The Black and Decker Manufacturing Company and subsidiaries at September 28, 1969,
and the consolidated results of their operations, the
changes in stockholders' equity, and source and application
of funds for the year then ended, in conformity with generally accepted accounting principles applied on a basis consistent with that of the preceding year.

Baltimore, Maryland
October 31, 1969   *Ernst + Ernst*

FIGURE 11-11

AUDITORS' REPORT

To the Shareholders and the Board of Directors of Stewart-Warner Corporation:

We have examined the consolidated statement of financial position of STEWART-WARNER CORPORATION (a Virginia corporation) AND SUBSIDIARY COMPANIES as of December 31, 1969, and the related consolidated statements of income, retained earnings, and funds for the year then ended. Our examination was made in accordance with generally accepted auditing standards, and accordingly included such tests of the accounting records and such other auditing procedures as we considered necessary in the circumstances. We were unable to obtain confirmation of receivables from government agencies; however, we have applied other auditing procedures with respect to such receivables. We have previously examined and reported on the consolidated financial statements for the preceding year.

We did not examine the consolidated financial statements of Thor Power Tool Company (summarized in Note 5), the investment in which represents approximately 10% of the assets of Stewart-Warner, but we were furnished with the report of other auditors thereon. The opinion of the other auditors, discussed in Note 5, was qualified as being subject to the ultimate adjustments arising from the disposition of Thor's inventories, and subject to the final outcome of the pending litigation and the assessment of additional Federal income taxes. However, in our opinion, the effect of these matters is not material in relation to Stewart-Warner's consolidated financial statements.

In our opinion, based upon our examination and the report of other auditors, the accompanying consolidated financial statements present fairly the financial position of Stewart-Warner Corporation and Subsidiary Companies as of December 31, 1969, and the results of their operations and the source and disposition of funds for the year then ended, in conformity with generally accepted accounting principles applied on a basis consistent with that of the preceding year.

Chicago, Illinois,   ARTHUR ANDERSEN & CO.
February 27, 1970.

(5) Throughout 1969 Stewart-Warner owned 81% of the outstanding shares of Thor Power Tool Company, compared to an average of approximately 69% for 1968. The only additional investment by Stewart-Warner in 1969 was the purchase of $125,000 principal amount of Thor Power Tool Company's 4⅞% convertible subordinated debentures at discounts from face value. At the year-end, the total investment, consisting of 589,532 shares of Thor's capital stock and $1,387,000 principal amount of Thor's 4⅞% convertible subordinated debentures, net of Stewart-Warner's share in Thor's earnings since December 31, 1965, aggregated $11,-855,185.

FIGURE 11-12

Accountants' Report

To the Board of Directors of
Granger Associates

We have examined the consolidated balance sheet of Granger Associates and Subsidiaries at August 31, 1969, and the consolidated statements of income and retained earnings, additional paid-in capital, and source and application of funds for the year then ended. Our examination was made in accordance with generally accepted auditing standards, and accordingly included such tests of the accounting records and such other auditing procedures as we considered necessary in the circumstances. It was not practicable in all cases to confirm by direct communication amounts due from the U.S. Government, as to which we satisfied ourselves by other auditing procedures.

We did not examine the financial statements of the consolidated foreign subsidiaries, Granger Associates, Limited, and Granger Associates Pty., Limited, which statements were examined by chartered accountants whose reports thereon have been furnished to us.

In our opinion, based upon our examination and the aforementioned reports of chartered accountants, the aforementioned financial statements present fairly the consolidated financial position of Granger Associates and Subsidiaries at August 31, 1969, and the consolidated results of their operations and the source and application of funds for the year then ended, in conformity with generally accepted accounting principles applied on a basis consistent with that of the preceding year.

San Francisco, California
October 15, 1969

FARQUHAR & HEIMBUCHER
Certified Public Accountants

FIGURE 11-13

Accountants' Report

Board of Directors
The Hoover Company
North Canton, Ohio

We have examined the consolidated balance sheet of The Hoover Company and subsidiaries as of December 31, 1969, and the related statements of consolidated income, stockholders' equity, and source and application of funds for the year then ended. Our examination was made in accordance with generally accepted auditing standards, and accordingly included such tests of the accounting records and such other auditing procedures as we considered necessary in the circumstances. The financial statements of certain subsidiaries were examined by other independent accountants whose reports thereon have been furnished to us.

In our opinion, based upon our examination and upon the aforementioned reports of other independent accountants, and subject to the ultimate effect of the tax examinations

referred to in Note C, the accompanying balance sheet and
statements of income, stockholders' equity, and source and
application of funds present fairly the consolidated financial position of The Hoover Company and subsidiaries at
December 31, 1969, and the consolidated results of their
operations, changes in stockholders' equity, and source and
application of funds for the year then ended, in conformity
with generally accepted accounting principles applied on a
basis consistent with that of the preceding year.

                                           ERNST & ERNST
Canton, Ohio
March 2, 1970

Note C—Income Taxes

Federal income tax returns filed by the Company for the years
1961 to 1966, inclusive, and returns filed by a domestic
subsidiary for the years 1963 to 1966, inclusive, were under
examination by representatives of the Internal Revenue
Service as of December 31, 1969. During 1968, the Company
and its subsidiary made partial payments, plus interest, in
advance of final settlement of their tax liabilities for such
years. The aggregate amount of such payments (less tax
benefits with respect to the interest paid), plus or minus
other amounts relating to subsequent adjustments arising
from such examinations, are included in deferred charges.
Subsequent to December 31, 1969, the aforementioned examinations were completed, subject to Internal Revenue Service
regional review procedures, and the companies have agreed
to certain additional adjustments and deficiencies which
have been proposed. With respect to a substantial portion of
amounts paid or payable, reserves previously have been
provided.

In addition, subsequent to December 31, 1969, the Company
and a director and former officer of the Company reached an
agreement, approved in principle by the Board of Directors,
relative to indebtedness arising out of facts and circum-

stances relating to a part of the aforementioned tax deficiencies. Final determination as to the amount of such
indebtedness, the items of expense to which it relates, and
the terms of payment have not yet been reached.

It is the present intention of Management to defer all
charges and credits in connection with the aforementioned
matters until final determination. At that time the earnings
of the years to which the net amounts are applicable will be
adjusted, unless such adjustments, if reflected in earnings
of the year in which all matters are finally settled, are not
deemed to have a significant effect on the consolidated results of operations for such year. In the opinion of Management, based upon the advice of counsel, the resolution of
these matters, however, will not have a material effect upon
the consolidated financial statements.

During the year, the tax liabilities of certain foreign subsidiaries were adjusted by local tax authorities and the
additional amounts resulting from such adjustments have been
charged to the current provision for foreign income taxes
in the accompanying statement of consolidated income.

The tax liabilities of certain other foreign subsidiaries
currently are being determined by local taxing authorities.
The additional amounts, if any, which ultimately may be
assessed are not determinable at this time.

At December 31, 1969, certain foreign subsidiaries had unused tax loss carry-forwards of approximately $2,400,000,
which may be used to reduce future taxable income of the
respective subsidiaries. Approximately $800,000 of the
loss carry-forwards will expire at various dates through
1974; the remainder will be available indefinitely.

The United States tax credit with respect to investment in
certain depreciable property amounted to $213,284 in 1969
and $132,129 in 1968, and has been reflected as a reduction
of federal income taxes currently payable in the respective
years.

OPINION MODIFICATION

"SUBJECT TO" MAJOR LOSSES

Figures 11-14 and 11-15 are both qualified "subject to" final determination of the loss on the sale of part of the business. In only one case is a dollar amount given for the estimated loss.

Questions

1 Why do you think the two reports differ in this respect?

2 Discuss the pro and con arguments for disclosure of a dollar amount for a loss which is the basis of a "subject to" opinion.

FIGURE 11-14

Accountants' Report

TOUCHE, ROSS, BAILEY & SMART

1380 First National Building
Detroit, Michigan 48226

November 18, 1968

To the Board of Directors and Stockholders,
American Motors Corporation,
Detroit, Michigan.

We have examined the accompanying consolidated balance sheet of American Motors Corporation and consolidated subsidiaries as of September 30, 1968, the related statement of net earnings, and the statement of sources and applications of working capital for the year then ended. Our examination was made in accordance with generally accepted auditing standards, and accordingly included such tests of the accounting records and such other auditing procedures as we considered necessary in the circumstances.

In our opinion, subject to the final determination of the loss on sale of the Appliance Division referred to in Note C, the financial statements referred to above present fairly the consolidated financial position of American Motors Corporation and consolidated subsidiaries at September 30, 1968, and the consolidated results of their operations and the sources and applications of working capital for the year then ended, in conformity with generally accepted accounting principles applied on a basis consistent with that of the preceding year.

Touche, Ross, Bailey & Smart

Certified Public Accountants

Note C—Sale of Appliance Division

As of July 3, 1968, the Corporation sold certain assets of its Appliance Division, including investments in appliance subsidiaries, for a price which is subject to independent determination. As of September 30, 1968, the final sales price had not been determined but an amount has been provided for the resulting loss on sale which, in the opinion of management, is considered adequate.

In order to provide meaningful information with respect to the automotive operations, the consolidated statements of net earnings and sources and applications of working capital are presented so as to exclude detailed transactions of the Appliance Division and to report the net loss of the division and its effect on working capital as separate items.

FIGURE 11-15

Accountants' Report

The Board of Directors
Hygrade Food Products Corporation:

We have examined the consolidated balance sheet of Hygrade Food Products Corporation and subsidiary companies as of November 1, 1969, and the related statements of operations, capital surplus and retained earnings for the fifty-two weeks then ended. Our examination was made in accordance with generally accepted auditing standards, and accordingly included such tests of the accounting records and such other auditing procedures as we considered necessary in the circumstances.

In our opinion, subject to the final determination of estimated expenses and losses in connection with the disposition of closed plants as discussed in note 2, the accompanying financial statements referred to above present fairly the financial position of Hygrade Food Products Corporation and subsidiary companies at November 1, 1969, and the results of their operations for the fifty-two weeks then ended, in conformity with generally accepted accounting principles, applied on a basis consistent with that of the preceding year.

Detroit, Michigan
December 12, 1969

PEAT, MARWICK, MITCHELL & CO.

(2) Reserve for Revaluation of Closed Plants
During the year the Company closed certain plants which proved to be unprofitable. Rec-

ognition has been given to these closed plant costs, in addition to costs applicable to announced plant closings, by an extraordinary charge to the statement of operations of $8,318,-000. Details of the charge are as follows:

Separation pay	$1,500,000
Payrolls, taxes, insurance, utilities, etc. of closed plant properties and incurred losses on their disposition	1,064,584
Provision for estimated future expenses of closed plant properties and estimated losses on their disposition	5,753,416
	$8,318,000
Credited to the reserve for revaluation of closed plants	$6,163,685
Credited to liability accounts	2,154,315
	$8,318,000

The provision for estimated future expenses of closed plant properties and estimated losses on their disposition has been computed by management based on probable proceeds and time required to effect disposals.

Expenses incurred and losses on disposition of closed plant properties charged to the reserve for revaluation of closed plants during the year ended November 1, 1969 amounted to $2,-479,485.

"SUBJECT TO" TAX CARRY-FORWARD

The report in Figure 11-16 appeared in the 1968 annual report of Allis-Chalmers Manufacturing Company. The opinion is qualified "subject to" realization of a tax loss carry-forward. *Statements on Auditing Procedure No. 33* discusses "subject to" opinions based on uncertainties as follows:

Unusual Uncertainties as to the Effect of Future Developments on Certain Items

45 *The management of a company ordinarily is expected to evaluate matters affecting financial position and results of operations. In cases where the probable effects of a matter are not reasonably determinable at the time of the opinion, such as in the case of certain lawsuits, tax matters, and other contingencies which may have a material effect upon the financial statements, and the final outcome is dependent upon the decision of parties other than management, the independent auditor should appropriately qualify his opinion. In such instances use of the phrase "subject to" is appropriate.*

46 *Occasionally, uncertainties arising from questions of valuation or realizability of assets dependent upon management's judgment may require a qualification of opinion. In such cases, use of the phrase "subject to" is also considered appropriate.*

47 *In some instances where the outcome of a matter is uncertain, the amount concerned may be so material that a qualified opinion is inappropriate. An example of such a situation would be a case in which the company is a defendant in a suit claiming damages of a very large amount in relation to the company's net assets and there is considerable uncertainty as to the outcome*

*of the suit. In such cases, the facts may be disclosed in a middle paragraph
of the independent auditor's report and the disclaimer of opinion may read
as follows:*

FIGURE 11-16

REPORT OF INDEPENDENT ACCOUNTANTS

To the Board of Directors of
Allis-Chalmers Manufacturing Company

We have examined the consolidated statement of financial
condition of Allis-Chalmers Manufacturing Company as of
December 31, 1968 and the related statement of consolidated
income (loss) and earnings retained for the year. Our examination was made in accordance with generally accepted
auditing standards and accordingly included such tests of
the accounting records and such other auditing procedures
as we considered necessary in the circumstances.

As explained in Note 3 to the financial statements, in the
last quarter of 1968 the Company recorded substantial
amounts associated with (a) reserves for anticipated costs
and losses, and (b) estimated income tax benefits expected
to be realized in the future. Although these reserves and
anticipated tax benefits reflect the best current judgment
of the Company's management, we cannot determine at this time
the amounts of costs and losses which ultimately will be
charged against the reserves, and the amounts of future tax
benefits which ultimately will be realized.

In our opinion, subject to the effect of any adjustments
which may result from ultimate determination of the matters
referred to in the preceding paragraph, the accompanying
consolidated financial statements examined by us present
fairly the financial position of Allis-Chalmers Manufacturing Company and its subsidiaries at December 31, 1968 and the
results of their operations for the year, in conformity with
generally accepted accounting principles applied on a basis
consistent with that of the preceding year, except for the
changes in accounting for depreciation and income taxes as
explained in Note 6 to the financial statements.

Milwaukee, Wisconsin   PRICE WATERHOUSE & CO.
March 26, 1969

NOTE 3—SPECIAL RESERVES AND INCOME TAXES / During the last
quarter of 1968 a major change took place in the Company's
management. The new management made an extensive study of the
Company's operations, products and markets. This study resulted in changes in Company philosophy and policies relating to organization, products and production facilities,
marketing and relations with dealers and customers. The
Company has estimated that implementation of these policy
changes will result in substantial costs and losses for (a)
parts replacement, warranty costs, repossession losses and
price allowances and (b) relocation and discontinuance of
facilities and products. Provisions were recorded in the
last quarter of 1968 to establish special reserves totaling
$68,754,410 for these anticipated costs and losses. Of this
amount, $28,494,304 ($13,437,093 net of taxes), associated
with relocation and discontinuance of products and facilities, is shown as an extraordinary charge in the consolidated
statement of income (loss). The remaining provisions,
totaling $40,260,106, were charged to sales ($5,627,178),
materials, plant payroll and services ($28,190,928) and
selling, general and administrative expenses ($6,442,000).

Although the costs and losses to be charged to the special
reserves cannot be finally determined at the present time,
management believes, based on the Company's extensive
studies and evaluations which were reviewed in depth by the
independent auditors, that the provisions recorded in 1968
represent a fair and reasonable determination of the amounts
required.

The net loss for the year has been determined after giving
recognition to income taxes recoverable ($14,345,721) from
carryback to prior years of operating losses and to estimated
future tax benefits ($50,900,000) of unused losses, includ-
ing $6,836,276 relating to an accounting change described
in Note 6 to the financial statements. The amounts recoverable from carryback to prior years are included in current
assets in the consolidated balance sheet together with 1968
tax refunds receivable of $3,970,000 and estimated future
income tax benefits of $17,303,304 relating primarily to
normal book-tax timing differences applicable to amounts
included in current assets and liabilities. The realization
of estimated future income tax benefits which total

$60,275,704 is dependent upon the Company's ability to generate future taxable income. This amount is included in the financial statements because, in the opinion of management, the realization of such tax benefits is assured beyond any reasonable doubt.

The Company has unrecorded investment tax credit carry-forwards of $6,098,722, applicable to the years 1962 through 1968, which may be used to reduce income taxes payable in future years.

Accounting Principles Board Opinion No. 11 explains the criteria for realization of tax loss carryforward as follows:

45 *The tax effects of loss carryforwards also relate to the determination of net income (loss) of the loss periods. However, a significant question generally exists as to realization of the tax effects of the carryforwards, since realization is dependent upon future taxable income. Accordingly, the Board has concluded that the tax benefits of loss carryforwards should not be recognized until they are actually realized, except in unusual circumstances when realization is assured beyond any reasonable doubt at the time the loss carryforwards arise. When the tax benefits of loss carryforwards are not recognized until realized in full or in part in subsequent periods, the tax benefits should be reported in the results of operations of those periods as extraordinary items.* [11]

46 *In those rare cases in which realization of the tax benefits of loss carryforwards is assured beyond any reasonable doubt, the potential benefits should be associated with the periods of loss and should be recognized in the determination of results of operations for those periods. Realization is considered to be assured beyond any reasonable doubt when conditions such as those set forth in paragraph 47 are present. (Also see paragraph 48.) The amount of the asset (and the tax effect on results of operations) recognized in the loss period should be computed at the rates expected* [12] *to be in effect at the time of realization. If the applicable tax rates change from those used to measure the tax effect at the time of recognition, the effect of the rate change should be accounted for in the period of the change as an adjustment of the asset account and of income tax expense.*

47 *Realization of the tax benefit of a loss carryforward would appear to be assured beyond any reasonable doubt when both of the following conditions exist: (a) the loss results from an identifiable, isolated and nonrecurring cause and the company either has been continuously profitable over a long period or has suffered occasional losses which were more than offset by*

---

[11] See APB Opinion No. 9, *Reporting the Results of Operations.*
[12] The rates referred to here are those rates which, at the time the loss carry*forward* benefit is recognized for financial accounting purposes, have been enacted to apply to appropriate future periods.

taxable income in subsequent years, and (b) future taxable income is virtually certain to be large enough to offset the loss carryforward and will occur soon enough to provide realization during the carryforward period.

Questions

1 Is a "subject to" qualification appropriate in this situation?

2 What alternative type of opinion might be rendered?

3 What argument could be used to justify the opinion actually rendered?

MULTIPLE QUALIFICATION

The opinion paragraph of Figure 11-17 differs in three major respects from the usual opinion in an unqualified short-form report.

Questions

1 What are the three major differences, and how would you describe the general nature of each item?

2 Are all three items qualifications?

3 Are qualifications cumulative?

FIGURE 11-17

OPINION OF INDEPENDENT CERTIFIED PUBLIC ACCOUNTANTS
ERNST & ERNST

Board of Directors
Infotronics Corporation
Houston, Texas

We have examined the consolidated balance sheet of Infotronics Corporation and its wholly-owned subsidiaries as of March 31, 1969, and the related consolidated statements of earnings and stockholders' equity for the year then ended. Our examination was made in accordance with generally accepted auditing standards, and accordingly included such tests of the accounting records and such other auditing procedures as we considered necessary in the circumstances. The financial statements of one foreign subsidiary, Infotronics Limited (Ireland), were not examined by us, but we were

furnished with the report of other independent accountants
thereon. Net assets of Infotronics Limited included in the
consolidated financial statements at March 31, 1969,
amounted to $184,106 and the net earnings for the year then
ended amounted to $146,828.

As described in Note B to the consolidated financial statements, the Company has deferred those research and development expenses relating to new products. The recoverability
of such expenses is dependent upon the development of marketable products.

In our opinion, based upon our examination and the aforementioned report of the other independent accountants,
subject to the ultimate realization of deferred research and
development expenses as mentioned in Note B, the accompanying statements identified above present fairly the consolidated financial position of Infotronics Corporation and
wholly-owned subsidiaries at March 31, 1969, and the consolidated results of their operations and changes in
stockholders' equity for the year then ended. In conformity
with generally accepted accounting principles applied on
a basis consistent with that of the preceding year as restated (see Note A) and after giving retroactive effect to
the inclusion of the accounts of the two foreign subsidiaries
as explained in Note A.

Houston, Texas
May 29, 1969   *Ernst + Ernst*

NOTE A—PRINCIPLES OF CONSOLIDATION

The accompanying consolidated financial statements include the accounts of the Company, its domestic subsidiaries (Datronics, Inc., Dohrmann Instruments Company and Loenco,
Inc.,) and effective for the year ended March 31, 1969, its two wholly-owned foreign subsidiaries, Infotronics Limited (Ireland) and Infotronics Corporation A.G. (Switzerland).
Amounts shown for the preceding year have been restated to include the accounts of 1) the
two foreign subsidiaries, the investments in which were previously carried at cost and 2)
Loenco, Inc. which was acquired in a pooling of interest transaction in August, 1968.

The accounts of the consolidated foreign subsidiaries, translated at appropriate rates of
exchange, are summarized as follows:

	March 31	
	1969	1968
Net current assets	$333,017	$163,714
Equipment and other assets	111,350	103,257
Net earnings (loss)	145,477	(39,630)

All material intercompany transactions have been eliminated.

NOTE B—DEFERRED RESEARCH AND DEVELOPMENT EXPENSES
In the year ended March 31, 1968, the Company initiated a policy of deferring research and development expenses directly related to its entry into the small computer and medical instrument markets, the principal projects being a small general purpose digital computer and data processing systems for clinical and analytical laboratories. These deferred expenses are amortized over a two-year period which begins upon customer acceptance of the first nonprototype unit of each new product. In the event that a lack of customer interest should be indicated in any product under development, the accumulated costs will be charged to current operations. All research and development expenses relating to these new products incurred after the date amortization begins will be expensed as sustaining engineering. The changes in deferred research and development expenses during the years ended March 31, 1969 and March 31, 1968 follows:

	Year Ended March 31	
	1969	1968
Balance at beginning of year	$179,483	$ —
Research and development expenses incurred	352,396	179,483
Amortization (deduction)	(21,989)	—
Balance at end of year	$509,890	$179,483

EXCEPTION TO FAIR PRESENTATION

Figure 11-18, concerning the Pacific Asbestos Corporation, includes an explanation that the company is insolvent and refers to the use of generally accepted accounting principles applicable to a going concern.

Questions

1 What type of opinion is this?

2 Explain the application of the generally accepted auditing standards of reporting to this report.

3 Of what significance is the reference to a "going concern" assumption: in his report, does he implicitly represent that the company will have profitable operations in the future?

4 Would this report be acceptable to the SEC?

5 Could this same exception lead to a qualified opinion?

FIGURE 11-18

Report of Independent Accountants

To the Shareholders and Board of Directors of
  Pacific Asbestos Corporation

  We have examined the financial statements and related
schedules of Pacific Asbestos Corporation listed in the

accompanying index. Our examination was made in accordance with generally accepted auditing standards and accordingly included such tests of the accounting records and such other auditing procedures as we considered necessary in the circumstances.

Current liabilities substantially exceed current assets; a substantial amount of indebtedness (including certain notes, the holders of which hold deeds of trust and chattel mortgages on the Company's properties as collateral) is in default; operating losses have continued and based on operating results since mining commenced, the carrying value of the Company's properties (cost less depreciation, depletion and amortization) will not be recovered. In these circumstances, we do not believe the use of generally accepted accounting principles applicable to a going concern, the basis on which the accompanying statements have been prepared, present fairly the financial position of the Company or the results of operations; therefore, we do not express an opinion on the accompanying financial statements. However, we believe that these statements have been prepared on the basis set forth in the preceding sentence, and the methods of application are consistent with the preceding year.

Price Waterhouse & Co.
(PRICE WATERHOUSE & CO.)

San Francisco, California
June 2, 1967

MULTIPLE EXCEPTIONS

Figure 11-19, concerning the Trans-Gulf Corporation, contains an explanatory middle paragraph which refers to two financial statement notes (not reproduced):

Questions

1 What type of report is this?

2 What is the general nature of the two exceptions referred to in the opinion paragraph?

3 In your opinion, why did the auditor issue this type of report?

FIGURE 11-19

LESLIE J. JEKO

Certified Public Accountant

Houston, Texas

To the Board of Directors
Trans-Gulf Corporation

I have examined the balance sheet of Trans-Gulf Corporation as of December 31, 1967, and the related statement of
loss and deficit for the six months then ended. My examination was made in accordance with generally accepted auditing
standards and accordingly included such test of the accounting records and such other auditing procedures as I considered necessary in the circumstances, except as noted in
the following paragraph.

As explained in Note 3 to the financial statements, the
ultimate value of the investment in non-producing gypsum
lease is not presently determinable. Also, as explained in
Note 6 to the financial statements detailed records underlying the cost and accumulated depreciation of plant and
equipment are not available. Therefore, I am unable to
satisfy myself that these accounts are properly stated.

Because of possible material effect on the financial
statements should it become necessary to charge off the
investment in non-producing gypsum lease, and because I am
unable to satisfy myself as to the fairness of presentation
of plant and equipment and the related accumulated depreciation, I am precluded from expressing an opinion on the
accompanying financial statements taken as a whole.

Leslie J. Jeko

Houston, Texas
January 31, 1968

OPINIONS ON OTHER INFORMATION

▷ ## FUNDS STATEMENT

Figures 11-20 and 11-21 both refer to the examination of the statement of source and application of funds. However, the opinion paragraph of Figure 11-21 does not contain any reference to the source and application of funds.

Questions

1 How do you account for this difference between the two reports?

2 Does the first generally accepted auditing standard of reporting apply to the statement of funds?

3 Can you suggest a third possible treatment for the expression of an opinion on the funds statement? Why was this third treatment not used in the two reports reproduced?

4 Is the funds statement a "basic financial statement"?

FIGURE 11-20

REPORT OF AUDITORS

TO THE SHAREHOLDERS OF NATIONAL BISCUIT COMPANY:

We have examined the balance sheet of National Biscuit Company and consolidated subsidiaries as of December 31, 1969, the related statement of income and retained earnings and the statement of source and application of funds for the year then ended. Our examination was made in accordance with generally accepted auditing standards, and accordingly included such tests of the accounting records and such other auditing procedures as we considered necessary in the circumstances. We were furnished reports of other public accountants upon their examinations of the financial statements of certain foreign subsidiaries. Our opinion expressed herein, insofar as it relates to the amounts included for such subsidiaries, is based upon such reports. We made a similar examination of the financial statements for the year 1968 and have previously reported thereon.

In our opinion, the aforementioned financial statements
present fairly the financial position of National Biscuit
Company and consolidated subsidiaries at December 31, 1969
and 1968, and the results of their operations and source and
application of funds for the years then ended, in conformity
with generally accepted accounting principles applied on a
consistent basis.

LYBRAND, ROSS BROS. & MONTGOMERY

February 6, 1970
2 Broadway
New York, New York 10004

FIGURE 11-21

Opinion of Independent Accountants

Board of Directors
Evans Products Company, Portland, Oregon

We have examined the accompanying consolidated balance sheet of Evans Products Company
and Subsidiaries as of December 31, 1968, and the related statements of earnings, additional
paid-in capital, retained earnings, and source and application of funds for the year then
ended. Our examination was made in accordance with generally accepted auditing standards,
and accordingly included such tests of the accounting records and such other auditing procedures as we considered necessary in the circumstances.

In our opinion, the financial statements referred to above present fairly the consolidated
financial position of Evans Products Company and Subsidiaries at December 31, 1968, and
the consolidated results of their operations for the year then ended, in conformity with generally accepted accounting principles applied, except for the change, which we approve,
referred to in Note 5 to the financial statements, on a basis consistent with that of the preceding year, as restated.

<table>
<tr><td></td><td>TOUCHE, ROSS, BAILEY & SMART</td></tr>
<tr><td>Portland, Oregon—March 7, 1969</td><td>Certified Public Accountants</td></tr>
</table>

5. EQUIPMENT HELD FOR LEASE

Leased railcars	$87,100,000
Less accumulated depreciation	13,951,000
	$73,149,000
Residual value of leased railcars accounted for under the finance method	2,276,000
	$75,425,000

The stock of United States Railway Equipment Company, a subsidiary primarily engaged in
the business of leasing reconstructed railcars, was acquired by the Company for cash in September, 1965. At that time the assets of the subsidiary were appraised in order to allocate the
purchase price. Until December 31, 1967, depreciation expense on railcars subject to this
appraisal was determined by lease-lot on the straight-line method. In 1968, the subsidiary
changed to a composite declining balance method of computing depreciation for these railcars to eliminate the uncertainty with respect to useful lives of individual cars and in the
opinion of the Company results in a better matching of costs and revenues. This change had
the effect of increasing net earnings for the year by $579,000 or $.18 per common share.

Other railcars are being depreciated over the estimated useful lives on the straight-line
method.

PROPERTY AND ACCUMULATED DEPRECIATION

Figure 11-22 on the financial statements of the Armco Steel Corporation includes an opinion on "the supplemental schedules of properties and accumulated depreciation."

Questions

1 How do the generally accepted auditing standards of reporting apply to an opinion on items of this sort?

2 In what other manner might the opinion on this item have been expressed?

FIGURE 11-22

HASKINS & SELLS

Certified Public Accountants   **One East Fourth Street**
                                              Cincinnati 45202

ACCOUNTANTS' OPINION

Armco Steel Corporation,
Its Shareholders and Directors:

We have examined the statement of consolidated financial
position of Armco Steel Corporation and subsidiary companies
as of December 31, 1969 and the related statements of consolidated income and shareholders' equity for the year then
ended, and the supplemental schedules of properties and
accumulated depreciation, and source and use of funds, as of
that date and for that year. We have also examined the statement of consolidated financial position of Armco/Boothe
Corporation and subsidiaries and the related statement of
consolidated income and income retained in the business for
the period from January 6, 1969 (date of inception) to December 31, 1969. Our examinations were made in accordance

with generally accepted auditing standards and accordingly included such tests of the accounting records and such other auditing procedures as we considered necessary in the circumstances. We did not examine the consolidated financial statements of HITCO and subsidiaries, but we were furnished with the report of other accountants on their examination of such statements for the year ended October 31, 1969. Our opinion expressed below, insofar as it relates to the amounts included for HITCO and subsidiaries, is based solely upon such report.

In our opinion, the accompanying financial statements and supplemental schedules present fairly (a) the financial position of Armco Steel Corporation and subsidiary companies at December 31, 1969 and the results of their operations and properties and accumulated depreciation and the source and use of funds for the year then ended and (b) the financial position of Armco/Boothe Corporation and subsidiaries at December 31, 1969 and the results of their operations for the period then ended, in conformity with generally accepted accounting principles applied on a basis consistent with that of the preceding year.

February 7, 1970   *Haskins & Sells*

COMPENSATION PLAN PROVISIONS

The 1968 annual report of the Boeing Company contained Figure 11-23, which includes a third paragraph appended to the standard short-form report.

Questions

1 What is the nature of the third paragraph?

2 Was inclusion of the third paragraph required by the generally accepted auditing standards of reporting? Explain.

3 Why do you believe the third paragraph was included?

FIGURE 11-23

Accountants' Report

TOUCHE, ROSS, BAILEY & SMART

1212 IBM Building
Seattle, Washington 98101

February 24, 1969

Board of Directors
The Boeing Company
Seattle, Washington

We have examined the accompanying consolidated balance
sheet of The Boeing Company and subsidiaries as of December
31, 1968 and the related consolidated statement of net
earnings and retained earnings for the year then ended. Our
examination was made in accordance with generally accepted
auditing standards, and accordingly included such tests of
the accounting records and such other auditing procedures
as we considered necessary in the circumstances.

In our opinion, the financial statements referred to above
present fairly the consolidated financial position of The
Boeing Company and subsidiaries at December 31, 1968 and the
consolidated results of their operations for the year then
ended, in conformity with generally accepted accounting
principles applied on a basis consistent with that of the
preceding year.

Also, in our opinion, the action of the Board of Directors
on February 24, 1969, in setting aside the sum of $2,300,000
for the year 1968 under the Incentive Compensation Plan for
Officers and Employees, is in conformity with the provisions
contained in the first paragraph of Section 2 of such plan.

Touche, Ross, Bailey & Smart

Certified Public Accountants

HISTORICAL FINANCIAL SUMMARIES

Figures 11-24 and 11-25 contain the expression of an opinion on data not usually included in an auditor's report—"the comparative statement of operations for the past ten years" and "the historical financial data."

Questions

1 How do the opinions expressed on this data differ from the opinions on financial position and results of operations?

2 Explain the application of the generally accepted auditing standards of reporting to Figures 11-24 and 11-25.

3 Why do auditors' reports not normally include opinions on such data?

4 What do you think the major problems are in evaluating the "fair presentation" of this data?

FIGURE 11-24

To the Stockholders of International Business Machines Corporation

In our opinion, the accompanying consolidated financial statements present fairly the financial position of International Business Machines Corporation and its subsidiaries at December 31, 1969, the results of their operations and the supplementary information on funds for the year, in conformity with generally accepted accounting principles applied on a basis consistent with that of the previous year. Also, in our opinion, the comparative statement of operations for the past ten years presents fairly the financial information included therein. Our examination of these statements was made in accordance with generally accepted auditing standards and accordingly included such tests of the accounting records and such other auditing procedures as we considered necessary.

Price Waterhouse & Co.
January 27, 1970
New York, New York

FIGURE 11-25

Opinion of Independent Accountants

To the Shareholders:

We have examined the financial statements of Caterpillar Tractor Co. and its subsidiaries for the year ended December 31, 1969. Our examination was made in accordance with generally accepted auditing standards and accordingly included such tests of the accounting records and such other auditing procedures as we considered necessary in the circumstances. We have made similar annual examinations since incorporation of the Company.

In our opinion, the accompanying statements present fairly (a) the financial position of Caterpillar Tractor Co. and consolidated subsidiaries at December 31, 1969, the results of their operations and the changes in their net current assets for the year, in conformity with generally accepted accounting principles applied on a basis consistent with that of the preceding year and (b) the historical financial data included therein.

Chicago, January 19, 1970   Price Waterhouse & Co.

EFFECTIVE INTERNAL CONTROL

The last paragraph of Figure 11-26 contains the expression of an opinion on the "effectiveness" of internal accounting controls.

Questions

1 How does the expression of an opinion on the internal control system differ from an opinion on financial statements?

2 Why do you think the opinion on internal control was expressed? How do investors, creditors, and management benefit from the opinion?

3 Are there any hazards associated with the expression of such opinions?

4 How do generally accepted auditing standards apply to such opinions?

5 Does the expression of an opinion on internal control extend the auditor's legal liability?

FIGURE 11-26

Opinion of Independent Accountants

Price Waterhouse & Co.
60 Broad Street, New York 10004

To the Board of Directors   January 23, 1970
and Stockholders of
Chemical New York Corporation

We have examined the consolidated statement of condition of
Chemical New York Corporation and its subsidiaries at
December 31, 1969, the related consolidated statements of
income and changes in capital for the year then ended and
the consolidated statement of condition of its wholly-owned
subsidiary, Chemical Bank and its subsidiaries, at December
31, 1969. Our examination was made in accordance with generally accepted auditing standards and accordingly included
such tests of the accounting records and such other auditing
procedures as we considered necessary in the circumstances.

As explained in Note 1, the consolidated financial statements for 1969 have been prepared in accordance with the
revised reporting requirements adopted in 1969 by bank
regulatory authorities.

In our opinion, the accompanying consolidated financial
statements present fairly the consolidated financial
position of Chemical New York Corporation and its subsidiaries at December 31, 1969, the results of their operations
for the year and the consolidated financial position of
Chemical Bank and its subsidiaries at December 31, 1969, in
conformity with generally accepted accounting principles
applied on a basis consistent with that of the preceding
year except for the changes in financial statements as
explained in Note 1.

Our examination included an evaluation of the effectiveness
of the internal accounting controls, including the internal
auditing. In our opinion, the procedures in effect, together
with the examinations conducted by the internal audit staff,
constitute an effective system of internal accounting control.

Price Waterhouse & Co.

PRO FORMA STATEMENTS

The third paragraph appended to the standard short-form report in Figure
11-27 contains the expression of an opinion on a *pro forma* balance sheet.

Questions

1 What are *pro forma* financial statements?

2 Is such an opinion in accordance with the Code of Professional Ethics of the
AICPA?

3 Has the *pro forma* balance sheet been "audited"?

FIGURE 11-27

Auditors' Report

Board of Directors
Computer Applications Incorporated
New York, N.Y.

We have examined the consolidated balance sheet of Computer Applications In-
corporated and subsidiaries as of September 30, 1968, and the related state-

ments of consolidated earnings and retained earnings for the year then ended. Our examination was made in accordance with generally accepted auditing standards, and accordingly included such tests of the accounting records and such other auditing procedures as we considered necessary in the circumstances.

In our opinion, subject to the recoverability of the deferred SPEEData development costs described in Note C, the accompanying balance sheet and statements of earnings and retained earnings present fairly the consolidated financial position of Computer Applications Incorporated and subsidiaries at September 30, 1968, and the consolidated results of their operations and changes in stockholders' equity for the year then ended, in conformity with generally accepted accounting principles applied on a basis consistent with that of the preceding year.

The pro forma consolidated balance sheet of Computer Applications Incorporated and subsidiaries as of September 30, 1968 is based upon the audited consolidated balance sheet at that date, adjusted to give effect to subsequent transactions enumerated in Note L to the financial statements, and in our opinion, such pro forma consolidated balance sheet has been prepared in accordance with generally accepted accounting principles reflecting such transactions as if they had occurred at September 30, 1968.

New York, N.Y.
January 17, 1969

Note L—Pro Forma Balance Sheet

The accompanying pro forma balance sheet gives effect to the following transactions which were consummated after September 30, 1968:

1 The receipt of $13,179,000 by the Company on October 17, 1968 representing the proceeds of sale of $15,000,000 principal amount of 5⅞% Convertible Subordinated Debentures due September 1, 1988, less underwriting discounts and commissions of $621,000.

2 The receipt of $1,146,000 by SPEEData on October 17, 1968 representing the proceeds of sale of 300,000 shares (representing a 19.4% stock interest) of its Common Stock, less underwriting discounts and commissions of $54,000.

3 The incurrence of liabilities of approximately $197,000 for professional and printing expenses applicable to the foregoing transactions. Of the total underwriting and other expenses incurred, $760,600 was charged to deferred financing expenses and the balance (applicable to the issuance of SPEEData common stock) was charged to the paid-in surplus of SPEEData. In addition, $1,200,000 representing the discount on sale of the Debentures, was also charged to deferred financing expenses.

4 The repayment of $4,505,000 on October 17, 1968 and $3,000,000 on December 2, 1968 of outstanding short-term bank loans pursuant to the Company's expressed intent as to use of proceeds from the Debenture offering.

5 The loan of $4,000,000 (eliminated in consolidation) to SPEEData on October 17, 1968.

PART FOUR

CONTEMPORARY
ISSUES
IN AUDITING

CHAPTER 12

TAX SERVICES: ETHICS AND
RESPONSIBILITIES

Until now, we have concerned ourselves directly with auditing. This chapter
and the next will depart from this central subject to present contemporary
issues in two other services offered by CPAs: tax and management services.

Accountants and lawyers have disagreed about the scope of accounting and
law in the overlapping area of tax practice. The controversy is currently dor-
mant but could reappear at any time. The following set of readings documents
the positions and solutions arrived at several years ago when the accountant-
lawyer disagreement reached its height. The first selection is composed of the
two viewpoints. Immediately following are two *Journal of Accountancy* edi-
torials with supplementary data pertinent to the problems.

THE TAX PRACTICE PROBLEM*

(1) A FURTHER LOOK AT LAWYERS AND ACCOUNTANTS

Erwin N. Griswold

For some months there has been a more or less open controversy
between organized accountants and organized lawyers. I think we
can all agree that this controversy has been unfortunate. As a matter
of fact, I think that its importance has been considerably exaggerated. Individual accountants and lawyers are going ahead doing their jobs as they have
been for many years in the past, working together, harmoniously and effectively. The overwhelming number of accountants have not been affected in
their activities. It would not be fair to call the dispute a tempest in a teapot.
But it really is fair to say that it is not worth the paper and time and effort that
have been spent on it. It is no doubt hard to do, but it would be a very fine
thing, it seems to me, if the organized accountants could be more philosophical about it, could recognize that they have certain formal disadvantages in
the area, and would accept the fact that their difficulties are probably going
to be worsened the more that attention is called to them.

In 1951, a very excellent Statement of Principles was adopted by a joint
conference of lawyers and accountants, and was approved by the American

* From *The Journal of Accountancy*, Vol. 100, No. 6 (December, 1955), pp. 29–43. Reprinted by permission
of the American Institute of Certified Public Accountants.

Institute of Accountants and the House of Delegates of the American Bar Association. Of course, on such a difficult and nebulous matter, this Statement of Principles does not give all the answers. But it does outline the approach which should dispose of many of the questions. Beyond that, the continuation of joint meetings between the representatives of the two professions should make it possible to wrestle with and probably to resolve specific questions which may hereafter arise.

In connection with the current controversy, the president of the American Bar Association has appointed a special committee on professional relations. This special committee has had several meetings with representatives of the certified public accountants. So far agreement has not been reached, which seems most unfortunate. It may perhaps be said that the position of the certified public accountants does not appear to have improved any during the year. I think they are about where they were. But where they were was really pretty good for them, and it would be a very fine thing indeed, it seems to me, if they would come to realize and accept that fact. No doubt, as I have indicated, they will have to be somewhat philosophical about their position, but if they are willing to do that, I think that they will find that they are not in fact materially hampered in carrying on their activities about as they have been carrying them on for a good many years.

The chairman of the special committee on professional relations is the former president of the American Bar Association, Mr. William J. Jameson. I do not see how the Association could have a better representative. He has been patient, fair, reasonable, pleasant, earnest, genial, firm, always willing to hear all sides, open-minded — in short, everything that the chairman of such a committee should be. Although there is close harmony between the members of the committee, I do not think that it can be said that there is close agreement among them on every aspect of the problem. Mr. Jameson has been particularly good, I think, in finding a fair consensus of the committee, and in presenting that view to the representatives of the accountants.

Last January, I undertook to make a speech in this area, because the problem has long interested me, and it was suggested that I might be able to make some contribution to it. I hope I may have contributed to discussion, at least. It is quite clear, of course, that I did not achieve a solution of the problem. There is one thing, though, which I suggested in that speech, and which has seemed to be even clearer to me since that time. Since this is primarily a meeting of lawyers, it may be well for me to undertake to make the point here, though it is very likely that many of my listeners will not agree with me. The point is this: The problem is often put in terms of "practice of law." Only lawyers can "practice law," it is said, and if what an accountant is doing is "practice of law" then he is acting improperly.

THE PRACTICE-OF-LAW APPROACH

I feel fairly sure myself that this is not a sound way to approach the problem. The trouble is that it really begs the question. If we start with that approach, then the conclusion is going to follow as surely as the night follows the day that much of what the accountants have long and customarily done is improper for them to do. The people who think in terms of "practicing law"—and this includes many of those who have been active on unauthorized practice committees—proceed from that major premise to a minor premise that if the problem involves a matter of law, such as the application of a statute or regulation or court decision, then it is "practice of law" and can only be done by a lawyer.

But this is surely too broad. Must all policemen be lawyers? They are surely involved in applying statutes, and regulations, and court decisions. Their actions are not merely ministerial by any means. Must all city clerks be lawyers? Must the doctors in health departments all be lawyers, too? Must all legislators be lawyers? Obviously, there are many things involving the law and its application which can and must be done by nonlawyers. The "practice of law" formula is not a safe and sound approach, it seems to me, if it is taken to include a rule that any matter involving application of statutes, regulations and court decisions can only be handled by a lawyer.

It would be my own view, for what it is worth, that this is the error into which the trial court has fallen, to some extent, in the well-known *Agran* case. The court has taken a too literal, or semantic, view of the concept of "practice of law," and has not recognized that there are many things that lawyers do which are properly also done by others. The concept of "practice of law" cannot be as exclusive as it sounds when put in those terms. There is a very considerable overlap at the edges, and injustice is done if that overlap is not recognized.

LAWYERS IN THE TAX FIELD

In this connection, it is well to remember that the overwhelming proportion of the government's employees actually administering the tax laws are not lawyers. Some people may deplore this. Nevertheless, I suggest that it would not be wise for lawyers to seek to obtain any change in this respect. At the present time, the Treasury Regulations go far to protect the position of lawyers in the tax field. The organized accountants have been seeking a change in these regulations, or to obtain from Congress a change in the statute law which would affect the position of lawyers. So far they have not been successful. For a century and a half, the admission to the practice of law in this country has been in the control of the states, and that system has worked well. This deep-seated tradition is a powerful factor in favor of lawyers in the present situation. It seems to me likely, though, that Congress and the Treasury have *power* to prescribe the requirements of practice before the Treasury if they choose to exercise it. So far they have left this to the states, and I hope they will continue to do so. But the surest way to lead Congress or the Treasury to exercise its power in this field, it seems to me, would be for the organized bar to take an extreme or unreasonable position on the matter.

The negotiations over the past year have been carried on with representatives of the American Institute of Accountants, which represents the certified public accountants. The certified public accountants are as a group the best qualified in the accounting field. But there are many public accountants and accountants and tax experts, and so on, who are not certified public accountants. For some reason, the certified public accountants have felt that they must seek to shelter all of these people under their wing. For example, the change in the Treasury Department Circular proposed by the American Institute of Accountants is applicable to all "agents"—which is the word used in the Treasury's Circular with respect to persons allowed to practice before it who are not lawyers. It might be that the lawyers would feel that some clarification should be adopted as to the position of certified public accountants, who have substantial standards, and have obtained a measure of professional status—though they are by no means subject to the same sort of discipline as are members of the bar. But it is very easy to see, I think, how no group of lawyers is going to agree to a change in the Regulations which is applicable to all "agents"—a term which includes persons of no qualification whatever.

For example, a disbarred lawyer might immediately qualify as an agent. Anyone can set himself up as an agent, without any professional status whatever. To me it seems quite clear, regardless of the scope of activity which might well be allowed to certified public accountants, that lawyers must be vigilant in the public interest to see that completely unqualified persons are not given what amounts to a federal license to carry on substantial legal activities in the federal tax area.

The problem is complicated by the fact that there are many public accountants who are well qualified, and who have high standing. It is difficult to see, however, how this problem can be effectively handled except in terms of groups with prescribed qualifications. It may be that the whole accounting area is too much in a stage of growth and development, and that the certified public accountants would be well advised not to seek to clarify their position until they have been able to take over the whole field, imposing their standards on all persons who seek to practice accounting. If that should ever come about, then it might be possible to deal with the certified public accountants more realistically than at present.

There are a number of problems in the area to which little attention has been given and which I have by no means been able to think through. I am going to try to suggest or outline some of these problems, but with no thought that I am saying the last word about them, or even that what I have to say may be very sound. Some of the matters may be somewhat controversial, and I want to make it plain that I would surely welcome discussion and further consideration of them by any persons who are interested.

At the outset, I will mention a problem that has puzzled me considerably. The accountant has many functions. One of them is to set up systems of accounts. Another is to carry out audits. In the latter capacity, the accountant is usually referred to as the "independent accountant." He puts his certificate on the company's balance sheets and published reports; and investors and bankers, the SEC and the stock exchange, and others, rely heavily on the accountant's independent judgment. In performing this function, the accountant acts in a very real sense judicially. He must decide questions, and he must be wholly free to decide questions against his client's interest if his investigation and judgment lead him to that conclusion.

My question is this, and it bothers me: Can this independent quasi-judicial function be properly performed by a person who also undertakes to act as advocate for the client? Suppose the accountant comes to the client and says: "I think I can get larger depreciation allowances for you." What then does he put into the company's published accounts to which he adds his signature? Does he put there what he thinks to be a sound depreciation allowance or what he thinks he can get the Treasury to allow? Many questions of this sort could be asked. The accountants have an important function in being independent examiners, and they have a long and honorable history in that work. Is this function really consistent with their acting as advocates for their clients before the Treasury? Perhaps they are able to rationalize this difficulty, but it seems to me that there is a problem here which requires some careful thinking.

Now let us look at some other problems.

THE WIDE RANGE OF TAX PRACTICE

There are a great many different sorts of activity in the tax field. There is first the making out of simple returns, including most of the returns for individuals. Accountants have long done much of this work. For the most part lawyers do not want to do it. It surely involves the application of statutes, and regulations, and court decisions, yet I would suppose that nearly everyone would agree that it is appropriate for accountants to do this work. Then there is the matter of corporate returns. Here there is much that only the accountant can do if the return is of any complexity. Taking the figures from the books, prescribing and keeping inventories, and so on, are clearly work for the accountant. A substantial corporate return, however, will almost always have involved in it some novel or difficult questions of law. It is a fact, I believe, that many such tax returns are now made out by accountants. Sometimes this is done in cooperation with lawyers, or sometimes the return is reviewed by lawyers, but often there is no lawyer in the picture at all at this stage. Although there may be some question here in some cases, I believe it is, as a practical matter, pretty well accepted that accountants may make out such corporate tax returns without the intervention of a lawyer except as the accountant or the client thinks it desirable to bring a lawyer in.

Beyond this, though, the problem gets more difficult. The next stage involves representation of the client before the Treasury Department when some question is raised about the return. Of course the question may be one of accounting only, or one that is essentially accounting. It is widely known that much of this representation has been done by accountants for a great many years, with a lawyer called in only when the accountant or the client thinks that to be desirable. It would be my own view that this system has in fact worked well. The accountant has kept the books and prepared the return. On many questions, he is the person who can handle the matter most simply, and often most effectively. As has been pointed out, the Treasury personnel who deal with these problems in the initial stages are not lawyers, and they often get their backs up if a lawyer comes into the picture. I have known of lawyers who, though giving advice, have had the corporation's treasurer carry on the negotiations with the revenue agent, because of a feeling on the lawyer's part that the treasurer can often get a better adjustment on routine matters, like repairs and bad debt reserves, than the lawyer can.

THE PROBLEM OF QUALIFICATION

At this point it is well to point out an important fact, which we lawyers should not forget in our consideration of this problem. That is the clear and undeniable fact that many lawyers are not qualified to practice tax law. Some of them know that, and some do not. But the mere fact that a man has been admitted to the bar does not mean that he is competent to handle or to advise on a tax matter.

This, I think, is one of the points that irritates the accountants most. We tend to say, sometimes, that only lawyers can practice law, and that this applies fully to tax law, making no distinctions among lawyers. Yet accountants know — and we lawyers know, too — that most accountants are much better qualified to handle the ordinary tax matter than are many lawyers. In many communities, the local lawyer habitually and willingly turns over all of the tax matters to the local accountant. Indeed the lawyer often has his own tax returns made out by the accountant. When a client comes in with a tax matter, many general practitioners simply throw up their hands and say, "Oh, you must take that to your accountant." The accountant is qualified to handle most of such tax questions which come to him. For the organized lawyers now to say that this is all improper, and that only a lawyer can handle what many lawyers are not competent to handle—matters which the accountant knows are habitually handled by the accountant with satisfaction to the client, and often to the local lawyer who has referred the matter to the accountant—this is understandably aggravating to the accountants. Moreover, it does not make sense as far as lawyers are concerned; and lawyers who are working on this problem must be careful not to overlook the fact, which I believe to be a fact, that many if not most accountants are better qualified to handle many tax questions than a very considerable proportion of the members of the bar are. If this is actually the fact, lawyers must be extremely careful in this area, and must not officially take positions which are simply not realistic in terms of the work as it is actually being done in many communities.

THE PROBLEM OF TAX PLANNING

There is another problem, however, which presents more serious difficulties. This is the matter of tax planning. This includes such things as corporate adjustments and reorganizations, family partnerships and trusts, and other aspects of estate planning, pension plans, deferred compensation plans, and so on. I suspect that a very large amount of this sort of work, including the drafting of often complicated instruments, has in fact been done over the past several years by accountants. I have grave doubts about the wisdom and propriety of this. It seems to me that the organized bar might well look into this aspect of the matter, and that it might well be able to work out a better case here, leading to a possible agreement with the American Institute of Accountants, than it can in the matter of practice which is actually before the Treasury Department.

My own observation leads me to think that many accountants have been very active in this area, and that they often do not use the restraint in advising clients which is customary among members of the bar. As an illustration, I recently heard that an accountant in my area was recommending to his clients, with respect to gifts to minors, that they should make the gift outright to the children's guardian, and then have the guardian create a trust with the funds extending beyond the children's minority. This was proposed as a means of obtaining the $3,000 or $6,000 exemption. Any lawyer would see, though, (1) that the guardian has no power to create such a trust, and (2) that the proposal comes pretty close, at least, to fraud on the Treasury.

I have no way of proving it, but I would venture the guess that three-fourths of the family partnership agreements were suggested and drafted by accountants, and often they did not work out very well for the clients. I think it likely, too, that many corporate adjustments of one sort or another have been suggested and carried out by accountants, and that many pension and profit-sharing plans have been drafted by accountants. Perhaps the lawyers and the American Institute of Accountants should give further consideration to this aspect of the problem.

A FURTHER BASIC ISSUE

Now I want to turn to some other questions. It may well be, it has seemed to me, that the basic issue in this field is not between the lawyers and the accountants, but is between the lawyers and the smaller firms of accountants on the one hand, and the great national accounting firms on the other.

Although the lawyers in this country have long practiced in partnership, and some few of the partnerships are rather large, they are almost all local in their activities. There are a few law firms which maintain Washington offices, and there are a few law firms which have partners in two or three cities. But, by and large, a New York firm, no matter how large, does its work in New York, and a Chicago firm does its work in Chicago, or elsewhere in Illinois. It may have correspondents in other states, but it does not have a formal relationship with these correspondents. Law practice is overwhelmingly individual and personal. Many lawyers practice by themselves as individuals, or in small partnerships. The large partnership is definitely the exception.

This is also true of a great many persons practicing in the accounting field. There are many persons practicing by themselves, or in small and local partnerships. However, among accountants, we have another phenomenon, namely, the huge nationwide or international accounting firm, with offices in a great many cities, both in this country and abroad. These are accounting factories far more extensive than any of the law firms which have been called law factories. Not only are they larger, but they are interstate and multistate in operations.

These huge organizations develop techniques and efficiencies which mean that large amounts of large business gravitate to a relatively small number of firms, to an extent, I expect, far more than is true among large law offices. Although there is much competition among these several large accounting firms, it seems clear that as a group they skim a very large part of the cream from the available accounting work. When these organizations then go on and handle large and complicated tax problems, the questions presented may well be different than those which arise with the individual or small accounting practitioner. The accounting factories develop a confidence in their own ability which makes them, I would guess, much less likely to call a lawyer into matters where a lawyer probably ought to be called in than is the case with the smaller accounting practitioner.

If these firms were just accountants, that would be one thing. Some of these firms, however, have, I am told, law departments, where legal advice is given. Sometimes these law departments do extensive tax planning. When the accountants working for this firm in Phoenix encounter what they feel to be a tax problem, they may not call in a Phoenix lawyer, but rather send the whole matter to their firm's legal department, which may be in New York. Thus we have something developing which is pretty close to the corporate practice of law, and I think it is bad. Perhaps this is a matter which is worth looking into.

LEGAL SERVICES AND ACCOUNTING FIRMS

This leads to a closely related question which is, I know, a very touchy one. Again I want to say that I know that I may not have thought of all aspects of the question. All I am trying to do is to raise the question for consideration. I am not making charges of any sort against anyone. I am merely saying that here is something that seems to me worth careful consideration.

What I have in mind is lawyers working for accounting firms. This divides into two aspects, I believe. There is, first, the accountant who practices as an accountant, but who is also a lawyer. There is, second—and this may be rare, but I am not sure that it does not exist—the lawyer who is hired as a lawyer by an accounting firm. My own present reaction is that the latter is an exceedingly doubtful practice. I have not been able to see myself why such employment is not unethical. Why does it not amount to solicitation of law business by the lawyer involved? He does not get his own business. The business is obtained by the accounting firm, a lay organization, and is then referred to him. Moreover, the accounting firm charges the client, and the lawyer often receives a salary. Insofar as the lawyer is performing legal services, and is hired because he is a lawyer—and this may well be a proper description of the handling of much tax work—is not such an arrangement a clear violation of the canons of professional ethics? It seems to me that the American Bar Association and the American Institute of Accountants might well examine this situation, and might clarify the present canons, and make it clear and explicit that a lawyer cannot properly be employed as a lawyer by an accounting firm.

Of course an accounting firm could hire a lawyer to advise it on its own legal problems. But that is not the situation to which I refer. What I have in mind are lawyers who perform legal services for clients of the accounting firm. This seems to me to be clearly improper, no matter how much indirection may be involved in doing it. This also applies to the legal departments of huge accounting firms, which render legal opinions, and make legal suggestions and draft papers, for the accounting firm's various local offices. It may be denied that this is done, or that such legal departments exist. No doubt they are not usually called that. I think the whole matter may warrant careful consideration, and the American Institute of Accountants should be as much concerned about it as the American Bar Association.

THE NEED FOR CLARIFYING STANDARDS

Now let me return to the matter of the accountant who is also a lawyer.

Here again, it seems to me, there may be a real problem, though perhaps not so clear and difficult a problem as the one to which I have referred. If a lawyer holds himself out as an accountant, too, is he in effect soliciting law business? Is he acting improperly if, when a clear legal question arises in his accounting practice, he renders a legal opinion, or takes the case into court, or drafts legal documents? I am not sure about this, but I think it is a very doubtful practice. I heard a while ago about a lawyer who was also an accountant and a partner in an accounting firm. He said that there was nothing wrong with what he did, because whenever he rendered a legal opinion, he always put it on a separate letterhead! I suspect that there may be a good deal of this sort of thing going on. It seems to me that here again it may well be worth looking into this problem, and clarifying the applicable rules and standards, preferably by action by both the American Institute of Accountants and the American Bar Association.

One suggestion occurs to me, which may or may not be practical. It is an analogy to a practice in the state of New South Wales, where they have both branches of the legal profession, the barristers and the solicitors. A person cannot be both at once, but there is considerable freedom in transferring from one branch of the profession to the other. If a solicitor wants to become a barrister, he has himself stricken from the roll of solicitors when he is admitted to the bar, and then he cannot practice as a solicitor. If, however, he does not find being a barrister to his liking, he can resign from the bar, and have his name restored to the list of solicitors. What is clear is that he cannot do both things at once.

SEPARATION OF LEGAL AND ACCOUNTING SERVICES

I wonder if something along the same line would not be useful here. It seems to me fairly clear, though there is certainly room for discussion, that a man should not practice both as an accountant and as a lawyer at the same time. Could we not work out a system under which an accountant-lawyer who wanted to practice as an accountant could have his membership in the bar suspended?

While it was suspended, he would not be a lawyer, and could not properly practice as a lawyer. On the other hand, if he preferred to be a lawyer, he could have his status as an accountant suspended. If his choice did not work out, he would be free to change from one to another, after a proper interval.

What is needed in this area, it seems to me, is a fairly complete separation between accountants and lawyers. An accounting firm should practice accounting, and by this I mean to include substantial activity in the tax field, but done as an accountant does it, by a person who holds himself out only as an accountant. An accounting firm should have no employed lawyers, and should not be in a position to represent directly or indirectly that it is able to provide legal opinions or to give the services of a lawyer. Similarly, lawyers' firms should not undertake to render the services of accountants—though I do not believe that they do now. If accounting firms really restricted their activities to accounting services, and were clearly debarred from the use of lawyers as employees or partners, then the public could choose the type of service it wants in a much more clear-cut way than is apparently the case at present. In my former speech on this subject, I included a sentence to the effect that it seemed to me that the matter between lawyers and accountants might well be left to the ordinary channels of competition, that is, that the clients might well be left to choose whether they wished to be served by an accountant or by a lawyer. In making that suggestion, however, I definitely had in mind that the choice should be between accounting services and lawyer's services, with no hybrid services to be offered, directly or indirectly, by the accounting firm.

Whether these observations add up to anything or not, I do not know. Some of the points made seem to me to be worth further consideration and perhaps investigation. Perhaps a resolution of some of these collateral questions might go far towards a solution of the basic problems which have been troubling the accountants and the lawyers over the past several years.

CONCLUSION

In closing, I would like to say again what I said at the beginning. It is a great mistake, I think, to blow this question up to too great importance. In my experience, lawyers and accountants have got along very well together, each performing a specialized service of complexity and importance to his clients. In the tax work I see being done, I know of very little friction between lawyers and accountants. If people would cease being excited, my guess is that the situation would move along with considerable satisfaction to the clients, and with little difficulty for the two professions, for a long time. It is my own conviction that it would be very wise if the American Institute of Accountants would relax and call off its activities, and let things go along for a while without much concern on its part. The Institute should always be free to bring to the attention of the Bar Association any situation where it really feels that its members are being improperly restricted, and the Bar Association should be prepared to act promptly and generously whenever any such situation is actually presented.

This is a great country, and I get the impression that accountants, with very few exceptions, are doing what they want to do without harassment. This is an area where it is extremely difficult to lay down explicit rules. Wouldn't we all be better off if we would just let well enough alone?

(2) A PROPOSED SOLUTION TO THE CONTROVERSY

MAURICE H. STANS

In the late spring of 1954, a decision [*Agran* v. *Shapiro*] by a lower court in California, involving a then obscure member of the accounting profession triggered a series of events that has occupied the time and thoughts of many accountants ever since. The court held that a CPA, enrolled to practice before the Treasury Department, was guilty of "unauthorized practice of law" in representing his client in a tax matter with the Treasury.

This decision, which has since been elaborated by a later decision upon remand and retrial, tends to nullify—at least within the area of the court's jurisdiction—the Treasury enrollment of the CPA. The court based its conclusions largely on the fact that the CPA consulted and reviewed statutes, regulations, rulings, and decisions. While the case was a local one, it took on added significance to accountants from the fact that it was backed by the California Bar Association. If its doctrine were extended to other jurisdictions it might remove the CPA entirely from the field of tax practice. Since there was growing evidence of a hostile attitude toward CPAs by unauthorized practice committees of many local bar associations in recent years, this whole matter took on the appearance of a formidable threat to the entire accounting profession. Many CPAs felt that they were the object of an organized campaign to push them out of a major part of their tax practice so that lawyers could take over. Their respect for the prestige, power and influence of the organized bar is great, and they were most uncomfortable in the belief that they were objects of its unfriendly attentions.

Something had to be done, and it was. The American Institute of Accountants undertook a carefully considered program designed to meet these fears. It requested legislative relief from the Congress; it supported the *Agran* case

to carry it on to appeal; it urged the Treasury Department to amend its regulations to make it clear that the results threatened by the *Agran* case were never
intended by the Treasury; and it met with the American Bar Association in a
series of conferences, hoping to find a solution to the problem that both professions would accept. None of these measures has as yet been successful.
However, the Institute believes that the problem imposed upon certified public
accountants by the *Agran* decision is now much better understood by lawyers,
by the Treasury, and by the business public than it was in 1954. The matter
of amending the regulations is now before the Treasury for determination.

Officially the two professions stand rather far apart: basically opposed positions have been taken by the Institute and the American Bar Association. Emo-
tion and professional pride have motivated some people and some groups to
express themselves on the problem without real knowledge of what it is about.
Yet underlying the situation are many factors that are promising. Individual
lawyers who work together with CPAs harmoniously and effectively show no
concern over what CPAs do in the tax field. The Treasury Department appears
to recognize that the outcome of the controversy can have a serious effect
on the collection of the revenues and is studying it fully. And now some individual lawyers who have deplored the differences between the two professions have taken the time to become better informed about them and have
spoken out publicly.

The latest of these is Dean Erwin N. Griswold of the Harvard Law School
who on August 21, 1955, spoke before the section on taxation of the American
Bar Association in Philadelphia. *In his speech, I think, lies the key to the solution of the entire controversy.*

This speech is even more significant than the earlier address by Dean Griswold in January 1955 (JofA, Apr.55), before the Association of the Bar of the
City of New York. In the interim Dean Griswold became a member of the committee on professional relations of the American Bar Association and participated in the latter stages of last winter's negotiations between that organization
and the Institute. Those negotiations succeeded in defining sharply the areas of
disagreement. Dean Griswold has now suggested a basis upon which they could
be reconciled.

A SOLUTION IS OFFERED

He says that it is unsound to approach the problem of tax practice by assuming
that general definitions of "practice of law" can be applied to CPAs in their
customary practice before the Treasury Department. He says, "The people who
think in terms of 'practicing law' . . . proceed from a major premise [that only
lawyers can practice law] to a minor premise that if the problem involves a

matter of law, such as the application of a statute or regulation or court decision, then it is 'practice of law' and can only be done by a lawyer." He goes on to point out that there are many things involving the law and its application which can and must be done by nonlawyers. "The 'practice of law' formula," he says, "is not a safe and sound approach, it seems to me, if it is taken to include a rule that any matter involving application of statutes, regulations and court decisions can only be handled by a lawyer."

Dean Griswold goes on to refer to two of the principles which are most relevant to this question. First, he points out that much of the representation of taxpayers before the Treasury Department has been done for a great many years by accountants. Of this he states: "It would be my own view that this system has in fact worked well." Secondly, Dean Griswold points out that this work, and indeed all of the activity of certified public accountants in the tax field, is a part of the practice of accounting.

THE HEART OF THE MATTER

If the American Bar Association would accept these principles and would agree that they should be spelled out in an authoritative manner, so that certified public accountants would no longer be in danger of being attacked in local courts for settling clients' tax liabilities with the Internal Revenue Service, as the Treasury authorizes them to do, there would be little need for further controversy. This is all that is involved in the whole matter.

All that the Institute has been seeking, in all of its activities since the *Agran* case, is confirmation of the right of certified public accountants to continue their customary practice before the Treasury Department, which until last year was generally assumed to be a natural and proper part of the practice of accounting. Dean Griswold frankly acknowledges the general competence of CPAs in most aspects of taxation. He also frankly recognizes that the mere fact that a man is admitted to the Bar does not endow him with competence in tax matters. He agrees that CPAs should not be prosecuted for "unauthorized practice of law" in the course of their ordinary tax work before the Treasury Department.

It can be stated with all possible emphasis that the Institute seeks no change which would broaden the present scope of CPAs. The Institute seeks no change which would adversely affect the position of lawyers. Its members do not want to practice law, or to interfere with the regulation of the practice of law. But neither do they want a substantial part of what has for over 40 years been accepted in this country (and for that matter in the rest of the world) as the practice of accounting, to be suddenly declared to be the practice of law because of an ambiguous clause in the Treasury regulations. They do not believe that the business public, or the Internal Revenue Service or, for that matter, the preponderant majority of lawyers really want CPAs to be expelled from this traditional tax practice. Yet the experience in California seems to show that it can happen anywhere and everywhere.

Dean Griswold's views, if applied, would solve the problem. Unfortunately, Dean Griswold does not suggest a means of implementing his views to make them effective in resolving things. Indeed, the Dean would seem to suggest that the working out of these problems should be left to the state courts. The obvious inadequacy of this method of handling the matter is highlighted by the *Agran* case and other state court decisions, which are inconsistent among themselves, and provide no uniform guide to practitioners concerned with federal tax matters in different states. Dean Griswold does not propose any remedy for this. On the contrary, he proposes that the accountants "be more philosophical" about the whole thing rather than continue to press the issue.

It is, of course, possible to be philosophical about anything in life, good or bad. A prisoner of war in Korea before a firing squad can be philosophical about his predicament, but most likely the only philosophy that would be comforting would be one of complete resignation to fate. To the accountants who view the *Agran* case as a gun at their heads, with the trigger ready to be pulled by any unauthorized practice committee before any court unschooled in the problem, that seems an unacceptable philosophy. They ask something more real, and that is understandable when their interests and the interest of their clients are so directly involved.

WORKING OUT THE SOLUTION

There are workable ways of making the Griswold principles operative with assurance and they could be applied quickly. The best and quickest way would be for the Treasury to promulgate an acceptable revision of the practice regulations in Circular 230, making it clear that what accountants do in Treasury tax work is within the proper practice of accounting and does not encroach on the practice of law. It would be highly desirable if the American Bar Association, before or after such a revision, would endorse the proposition, because such an endorsement would set the stage for the renewal of cooperative relations between the two professions.

There seems little doubt that the Treasury has the power to prescribe the requirements of practice before the Treasury Department. If the Treasury Department makes it clear that it is the intent of its regulations that a certified public accountant, enrolled to practice before the department, may continue to settle clients' tax liabilities with the Internal Revenue Service, as the Treasury has always permitted them to do, then the state courts would not be likely to interfere.

If the Treasury Department would clear up this misunderstanding, there would appear to be no further reason to seek federal legislation in this area, nor to carry the *Agran* decision to the United States Supreme Court. The Treasury, which has the power to do so, would then have settled the matter.

However, it seems to me that a favorable attitude of the American Bar Association is essential, even if the Treasury regulations are amended to meet the problem. It puzzles and disturbs the accounting profession that the American Bar Association has opposed its efforts to clarify the real meaning of the Treasury Department regulations. Twenty-two different variations in proposed amendments have been offered which would satisfy the Institute, but the Bar Association has said "no" to all of them. It seems to insist that the ambiguity and uncertainty be preserved. This encourages the fear among CPAs that some elements of the organized bar want to take further advantage of the uncertainty.

It is obvious that there must be a difference of opinion within the Bar Association. Dean Griswold hints at this when he says, "Although there is close harmony between the members of the committee, I do not think that it can be said that there is close agreement among them on every aspect of the problem." As a matter of fact, the Institute's negotiators were convinced at an early stage of the discussions that the members of the Bar Association committee would accept a solution consonant with the point of view now expressed by Dean Griswold. This would have been perfectly satisfactory to the Institute. But later, apparently after consultation with other Association officials, the committee's attitude changed. The dogmatic view seems to have prevailed that anything involving the interpretation of statutes or regulations or court decisions, even in determining and settling tax liabilities, must be considered the practice of law, regardless of whether lawyers generally are competent to do it.

THE NEED FOR A SOLUTION

So, as things stand, certified public accountants are continuing their customary tax practice only because, for the moment, *there is no agressive effort to prevent them from doing so.* But in California, where the *Agran* case was decided, it must be remembered that the California State Bar provoked the decision which put the fat in the fire. It must also be remembered that the unauthorized practice committee of this same California State Bar has repudiated the Statement of Principles promulgated by the National Conference of Lawyers and Certified Public Accountants, which Dean Griswold refers to with approval.

The committee proposed instead a standard of behavior for accountants from which the following is an excerpt:

Upon the instigation of an audit, it is recommended that an accountant should advise the retention of an attorney; and upon the issuance of a 30-day letter by the Treasury Department, an accountant shall do nothing further in the matter except under the supervision of and in aid of an attorney.

The second decision of the trial court in the *Agran* case was squarely in accordance with the proposal of the unauthorized practice committee of the California State Bar.

So far as the Institute can see, only amendment of the Treasury Department regulations, or an Act of Congress, or a reversal of the *Agran* decision can assure taxpayers that they may continue to employ CPAs in tax matters and will not be forced to employ lawyers whether they want them or not. If the bar can propose any other assurance against charges of "unauthorized practice of law" against CPAs in tax work, the Institute would be very glad to consider it.

"COOPERATIVE MACHINERY"

But the bar proposes only "cooperative machinery" to discuss the problems and try to settle specific complaints. The Institute favors cooperative machinery, but certified public accountants must first know which philosophy will govern the consideration of complaints—Dean Griswold's approach, or the approach of the California State Bar. If the Treasury Department would make Dean Griswold's point of view effective, the cooperative machinery would work. But if it must start with the assumption that interpretation of the tax law, regulations, and decisions for the purpose of determining and settling tax liabilities is a function exclusively reserved for lawyers, then the cooperative machinery will surely break down on the first case it encounters.

This all adds up to the fact that a real problem exists, that a solution is mandatory, that a solution can be formulated from the principles suggested by Dean Griswold, and that such a solution is workable.

THE FRINGE QUESTIONS

In his speech, Dean Griswold deals relatively briefly with the main point that the accountants are concerned about in the present state of affairs—the question of their right to practice before the Treasury Department. More than half of his comments are directed toward what I would like to call, using a term of common usage today, "fringe issues." As has been generally demonstrated in the labor-management arena, fringe issues that are once raised can seldom be ignored or even given less attention than the main propositions in a negotiation. Many times they carry emotional impacts on one side or another that delay agreement on matters of much greater significance. Once these side issues are cleared up, the main problem frequently yields to a ready solution.

That may be the case here, and Dean Griswold may have performed an important service in bringing these questions into the open. Accountants who are really interested in finding an accord with the lawyers should not resent them. They should welcome the opportunity of finding ways of removing any obstacles, imaginary or real, that, in the minds of any group or individuals among the lawyers, inhibit an understanding between the two professions in the major areas. It must be assumed that the questions raised by Dean Griswold do exist in the minds of some lawyers, that they have been conveyed to him on occasions sufficiently numerous to cause him to believe that collectively they constitute a barrier of some size to mutual understanding, that he hopes they can be answered or dealt with in ways that exhibit good faith on the part of the accountants, and that the chances of harmonious relations between the two professions will then be greatly enhanced.

On that basis, we ought to analyze his "fringe" questions very carefully. As he says, it would do no good for us simply to deny them, because this is expected. In any event, categorical denial would subtract nothing from any present misunderstanding. What is needed is real light in the form of factual and rational information sufficient to establish fully the answers to his questions, and then a determination of whether anything ought to be done about any of them.

Here are the six fringe issues raised by Dean Griswold. I have paraphrased them into the form of questions, since he makes it clear that he considers them to be just that and not accusations or charges.

1 Why does the American Institute of Accountants, the national organization of certified public accountants, seek to shelter under its wing other groups ("public accountants and accountants and tax experts") who are not certified public accountants?

2 Can an independent accountant, who certifies to the correctness of a client's financial statements after an examination in which he must in a sense act quasi-judicially on the questions and facts disclosed by his audit, also act as "advocate" for the same client in a tax matter?

3 Do accountants, under the guise of tax planning, frequently draft complicated legal instruments for their clients (in such areas as corporate adjustments and reorganizations, family partnerships and trusts, pension plans, deferred compensation plans, and so on)?

4 Do the large national accounting firms, or some of them, have law departments,

which give legal advice to their clients, render legal opinions, make legal suggestions, and draft papers, for the accounting firms' various local offices (to the exclusion of local lawyers)?

5 Should accounting firms hire lawyers and then offer their services as lawyers to clients?

6 Should an accountant who is also a lawyer practice both professions at the same time, or should he be required to choose one or the other?

These questions cover a wide range of subject matter and must for that reason be dealt with individually.

THE INSTITUTE AND CPAs

On the first of these questions, there is a profound misunderstanding that can be cleared up right away. The Institute speaks only for certified public accountants. It admits to membership only certified public accountants. It takes no others under its wing. It is true that in one case involving the question of unauthorized practice of law by a self-designated tax expert (*Gardner* v. *Conway*), the Institute appeared and filed a brief as amicus curiae; however, that was done for the sole and specific purpose of urging the court to do, in its opinion, what Dean Griswold believes the Institute should now do—to differentiate between the proper place of the CPA in tax practice and the place of the obviously less qualified practitioner.

Dean Griswold feels that the Institute is making a mistake in urging that the Treasury amend its Circular 230 in terms which would establish a uniform status for all "agents" enrolled to practice before it. He says that the designation "agent" includes persons of no qualifications whatever, and goes on to add: "For example, a disbarred lawyer might immediately qualify as an agent. Anyone can set himself up as an agent, without any professional status whatever."

Can he here be confusing the enrolled Treasury agent with the so-called "tax expert" who prepares tax returns in barber shops and real estate offices, with no professional status and no standard of qualifications?

Such persons are today not registered or regulated in any way. Perhaps they should be, but that is clearly another subject. The enrolled "agent" authorized to represent taxpayers before the Treasury, on the other hand, must meet a high standard. Lawyers and certified public accountants are admitted to practice without examination, as are a few former employees of the Internal Revenue Service of high rank. Any other applicants for enrollment must pass a written examination given by the Treasury itself, and this examination at the present time includes the accounting section of the uniform CPA examination.

Once admitted, all agents must conform with the rules of conduct of the accounting profession and certain stipulated rules set forth in Circular 230. A lawyer or a certified public accountant will not be given a Treasury card unless he is in good standing in his profession in his own state.

The Institute has felt all along that it cannot seek special privileges for certified public accountants so long as the Treasury admits others to practice before it as agents, under standards which the Treasury considers adequate for the representation of taxpayers in tax controversies. The Institute has been ready to concede that the Treasury is in the best position to judge who should be admitted to represent taxpayers and what those admitted should be allowed to do. It has no indication that the Treasury has the present right or power to create new distinctions among those already admitted as agents, even if it wanted to do so. (Perhaps in the course of years the standards of admission will warrant reconsideration, but again this is a matter not germane to the present question.)

THE CPA AS ADVOCATE

Dean Griswold raises the question as to whether the position of the certified public accountant in certifying financial statements as independent auditors can be reconciled with his representation of a client in a tax matter.

There does not seem to me to be any real difficulty here. The fact that a CPA presents independent findings to his client or to third parties on financial matters doesn't require him to remain aloof on other proper ways of serving his client, so long as he does nothing to prejudice his independence of views on the financial statements. Nor is there anything unique about the role of the certified public accountant as an independent adviser. A lawyer who gives an opinion as to the validity of a proposed issue of securities for inclusion in a prospectus is functioning no less as an independent expert than the certified public accountant who gives an opinion on the financial statements included in the same prospectus. Like the lawyer, the certified public accountant can properly perform other functions in addition to giving independent opinions. He can and does install accounting and cost systems; he can and does advise on accounting questions, on financial matters, and on accounting and financial personnel, for example. In tax work he is particularly well qualified to defend his client's positions before the Treasury representative, because he is aware of the income data shown by the records, the variations between book income and taxable income permitted or required by tax law, and so on. When he expresses an opinion that financial statements fairly present the financial position and results of operation of a business, he is guided by generally accepted accounting principles. If the Internal Revenue Code accepts a greater deduction for depreciation in any year than that which would be permissible under generally accepted accounting principles—and there are many cases when this is the situation—there is no reason why he shouldn't advise the taxpayer to take the greater deduction in his tax return. No one expects income tax returns and certified income statements to be identical. In many cases the tax law requires them to be different, and the skill of the CPA in this field makes him peculiarly competent to see that his client's reporting for tax purposes is properly done in the first instance and is then properly defended before the Treasury. On this point of competence, Dean Griswold seems to agree. As I have indicated earlier, he says the system of representation before the Treasury by CPAs "has in fact worked well."

DRAFTING LEGAL INSTRUMENTS

The third question carries with it implications, and some passing estimates by Dean Griswold, that if true would well justify censure of accountants for improper practices. He "suspects" that a large amount of tax planning of corporate adjustments and reorganizations, family partnerships and trusts, and other aspects of estate planning, pension plans, deferred compensation plans, and so on, *including the drafting of often complicated instruments,* has been done over the past several years by accountants. He ventures the "guess" that three-fourths of the family partnership agreements were suggested *and drafted* by accountants. He thinks it "likely" that many corporate adjustments of one sort and another were suggested *and carried out* by accountants, and that many pension and profit-sharing plans *have been drafted* by accountants.

These are serious conclusions, and it would be helpful to have available some of the evidence upon which Dean Griswold bases them. To deny them, and then seek to prove the correctness of the denial, involves the difficult feat of attempting to prove a negative. It is not effective, of course, for the Institute to say that it just does not believe these conclusions to be justified.

There are two propositions involved here. One is that accountants have undertaken to plan these transactions. The other is that they have carried them out and have prepared the required legal documents. I do not believe that Dean Griswold or many other lawyers will object to a CPA's suggesting any of these matters to a client for consideration, even with proposals as to ways of effecting them. In many cases, the CPA is in the best position and has the best opportunity to originate such advice. The criticism involved in Dean Griswold's assumptions must be against the CPA undertaking to carry them out without calling in a lawyer.

On this point of principle, the Institute agrees with him completely. It has specifically disapproved drafting of legal instruments of any kind by CPAs and would discipline members who did so in any case that came to its attention. It is ready to meet the test of good faith on this by dealing specifically with any such instances that are reported to it by any member of the bar. It would, I believe, be willing to strengthen its disciplinary procedures if it found that violations anywhere near the extent estimated by Dean Griswold actually did exist.

I cannot leave this question, however, without stating my own feelings that it has an aura of unreality. Tax planning in the kind of situations referred to just doesn't happen that way. In the high proportion of cases where involved questions and substantial amounts are present, both lawyers and certified public accountants have a voice. I believe the number of violations of this premise is extremely small. Dean Griswold would do a service to both professions if he were to urge his informants that any unsatisfactory cases be brought to the Institute's attention promptly.

LEGAL DEPARTMENTS IN CPA FIRMS

I know that Dean Griswold would not have said that some lawyers think that CPA firms maintain legal departments unless some lawyers actually think so. But here again it is unfortunate that the experiences which lead them to this conclusion are not available for investigation. Here again CPAs are asked to prove a denial of something which, to the very best of my knowledge, is not true.

The growth of national and international accounting firms, much larger than most law firms, was necessary to meet the requirements of large national and international corporations, whose accounts must be audited and whose inventories, properties, and other assets must be inspected at widely separated locations. These accounting firms habitually work closely with lawyers in tax matters and in many other corporate problems. I am sure that many, many lawyers would testify to that, and would say that their relations with the accountants they know are eminently satisfactory.

Any of the large accounting firms would welcome a visit from Dean Griswold and would be glad to show him their offices and introduce him to members of their partnership and staff who deal with tax matters. They would be glad to tell him the kind of work they do and the circumstances under which they do it. If that were done, and assuming that he applied the same yardstick of proper accounting practice that he adopts in his speech, I do not believe he would find anything that he would consider improper.*

* Editor's Note: Dean Griswold's question led The Journal to query 15 of the largest accounting firms on whether or not they maintain law departments which offer legal advice to clients, draft legal papers, etc. All 15 emphatically replied that there was nothing in their own practices to justify such a statement.

CPAs HIRING LAWYERS?

The employment of lawyers by accounting firms is the subject of the next question. The Institute agrees completely that no accounting firm should offer to render legal services to its clients or to permit lawyers on its staff to do anything which certified public accountants are not authorized to do. It does not believe that this standard is violated very frequently. Accountants are quite often employed by law firms, and most lawyers agree that they should not be used to render accounting services to clients. Several years ago we proposed to the National Conference of Lawyers and CPAs that it adopt these mutual propositions. They are still acceptable to the Institute.

On the subject of joint practice of the two professions by an individual who is both a lawyer and CPA, or by a firm composed of such individuals, the Institute has never adopted an official policy. It agrees that this is a matter worth studying by the national organizations of the two professions. It understands that there are differences of opinion among lawyers as to whether joint practice is in any way improper. Certainly this is not a matter which need impede or delay a mutual understanding on the rightful place of the two professions in the tax field.

CONCLUSIONS

We are getting much closer to a solution of our problem when the discussions "come to grips with specific propositions." The accounting profession and the legal profession are both indebted to Dean Griswold for his contribution. It is to be hoped now that others among the lawyers will adopt his reasoned point of view and thereby set the stage for a meeting of the minds and a resumption of cooperative relations.

There is accumulating evidence that his basic views are shared by a growing number of thoughtful lawyers. For example, in a round table conducted by the *Journal of Public Law* this year there appear these significant comments on the subject of administrative practice by nonlawyers:

Morris Ernst, New York attorney: "Some bar groups are worried about loss of clients because of the recent promotion of bookkeeping to certified public accountancy. It is true that every tax return—even the simplest—requires interpretation of a revenue statute. But it is equally true that every tax return of corporate complexity requires knowledge of the choices and vagaries of double entry bookkeeping—a magic untaught at law schools. The two professions have lived together in substantial good will. But now accountants are entrapped by law associations; entrants to the bar are asked to sign pledges that they will never practice accountancy; and some lawyers—following the worst of trade-union practices—are intent on pre-empting for lawyers alone appearances before administrative tax authorities."

J. A. McClain, Jr., Dean of the School of Law, Duke University: "When we consider the criticism—against trade-union tactics among the bar, it would seem that . . . . competition in the market place will eventually decide this question: and no self-protective trade-union concept held by the bar will prevent the public from accepting the most economical and efficient way of handling these problems, regardless of what they may be."

Elliott E. Cheatham, Professor of Law, Columbia University: "Increased efforts toward the clarification of business conditions have created the statistician and the accountant. . . . The bar is under the necessity of coming to terms with these new groups. So far the bar has dealt with these new groups through its committees on the unauthorized practice of law. At an earlier time, it is true, the challenges to the established work of the bar came merely from petty poachers, persons obviously unqualified to do the work. Now the problem has largely changed its character. No longer is the petty poacher the major challenger. The challenger is the man who offers or seems to offer something the lawyer does not offer and who gives his services with greater efficiency and economy. The test, 'unauthorized practice of law,' is antiquated and inadequate. The new groups cannot rightly be regarded merely as rivals for work which are to be combatted or whose fields must be rigidly delimited. They must be recognized for what they are, collaborators in the common task of advising and guiding clients. The bar should take measures to examine the whole situation afresh and to see to it that this new expertness is made available to clients who need it in a way which does not involve burdensome and unnecessary fees."

These comments may be merely straws in the wind, but they tell us something that may be very important. To me they say, when added to the proposals of Dean Griswold: "Here is evidence of reasoned thinking. Here is hope for a rational and reasonable understanding. Here is hope for a new peace between our two great professions."

The steps are simple. I propose and urge that:

1 The Treasury conform its regulations to the actual practice before the Department and the principles suggested by Dean Griswold.

2 The American Bar Association approve such an amendment to the Treasury regulations.

3 The Institute consider amending its code of ethics to provide that accountants may not prepare legal documents on any occasion and that accountants may not employ lawyers and hold out their services as lawyers.

4 Cooperative machinery be established between the two organizations to deal

with all complaints of members of one against members of the other, within the spirit of the Statement of Principles adopted by them several years ago.

We need now only to bring to bear the statesmanship and leadership that both professions possess in full measure. I urge upon both the sensible fact that they owe it to their own futures and to the interests of the public to adopt such a course by whatever means seem feasible.

To seek to solve differences peaceably is not appeasement and it is not surrender of principle. It is the challenge of today—in this era of relaxed tensions in the world and of new statesmanship among peoples. And every solution that is reached which dispels the emotions of controversy adds to the stature of man.

EDITORIAL—PRACTICE BEFORE TREASURY DEPARTMENT CLARIFIED*

Last month we published a statement released by the Secretary of the Treasury January 30, 1956, interpreting parts of Treasury Department Circular No. 230 relating to practice before the Treasury Department by enrolled attorneys and agents (JofA, Mar.56, p. 6). . . .

Meanwhile, counsel for the American Institute of Accountants has prepared an opinion on the legal effect of the statement, which appears . . . immediately following this editorial. This opinion deserves careful study.

The Treasury Department statement must be appraised in the light of recent events which led up to its issuance.

For many years certified public accountants have represented their clients fully before the Treasury Department to the apparent satisfaction of all concerned. Recently it has been contended that some phases of practice before the Department constituted the "practice of law;" that the state courts had power to regulate the practice of law; and that the state courts, therefore, could properly prevent nonlawyers from doing things, in representing taxpayers before the Treasury Department, which the courts held to be within the exclusive domain of lawyers.

The Treasury Department statement of January 30th seems clearly to confirm the long-established practice of enrolled agents before the Department and to make it clear that regulation of practice before the Department is within the exclusive province of the Secretary. But the Department warns both enrolled agents and attorneys that if the two groups do not respect the appropri-

*From *The Journal of Accountancy*, April, 1956, pp. 29–33. Reprinted by permission of the American Institute of Certified Public Accountants.

ate fields of each, as a matter of professional responsibility, the Department may find it necessary to define the appropriate scope of activity of members of each profession in Treasury practice, as it unquestionably has the power to do.

The Treasury Department refers to the "Statement of Principles Relating to Practice in the Field of Federal Income Taxation," approved by the governing bodies of the American Bar Association and the American Institute of Accountants in 1951, in connection with its references to professional responsibility. The "Statement of Principles" thereby acquires additional prestige, and for this reason we are reprinting it. . . .

We are gratified to report these developments. They should provide a basis for ending the unfortunate controversies about tax practice to which we have had to devote so much space in these pages in recent years. With the new assurance that certified public accountants may continue their customary practice before the Treasury Department without fear of harassment, other problems with which the legal and accounting professions are mutually concerned should yield to friendly negotiations.

"Ground rules" more specific in some respects than the "Statement of Principles" may be needed as a guide to both lawyers and accountants in observing the Treasury's admonition not to undertake work outside the field of their professional competence. Surely the American Bar Association and the American Institute of Accountants will prefer to establish such standards for themselves by voluntary cooperative effort. It is clear that the Treasury Department prefers to leave the task to them if they will do it.

Relations between lawyers and certified public accountants in actual practice have normally been friendly and cooperative. Members of both professions will welcome the opportunity now presented for resumption of the same relationship between their professional organizations.

OPINION OF COUNSEL ON TREASURY STATEMENT*

American Institute of Accountants
270 Madison Avenue
New York 16, N.Y.

Dear Sirs:

You have asked our opinion as to the permissible scope of practice before the Treasury Department by enrolled agents under Treasury Department Circular

---

* Ibid.

230 and the official interpretation of Section 10.2 thereof promulgated by the Secretary of the Treasury January 30, 1956.

The Secretary of the Treasury has been given the power by Congress to regulate fully practice before the Department.

The Secretary of the Treasury has been expressly authorized by Congress to prescribe rules and regulations governing the recognition of "agents, attorneys, or other persons representing claimants before his Department . . ." 5 U.S.C., §261. This statute constitutes a valid delegation of power by Congress to the head of an executive department. *Goldsmith v. United States Board of Tax Appeals,* 270 U.S. 117 (1926).

To the extent that the Secretary prescribes regulations governing practice before his Department, such regulations pre-empt the field. Under the Supremacy Clause of the Constitution, they supersede any state law which might have been applicable to the activities governed by the regulations if the regulations had not been issued. United States Constitution, Article VI; *Auerbacher v. Wood,* 139 N.J. Eq. 599, 53 A. 2d 800 (Ch. 1947), aff'd, 142 N.J. Eq. 484, 59 A. 2d 863 (Ct. Err. & App. 1948). *DePass v. B. Harris Wool Co.,* 346 Mo. 1038, 144 S.W. 2nd 146 (1940).

Varying interpretations of Treasury Circular 230 had raised some question as to whether the Secretary had fully exercised the power to regulate the scope of practice before the Department.

The Secretary of the Treasury has issued regulations governing practice before the Department and these are set forth in Treasury Department Circular No. 230. 31 C.F.R., Subtitle A, Part 10. The scope of the practice thus regulated is dealt with in Section 10.2 of these regulations, particularly in Subsections 10.2(b) and 10.2(f).

Subsections 10.2(b) and 10.2(f) read:

> *10.2(b): Practice before the Treasury Department shall be deemed to comprehend all matters connected with the presentation of a client's interests to the Treasury Department, including the preparation and filing of necessary written documents, and correspondence with the Treasury Department relative to such interests. Unless otherwise stated the term 'Treasury Department' as used in this paragraph and elsewhere in this part includes any division, branch, bureau, office, or unit of the Treasury Department, whether in Washington or in the field, and any officer or employee of any such division, branch, bureau, office, or unit.*

> *10.2(f): Rights and duties of agents. An agent enrolled before the Treasury Department shall have the same rights, powers, and privileges and be subject to the same duties as an enrolled attorney: Provided, That an enrolled agent shall not have the privilege of drafting or preparing any written instrument by which title to real or personal property may be conveyed or transferred for the*

purpose of affecting Federal taxes, nor shall such enrolled agent advise a client as to the legal sufficiency of such an instrument or its legal effect upon the Federal taxes of such client: And provided further, *That nothing in the regulations in this part shall be construed as authorizing persons not members of the bar to practice law.*

While the second proviso of Subsection 10.2(f) has long been part of the regulations, it received virtually no attention or comment until relatively recently, although one court during this early period did uphold the right of accountants to practice fully before the Treasury Department. *Richter* v. *Moon,* (Pa. Ct. of Cm. P. 1939), JofA, Nov.42, p. 470. In this earlier period, at least one Bar Association spokesman interpreted this proviso as having the effect only of prohibiting enrolled agents who were not members of the bar from holding themselves out as attorneys by virtue of their authorization to practice before the Department. He stated that the proviso did not limit in any way the scope of practice permitted to enrolled agents by the regulation. Julius Henry Cohen, 9 ICC, Practitioners' Journal 874.

More recently, Section 10.2(f) and, in particular, the second proviso of that section, has been considered and interpreted for the first time by a state court. In *Agran* v. *Shapiro,* 127 Cal. App. 2d 807, 273 P. 2d 619 (1954), the Superior Court of California held that this second proviso constituted a "disavowal" by the Secretary of the Treasury of any intention to authorize enrolled agents to engage in activities which might constitute the unauthorized practice of law in the particular state in which they took place. In effect, the court held that the scope of practice authorized by the regulations was, by the terms of the regulations themselves, limited by the state law of unauthorized practice of law of the various states in which representation of clients before the Treasury Department was carried on by enrolled agents.

On the other hand, more recently the Supreme Court of Georgia upheld the claim of an enrolled agent for a fee for services consisting of the representation of his client before the Treasury Department on the ground that under the regulations of the Department he was authorized to practice there. *Irwin* v. *Young,* 90 S.E. 2d 22 (1955).

The Treasury Department's Interpretation of Circular 230 published January 30, 1956, makes it clear that in Circular 230 the Secretary intended to and did exercise fully his power to regulate the scope of practice before the Department.

The Secretary of the Treasury has now issued an interpretation of the rules and regulations relating to practice set forth in Circular 230 directed specifically to Section 10.2 of the circular.

The interpretation calls attention to the provisions of Section 10.2(b) which state that the scope of practice (of agents, as well as attorneys) before the Department comprehends "all matters connected with the presentation of a client's interest to the Treasury Department." The interpretation goes on to note that enrollees, "whether agents or attorneys," had been "satisfactorily fully representing clients before the Department for many years." The interpretation states that the Department believes this to have been beneficial to taxpayers and to the government and that "there presently appears no reason why the present scope and type of practice should not continue as it has in the past."

The interpretation then goes on to state that the attention of the Department has been called to "the decisions of certain state courts and to statements which suggest varying interpretations of §10.2(f) of the circular."

The interpretation summarizes the provisions of Section 10.2(f), including the second proviso of that section. It then goes on to state as follows:

> *The uniform interpretation and administration of this and other Sections of Circular 230 by the Department are essential to the proper discharge of the above responsibility imposed on it by the Congress.*
>
> *It is not the intention of the Department that this second proviso should be interpreted as an election by the Department not to exercise fully its responsibility to determine the proper scope of practice by enrolled agents and attorneys before the Department.*

This statement constitutes the clearest possible statement of the intention of the Secretary of the Treasury to pre-empt control over the determination of the scope of practice before the Department by enrolled agents—and by enrolled attorneys as well. Since the Secretary is the officer to whom Congress has delegated the power to regulate practice before the Department, his official statement as to the meaning of the regulations he has published is conclusive.

It follows that the Secretary, by the regulations governing practice contained in Circular 230, has pre-empted wholly the matter of determining the proper scope of practice before the Treasury Department by enrolled persons. This being so, it follows as a matter of constitutional law that no state has the power through its courts, or otherwise, to modify, limit or otherwise determine the proper scope of practice before the Treasury Department whether by enrolled agents or enrolled attorneys. Cft. *Selling* v. *Radford,* 243 U.S. 46 (1917), and authorities cited *supra.*

This does not mean that there are no limitations whatever upon the scope of practice by enrolled agents or by enrolled attorneys before the Treasury Department. It simply means that the scope of such practice is not subject to limitations imposed by state courts applying state unauthorized practice of law statutes or principles or, for that matter, state statutes prohibiting the practice of accounting by unlicensed persons.

The interpretation makes it clear that the Department contemplates that in certain situations enrolled agents and enrolled attorneys should obtain the assistance of a member of the other profession. At the present time the Department has not attempted to determine or define these situations. Instead, it has, as the interpretation notes, "properly placed" the responsibility for making this determination in any specific situation "on its enrolled agents and enrolled attorneys."

In this connection the interpretation draws attention to the provisions of Section 10.2(z) which require enrolled attorneys to "observe the canons of ethics of the American Bar Association and enrolled agents must observe the ethical standards of the accounting profession." Also, in this connection, the Department in the interpretation notes with gratification the extent to which the two professions over the years have made progress toward "mutual understanding of the proper sphere of each, as exemplified in the joint 'Statement of Principles Relating to Practice in the Field of Federal Taxation'" [reproduced in full below].

The interpretation closes on a somewhat admonitory note. The Department states that the question of Treasury practice will be kept under surveillance. If it is found at any time that the professional responsibilities of enrolled agents or enrolled attorneys are not being properly carried out or that enrolled agents and enrolled attorneys are not "respecting the appropriate fields of each" in accordance with the Statement of Principles then, the interpretation states, the matter can be reviewed to determine whether it is necessary to amend the provisions of the circular or "take other appropriate action."

The interpretation makes it clear that Circular 230 is not intended to affect practice by accountants or lawyers in any part of the tax field other than Treasury practice.

The interpretation makes it clear that the Department does not regard itself as having either the responsibility or the authority to regulate the professional activities of lawyers and accountants "beyond the scope of their practice before the Department as defined in Section 10.2(b)."

In short, Circular 230 and the recently published interpretation of the circular deal only with practice before the Treasury Department and not with any other aspect of Federal tax practice.

Yours truly,

Cahill, Gordon, Reindel & Ohl
By: Mathias F. Correa

February 23, 1956

STATEMENT OF PRINCIPLES RELATING TO PRACTICE IN THE FIELD OF FEDERAL INCOME TAXATION*

PROMULGATED BY THE NATIONAL CONFERENCE OF LAWYERS AND CERTIFIED PUBLIC ACCOUNTANTS

Preamble

In our present complex society, the average citizen conducting a business is confronted with a myriad of governmental laws and regulations which cover every phase of human endeavor and raise intricate and perplexing problems. These are further complicated by the tax incidents attendant upon all business transactions. As a result, citizens in increasing numbers have sought the professional services of lawyers and certified public accountants. Each of these groups is well qualified to serve the public in its respective field. The primary function of the lawyer is to advise the public with respect to the legal implications involved in such problems, whereas the certified public accountant has to do with the accounting aspects thereof. Frequently the legal and accounting phases are so interrelated and interdependent and overlapping that they are difficult to distinguish. Particularly is this true in the field of income taxation where questions of law and accounting have sometimes been inextricably intermingled. As a result, there has been some doubt as to where the functions of one profession end and those of the other begin.

For the guidance of members of each profession the National Conference of Lawyers and Certified Public Accountants recommends the following statement of principles relating to practice in the field of federal income taxation:

1. Collaboration of Lawyers and Certified Public Accountants Desirable. It is in the best public interest that services and assistance in federal income tax matters be rendered by lawyers and certified public accountants, who are trained in their fields by education and experience, and for whose admission to professional standing there are requirements as to education, citizenship, and high moral character. They are required to pass written examinations and are subject to rules of professional ethics, such as those of the American Bar Association and American Institute of Accountants, which set a high standard of professional practice and conduct, including prohibition of advertising and solicitation. Many problems connected with business require the skills of both lawyers and certified public accountants and there is every reason for a close and friendly cooperation between the two professions. Lawyers should encourage their clients to seek the advice of certified public accountants when-

* Ibid.

ever accounting problems arise and certified public accountants should encourage clients to seek the advice of lawyers whenever legal questions are presented.

2. Preparation of Federal Income Tax Returns. It is a proper function of a lawyer or a certified public accountant to prepare federal income tax returns.

When a lawyer prepares a return in which questions of accounting arise, he should advise the taxpayer to enlist the assistance of a certified public accountant.

When a certified public accountant prepares a return in which questions of law arise, he should advise the taxpayer to enlist the assistance of a lawyer.

3. Ascertainment of Probable Tax Effects of Transactions. In the course of the practice of law and in the course of the practice of accounting, lawyers and certified public accountants are often asked about the probable tax effects of transactions.

The ascertainment of probable tax effects of transactions frequently is within the function of either a certified public accountant or a lawyer. However, in many instances, problems arise which require the attention of a member of one or the other profession, or members of both. When such ascertainment raises uncertainties as to the interpretation of law (both tax law and general law), or uncertainties as to the application of law to the transaction involved, the certified public accountant should advise the taxpayer to enlist the services of a lawyer. When such ascertainment involves difficult questions of classifying and summarizing the transaction in a significant manner and in terms of money, or interpreting the financial results thereof, the lawyer should advise the taxpayer to enlist the services of a certified public accountant.

In many cases, therefore, the public will be best served by utilizing the joint skills of both professions.

4. Preparation of Legal and Accounting Documents. Only a lawyer may prepare legal documents such as agreements, conveyances, trust instruments, wills, or corporate minutes, or give advice as to the legal sufficiency or effect thereof, or take the necessary steps to create, amend, or dissolve a partnership, corporation, trust, or other legal entity.

Only an accountant may properly advise as to the preparation of financial statements included in reports or submitted with tax returns, or as to accounting methods and procedures.

5. Prohibited Self-Designations. An accountant should not describe himself as a "tax consultant" or "tax expert" or use any similar phrase. Lawyers, similarly, are prohibited by the canons of ethics of the American Bar Association and the opinions relating thereto, from advertising a special branch of law practice.

6. Representation of Taxpayers Before Treasury Department. Under Treasury Department regulations lawyers and certified public accountants are authorized, upon a showing of their professional status, and subject to certain limitations as defined in the Treasury rules, to represent taxpayers in proceedings before that Department. If, in the course of such proceedings, questions arise involving the application of legal principles, a lawyer should be retained, and if, in the course of such proceedings accounting questions arise, a certified public accountant should be retained.

7. Practice Before the Tax Court of the United States. Under the Tax Court rules nonlawyers may be admitted to practice.

However, since upon issuance of a formal notice of deficiency by the Commissioner of Internal Revenue a choice of legal remedies is afforded the taxpayer under existing law (either before the Tax Court of the United States, a United States District Court, or the Court of Claims), it is in the best interests of the taxpayer that the advice of a lawyer be sought if further proceedings are contemplated. It is not intended hereby to foreclose the right of nonlawyers to practice before the Tax Court of the United States pursuant to its rules.

Here also, as in proceedings before the Treasury Department, the taxpayer, in many cases, is best served by the combined skills of both lawyers and certified public accountants, and the taxpayers, in such cases, should be advised accordingly.

8. Claims for Refund. Claims for refund may be prepared by lawyers or certified public accountants, provided, however, that where a controversial legal issue is involved or where the claim is to be made the basis of litigation, the services of a lawyer should be obtained.

9. Criminal Tax Investigations. When a certified public accountant learns that his client is being specially investigated for possible criminal violation of the Income Tax Law, he should advise his client to seek the advice of a lawyer as to his legal and constitutional rights.

Conclusion

This statement of principles should be regarded as tentative and subject to revision and amplification in the light of future experience. The principal purpose is to indicate the importance of voluntary cooperation between our professions, whose members should use their knowledge and skills to the best advantage of the public. It is recommended that joint committees representing the local societies of both professions be established. Such committees might well take permanent form as local conferences of lawyers and certified public accountants patterned after this conference, or could take the form of special committees to handle a specific situation.

EDITORIAL — THE AGRAN CASE IN PERSPECTIVE*

The American Institute of Accountants and the California Society of Certified Public Accountants have decided to drop the *Agran* case. Since this case has become something of a *cause celebre,* an explanation of the circumstances seems in order.

Agran, a certified public accountant, enrolled to practice before the Treasury Department, sued a client, Shapiro, for a fee for services rendered, including settlement of tax liability with an Internal Revenue agent. He won the suit in Municipal Court and was awarded the full amount of the fee claimed.

On appeal, the Appellate Department, Superior Court of Los Angeles County, California, held that Agran's work in part constituted the unauthorized practice of law, and remanded the case to the lower court for decision as to how much fee he was entitled to for that part of his work which was not considered the practice of law (JofA, Aug. 54, p. 219). A representative of the unauthorized practice committee of the California State Bar had appeared against the certified public accountant before the Appellate Court.

This case followed on the heels of the *Bercu* case in New York, the *Conway* case in Minnesota, and others of less importance in other states, in which unauthorized practice committees of local bar associations had charged that various activities of accountants in the field of tax practice constituted unauthorized practice of law.

But the *Agran* case was the first in which a CPA who held a Treasury card had been attacked apparently for doing only what the Treasury authorized him to do. The accounting profession felt that a pattern of judge-made law was developing which might curtail drastically the extent to which certified public accountants could assist taxpayers. The implications of the *Agran* decision seemed so ominous that the Council of the American Institute of Accountants resolved to ask the Treasury Department to clarify the right of enrolled certified public accountants to represent their clients before the Department; to support legislation in Congress that would have the same effect; and to support retrial of the *Agran* case, so that it might be appealed to the United States Supreme Court if necessary. It was recognized that if the Treasury Department clarified the position of CPAs, the other steps might not be necessary.

These efforts of the Institute attracted public attention. Many leaders of the organized bar, in the belief that a quarrel between the two professions should be avoided if possible, made public statements indicating a much more sympathetic attitude than official bar spokesmen had theretofore evinced.

* From *The Journal of Accountancy,* December, 1956, pp. 29–31. Reprinted by permission of the American Institute of Certified Public Accountants.

These statements gave hope that the organized bar would not seek radical changes in the customary scope of tax practice by certified public accountants. See, for example, the comments of Dean Erwin N. Griswold, which appeared in *The Journal* (JofA, Apr.55, p. 33, and Dec.55, p. 29). Co-operative committees of the American Bar Association and the American Institute of Accountants were re-established, and after a number of meetings found themselves generally in agreement on the fundamental issues.

On January 30, 1956, the Secretary of the Treasury issued an interpretation of the regulations governing practice before the Treasury Department (JofA, Mar.56, p. 6). Lawyers have differed as to the precise extent of the legal protection this interpretation provides to certified public accountants in representing clients before the Department, but it seems clear to the Institute that the Treasury Department desires CPAs to continue to practice before it as they have done in the past, and the American Bar Association has not challenged this position.

In the light of the improved relations with the organized bar, and the Treasury interpretation of its regulations, the Council of the American Institute of Accountants at its April 1956 meeting decided that there was no necessity to participate further in the *Agran* case, which in the meantime had been retried, with a decision adverse to the CPA plaintiff (JofA, July55, p. 72).

The California Society of Certified Public Accountants, however, in response to the desire of many of its members and on the advice of its counsel that the status of CPAs in Los Angeles County should be clarified, decided to support an appeal from the decision on retrial. The final decision of the Appellate Department of the Superior Court of Los Angeles County was handed down September 20, 1956 (JofA, Nov.56, p. 75). It was again adverse to the CPA plaintiff.

However, this latest decision is far from clear. It appears that the Court may have been under some misconception as to the scope of the practice involved in the case before it. The first and second decisions of the Superior Court are not consistent, although the second decision expressly affirms the first. The criteria of what constituted the unauthorized practice of law, as suggested in the series of decisions, are so vague and indefinite as to be almost impossible of application to another set of facts.

The latest decision makes no reference to the interpretation of Circular 230 issued by the Secretary of the Treasury. Instead the California Court seems to take the position that the Treasury Department may not confer upon persons who are not members of the bar authority to perform services within a state which under its laws constitute the practice of law in violation of that state's laws. This appears to create a direct conflict between federal and state powers, which the weight of authority suggests would be resolved in favor of the federal government.

However, due to the peculiar structure of the California judicial system, this case cannot be appealed to the Supreme Court of California. The only appeal available is to the Supreme Court of the United States, and there is reason for serious doubt that the United States Supreme Court would undertake to review such a case, originating in a fee suit, from a court of inferior jurisdiction.

Additional doubt arises from the fact that the case was tried and the record created before the Treasury interpretation was issued. While the interpretation was brought to the attention of the Superior Court of Los Angeles County at the last minute, in conjunction with the final appeal, the fact that the Court's decision made no reference to the interpretation may suggest that the Court considered it not applicable retroactively to the transactions in litigation.

Again, the essential issues may be obscured by the testimony of the CPA in the original suit for his fee, to the effect that he had dealt with a "question of law" and had spent a good deal of time in a "law library," which clearly influenced the Superior Court's view of the case.

Altogether this case seems to fall short of a fully satisfactory basis on which to ask the highest court of the land to rule on the position of certified public accountants in Treasury practice.

If it were immediately necessary to seek such a ruling, there would be no choice but to proceed. However, since the suit was a fee suit, and no one has been enjoined from doing anything, the decision, in the opinion of outstanding lawyers, does not prevent anyone in Los Angeles or elsewhere from continuing to practice before the Treasury Department if the Treasury authorizes him to do so. The decision deals with the facts of the case before it, and, according to high legal authority, does not in any broad sense create new law.

The net effect appears to be that while the decision is an unpleasant and annoying one, it does not prevent CPAs of Los Angeles from continuing their customary tax practice without legal jeopardy or moral stigma. If in another case an effort is made to restrict such practice the issue may have to be litigated again, perhaps under circumstances more favorable to certified public accountants. Meanwhile, counsel advises that the *Agran* decision is not a serious precedent in other states, and in the improving climate of relations between the legal and accounting professions it seems not nearly so likely to be used against CPAs as it appeared to be two years ago. In any event, there seems to be nothing to lose by waiting and giving the favorable trends an opportunity to gain momentum.

It was with these considerations in mind that the executive committee of the American Institute on October 31st, and the board of directors of the California Society of Certified Public Accountants on November 5th, decided not to make any effort to have the *Agran* decision reviewed by the United States Supreme

Court. This by no means signifies acquiescence in the decision. Rather it suggests that in the light of current developments the decision is no longer regarded as of major significance.

If CPAs in Los Angeles or elsewhere were prevented by local authorities from continuing to do what the United States Treasury Department authorized them to do, the Institute and the California Society would certainly do everything in their power to have the conflict of authority resolved—in the interests of taxpayers and the government as well as of certified public accountants themselves.

However, in the long run, lawyers and certified public accountants can and must learn to live together in tax practice without stepping on each other's toes. This happy day will come sooner if litigation and other public conflict can be avoided. We earnestly hope that the two professions in California and all other states can resolve any future differences in the same spirit of mutual respect and tolerance, and with the same concern for the public interest, which characterizes the current relations of the American Bar Association and the American Institute of Accountants.

The tax practice problem has not been completely solved. Raby presents evidence of this fact in the following paper. Suggestions for operating an ethical tax practice by an audit firm are presented.

ETHICS IN TAX PRACTICE
William L. Raby*

Let us start out by exploring two frequently expressed points of view towards the ethical problems of tax practice. First, there is the point of view which says that there are no problems of ethics in tax practice which cannot be solved by application of standards of personal ethical conduct. The second point of view is that the problems of ethics in tax practice can be solved entirely within the framework of professional ethics as developed by the CPA profession in connection with its auditing activities.

* From *The Accounting Review,* Vol. XLI, No. 4 (October, 1966), pp. 714–720. Reprinted by permission of the American Accounting Association.

PERSONAL ETHICS

When we talk about personal ethics, we are talking about the individual's system of values, his moral code. To a great extent, one's individual moral code is shaped by what he conceives to be expected of him. The CPA may perceive that his wife, his children, his partners, and his business associates measure his success by the amount of money and time that he lavishes on them and on the things that they observe (e.g., house, car, travel, etc.). Most of the correspondence he gets from his professional societies either pleads for his time or his money, or a combination of the two. These requests for his time and money are all for worthy purposes, including his own professional self-development; but nevertheless it is time and money that he is apt to feel is constantly demanded of him.

To many such a CPA, then, personal ethics will simply be that approach to things which produces the most successful pecuniary results. If "due diligence" in preparing returns proves profitable, then "due diligence" he will use. If hiring part-time workers during tax season, preparing returns on an assembly-line basis with no adequate review of the basic data, and handling tax problems superficially appears most profitable, then that may well be the course followed. Whatever will, or will appear, to produce optimum results in terms of time and money will be the route taken.

There are many forces that intrude to shape codes of personal conduct away from the "expectations of others" pattern. Some of these are religious, some philosophical, some the result of overwhelming influences on a person during his developmental years. The individual may well perceive that the kind of personality he has depends upon the "moral-decision diet" that he feeds himself. He may see, for instance, that living solely within a value framework built upon the expectations of others seriously cripples his freedom. He may realize that given a set of values and a certain amount of information in a situation calling for a decision, the general nature of that decision has been pretty well predetermined. Increasing his knowledge about the problem increases his freedom of choice. "The truth shall set you free." But for some types of problems, there is little he can do to increase his knowledge. And even where he can increase his knowledge, there are limits to what he can know and to how sure he can be of what he knows. Building a value system that is his own, and not one foisted upon him by the expectations of others, is his ultimate freedom, however.

The intensely personal nature of value systems means that an *act* cannot be judged "good" or "bad" by virtue of *what* it is. It could only be judged if we knew the intentions of the person involved, the knowledge possessed by the person, the problem that he thought he faced, the value system out of which his action flowed. Thus, we will find that at the most personal ethics can handle only a limited and general area of tax ethic problems. This will be clearer if we examine the environment of tax practice.

TAX PRACTICE ENVIRONMENT

Some 67,000,000 individual, corporation, estate, and gift tax returns were filed in the fiscal year ending in 1964. A total of 3.6 million of these returns were examined, and an average of $704 in additional tax and penalties was recommended per examined return. Statistics are not readily at hand on the number of cases taken to what was then the Informal Conference and is now the District Conference, although the figure is probably in the neighborhood of 150,-000. Some 21,000 cases could not be resolved at the agent or Informal Conference (now District Conference) level, and were protested to the Appellate Division (the highest appeal level within the Treasury Department). More than two thirds of the pre-docketed cases disposed of by the Appellate Division resulted in agreements with the taxpayer. The revenue agent's report originally proposed $415,000,000 of tax deficiency in these cases settled by agreement, while the Appellate Division actually settled the cases for $141,000,000, or 34% of the amounts originally proposed. During the same year, the Appellate Division disposed by stipulation of over 5,000 cases which had been docketed with the Tax Court. The tax deficiencies involved in these cases amounted to $387,000,000, and were settled for $95,000,000, or about 25% of the deficiency originally proposed. Of the 867 cases that were actually decided on their merits by the Tax Court, taxpayers wound up having to pay 52%, or $25,-000,000 out of $48,000,000 in deficiencies originally proposed. In the same year, in the Court of Claims the taxpayer won part or all of what he was contending for in 21 out of 36 tax cases, a 58% record; while in the District Courts the taxpayer won part or all of what he was contending for in 225 out of 452 tax cases, a batting average of slightly under 50%. On the other hand, the average in the Courts of Appeals was very much in favor of the government, with 67% of the appeals taken from Tax Court decisions being favorable to the government. Sixty-three per cent of the appeals taken from District Court decisions were decided favorably for the government.

The tax practitioner faces a dilemma as the result of this lack of certainty as to the actual tax liability of a given taxpayer. The complexity of the law requires that he research most problems with painstaking care. The economics of tax practice are such that it is impossible for him to get most clients to pay reasonable fees for this ultimate degree of service. The relatively small number of returns audited (about 5%) inspires some degree of chance taking, where some tax practitioners will resolve the question the way the client wants it, since the return probably won't be audited anyway. On the other hand, pride in his own reputation, and a feeling that he is to function as independently in the tax area as he does in the audit area, may stimulate an overly conservative attitude which will result in the practitioner's resolving most doubts against his client.

It seems obvious that an attitude of independence is inappropriate in tax matters, inasmuch as clients may often be better served by adopting the position which is most favorable to them. Our present environment of tax practice is one in which it is the norm to have deficiencies when returns are audited and to have compromises when deficiencies are protested. However, the route of solution to the ethical dilemma that this poses is one already familiar to the CPA. It lies in full disclosure. It is thus that we resolve similar problems in audit situations, disclosing the relevant facts so that the reader of the financial statements will not be misled. A direct analogy with the audit situation would indicate disclosure of all relevant facts to the government; but the tax practice situation, as we shall discuss in a moment, is one of advocacy rather than of independence. The practitioner's requirement is, thus, full disclosure to the client.

THE BASIC ETHICAL REQUIREMENT

Both the taxpayer and the tax-return preparer take responsibility for the return and for the positions subsequently taken in controversy. As the expert, the tax practitioner must indicate to the client the relevant alternative tax treatments and the possible results if they are adopted. But the taxpayer must be allowed to make the final decisions. The practitioner has no moral right to substitute his own scale of values for the client's scale of values. If the client reaches a decision based on reasonable knowledge of the probable effects of the alternatives he could adopt, the decision he has reached is rational and the tax practitioner has fulfilled his function as an expert. If the practitioner finds that the client's decision is personally unsatisfactory to him, his recourse is to cease representing that client. Not only is this the ethically proper course of action, but it should improve the relationship between the client and the practitioner, since the client will not feel that assessment of a deficiency is the result of an error of judgment on the part of the practitioner.

PROFESSIONAL ETHICS

What we have said so far deals essentially with personal ethics. But personal ethics alone are not sufficient in the area of tax practice. Society as a whole has conferred upon CPAs the right to engage in tax practice. It has done this through giving them the right to use the title of CPA, and more recently through Congressional action recognizing their right to practice before the Treasury Department. Such privileges as are conferred upon CPAs are not conferred in order to provide them with a monopoly position in tax practice; they are conferred because it is felt that they promote the public interest. In the same fashion, the rules of professional conduct are justified only so long as they are in the best interest of the public that is being served. The economic self-interest of the members of the profession is not alone a valid basis for rules of professional ethics, although it should also be recognized that an economically weak profession cannot serve the public well.

AUDIT ETHICS

At the other end of the spectrum from the approach of personal ethics, we have the approach that there are no problems peculiar to tax practice, but that the ethical standards devised to govern our audit practice should apply to tax work as well. The simple answer to this is that in the audit situation we are acting as independent auditors, with our primary point of reference being a fair presentation for the benefit of third parties. In the tax situation, we are acting as advocates of the client's interest in his relationship with the Federal government. That we are acting as advocates does not condone a lower standard of behavior, but rather indicates a *different point of view.* In acting as an independent auditor, our position is normally one of conservatism, and we frequently tend to resolve doubts against the client. As an advocate of our client's interest, our responsibility in tax practice is to put our client's best foot forward, with candor and with fairness.

How we exercise that responsibility must be left somewhat to the judgment of the individual practitioner, within the general framework of prevailing practices. It is to be expected that the American Institute of CPAs, through the Committee on Federal Taxation's program on statements of responsibilities in tax practice, will increasingly clarify the responsibility of the CPA in tax practice. Such clarification will undoubtedly enlarge the legal liability of the practitioner for his actions, since standards will then exist to which he can be held accountable. We can expect that the rules that will be propounded in the future, like the existing rules incorporated in the Opinions of the Committee on Professional Ethics and in the Treasury Department's Circular 230, will fall into one of three categories: (1) Behavior that is personally unethical and which is universally frowned upon [e.g., knowingly suggesting an illegal tax evasion plan]; (2) Behavior that is not personally unethical, but is deemed to be professionally unethical because it is not in the public interest [e.g., solicitation of clients, which is against the public interest because it undermines the professional independence a tax practitioner needs and instead puts the practitioner into the subservient role of a supplicant who will be tempted to substitute the client's conscience for his own professional conscience]; and, (3) Behavior that is not personally unethical nor itself clearly against the public interest, but which is deemed professionally unethical because its potential abuses would not be in the public interest [e.g., representing before the Treasury Department on a wholly contingent fee basis, clients who are able to pay, which would not violate the AICPA rules, but which would violate Circular 230].

It should thus be apparent that we operate under several different sets of rules. These are basically:

1 Rules of conduct, promulgated by State Boards of Accountancy;

2 The rules of Treasury Department Circular 230; and

3 The rules of state CPA societies and of the American Institute.

Since state boards and state societies vary, but tend to follow the American Institute of CPAs, we really have two sets of rules with which to concern ourselves. And since Circular 230, in effect, incorporates the standards of the accounting profession and thus, presumptively, the Institute rules, we can say that the Institute rules provide the basic fabric, with Circular 230 simply providing additional restrictions in some areas. The major AICPA pronouncements are found in the numbered opinions of the Committee on Professional Ethics:

1 Tax booklets cannot be imprinted with the CPA's name when prepared by others.

2 A bank or trade association cannot be utilized, even on an unpaid basis, to "drum up" tax business.

3 Tax files cannot be transferred to the purchaser of a practice, without first obtaining client permission.

4 Writing tax articles and books is encouraged, but promotion must be in good taste.

5 Self-designations (e.g., "tax consultant," "tax specialist") are prohibited.

6 Fees cannot be shared with persons not engaged in public accounting.

9 Distribution of firm tax publications is limited to staff members, clients, lawyers of clients, bankers, and "others with whom professional contacts are maintained."

10 Neither stationery nor business cards nor directory listings may indicate any tax specialization. Help wanted ads should not imply that specialized services are rendered.

12 Tax practice does not impair audit independence "so long as (the CPA) does not make management decisions or take positions which might impair that objectivity."

13 A tax return is not a financial statement that requires either an opinion or a disclaimer. Further, the CPA may "resolve doubts in favor of his client as long as there is reasonable support for his position."

If one wants to deal with the "spirit" of professional ethics as though it represented a "pure" or pristine guide to conduct, then the message of these opinions would be that anything which called attention to the practitioner or distinguished him from his fellow practitioners would be unethical conduct. In its pure form, this is exemplified by the position of the bar that an attorney cannot, on his letterhead or business card, indicate the degrees he possesses, whether they are law degrees (LL.B., J.D., LL.M., J.S.D., etc.) or other degrees (B.A., M.B.A., Ph.D., C.P.A., etc). The Institute has not yet gone this far.

But the rules of professional ethics are more like tax legislation than like moral imperatives. Congress does not say in Sec. 341 that corporations cannot be used to transmute what would otherwise be ordinary income into capital gain. Rather it defines, albeit with some ambiguity (e.g., "realized a substantial part of the income to be derived"), when you can perform this alchemy. Similarly, our rules do not prevent all action that distinguishes one practitioner from another. I cannot take out a newspaper ad saying that I am a tax expert, but I can write a tax column for my local newspaper. I cannot accost people and solicit their business, but I can join a Kiwanis Club where I will meet and get acquainted with prospective clients. I cannot ask my clients to solicit business for me, but I can hope that I so persuade them of the value of my services that they will urge their friends to see me when they have problems.

We do not say that all contingent fees are improper, but only certain types. We do not say that referral fees cannot be paid, but only that they cannot be paid to the laity. We do not even prohibit partnerships with non-CPAs, although the partnership renders services of a type normally rendered by CPAs.

Rules of conduct for CPAs are evolving toward barring any action distinguishing one from another. The areas not yet blotted out are mainly those in which it is deemed that either or both the public interests or the interests of the profession as a whole are served by the conduct involved. Thus, the publication of articles serves to educate the public and help build the image of the profession. These justify the incidental benefits, if any, to the individual author. In a sense, the mention of his name is compensation for his public service and his service to his professional brethren.

It is likely that in the years to come, there will be a great deal of crystaliza-tion of rules of conduct in the area of professional ethics. There is a danger that in formulating such rules we will deal with specific problems in a specific way, and not formulate broad rules of general application. The problems that we face are far from simple, and the formulation of broad rules of general ap-plication would frequently challenge the wisdom of a Solomon; yet the attempt must be made. Without trying to propound answers let me pose some common situations to illustrate the complexity to which I refer.

Example 1   "This is a debatable item," says Mr. Conservative CPA. "There is a good chance that if I file the return and claim this as a deduction, it will go through all right. There is a slight chance that it will not go through and my client will get involved in a controversy. Even if we win the controversy, he will still feel that the whole problem was due to my negligence and be reluctant to pay a fee for the tax controversy." Whereupon Mr. Conservative CPA con-cludes that it is better to decide the doubt against the client, and then prepare and file a refund claim. "A successful refund claim brings money to the client, and he then doesn't mind paying the fee!"

From our previous discussion about personal ethics, we might conclude that Mr. Conservative CPA is violating a fundamental tenet of ethical tax practice — that of letting the client make the decision. He is substituting his value sys-tem for that of his client. He is generating more income for himself and more expense for his clients, because the chances of a refund claim being audited by IRS are substantially greater than that of a return being audited. Yet he has violated no rule of professional ethics. In fact, there are many persons involved in tax work (especially on the academic side) who might well feel that his action is, on the whole, more in the public interest than would be the opposite policy of resolving all doubts in favor of the taxpayer.

Example 2   "IRS is making a tax audit of the X Corporation," Mr. CPA tells a staff man. "We don't make an audit of X, so you'd better check their minute book and see that everything is properly authorized. Agents seem to be getting into minutes more than they used to." Now what is Mr. CPA to do when the re-port comes back that no minutes have been written for the past three years? First of all, we can state as dicta that he is not going to create any minutes himself. This would violate the 1951 Statement of the National Conference of Lawyers and CPAs, if for no other reason. Let's say that he first discusses the situation with the client.

"Can we make up some back-dated minutes?" asks the client. Mr. CPA explains that all minutes are literally backdated, in the sense that they are written up after the meeting took place. He also points out to the client that some sort of authorization of salaries, leases, etc. must have taken place, albeit somewhat informally. This type of thing, he tells the client, is essentially a legal matter. He furnishes the client with a list of the transactions for which proper corporate authorization would be desirable, and sends him trotting off to see the lawyer. When the agent comes in to conduct his examination, the corporate minutes are all neatly up to date.

The courts have frequently recognized that in a small corporation the same degree of formality is not to be expected as in the large. IRS now recognizes that a plan under Section 337 can be adopted without the formality of a meeting. Yet the CPA is also aware that the minutes that are now in the minute book were not there previously, and that he was at least partially instrumental in bringing them into existence. Could he do less than he did and still be adequately serving his client? Yet is what he did just skirting the borderline of creating evidence to fit the need of the moment? Perhaps the ultimate answer is that even though no audit is made, "due diligence" still requires annual review of the existence and adequacy of corporate minutes.

Example 3   Mr. Able and Mr. Baker are equal partners in a chain of novelty stores. Mr. CPA suggests to them, at a tax planning conference, that they need to incorporate and that perhaps each separate store should be a separate corporation. After a great deal of discussion, all agree that the tax consequences are much to be desired and that the nature of the store operations makes it feasible for each store to function as a separate corporation.

"Now," Mr. CPA says, "let's think up the good business reasons that will justify having each one of these stores as a separate corporation!"

Is such a question improper? Unethical?

A discussion then develops of what non-tax advantages separate corporations might have. Each store has a manager, and the profitability of the store is largely the result of his ability. Some managers have indicated that they would like an ownership interest and/or profit-sharing bonus. It is concluded that the managers should be given stock options, and that all employees of each store (excluding part-time workers and those with less than five years of service) should participate in a tax-qualified pension plan. Emphasis is also laid on the compartmentalization of liability on long-term leases resulting from separate corporations, as well as the relative ease of selling off individual units when they are separate corporations.

When the decision is finally reached, who is to say that *the* major purpose

(IRC 269) was the obtaining of tax benefits? Many a man who has been first attracted to a girl by her personal appeal marries her for such a complex of reasons that the original attracting reason may well be almost minor in the scales in which the final decision is weighed.

CONCLUSION

The fundamental ethical rule in tax practice at the level of personal ethics is that the tax practitioner must allow the client to make the final decisions. The practitioner has no right to substitute his scale of values for that of the client.

Beyond that, the practitioner must recognize a positive responsibility not to provide false or misleading information to the government. This responsibility is imposed on him by Circular 230 and by the Code of Professional Ethics of the AICPA.

But within the framework of the Code and the Circular, it seems clear that the practitioner is concerned with protecting and advancing the interests of his client and not that of the Internal Revenue Service. If the client has a right (e.g., to take an advantage in an open year when the government's offsetting adjustment is barred because of a closed year and IRC 1311 does not apply), then the practitioner would be derelict in not advising him as to that right and assisting him in asserting it. If this attitude of advocacy rather than of independence creates a situation in which both tax advocacy and audit independence are incompatible, then the practitioner owes a duty to the client to recommend that he either obtain a new tax advisor or a new independent auditor. The public expects advocacy from the CPA in tax matters; no rule of professional conduct requires otherwise; and it would appear unethical to not offer the client a service primarily geared to protecting his interests.

Apply the Code of Professional Ethics of the AICPA to the following questions and, at the same time, judge the merits of Raby's suggestions for an ethical CPA tax practice.

Apply the Code of Professional Ethics of the AICPA to the questions on the following page and, at the same time, judge the merits of Raby's suggestions for an ethical CPA tax practice.

THE CPA's RESPONSIBILITY FOR FEDERAL INCOME TAX RETURNS

 Federal income tax returns provide for the signature of the individual or firm preparing the tax return.

Required

Discuss whether a CPA is required to sign the tax return in each of the following independent situations:

1 The tax return was prepared by the CPA without compensation.

2 The tax return was prepared by the CPA who had rendered an adverse opinion in his auditor's report on the taxpayer's financial statements.

3 The tax return was prepared by the taxpayer's chief accountant who later submitted the return to the CPA for his recommendations. The CPA recommended substantial changes which were adopted.

(AICPA)

CHAPTER 13

MANAGEMENT SERVICES: ETHICS AND RESPONSIBILITIES

The controversy that has surrounded the offering of consulting services by CPAs has centered around the compatibility of these services with auditing. The "CPA Invasion" documents the scope of management services and the central feature of the issue: independence.

CPA INVASION
Ed Cony*

When Lockheed Aircraft Corp. set out to slash costs in its white collar departments, it called in an outside consultant. With this aid, new work standards were set up for office employes and a more efficient flow of paperwork assignments was achieved. Result: $3 million was saved in the first year under the program.

Similarly, Pittsburgh & West Virginia Railway turned to outside help in launching a general company-wide cost cutting program which is expected to pare expenses $1,038,000 this year.

In neither case were conventional management consulting firms employed. Lockheed called on Arthur Young & Co., its regular accounting firm. And Pittsburgh & West Virginia also used the firm that audits its books, Price Waterhouse & Co.

HELP PLAN PRODUCTS

Much to the distress of management consultants, an increasing volume of consulting work of all sorts is now flowing to the accountants. Some of this advice-giving is far removed from matters directly related to the corporate balance sheet. Accounting firms now stand ready to help their clients plan the layout of a new factory, develop new products and work out marketing programs. In some cases, they may even sit in on labor negotiations.

Ernst & Ernst has "over 250" staff men in its "management services" divi-

* From *The Wall Street Journal*, Vol. 1, CLVIII, No. 84 (October 30, 1961), p. 1. Reprinted by permission of *The Wall Street Journal*.

sion, which on a manpower basis puts it on a par with all except the very largest conventional management consulting firms. In 1952 Peat, Marwick, Mitchell & Co. had a dozen people in its then new "management controls" department; today it has 200 professional people in this department. Arthur Young & Co.'s consulting staff has spiraled from about 12 in 1954 to "well over 100" today, according to an official of the firm. A fourth member of the "Big Eight," as the largest CPA firms are called, says income from its management consulting department has "grown tenfold in a matter of eight years."

"The future of management consulting belongs to the accounting firms because of our continuing, close, confidential relationship with our clients," declared Kenneth S. Axelson, a Peat, Marwick, Mitchell partner who heads his firm's management consulting department.

NO CORPORATE SECRETS

He explains: "We know things about a company that perhaps only one or two company executives know. There can't be any secrets from us—or we won't sign the financial statement."

Mr. Axelson's confident prediction of the eventual dominance of accountants in the consulting field, of course, would be hotly disputed by many management consultants. In similar fashion, a "boundary dispute" has been simmering for years between lawyers and accountants over the giving of tax advice.

A few of the older partners of accounting firms, it must be said, also look askance at a good deal of the non-accounting consultant work being conducted by members of their profession. In their view, much work raises some rather delicate ethical questions about the propriety of an accounting firm wearing two hats: As a supposedly independent auditor or reviewer of a company management's financial practices while at the same time becoming closely involved with the same management by advising it how to run the business.

Nevertheless, there seems little likelihood of the accounting firms pulling out of the lucrative consulting business. In fact, the buildup of their staffs to include marketing and production specialists, psychologists for personnel work and others with skills outside of accounting points to greater consulting activity as time goes on. Some of the old-line auditing firms are even taking on executive recruiters to find top management talent for their clients.

CPA firms are chary about giving the precise amount of business they now derive from consulting, but one partner in a Big Eight firm makes this "educated guess": "Among the Big Eight, management consulting now accounts for from 4% to 30% of the firms' total revenues."

TAKING A PLUNGE

Smaller CPA firms are taking the plunge too. One medium-sized firm is now said to get over 50% of its revenues from management consulting. "Right here in New York we have some small CPA firms which won't take any audit work at all now," says Robert Ettlinger of the American Institute of Certified Public Accountants. These firms—usually one, two, or three man operations—normally specialize "in one or two areas of management services such as electronic data processing," he explains.

The Institute employs Mr. Ettlinger, a former controller of the Papermate Division of Gillette Co., to stimulate smaller CPA firms to get into, as Mr. Ettlinger phrases it, "this hifalutin field of management advisory services."

A few examples of work being done by accounting firms suggests the broad scope of their "management services" work.

Lybrand, Ross Brothers & Montgomery is deep into operations research, a system which borrows from the disciplines of many sciences, including physics and higher mathematics, to solve management problems. One client is confronted with this situation: It has a multiple product line of more than 200 products, manufactured in 12 plants and eventually shipped to about 200 warehouses. Each plant has different costs for each product and each factory can produce a variety of products. Currently, Lybrand is trying to minimize the cost of producing and transporting every one of the 200-odd products, by using operations research.

Says Felix Kaufman of the accounting firm's management consulting services: "The range of possibilities in allocating production and distribution is in the range of one million. We think we've conjured up a technique, using computers, which will give us the answers." Mr. Kaufman says costs could be cut "by millions of dollars" as a result of the current study.

The computer field is a rich one for accountants giving advice to companies. Peat, Marwick, Mitchell is currently working with a client to help him use his computer to forecast sales much more accurately than he could in the past. "Already—and we aren't nearly through yet—the company thinks it can reduce its inventory by as much as 75%," says an official of Peat, Marwick.

Price Waterhouse recently worked closely with a client's own personnel to "revitalize the company's financial department," says Arthur Toan, senior partner in charge of Price Waterhouse's management advisory services department. He describes the results: "The company replaced people, changed the organization of the department, came up with a whole new approach to providing financial information to top executives. They're getting fewer figures, more highlights. They now report, for instance, the percentage of the market which the company enjoys." He adds that in the process the company has "made very substantial clerical savings—hundreds of thousands of dollars annually."

White-collar costs are a price target of accountants turned consultants. Establishing work standards for white-collar workers accounts for about 40% of Arthur Young's work in management services, says Ralph Lewis, who heads the department. For years manufacturers have had good performance standards in production lines, he says, "but typically we find the white-collar worker is working at 60% of capacity—mostly because of bad loading assignments from his immediate supervisory."

After Arthur Young helped Lockheed set up work standards for its white-collar workers, a Lockheed accounting official reported: "Many of our (clerical) organizations which were operating at between 60% and 70% (of capacity), today are operating close to or at 100%." Among others with whom Arthur Young has worked in this field are: Sinclair Oil Corp., Continental Baking Co. and Encyclopaedia Britannica, Inc.

Manufacturing costs occupy CPAs also. Fred Sengstacke, a partner of Scovell, Wellington & Co., tells of this case: "We had one client in a heavy industry who was very enthusiastic about sales of a new product. We went in and found that actually they were losing money on it, because they had incorrectly analyzed the costs involved. The last we heard, they'd pretty much decided to discontinue the product."

HEAD-HUNTING FOR EXECUTIVES

Analyzing costs is not a big departure from traditional accounting. But some new CPA activities are considered "far out." Arthur Young, for instance, now employs four full-time executive recruiters, or "head-hunters." Recently they found an administrative vice president for a top company, a position which commands $50,000 a year, plus stock options.

Ernst & Ernst does a variety of personnel work for clients. "Professional trained psychologists" on E&E's staff interview clients' employees, give them batteries of tests and make appraisals of the individuals which E&E says "are designed for constructive guidance in matching the man and his abilities with the requirements of a particular job."

Actually, CPAs insist they have been giving management advice, on a limited scale, for a good many years. Mr. Toan of Price Waterhouse says he has in his files a consulting job dated in 1898. "And you could lift out some of our recommendations and use them today," he adds.

Peat, Marwick, Mitchell did some consulting work at the birth of General

Electric "when several companies were put together," says Mr. Axelson. Scovell Wellington participated in a massive "systems and procedures" study for U.S. Steel in the 1930s, says Mr. Sengstacke. And Ralph Kent, managing partner of Arthur Young, says: "We've always had calls to help clients with budget services and accounting systems. The partner in charge of the audit used to handle such chores himself. But after World War II, we set up a separate department of experts in the management services field."

A POSTWAR PHENOMENON

Most accountants agree the spurt in their consulting work has been a post-World War II phenomenon. They cite a variety of reasons for the rapid growth and for their expectation it will continue. Since the war business has become more complex, more highly mechanized and more competitive, say the CPAs. All these factors have contributed to management's increasing interest in "how to run a business scientifically," says Mr. Ettlinger of the CPA institute.

One prominent member of a Big Eight firm says with candor: "After World War II, we saw management consultants putting in cost accounting, budgeting systems, even general accounting systems for our clients. We saw them collecting big fees on the order of $100,000 when perhaps our clients were paying us only $10,000 for auditing the books. Our partners were upset by this invasion of a field we regarded ourselves as particularly qualified in."

The CPA firms, while careful not to knock the ability or work of outside management consulting firms, are fond of talking about the high quality of the work CPA firms do. A typical comment: "The client knows we'll do as good a management consultant job as we can. With us, it's not a one-shot proposition. We'll be coming back next year for an audit exam. We have a continuing stake in the company."

But this is just the point that worries some of the older, more conservative audit partners. They fear that a management consultant job may turn sour and cause the client to turn over his auditing and accounting work to a rival CPA firm.

Another problem: "If an auditing partner has been auditing a firm 15 to 20 years, and we're going in to make an organizational study, some of the people he has come to know in the company may get hurt. So he worries about the good relations he's built up over the years," says a senior man in one accounting firm.

Some old-line partners also worry that the consulting business endangers the independence of the accounting firm. One man states this point of view as follows: "We are supposed to audit the books at arm's length, but aren't we auditing our own work in some cases a year or two after our consulting people have reorganized a department?"

Some management consultants believe the accounting firms may be stretching their available talents a bit thin when they venture far from "financial facts and figures work." Says one consultant: "One of the Big Eight CPA firms has done some pretty bad work in production planning and control. I know of several instances where companies had to call in a management consulting firm to undo the damage."

As the management services controversy has gained momentum, more parties have offered positions on it. At one point, the AICPA invited and published the following viewpoints: an outside observer, a financial statement user, and a CPA. No solution to the problem has yet been found; the matter stands substantially as it did at the time of the publication of the following set of positions.

COMPATIBILITY OF AUDITING AND MANAGEMENT SERVICES
Arthur A. Schulte, Jr. (I), Frank J. Hoenemeyer (II), and Malcolm M. Devore (III)*

I. THE VIEWPOINT OF AN OUTSIDE OBSERVER

Is the independence of a CPA as auditor jeopardized when he also performs management services for the same client? The question is really twofold, since the auditor not only must be independent in fact but also must appear independent in the eyes of others.

In presenting my view of this question, that of an outside observer, I will use Opinion No. 12 of the American Institute's committee on professional ethics as the main point of reference, since this seems to be the profession's most authoritative statement on the matter (see box on page 30 for the pertinent excerpt from the opinion).

In this opinion the committee states that, where independence in fact is concerned, there are potential conflicts of interest when a CPA performs both

* From *The Journal of Accountancy,* Vol. 124, No. 6 (December 1967), pp. 29–39. Reprinted by permission of The American Institute of Certified Public Accountants.

auditing and management services for the same client. For example, in acting as a consultant, he may make management decisions, or he may become in effect an employee of the client. In either case his independence as auditor would be impaired. But if the CPA avoids these situations, the committee can discern no likelihood of a conflict of interest.

Concerning the appearance of independence, the committee simply states, without offering any empirical evidence, that an auditor's rendering of management services does not suggest to a reasonable observer a conflict of interest. Thus, the committee does not see the performance of management services as a challenge to either the actual or the apparent independence of auditors.

Let us evaluate these two statements.

As to independence in fact, this is essentially a state of mind, having two equally important meanings. These are summarized by Messrs. Carey and Doherty as follows:

> It is most important not only that the CPA shall refuse consciously to subordinate his judgment to that of others, but also that he avoid relationships which would be likely to warp his judgment even subconsciously in reporting whether or not the financial statements he has audited are in his opinion fairly presented. Independence in this sense means avoidance of situations which would tend to impair objectivity or create personal bias which would influence delicate judgments.[1]

Now let us look at the CPA in his role of professional consultant. What professional relationships are established when he undertakes a consulting job?

First, the consultant participates in all of the steps in the decision process except the final choice. That is, he helps define the problem, gets facts, analyzes the consequences of alternative courses of action and makes recommendations. Then there is a choice. This alone is management's prerogative.

Second, the consultant's advice and services must be integral to the decision process to be considered truly professional. This is self-evident.

Third, the consultant becomes logically and emotionally involved with management in developing solutions to a problem.

Fourth, he is inherently an advocate. It is part of his job to persuade management to choose what he thinks is the best solution to the problem.

Fifth, the consultant puts his reputation on the line in any engagement.

Sixth, the CPA as consultant has a direct social responsibility to his client and an indirect social responsibility to third parties and to the public. This is entirely different from his responsibility as auditor.

[1] John L. Carey and William O. Doherty, *Ethical Standards of the Accounting Profession*, American Institute of Certified Public Accountants, New York City, 1966, p. 19.

The CPA's participation in the decision-making process in his role of consultant creates two potential sources of conflict with his independence as auditor.

On the one hand, management might surrender to the CPA its authority to choose among the alternative decisions. The CPA might accept this authority and make the decision by default. Maybe he is the only one with the expertise to make the decision. In such a case, he becomes a decision-maker and thereby forfeits his independence.

On the other hand, even if the manager does not surrender his authority to make the decision, the very involvement of the CPA in the decision process generates pressures which may lead to an impairment of his independence. These pressures include the degree of closeness between the CPA and the client which management consulting establishes, the amount of persuasion necessary to influence the client toward a particular course of action, and the financial stake the CPA inevitably has in the outcome of the decision.

There is another area of potential conflict. In a management consulting engagement the CPA may become an advocate for his client. He would naturally become patently partisan. Therefore, it might be difficult for him later to assume the quasi-judicial position of independent auditor.

It is clear then that management consulting may produce a potential conflict of interest with the CPA's factual independence. This danger is greater than is generally recognized. The AICPA committee on professional ethics mentions only the conflicts that would result if the CPA made management decisions or took an employee position. In limiting itself to these two readily identifiable sources of potential conflict, the committee has overlooked other possible conflicts, which, although not as readily identifiable, are nonetheless real.

Now let me turn to the committee's contention regarding the appearance of independence when an auditor performs management services. Does the rendering of such services really suggest a conflict of interest to a reasonable observer? To find an answer to this question I conducted a survey of a substantial cross section of "reasonable observers." The results of this study were published in the July 1965 issue of *The Accounting Review*.

A research population was defined in terms of four important groups of third parties who rely on CPA audit reports in making investment and credit decisions. These four groups were (1) research and financial analysts of brokerage firms, (2) commercial loan and trust officers of banks, (3) investment officers of insurance companies, both life and fire and casualty, and (4) investment officers of domestic mutual funds.

From these groups I drew two samples. I chose the first from the largest institutions of this population and the second from all the others.

A representative sample of 635 financial executives responded to the questionnaire. An analysis of their responses reveals the following points.

About 9 per cent of the third parties possess a definite conviction and 34 per cent a fairly definite conviction that management consulting does not impair audit independence. Thus 43 per cent see no problem.

These respondents were consistent in their answers because they said that their confidence in no way had been affected by the performance of management services by the auditor-CPA. Some 20 per cent said that their confidence had even been increased. The reasons given for this belief were in this order: (1) management services is essentially an advisory and not a decision-making function; (2) they had faith in the integrity of the CPA and believed that if his independence was in doubt, he would withdraw from one of the engagements; and (3) intelligent self-interest would prevail, because the CPA knows he is legally liable for any encroachment on his independence.

About 5 per cent of the financial executives indicated a definite conviction and 28 per cent indicated a fairly definite conviction that management consulting does impair the CPA's audit independence. Thus, to 33 per cent the performance of auditing and management services does suggest a conflict of interest, and these executives were also consistent in their replies.

Moreover, they indicated that their confidence in the CPA's audit report would have been less as a result of his management consulting activities. Again, they give the reasons for their concern: the closeness of the relationship between the consultant and management, the advocacy role that he plays, and the inevitable stake he has in the outcome of the engagement.

The remaining 24 per cent expressed no definite opinion.

If the 43 per cent of the respondents who see no problem are combined with the 24 per cent who hold no firm conviction, we see that a majority of 67 per cent do not believe management consulting has serious implications for the CPA's audit independence and 33 per cent believe that it does.

This 67-33 split was for all classifications of third parties except those from the largest brokerage houses and banks. In that group 83 per cent of the bankers saw no problem, whereas only 17 per cent did; among the largest brokerage houses 78 per cent saw no problem and 22 per cent did.

This difference may be due to the fact that third parties from the largest financial institutions tend to deal more with larger CPA firms, in which auditing and management services are performed by separate departments and personnel.

This point was discussed by C. E. Graese, who said that this difference between these groups may also be due to the fact "that these loan officers and financial analysts are better informed as to the nature of management services work as performed by CPAs and have probably given further thought to the factors which are significant in the matter of independence and reliability of the auditor's opinion."[2]

Messrs. Carey and Doherty, in "The Concept of Independence—Review and Restatement" (JofA, Jan.66, p.38) criticized my use of the rather emotionally charged term "management consulting" instead of "management services." They believed that respondents may have read too much into the term and that the results may therefore be misleading.

The only way to prove this would be to design another questionnaire that uses the term "management services," and see if there is any difference in the results. In this connection, I would like to mention another study which was carried out by Professor Abraham Briloff and published in the July 1966 issue of *The Accounting Review*. He used the term "management services" and his findings indicate that 58 per cent feel that management services and auditing are incompatible.

Messrs. Carey and Doherty also criticize my use of the general phrase "managerial consulting type of services" without specifying the types of management services CPAs normally perform. I did not specify types of management services because the Institute itself has not delineated the services CPAs perform. They are encouraged to practice the entire range of management services, limited only by their own competency and legal barriers. It would have been presumptuous of me, therefore, to say what CPAs may and may not do.

There is, of course, disagreement within the profession about the scope of management services. Some maintain that the function should be confined to certain accounting-related services. Others say that CPAs should be free to render all management services. I did not specify the types of services rendered because I did not think that this was a critical factor in deciding the question.[3]

When a CPA is engaged to consult on financial, personnel, production or other business problems, he becomes a management consultant. Therefore, the essential question is whether the nature and characteristics of management consulting give rise to relationships conflicting with his independence as auditor or which suggest such a conflict to a reasonable observer.

Mr. Graese criticized one of the key questions in my questionnaire on the ground that it may have biased the responses.[4] The question read as follows: "To what degree do you believe that CPAs can perform the managerial consulting type of services to management on a fee basis and still remain com-

---

[2] Clifford E. Graese, CPA, "Management Services and the Independence Issue," *The New York Certified Public Accountant,* June 1967, p. 434.
[3] See my correspondence with Messrs. Carey and Doherty on this point: JofA, Apr.66, p. 32.
[4] Clifford E. Graese, *op. cit.,* p. 434.

pletely independent?" Mr. Graese thought that different responses would have been elicited if the word "completely" had not been used.

Again, this objection can only be met by replacing the question and omitting the word "completely." However, in our final test of the questionnaire this problem did not arise. The respondents did not think the word was ambiguous and understood it in its context.

In the Briloff study, a question similar to mine was used, and the results were consistent with mine. Graese also indicated that my findings, like those of the Briloff study, were static data and that trend data were needed. I agree. We are not making final conclusions yet. We are still in the stage of examining the total problem.

The Institute's new *ad hoc* committee on independence will undoubtedly study further the attitudes of third parties.

In summary, I'd like to say, from an outsider's point of view, that there should be concern about the validity of Opinion 12. If audit independence is a state of mind, then the profession ought to recognize all the influences on the CPA's state of mind which the performance of management services establishes, subtle though that may be. Independence can be impaired, even though the auditor does not make management decisions or assume an employee status. It is apparent that the Institute's ethics committee acted on its own assumption, rather than on any inquiry, when it categorically stated that the rendering of management services by an auditor would not suggest a conflict of interest to a reasonable observer.

II. THE VIEWPOINT OF A USER
OF FINANCIAL STATEMENTS

Investment analysts owe a great deal to the CPA profession. Investment analysis is mostly art and a little science. If we didn't have certified financial statements to rely on, our work would be all art and no science.

From time to time Prudential makes investments in countries in which the auditing and accounting standards leave much to be desired. This is like being adrift in a small boat in the middle of the ocean with a compass that doesn't work. You don't know where you have been and you haven't any idea where you are going. This kind of situation makes us realize how lucky we are that most of the time we are dealing with financial statements that we can rely on.

At Prudential we place so much emphasis on these statements that we will not invest in the securities of any company unless we have statements that bear an unqualified opinion.

As a matter of fact, we may rely too much on these statements. The reputation of CPAs is so good that we fail to realize that they do have some faults, that they do make mistakes and that they have difficulty in hiring and keeping competent people, just as we do. As a result, we sometimes make less than adequate investigations on our own and are occasionally shocked when subsequent developments prove that all was not as reported.

When I was first asked whether I believed that CPAs, by providing management services, created a conflict of interest that impaired their objectivity as auditors, I thought it was a trivial matter, and I could not understand why there was so much concern about it. However, I have come to realize that it is a larger problem than I had at first thought. In fact, I have been led to review all of my ideas on independence and now more than ever I feel this is the keystone of the CPA profession, and it is reassuring to me as a user of financial statements to see how seriously the question is considered.

I am not an expert in accounting. Although I use financial statements every day and I believe I know what is involved in their preparation and what they mean, there are a lot of technical points that I do not understand. I mention this because my comments may not be correct on technical points. My purpose is to reflect the thoughts and attitudes of the nontechnician.

In our security analysis at Prudential, whether we are analyzing debt or equity securities, 90 per cent of our investigation is on earning power. We are interested in the past level of earnings, the current earnings and the trend of earnings so that we can arrive at an estimate of earnings in the four or five years in the future. To make such an estimate we need to know where the earnings are being generated.

That is, we would like a breakdown of earnings by product lines. More emphasis is being given to this with the rise of conglomerates. However, we have been interested in it for a long time because most corporations today are in at least two different businesses.

A breakdown of earnings is not always available, but it occasionally is, especially where we are buying securities on a private placement basis. There are indications that this information will be more generally available as time goes on.

I should now like to make clear my understanding of what is meant by management services and what is the difference between management services and a manager. To me, management services and management consulting are synonymous. As I see it, the management consultants are those who are rendering management services. That is, they do everything except make the final decision.

They gather all the statistics and facts, discard some as irrelevant or unimportant, organize the material, and present a recommendation, but they do not decide. Management decides. Often just a listing of the pros and cons makes a decision obvious. Or a biased presentation can make the decision seem obvious. Nevertheless, there is, in my opinion, a definite distinction between management and those providing management services.

At the same time I feel that management consultants have a strong interest in seeing that their recommendations are accepted and proved sound. After all, when a consultant makes a recommendation, he puts his reputation on the line.

After considering all the pros and cons, I believe that the rendering of management services by CPAs *could* lead to a loss of their independence. But I would like to emphasize the following:

First, I used the word "could" and not "would."

Second, some of the functions which a CPA now performs, and which are not being questioned, are more likely to lead to a loss of independence.

Third, so far as appearance of independence is concerned, it is more important to solve the problem of what I call multiple-choice or flexible accounting.

Fourth, the biggest problem, so far as independence is concerned, is that CPAs are selected and paid by the management they are supposed to check on.

I would like to explain why I said that some of the functions now performed by CPAs could lead to a loss of independence. One typical management consulting engagement involves advice on whether or not a company should be acquired. In this kind of engagement, the consultant would investigate the company to be acquired. His investigation would cover its management, the condition of its plant, its production efficiency, the demand for its products, the quality of its products and its earnings. Some forecast of future earnings would be made.

Let us assume that on the basis of the consultant's recommendations the acquisition is made and that a competitor enters the market with an improved product that no one had known about before the acquisition. As a result, earnings take a sharp turn downward. The CPA-management consultant might be tempted to hide the fact that earnings of the acquired company had declined.

He might not go so far as to agree to an overstatement of the consolidated earnings, but he might want to see the earnings of the acquired company higher and those of another company or division lower. Management would also be biased in this direction since it would reflect on their judgment if they had to report to stockholders that a company they had just acquired showed a downward trend in earnings. This, as I see it, is one case of how a conflict of interest could arise when a CPA functions as a management consultant and as an independent auditor of the company's statements.

But let me assume that instead of being asked to give advice, the CPA is asked to determine whether or not the statements of the company to be acquired fairly present its financial condition. This would surely be considered a proper function of the CPA.

Let us assume again that the acquisition is made and that earnings again decline. However, this time the decline was due to the fact that after the acquisition, it was found that some of the previous accounting procedures for the company acquired were incorrect. When correct procedures were used the earnings before the acquisition were found to be much lower than reported. The CPA would again be in a spot in that he would like to overstate the earnings, and thus his objectivity would presumably be impaired.

However, in my mind the conflict of interest would be much greater in the second case. In the first situation it would not be fair to criticize the management consultant since there was presumably no way for him to know what some competitor was doing secretly. But in the second case I think the CPA was plainly incompetent. However, it is currently widely accepted that a CPA may check on the financial statements of a company being acquired and that this does not result in any impairment of his independence.

Let me give another illustration. A CPA might be asked how a transaction should be handled so that it would be treated as a capital gain rather than ordinary income. After his advice is followed, subsequent developments might indicate that the transaction would most likely be treated as ordinary income. However, the CPA has prepared the income tax return treating the item as being subject to capital gains.

In certifying the financial statements he is, of course, required to pass upon the adequacy of the income tax reserve. Thus a conflict of interest arises in that he now believes the reserve is inadequate. This conflicts with his advice on how the transaction should have been handled. The cost of such faulty advice could be substantial and the blame could easily be traced to the accountant.

Yet it is generally conceded that the preparation of income tax returns is a proper function of the independent accountant. In fact, most people, and I include myself, feel that an income tax return prepared by a CPA is more likely to be completely accurate.

Another activity that has been criticized is executive recruitment. If an accounting firm acting as an executive recruiter for a client recommends a treasurer and the man turns out to be incompetent, the accounting firm, acting as auditors, will be less likely to bring this to the attention of management. I will agree there could be a conflict of interest, but it seems to me that it makes no difference whether or not the CPA receives a fee for this service. Again, the CPA's judgment is at stake whether or not there was a fee.

Yet most people in management recognize the difficulty of successfully hiring someone at a high level. Despite all types of testing and outside recommendations, a man still may not be just the right one for the job. I would be a lot less critical of a CPA-management consultant if he recommended a poor sales vice president than if I hired an incompetent treasurer after he had been interviewed and appraised by the CPA.

Another example of management consulting that has been cited as potentially leading to a loss of independence is market surveys to determine the potential demand for a product or service. Relying on a survey that showed an increasing demand, the client might decide to enter a new field or expand its activity in an existing field. If the demand did not materialize as forecast by the CPA-management consultant, earnings of this division would be depressed. In this kind of situation the CPA would be under pressure to have the division show better earnings.

Let us consider a management consulting engagement involving a recommendation on plant layout. On the consultant's advice the company rearranged its plant but then experienced an increase rather than a decrease in costs. Again, there would be pressure on the CPA to improve the picture somehow.

But I would like to contrast these examples with an accounting firm that might be setting up a system of cost control. Suppose this system made it appear that one segment of the business was particularly profitable and, as a result, the client expanded in that field. Later it was determined that the system was incorrect and the product line that was expanded should have higher costs assigned to it.

Here again there arises a conflict of interest and, if the plant expansion program was a large one, the cost to the client could be substantial and the independent accountant could be under great pressure not to change the cost system.

Some of the surveys on the question of whether CPAs should provide management services tend to support the argument that the rendering of management services impairs the auditor's independence, or at least his appearance of independence. However, I would like to give my reaction to such surveys as they apply to loan officers and investment analysts.

First of all, many of these men have very little accounting background. Their lack of knowledge in this field is astounding. In hiring men for our securities investment departments—and we try to hire the same ones that the banks, brokerage houses and investment bankers do—we rely mainly on those with a master's degree in business administration.

Normally we are not successful in attracting someone who has majored in accounting, but a surprising number of those we interview, who eventually end up in the financial field—at Prudential or with one of our competitors—have had little accounting. Often they have had less than a year or at most a year in their entire undergraduate studies.

My point is that I don't think loan officers and investment analysts fully appreciate the role of the independent accountant, even after they have been in business for a number of years and should have learned a lot. Also, when analyzing these surveys we should keep in mind that investment analysts have been critical of the independent accountants for so-called multiple-choice accounting.

I think there is a widespread feeling among us that CPAs in some cases follow their clients' accounting procedures even though they disapprove of them. Also, in the case of lending officers, there have been examples in recent years of incompetency on the part of the CPAs and, as a result, lenders have suffered substantial losses.

In this kind of circumstance and in this frame of mind, the lender naturally blames the other fellow rather than himself, and he might feel that his loss was due to the accountant's lack of independence rather than his incompetence. This is why I stated as the third point in my opinion that there would be little question about the effect of management services on independence if all audits were done perfectly and there was much less multiple-choice accounting. I should, of course, recognize that CPAs are making real progress in narrowing areas of difference in accounting principles.

One of the factors which led me to state that the rendering of management services *could* lead to a loss of independence but *would* not lead to it is my understanding that management services are secondary to the auditing function. By this I mean that the fees produced by the performance of management consulting are less than those from the auditing function. As I view it, the CPA firm gets its management service engagements because it is the company's CPA and it is selected as a CPA because it is independent. Another way of stating this is that if the CPA firm lost its reputation of being independent, it would not then be the auditor and would not then be hired as a management consultant.

If management services should grow to the point where they are the tail that wags the dog, there would be a real impact on my thinking.

In conclusion, I feel that the greatest threat to CPA independence is the fact that CPAs are selected and paid by the management they are supposed to check. However, I don't mean to imply that there is a lack of independence.

Further, I am more concerned with the problem associated with flexible accounting principles than I am with the rendering of management services. In the case of questionable multiple-choice decisions, the CPA can be under great pressure to agree with the management that hired him. In the case of management services, it seems to me much more likely that the management in effect will be checking on the CPA's performance.

All things considered, I believe CPAs have done an excellent job of maintaining their independence and retaining the confidence of the investing public.

III. A VIEWPOINT FROM WITHIN THE PROFESSION

This article is essentially a report on the activities of the American Institute's *ad hoc* committee on independence. It is a progress report because we are not through with our deliberations.

The committee was appointed to study questions which have been raised challenging the CPA's audit independence. Serving on the committee are members drawn from other Institute committees dealing with auditing, taxation, management services and ethics. The committee has met with academicians, Securities and Exchange Commission personnel and with various users of financial statements—bankers, corporate financial executives and financial analysts.

From the beginning we agreed that we would do our best to keep an open mind in our discussions and conclusions. It must be admitted that this is not easy because when one is belabored by critics from the outside, one's natural inclination is to flare back at them on the ground that they don't understand the problem. But we feel that unless we can keep an open mind, we are not likely to come up with the lasting solution we want.

Before getting into the work of the committee, I would like to make six statements which are related to our problem and which are essentially non-controversial.

1 Management services are useful to clients. This is self-evident; otherwise they wouldn't be asking us to render such services.

2 Such services have improved methods, procedures and controls and have assisted clients in improving their operations. They have consequently strengthened the companies to the benefit of stockholders and creditors.

3 Independence is essential to our attest function, and we should do nothing to impair it.

4 If, in rendering management services, we should impair our independence as auditors, we must either cease our auditing work or withdraw from the management services, since our Code of Professional Ethics prohibits us from taking a position that might impair our independence as auditors.

5 CPAs do have a remarkable reputation for integrity and independence.

6 We can err in our observance of rules just as surely in the field of management services as we can in the field of auditing.

Now I would like to discuss briefly the work of our *ad hoc* committee.

First, we have found no substantive evidence that the rendering of management services has, in fact, impaired independence. There is one aspect of his study which Dr. Schulte did not mention. He addressed inquiries to the state boards of accountancy, asking whether they had ever had a case where a CPA had violated his audit independence in conjunction with the fact that he had rendered management services to the same client. All 44 respondents said they had never had any such cases. That is compelling evidence.

Our committee wrote to various persons who had written articles of any note on this subject and asked them this question: "Do you know of any instance in which independence has been impaired where management services have been involved?" We received no substantive evidence of any such problems there.

As indicated, we have talked to representatives of the SEC. They also do not know of any cases in which independence has been impaired.

We were aware of the work done in California with the Savings and Loan Commissioner of that state, where the propriety of an auditor's rendering management services had been under discussion. There again, in response to our inquiry, no evidence was unearthed to indicate that independence had in fact been impaired.

To say that we have found no such evidence does not mean that none exists. Still, if the fears of our critics are valid, it would seem that somewhere along the line we should have been able to find some evidence that our system had broken down.

However, we do know that some users of financial statements believe that management services *could* impair independence. And, so long as a significant minority holds this view—I think it immaterial whether their view be well- or ill-founded—the profession has a problem and cannot ignore it.

One other thing did come out of our studies: There is substantial misunderstanding on the part of users of financial statements of the nature of the management services rendered by CPAs and the manner in which they are rendered.

This became apparent when the committee sought the assistance of those invited to take part in our discussions. We asked them to fill out a questionnaire used by Professor Briloff. This questionnaire asked respondents whether or not they were aware of the fact that CPAs rendered the indicated management services; it also asked the respondents whether or not, in their opinion, CPAs ought to render such services.

I think it took about as long as 60 seconds for some of them to raise their hands and say, "We don't understand this question. Will you clarify it?" and we said, "No, we will not clarify it, because we want you to respond to the questionnaire in exactly the same fashion as those who responded to Professor Briloff's questions. We want you to go down the line and give us an answer. If you think a CPA should not render this service, we want you to tell us why." We had someone say, "Well, I have checked that I don't think he should do it." We asked, "Why?" "Well, I just don't think he is competent to do that."

"That may be so, but what we are really trying to find out is whether or not the rendering of that service would impair independence," so a second factor appears: There seems to be confusion in the minds of some people responding to the questionnaire as to competency and independence.

Then our committee concluded that part of our problem in using this questionnaire may well have been its wording, because there were verbs such as "determine" and "develop," whereas verbs such as "advise" and "consult" more appropriately state the role of the CPA-consultant. So we reworded the questionnaire to better spell out what a CPA does and how he does it and also to make it clear we were talking only about independence and not about competence.

Then on a later group of invited guests we tried out the reworded questionnaire. Almost immediately we were surprised for we continued to get some adverse answers. We asked, "Why?" Then the statement was made, "Well, your question asks, 'If you did these things, *could* independence be impaired.' Our interpretation of the verb 'could' is that it is possible, it might happen and so we answered, 'Yes.' But if you were to change the verb 'could' to 'would,' then we would have said, 'No.'"

In other words, the change of a single word in our carefully contrived, reworded questionnaire completely changed the results. As a result of these experiences our committee seriously questions the value of questionnaires in this seemingly esoteric field. In saying this, we are not being critical of Professor Briloff and Dr. Schulte and others. We think this is a limitation necessarily inherent in the questionnaire approach.

The limitation arises from the present substantial misunderstanding of the nature of management services, misunderstanding as to how CPAs perform these services, and the incredibly difficult art of communication. And of course any questionnaire is essentially one-way communication since there is no opportunity for dialogue.

Nonetheless, even recognizing the problem and the necessary limitations, our committee is now considering an additional questionnaire which we hope, with Dr. Schulte's co-operation, to send to the population to which Dr. Schulte addressed his questionnaire. We hope through this process to accumulate further data that will be helpful.

An observation of our committee is that the rendering of management services seems to be not a problem of lack of independence in *fact* but to some the *appearance* of lack of independence. This suggests that the profession should outline more clearly what management services are and particularly how the CPA performs in this field. We should continue to educate users of financial statements as to these matters, the caveats of competence, and our ethical proscription regarding the making of management decisions or taking positions which might impair our objectivity as independent auditors.

Since Manuel F. Cohen, Chairman of the SEC, in his talk at Boston last year (JofA, Dec.66, p.56) raised some questions about audit independence, our committee discussed his views. In his talk he cited (as illustrative of his concern) four management services (which I will call peripheral services)—market surveys, factory layout, psychological testing and public opinion polls. Our committee found that few CPAs perform these services. Also the cited services, of themselves, did not seem to the committee to really pose any significant threat to the auditors' independence.

This suggested that one solution to the problem might be simply to say, "Well, we won't do any of this work." It would be no great hardship either to the profession or to our clients to give up something we really are not doing anyway. Maybe we should voluntarily do this, but our committee didn't think so unless we could develop a sound rationale as to just why we should not perform such services.

Executive recruitment for a fee, also mentioned by Mr. Cohen as of concern, is more widespread among some firms, and our committee is still struggling with this problem. It appears, however, that only a few firms have formally created departments—utilizing executive-search personnel—to render this service.

Our committee recognizes there is no such thing as absolute, pure independence. If the profession were to eliminate management services and confine its efforts solely to the attest function, I feel sure that there would be some who would challenge our independence on the basis that we received a fee for our services.

Also, few people recognize the powerful countervailing forces that help to protect a CPA's independence and keep him on the straight-and-narrow path. The first is personal integrity, which we recognize as the foundation stone of the profession. The second is possible legal liability. The third is possible loss of the CPA certificate. Fourth is the possible loss of clients; I think that many of our clients would say they could not afford to have us as auditors if we were found, even in other cases, to have been lacking in independence. In short, we really can't afford not to be independent.

Here are some preliminary observations and recommendations in connection with our continuing study:

1 So long as a significant minority of users of financial statements are concerned that management services may pose a threat to our independence, the profession has a problem which cannot be ignored.

2 Our profession should proceed as soon as practicable to issue statements as to the nature of management services rendered by CPAs and the appropriate role of CPAs in rendering these services.

3 The profession should continue to confer with representatives of user groups in order to clarify positions. And I think it is a natural corollary that if these discussions indicate a continuing concern—again this is my own opinion—then the profession has to take whatever action seems to be appropriate, including possible proscription of some services.

4 CPAs should recognize that there are practical limitations in the management services field. With the complexity of public accounting practice today, many CPAs are hard-pressed to stay abreast of current developments in accounting, auditing and taxation; and any extension of their services into the management services area may dilute the quality of their services in the traditional fields and possibly should be avoided for that reason alone. I think this applies particularly to small firms and individuals but should also be considered by firms of any size.

5 I think we have to recognize that the performance of peripheral services—i.e., those not "related logically to the financial process or to broadly defined information and control systems"[1] is raising questions in some quarters, not so much that they may possibly impair independence as that they seem foreign to the accepted concept of what a CPA does. Most people would recoil, I think, at the thought of a CPA's going in for psychological testing. This also raises, in their minds, the question of competence, and, whether or not these views are well- or ill-founded, the question exists.

Our committee has found no substantive evidence that peripheral services (or any other management services) have impaired independence, and also there is a lack of a sound rationale as to why peripheral services should be proscribed. Nonetheless, quite possibly we should voluntarily refrain from holding ourselves out as rendering these services of and by themselves; although if they arise as an incident to other services, and the CPA is competent, the extended services might be appropriate.

For example, if a CPA assists a client in the development and installation of a production control system and some collateral rearrangement of machines seems to be desirable, I don't think there would be any objection to the CPA's advising him on this.

[1] Manuel F. Cohen, Chairman of SEC, in a speech at the 1966 annual meeting of the AICPA.

6 In view of the questions raised by critics as to possible impairment of an auditor's independence through the rendition of management services, our committee believes that better assurance might be given to users of financial statements that such impairment does not exist if use is made of "audit committees" like those recently recommended by the AICPA executive committee (JofA, Sept.67, p. 10). Such "audit committees," desirably consisting of directors who are not officers or employees, ordinarily recommend the appointment of the company's auditors.

Accordingly we are presently of the opinion that if a CPA is going to render a management service which appears to involve a material business decision —say, in the acquisition of another company or a substantial expansion (or contraction) of product lines—he should first be required to get approval of his engagement, and the scope thereof, from the company's audit committee.

If the audit committee, knowledgeable of the contemplated service and recognizing the need for the CPA to be considered to be independent in the subsequent audit of the company's financial statements, were to approve the management service (possibly with limitations as to the CPA's role), such action should give greater assurance to users of financial statements as to the independence of the CPA. This would be powerful support for us.

We also think it might be desirable for the CPAs to report periodically to the audit committee concerning all services rendered so that all the cards are on the table. If this is to be considered, it should be done prior to the time the audit committee recommends to the board of directors whether or not that firm should be reappointed as auditors.

In concluding, I would like to say we are under no illusions that we have solved our problems. We are suggesting no final answers. This is a progress report on a continuing study.

Even though the compatibility of management services and auditing has not been totally resolved to the satisfaction of all concerned, CPAs must face situations like the following one.

MARK CORPORATION

▷ During 19X6 your client, Mark Corporation, requested that you conduct a feasibility study to advise management of the best way the Corporation can utilize electronic data processing equipment and which computer, if any, best meets the Corporation's requirements. You are technically competent in this area and accept the engagement. Upon completion of your study the Corporation accepts your suggestions and installs the computer and related equipment that you recommended.

Discuss the effect the acceptance of this management services engagement would have upon your independence in expressing an opinion on the financial statements of the Mark Corporation.

(AICPA adapted)

CHAPTER 14

THE ATTEST FUNCTION:
APPLICATIONS OF
ACCOUNTING PRINCIPLES

The audit profession has been under fire for many years on many fronts, but applications of accounting principles is perennially the chief area of attack. The following selection presents the problem and its manifestations.

ACCOUNTANTS TURN TOUGHER
(Anon.)*

In the popular mind, accountants are precise, logical people—flinty-eyed men wearing green eyeshades who toil over dusty ledgers searching for errant numbers. But far from being models of precision, accountants have gotten into hot water in recent years because they have failed to be precise enough.

More and more, they have found themselves differing over what constitutes "generally accepted accounting principles"—the yardstick that each accountant uses in passing judgment on a corporation's financial records. In theory, the American Institute of Certified Public Accountants keeps its 65,000 members marching in step, eliminating conflicts and changing standards when necessary. But AICPA debates tend to drag on for years. As the discussions continue, ambiguities multiply, and the rules accountants live by fall out of date.

Suddenly, in the face of a crescendo of complaint that has rocked the accounting profession right down to its toes, all that is changing. For one thing, there are more investors—and more sophisticated ones, at that—poking into corporate financial statements. For another, the nature of corporate financing has changed dramatically. The rise of the conglomerate, and of conglomerate-style accounting, has brought cries for new standards from both the Securities & Exchange Commission and harried Wall Street analysts. A rash of lawsuits aimed at some of the biggest and most prestigious accounting firms has forced the profession to grapple not only with accounting standards but also with such thorny issues as the potential conflict of interest that exists because an accountant's fees are paid by the same management whose books he audits.

---

* Reprinted from the October 18, 1969 issue of *Business Week* by special permission. Copyrighted © 1969 by McGraw-Hill, Inc.

NEW DAY

Nothing shows the change more clearly than a proposal made a few weeks ago by the rule-making Accounting Principles Board of the AICPA to outlaw the "pooling of interest" method in merger accounting. Using that approach, the acquiring company can show "instant growth" by adding the acquired company's earnings and assets to its own, as though the two had never been apart. The alternative to pooling of interest is "purchase" accounting, in which the acquired company's earnings and assets are counted only from the date of merger.

Conglomerates have grown huge almost overnight by using the pooling-of-interest method. If the SEC and much of Wall Street question the technique, it obviously has powerful advocates. In tackling the pooling-of-interest concept, the APB has launched what promises to be the bitterest fight in the board's 10-year history.

Beyond that, the APB in just a few months has:

Laid groundwork to require that goodwill (the difference between a property's book value and the price paid for it) be written off the balance sheet over a period of time by deducting a portion of it each year.

Required companies to start reporting an earnings-per-share figure that includes the potential dilution from all outstanding convertible securities.

Helped federal bank regulators devise a new method of computing bank earnings. Instead of showing net operating earnings, banks now must report a net income figure that includes operating earnings, loan losses, and results from sales of securities.

Occasionally, when the APB fails to move, others step in. When the accountants dragged their feet on an SEC request that they propose standards of reporting divisional sales and earnings of diversified corporations, the agency asked the Financial Executives Institute to do the job. Rules based on the FEI study went into effect two months ago. They apply only to SEC registration statements.

The aim of the APB is to hush some of the controversy by narrowing the bookkeeping alternatives open to companies. While the APB has changed many standards in the past, it never before has delved into so many highly controversial areas in so short a time — a clear indication of the pressures the profession is under.

But even if the APB does come up with a clear set of standards that accountants can follow, it still would not silence all of the critics. The touchy issue of the dual role that accountants play would remain, and here the going is very slow.

CONFLICT

In theory, the basic job of an accountant is to audit a corporation's books for the enlightenment and protection of shareholders and the investing public. In that sense, an accountant is looked upon as an independent seeker of truth. But in fact, accountants are hired by management, and while shareholders must then pass judgment on management's choice, they seldom, if ever, balk.

There have been few cases of fraud involving accountants. But given the nature of the role, there always is a question as to how much scope an accountant has for outright independence, particularly when he serves not merely as an auditor but also as a management consultant to the client. It is common for an accounting firm to play both roles — meaning that the accountant often is asked to pass judgment on the results of his own recommendations.

"Some firms," says the senior partner of a big New York accounting firm, "say they draw the line against consulting that involves them in management decision-making. But don't let anybody fool you. We take on any job."

STANDARDS

Foremost among accounting notions is the tradition, borrowed from the British, that the client — not the auditor — knows best how to present his own financial statements and which accounting principles should be used in drawing up a balance sheet. The corporation prepares the financial statement; the auditor checks to see if acceptable accounting principles and procedures have been used.

No less a tradition — indeed, it is part of the AICPA's code of ethics — is the confidential relationship that is supposed to exist between the auditor and his client. This sometimes brings on agonizing decisions. The New York accounting firm of Peat, Marwick, Mitchell & Co. faced such an experience several years ago when it learned that annual reports it had certified for Yale Express Co. were false and misleading. Peat, Marwick, when sued by Yale stockholders, maintained it had no ethical duty to disclose the facts publicly. Then the SEC jumped in saying prompt public disclosure was called for.

Recently, the AICPA moved to clear up the issue by ruling that accountants are obliged to flag the SEC and appropriate stock exchanges when they determine that certified statements are false and management will not publicize the fact. While that clears up one issue, it hardly comes to grips with the conflict-of-interest question.

OVER THE SHOULDER

Worrying accountants today is the threat of federal rulemaking, a hazard the profession thought it had buried after the 1929 market collapse. At that time, accountants were unable to stop Congress from handing the SEC powers to make accounting rules, but they did wangle an important concession. Public financial statements filed with the SEC would be audited by independent accountants and not, as Congress had considered, by federal employees.

In the years since, the relationship between SEC and accountants has blown hot and cold, and on some occasions the SEC has felt accountants were not holding up their end of the bargain.

Finally, in 1959, the Accounting Principles Board was established. Basically, its mandate was the same as that of a predecessor, the Committee on Accounting Procedure, which in 20 years made little progress in imposing more uniformity on business accounting practices. The APB, though, was to have moved faster.

But now, after 10 years, the APB has come under the same pressure for accounting reforms as did the CAP. Whether it can stand the pressure or be toppled, as was its predecessor, is an open question. "The foremost obstacle," the AICPA's executive director Leonard Savoie said earlier this year, "is the complexity of the problems the board is facing."

ROLE

On the APB falls the responsibility of establishing accounting principles that American business follows. While the board has no legal authority, its decisions are binding on CPAs, and they must take exception in a company's certificate if it fails to follow the board's principles.

The board's members, 15 practicing CPAs, two businessmen, and one university professor, are among the elite of the profession. They also represent the views and desires of their accounting firms, which include the Big Eight that audit most companies listed on stock exchanges. Price Waterhouse & Co. is the biggest, followed by Arthur Andersen & Co.; Peat, Marwick, Mitchell & Co., Lybrand, Ross Bros. & Montgomery, Haskins & Sells, Ernst & Ernst, Arthur Young & Co., and Touche, Ross, Bailey & Smart.

Despite the fact that these firms and the AICPA have spent millions on the board and its work, the APB has a spotty record in trying to formulate accounting principles. One of the problems, says John Queenan, senior partner of Haskins & Sells who recently finished a six-year term on the board, is that the board "always ended up fighting brush fires."

On its first major issue in 1963, accounting for investment tax credit, the board split badly. The APB wanted companies to take the credit into income over a period of years; most companies, however, wanted to take it all in one year and give earnings a boost. Business put intense pressure on the accounting firms, and three of the Big Eight—Price, Waterhouse; Haskins & Sells, and Ernst & Ernst—decided to ignore the APB ruling. Then the SEC showed no interest in backing the board. Finally, the APB backed down and said that both ways of figuring the credit would be acceptable.

FULL LOAD

Since then, the board has handled a host of issues. Opinions have gone out on accounting for pension costs, and on reporting of leases by both lessors and lessees. The board has tackled the question of resolving differences that arise in using one form of depreciation on tax returns and another on annual reports, and it has made companies separate earnings from other activities, such as gains in the sale of a plant, in the reports.

But some of these and other opinions left unanswered many questions, and on several occasions the board had to go back and make revisions. In 1967, a ruling on convertible bonds created a furor. The APB held that since investors were willing to buy convertibles at rates lower than those for conventional bonds, the discount represented the value of conversion to investors. The board wanted companies to capitalize this value and amortize it over the bond's life.

The opinion created a storm. Investment bankers said it was impossible to fix the value of the conversion feature. Businesses worried about the impact on earnings, especially because the amortization charges were not deductible. Finally, a few months ago, the ruling was killed except where bonds are issued with warrants, which have market value.

LISTENING FIRST

These days, the board seeks advice from businessmen before issuing an opinion. It works closely with the Financial Executives Institute, whose members are largely company treasurers and controllers, and with other groups such as the National Assn. of Accountants, the Financial Analysts Federation, and the American Assn. of Accountants.

These groups do not always see eye-to-eye with the board and sometimes oppose its opinions. In July, the NAA organized its own Management Accounting Practices Committee. However, I. Wayne Keller, chairman of the group and Armstrong Cork's general manager of international operations, said the committee would work to reconcile differences with the APB before taking a stand.

One reason outsiders want a bigger say in the board's decision-making is that it appears to deal with issues that directly affect corporate earnings reports. For management, earnings per share are sacred, and often go far to determine market value of stock. But in recent years, accountants have worried that investors were relying too much on the per-share figures and failing to take into account the potential for dilution represented by convertible securities issued in mergers.

In 1967, accountants required companies to report two per-share earnings figures: the conventional amount, based on the average number of common shares outstanding and another to show potential dilution. But business claimed the rule posed too complex a formula, and they got around it by issuing warrants and stock options in mergers, both of which were exempt from the rule. But this year, accountants came back with a new opinion, and this time warrants and options were included as convertible securities.

The latest ruling also banned the use of traditional earnings-per-share figures altogether, and that angered companies. "There is considerable investor confusion over just what an earnings-per-share figure means," says John Hangen, chairman of the FEI's Corporate Reporting Practices Committee. But while accountants still may be forced to reopen the question of earnings dilution, another hassle appears settled for good.

BATTLE

For years, banks resisted the contention that they should include loan losses and results of portfolio transactions in earnings figures. Instead, they reported results of these operations separately. At first, accountants did not press the issue hard because banks, like other regulated businesses, follow accounting rules laid down by federal and state agencies. But when banks began listing their shares on stock exchanges, a fight began.

The APB made ready to rule on the question, but banks resisted. The American Bankers Assn. went so far as to advise banks to ignore the accountants, even if it meant having their auditor take exception to their financial statements. Finally, banks capitulated, but only after a heavy bargaining session in Washington that involved the ABA, SEC, AICPA, the Federal Reserve, and other bank regulatory agencies. The banks, however, were allowed to report a five-year average of annual provisions for loan losses, rather than the actual provision each year.

Even with aid from federal agencies, the bank earnings question was rough enough. But in the pooling-of-interest hassle, the APB may stand alone. The issues may be too hot for even the SEC.

The pooling idea—simply adding together companies' assets and liabilities in a merger—was practically unknown before the great merger movement of the 1960s. But the practice suited conglomerates perfectly, and they quickly made it the most controversial of all accounting procedures.

With pooling, last-minute mergers could be made, and the earnings of the acquired company added retroactively to those of the conglomerate. But the accounting mechanics in pooling left no clue as to how well, or poorly, the companies had performed separately. Poolings also avoided an unpleasant alternative: the transaction which resulted in a large amount of goodwill popping up on the balance sheet. Not only do creditors deduct goodwill from a company's net worth in determining how much money to lend, but the possibility has existed that accountants might require it be written off.

Accountants debated long and hard on whether poolings were a legitimate bookkeeping practice, even though they continued to approve it. Meanwhile, protests were mounting from investors and others that poolings were being abused. At one point, trustees of Westec Corp. sued Ernst & Ernst, the company's auditors, accusing them, among other things, of allowing Westec to report dramatic earnings increases that, for technical reasons it was claimed, should not have been approved.

STAND

When APB finally looked hard at the pooling concept, which wasn't until this fall, the majority could see no justification at all for allowing the practice. Next week the APB will have an opportunity to defend that position. Starting Oct. 22, the board begins a four-day session in New York at which it hopes to reach a final decision. The session opens with an all-day symposium on the pooling question, with the SEC and business and professional organizations.

No matter what the outcome, says LeRoy Layton, the APB's chairman and partner at Main Lafrentz & Co., board members feel APB will survive. Even though it has quarreled with business, it remains the major bulwark against a government takeover of accounting rule-making. Further, organizations such as the Financial Executives Institute and National Assn. of Accountants are not trying to take the APB's place. Both want the board to keep the rule-making role.

The accountants still face potentially controversial issues in the next year. Questions include how companies should handle research and development costs and the reporting of equity and earnings in unconsolidated subsidiaries.

While the SEC's stand on poolings is not known, the board has the agency's strong backing in what Savoie calls the board's "integral part of the regulatory process."

"The SEC," says Andrew Barr, the agency's chief accountant, "still looks to the accountants to deal with problems of principles and procedures."

In the face of much criticism, the AICPA took a step toward control of the situation. The following pronouncement was designed to reduce the number of alternative accounting practices in areas on which the AICPA had taken a position. As we shall soon discover, the pronouncement was only minimally successful.

SPECIAL BULLETIN—DISCLOSURE OF DEPARTURES FROM OPINIONS OF ACCOUNTING PRINCIPLES BOARD*

TO MEMBERS OF THE AMERICAN INSTITUTE OF CERTIFIED PUBLIC ACCOUNTANTS

The Council of the Institute, at its meeting October 2, 1964, unanimously adopted recommendations that members should see to it that departures from Opinions of the Accounting Principles Board (as well as effective Accounting Research Bulletins issued by the former Committee on Accounting Procedure) are disclosed, either in footnotes to financial statements or in the audit reports of members in their capacity as independent auditors.

This action applies to financial statements for fiscal periods beginning after December 31, 1965.

The recommendations adopted by Council are as follows:

1 "Generally accepted accounting principles" are those principles which have substantial authoritative support.

2 Opinions of the Accounting Principles Board constitute "substantial authoritative support."

3 "Substantial authoritative support" can exist for accounting principles that differ from Opinions of the Accounting Principles Board.

---

* American Institute of Certified Public Accountants, October 1964. Reprinted by permission of the American Institute of Certified Public Accountants.

4 No distinction should be made between the Bulletins issued by the former Committee on Accounting Procedure on matters of accounting principles and the Opinions of the Accounting Principles Board. Accordingly, references in this report to Opinions of the Accounting Principles Board also apply to the Accounting Research Bulletins.[1,2]

5 If an accounting principle that differs materially in its effect from one accepted in an Opinion of the Accounting Principles Board is applied in financial statements, the reporting member must decide whether the principle has substantial authoritative support and is applicable in the circumstances.

  a If he concludes that it does not, he would either qualify his opinion, disclaim an opinion, or give an adverse opinion as appropriate. Requirements for handling these situations in the reports of members are set forth in generally accepted auditing standards and in the Code of Professional Ethics and need no further implementation.

  b If he concludes that it does have substantial authoritative support:

    1 he would give an unqualified opinion and

    2 disclose the fact of departure from the Opinion in a separate paragraph in his report or see that it is disclosed in a footnote to the financial statements and, where practicable, its effects on the financial statements.* Illustrative language for this purpose is as follows:

The company's treatment of (describe) is at variance with Opinion No. _____ of the Accounting Principles Board (Accounting Research Bulletin No. _____ of the Committee on Accounting Procedure) of the American Institute of Certified Public Accountants. This Opinion (Bulletin) states that (describe the principle in question). If the Accounting Principles Board Opinion (Accounting Research Bulletin) had been followed, income for the year would have been increased (decreased) by $_____, and the amount of retained earnings at (date) increased (decreased) by $_____. In our opinion, the company's treatment has substantial authoritative support and is an acceptable practice. . . .

If disclosure is made in a footnote, the last sentence might be changed to read: In the opinion of the independent auditors, _____, the company's treatment has substantial authoritative support and is an acceptable practice.

6 Departures from Opinions of the Accounting Principles Board which have a material effect should be disclosed in reports for fiscal periods that begin:

  a After December 31, 1965, in the case of existing Bulletins and Opinions;

---

[1] This is in accord with the following resolution of the Accounting Principles Board at its first meeting on September 11, 1959:

"The Accounting Principles Board has the authority, as did the predecessor committee, to review and revise any of these Bulletins (published by the predecessor committee) and it plans to take such action from time to time.

"Pending such action and in order to prevent any misunderstanding meanwhile as to the status of the existing accounting research and terminology bulletins, the Accounting Principles Board now makes public announcement that these bulletins should be considered as continuing in force with the same degree of authority as before."

[2] The Terminology Bulletins are not within the purview of the Council's resolution nor of this report because they are not statements on accounting principles.

* In those cases in which it is not practicable to determine the approximate effect on the financial statements, this fact should be expressly stated.

b After the issue date of future Opinions unless a later effective date is specified in the Opinion.

7 The Accounting Principles Board should review prior to December 31, 1965, all Bulletins of the Committee on Accounting Procedure and determine whether any of them should be revised or withdrawn.

8 The Accounting Principles Board should include in each Opinion a notation that members should disclose a material departure therefrom.

9 The failure to disclose a material departure from an Accounting Principles Board Opinion is deemed to be substandard reporting.† The Practice Review Committee should be instructed to give its attention to this area and to specifically report to Council the extent of deviations from these recommendations.

10 The Committee on Professional Ethics and the Institute's legal counsel have advised that the present By-Laws and Code of Professional Ethics would not cover an infraction of the above recommendations. Whether the Code of Professional Ethics should be amended is a question which should be studied further. . . .‡

As indicated in the above text, Council's action is not intended to have the force and effect of a rule of ethics, but rather that of a standard of reporting practice, deviations from which should have the attention of the Practice Review Committee.

Yours truly,

Thomas D. Flynn, President

†In discussion at the Council meeting it was explained that the phrase "substandard reporting" was used in the sense of reporting practices not in conformity with recommendations of the Council.
‡By order of the Council a special committee is now reviewing the entire matter of the status of Opinions of the Accounting Principles Board, and the development of accounting principles and practices for the purpose of recommending to Council a general statement of philosophy, purpose and aims in this area.

The following press report appeared almost two years after the Special Bulletin. Its appearance bore witness to the vitality of the accounting principles controversy in spite of preliminary efforts by the AICPA to solve the problem.

ACCOUNTING REFORM
Frederick C. Klein*

Pressured from within and without, the accounting fraternity is likely to adopt important reforms soon — producing some handsome dividends for stockholders everywhere.

* Reprinted by permission from *The Wall Street Journal*, Vol. XLVI, No. 151 (May 16, 1966), p. 2.

The benefits won't be in cash, but in the form of clearer and more copious information in company financial reports. Some of the changes the public accountants envision will arbitrarily settle honest differences of opinion on technical accounting principles. Others may rule out practices that now tempt some managements to manipulate figures in such a way as to mislead investors. Still other changes could help prevent outright fraud.

Basically, the accountants will try to give more meaning to the standard declaration included in annual reports. In all but those very few cases where the auditors take serious exception to the financial data as presented by the company, these declarations have an identical and reassuring ring; they attest that the auditors find the financial statements "present fairly" the company's condition "in accordance with generally accepted accounting principles."

"A ROULETTE WHEEL"

But these "generally accepted" principles are so varied, and can be applied so flexibly, that investors can hardly be blamed for sometimes throwing up their hands in confusion when trying to compare a company's current results with past performance, or with the results of a competitor. Some leading accountants feel it's high time that the investor got a better break. Leonard Spacek, senior partner of Arthur Andersen & Co., a major accounting firm, declares: "My profession appears to regard a set of financial statements as a roulette wheel for investors—and it's their tough luck if they don't understand the risk that's involved in interpreting any accounting report."

Some certified public accountants (CPAs) are arguing for a go-slow approach to new rule-making, but the pressures for change appear so strong that their objections will be unheeded—in part because the profession is feeling the heat of outside criticism as well as demand for reforms by its own practitioners.

Banks want to see some changes made, and fast. Recently J. Howard Laeri, vice chairman of giant First National City Bank of New York, coupled a plea for more accountant-banker cooperation with an attack on what he called "the audit gap." Under present accounting procedures, he said, "the investor or lender . . . is very much like the navigator who would have to pilot" a drifting beacon.

UNDER LEGAL FIRE

The accounting profession has also been hit with a rash of lawsuits (some filed by banks) charging that accounting firms have permitted dissemination of misleading information about companies' financial condition. The American Institute of Certified Public Accountants (AICPA) doesn't know precisely how many such suits are outstanding but estimates that about 50 "cases" (several suits may be filed under a single case) may now be up for litigation. This is a sharp increase from prior years, and the AICPA last year set up a special committee on accountants' liability to study the problem.

Last year the Securities and Exchange Commission initiated a major change in accounting procedure on its own, without prior action by the profession — the first time in years such a step had been taken. The commission ruled that companies which list the uncollected portion of installment receivables as a current asset must also list the resulting deferred tax as a current liability. The ruling was designed to halt the spreading practice of listing the deferred tax as a noncurrent item. This artificially inflated "working capital" (current assets minus current liabilities), a key credit rating factor.

BOARD RULINGS EXPECTED

Thus prodded from several directions, the AICPA now is ready to act through its accounting principles board, a body known principally for its lethargy during the six years since its formation. It has issued only six opinions on specific matters, and "none of these . . . served to narrow the areas of difference and inconsistency in practice," according to one board member.

This year, however, it's considered almost certain that a revitalized board will take steps to bring about more conformity in at least two areas — accounting for pension costs and for the report of "special items" affecting earnings. In the latter case, it's expected the board will require a two-part income state-ment — one part dealing with operating earnings only, and the other with items of non-recurring gain or loss.

This would be a radical departure from past practice for many companies. A recent AICPA survey of a sample of 600 companies revealed that 60% of 252 "unusual" items of income and expense they reported in 1964 were lumped into the reported net income figure for the year, which in turn was used to com-pute earnings per share. Only 16% of these special items were reported as such and listed separately after the net income figure. The remainder was taken directly to retained earnings and did not show up in the year's profit statement at all.

This lack of consistent treatment of non-operating items of gain and loss is a prime source of stockholder confusion. Companies sometimes highlight these special items one year and ignore them the next, making comparisons of year-to-year performance difficult for those without a practiced eye.

Consider Firth Sterling, Inc., a maker of specialty steels and tungsten car-bide based in McKeesport, Pa. In 1964, when earnings from operating dipped to 19 cents a share from 32 cents the previous year, the company featured prominently in its annual report an additional special profit of 8 cents a share realized from investment tax credits. This gain was mentioned in five separate places in the report, including a "highlight" table and the president's letter to stockholders.

In 1965, however, Firth Sterling's earnings from operations bounced back to 31 cents a share and readers of this annual report had to search hard to find any reference to the 1964 special gain. It was recognized only once—in a source-and-use-of-funds table deep in the report—and the source of the gain wasn't spelled out anywhere. All this, of course, made Firth Sterling's earnings compare more favorably year to year than would otherwise have been the case.

Varying accounting practices among different companies in the same industry also create confusion. Last year, for example, reported net income of Inland Steel Co. dropped 4% from 1964. But unlike most of its competitors, Inland prorates its 7% investment tax credit over the depreciable life of new equipment. If Inland had emulated other steelmakers and taken the full credit each year, its 1965 net income would have shown a gain of 7% over 1964 instead of a 4% drop.

Similar confusion has arisen over the handling of damage suit payouts by General Electric Co. and Westinghouse Electric Corp.; GE has reduced its profits by the amount of the payouts in the years they were made, but Westinghouse has elected to write them off against retained earnings, not current profits.

The current state of accounting for pension costs is described as "chaotic" by Clifford V. Heimbucher, a San Francisco CPA and current chairman of the accounting principles board of AICPA. Companies currently use at least three widely divergent methods of accounting for these costs, and auditors can take exception to them only if a company changes from one to another in the midst of a year.

"EVERYONE WON'T LIKE IT"

To clear up the chaos, the board is expected to establish a single method of accounting for pension costs. "Everyone won't like it, but it's an area where we must take a stand," says Mr. Heimbucher.

The principles board has other thorny items on its docket, including measures to bring more conformity to accounting for the allocation of some taxes, the handling of treasury stock, changes in price levels, and research and development costs. The latter is an area where particularly divergent practices now exist.

Any decisions the board comes to will undoubtedly be widely followed by companies and accounting firms. Before 1964, board rulings were only one source of "authoritative support" for a given accounting procedure. Others included textbooks, opinions of leading CPAs or simply widespread use of a method. In 1964, however, the governing council of the AICPA resolved that effective with statements for fiscal years beginning after Dec. 31, 1965, departures from board opinions would have to be disclosed in footnotes to financial statements or in the standard auditor's opinion at the back of annual reports. Also, the effect of such departures on per-share earnings would have to be stated.

Compliance by member accounting firms is now voluntary, but the AICPA expects that few, if any, will choose to disregard the council's resolution. If that should occur, however, the AICPA could insert the resolution in its code of ethics; a member firm breaking this code could be subject to expulsion from the AICPA.

ENCOURAGING CONFORMITY

This ruling on exceptions "makes the board more a judicial than an educational body," says John L. Carey, executive director of AICPA. Corporation executives agree it can only encourage greater accounting conformity. "The last thing any company wants is an auditor's exception," says the president of a big Eastern manufacturing concern. "It guarantees a lively annual meeting."

In addition to the board's work, the AICPA itself is deep in study of the internal auditing methods of public warehouses; the data gathered could be used to help prevent the type of manipulations involved in Allied Crude Vegetable Oil Refining Corp. salad oil scandal. Guidelines to be used by auditors in checking warehouse inventories are expected to result from the study.

More often now, individual accounting firms are amplifying their written opinions when they feel a company's report requires further interpretation. Last year, for example, Price Waterhouse & Co. included a clarification of per-share earnings of Unexcelled Chemical Corp. in the auditor's statement in that company's annual report. Unexcelled Chemical had listed separately both a charge and a credit affecting profit, and Price Waterhouse apparently felt this might confuse some stockholders. Says the AICPA's Mr. Carey: "There's a growing feeling in the profession that the auditor should give his opinion when he feels something needs to be said."

THE LIABILITY QUESTION

Though the accountants won't say so outright, it's understood that the current rash of lawsuits against them has helped speed reform. Broadly speaking, accountants are liable for damages when company statements come up wrong if they are found to have participated in a fraud, or if they are judged negligent in exercising normal professional care in approving a company's statements.

CPAs are quick to point out that their statements are no guarantee against fraud; their checks are made on a sample basis, and they must rely heavily on company representations of the facts. This was brought home recently when Frank G. Shattuck Co., New York, disclosed its earnings from 1965 and 1964 were overstated by a total of about $600,000, primarily because of "collusive fabrication of fictitious invoices" and other accounting records by certain department heads of the company's W. F. Schrafft & Sons Corp. subsidiary in Boston.

Peat, Marwick, Mitchell & Co. was the auditor. Walter E. Hansen, senior partner, calls the case "a perfect example of what can happen when top people in a company or division operate collusively" to falsify records. Discrepancies resulting from such collusion "come out sooner or later when figures get out of line," says Mr. Hansen, but they are "virtually impossible" to detect immediately in the course of a normal audit.

"ABSOLUTELY BLAMELESS"

Edward E. Butler, group vice president of Shattuck, says his company feels Peat-Marwick is "absolutely blameless" in the matter. The firm was of "great assistance" in uncovering the collusion, he declares, and adds that "in the light of all the circumstances, the auditors had no way of knowing what had taken place" in time to prevent the misstatements.

Such arguments evidently cut no ice with plaintiffs in the many suits filed against accountants. As it happens, Peat-Marwick has been charged in some of the larger more publicized actions. In San Francisco, four banks are suing the firm for more than $6 million in connection with the 1963 bankruptcy of Otis, McAllister & Co., a coffee importer. The suits charge that financial statements of the company from 1958 through 1960, audited by Peat-Marwick, were "misleading." A Peat-Marwick spokesman says his firm refused an offer from the banks calling for an out-of-court settlement for $1.3 million, and will "have the matter litigated on its merits."

Peat-Marwick is also the target of more than a dozen suits filed in connection with the 1965 bankruptcy of Yale Express System, Inc. The accounting firm claims that information was withheld by accounting personnel of Yale Express and that under assets the company listed receivables it never got around to collecting.

Is the following type of report indicative of those that have provoked the accounting controversy? You will of necessity answer this question in the course of your analysis.

RED BAG CEMENT COMPANY

 Following is the 1968 Annual Report of Red Bag Cement Company. This is the only report of this entity issued during its short life, and it is reproduced in its entirety.

Read and analyze the entire report with the following questions in mind:

1 What was the ultimate objective of the numerous adjustments made to the statements of the company? Support any conclusions with appropriate figures.

2 Comment on the propriety of the auditor's opinion noting any deficiencies therein. Note the reasons for any deficiencies you believe exist.

3 What changes in the auditor's opinion would you make in order for the opinion to conform to today's standards?

RED BAG CEMENT COMPANY
Steel City, Pennsylvania

TO WHOM IT MAY CONCERN:

This report covers the operations in 1968 of Red Bag Cement Company of Steel City, Pennsylvania, which operates a cement producing plant located in the Steel City area. Balance Sheet as at December 31, 1968, and the related Statements of Income and Income Retained in the Business for the year then ended are included. Report of Potter and Pepper, Certified Public Accountants, is appended.

From 1929 until December 21, 1967, Steel City Coke & Chemical Company was engaged in the production and sale of cement through its Red Bag Division. On that date Steel City Coke & Chemical and Red Bag, by proper corporate action, authorized the transfer of the plant and business of its Cement Division to Red Bag in exchange for all of the capital stock of Red Bag.

Red Bag Cement Company was a wholly owned subsidiary of Steel City Coke & Chemical Company. Both are Pennsylvania

corporations. On December 5, 1968, Wisconsin Cement Manufacturing Company of Port City entered into an agreement
with Steel City Coke & Chemical to acquire all of the capital
stock of Red Bag in exchange for the issuance to Steel City
Coke & Chemical of 150,000 Wisconsin common shares.

Formal exchange between Steel City Coke & Chemical and
Wisconsin of all the capital stock of Red Bag for 150,000
Wisconsin common shares took place on January 17, 1969. These
shares were acquired by Steel City Coke & Chemical as an
investment.

Respectfully submitted,

/s/ L. L. Wall

March 20, 1969   Vice President

POTTER & PEPPER   1 Center Tower
Certified Public Accountants   Steel City
                                             March 20, 1969

The Board of Directors of
Red Bag Cement Company

We have examined the accompanying balance sheet of Red Bag
Cement Company (a subsidiary of Steel City Coke & Chemical
Company) as of December 31, 1968, and the related statement
of income and income retained in the business for the year.
Our examination of these statements was made in accordance
with generally accepted auditing standards, and accordingly
included such tests of the accounting records and such other
auditing procedures as we considered necessary in the
circumstances.

Under the terms of an agreement dated November 4, 1968, Steel
City Coke & Chemical Company, on January 17, 1969, exchanged
all of the capital stock of Red Bag Cement Company for
150,000 shares of the common stock of Wisconsin Cement
Manufacturing Company. In closing the books of Red Bag at
December 31, 1968, certain adjustments were recorded in
order to state the accounts at amounts suitable for inclusion in the consolidated financial statements of Steel
City Coke & Chemical. Two of these adjustments were the
elimination of the reserve for doubtful accounts and the
reserve for plant shutdown expenses to reflect the fact that

Red Bag was no longer on a "going concern" basis as far as
Steel City Coke & Chemical was concerned. In addition, an
election was made in 1968 to price the finished cement inventory at standard costs which approximate current costs
in lieu of the lifo method previously used. The balance in
the lifo reserve of $65,942 at January 1, 1968, was accord-
ingly eliminated. These three adjustments are shown in the
accompanying statement of income and income retained in the
business as special credits and are detailed as follows:

	Gross adjustment	Income tax effect	Net special credits
Elimination of reserve for doubtful accounts	$ 5,728	_____	$ 5,728
Elimination of reserve for plant shutdown expenses	270,637	$106,122	164,515
Elimination of lifo reserve	65,942	35,609	30,333
	$342,307	$141,731	$200,576

The reserve for doubtful accounts at January 1, 1968, was
$20,000, which was eliminated during the year by charges
for bad debts written off totaling $14,272 with the balance
of $5,728 credited as a special item as noted above. It is
estimated that, on a "going concern" basis, the balance
in this reserve account at December 31, 1968, should probably
have been approximately equivalent to the balance at January
1, 1968.

In previous years, it was the consistent practice of Steel
City Coke & Chemical to provide a reserve for expenses to be
incurred when the cement plant was shut down for major repairs. These shutdowns were scheduled at approximately
18-month intervals. Since these repairs after December 31,
1968, are the responsibility of Wisconsin as the parent
company of Red Bag, rather than Steel City Coke & Chemical,
the balance in the reserve at December 31, 1968, totaling
$270,637 was eliminated when the accounts were finally
closed for the year. However, if accounts of Red Bag were
to be issued on a "going concern" basis, a reserve should
be provided for in the December 31, 1968, financial state-

ments. The portion of this reserve provided in 1968 has been
considered as a deduction in computing taxes on income of
$288,029 and the special credit has therefore been reduced
by the equivalent tax effect amounting to $106,122.

Present plans contemplate the replacement by Wisconsin of
certain portions of the existing plant with modern facilities. It is not possible at this time to estimate what loss,
if any, would be incurred with regard to the operating
supplies inventory and fixed assets if these plans are
carried out.

Prior to 1968, the cement plant of Steel City Coke & Chemical
Company was operated as a division of the company. On
December 31, 1967, this division's assets and business were
transferred to Red Bag Cement Company, a previously inactive
subsidiary. Because of this transfer, facilities acquired
from 1963 through 1967 for which the sum of the years-digits
method of calculating depreciation had been used, were considered to be second hand facilities to Red Bag effective
January 1, 1968. As a result, 1968 depreciation on these
items was calculated using the straight-line method and
depreciation charged to expense was approximately $37,000
less than it would have been had the sum of the years-digits
method been continued for these facilities.

Employees of Red Bag, upon retirement, are entitled to
pensions under noncontributory pension plans. These plans
are to be continued by Wisconsin. In the period when Red Bag
was a subsidiary of Steel City Coke & Chemical, the current
actuarially estimated cost of pensions was charged to
operating expense of Steel City Coke & Chemical as each
employee became eligible to retire and the pensions funded
over a five-year period from that date. Under this method,
no pension provision was necessary for Red Bag employees in
1968.

Prior to 1968, general management expenses of Steel City
Coke & Chemical were not allocated to the several divisions
of the company. However, a portion of such expenses amounting
to approximately $154,000 was allocated to Red Bag in 1968

and is included in the accompanying statement of income and income retained in the business. The allocated portion of these expenses was, of necessity, based upon estimates, since the nature of these expenses are such that they could not be precisely accounted for as relating to specific subsidiaries or divisions of Steel City Coke & Chemical.

In accordance with the agreement between Steel City Coke & Chemical and Wisconsin, a dividend of $415,635 was paid by Red Bag to its shareholder, Steel City Coke & Chemical, on January 16, 1969.

In view of the materiality of the matters referred to above, we are unable to express an opinion on the appended financial statements as a whole. Except for these matters, we believe that the statements are presented in conformity with generally accepted accounting principles.

/s/ POTTER & PEPPER

RED BAG CEMENT COMPANY (A SUBSIDIARY OF STEEL CITY COKE & CHEMICAL COMPANY)

Balance Sheet
December 31, 1968
(See Report of Potter and Pepper)

Assets:

Cash		$ 180,259
Accounts receivable:		
Customers	$156,165	
Steel City Coke & Chemical Company and subsidiaries	90,366	
Employees	12,920	259,451
Inventories, principally at current cost:		
Finished goods	$335,166	
Work in process	257,380	
Raw materials	57,140	
Operating supplies	562,141	1,211,827
Property, plant and equipment at cost, less accumulated depreciation of $2,909,993		2,059,560
Prepaid expenses and deferred charges		8,247
		$3,719,344

RED BAG CEMENT COMPANY (A SUBSIDIARY OF STEEL CITY COKE & CHEMICAL COMPANY) BALANCE SHEET (CONT'D)

Liabilities and Shareholders' equity:

Accounts payable:

Trade	$159,530	
Steel City Coke & Chemical Company and subsidiaries	200,415	$ 359,945
Salaries, wages and vacation pay		96,651
Federal and state income taxes		279,760
Other accrued liabilities		18,007
Total liabilities		$ 754,363
Capital stock, authorized 1,000 shares, issued 50 shares at stated value of		2,502,448
Income retained in the business		462,533
Total shareholders' equity		$2,964,981
		$3,719,344

Statement of Income and Income Retained in the Business
Year Ended December 31, 1968

Net Sales	$5,283,295
Costs and expenses:	
Cost of sales and operating expenses	3,863,975
Depreciation	183,978
Selling and administrative	607,208
Taxes, other than income taxes	37,313
Other	40,766
	$4,733,240
Income before taxes on income	$ 550,055
Provision for income taxes	288,029
Income for the year	$ 262,026
Special credits net of related income taxes payable of $141,731	200,576
Income for the year and special credits	$ 462,602
Income (deficit) retained in the business:	
Balance at beginning of year	(69)
Balance at end of year	$ 462,533

CHAPTER 15

EXTENSION OF THE ATTEST FUNCTION

Auditors apply the attest function almost wholly to historical financial statements. Chapter 11 presented a few examples of departures from this practice, but the fact remains that departures are rarities. The following readings suggest new applications of the attest function. It is proposed that auditors consider attesting to overall operations of an organization, management performance, and budgets.

OPERATIONAL AUDITS BY PUBLIC ACCOUNTANTS
J. W. Buckley*

The earliest public accountants were, in fact, business consultants. They advised clients regarding most business matters. Businesses were small and relatively uncomplicated. Services rendered were to the proprietor, and the concept of third-party responsibility was virtually nonexistent. There was no accounting profession in those days; no formal requirements in accounting education; no qualifying examinations. The relationship between the businessman and his accountant was a very personal one — independence was not a primary issue.

The last decades of the nineteenth century brought about many changes in the nature and scope of public accountancy. A profession was born. Extensive educational programmes were developed. Stringent requirements regulated admission to practice. The concepts of 'third-party responsibility' and 'independence' became the hallmarks of accounting professionalism. For many reasons it became necessary to confine practice narrowly to the areas of auditing and tax, sorting out accounting problems resulting from business failures, and fiduciary relationships.

The prognosis is for a reversal of this trend during the latter half of the twentieth century. Since the 1950s, public accounting firms have developed an increasing capacity in 'management services'.[1] More recently they have turned

---

* First published in *Abacus*, Vol. 2, No. 2 (December, 1966), pp. 159–171, and reproduced here by permission of Sydney University Press and the author.
[1] Surveys in the United States show that the major CPA firms obtain as much as 26% of their current revenues from management services: John W. Buckley, *Extended Services of Certified Public Accountants: An Investigation of Management Services and Management Audits*, unpublished doctoral dissertation, Seattle: University of Washington, June 1964; American Institute of Certified Public Accountants, *Revenue and Expenses of Accounting Firms*, A Management of Accounting Practice Bulletin, Map 14b, Second Annual Survey, 1963; Committee on Management Services: The Georgia Society of Certified Public Ac-

their attention to 'management' or 'operational' auditing. These programmes reestablish the role of the public accountant as a business consultant; but it would be naive to propose that this emergent role bears any resemblance to the archaic one described previously.

What is 'operational auditing'? How does it differ from conventional auditing? How does it differ from 'management services'? What are the design and operative requirements of operational auditing? It is to these questions that we direct our attention.

OPERATIONAL AUDITING DEFINED

An operational audit has been defined as

> a comprehensive and constructive examination of an organizational structure of a company, institution, or branch of government, or of any component thereof, such as a division or department, and its plans and objectives, its methods of control, its means of operation, and its use of human and physical facilities.[2]

Conceptually the operational audit is a 'complete' audit—it examines all of the interrelated aspects of a problem.

Some implicit assumptions of operational auditing include the recognition that non-fiscal as well as fiscal data are important to management decisions; a notion of the firm as being a person-oriented and -directed system; and a belief that the 'management by exception' strategy is an insufficient administrative device. Operational auditors subscribe to the philosophy that the grey areas of marginal efficiency are as critical to the success of business operations in the long run as are problems of the acute and cognizable variety.

The objective of operational auditing is to appraise management organization, techniques and performance with a view toward improvement. In this sense it may be thought of as being a *constructive* audit.

Operational auditing may be developed as an extension of the internal audit[3] or it may be performed by independent analysts;[4] in either case the

---

countants, 'Management Services Survey,' *The Georgia CPA,* Vol 2, No 2, Fall 1960, pp. 8–11; and James E. Redfield, *A Study of Management Services by Certified Public Accountants,* Austin, University of Texas 1961.

[2] William P. Leonard, *The Management Audit,* Englewood Cliffs, New Jersey, Prentice-Hall 1963, p. 35. It should be noted that the terms 'management auditing' and 'operational auditing' are used synonymously in the literature.

[3] An extensive and illustrative treatment of the expansion of the internal audit function is contained in Francis J. Walsh, Jr., *Internal Auditing,* No. 111, National Industrial Conference Board, 1963.

[4] External analysts include business consulting firms, governmental operational auditors of which the General Accounting Office in the United States is typical, bank loan officers, e.g., The National Association of Bank Loan Officers and Credit Men, *How to Appraise Management—A Check List,* 39th Annual Conference, Atlantic City, October 1953; organizations whose primary interest is operational auditing, e.g., The American Institute of Management, and public accounting firms.

basic principles are consistent. External operational auditing is used where management has insufficient resources to support an internal programme; where independent, objective appraisal is preferred *in lieu* of internal operational auditing; or where external appraisal is applied in addition to the internal audit. Our particular focus here is on external operational auditing.

OPERATIONAL vs. CONVENTIONAL AUDITING

The conventional audit is concerned primarily with the fiscal record. Its objectives are to confirm a state of financial affairs, to verify that generally accepted principles have been applied with consistency, and to express an opinion on fiscal stewardship. The conventional audit has many shortcomings from a managerial viewpoint: it fails to measure progress toward enterprise objectives; it fails to account for the non-fiscal essentials of business management; it orients toward the past rather than the future; it fails in comparative analysis, i.e., in evaluating the effectiveness of the client's plans, procedures and operations vs. those of competitors; it fails in integrative analysis, i.e., in evaluating the efficiency of functional interaction within the firm; and it fails in interpretative analysis, e.g., in relating fiscal data to current decisions.

The comparison of these two auditing techniques might be summarized as follows:

A COMPARISON: CONVENTIONAL vs. OPERATIONAL AUDITING

Characteristic	Conventional Auditing	Operational Auditing
1. Purpose	Express an opinion on financial condition and on stewardship	Appraise and improve management methods and performance
2. Scope	The fiscal record	Interrelated business functions
3. Method	Emphasis on accounting skills	Emphasis on interdisciplinary skills
4. Time-orientation	To the past	To the future
5. Precision	Absolute	Relative
6. Recipients	External — stockholders, government, public	Internal — management
7. Realization	Actual	Potential
8. Necessity	Legally required	Optional
9. Practice	Archaic	Recent
10. Catalyst	Tradition	Executive intuition

These differences are emphasized repeatedly in the literature, e.g.:[5]

While the accounting audit looks backward into the accounting transactions that have already taken place, the management audit looks forward. It is concerned with ways and means of improving future business operations. It is not concerned with past malfeances or misfeances. It is distinctly constructive in concept. It aims to insure better results — to assist management in bettering the position of the business.

Of course, it is not implied that operational auditing should supplant conventional auditing. On the contrary, the programmes are supplementary. In fact, the operational audit can be a natural extension of the conventional audit, as noted by Worthy:[6]

Implicit (and sometimes explicit) in discussions of the management audit idea is the aspiration that in due course the management auditor can achieve a degree of status and recognition not different in kind from that enjoyed by the accountant. Indeed, the management audit evolved in important part from the internal audit, which was a gradual extension of the traditional work of accountancy. It is not strange, therefore, that parallels should be drawn between public accounting and what the management audit might be developed into.

The public accountant is in an optimum position to persuade management of the benefits of extending the audit function to overall business operations. His chief selling point is that *prevention* is better than *cure*. Through operational auditing he may detect danger signals that portend serious trouble in the future and thereby promote early corrective action. It is often the medium and small business that could benefit most from on-going appraisal, as noted by Larke:[7]

The really big companies usually keep enough industrial medicine men in attendance so that they're able to get an outsider's view of what they're doing often enough to remain realistic. Too often the medium and small plant can't afford expert care until it is in extremis. As rigor mortis is about to set in, the owners cry 'Doc, save us!' And, amazingly, the management consultants often do.

Even though the operational audit may not reveal any ghosts in the closet, it may still have salutory benefits, e.g., it may create a feeling of satisfaction on the part of management by assuring it that its house is in order; it has an effect similar to favourable reports on routine medical check-ups.

---

[5] Arthur P. Wilson, 'The Management Audit Comes of Age,' *The Controller*, September 1950, p. 411.

[6] James C. Worthy, 'The Management Audit,' *Proceedings of Annual Meeting*, 1962, American Academy of Management, pp. 176–178.

[7] Alfred G. Larke, 'Management Self-Audit for Smaller Companies,' *Dunn's Review and Modern Industry*, March 1955, p. 40.

MANAGEMENT SERVICES AND OPERATIONAL AUDITING

In discussing the extended services of public accountants, it is useful to distinguish between the two emerging areas of practice: *management services* and *operational auditing*. The line between these practices may be narrow, but there is a significant theoretical difference. Essentially, management services denote activities that provide *assistance to* management on *specific* problems, while operational auditing is related to the *appraisal of* management from a *general* viewpoint. The comparison of these two practices may be extended as follows:

A COMPARISON: MANAGEMENT SERVICES vs. OPERATIONAL AUDITING

Characteristic	Management Services	Operational Auditing
1. Purpose	Assist Management	Appraise Management
2. Scope	Tends toward the specific	Tends toward the general
3. Method	Non-standardized—is designed for the specific task	Utilizes standardization—in the use of questionnaires, checklists, etc.
4. Orientation	To the task	To the individual
5. Repetition	Seldom. Limited to completion of specific task	Frequent. Promotes periodic appraisal

Conceptual differences in the fundamental orientation of management services vs. operational auditing appear to include the following:

FUNDAMENTAL ORIENTATION: MANAGEMENT SERVICES

1 Management requires specific assistance at specific times to meet specific needs. Often the problem is immediate—it cannot wait for the occurrence of a routine audit.

2 Management recognizes that some business problems are more critical than others, and believes that careful attention to these problems may be all that is needed to raise total performance to a desired level.

3 Management at times requires specialists for in-depth attention to specific problems. Highly-trained analysts of this type have different training and experience from the inter-disciplinarians who engage in operational auditing.

4 If problems were known to be of the continuing type that materially affect the well-being of the firm, management would recruit and retain staff personnel to cope with the problem. Hence their principal reason for securing external assistance would be in connection with the unexpected, non-repetitive-type problem.

FUNDAMENTAL ORIENTATION: OPERATIONAL AUDITING

1 There is an interrelationship between all business functions. While there is a need for the specialist who examines one problem in particular, there is an equal need for the analyst who can review the whole business systematically and examine the efficiency of functional interaction.

2 If management adopted the systematic review and appraisal of its overall operations, acute problems would be minimized. And in terms of reducing costs and promoting efficiency, preventative action, where possible, is superior to therapeutic action.

3 It is probably more effective to have one group of analysts perform the review and appraisal of the whole business, than it would be to have a number of independent specialists attempt to isolate and examine separately problems that are inextricably tied together.

4 Business management cannot be separated from businessmen, i.e., from the people who run the business. Any audit or consulting programme that fails to recognize the person-oriented and -directed nature of a firm will fail also to grasp the full reality of a particular situation. Operational auditing is, by design, a person-oriented programme. Its chief concern is the 'who' in administration.

Once again, the discussion of these differences should not lead one to conclude that these programmes are intrinsically competitive or even mutually exclusive. On the contrary, there can be a very natural interaction not only between management services and operational auditing, but also between these programmes and conventional auditing. If we view management services as being directed primarily at specific problem-solving tasks, conventional auditing as being mainly concerned with the accounting overview, and operational auditing as being mainly concerned with the organizational overview, it is not difficult to perceive a work-flow system in which the specific accounting-oriented problems arising from the conventional audit, and the specific managerial problems arising from the operational audit, may be referred to management services personnel for in-depth attention. This work-flow system may be illustrated as follows (see below).

If separate departments, i.e., separate personnel, operate in these several areas, qualitative feedback and evaluation are possible. It is believed in the U.S.A. that independence can be retained between the public accounting firm and the client by maintaining the independence of operational areas; an analogous reference is the independence that exists between the internal and operating departments within the firm.

The importance of distinguishing between these areas of practice has

A WORK-FLOW SYSTEM DEMONSTRATING THE COMPLEMENTARY RELATIONSHIP OF CONVENTIONAL AUDITING, OPERATIONAL AUDITING, AND MANAGEMENT SERVICES

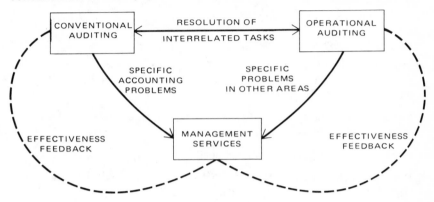

CONTEMPORARY ORGANIZATION OF A TYPICAL MAJOR CPA FIRM

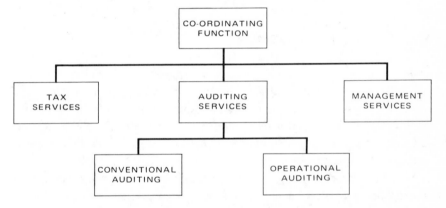

induced changes in the organizational structure of the major CPA firms in the United States. In several instances, the operational auditing programme is being developed as a division of the conventional auditing department, while management services are performed generally by a separate department.[8] Typically, the organization arrangement is as above.

In the United States, staffing for operational auditing, and to a greater extent management services, has involved recruiting personnel with non-accounting specialties. In some instances from 24% to 26% of the professional staff consist of non-accountants. The repercussions of this organizational change have yet to be analysed.

---

[8] The extent to which separate departments have been created for management services is reported by Buckley, op. cit., pp. 30–36. (80% of firms with a professional staff of 26 persons or more had separate departments for management services); American Institute of Certified Public Accountants, *How to Get Started in Management Services*, 1963, pp. 22–23; and Redfield, op. cit., p. 53.

DESIGN OF OPERATIONAL AUDITING

The basic operational auditing format typically includes the following steps:

1 Identifying management criteria.

2 Preparing for the operational audit: a. Environmental introduction. b. Relating established criteria to the particular situation. c. Confirming the scope of the engagement.

3 Conducting the operational survey: a. Selection of survey technique: questionnaire or memorandum. b. Evaluating the operational survey.

4 Conducting the in-depth operational audit.

5 Reporting on the operational audit: a. Reporting results of the operational survey. b. Reporting results of the in-depth operational audit.

6 Follow-up of the operational audit: a. Follow-up in subsequent periods. b. Follow-up in specific problem areas.

IDENTIFYING MANAGEMENT CRITERIA

A basic premise in the design of operational auditing is the concept that there are common denominators of good management that have relevance to all types of business organizations.[9] The audit programme begins with an identification of these key managerial elements. To accomplish this, some operational auditors use a horizontal or inter-functional approach,[10] while others use a vertical or functional approach.[11]

A typical horizontal approach would recognize key elements relating to management objectives, e.g., quality of management, qualified personnel, sound plans, policies and procedures. A typical vertical approach would recognize key elements relating to management functions, marketing, purchasing, e.g., industrial relations, research and engineering.

The reason for selecting management criteria is to improve the comparison of organizations, i.e., one organization with another, or the same organization over time. Arguments favouring comparative inter-organizational financial statements could be used in defense of this approach. Some proponents of the

---

[9] The principles or organization developed in the management theory literature form the basis, in most instances, for identifying the inter-organizational management criteria.

[10] Larke, op. cit., p. 40, and Charles J. Berg, Jr., 'Management Audits as an Effective Analysis Tool,' *Ideas for Management,* Systems and Procedures Association, Cleveland, Ohio, 1964, pp. 27–28.

[11] American Institute of Management, *Appraising A Management,* New York, 1955, and The National Association of Bank Loan Officers and Credit Men (Robert Morris Associates), 'How to Appraise Management — A Check List,' *39th Annual Conference,* October 1953, pp. 25–35.

operational audit suggest that the identification of common management criteria enables managerial comparison even where financial comparison is impractical.[12]

PREPARING FOR THE OPERATIONAL AUDIT

The first step in preparing for the particular assignment consists of the *environmental introduction,* i.e., where the operational auditors physically survey the subject organization and meet with its personnel. This phase is important because it gives the auditor an opportunity to gauge the interest of operating personnel in the programme, and to obtain some indication of the degree to which they will cooperate with the audit. Without the direct interest and cooperation of key personnel in the organization much of the programme's value will be lost. Because of the dubious ends for which some operational audits have been used, e.g., building a case for personnel action (hiring, firing, promoting or transferring), it may be necessary to reiterate the constructive nature of the programme in order to minimize the threat to individual security. The reluctance of employees to recognize the need for adaptation by the organization may be countered by forthright assertion that a primary purpose of the audit is the correction of employee deficiencies with a view to continued employment within an organization which will have become more economically viable.

[12] For example, commercial enterprises and non-profit organizations may be compared managerially even where substantive differences in financial accounting practice make financial comparison difficult. As a case in point, the American Institute of Management consistently appraises management performance in diverse industry types on the basis of the same management criteria. See *Manual of Excellent Managements,* published annually by the Institute. With regard to non-profit organizations *per se,* the managerial functions are given different titles and weights than is the case with profit organizations:

Commercial Management Functions		Non-Profit Management Functions	
Category	Weight	Category	Weight
Economic Function	1,000	Social Function	1,000
Corporate Structure	500	Organization Structure	800
Health of Earnings	600	Growth of Facilities	500
Service to Stockholders	700	Membership Analysis	1,300
Research and Development	800	Development Programme	800
Directorate Analysis	800	Fiscal Policies	800
Fiscal Policies	1,000	Trustee Analysis	800
Production Efficiency	1,100	Operating Efficiency	700
Sales Vigour	1,300	Administrative Evaluation	1,200
Executive Evaluation	2,200	Effectiveness of Leadership	2,100
	10,000		10,000

For an example of their non-profit operational audits, see *The Roman Catholic Church,* American Institute of Management, 1956, 1960 and 1962.

The next preparatory step consists of determining whether or not the standardized management criteria are valid in the particular circumstances. For example, criteria developed for the audit of a large business may be unsuitable when applied to a small business; or criteria developed for a whole company may be invalid when applied to a single department. To minimize field adjustments, several operational auditing firms have developed a number of alternative programmes based on company size, type, departmental structure, and so forth.

The third preparatory step is to confirm the engagement. The operational audit is an exercise in co-operation, so the role of each party must be set forth clearly. Because management will often expect more from the audit than it is possible to accomplish with economy, it is necessary precisely to define the nature and scope of the audit in the contractual documents.

CONDUCTING THE OPERATIONAL SURVEY

The operational survey is intended to be comprehensive; it should cover all of the important aspects of the audit unit. There are two basic approaches to obtaining survey information: (a) the questionnaire approach, or (b) the memorandum approach.[13]

To survey the organizational management of a company, for example, the questionnaire approach may be illustrated as follows:

	YES	NO	NOT APPLICABLE
1 Does the company have a current organization chart in effect?			
a For the entire company?			
b For each department?			
2 Have job descriptions been prepared for all key positions?			
a At top management level?			
b At middle management level?			
c At supervisory level?			

[13] For a critical evaluation of these optional techniques see Henry De Vos, ed, 'Pros and Cons of Using a Management Control Questionnaire,' *The Journal of Accountancy,* September 1964, pp. 83–84. For sample questionnaire see Henry De Vos, ed, *Management Services Handbook,* New York, American Institute of Certified Public Accountants, 1964, pp. 31–50; and *The Review of the Management Controls of the Small Business,* No. 6 in the Series, *Management Services by CPA's,* New York, American Institute of Certified Public Accountants, 1961.

The memorandum approach, on the other hand, would obtain information this way:

1 Obtain a copy of the current organization chart(s).
   a List persons who appear to be the effective decision-makers.
   b Comment on the relationship between the formal organization chart(s) and the perceived roles of authority.

2 Obtain copies of job descriptions of key positions at the various management levels.
   a Comment on the adequacy of the job descriptions.
   b Comment on the extent to which existing personnel perform the tasks in accordance with the job descriptions.

Some management audit programmes use a combination questionnaire-memorandum approach. See figure on next page.

The purpose of the operational survey is twofold: (a) to obtain a measure of the overall effectiveness of the organization, and (b) to uncover specific operational problem areas. The above-mentioned approaches are the mechanical means by which survey information is obtained. The survey questionnaire and/or memorandum is augmented by physical observations, programmed interviews, plant tours and whatever other means are necessary to secure sufficient substantive information.

COMBINATION QUESTIONNAIRE-MEMORANDUM

	YES	NO	NOT APPLICABLE
1 Does the company have a current organization chart in effect?			
a Obtain a copy of the current organization chart.			
b Does the organization chart reflect existing lines of authority?			
c If not, describe the organization relationships as you perceive them.			
2 Have job descriptions been prepared for all key personnel?			
a Obtain copies of the job descriptions.			
b Does actual performance have relevance to the job descriptions?			
c If not, comment on the nature in which performance varies from the job description(s).			

CONDUCTING THE IN-DEPTH OPERATIONAL AUDIT

The in-depth operational audit is the problem-solving phase of the programme. Major problems observed in the course of the operational survey are investigated in detail. If problem solution rests within the limits of the technical competence of the operational audit staff, no effort is made to refer the assignment to others. On the other hand, where special skills are required, the assignment may be transferred to specialists in the field. In the case of public accounting firms, the assignment would be transferred to the management services staff.

REPORTING ON THE OPERATIONAL AUDIT

The results of the operational survey may be reported in a number of ways. In some instances specific reporting categories are developed, e.g.:[14]

AUDIT AREA: COMPANY POLICY

AUDIT AREA: COMPANY POLICY

Progressive	Average	Weak
1 Policies and objectives are clearly defined and understood by all.	1 Policies not clearly defined nor understood.	1 No general policy except to carry on tradition.
2 All current and potential economic factors recognized in overall company planning.	2 Sporadic consideration of potential economic factors in company planning.	2 Planning done under impulse.
3 Aggressive participation in trade and business associations.	3 Interest in trade and business associations limited.	3 Trade and business associations regarded as a necessary evil.

The most accurate statement in each case may be designated by a 'check mark', or if greater precision is needed, weighted numerical values could be assigned to the various statements.

The American Institute of Management's report consists, in part, of a numerical rating scale:[15]

[14] Adapted from Howard Ellsworth Sommer, 'How to Analyze your own Business,' *Management Aids for Small Manufacturers No. 46*, Washington, D.C., Small Business Administration.

[15] The American Institute of Management's audit reports are published periodically in its *Manual of Excellent Managements*, New York, American Institute of Management. The eighth edition, for example,

Category	Optimum Rating	Minimum for Excellence	Actual Rating
Economic Function	1,000	750	1,000
Corporate Structure	500	375	470
Health of Earnings	600	450	580
Service to Stockholders	700	525	640
Research and Development	800	600	770
Directorate Analysis	800	600	760
Fiscal Policies	1,000	750	1,000
Production Efficiency	1,100	825	1,000
Sales Vigour	1,300	975	1,200
Executive Evaluation	2,200	1,650	2,100
Total	10,000	7,500	9,520

This method attempts to appraise managerial effort in quantitative terms; a detailed questionnaire provides the basic data. Criticisms of this approach centre on the dubious reliability of the weight index used to differentiate management functions, and on the implied precision by which some highly subjective conclusions are measured.

Reports of the foregoing type are usually accompanied by descriptive text which explains the rationale employed in arriving at the indicated conclusions. Some operational audit reports are entirely descriptive and do not attempt to place a numerical value on management performance in specific areas. In any event, the basic objective of the report is to convey an overall impression of the situation as the auditor sees it; including reference to areas where excellence is observed, to areas where slight improvement is indicated, and to those areas where considerable improvement is needed.

A specific report should be prepared for each in-depth operational audit conducted. The report should indicate the nature of the problem investigated and its disposition. The report is intended as a basis for managerial action, and should not reduce management's own decision-making responsibility.

listed 524 companies in 72 industrial groups as being 'excellently managed'. Reference to methodology employed by the Institute may be obtained from Jackson Martindell, The Scientific Appraisal of Management, New York, Harper 1950, and The Appraisal of Management, New York, Harper 1962.

FOLLOW-UP OF THE OPERATIONAL AUDIT

An important characteristic of the operational survey is its periodicity. The appraisal of management performance in consecutive periods by means of consistent criteria promotes comparative analysis and the measurement of progress toward designated objectives. Knowledge of periodic appraisal may also induce a striving for excellence on the part of corporate personnel.

Similar follow-up activities should be undertaken in connection with the in-depth operational audits. This is particularly important in those instances where problems have been assigned to others. Problem solutions should be evaluated in the abstract as well as in the operating context. The impact of certain problem solutions on the environment must be the subject of careful review. Some remedies require such drastic changes in surrounding functions as to render implementation infeasible.

THE PUBLIC ACCOUNTING ROLE
IN OPERATIONAL AUDITING

Public accountants have extended their consulting services partly because they believe their services to be different and often complementary to those of other business consultants, and partly because they believe that they can perform better services for their clients for the following reasons:

1 They are already familiar with the client's organization, operations and personnel.

2 They are better able to perceive the tax and audit implications of their recommendations.

3 Their income is not based entirely on management services or operational auditing. This spreads office overhead over the several activities of the firm.[16]

4 Retention of their tax and audit work depends upon the manner in which they perform extended services for the same client. (This interrelationship of functions promotes a striving for excellence in the several services in order to retain any of them.)

Typical progression into operational auditing begins with the examination

---

[16] Perrin Stryker, 'The Ambitious Consultants,' *Fortune*, May 1954, pp. 82ff, notes that management consulting firms often have difficulty in keeping their people busy and appear to be able to bill an average of only about 60 per cent or 150 days out of a 260-day working year'. Accounting firms, on the whole, are able to do much better than this. Also, because they have corresponding practices in auditing and taxes, they are able to allocate office overhead to all of their activities.

of problem areas related to the conventional audit programme.[17] As experience is gained, and as management is made aware of the benefits of operational auditing as a problem-solving, money-saving programme, the audit is expanded into functional areas, and finally, is applied to all management levels.

There is ample evidence that accountants are being encouraged to develop operational audit programmes. In fact, statements on record suggest that, in time, public accountants may 'attest' to management performance in terms of stated objectives and responsibilities in a manner similar to the present attestation of financial reports:[18]

> *The question to be considered here is whether it is possible that CPAs may be asked to attest to data which would provide a basis for judging the performance of corporate management in the public interest. To many readers this question may seem wholly remote from reality. But the subject of corporate accountability is being discussed so widely in economics and social literature that CPAs would be unwise to ignore it.*

> *If the independent CPA in public practice becomes more deeply involved with the internal information systems of his clients, his attest function might be extended in a number of ways. He might express opinions providing assurance to top management that the data which it was receiving for various purposes were reliable, or that projections were well founded, or that decisions were being made upon sound modern theoretical and procedural bases. CPAs might develop standards and criteria which would enable them to attest that an organization did or did not follow 'generally accepted managerial standards' in deciding among alternative courses of action.*

In the meantime, nearer at hand, is a continually improving literature on ways and means of initiating and sustaining operational auditing programmes. The extension of accounting practice will have a profound influence on the education and certification of accountants, and professional accounting bodies are giving preferential consideration to these matters.[19]

---

[17] A number of major CPA firms have initiated their operational auditing programmes by conducting pilot projects for certain clients on an experimental and non-fee basis.

[18] John S. Carey (Executive Director of the American Institute of Certified Public Accountants), *The CPA Plans for the Future,* New York, The American Institute of Certified Public Accountants, 1965, pp. 202 and 238 respectively.

[19] Indicative of this interest is the establishment of the *Study Committee on The Common Body of Knowledge for CPAs* under the joint sponsorship of the Carnegie Corporation and the American Institute of Certified Public Accountants. The development of specific educational programmes, standards, examinations, and credentials directly related to accounting and management consulting services are noted particularly in the United Kingdom and in Canada, see, for example, 'Management Accounting Diploma in United Kingdom,' *The Canadian Chartered Accountant,* July 1964, p. 8; 'Management Consultancy Ethics,' *The Accountant,* March 13, 1965, p. 360; 'Certificate in Management Information: Courses in Oral Tuition,' *The Accountant,* July 10, 1965, p. 61; and 'The Certificate in Management Information: Institute Conferences in London,' *The Accountant,* May 29, 1965, pp. 751–752.

MANAGEMENT AUDITING
John C. Burton*

In the coming decade, it seems very likely that there will be increasing demand for information about corporate performance. In part, this will manifest itself in additional requirements for disclosure of historical financial data. In addition, however, there may well be demand for some impartial evaluation of management performance beyond that implicitly provided by historical results reported in conformity with generally accepted accounting principles.

This demand may come from several sources. Investment analysts today recognize that the evaluation of management is of crucial importance and, at the same time, extremely difficult for any outsider. They may require managements to submit more data on this subject. Similarly, stockholders — particularly those who control large holdings in trust for others — may want more assurance that their capital is being effectively used. Finally, there is an increasing tendency for the public to feel that corporate management has the responsibility of using assets under its control effectively as a service to society as well as to its own stockholders. Several different groups might argue for some appraisal of management beyond conventional financial statements.

If some auditor in the future is to be asked to attest not only to financial results but also to the effectiveness of management's stewardship, it is important to consider what the nature of the "management audit" will be and how this auditor is to be qualified. Although there has been some writing on this subject, to date there has been no attempt to construct a total framework for the management audit.

In developing such a framework, four areas must be examined. First, the criteria for a management audit must be considered. Second, standards of managerial performance must be developed if the evaluation of management stewardship is to have meaning. Third, a method of reporting must be established so that the auditor can have a structured means of disclosing the results of his examination. Finally, it will be necessary to develop management auditing procedures and standards of documentation to support the report given.

Turning first to the criteria underlying the management audit, it seems that three premises may be established:

1 The audit must deal with the objective and the measurable.

2 It must deal with the present and the past and not with the future.

* From *The Journal of Accountancy*, Vol. 125, No. 5 (May, 1968), pp. 41–54. Reprinted by permission of the American Institute of Certified Public Accountants.

3 It must produce a result which is understandable and usable by the various interested publics.

The first of these criteria has always created problems for the advocate of management auditing. This is because the accountant has traditionally thought of measurability and objectivity in terms of countability and the ability to recount. It seems clear, however, that measurement need not imply the tally clerk's precision and that objectivity does not require that an identical answer always be derived from the same data. Objective is defined as detached, impersonal and unprejudiced. This definition can surely be met by a trained auditor exercising professional judgment on the effectiveness of managerial stewardship. Two separate auditors might emerge from an audit with slightly different results, but the variation should not exceed that attributable to normal sampling errors if due professional care is used.

The second criterion for a management audit indicates that the auditor must examine that which exists and has existed rather than that which it is hoped will develop. Almost by definition an audit cannot be a forecast and, accordingly, it is clear that a management audit will not supplant the investor's task of forecasting the relative success or failure of enterprises. Rather, it will improve data so that the marketplace will be better informed and the analyst will be able to make a more reasoned forecast based upon his own expectations of movements within the economy.

The elimination of forecasting from the audit function, however, does not mean that the future will be totally ignored. Management's present outlook is primarily future-oriented and, therefore, in evaluating the management of the present, the future must be implicitly considered. What the auditor must do, therefore, is to measure and evaluate whether or not management is currently performing its future-oriented function appropriately. This implies an audit of procedures, which is clearly part of the management audit.

At the same time, part of the auditing procedure must concern itself with the past since the results of past decisions may be the best means of estimating future results. The second part of the management audit, therefore, will be reporting on and evaluation of the results of the past.

Finally, the management audit must produce a result which is understandable and usable by the interested publics. The users of the audit must know what has been done and be aware of the significance of it. It has been charged by some that the auditor of today has failed in this respect even in regard to the financial audit, and it is most important that a similar failing does not occur if an expansion of the audit function takes place. This implies reporting needs, which will be discussed later.

DEVELOPMENT OF PERFORMANCE STANDARDS

If the first two criteria for a management audit are to be met, one prerequisite is the development of standards of managerial performance that can be expressed in specific terms. These standards are needed to evaluate both procedures and results. In the procedural area, the principal objective normally sought by the management of a firm is effective managerial control over the operations of the business. In order to achieve this control, management conventionally sets up a series of procedures. While it is true that procedures alone do not create control, it still appears plausible to evaluate the effectiveness of management control through the appraisal of the existence and use of the control procedures which the firm has established.

A first approach to the development of a control measure might be to identify the various areas of managerial control within the firm. One possible classification would be as follows:

1 Organization control
    a Chart of organization
    b Job descriptions
    c Procedure manuals
    d Stated corporate objectives

2 Planning and information systems
    a Long-range planning—strategic and operational
    b Operating budgets
    c Cost accounting systems
    d Cost controls

3 Asset management
    a Liquid asset control
    b Credit and receivable control
    c Inventory control
    d Capital budgeting system

4 Marketing system
    a Product planning
    b Market research
    c Sales forecasting
    d Sales analysis

5 Production system
    a Production planning
    b Quality control
    c Labor relations
    d Purchasing and procurement

Within each of these areas, it may be possible to identify the various procedures which are most significant in improving the quality of managerial control.

Relative "quality points" might then be assigned reflecting the existence and effective use of these procedures in each area and, by totaling these quality points, an overall index of the quality of control procedures might be developed which would serve as a basis for comparison among firms.

Considerable research is needed in determining what these quality points should be, and it may be that no quantitative evaluation of this sort is possible. Nevertheless, the evaluation of the adequacy of procedures and controls within each of these areas, even if performed on a nonquantitative basis, may be of significance in the evaluation of the management of the firm.

Beyond procedural standards, it is necessary to develop financial standards to evaluate the performance of the firm. Some bench marks are needed to supplement conventional net income which is the figure commonly used today. These might include the development of additional absolute figures, such as income exclusive of holding gains and charges related to future activities (like most research expenses), though the major financial standards will be relative ones. Reported achievements must be related to the industry and economic environment in which the firm operates, to the prior performance of the firm and to the prior plans of the corporation.

As an example of the type of approach that could be used, the following are possible measures of relative success:

1 Ratio of operating return on sales earned by the company compared to the return earned by the industry

2 Ratio of operating return on long-term capital earned by the company compared to the return earned by the industry

3 Comparative variability in return compared to average industry variability

In addition to standards for annual or periodic corporate data, financial standards might also encompass the comparison of results with expectations on a major project basis. There seems to be an increasing tendency today for firms to control operations not only by the calendar period but by major projects of a strategic nature. As information systems are improved, it is likely that the interpretation of corporate results will require an analysis of projects as well as of periods. In this way, past strategic decisions of the management can be evaluated as evidence develops relating to their success. While this will not be definitive evidence of the effectiveness of current strategic planning, it may be of some help to the investor to see the varying major decisions of corporate management identified and their results reported on as well as having successes and failures combined into a single net income figure.

REPORTING ON THE MANAGEMENT AUDIT

The third principal problem associated with the development of the management auditing framework is the establishment of the method of reporting to be used in connection with the audit performed. First, the recipient of the report must be identified. It is conceivable that management might seek a management audit from independent auditors and wish to be the only party receiving the auditor's report. Similarly, the directors might commission the audit and wish the report to be made solely to them. If the management audit develops to meet the needs mentioned above, however, the report must ultimately be available to stockholders and to the public.

The format of such a report will require considerable thought. It seems obvious that the report will bear little similarity to the standard short-form auditor's report which is predominant today. It is impractical to expect the auditor to report simply that management is following "generally accepted standards of management" and leave it at that. Such a report would tend to become a formality as indeed reports following this approximate wording seem to have become in certain European countries. What will be needed, therefore, is a longer and less standard statement.

It is premature to suggest the exact appearance of this report, but one approach might be to include three basic sections: first, a scope section where the auditor would describe the nature of his examination; second, a section in which the auditor evaluated the past performance of the company, perhaps including a variety of measures of performance in both absolute and comparative terms; and finally, a section in which the auditor evaluated the current management procedures of the corporation, perhaps including a "management control score." In all, a management audit report might take two or three pages in an annual report to stockholders.

Supplementing this report, there might be made available to management and to the directors a more detailed discussion of corporate results and controls and recommendations for improvements in the management system of the corporation. The auditor might also complete a management questionnaire which would be submitted to the directors and perhaps made available to the public through filing with the Securities and Exchange Commission.

MANAGEMENT AUDITING PROCEDURES

The final part of the management audit framework that must be developed is the determination of the auditing procedures associated with this audit and the documentation which is necessary to support the auditor's opinion. Today's auditing procedures provide a reasonable starting point. In connection with his examination of financial statements, today's auditor must develop a thorough understanding of the business enterprise. A major part of the audit today is the review of internal control and, in the expansion of the audit function, this is the area to which the greatest attention will have to be paid.

The current review of internal control normally focuses upon accounting controls. Under management auditing, however, the review of management controls will take on an enormously greater importance. This review today is normally performed on an occasional but not an intensive basis. The auditor generally has an organization chart in his working papers, but he does not spend a great deal of time on the planning side of the business. His analysis of the financial information system is more geared to satisfying himself about its reliability than to determining whether it produces appropriate information for the management of the firm. In a management audit, this emphasis will be changed. The auditor will look to see whether management is getting information relevant to the decisions and actions which it must take. This will require a much more intensive analysis of information needs and the efficiency of the existing system in meeting them. In the marketing and production areas particularly it is likely that the auditor will have to develop increased familiarity with the information needed to make decisions, including that which is not part of the conventional books of account. The auditor will not have to decide whether management is making the *right* strategic and operative decisions but rather whether management has available to it and is using the relevant information and techniques necessary to evaluate rationally the various alternatives that exist.

The procedures associated with the management audit, therefore, will include a substantial increase in the amount of time spent in evaluating internal control. They will include increasing reliance upon interviews with corporate managers, and they will require a study of the information system of the firm with new objectives in mind.

The second part of the management audit will require the auditor to undertake a financial analysis of the company in order to compare its results with the appropriate financial standards of performance. In this connection, the auditor must consider the operating results of the various parts of the firm. He must select that data which are most significant in the evaluation of corporate performance and array them in an understandable fashion so that the investor and the outside analyst can use such data for their purposes. In this connection, data will have to be accumulated about the company and its environment from the accounting and other records of the firm and from outside industry and government sources.

The increased scope of the management audit will create problems of audit documentation, although the changes in this area will not be as great as the changes in reporting on the audit. Presumably, the working papers of the auditor will include copies of the procedural manual of the firm and sample copies of the varying reports used by management to run the business, together with interview data indicating the extent to which formal procedures are actually used. There will be flowcharts of the information system, a description of the corporate planning process, and a record of the varying interviews and tests undertaken during the audit.

To support the financial analysis, there will be a compilation of the firm's operating data, a description of industry and government data sources and a record of calculations made. In addition, there might be a questionnaire designed to elicit from management the most significant facts for performance evaluation.

While the volume of documentation may not be great, there will be a need for an increased number of memorandums outlining in a reasoned manner the various judgments made in connection with the audit, and the logic supporting them. There will be relatively few schedules supplying arithmetic support, since the final judgments will not be verifiable by counting in the way an inventory may be checked today.

IMPLICATIONS FOR THE PUBLIC ACCOUNTING PROFESSION

In this discussion, it has been tacitly assumed that the management audit would develop out of today's financial audit. Certainly the CPA has a reasonable claim to be the most qualified management auditor. His current function requires that he be thoroughly familiar with the business of his client. He has traditionally given business advice, and in recent years his management consulting function has been growing rapidly. On the other hand, this function would require major changes in the reporting philosophy moving away from the increasingly standardized reports which are being given to the public today. There will be significant implications in the areas of competence, independence and legal liability which must be considered carefully before deciding whether management auditing should represent a major part of the activity of the public accounting profession.

If the measurement function of the public accountant is to be dramatically expanded, it is essential that the profession recruit and develop a cadre of people with competence in this form of measurement. This will require an increasing number of specialties within the profession and it will require a significant upgrading in the quality of personnel recruited. The public accounting firm will need specialists in production and marketing as well as financial information specialists in order to perform the management audit.

In part, this competence is currently being developed in management consulting divisions of the larger firms. The development of management auditing will put tremendous demands on these divisions since the skills they possess will initially be in short supply within the firm. This will require increasing integration between the audit function and the consulting function in firms since a management auditing engagement requires many of the people who are now used primarily in consulting work.

An additional implication which must be considered is the perennial problem of independence. The management auditor will start with fewer rules than govern the performance of the conventional financial audit. In the absence of generally accepted principles and standards, the auditor will have to feel his way. He will have to measure in an area where there is little precision. Given the increasing difficulty of measurement and the lack of fixed standards, the importance of independence of outlook becomes of increasing significance. The faith of the public in the integrity and ability of the auditor must be very great as the element of professional judgment in measurement becomes more significant.

The problem of independence will be particularly acute in the consulting area. If an auditor is to evaluate and report specifically on the procedures of a firm, is he barred from making recommendations for improvements? If he has suggested procedures which have been adopted, can he then independently review them? On the other hand, can one audit procedures without at least implicitly recommending change, except in the unusual case where perfection has been achieved? These are questions which will certainly become increasingly heard with the development of management audits, and no simple solutions are apparent.

The third implication that must be considered in connection with the management audit is that of the auditor's legal liability. As the management audit grows in stature and investors and other parties put increasing reliance upon this report of the public accountant, the potential for damage claims increases. The degree of responsibility which an auditor takes in his management attestation must be spelled out. Since errors in judgment can be increasingly costly, it must be clear that the auditor is not guaranteeing the future in his attestation. Rather he must be charged with the responsibility of justifying a professional opinion on the adequacy of current management procedures and past management performance. This, it would seem, presents no insurmountable difficulty if audit documentation has been properly prepared.

A FORECAST

Despite these problems the existence of the need for the attestation of corporate performance makes it likely that the management audit in some form
will come to be. While it appears that the public accounting profession is in
the best position to serve this function, if the profession declines to expand
its attest function beyond what it currently undertakes, then some other professional or governmental group might well perform the task required.

The management audit will not develop overnight. Rather it is more likely
that it will come from an evolution perhaps already under way. Two examples
of this trend are the use of auditors in pre-acquisition investigations and the
engagement of CPAs to attest to the existence of controls against conflict of
interest situations arising in a corporation. The next step might well be the
evolution of the internal control letter to management into the expression of
an opinion on efficiency. From this point it would not be difficult to develop
a routine for reporting on managerial effectiveness to directors.

Once such a trend starts, it is likely that it will grow since most outside
boards feel somewhat vulnerable in the absence of significant external review
of corporate management's activity.

Once managements and directors begin receiving regular opinions on the
efficiency of management performance, it will not be long before principal
creditors will demand such opinions as well. There is already evidence that
some creditors feel such information should be made available to them. Once
creditors have this information, it would not be surprising to see the managements of one or two corporations begin to publish such attestations in the
annual report to stockholders and at that point pressure on other managers
to do likewise would no doubt grow. Thus, the evolution of the management
audit might well take place without the force of law ever being invoked.

An alternative means of meeting the information need implied by the management audit would be by act of law. Congress might require that an independent appraisal of management be performed either by an independent
auditor or by a government agency. Such an act might require regular filing
of management audit reports so that such information would be available
to investors and potential investors.

Whatever the route, however, it seems logical to assume that this need
for additional information about the performance of management will be met
and in the not-too-distant future. It is incumbent upon the public accounting
profession to prepare itself to meet this demand.

ON BUDGETING PRINCIPLES
AND BUDGET-AUDITING STANDARDS
Yuji Ijiri*

PROPOSALS FOR BUDGET DISCLOSURE

As one way of providing more useful information to stockholders and investors of a firm, there have been growing attentions on budget disclosure. According to Cooper, Dopuch, and Keller [4], a proposal for budget disclosure was first introduced in accounting literature in 1947 by Stuart A. Rice at the Sixtieth Annual Meeting of the American Institute of (Certified Public) Accountants [7]. More than a decade later, a number of articles followed this proposal.

For example, Nielsen stated:

> The predictive quality of budgetary information is one of its most important characteristics. The very problem of integrating the components of projections tends to disclose what is necessary in order to achieve harmony in an operation so that the maximum benefits to the firm may result. The disclosure achieved by such projections tends to show what is necessary in order to maximize benefits accruing from the total operation of the firm. [6, p. 586].

Similarly, Bevis considered certification of business planning (prospective accounting) as being one of the important areas where the CPA's attest function would be valuable and stated:

> Since budgetary control already is oriented to the prospective view, it is suggested that this would be as excellent an avenue as any to commence auditing's new future in this field of business planning. [2, p. 34].

Birnberg and Dopuch, in discussing the need for a new framework of disclosure, expressed their opinion as follows:

> In order to inform the external parties of what they anticipate the future to hold for the entity, management must provide the investor with the information on three types of expectations. 1. Prospects for the economy. 2. Prospects for the industry and the enterprise as a member of that subset. 3. The specific expectations which underlie the major investments made in resources and the projects undertaken in attempting to achieve the enterprise's goals. [3, p. 58].

Lazarsfeld, an eminent sociologist, emphasized at a meeting of the Long-Range Objective Committee of the AICPA the budget function as an important future area of possible accounting practice and as an example he stated:

* From *The Accounting Review*, Vol. XLIII, No. 4 (October, 1968), pp. 662–667. Reprinted by permission of the American Accounting Association.

An article in the Public Opinion Quarterly *titled "Dollars and Sense" has pointed out that budgeting and auditing of scientific research projects is a completely new problem in our society. This is true for both physical and social science research. At the present time governments and foundations do not know how to budget research projects and they do not know how to audit research budgets submitted to them.* [1, p. 5].

Similarly, Solomon pointed out forecasting as one of the major scopes of the accounting function and "hence the scope of his education and his thinking." [8, p. 24].

Wilkinson and Doney [9] followed Bevis in advocating that auditing and reporting boundaries be extended to include budget auditing, and analyzed the effects of budget disclosure and budget auditing on management, stockholders and investors, creditors, competitors, the government, and independent auditors.

Cooper, Dopuch, and Keller [4] have gone farther to analyze "how a budgetary framework of disclosure brings into a new perspective several of the recent proposals for altering the historical cost basis of accounting reports."

From an analytical viewpoint, Ijiri, Kinard, and Putney [5] explored budget incentive systems which will stimulate reasonable forecasts on goal levels in profit, sales, etc., that management expects to attain and, at the same time, will stimulate better performance over and beyond estimated goal levels whenever possible. The attempt was to solve the problem that the discrepancy between estimated and actual goal levels cannot be the only basis of reward or penalty if efforts to attain better goal levels should always be stimulated irrespective of the estimates.

Following these efforts for budget disclosure and budget auditing, this present paper tries to move a step toward its implementation. In particular, the author will attempt to analyze the nature of budget audits and outline some essential factors in the generally accepted budgeting principles and procedures as well as the generally accepted budget-auditing standards and procedures. (For simplicity the term "generally accepted" will be omitted throughout this paper.) It will also discuss the contents of budget-audit reports as well as the responsibility of auditors concerning budget auditing.

Although budgets may be prepared and reported in various forms, it will be assumed for purposes of this discussion that firms publish financial statements in the following form and auditors are asked to express their opinions on such statements. For example, financial statements as of December 31, 1968 include actual figures for 1968 and estimated figures for 1969 where estimates are made based on the data available at the time the financial statements are prepared. For comparative purposes, they also include actual figures

COMPARATIVE FINANCIAL STATEMENTS
XYZ CORPORATION
AS OF DECEMBER 31, 1968

Account Names	1967 Actual	1968 Estimate	1968 Actual	1969 Estimate
xxx	xxx	xxx	xxx	xxx
xxx	xxx	xxx	xxx	xxx

for 1967 and estimated figures for 1968 which have been reported in the previous financial report.

This method of reporting budgets has an advantage over other methods in that budgets are directly tied in with the financial statements for the past periods. This allows a direct comparison between estimates and actual in order to determine the reliability of past estimates.

THE NATURE OF BUDGET AUDITS

Budget audits are similar to audits on audits in the sense that the central task of both types of audits is to check whether reasonable inferences were made in preparing budgets or in preparing audit reports, and not to make inferences by the auditors themselves.

In ordinary financial-statement audits, auditors gather evidence to infer the existence or non-existence of certain factors in the operations or in the financial state of the firm as well as in their accounting records in the period under examination. For example, auditors examine purchase orders, material-receiving slips, invoices, cancelled checks, etc., to infer material purchases and the procedures taken to record them. Cash count and reconciliations are means to infer the balance of cash at the end of the period examined as well as the effectiveness of the surveillance on cash.

However, no matter how painstakingly auditors gather and examine the evidence, they cannot be 100 per cent certain that they have made correct inferences, since there always exist possibilities, however small, that the evidence auditors examined may have been falsely produced. Therefore, in evaluating auditors' work, what is significant is whether the auditors' inferences are "reasonable" or not. This is exactly the point that partners of a CPA firm check when they review audit working papers prepared by field auditors. That is, the auditors' task in reviewing audits made by others (namely, audits on audits) is to see whether original auditors' inferences are "reasonable"; patently their task is not to make such inferences by themselves.

Similarly, in preparing budgets the management must make inferences on various factors in the future based on clues that are available at the time of the prediction. Therefore, the essential of budget audits lies in checking whether the inferences that the management made in preparing the budgets are reasonable or not.

This is analogous to the so-called "beyond-reasonable-doubt" notion in legal processes. A cautious juror may not be able to reach a conviction without any doubts whatsoever, but he is nonetheless supposed to avoid "unreasonable doubts." However, there are no natural and absolute standards to be used in distinguishing between reasonable and unreasonable doubts; the distinction is a social one, hence it depends upon time and places.

Therefore, in such situations, it is important to provide explicitly a set of standards by which members of the society understand what are considered to be "reasonable" doubts or "reasonable" inferences. In this sense, the most requisite step toward the implementation of budget disclosure and budget auditing is to develop a set of budgeting principles and procedures as well as a set of budget-auditing standards and procedures.

BUDGETING PRINCIPLES AND PROCEDURES

First, a set of budgeting principles and procedures must be prepared after a thorough investigation of what are involved in actual budgeting processes in various types of industries. It is hardly possible to elaborate on the components of the principles and procedures in detail here. The following discussion is intended to be only an outline of what are essential to the formulation of the budgeting principles and procedures.

The budgeting principles and procedures can be divided into two parts, one concerning the predictions of events and the other the recording of predicted events. The latter deals with the ordinary accounting procedures after certain events are predicted according to the former. Therefore, if the budgets are to be reported in the form of projected financial statements, we may simply quote the generally accepted accounting principles and procedures and state that the predicted events must be recorded according to them. Thus, the cost principle, the realization principle, the matching principle of revenue and costs, etc., will all be observed. Of course, it is possible to set up a different set of accounting principles and procedures for the recording of predicted events, allowing, for example, the firm to evaluate assets by factors other than their acquisition costs. However, unless they are also accepted in the preparation of ordinary financial statements, such dual principles and procedures would simply result in confusion and lack of comparability between budget and actual.

Two basic principles will govern the prediction of events. One is to make the inference process explicit. Just as auditors are required to prepare audit working papers as supporting documents of their inference processes, the management is asked to prepare "budget working papers" so that the processes of preparing the projected financial statements are made clear and explicit. This is essential since if the budgets are made by somewhat mysterious implicit hunches of management, there is no way to make an independent investigation on the budgets.

A second principle which will govern the prediction of events is consistency. The consistency principle covers a broad area of prediction. It may be divided into internal consistency and external consistency. Internal consistency deals with the data internal to the firm that are used in budgeting. It has two aspects: historical consistency, i.e., consistency between current estimates and estimates made in the past, and current consistency, i.e., consistency among current estimates. If a firm estimated the production capacity as 40,000 units a year in preparing a budget for 1968, the same number of units should be used in preparing a budget for 1969, unless there have been explainable changes in the factors related to the production capacity. This is historical consistency. Furthermore, estimates for 1969 should be mutually consistent. If the sales figure is estimated based on the production capacity of 50,000 units, and the production cost is estimated based on the production capacity of 30,000 units, the estimates lack current consistency. Similarly, if the cost of Product A is estimated based on the assumption that the plant will be expanded by the end of June 1969 whereas the cost of Product B that is produced by the same plant is estimated based on the assumption that the plant will not be expanded by the end of June 1969, the estimates lack current consistency.

Contrary to internal consistency, external consistency deals with consistency of budget estimates with estimates on industry and general economic factors. For example, if it is clear that the demand for the industry is going to be cut in half for the coming year because of the defense cut-back, it is inconsistent with external factors if the firm does not take into account this effect in preparing budget estimates. It is also inconsistent with external factors to make budget estimates based on the assumption that the price of the products will be doubled when industry economic forecasts see only moderate increases in prices. Of course, the firm's estimates may turn out to be correct, but the point is that in such cases the firm must explain why their estimates are more reliable than others.

BUDGET-AUDITING STANDARDS AND PROCEDURES

In addition to budgeting principles and procedures, a set of budget-auditing standards and procedures must be prepared in order to define methods of examining budget working papers and related evidence which support the inferences as well as the extent of examination. They must also provide reporting standards for budget audits.

The main purpose of budget audits is to make sure that the budgeting processes are carried out as specified by the budgeting principles and procedures.

In particular, budget-auditing standards and procedures must specify the extent to which auditors are asked to check internal and external consistency of budget estimates. For example, it may be required that auditors seek some external evidence in trade journals, government and other reputable sources of economic indicators, etc., to satisfy themselves as to external consistency of budget estimates.

The budget-auditing standards and procedures must also specify the types of budget-audit reports that auditors are supposed to provide. Since such a budget-audit report will be published together with the firm's financial statements (actual and projected), care should be taken not to mislead the readers as to the nature of budget audits and budget-audit reports. Auditors' responsibility should be clearly spelled out in the budget-auditing standards and procedures so that there will not be any misunderstanding by the readers. Since this topic of budget-audit reports and auditors' responsibilities is important, it will be elaborated in more detail below.

BUDGET-AUDIT REPORTS
AND AUDITORS' RESPONSIBILITIES

As in audits on ordinary financial statements, auditors should be required to state in their budget-audit reports whether their budget audits are done in accordance with the budget-auditing standards and procedures. If not, they should state the reason why adherence to them was not possible, and what alternative procedures they have adopted to supplement the procedures not followed.

Auditors should in addition be required to state whether or not, in their opinion, the firm's budgets have been prepared under the budgeting principles and procedures. They should also be asked to disclose any significant deviation from them in the firm's budget preparation. Especially, any inconsistency in prediction, external or internal, current or historical, should be reported together with their effects upon the budgets. Any significant deviation from the accounting principles and procedures in recording the predicted events, including inconsistent treatment of predicted events, should also be reported, together with their effects upon the budgets.

In the budget-auditing standards and procedures, it may be appropriate to require auditors to express their opinion if they feel that the budget estimates are extremely optimistic or extremely pessimistic, although within the boundary of being consistent estimates, and approximately by how much they deviate from what the auditors consider to be reasonable. Auditors should also be allowed to remind the readers of the financial statements as to how deviations existed between estimated and actual figures during the last few periods. These are necessary safeguards against the possibilities of misleading the readers due to the fact that there may be a wide range of estimates which are consistent.

In addition, the budgeting principles and procedures as well as the budget-auditing standards and procedures should state specifically the condition under which the firm and/or the auditors are required or allowed to report any major uncertain factors upon which the budget estimates critically depend. Examples of such factors are major government contracts which the firm may or may not get, major expansion plans which may be delayed because of financial arrangements with banks, major investment in oil well drilling, etc. Of course, the interest of the firm in keeping managerial secrets must be preserved. However, since these are important factors which materially affect the projected financial statements, the readers should be informed as to how these uncertain factors are treated (e.g., optimistically or pessimistically) and how the financial statements should be modified in the event that they do not turn out as expected.

The four types of audit reports in the case of audits on ordinary financial statements can also be applied to budget-audit reports, namely reports with unqualified, qualified, and adverse opinions as well as opinion-disclaimed reports. In addition, a long-form and a short-form budget-audit report may be prepared as in audits on ordinary financial statements.

Auditors' responsibility should be judged primarily based upon whether they have followed the budget-auditing standards and procedures and have done the budget audit with "due professional care." The firm is the one who is primarily responsible for the budgets and the auditors' responsibility is secondary as in the case of ordinary financial statements. It is possible that the firm may be held responsible for improper budgets if they neglect or conceal major factors which had become certain "beyond reasonable doubt" by the time the budgets were prepared and if they would materially affect the projected financial statements. Similarly, it is possible that the auditors may be held responsible for the negligent failure to detect an obvious and serious inconsistency in the projected financial statements. Contrary to the penalty on estimated income tax that is underestimated beyond a given percentage limit, it would be unreasonable to state admissible error ranges quantitatively until the system of budget auditing is developed substantially. However, any major deviation from actual figures would require the firm's and, in some cases, the auditors' explanation.

CONCLUSIONS

Although, as pointed out by the articles cited earlier, the usefulness of budget disclosure to stockholders and other investors is unquestionable, the implementation of budget disclosure must be supported by effective budget auditing in order to insure the reliability of the budgets. For this purpose, it becomes crucial to develop a set of generally accepted budgeting principles and procedures and a set of generally accepted budget-auditing standards and procedures so that firms and auditors have some frameworks to rely upon in developing budgets and in performing budget audits.

Coordinated research efforts by accounting institutions and associations to develop such principles, standards, and procedures will be the most needed and fruitful step toward expanding the traditional boundaries of accounting and auditing.

References

1 American Institute of Certified Public Accountants—Long-Range Objective Committee, **Profile of the Profession: 1975.** "From the Viewpoint of a Sociologist," prepared by N. M. Bedford in consultation with Paul F. Lazarsfeld of Columbia University.

2 Bevis, Herman W., "The CPA's Attest Function in Modern Society," **The Journal of Accountancy,** (February 1962), pp. 28–35.

3 Birnberg, J. G. and N. Dopuch. "A Conceptual Approach to the Framework for Disclosure," **The Journal of Accountancy,** (February 1963), pp. 56–63.

4 Cooper, W. W., N. Dopuch, and T. F. Keller, "Budgetary Disclosure and Other Suggestions for Improving Accounting Reports," (October 1968), pp. 640–648.

5 Ijiri, Y., J. C. Kinard, and F. B. Putney, "An Integrated Evaluation System for Budget Forecasting and Operating Performance—With a Classified Budgeting Bibliography," **Journal of Accounting Research,** (Spring 1968), pp. 1–28.

6 Nielsen, Oswald, "New Challenges in Accounting," **The Accounting Review,** (October 1960), pp. 583–89.

7 Rice, S. A. "Uses of Accounting Data in Economics and Statistics," in **Chal-**

lenges to the Accounting Profession, 1947. (American Institute of Accountants 1947).

8 Solomon, Ezra, "Accounting in the Next Decade," **The Journal of Accountancy,** (January 1965), pp. 22–26.

9 Wilkinson, J. R. and L. D. Doney, "Extending Audit and Reporting Boundaries," **The Accounting Review,** (October 1965), pp. 753–56.

Another, and final, application of the attest function gained considerable attention during the 1964 United States presidential campaign. Opinions were rendered on the personal financial statements of some of the candidates. A comparison of two such reports follows, along with an argument supporting one approach over the other. Make your own analysis of the two approaches and support your choice.

AUDITED PERSONAL FINANCIAL STATEMENTS
James F. Pitt and E. Palmer Tang*

Presidential Campaign 1968 is over and the votes tallied. Fading into history are the primaries, platforms, promises and platitudes. We wonder, however, how many noticed the conspicuous absence of the CPA's opinion on personal financial statements published in connection with this campaign.

Having been personally involved with the statements of one candidate in 1964 who ran for top honors in 1968, we waited anxiously to see how the profession would resolve the controversies generated in 1964 among professional and academic people. But in contrast to 1964, when it was the vogue to issue audited personal financial statements, the CPA's opinion did not accompany the candidates' financial statements published in 1968.

What happened? Was the audited personal statement a fleeting fancy, or has the accounting profession been so unrealistic in its pronouncements in this area that the disclaimer of opinion, now required in virtually every case, offers little appeal to the potential buyer of our services?

Accounting Research Bulletins issued by the American Institute of CPAs have been specifically directed to "accounting practices reflected in financial statements and representations of commercial and industrial companies" and

* From *Tempo,* Vol. 14, No. 4 (December 1968), pp. 4–7. Reprinted by permission of Touche Ross & Co.

not to "accounting problems or procedures of religious, charitable, scientific, educational, and similar non-profit institutions, municipalities, professional firms, and the like."[1] Until 1968 virtually no printers' ink had been consumed in defining the standards for personal financial statements.

Banks have long required personal balance sheets from their personal borrowers and from guarantors, but, since audited statements were hardly ever required, the certified public accountant has exerted little or no influence over their form and content or the method of reporting.

In most instances, the forms provided by banks to personal borrowers for reporting upon their financial position have provided specifically for reporting assets at fair market value, without regard to historical cost. While this method of reporting assets has long been considered unacceptable for commercial and industrial enterprises, it has been used almost exclusively by investment companies and stock brokers.

Much like an individual, these companies emphasize financial condition in their reports rather than the matching of revenues and expenses. Market values, therefore, provide the most timely criteria of that condition. Market values also provide comparability for measurement of total investment performance by including the effect of realized gains (dividends on income stocks) and unrealized gains (appreciation on growth stocks).

The financial statements published by the 1964 candidates were not models of consistency—which is quite natural considering the previous lack of attention to this subject. Perhaps the greatest divergency existed between the statements of President Johnson, which were basically at cost, and those of Vice President Humphrey, which were basically at market.

At any rate these divergencies, particularly the basis of reporting, caused the greatest furor within professional and academic circles. Important differences in the form and content of these two reports and financial statements are shown here.

In an attempt to clarify some of the more controversial questions posed by the inconsistencies enumerated, an ad hoc committee on personal financial statements was appointed by the American Institute of CPAs. In June 1968 this committee issued an audit guide entitled "Audits of Personal Financial Statements."

In summary, the guide sets forth the following recommendations:

1 Ordinarily a combined statement of assets and liabilities of both spouses, and possibly those of minor children, will be the most appropriate representation.

2 The title of personal financial statements should be "Statement of Assets and Liabilities," instead of the more traditional "Balance Sheet" or "Statement of

---

[1] Accounting Research Bulletin No. 43, American Institute of Certified Public Accountants, 1953, page 8.

	President Johnson	**Vice President Humphrey**
Family members included in the financial statements	President and Mrs. Johnson and daughters	Vice President and Mrs. Humphrey
Titles of the financial statements	Statement of assets and liabilities; statement of capital	Statement of financial conditions
Basis of reporting assets	Cost (stock in family corporation reported at cost plus share of retained earnings, reduced by applicable capital gains taxes)	Present market value (stock in family corporation reported at share of book net equity; deferred taxes reported as liability)
U.S. government pension fund	Not included	Included
Assets in trust	Included	Not included; disclosed by footnote
Household goods and personal effects	Not included	Included
Personal documents and memorabilia	Not included	Not included
Designation of excess of assets over liabilities	Capital	Net assets
Auditors' scope paragraph	Substantially standard	Substantially standard, with two additional sentences: "In this connection we have received and relied upon appraisals by real estate agents as to the present market value of real estate and upon representations from the principals as to the present market value of household goods and personal effects. We have also received and relied upon representations from the

		principals as to the completeness of the statements."
Auditors' middle paragraph	Explains basis of reporting stock in family corporations and real estate; specifically disclaims any representation that reported amounts are representative of present market values	Explains that assets are reported at present market values and recites auditors' approval of that method of reporting
Auditors' opinion paragraph	Substantially standard	Substantially standard except no reference to consistency

Financial Condition," and "Statement of Changes in Net Assets," instead of other customary descriptions.

3 The accrual method of reporting should be employed.

4 Assets should be reported primarily on a cost basis, but preferably in columnar form with present market values shown also. Apparently, however, the committee takes the position that absence of the cost column would require an auditor's exception while absence of the present market value column would not.

5 Business interests of significant size, whether corporate shares, partnership interest, or single proprietorship, should be reported as a single line item. Stocks in corporations should be reported at cost and, except for corporations maintaining Subchapter S elections, should not reflect earnings retained since acquisition of the shares.

6 Cost is defined substantially the same as basis for federal income tax purposes, except that property acquired by gift or by nontaxable exchange is regarded as having a cost equal to the value when received.

7 Vested rights in pension or profit sharing funds, deferred compensation plans and property residuals should be reported in the financial statements in the absence of unusual circumstances. Non-vested interests and those subject to indefinite restrictions should be disclosed by footnote but should not be reported as assets.

8 Household goods, personal effects, etc. may be omitted, or reported at a nominal amount, unless such items are material in relation to total assets.

9 The excess of assets over liabilities should be designated in just those words, and not as "capital" or "net assets."

10 Internal control is a prerequisite in the case of personal financial statements,

no less than those of business enterprises, and the absence of reliable control requires the auditor to disclaim an opinion.

11 Formal representations from the principals should be procured but should not be regarded as satisfying any of the auditor's procedural responsibilities.

12 When the auditor is unable to satisfy himself as to the existence of unreported assets or liabilities, he should disclaim an opinion.

13 A separate expression should be given by the auditor with respect to the "present market value" column of the financial statements.

While this guide represents a valuable addition to accounting literature, we take issue with several major areas.

In the first place, we disagree strongly with the recommendation that the historical cost basis of reporting should be regarded as a primary reporting method. We feel that personal financial statements are more comparable with those of investment companies, where assets are customarily included at present market value, rather than with those of typical commercial and industrial enterprises, where assets are customarily included at historical cost.

We feel that the dual basis of reporting serves a sound transitional purpose, but we disagree that cost data, without present value data, should be regarded as being in conformity with generally accepted accounting principles. On the contrary, we feel that the generally accepted reporting practice today is the one bankers have established over a long period of time—namely present market values—and that the omission of cost data would be much less critical than the omission of present market values.

We feel the committee's approach to internal control is impractical, self-defeating and out of touch with reality. Few individuals, even with sophisticated records, maintain effective internal control as that term is defined in our literature. Therefore, if we are to follow the guide with integrity, we must disclaim an opinion in virtually every case. And this practice can only lead to the discontinuation of our services in this area. Could the absence of auditors' opinions on financial statements published by the 1968 Presidential and Vice-Presidential candidates be the beginning of such a trend?

No system of internal controls, however elaborate, could prevent an individual from secretly acquiring valuable property on credit, thereby creating both a material asset and a material liability. Further, no practicable audit procedures can be devised which will disclose such a transaction in the face of an effort to suppress it. An auditor is not charged with procedures which are impossible or impractical to perform, and therefore it is an unfortunate fact of life that he must rely on representations from the principals as to the completeness of personal financial statements.

Yet this need not be fatal to the expression of an opinion. There are responsible ways in which to express the nature and results of an auditor's work in the examination of personal financial statements without resorting to stereotyped terminology which evolved from completely different facts and circumstances. We feel that the committee's energies would have been more fruitful if they had been pointed in that direction.

We also take issue with the committee's suggested language for the auditor's report on the present market value data in the statement of assets and liabilities. The committee suggests a sentence beginning: "We have also determined that the additional information set forth in the accompanying statements on the estimated value basis. . . ."

Must we regress!

"We have determined" is only a whisper away from "We hereby certify," the phrase we abandoned long ago on advice of counsel. We would substitute simply: "Further, in our opinion, the additional information set forth . . ."

Last, and perhaps least important, we feel there is a confusing inconsistency in recommended reporting terminology. On the Statement of Assets and Liabilities, the committee uses the caption "Excess of Assets Over Liabilities." Yet the recommended title for the related statement which reconciles the beginning and ending amounts so reported is "Statement of Changes in Net Assets." Nowhere else is the term "net assets" suggested. We think there should be consistency here.

This item should be identified in the Statement of Assets and Liabilities as "net assets" or else the caption of the related statement should be "Statement of Changes in Excess of Assets Over Liabilities." Our preference is rather obvious, although "net equity" also would be quite acceptable.

The many excellent recommendations made by the committee should not be obscured by our criticisms.

We believe, however, that corrective action should be taken in the areas discussed and a new committee appointed by the AICPA to restudy the entire area. Certainly the public interest would be served best by a realistic approach to reporting on personal financial statements.

Such an approach must recognize that internal controls for an individual cannot be measured against those of the behemoths of industry. Further, it must recognize that an individual thinks of his worldly goods in terms of today's market values, not historical costs.

Looking forward to Campaign 1972, as well as everyday service in an important field, we must be able to report on personal financial statements after performing realistic audit steps. We accomplish nothing for the profession or for those using our services by establishing artificial criteria which virtually negate the opportunity for service. We believe that there is a "place in the sun" for auditors' reports on personal financial statements. But in our opinion, the existing guide puts it many moons away.

Within the mass of material published on management auditing, the following article is singular in questioning the appropriateness of extending the attest function in this direction. Formulate your own answer to each of the ten questions along with a brief statement of support.

SOME HARD QUESTIONS ON MANAGEMENT AUDITS
D. R. Carmichael*

With the literature on management audits being churned out at a merry pace, there is a danger that the desirability of management audits may become generally accepted by default. In the current vocabulary of accounting, the management audit is a *progressive* idea — a virtue that is difficult to oppose. However, the time has come to pause and ask some rather searching questions about management audits.

1 **Do the advocates of management auditing propose an independent attestation of management performance for the benefit of third parties?** Actually, some people advocating management audits do propose an independent attestation of management, while others have in mind no more than a management services type engagement to evaluate operations for management. Audits made for management's benefit raise few serious problems. Independence is not a key factor, the public interest is not involved, and, if management is willing to pay for the service, the independent auditor is but one of a number of professionals available.

The purpose of this article is to ask some searching questions of those who do propose independent attestation of management — and there are many who do. The management audit is proposed as a natural and desirable extension of the attest function. However, the prestige of the public accounting profession has been based largely upon independent audits — an expert opinion on financial position and results of operations. If the profession *unduly* extends the

* From *The Journal of Accountancy*, Vol. 129, No. 2 (February 1970), pp. 72–74. Reprinted by permission of the American Institute of Certified Public Accountants.

attest function, severe damage may be done to the reputation established for the traditional area of expertise.

2 Can the concept of independent attestation of management be crystallized in an intelligible report? The traditional short-form report is the end product of the audit process. It is the auditor's attestation to the public. Within the report are found concise summaries of the work the auditor did and the conclusions he formed. Before such a report could be developed the accounting profession had to have a rather firm idea of what work was involved in an audit and what conclusions could be expressed.

On the other hand, in all of the many articles written on management auditing not one author has suggested an appropriate report for expressing an independent attestion on management. Some have suggested that the management audit report would need to be longer and have a less standard format than the report on financial statements. That makes sense. But why has not one example of such a report been given?

Could it be that the management audit is such a loosely defined and abstract concept that the actual writing of a concrete report has not been attempted? The time has come for the advocates of management auditing to be specific. A report should be proposed so that it can be evaluated on its merits.

3 Just exactly what are management representations? The attest function has generally been interpreted to mean assumption of responsibility for the credibility of representations of others for the benefit of third parties. This idea has been adapted by advocates of management audits who believe that an independent attestation of management should involve assumption of responsibility for the credibility of management representations. However, the concept of management representations is not very concrete.

In fact, in a recent article in *The Accounting Review,* Harold Q. Lagenderfer and Jack C. Robertson offer a rather involved postulational system for management audits which relies on management representations as a fundamental concept, yet not one example of a management representation is given. Certainly, before the desirability of management audits can be realistically evaluated, some specific examples of management representations must be made available.

In addition to a specific definition of management representations, some criteria for evaluation of these representations must be developed, but even this difficult task cannot begin until we know what management representations are.

4 Can the notion of "fair presentation" be applied to representations other than the basic financial statements? The notion of "fair presentation" applied to representations other than those in the basic financial statements has no settled and well-understood meaning. A grave hazard is presented by the ambiguity which may result if the term is applied to representations other than financial position and results of operations.

Since there would be lack of certainty concerning the meaning of "fair presentation" applied to management representations, there would be some risk of misunderstanding and consequent liability, and the exact extent of such risk would be difficult to determine.

The auditor's opinion on financial statements relates to the fair presentation of the *overall* statements. The limited use of piecemeal opinions is testimony to the difficulty of expressing an opinion on the fair presentation of even isolated components of financial statements. Auditors have shown great reluctance to express opinions on condensed financial statements and interim financial statements. Can the application of "fair presentation" to data even further removed from the frame of reference of the overall presentation of financial position and results of operations be seriously considered?

5 Can data be audited that are obtained from records which are not an integral part of the financial accounting process and not subject to the internal controls of the formal accounting system? A portion of the auditor's assurance concerning the overall fairness of financial statements stems from an analytic review of the data (ratio and trend analysis), which is based on the dual nature of accounting transactions, reflected in the double-entry bookkeeping system, and the natural interrelationships among the variables of the accounting process. Verification of data outside this framework cannot rely upon this important characteristic of accounting data.

Perhaps the representations made about other data could be reasonably verified. However, the problems of understatements in data presented or omission of important data would remain. Consider the proposal to audit backlog information, a much more modest task than the audit of management. Since backlog information is not part of the double-entry bookkeeping system and it is not subject to the internal controls of the formal accounting system, there would be little assurance that all contracts were included in backlog information. The audit of management would present even more significant verification problems.

In summary, if some of the auditor's verification methods are peculiarly suited to the verification of accounting information, can the verification process be transferred with reliance to other types of data?

6 Are the evidence gathering methods of auditing appropriate to any type of data merely because auditors are capable of counting, reading, observing, or performing other applicable functions? Observing and asking questions are universal methods of acquiring knowledge. Almost everyone can see, hear and touch, and auditors are no exception. Yet, is the auditor's presence on the scene and his previous association with attestations on financial statements sufficient justification for extending attestation to nonaccounting information?

While it is quite true that auditing is a separate discipline and not a subdivision of accounting, still one can have competence as an auditor only if he has competence as an accountant. The auditor's opinion on the financial statements is valuable because he is an expert in the subject matter of the statements.

Many of the auditor's conclusions on the propriety of the data examined are based on his knowledge of appropriate accounting methods. Although the auditor uses many common methods of acquiring knowledge, the knowledge acquired is viewed from the perspective of its accounting implications. For example, an auditor normally reads the minutes of the meetings of the board of directors, noting such things as the declaration of dividends and authorization of fixed asset expenditures. The data are important to the auditor because of their implications for the financial statements. He is not asked for his opinion on the legality of the actions taken, because legal judgments fall outside the auditor's area of expertise. The ability to read the minutes has no particular significance as an investigative method outside the expert's frame of reference.

If the representation in question involves no particular area of expertise, is it a legitimate subject for attestation by the independent auditor? Might not such attestations raise questions about the real significance of an auditor's opinion?

7 Is the independent auditor respected more for his competence or his independence? While almost no one would challenge the *necessity* of independence in performance of the attest function, competence is also an indispensable quality. One cannot verify accounting data unless he has a sound knowledge of all aspects of the accounting process — accumulation, classification, summarization and presentation. Competence in accounting is a necessary background for auditing work.

Users of financial statements have come to value the opinions of public accountants because of the accountant's expertise in the subject matter of the statements. In emphasizing the importance of independence to attestation, we must not lose sight of the fact that competence played a critical role in making the attest function what it is today. While no definitive answer can be given to the relative importance of competence versus independence, since both are necessary, too little attention has been given to the integral role that competence in accounting has in the attest function.

8 Does competence as an independent auditor have relevance to audits of management? Advocates of management auditing have been willing to admit that CPAs may not be competent to perform management audits. In most cases they leave unanswered the question of who should perform management audits and imply that the area is open to CPAs if they will only equip themselves to perform management audits.

Despite the concessions made on the present inability of CPAs to perform such audits, advocates of management auditing have almost wholeheartedly appropriated the concepts of financial auditing without considering the questions posed in this article concerning the applicability of these concepts. Management representations, "fair presentation," and an attestation type report with scope and opinion sections are examples of financial auditing concepts adapted to management auditing, all without the development of concrete examples for evaluation and thoughtful consideration.

Without detailed specification of the concepts enumerated above, it is difficult to evaluate the independent auditor's ability to audit and report on management auditing data; however, some verification methods of auditing may be inextricably tied to accounting data. Other verification methods are general ways of acquiring knowledge possessed by everyone with no particular significance outside the frame of reference of accounting information. Certainly, advocates of management auditing must address themselves to these questions.

9 Do investors need or want independent attestations on management? To my knowledge, no surveys of investors have indicated a desire for opinions on management. No analytic models of investor decision-making have management characteristics as a variable. If investors were given a choice between accurate forecasts of earnings and accurate evaluations of management, which would they choose?

Before devoting the scarce intellectual resources of the profession to theorizing on independent attestations of management, would it not be better to consider the real need for such opinions and other possible extensions of the attest function which may be not only more responsive to investor needs, but more capable of accomplishment?

10 Are there not other more appropriate areas for extending the attest function? In contrast to the lack of expressed desire for attestations on management, investors have expressed a desire for earnings forecasts and bankers have expressed a desire for reports on internal control. In addition, certain unaudited financial information, such as capsule earnings summaries and backlog information, appears regularly in annual reports. The problems of auditing and reporting on such information are more immediate and concrete than the problems of management auditing and may also be more worthy of attention. Should not our sense of priorities direct primary attention to extensions of the attest function other than management auditing?

Summary

Before serious evaluation of proposals to audit management can begin, attention must be given to certain critical questions. Detailed specification of the concepts of management representations, fair presentation of such representations, and an attestation type report with scope and opinion sections on management performance must be offered for evaluation. In addition, the applicability of the traditional verification methods of auditing to nonaccounting information must be critically evaluated. Finally, the real need for attestations on management and the priority of various possible extensions of the attest function must be assessed.